DIMENSIONS OF
HUMAN BEHAVIOR

Person and Environment

FIFTH EDITION

Elizabeth D. Hutchison
Virginia Commonwealth University, Emerita
and Contributors

Los Angeles | London | New Delhi
Singapore | Washington DC

Los Angeles | London | New Delhi
Singapore | Washington DC

FOR INFORMATION:

SAGE Publications, Inc.
2455 Teller Road
Thousand Oaks, California 91320
E-mail: order@sagepub.com

SAGE Publications Ltd.
1 Oliver's Yard
55 City Road
London, EC1Y 1SP
United Kingdom

SAGE Publications India Pvt. Ltd.
B 1/I 1 Mohan Cooperative Industrial Area
Mathura Road, New Delhi 110 044
India

SAGE Publications Asia-Pacific Pte. Ltd.
3 Church Street
#10-04 Samsung Hub
Singapore 048763

Printed in the United States of America

Library of Congress Cataloging-in-Publication Data

Hutchison, Elizabeth D.

Dimensions of human behavior : person and environment / Elizabeth D. Hutchison, Associate Professor Ermerita, Virginia Commonwealth University, and contributing authors. — Fifth edition.

pages cm
Includes bibliographical references and index.

ISBN 978-1-4833-0391-8 (pbk. : alk. paper)

1. Social psychology. 2. Human behavior. 3. Social structure.
4. Social service. I. Title.

HM1033.D56 2015
302—dc23   2014021700

This book is printed on acid-free paper.

Acquisitions Editor: Kassie Graves
Digital Content Editor: Lauren Habib
Editorial Assistant: Carrie Baarns
Production Editor: Jane Haenel
Copy Editor: Mark Bast
Typesetter: C&M Digitals (P) Ltd.
Proofreader: Scott Oney
Indexer: Terri Corry
Cover Designer: Michael Dubowe
Marketing Manager: Shari Countryman

Certified Chain of Custody
Promoting Sustainable Forestry
www.sfiprogram.org
SFI-01268

SUSTAINABLE FORESTRY INITIATIVE

SFI label applies to text stock

14 15 16 17 18 10 9 8 7 6 5 4 3 2 1

BRIEF CONTENTS

DETAILED CONTENTS

▶ # PART I

A Multidimensional Approach for Multifaceted Social Work   1

▶ PART II

The Multiple Dimensions of Person 77

▶ PART III

The Multiple Dimensions of Environment   223

CASE STUDIES

(Continued)

PREFACE

In the preface to the first edition of this book, I noted that I have always been intrigued with human behavior. I didn't know any social workers when I was growing up—or even that there was a social work profession—but I felt an immediate connection to social work and social workers during my junior year in college when I enrolled in an elective entitled Introduction to Social Work and Social Welfare. What attracted me most was the approach social workers take to understanding human behavior. I was a sociology major, minoring in psychology, and it seemed that each of these disciplines—as well as disciplines such as economics, political science, and ethics—added pieces to the puzzle of human behavior; that is, they each provided new ways to think about the complexities of human behavior. Unfortunately, it wasn't until several years later when I was a hospital social worker that I began to wish I had been a bit more attentive to my course work in biology, because that discipline increasingly holds other pieces of the puzzle of human behavior. But when I sat in that Introduction to Social Work and Social Welfare course, it seemed that the pieces of the puzzle were coming together. I was inspired by the optimism about creating a more humane world, and I was impressed with an approach to human behavior that clearly cut across disciplinary lines.

Just out of college, amid the tumultuous societal changes of the late 1960s, I became an MSW student. I began to recognize the challenge of developing the holistic understanding of human behavior that has been the enduring signature of social work. I also was introduced to the tensions in social work education, contrasting breadth of knowledge versus depth of knowledge. I found that I was unprepared for the intensity of the struggle to apply what I was learning about general patterns of human behavior to the complex, unique situations that I encountered in the field. I was surprised to find that being a social worker meant learning to understand my own behavior, as well as the behavior of others.

Since completing my MSW, I have provided services in a variety of social work settings, including a hospital, nursing homes, state mental health and mental retardation institutions, a community mental health center, a school-based program, public child welfare programs, and a city jail. Sometimes the target of change was an individual, and other times the focus was on bringing about changes in dyadic or family relationships, communities, organizations, or social institutions. I have also performed a variety of social work roles, including case manager, therapist, teacher, advocate, group facilitator, consultant, collaborator, program planner, administrator, and researcher. I love the diversity of social work settings and the multiple roles of practice. My varied experiences strengthened my commitment to the pursuit of social justice, enhanced my fascination with human behavior, and reinforced my belief in the need to understand human behavior holistically.

For almost 30 years, I taught courses such as Human Behavior in the Social Environment to undergraduate students, MSW students, and doctoral students. The students and I struggled with the same challenges I encountered as a social work student in the late 1960s: the daunting task of developing a holistic understanding of human behavior, the issue of breadth versus depth of knowledge, and discovering how to use general knowledge about human behavior in unique practice situations. Increasingly, over time, my students and I also recognized a need to learn more about human and social diversity, and to build a knowledge base that provided tools for promoting social justice. My experiences as student, practitioner, and teacher of human behavior led me to write this book.

MULTIDIMENSIONAL UNDERSTANDING OF HUMAN BEHAVIOR_____

Social work has historically used the idea of person-in-environment to develop a multidimensional understanding of human behavior. The idea that human behavior is multidimensional has become popular with most social and behavioral science disciplines. Recently, we have recognized the need to add the aspect of time to the person–environment construct, to capture the dynamic, changing nature of person-in-environment.

The purpose of this book is to help you to breathe life into the abstract idea of person-in-environment. As I did in the first four editions, I identify relevant dimensions of both person and environment, and my colleagues and I present up-to-date reports on theory and research about each of these dimensions. All the while, we encourage you to link the micro world of personal experience with the macro world of social trends—to recognize the unity of person and environment. We help you make this connection by showing how several of the same theories have been used to understand dimensions of both person and environment. A companion volume to this book, *The Changing Life Course*, builds on the multiple dimensions of person and environment analyzed in this book and demonstrates how they work together with the dimension of time to produce patterns in unique life course journeys.

BREADTH VERSUS DEPTH_____

The most difficult challenge I have faced as a student and teacher of human behavior is to develop a broad, multidimensional approach to human behavior without an unacceptable sacrifice of depth. It is indeed a formidable task to build a knowledge base both wide and deep. After years of struggle,

I have reluctantly concluded that although both breadth and depth are necessary, it is better for social work to err on the side of breadth. Let me tell you why.

Social workers are doers; we use what we know to tell us what to do. If we have a narrow band of knowledge, no matter how impressive it is in its depth, we will "understand" the practice situations we encounter from this perspective. This will lead us to use the same solutions for all situations, rather than to tailor solutions to the unique situations we encounter. The emerging risk and resilience literature suggests that human behavior is influenced by the many risk factors and protective factors inherent in the multiple dimensions of contemporary social arrangements. What we need is a multidimensional knowledge base that allows us to scan widely for, and think critically about, risk factors and protective factors and to craft multi-pronged intervention programs to reduce risks and strengthen protective factors.

To reflect recent developments in the social and behavioral sciences, this book introduces dimensions of human behavior not covered in similar texts. Chapters on the biological and spiritual dimensions of person, the physical environment, social institutions, and social movements provide important insights into human behavior not usually covered in social work texts. In addition, we provide up-to-date information on the typically identified dimensions of human behavior.

GENERAL KNOWLEDGE AND UNIQUE SITUATIONS _____

The purpose of the social and behavioral sciences is to help us understand *general patterns* in person–environment transactions. The purpose of social work assessment is to understand *unique configurations* of person and environment dimensions. Those who practice social work must interweave what they know about unique situations with general knowledge. To assist you in this process, as we did in the first four editions, we begin each chapter with one or more case studies, which we then interweave with contemporary theory and research. Most of the stories are composite cases and do not correspond to actual people known to the authors. In this fifth edition, we continue to expand on our efforts in the last four editions to call more attention to the successes and failures of theory and research to accommodate human diversity related to gender, class, race and ethnicity, culture, sexual orientation, and disability. More important, we have extended our attention to diversity by being very intentional in our effort to provide a global context for understanding person–environment transactions. The attention to the global world has once again expanded in this edition. The most significant change in this fifth edition is the greatly increased content on the impact of new technologies on all dimensions of the person and environment. These new technologies are driving change at all levels.

ABOUT THIS BOOK

The task of developing a solid knowledge base for doing social work can seem overwhelming. For me, it is an exciting journey, because I am learning about my own behavior as well as the behavior of others. I love it that knowledge development and cultural change are happening at such a fast clip that I learn something new every day about the influences on human behavior. What I learn enriches my personal life as well as my professional life. My colleagues and I wanted to write a book that gives you a state-of-the-art knowledge base, but we also wanted you to find pleasure in your learning. We have tried to write as we teach, with enthusiasm for the content and a desire to connect with your process of learning. We continue to use some special features that we hope will aid your learning process. As in the first four editions, key terms are presented in bold type in the chapters and defined in the Glossary. As in the second, third, and fourth editions, we present orienting questions at the beginning of each chapter to help you begin to think about why the content of the chapter is important for social workers. Key ideas are summarized at the beginning of each chapter to give you an overview of what is to

come. Critical thinking questions are presented throughout all chapters. Active learning exercises are presented at the end of each chapter.

The bulk of this fifth edition will be familiar to instructors who used earlier editions of *Dimensions of Human Behavior: Person and Environment*. Many of the changes that are included came at the suggestion of instructors and students who have been using the fourth edition. To respond to the rapidity of changes in complex societies, all chapters have been comprehensively updated. As the contributing authors and I worked to revise the book, we were surprised to learn how much the knowledge base had changed since we worked on the fourth edition. We had not experienced such major change between editions in the past, and this led us to agree with the futurists who say that we are at a point where the rate of cultural change will continue to accelerate rapidly. You will want to use the many wonders of the World Wide Web to update information you suspect is outdated.

NEW IN THIS EDITION

The more substantial revisions for this edition include the following:

- Even more content has been added on globalization.
- Even more attention has been given to the impact of the severe global economic recession that began in late 2007.
- Even more content has been added on human diversity.
- More attention is given to postmodern culture and postmodern approaches to understanding human behavior.
- Significantly more content has been added on the impact of the new information and communication technologies on person and environment.
- New content on environmental and ecological justice has been added to the chapter on the physical environment.
- Visual metaphors are used to represent the major theoretical perspectives used in the book.
- Some new exhibits have been added and others updated.

- Several new case studies have been added to reflect contemporary issues.
- The number of critical thinking questions is increased in every chapter.
- Web resources have been updated.

ONE LAST WORD_____

I imagine that you, like me, are intrigued with human behavior. That is probably a part of what attracted you to social work. I hope that reading this book reinforces your fascination with human behavior. I also hope that when you finish this book, and in the years to come, you will have new ideas about the possibilities for social work action.

Learning about human behavior is a lifelong process. You can help me in my learning process by letting me know what you liked or didn't like about the book.

—Elizabeth D. Hutchison
Rancho Mirage, CA
ehutch@vcu.edu

ACKNOWLEDGMENTS

A project like this book is never completed without the support and assistance of many people. A fifth edition stands on the back of the first four editions, and over the years since I started work on the first edition of this book in the mid-1990s, a large number of people have helped me keep this project going. I am grateful to all of them, some of them known to me and others working behind the scenes in a way not visible to me.

Steve Rutter, former publisher and president of Pine Forge Press, shepherded every step of the first edition and provided ideas for many of the best features of the second edition, which are carried forward in the third, fourth, and now this, the fifth, edition. Along with Paul O'Connell, Becky Smith, and Maria Zuniga, he helped to refine the outline for the second edition, and that outline continues to be used in this book. I am especially grateful to Becky Smith, who worked with me as a developmental editor for the first two editions. She taught me so much about writing, and I often find myself thinking "How would Becky present this?"

The contributing authors and I are grateful for the assistance Dr. Maria E. Zuniga offered during the drafting of the second edition. She provided many valuable suggestions for how to improve the coverage of cultural diversity in each chapter. Her suggestions improved the second edition immensely and have stayed with us as lasting lessons about human behavior in a multicultural society.

I am grateful once again to work with a fine group of contributing authors. They were gracious about timelines and incorporating feedback from reviewers. Most important, they were committed to providing a state-of-the-art knowledge base for understanding the multiple dimensions of human behavior across the life course. I am also grateful for colleagues who have provided rich case studies for Chapters 1 and 9.

We were lucky to be working again with the folks at SAGE. It has been wonderful to have the disciplined and creative editorial assistance of Kassie Graves again. Kassie came on board at SAGE while I was working on the third edition, and she has been a delight to work with over the last three editions. She is dependable, thoughtful, collegial, and a lot of fun. She has been supportive when life events have complicated my deadlines. Maggie Stanley and Liz Luizzi assisted me in numerous ways to get work on the fifth edition up and running. Carrie Baarns came on board in time to shepherd me through the various stages of editing and putting the book into production. She is a jewel. Once the drafting was done, Mark Bast came into my life as copy editor extraordinarie. He caught our mistakes and offered improved language, and he did it with such a delightful sense of humor. Jane Haenel came on board as production editor for this fifth edition and has contributed reader-friendly design features while helping us manage tight deadlines. She and her assistants have turned words and ideas into a book.

I am grateful to my former faculty colleagues at Virginia Commonwealth University (VCU), who set a high standard for scientific inquiry and teaching excellence. They also provided love and encouragement through both good and hard times. My conversations about the human behavior curriculum with colleagues Rosemary Farmer, Stephen Gilson, Marcia Harrigan, Holly Matto, Mary Secret, and Joe Walsh over many years have stimulated much thinking and resulted in many ideas found in this book.

My students over almost 30 years also deserve a special note of gratitude. They taught me all the time, and many things that I have learned in interaction with them show up in the pages of this book. They also provided a great deal of joy to my life journey. Those moments when I learn of former students doing informed, creative, and humane social work are special moments, indeed, and I am happy to say there are many such moments. I have also enjoyed receiving e-mails from students from other universities who are using the books, and I have found their insights to be very helpful.

My deepest gratitude goes to my husband, Hutch. Since the first edition of this book was published, we have weathered several challenging years and experienced many celebratory moments. He is a kind, generous, patient man, and his technical assistance on my writing projects is a major reason I can meet writing deadlines. But, more important, he makes sure that I don't forget that life can be great fun. What a joy it has been to travel so much of my life journey with him.

Finally, I am enormously grateful to a host of reviewers who thoughtfully evaluated the fourth edition and provided very useful feedback about how to improve it. Their ideas were very helpful in framing our work on this fifth edition.

Billy P. Blodgett
West Texas A & M University

Diane Calloway-Graham
Utah State University

Carol S. Drolen
University of Alabama

Nicole Dubus
Wheelock College

Patti Gross
CUNY: College of Staten Island

Laurel Iverson Hitchcock
University of Montevallo

Ski Hunter
University of Texas at Arlington

Stacie McGee
Texas State University–San Marcos

Carla Mueller
Lindenwood University

Fay Roseman
Barry University

Johanna Slivinske
Youngstown State University

Donna Taylor
University of Arkansas at Monticello

George S. Tsagaris
Cleveland State University

Karla T. Washington
University of Louisville

*To all the advocates working on environmental justice
issues for East Coachella Valley. Your tireless efforts have inspired
me throughout the months I have worked on this book. Mantener viva la esperanza.*

PART I

A Multidimensional Approach for Multifaceted Social Work

- Devyani Hakakian is beginning her workday at an international advocacy organization devoted to women's rights.
- Sylvia Gomez and other members of her team at the rehabilitation hospital are meeting with the family of an 18-year-old male who is recovering from head injuries sustained in a motorcycle accident.
- Mark Bernstein is on the way to the county jail to assess the suicide risk of an inmate.
- Caroline O'Malley is knocking at the door of a family reported to her agency for child abuse.
- Helen Moore is preparing a report on environmental justice for a legislative committee.
- Juanita Alvarez is talking with a homeless man about taking his psychotropic medications.
- Stan Weslowski is meeting with a couple who would like to adopt a child.
- Andrea Thomas is analyzing the results of a needs assessment recently conducted at the service center for older adults where she works.
- Anthony Pacino is wrapping up a meeting of a cancer support group.
- Sam Belick is writing a social history for tomorrow's team meeting at the high school where he works.
- Sharlena Cook is preparing to meet with a group of Head Start parents to discuss parenting issues.
- Sarah Sahair has just begun a meeting of a recreational group of 9- and 10-year-old girls.
- Jane Kerr is facilitating the monthly meeting of an interagency coalition of service providers for substance-abusing women and their children.
- Ann Noles is planning a fund-raising project for the local Boys' and Girls' Club.
- Meg Hart is wrapping up her fourth counseling session with a lesbian couple.
- Chien Liu is meeting with a community group concerned about youth gang behavior in their neighborhood.
- Mary Wells is talking with one of her clients at the rape crisis center.
- Nagwa Nadi is evaluating treatment for post-traumatic stress disorder at a Veteran's Administration hospital.

What do these people have in common? You have probably guessed that they all are social workers. They work in a variety of settings, and they are involved in a variety of activities, but they all are doing social work. They all are involved in activities to assess and influence human behavior. Social work is a multifaceted profession, and because it is multifaceted, social workers need a multidimensional understanding of human behavior. This book provides such an understanding. The purpose of the two chapters in Part I is to introduce you to a multidimensional way of thinking about human behavior and to set the stage for subsequent discussion. In Chapter 1, you are introduced to the multiple dimensions of person, environment, and time that serve as the framework for the book, and you are introduced to social work's emphasis on diversity, inequality, and social justice. You also are given some tools to think critically about the multiple theories and varieties of research that make up our general knowledge about these dimensions of human behavior. In Chapter 2, you encounter eight theoretical perspectives that contribute to multidimensional understanding. You learn about their central ideas and their scientific merits. Most important, you consider the usefulness of these eight theoretical perspectives for social work.

1

Human Behavior

A Multidimensional Approach

Elizabeth D. Hutchison

Chapter Outline

Key Ideas

As you read this chapter, take note of these central ideas:

1. This book provides a multidimensional way of thinking about human behavior in terms of changing configurations of persons and environments.

2. Although person, environment, and time are inseparable, we can focus on them separately by thinking about the relevant dimensions of each.

3. Relevant personal dimensions include the biological, the psychological, and the spiritual.

4. Nine dimensions of environment that have relevance for social work are the physical environment, culture, social institutions and social structure, dyads, families, small groups, formal organizations, communities, and social movements. These dimensions have been studied separately, but they are neither mutually exclusive nor hierarchically ordered.

5. Social work puts special emphasis on diversity, inequality, and the pursuit of global social justice.

6. Knowledge about the case, knowledge about the self, values and ethics, and scientific knowledge are four important ingredients for moving from knowing to doing.

7. This book draws on two interrelated logical and systematic ways of building scientific knowledge: theory and empirical research.

CASE STUDY

Manisha and Her Changing Environments

Manisha is a 61-year-old Bhutanese woman who resettled in the United States in early 2009. She describes her childhood as wonderful. She was the youngest of seven children born to a farming family in a rural village of Bhutan. Although there was little support for education, especially for girls, Manisha's parents valued education, and she was one of five girls in her village school, where she was able to finish the second grade. As was tradition, she married young, at age 17, and became a homemaker for her husband, who was a contractor, and the four sons they later had. Manisha and her husband had a large plot of farmland and built a good life. They were able to develop some wealth and were sending their children to school. They were managing well and living in peace.

In 1988, the political climate began to change and the good times ended. Manisha says she doesn't really understand how the problem started because in Bhutan, women were excluded from decision making and were given little information. As she talks, she begins to reflect that she has learned some things about what happened, but she still doesn't understand it. What she does recall is that the Bhutanese government began to discriminate against the Nepali ethnic group to which she belongs. News accounts indicate that the Druk Buddhist majority wanted to unite Bhutan under the Druk culture, religion, and language. The Nepalis had a separate culture and language and were mostly Hindu, while the Druks were Buddhist. Manisha says she does not know much about this, but she does recall that suddenly Nepalis were denied citizenship, were not allowed to speak their language, and could no longer get access to jobs. Within a family, different family members could be classified in different ways based on ethnicity.

Manisha recalls a woman who committed suicide as the discrimination grew worse. She also remembers that the Nepali people began to raise their voices and question what was happening. When this occurred, the Bhutanese government sent soldiers to intimidate the villagers and undermine the Nepali resistance. Manisha tells about cases of rape of Nepali women at the hands of the Bhutanese soldiers and recalls that the soldiers expected Nepali girls and women to be made available to them for sexual activity. She reports that government forces targeted Nepali families who had property and wealth, arresting them in the middle of the night and torturing and killing some. Families were forcefully evicted from their property.

One day when Manisha was at the market, the soldiers arrested her husband and took him to jail; she didn't know where he was for 2 days. He was in jail for 18 months. She remembers that she and her sons would hide out, carefully watch for soldiers, and sneak back home to cook. She was afraid to be at home. Finally, one day she was forced to report to the government office and there was told to leave and go to Nepal. She told the government representative that she couldn't leave because her husband was in jail and she needed to care for her children. She tried to survive, living with other families, and she managed to live that way for a year.

Finally, Manisha heard that her husband would be released from jail on condition that he leave the country. By this time, neighbors had started to flee, and only four households were left in her village. She sent her youngest son with friends and neighbors who were fleeing. A few days later, her husband was released. He said he was too afraid to stay in their home, and they too had to flee. Manisha did not want to leave, and she still talks about the property they had to leave behind. But the next morning, she and her husband and their other three sons fled the country. It was a 3-day walk to the Indian border, where Manisha and her family lived on the banks of a river with other Nepalis who had fled. Her sons ranged in age from 6 to 19 at this time. Manisha recalls that many people died by the river and that there was "fever all around."

After 3 months, Manisha and her family moved to a refugee camp in Nepal, the largest of seven Nepali refugee camps. They spent 17 years in this camp before coming to the United States. The 18 months of imprisonment affected her husband such that he was not able to tolerate the close quarters of refugee camp living; he lived and worked in the adjacent Nepali community and came to visit his family. The four boys were able to attend school in the camp.

The camp was managed by the United Nations High Commissioner for Refugees (UNHCR), whose representatives started to build a forum for women. Manisha says that many of the women were, like her, from rural areas where they had been self-reliant, eating what they grew and taking care of their families. Now they were dependent on other people. The facilities at the camps were closely built and crowded. There was always a need for cash; the refugees were given food, but money was needed for other things, like clothes and personal hygiene items. Oxfam, an international aid organization, started a knitting program, and the women were able

(Continued)

(Continued)

to sell their knitted items, which provided much-needed cash. Manisha began to provide moral support to other women and to disabled children, and she worked as the camp's deputy secretary for 3 years.

Manisha's family wanted desperately to get back to Bhutan, but they began to realize that that would not happen. They also learned that Nepal would not give citizenship to the refugees even though they had a shared culture. So, Manisha and her family decided to resettle in the United States, where they had been assured by UNHCR workers that they would have a better life. The family resettled in three stages. First, Manisha and her husband came to the United States along with their youngest son and his wife. The older sons and their families resettled in two different waves of migration. They all live in close proximity. All of Manisha's sons and daughters-in-law are working, but some have only been able to find part-time work. They work in retail; hotel, hospital, and school housekeeping; and school food services. Her youngest son works at Walmart as a customer service manager and takes online college courses. Her grandchildren are all thriving and doing well in school. Manisha is pleased that they learned English so quickly.

In the camp in Nepal, Manisha had been working and was on the go. In her first year in the United States, she felt lonely, describing her life as "living behind closed doors." She and her husband took English as a second language (ESL) classes, but she felt strongly that she needed to be out at work so that she would have a chance to practice English. Four years after arriving in the United States, Manisha says that everything was so strange at first, and she found it difficult to adjust. For the past 3 years, she has worked part-time in a public school cafeteria, and this semester she is taking a citizenship preparation class. Her husband is not working, and he dropped out of the citizenship preparation class after a few weeks. English is still very hard for her, but her friends at work help her with the language. She has both American and Nepalese friends, and her friends are an important part of her life. She and her husband continue to practice their Hindu faith at home, but they are not able to attend the nearest Hindu Center, which is about 20 miles from their apartment, as often as they would like. The social worker at the refugee resettlement program is pleased that Manisha has found dignity and purpose in resettlement, but he continues to be concerned about other refugee men and women who are isolated and unhappy.

—Beverly B. Koerin and Elizabeth D. Hutchison

HUMAN BEHAVIOR: INDIVIDUAL AND COLLECTIVE

As eventful as it has been, Manisha's story is still unfolding. As a social worker, you will become a part of many unfolding life stories, and you will want to have useful ways to think about those stories and effective ways to be helpful to people like Manisha and her community of Bhutanese refugees. The purpose of this book and its companion volume, *Dimensions of Human Behavior: The Changing Life Course*, is to provide ways for you to think about the nature and complexities of the people and situations at the center of social work practice.

As you think about Manisha's story, you may be thinking, as I was, not only about Manisha but also about the different environments in which she has lived and the ways in which both Manisha and her environments have changed over time. Historically, both the person and his or her environments have been essential considerations in social work practice. Individual behavior has been understood in the context of the various natural and social environments in which the behavior occurs. This continues to be the case; the most recent Educational Policy and Accreditation Standards of the Council on Social Work Education (2008) instructs that social work practice is guided by a "person and environment construct" (p. 1). The person and environment construct is an old idea in social work, but it still is a very useful way to think about human behavior—a way that can accommodate such contemporary themes in human life as the emotional life of the brain, human-robot relationships, social media, human rights, economic globalization, and environmental justice. This book elaborates and updates the person and environment construct that has guided social work intervention since the earliest days of the profession. The element of time is added to the person and environment construct to call attention to the dynamic nature of both people and environments. This is important in rapidly changing societies around the world. Early social workers could not have imagined television and air travel, much less cell phones, Facebook, Instagram, Twitter, Tumblr, or online courses. And, no doubt, the world 50 years from now would seem as "foreign" to us as the United States seemed to Manisha and her family when they first arrived here.

As they live their lives in the natural environment, humans join with other humans to develop physical landscapes and structures, technologies, and social systems that form the context of their lives. These landscapes, structures, technologies, and systems are developed by collective action, by humans interacting with each other. Once developed, they then come to shape the way humans interact with each other and their natural environments. Structures, technologies, and systems can support or deter individual and collective well-being. Usually, they benefit some individuals and groups while causing harm to others. Social workers are concerned about both individual and collective behavior and well-being. When I talk about human behavior, I am referring to both the individual and collective behavior of humans. Sometimes we focus on individual behavior, and other times we are more concerned about the social systems created by human interaction.

This book identifies multiple dimensions of both person and environment and draws on ongoing scientific inquiry, both conceptual and empirical, to examine the dynamic understanding of each

dimension. Special attention is paid to globalization, diversity, human rights, and social and economic justice in examination of each dimension. In this chapter, a multidimensional approach to person and environment is presented, followed by discussion of diversity, inequality, and the pursuit of social justice from a global perspective. After a brief discussion of the process by which professionals such as social workers move from knowing to doing, the chapter ends with a discussion of how scientific knowledge from theory and research informs social work's multidimensional understanding of human behavior.

A MULTIDIMENSIONAL APPROACH

Social work's person and environment construct has historically recognized both person and environment as complex and **multidimensional**, that is, as having several identifiable dimensions. A **dimension** refers to a feature that can be focused on separately but that cannot be understood without also considering other features. This last piece is really important: Although we can focus on one dimension of a human story to help us think about it more clearly, no one dimension can be understood without considering other dimensions as well. With an explosion of research across a number of disciplines in the past few decades, the recent trend has been to expand the range of dimensions of both person and environment folded into the person and environment construct. Time too can be thought of as multidimensional. Let's look at some of the dimensions of person, environment, and time in Manisha's story.

If we focus on the *person* in Manisha's story, it appears that she was born with a healthy biological constitution, which allowed her to work in the family gardens and care for four sons. She describes no difficulty in managing the strenuous 3-day walk to the Indian border as she fled Bhutan. She survived while many people died by the river, and later, in the refugee camp, she survived and found new purpose when many others died of damaged bodies or broken spirits. Manisha appears to have emotional resilience, and she has maintained a belief in her ability to find dignity and purpose in life in the United States. She is able to learn a new language and culture, and plan for the future. Her Hindu faith has been a source of comfort for her as she has adapted to different environments.

If we focus on the *environment*, we see many influences on Manisha's story. Consider first the physical environment. Manisha lived in relative comfort, first on her father's and then her husband's farm, for almost 40 years, where she was able to spend much of her day outside helping to turn gardens into food for her family. From there, she endured a long hike and a few months of survival in a poorly sheltered camp by the river. Her next stop was a crowded refugee camp. After 17 years, she and her family left the camp to establish a new life in the United States, where she lives with her husband in a small apartment that at first left her feeling isolated.

Culture is a dimension of environment that exerts a powerful influence in Manisha's story. Culture influenced the fact that she received limited, if any, education and that she be married at what may appear to us to be an early age. Her culture also held that women lack power and influence and are not involved in affairs outside the home, and yet Manisha assumed a powerful role in holding her family together after her husband was imprisoned. She also developed a very public role in the refugee camp and, upon first coming to the United States, grieved the loss of that role. Although there were many challenges in the camp, she was living among people who shared her culture, language, and religion. She is adapting to a new, fast-moving culture where language is a constant barrier and her religious beliefs are in the minority. But culture is an important part of Manisha's story in another way. Culture clash and cultural imperialism led the Bhutanese government to discriminate against and then banish the Nepali ethnic group. Such cultural conflict is not new; historical analysis suggests that intercultural violence has actually declined in recent times (Pinker, 2011), but it continues to be a source of great international upheaval.

Manisha's story has been powerfully influenced by the geopolitical unrest that began just as she was entering middle adulthood. Her relationships with social institutions have changed over time, and she has had to learn new rules based on her changing place in the social structure. Prior to 1988, she enjoyed high status in her village and the respect that comes with it. She lived in peace. She still does not understand why the Bhutanese government suddenly began to discriminate against her ethnic group, and she grieves the loss of property, status, and homeland that came out of this unrest. She is grateful to the United Nations for their support of the Bhutanese refugees and to the United States for welcoming some to resettle here. Unfortunately, she and her family resettled in the United States in the midst of the worst global economic recession since the Great Depression of the 1930s. They struggled to find work that would allow them to have some of the self-reliance they experienced in Bhutan.

Another dimension of the environment, family, is paramount to Manisha. She is lucky to have her husband living with her again and all of her children nearby. None of her siblings was resettled in the same city, however, and they are spread across several countries at this time. She is not even sure what has happened to much of her large extended family. Manisha's children and grandchildren are central to her life, and they give her hope for the future. Manisha and her husband are devoted to each other but had to adjust to living together again after living in separate quarters for many years. In some ways, Manisha led a much more independent life in the refugee camp than back in Bhutan, and she came to value that independence. She and her husband are still negotiating this change from traditional gender roles.

Small groups, organizations, and communities have been important forces in Manisha's life, but she has had little direct contact with social movements. In the refugee camp, she participated in some focus groups that the UNHCR conducted with the women in the camps. She is enjoying the relationships she is developing with her ESL class and her citizenship preparation class; she draws courage from the companionship and the collegial sense of "we are all in the same boat" that she gets from the weekly classes. She also has warm relationships with the other cafeteria workers at the school.

Several organizations have been helpful to Manisha and her family since they fled Bhutan. First, she is grateful for the UNHCR for all of the resources they put into running the Nepali refugee camps. Second, she has high praise for Oxfam International, which started the knitting program in the camps. In the United States, she is grateful for the assistance of the refugee resettlement program that sponsored her family and is especially appreciative of the ESL program they run and the moral support provided by the social worker. She is learning to work within the context of the public school bureaucracy. She would like to have more contact with the Hindu Center, but the distance does not make that easy.

Manisha has adapted her behavior to live within four different types of communities. In her Bhutanese farming village, she was surrounded by open land, extended family, and long-term friends. In the poorly sheltered camp by the river, fear and confusion were the driving force of relationships, and loss of loved ones was a much too common occurrence. In the crowded refugee camp, disease and despair were common, but she also found her voice and played an important role in helping other women and their children. She enjoyed her leadership position as deputy secretary of the camp and liked the active life she created in this role. Now, she has moved to a suburb of a U.S. city where she lives in a small apartment in a neighborhood with many other Bhutanese refugees. Suburban life is a new experience for her, and she has had many new behaviors to learn, such as how to use unfamiliar appliances, how to cook with unfamiliar foods, and how to navigate public transportation.

Manisha is aware that some members of her Nepali ethnic group developed a resistance social movement when the Bhutanese government began to discriminate against them. She is also aware that some refugees in the Nepali refugee camps resisted the idea of resettlement in the United States and other countries because they thought resettlement would dilute the pressure on Bhutan to repatriate the Nepalis. As much as Manisha would love to be repatriated, she and her family decided that resettlement in the United States was their best chance for a good future.

Time is also an important part of Manisha's story. Her story, like all human stories, is influenced by the human capacity to live not only in the present time but also in past and future times. Discrimination, imprisonment, escape, crowded camps, and resettlement are past events in her family's life and can be vividly recalled. The language barrier takes on special meaning because it reminds them of the time when the Bhutanese government prohibited the use of the Nepali language in schools. There have been times in Manisha's life when she needed to focus on future possibilities with questions such as "Should we leave Bhutan or stay?" and "Should we resettle in the United States or continue to try to return to Bhutan?" This future thinking has had an enormous impact on the current circumstances of the family's lives. Manisha's husband spends a lot of time thinking about his past life in Bhutan and all that has been lost, but she likes to think about the pleasant aspects of her past life. Manisha sees that her children and grandchildren are living largely in the present while also imagining possibilities for their future life in the United States, and she is trying to do that as well.

Manisha's story is also influenced by the historical times in which she has lived and is living. If she had been born 50 years earlier, it is possible that she could have lived out life peacefully in her farm village. On the other hand, the UNHCR, which was so instrumental to her family's survival, was not established until December 1950, 2 years before her birth, and she is lucky to have lived in an era of international support for refugees. The family's adjustment to life in the United States was hampered in the early days by the global economic recession of the time. Her youngest son benefits from living in an era when college credits can be earned by online study. The times in which we live shape our behaviors in many ways.

Another way to think about the role of time in human behavior is to consider the way in which age, or life stage, influences behavior. Manisha notes that learning English and adapting to their new life in the United States is so much easier for her children and grandchildren than it is for her and her husband. She is enjoying the grandparent role that is a large part of her focus in this life stage. She is happy to have a job rather than spending all day in the small apartment, but she hopes that she and her husband will stay well enough for her to continue to work for many more years.

As suggested, social work has historically recognized human behavior as an interaction of person with environment. The earliest social work practice book, *Social Diagnosis*, written by Mary Richmond in 1917, identified the social situation and the personality of the client as the dual foci of social work assessment. The settlement house movement put heavy emphasis on the environmental elements of person–environment interactions, but environment was de-emphasized and intrapsychic factors were emphasized when social work began to rely on psychodynamic theory in the 1920s. In the late 1960s, however, social work scholars began to focus on the environment again when general systems theory, and later ecological theory, was incorporated into the way social work scholars think about human behavior (Kondrat, 2008). The multidimensional approach of this book is rooted in the systems perspective.

Today, a vast multidisciplinary literature is available to help us in our social work efforts. The good news is that the multifaceted nature of this literature provides a broad knowledge base for the varied settings and roles involved in social work practice. The bad news is that this literature is highly fragmented, scattered across a large number of fields. What we need is a structure for organizing our thinking about this multifaceted, multidisciplinary, fragmented literature.

The multidimensional approach provided in this book should help. This approach is built on the person–environment–time model described earlier. Although in this book we analyze specific dimensions of person and environment separately, including information on how our understanding of these dimensions has changed over time, keep in mind that *dimension* refers to a feature that can be focused on separately but cannot be understood without considering other features. The dimensions identified in this book were traditionally studied as detached or semidetached realities, with one dimension characterized as causing or leading to another. In recent years, however, behavioral science scholars have begun to collaborate across disciplines, leading to exciting new ways of thinking about human behavior, which the contributing authors and I share with you. I want to be clear that I do not see the dimensions analyzed in this book as detached realities, and I am not presenting a causal model. I want instead to show how these dimensions work together, how they are interwoven with each other, and how many possibilities are opened for social work practice when we think about human behavior in a multidimensional way. I am suggesting that humans engage in **multidetermined behavior**, that is, behavior that develops as a result of many causes. I do think, however, that focusing on specific dimensions one at a time can help to clarify general, abstract statements about person and environment—that is, it can put some flesh on the bones of this construct. Exhibit 1.1 is a graphic overview of the dimensions of person, environment, and time discussed in this book. Exhibit 1.2 defines and gives examples for each dimension.

Critical Thinking Questions 1.1

What courses have you taken in the past that added to your understanding of human behavior? How does content from any of these courses help you to understand Manisha's story and how a social worker might be helpful to Manisha and her family? Do you agree that the person and environment construct is still useful for social work? Explain your answer.

Exhibit 1.1   Person, Environment, and Time Dimensions

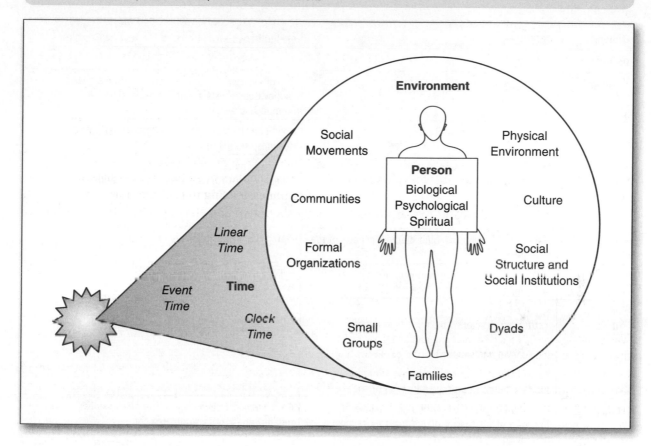

Personal Dimensions

Any story could be told from the perspective of any person in the story. The story at the beginning of this chapter is told from Manisha's perspective, but it could have been told from the perspectives of a variety of other persons such as the Bhutanese king, Manisha's husband, one of her children, one of her grandchildren, a UNHCR staff member, one of the women supported by Manisha in the camp, the social worker at the refugee resettlement agency, or one of her co-workers. You will want to recognize the multiple perspectives held by different persons involved in the stories of which you become a part in your social work activities.

You also will want tools for thinking about the various dimensions of the persons involved in

these stories. When the person and environment construct has been criticized, the criticism often focuses on some dimension of either person or environment that has not received adequate coverage. For many years, social work scholars described the approach of social work as *psychosocial*, giving primacy to psychological dimensions of the person. Personality, ego states, emotion, and cognition are the important features of the person in this approach. In the 1980s, the social work literature began to be critical of the psychosocial approach to person and environment, arguing that it failed to pay attention to the important role that biology plays in human behavior. These critics recommended a **biopsychosocial approach** that recognizes human behavior as the result of interactions of integrated biological, psychological, and social

Exhibit 1.2 Definitions and Examples of Dimensions of Person, Environment, and Time

Dimension	Definition	Examples
Person		
Biological	The body's biochemical, cell, organ, and physiological systems	Nervous system, endocrine system, immune system, cardiovascular system, musculoskeletal system, reproductive system
Psychological	The mind and the mental processes	Cognitions (conscious thinking processes), emotion (feelings), self (identity)
Spiritual	The aspect of the person that searches for meaning and purpose in life	Themes of morality; ethics; justice; interconnectedness; creativity; mystical states; prayer, meditation, and contemplation; relationships with a higher power
Environment		
Physical	The natural and human-built material aspects of the environment	Water, sun, trees, buildings, landscapes
Culture	A set of common understandings, evident in both behavior and material artifacts	Beliefs, customs, traditions, values
Social structure and social institutions	Social structure: a set of interrelated social institutions developed by humans to impose constraints on human interaction for the purpose of the survival and well-being of the collectivity Social institutions: patterned ways of organizing social relations in a particular sector of social life	Social structure: social class Social institutions: government, economy, education, health care, social welfare, religion, mass media, and family
Formal organizations	Collectivities of people, with a high degree of formality of structure, working together to meet a goal or goals	Civic and social service organizations, business organizations, professional associations
Communities	People bound either by geography or by network links (webs of communication), sharing common ties, and interacting with one another	Territorial communities such as neighborhoods; relational communities such as the social work community, the disability community, a faith community, a soccer league
Social movements	Large-scale collective actions to make change, or resist change, in specific social institutions	Civil rights movement, poor people's movements, disability movement, gay rights movement
Small groups	Two or more people who interact with each other because of shared interests, goals, experiences, and needs	Friendship group, self-help group, therapy group, committee, task group, interdisciplinary team
Families	A social group of two or more persons, characterized by ongoing interdependence with long-term commitments that stem from blood, law, or affection	Nuclear family, extended family, chosen family
Dyads	Two persons bound together in some way	Parent and child, romantic couple, social worker and client
Time		
Linear time	Time in terms of a straight line	Past, present, future
Historical era	A discrete block of time in human history	Progressive Era, the Great Depression, 1960s
Chronological age	Age of a person measured in years, months, and days from the date the person was born; may also be described in terms of a stage of the human life course	Six months old (infancy), 15 years old (adolescence), 80 years old (late adulthood)

systems (see Melchert, 2013). In this approach, psychology is seen as inseparable from biology; emotions and cognitions affect the health of the body and are affected by it (Smith, Fortin, Dwamena, & Frankel, 2013). Neurobiologists are identifying the brain circuitry involved in thoughts and emotions (Davidson & Begley, 2012; Kurzweil, 2012). They are finding evidence that the human brain is wired for social life (Lieberman, 2013). They are also finding that the social environment has an impact on brain structure and processes and that environments actually turn genes on and off. Environments influence biology, but the same environment acts on diverse genetic material (Hutchison, 2014).

In recent years, social work scholars and those in the social and behavioral sciences and medicine have argued for greater attention to the spiritual dimension of persons as well (see Crisp, 2010). Developments in neuroscience have generated new explorations of the unity of the biological, psychological, and spiritual dimensions of the person. For example, recent research has focused on the ways that emotions and thoughts, as well as spiritual states, influence the immune system and some aspects of mental health (Davidson & Begley, 2012). One national longitudinal study examined the role of spirituality in physical and mental health after the collective trauma of the 9/11 attacks and found that high levels of spirituality were associated with fewer infectious ailments, more positive emotions, and more immediate processing of the traumatic event in the 3 years following the attacks (McIntosh, Poulin, Silver, & Holman, 2011). In this book, we give substantial coverage to all three of these personal dimensions: biological, psychological, and spiritual.

Environmental Dimensions

Social workers have always thought about the environment as multidimensional. As early as 1901, Mary Richmond presented a model of social work case coordination that took into account not only personal dimensions but also family, neighborhood, civic organizations, private charitable organizations, and public relief organizations. Several models for classifying dimensions of the environment have been proposed since Mary Richmond's time. Among social work scholars, Ralph Anderson and Irl Carter made a historic contribution to systemic thinking about human behavior with the first edition of their *Human Behavior in the Social Environment: A Social Systems Approach* (1974), one of the earliest textbooks on human behavior authored by social workers. Their classification of environmental dimensions has had a significant impact on the way social workers think about the environment. Anderson and Carter divided the environment into five dimensions: culture and society, communities, organizations, groups, and families. Social workers (see, e.g., Ashford, LeCroy, & Lortie, 2010) have also been influenced by Uri Bronfenbrenner's (2005) ecological perspective, which identifies the five interdependent, nested categories or levels of systems presented in Exhibit 1.3 (by adding

Exhibit 1.3   Five Categories or Levels of Systems as Presented by Uri Bronfenbrenner

1. *Microsystems* are those that involve direct, face-to-face contact between members.

2. *Mesosystems* are networks of microsystems of a given person.

3. *Exosystems* are the linkages between microsystems and larger institutions that affect the system, such as the family system and the parent's workplace or the family system and the child's school.

4. *Macrosystems* are the broader influences of culture, subculture, and social structure.

5. *Chronosystems* are systems of time and history.

chronosystems in his later work, Bronfenbrenner was acknowledging the importance of time in person–environment transactions). Some social work models have included the physical environment (natural and built environments) as a separate dimension (see Norton, 2009). There is growing evidence of the impact of the physical environment on human well-being.

To have an up-to-date understanding of the multidimensional environment, I recommend that social workers have knowledge about the eight dimensions of environment described in Exhibit 1.2 and presented as chapters in this book: the physical environment, culture, social structure and social institutions, families, small groups, formal organizations, communities, and social movements. We also need knowledge about dyadic relationships—those between two people, the most basic social relationship. Dyadic relationships receive attention throughout the book and are emphasized in Chapter 5, which focuses on the psychosocial person. Simultaneous consideration of multiple environmental dimensions provides new possibilities for action, perhaps even new or revised approaches to social work practice.

These dimensions are neither mutually exclusive nor hierarchically ordered. For example, a family is sometimes referred to as a social institution, families can also be considered small groups or dyads, and family theorists write about family culture. Remember, dimensions are useful ways of thinking about person–environment configurations, but we should not think of them as detached realities.

Time Dimensions

When I was a doctoral student in a social work practice course, Professor Max Siporin began his discussion of social work assessment with this comment: "The date is the most important information on a written social work assessment." This was Siporin's way of acknowledging the importance of time in human behavior, of recognizing the ever-changing nature of both person and environment. The importance of time in human behavior is reflected in the finding that *time* is the most commonly used noun

in print in the English language; *person* is the second most common (BBC News, 2006).

There are many ways to think about time. Physics is generally seen as the lead discipline for studying time, and quantum physics has challenged much about the way we think about time. Various aspects of time are examined by other disciplines as well, and there are a number of different ways to think about time. In this book and the companion volume *Dimensions of Human Behavior: The Changing Life Course*, we examine three dimensions of time that have been studied by behavioral scientists as important to the understanding of human behavior: linear time, historical era, and chronological age.

Linear time—time ordered like a straight line from the past through the present and into the future—is the most common way that humans think about time. Although it is known that people in some cultures and groups think of time as stationary rather than moving (Boroditsky, Fuhrman, & McCormick, 2011), contemporary behavioral science researchers are interested in what they call "mental time travel," the human ability to remember events from the past and to imagine and plan for the future (Eacott & Easton, 2012). The research on "mental time travel" has focused on the conscious processes of reminiscence and anticipation, but there is also considerable evidence that past events are stored as unconscious material in the brain and the body and show up in our thoughts and emotions (see Davidson & Begley, 2012; Kurzweil, 2012). Traces of past events also exist in the natural and built environments, for example, in centuries-old buildings or in piles of debris following a hurricane or tornado.

Linear time is measured by clocks and calendars. When I think of time, I tend to think of clocks, calendars, and appointments. And I often seem to be racing against time, allowing the clock to tell me when an event should begin and end. This is the way most people in affluent countries with market economies think of time. This approach to time has been called *clock time* (Zimbardo & Boyd, 2008). However, this approach to time is a relatively new invention, and many people in the contemporary

Photo 1.1 Three dimensions of human behavior are captured in this photo—person, environment, and time.

© John Foxx/Stockbyte/Thinkstock

world have a very different approach to time. In nonindustrialized countries, and in subcultures within industrialized countries, people operate on *event time*, allowing scheduling to be determined by events. For example, in agricultural societies, the most successful farmers are those who can be responsive to natural events—sunrise and sunset, rain, drought, temperature—rather than to scheduled events (Zimbardo & Boyd, 2008). Manisha's life was organized around cues from the natural world rather than the clock when she lived in Bhutan, just as my grandfather's was on his farm in rural Tennessee.

Clock time cultures often use the concept of **time orientation** to describe the extent to which individuals and collectivities are invested in the three temporal zones—past, present, and future.

Research indicates that cultures differ in their time orientation. In most cultures, however, some situations call for us to be totally immersed in the present, others call for historical understanding of the past and its impact on the present, and still others call for attention to future consequences and possibilities. Psychologists Philip Zimbardo and John Boyd (2008) have been studying time orientation for more than 30 years and have identified the six most common time perspectives held in the Western world. They call these the *past-positive* (invested in the past, focused on its positive aspects), *past-negative* (invested in the past, focused on its negative aspects), *present-hedonistic* (invested in the present, focused on getting as much pleasure as possible from it), *present-fatalistic* (invested in the present, sees life as controlled by fate), *future* (invested in the future, organizes life around future goals), and *transcendental-future* (invested in the future, focuses on new time after death). Zimbardo and Boyd's research using the Zimbardo Time Perspective Inventory (ZTPI) in a number of Western societies indicates that human well-being is maximized when people in these societies live with a balance of past-positive, present-hedonistic, and future perspectives. People with biases toward past-negative and present-fatalistic perspectives are at greater risk of developing physical and mental health problems. Zimbardo and Boyd's (2008) book *The Time Paradox* suggest ways to become more past-positive, present, and future oriented to develop a more balanced time orientation. You might want to visit www.thetimeparadox.com and complete the ZTPI to investigate your own time orientation.

Photo 1.2 Time is one of the three elements outlined in this text for studying human behavior. It recognizes that people and environments are ever changing, dynamic, and flowing.

© Comstock/Thinkstock

Zimbardo and Boyd have carried out their research in Western societies and acknowledge that the ZTPI may not accurately reflect time orientation in other societies. They make particular note that their description of present-hedonistic and present-fatalistic does not adequately capture the way Eastern religions think about the present. Recently, Western behavioral scientists have begun to incorporate Eastern mindfulness practices of being more fully present in the current moment (present orientation) to help people buffer the persistent stresses of clock time and goal monitoring (future orientation) (Davidson & Begley, 2012). Research also indicates age-related differences in time orientation, with older adults tending to be more past oriented than younger age groups (Yeung, Fung, & Kam, 2012). Women have been found to be more future-oriented and men more present-oriented (Zimbardo & Body, 2008). Researchers have found that trauma survivors who experienced the most severe loss are more likely than other trauma survivors to be highly oriented to the past (Martz, 2004). Zimbardo and Boyd (2008) suggest that trauma survivors may need assistance to think in different ways about past trauma and to enhance their capacity for present and future thinking. This is something to keep in mind when we interact with refugees, military men and women who have served in war zones, and other groups who have an increased likelihood of having a history of trauma. It is also important for social workers to be aware of the meaning of time for the individuals and communities they serve.

Two other dimensions of time have been identified as important to the understanding of human behavior. Both of these dimensions are aspects of linear time but have been separated out for special study by behavioral scientists. The first, *historical era*, refers to the specific block or period of time in which individual and collective lives are enacted. The historical era in which we live shapes our environments. The economies, physical environments, institutions, technologies, and geopolitical circumstances of a specific era provide both options for and constraints on human behavior. The second, *chronological age*, seems to be an important variable in every society. How people change at different ages and life stages as they pass from birth to death has been one of the most enduring ways of studying both individual and collective behavior. Historical era is examined throughout this book and its companion book *The Changing Life Course*, and chronological age is the organizing framework for *The Changing Life Course*.

Critical Thinking Questions 1.2

How would our understanding of Manisha's story change if we had no knowledge of her prior life experiences in Bhutan and the Nepali refugee camp—if we only assessed her situation based on her current functioning? What personal and environmental dimensions would we note in her current functioning?

DIVERSITY, INEQUALITY, AND THE PURSUIT OF SOCIAL JUSTICE: A GLOBAL PERSPECTIVE

The Council on Social Work Education requires that social work educational programs provide a global perspective to their students. I think this is a great idea, but what exactly does it mean, and why is it valued? We are increasingly aware that we are part of an interconnected world, and Manisha's story is one reminder of this. But just how connected are we? In her book *Beyond Borders: Thinking About Global Issues*, Paula Rothenberg (2006) writes, "A not so funny, but perhaps sadly true, joke going around claims that people in the United States learn geography by going to war" (p. xv). Certainly, we learned something about the maps of Afghanistan and Iraq in the past decade, but what do we know about the map of Bhutan? A global perspective involves much more than geography, however. Here are some aspects of what it means to take a global perspective:

- To be aware that my view of the world is not universally shared, and others may have a view of the world that is profoundly different from mine
- To have a growing awareness of the diversity of ideas and cultural practices found in human societies around the world
- To be curious about conditions in other parts of the world and how they relate to conditions in our own society
- To understand where I fit in the global social structure and social institutions
- To have a growing awareness of how people in other societies view my society
- To have a growing understanding of how the world works, with special attention to systems and mechanisms of inequality and oppression around the world

We have always been connected to other peoples of the world, but those connections are being intensified by **globalization**, a process by which the world's people are becoming more interconnected economically, politically, environmentally, and culturally. It is a process of increased connectedness and interdependence that began at least 5 centuries ago but has intensified in recent times and is affecting people around the world (C. Mann, 2011). This increasing connectedness is, of course, aided by rapid advancements in communication technology. There is much debate about whether globalization is a good thing or a bad thing, a conversation that is picked up in Chapter 9 as we consider the globalization of social institutions. What is important to note here is that globalization is increasing our experiences with social diversity and raising new questions about inequality, human rights, and social justice.

Diversity

Diversity has always been a part of the social reality in the United States. Even before the Europeans came, the Indigenous people were divided into about 200 distinct societies with about 200 different languages (Parrillo, 2009). Since the inception of the United States of America, we have been a nation of immigrants. We value our nation's immigrant heritage and take pride in the ideals of equality of opportunity for all who come. However, there have always been tensions about how we as a nation handle diversity. Are we a *melting pot* where all are melted into one indistinguishable model of citizenship, or are we a *pluralist society* in which groups have separate identities, cultures, and ways of organizing but work together in mutual respect? Pioneer social worker Jane Addams (1910) was a prominent voice for pluralism during the early 20th century, and that stance is consistent with social work's concern for human rights.

Even though diversity has always been present in the United States, it is accurate to say that some of the diversity in our national social life is new. Clearly, there is increasing racial, ethnic, and religious diversity in the United States, and the mix in the population stream has become much more complex in recent years (Parrillo, 2009). The United States was 87% White in 1925, 80% White in 1950, and 72% White in 2000; by 2050, it is projected that we will be about 47% White (Taylor & Cohn, 2012). Why is this happening at this time? A major driving force is the demographic reality that native-born people are no longer reproducing at replacement level in the wealthy postindustrial nations, which, if it continues, ultimately will lead to a declining population skewed toward advanced age. One solution used by some countries, including the United States, is to change immigration policy to allow new streams of immigration. The current rate of foreign-born persons in the United States is lower than it has been throughout most of the past 150 years, but foreign-born persons are less likely to be White than when immigration policy, prior to 1965, strictly limited entry for persons of color. With the recent influx of immigrants from around the globe, the United States has become one of many ethnically and racially diverse nations in the world today. In many wealthy postindustrial countries, including the United States, there is much anti-immigrant sentiment, even though the economies of these countries are dependent on such migration. Waves of immigration have historically been accompanied by anti-immigrant sentiment. There appear to be many reasons for

anti-immigrant sentiment, including fear that new immigrants will dilute the "purity" of the native culture, racial and religious bias, and fear of economic competition. Like other diverse societies, we must find ways to embrace the diversity and seize the opportunity to demonstrate the human capacity for intergroup harmony.

On the other hand, some of the diversity in our social life is not new but simply newly recognized. In the contemporary era, we have been developing a heightened consciousness of human differences—gender differences, racial and ethnic differences, cultural differences, religious differences, differences in sexual orientation, differences in abilities and disabilities, differences in family forms, and so on. This book intends to capture the diversity of human experience in a manner that is respectful of all groups, conveys the positive value of human diversity, and recognizes differences *within* groups as well as *among* groups.

As we seek to honor differences, we make a distinction between heterogeneity and diversity. We use **heterogeneity** to refer to individual-level variations—differences among individuals. For example, as the social worker whom Manisha consults, you will want to recognize the ways in which she is different from you and from other clients you serve, including other clients of Bhutanese heritage. An understanding of heterogeneity allows us to recognize the uniqueness of each person and situation. **Diversity**, on the other hand, is used to refer to patterns of group differences. Diversity recognizes social groups, groups of people who share a range of physical, cultural, or social characteristics within a category of social identity. As a social worker, besides recognizing individual differences, you will also want to be aware of the diversity in your community, such as the distribution of various ethnic groups, including those of Bhutanese heritage. Knowledge of diversity helps us to provide culturally sensitive services.

I want to interject a word here about terminology and human diversity. As the contributing authors and I attempted to uncover what is known about human diversity, we struggled with terminology to define identity groups. We searched for consistent language to describe different groups, and we were dedicated to using language that identity groups would use to describe themselves. However, we ran into challenges endemic to our time related to the language of diversity. It is not the case, as you have probably observed, that all members of a given identity group at any given time embrace the same terminology for their group. As we reviewed literature from different historical moments, we recognized the shifting nature of terminology. In addition, even within a given historical era, we found that different researchers used different terms and had different decision rules about who composes the membership of identity groups. Add to this the changing way that the U.S. Census Bureau establishes official categories of people, and in the end, we did not settle on fixed terminology to consistently describe identity groups. Rather, we use the language of individual researchers when reporting their work, because we want to avoid distorting their work. We hope you will not find this too distracting. We also hope that you will recognize that the ever-changing language of diversity has both constructive potential to find creative ways to affirm diversity and destructive potential to dichotomize diversity into *the norm* and *the other*.

Inequality

Attending to diversity involves recognition of the power relations and the patterns of opportunities and constraints for social groups. If we are interested in the Bhutanese community in our city, for example, we will want to note, among other things, the neighborhoods where they live, the access to community resources and quality of the housing stock in those neighborhoods, the comparative educational attainment in the community, the occupational profile of the community, the comparative income levels, and so on. When we attend to diversity, we not only note the differences between groups but also how socially constructed hierarchies of power are superimposed on these differences.

Recent U.S. scholarship in the social sciences has emphasized the ways in which three types of categorizations—gender, race, and class—are used to develop hierarchical social structures that influence social identities and life chances (Rothenberg, 2010; Sernau, 2014). This literature suggests that these social categorizations create **privilege**, or unearned advantage, for some groups and disadvantage for other groups. In a much-cited article, Peggy McIntosh (2007) has pointed out the mundane daily advantages of White privilege that are not available to members of groups of color, such as assurances "that my children will be given curricular materials that testify to the existence of their race," and "Whether I use checks, credit cards, or cash, I can count on my skin color not to work against the appearance of financial reliability." We could also generate lists of advantages of male privilege, adult privilege, upper-middle-class privilege, heterosexual privilege, ability privilege, Christian privilege, and so on. McIntosh argues that members of privileged groups benefit from their privilege but have not been taught to think of themselves as privileged. They take for granted that their advantages are normal and universal. For survival, members of nonprivileged groups must learn a lot about the lives of groups with privilege, but groups with privileged status are not similarly compelled to learn about the lives of members of nonprivileged groups.

Michael Schwalbe (2006) argues that those of us who live in the United States also carry "American privilege," which comes from our dominant position in the world. (I would prefer to call this "U.S. privilege," since people living in Canada, Ecuador, and Brazil also live in America.) According to Schwalbe, among other things, American privilege means that we don't have to bother to learn about other countries or about the impact of our foreign policy on people living in those countries. Perhaps that is what Rothenberg (2006) was thinking of when she noted ignorance of world geography among people who live in the United States. American privilege also means that we have access to cheap goods that are produced by poorly paid workers in impoverished countries. As Chapter 9 shows, the income and wealth gap between nations is mind-boggling. Sernau (2014) reports that the combined income of the 25 richest people in the United States is almost as great as the combined income of 2 billion of the world's poorest people. In 2011, the average per capita income in Bhutan was $2,346 in U.S. dollars, compared with $48,112 in the United States (World Bank, 2013a). It is becoming increasingly difficult to deny the costs of exercising American privilege by remaining ignorant about the rest of the world and the impact our actions have on other nations.

As the contributing authors and I strive to provide a global context, we encounter current controversies about appropriate language to describe different sectors of the world. Following World War II, a distinction was made between First World, Second World, and Third World nations, with *First World* referring to the Western capitalist nations, *Second World* referring to the countries belonging to the socialist bloc led by the Soviet Union, and *Third World* referring to a set of countries that were primarily former colonies of the First World. More recently, many scholars have used this same language to define global sectors in a slightly different way. *First World* has been used to describe the nations that were the first to industrialize, urbanize, and modernize. *Second World* has been used to describe nations that have industrialized but have not yet become central to the world economy. *Third World* has been used to refer to nonindustrialized nations that have few resources and are considered expendable in the global economy. However, this approach has begun to lose favor in the past few years (Leeder, 2004). Immanuel Wallerstein (1974, 1979) uses different language but makes a similar distinction; he refers to wealthy *core* countries, newly industrialized *semiperiphery* countries, and the poorest *periphery* countries. Other writers divide the world into *developed* and *developing* countries, referring to the level of industrialization, urbanization, and modernization. Still others divide the world into the *Global North* and the *Global South*, calling attention to a history in which the Global North colonized and exploited the resources of the Global South. Finally, some writers talk about the *West* versus the *East*, where the distinctions are largely cultural. We recognize that such categories carry great symbolic meaning and can mask systems of power and exploitation. As with diversity, we attempted to find a respectful language that could be used consistently throughout the book. Again, we found that different researchers have used different language and different characteristics to describe categories of nations, and when reporting on their findings, we have used their own language to avoid misrepresenting their findings.

It is important to note that privilege and disadvantage are multidimensional, not one-dimensional. One can be privileged in one dimension and disadvantaged in another; for example, I have White privilege but not gender privilege. As social workers, we need to be attuned to our own *social locations*—where we fit in a system of social identities, such as race, ethnicity, gender, social class, sexual orientation, religion, ability/disability, and age. We must recognize how our own particular social locations shape how we see the world, what we notice, and how we interpret what we "see."

It is important for social workers to acknowledge social inequalities because our interactions are constantly affected by inequalities of various types. In addition, there is clear evidence that social inequalities are on the rise in the United States. Although income inequality has been growing in all of the wealthy nations of the world over the past 2 decades, the United States gained the distinction as the most unequal wealthy nation in this period, and the gap has continued to widen since the deep economic crisis that began in 2008 (Organisation for Economic Co-operation and Development, 2011).

The Pursuit of Social Justice

There is another important reason why social workers must acknowledge social inequalities. The National Association of Social Workers (NASW) Code of Ethics identifies social justice as one of six core values of social work and mandates that "Social Workers challenge social injustice" (NASW, 2008). To challenge injustice, we must first recognize it and understand the ways it is embedded in a number of societal institutions. That is the subject of Chapter 9 in this book.

Suzanne Pharr (1988) has provided some useful conceptual tools that can help us recognize injustice when we see it. She identifies a set of mechanisms of oppression, whereby the everyday arrangements of social life systematically block opportunities for some groups and inhibit their power to exercise self-determination. Exhibit 1.4 provides an overview of these mechanisms of oppression. As you review the list, you may recognize some that are familiar to you, such as stereotyping and perhaps blaming the victim. There may be others that you have not previously given much thought to. You may also recognize, as I do each time I look at the list, that while some of these mechanisms of oppression are

Exhibit 1.4   Common Mechanisms of Oppression

Economic power and control	Limiting of resources, mobility, education, and employment options to all but a few
Myth of scarcity	Myth used to pit people against one another, suggests that resources are limited and blames people (e.g., poor people, immigrants) for using too many of them
Defined norm	A standard of what is good and right, against which all are judged
The other	Those who fall outside "the norm" but are defined in relation to it, seen as abnormal, inferior, marginalized
Invisibility	Keeping "the other's" existence, everyday life, and achievements unknown
Distortion	Selective presentation or rewriting of history so that only negative aspects of "the other" are included
Stereotyping	Generalizing the actions of a few to an entire group, denying individual characteristics and behaviors
Violence and the threat of violence	Laying claim to resources, then using might to ensure superior position
Lack of prior claim	Excluding anyone who was not originally included and labeling as disruptive those who fight for inclusion
Blaming the victim	Condemning "the others" for their situation, diverting attention from the roles that dominants play in the situation
Internalized oppression	Internalizing negative judgments of being "the other," leading to self-hatred, depression, despair, and self-abuse
Horizontal hostility	Extending internalized oppression to one's entire group as well as to other subordinate groups, expressing hostility to other oppressed persons and groups rather than to members of dominant groups
Isolation	Physically isolating people as individuals or as a "minority" group
Assimilation	Pressuring members of "minority" groups to drop their culture and differences and become a mirror of the dominant culture
Tokenism	Rewarding some of the most assimilated "others" with position and resources
Emphasis on individual solutions	Emphasizing individual responsibility for problems and individual solutions rather than collective responsibility and collective solutions

SOURCE: Adapted from Pharr, 1988.

sometimes used quite intentionally, others are not so intentional but occur as we do business as usual. For example, when you walk into your classroom, do you give much thought to the person who cleans that room, what wage this person is paid, whether this is the only job this person holds, and what opportunities and barriers this person has experienced in life? Most likely, the classroom is cleaned in the evening after it has been vacated by teachers and students, and the person who cleans it, like many people who provide services that make our lives more pleasant, is invisible to you. Giving serious thought to common mechanisms of oppression can help us to recognize social injustice and think about ways to challenge it.

In recent years, social workers have expanded the conversation about social justice to include *global* social justice. As they have done so, they have more and more drawn on the concept of *human rights* to organize thinking about social justice (see Mapp, 2008; Reichert, 2006; Wronka, 2008). In the aftermath of World War II, the newly formed United Nations (1948) created a Universal Declaration of Human Rights (UDHR), which spelled out the rights to which all humans were entitled, regardless of their place in the world, and this document has become a point of reference for subsequent definitions of human rights. Cox and Pawar (2013) identify eight philosophical values suggested by the UDHR: life (human and nonhuman); freedom and liberty; equality and nondiscrimination; justice; solidarity; social responsibility; evolution, peace, and nonviolence; and relationships between humankind and nature.

A number of theories of social justice have been proposed. Probably the most frequently cited theory of social justice in the social work literature is John Rawls's (1971, 2001) theory of justice as fairness. In the past decade or so, some social work scholars (Banerjee & Canda, 2012; Morris, 2002) have recommended the capabilities approach to social justice, originally proposed by Amartya Sen (1992, 2009) and revised by Martha Nussbaum (2011). The capabilities approach draws on both Western and non-Western thinking. In this approach, capabilities are, in simplest terms, opportunities and freedoms to be or do what we view as worthwhile; justice is served when people have such opportunities and freedoms. Nussbaum carries the capabilities approach a step further and identifies 10 core capabilities that all people in all societies must have to lead a dignified life. She asserts that promotion of social justice involves supporting the capabilities of people who are denied opportunities and freedoms related to any of the core capabilities. See Exhibit 1.5 for an overview of the core capabilities identified by Nussbaum.

Critical Thinking Questions 1.3

What impact is globalization having on your own life? Do you see it as having a positive or negative impact on your life? What about for Manisha? Do you think globalization is having a positive or negative impact on her life? Do you agree with Martha Nussbaum that it is important for all people to have opportunities and freedoms in relation to the 10 core capabilities she identifies? How do you see Manisha in relation to these core capabilities?

KNOWING AND DOING

Social workers, like other professional practitioners, must find a way to move from knowing to doing, from "knowing about" and "knowing that" into "knowing how to" (for fuller discussion of this issue, see Hutchison, Charlesworth, Matto, Harrigan, & Viggiani, 2007). We *know* for the purpose of *doing*. Like architects, engineers, physicians, and teachers, social workers are faced with complex problems and case situations that are unique and uncertain. You no doubt will find that social work education, social work practice, and even this book will stretch your capacity to tolerate ambiguity and uncertainty. That is important because, as Carol Meyer (1993) has suggested, "There are no easy or simple [social work] cases, only simplistic perceptions" (p. 63). There are four important ingredients of "knowing how" to do social work: knowledge about the case, knowledge about the self, values and ethics, and scientific knowledge. These four ingredients are intertwined in the process of doing social work. The focus of this book is on scientific knowledge,

Exhibit 1.5   Nussbaum's 10 Core Capabilities

Capability	Definition
Life	To live to the end of a normal life course
Bodily health	To have good physical health and adequate nourishment and shelter
Bodily integrity	To exercise freedom of movement, freedom from assault, and reproductive choice
Senses, imagination, and thought	To have pleasant sensory experiences, pain avoidance, adequate education, imagination, free self-expression, and religious freedom
Emotion	To experience a full range of emotion and to love and be loved
Practical reason	To think critically and make wise decisions
Affiliation	To live with others with empathy and compassion, without discrimination
Concern for other species	To show concern for animals, plants, and other aspects of nature
Play	To laugh and play and enjoy recreational activities
Control over one's political and material environment	To participate freely in the political process and have equal access to employment and property

SOURCE: Nussbaum, 2011.

but all four ingredients are essential in social work practice. Before moving to a discussion of scientific knowledge, I want to say a word about the other three ingredients.

Knowledge About the Case

I am using *case* to mean the situation at hand, a situation that has become problematic for some person or collectivity, resulting in a social work intervention. Our first task as social workers is to develop as good an understanding of the situation as possible: Who is involved in the situation, and how are they involved? What is the nature of the relationships of the people involved? What are the physical, societal, cultural, and community contexts of the situation? What are the contextual constraints as well as the contextual resources for bringing change to the situation? What elements of the case are maintaining the problematic situation? How have people tried to cope with the situation? What preferences do the involved people have about the types of intervention to use? What is the culture, and what are the social resources of the

social agency to whose attention the situation is brought? You might begin to think about how you would answer some of these questions in relation to Manisha's situation.

It is important to note that knowledge about the case is influenced by the quality of the relationship between the social worker and client(s). There is good evidence that people are likely to reveal more aspects of their situation if they are approached with commitment, an open mind, warmth, empathic attunement, authentic responsiveness, and mutuality (Hepworth, Rooney, Rooney, & Strom-Gottfried, 2013). For example, as Manisha became comfortable in the interview, feeling validated by both the interviewer and the interpreter, she began to engage in deeper reflection about what happened in Bhutan. At the end of the interview, she expressed much gratitude for the opportunity to tell her story, noting that it was the first chance she had to put the story together and that telling the story had led her to think about some events in new ways. This can be an important part of her grieving and adjustment process. The integrity of knowledge about the case is related to the quality of the relationship, and the capacity for relationship is related to knowledge about the self.

But knowledge about the case requires more than simply gathering information. We must select and order the information at hand and decide if further information is needed. This involves making a series of decisions about what is relevant and what is not. It also involves searching for recurring themes as well as contradictions in the information. For example, it was important for the refugee resettlement social worker to note a strong theme of the desire for purpose and self-respect in Manisha's story in her early months in the United States. Equally important was the information that Manisha shared about the knitting project sponsored by Oxfam. This could provide a clue for further program development to meet the needs of the community of Bhutanese refugees. It was also important to note Manisha's lingering confusion about why her peaceful world in Bhutan got turned upside down. This suggests that Manisha and other Bhutanese refugees might benefit from narrative exercises that help them to make sense of these experiences.

To assist you in moving between knowledge about the case and scientific knowledge, each chapter in this book begins, as this one does, with one or more case studies. Each of these unique stories suggests what scientific knowledge is needed. For example, to work effectively with Manisha, you will want to understand some things about Bhutan, the Nepali ethnic group, Hinduism, grief reactions, the acculturation process, challenges facing immigrant families, and cross-cultural communication. Throughout the chapters, the stories are woven together with relevant scientific knowledge. Keep in mind that scientific knowledge is necessary, but you will not be an effective practitioner unless you take the time to learn about the unique situation of each person or collectivity you serve. It is the unique situation that guides what scientific knowledge is needed.

Knowledge About the Self

In his book *The Spiritual Life of Children*, Robert Coles (1990) wrote about the struggles of a 10-year-old Hopi girl to have her Anglo teacher understand Hopi spirituality. Coles suggested to the girl that perhaps she could try to explain her tribal nation's spiritual beliefs to the teacher. The girl answered, "But they don't listen to hear *us*; they listen to hear themselves" (p. 25, emphasis in the original). This young girl has captured, in a profound way, a major challenge to our everyday personal and professional communications: the tendency to approach the world with preconceived notions that we seek to validate by attending to some information while ignoring other information (Kahneman, 2011). The capacity to understand oneself is needed in order to tame this very human tendency.

Three types of self-knowledge are essential for social workers: understanding of one's own thinking processes, understanding of one's own emotions, and understanding of one's own social location. We must be able to think about our thinking, a process called *metacognition*. We all have biases that lead to thinking errors, and it is very difficult to get control of our biases. As Daniel Kahneman (2011) suggests in his book *Thinking Fast and Slow*, constant questioning of our own thinking can become tedious and immobilize us. The best we can do, therefore, is to understand the types of situations in which we are likely to make mistakes and slow down and use multiple sources of information to help correct for our biases. We also must be able to recognize what emotions get aroused in us when we hear stories like Manisha's and when we contemplate the challenges of the situation, and we must find a way to use those emotions in ways that are helpful and avoid using them in ways that are harmful. Although writing about physicians, Gunnar Biorck (1977) said it well when he commented that practitioners make "a tremendous number of judgments each day, based on inadequate, often ambiguous data, and under pressure of time, and carrying out this task with the outward appearance of calmness, dedication and interpersonal warmth" (p. 146).

In terms of social location, as suggested earlier, social workers must identify and reflect on where they fit in a system of social identities, such as race, ethnicity, gender, social class, sexual orientation, religion, ability/disability, and age. The literature on culturally sensitive social work practice proposes that a strong personal identity in relation to important societal categories, and an understanding of the impact of those identities on other people, is essential for successful social work intervention across cultural lines (see Lum, 2011). This type of self-knowledge requires reflecting on where one fits in systems of privilege.

Values and Ethics

The process of developing knowledge about the case is a dialogue between the social worker and client system, and social workers have a well-defined value base to guide the dialogue. Six core values of the profession have been set out in a preamble to the Code of Ethics established by the National Association of Social Workers (NASW) in 1996 and revised in 2008. These values are service, social justice, dignity and worth of the person, importance of human relationships, integrity, and competence. The value of social justice was discussed earlier in the chapter. As demonstrated in Exhibit 1.6, the Code of Ethics articulates an ethical principle

for each of the core values. Value 6, competence, requires that we recognize the science available to inform our work. It requires understanding the limitations of the available science for considering the situation at hand but also that we use the strongest available evidence to make practice decisions. This is where scientific knowledge comes into the picture.

Critical Thinking Questions 1.4

If you were the social worker at Manisha's refugee resettlement program when she first arrived in the United States, what "knowledge about the case" would you like to have? What information would you find most important? What emotional reactions did you have to reading Manisha's story? What did you find yourself thinking about her story? Where do you see Manisha fitting in systems of privilege? Where do you see yourself fitting? How might any of this impact your ability to be helpful to Manisha?

Exhibit 1.6   Core Values and Ethical Principles in the NASW Code of Ethics

1. **Value:** Service

   Ethical Principle: Social workers' primary goal is to help people in need and to address social problems.

2. **Value:** Social justice

   Ethical Principle: Social workers challenge social injustice.

3. **Value:** Dignity and worth of the person

   Ethical Principle: Social workers respect the inherent dignity and worth of the person.

4. **Value:** Importance of human relationships

   Ethical Principle: Social workers recognize the central importance of human relationships.

5. **Value:** Integrity

   Ethical Principle: Social workers behave in a trustworthy manner.

6. **Value:** Competence

   Ethical Principle: Social workers practice within their areas of competence and develop and enhance their professional expertise.

SOURCE: National Association of Social Workers, 2008.

SCIENTIFIC KNOWLEDGE: THEORY AND RESEARCH

Ethical social workers are always searching for or recalling what is known about the situations they encounter, turning to the social and behavioral sciences for this information. Scientific knowledge serves as a screen against which the knowledge about the case is considered. It suggests **hypotheses**, or tentative statements, to be explored and tested, not facts to be applied, in transactions with a person or group. Because of the breadth and complexity of social work practice, usable knowledge must be culled from diverse sources and a number of scientific disciplines. **Science**, also known as scientific inquiry, is a set of logical, systematic, documented methods for answering questions about the world. Scientific knowledge is the knowledge produced by scientific inquiry. Two interrelated approaches to knowledge building, theory and empirical research, fit the scientific criteria of being logical, systematic, and documented for the public. Together, they create the base of knowledge that social workers need to understand commonalities among their clients and practice situations. In your coursework on social work research, you will be learning much more about these concepts, so I only provide a brief description here to help you understand how this book draws on theory and research.

Theory

Social workers use theory to help organize and make sense of the situations they encounter. A **theory** is an interrelated set of concepts and propositions, organized into a deductive system, that explains relationships among aspects of our world. As Elaine Leeder (2004) so aptly put it, "To have a theory is to have a way of explaining the world—an understanding that the world is not just a random series of events and experiences" (p. 9). Thus, theory gives us a framework for interpreting person and environment and planning interventions. It seems to be human nature to develop theories to make sense of the world. As social workers we put our personal theories of the world to the test by studying theories proposed by serious scholars of human behavior. I want to emphasize that theories allow us to organize our thinking, but theories are not "fact" or "truth."

Other terms that you will often encounter in discussions of theories are *model*, *paradigm*, and *perspective*. *Model* usually is used to refer to a visual representation of the relationships between concepts, *paradigm* most often means a way of seeing the world, and *perspective* is an emphasis or a view. Paradigms and perspectives are broader and more general than theory.

If you are to make good use of theory, you should know something about how it is constructed. **Concepts** are the building blocks of theory. They are symbols, or mental images, that summarize observations, feelings, or ideas. Concepts allow us to communicate about the phenomena of interest. Some relevant concepts in Manisha's story are culture, Hinduism, Buddhism, cultural conflict, refugee, resettlement, acculturation, loss, and grief.

Theoretical concepts are put together to form **propositions**, or assertions. For example, loss and grief theory proposes that the loss of a person, object, or ideal leads to a grief reaction. This proposition, which asserts a particular relationship between the concepts of loss and grief, may help the refugee resettlement social worker understand some of the sadness, and sometimes despair, that she sees in her work with Bhutanese refugee families. They have lived with an accumulation of losses—loss of land, loss of livelihood, loss of roles, loss of status, loss of extended family members, loss of familiar language and rituals, and many more.

Theories are a form of **deductive reasoning**, meaning they lay out general, abstract propositions that we can use to generate specific hypotheses to test in unique situations. In this example, loss and grief theory can lead us to hypothesize that Bhutanese refugees are grieving the many losses they have suffered, but we should understand that this may not be the case with all Bhutanese refugees. Theory is about likelihood, not certainty.

Social and behavioral science theories are based on **assumptions**, or beliefs held to be true without testing or proof, about the nature of human social life. These theoretical assumptions have raised a number of controversies, three of which are worth introducing at this point.

1. Do the dimensions of human behavior have an **objective reality** that exists outside a person's consciousness, or is all reality based on personal perception (**subjective reality**)?

2. Is human behavior determined by forces beyond the control of the person (**determinism**), or are people free and proactive agents in the creation of their behavior (**voluntarism**)?

3. Are the patterned interactions among people characterized by harmony, unity, and social cohesion or by conflict, domination, coercion, and exploitation?

The nature of these controversies will become more apparent to you in Chapter 2. The contributing authors and I take a middle ground on all of them: We assume that reality has both objective and subjective aspects, that human behavior is partially constrained and partially free, and that social life is marked by both cohesion and conflict.

Empirical Research

Traditionally, science is equated with empirical research, which is widely held as the most rigorous and systematic way to understand human behavior. Research is typically viewed, in simple terms, as a problem-solving process, or a method of seeking answers to questions. If something is empirical, we experience it through our senses, as opposed to something we experience purely in our minds. The process of **empirical research** includes a careful, purposeful, and systematic observation of events with the intent to note and record them in terms of their attributes, to look for patterns in those events, and to make our methods and observations public. Each empirical research project is likely to raise new questions, often producing more questions than answers. The new questions become grist for future research. Like theory, empirical research is a key tool for social workers. It is important to understand, however, that empirical research informs us about probabilities, not certainties (Firestein, 2012). For example, research can tell us what percentage of parents who were abused as children will become abusive toward their own children, but it cannot tell us whether a specific parent who was abused as a child will become abusive toward his or her children. Social workers, of course, must make decisions about specific parents, recognizing the probabilities found in research as well as considering the knowledge about the case.

Just as there are controversies about theoretical assumptions, there are also controversies about what constitutes appropriate research methods for understanding human behavior. Modern science is based on several assumptions, which are generally recognized as a **positivist perspective**: The world has an order that can be discovered, findings of one study should be applicable to other groups, complex phenomena can be studied by reducing them to some component part, findings are tentative and subject to question, and scientific methods are value-free. **Quantitative methods of research** are preferred from the positivist perspective. These methods use quantifiable measures of concepts, standardize the collection of data, attend only to preselected variables, and use statistical measures to look for patterns and associations (Engel & Schutt, 2013).

Over the years, the positivist perspective and its claim that positivism = science have been challenged. Critics argue that quantitative methods cannot possibly capture the subjective experience of individuals or the complex nature of social life. Although most of these critics do not reject positivism as *a way* of doing science, they recommend other ways of understanding the world and suggest that these alternative methods should also be considered part of science. Various names have

Photo 1.3 Theories and research about human behavior are boundless and constantly growing. Active readers must question what they read.

© iStockphoto.com/Udo Weber

been given to these alternative methods. I refer to them as the **interpretist perspective**, because they share the assumption that reality is based on people's definitions of it and research should focus on learning the meanings that people give to their situations. This is also referred to as a *constructivist perspective*.

Interpretists see a need to replace quantitative methods with **qualitative methods of research**, which are more flexible and experiential and are designed to capture how participants view social life rather than to ask participants to respond to categories preset by the researcher (Engel & Schutt, 2013). Participant observation, intensive interviewing, and focus groups are examples of qualitative methods of research. Interpretists assume that people's behavior cannot be observed objectively,

that reality is created as the researcher and research participants interact. Researchers using qualitative methods are more likely to present their findings in words than in numbers and to attempt to capture the settings of behavior. They are likely to report the transactions of the researcher and participant as well as the values of the researcher, because they assume that value-free research is impossible.

In this controversy, it is our position that no single research method can adequately capture the whole, the complexity, of human behavior. Both quantitative and qualitative research methods have a place in a multidimensional approach, and used together they may help us to see more dimensions of situations. This view has much in common with postpositivism, which developed in response to criticism of positivism. **Postpositivism** is a philosophical position that recognizes the complexity of reality and the limitations of human observers. It proposes that scientists can never develop more than a partial understanding of human behavior (Engel & Schutt, 2013). Neuroscientist Stuart Firestein (2012) reminds us that we must learn to live with "unknowable unknowns" (p. 30) and become capable of working with uncertainties. Nevertheless, science remains the most rigorous and systematic way to understand human behavior.

Critical Use of Theory and Research

You may already know that social and behavioral science theory and research have been growing at a fast pace in modern times, and you will often feel, as McAvoy (1999) aptly put it, that you are "drowning in a swamp of information" (p. 19), both case information and scientific information. Ironically, as you are drowning in a swamp of information, you will also be discovering that the available scientific information is incomplete. You will also encounter contradictory theoretical propositions and research results that must be held simultaneously and, where possible, coordinated to develop an integrated picture of the situation at hand. That is, as you might guess, not a simple project. It involves weighing available evidence and analyzing its relevance to the situation at hand. That requires critical thinking. **Critical thinking** is a thoughtful and reflective judgment about alternative views and contradictory information. It involves thinking about your own thinking and the influences on that thinking, as well as a willingness to change your mind. It also involves careful analysis of assumptions and evidence. Critical thinkers also ask, "What is left out of this conceptualization or research?" "What new questions are raised by this research finding?" Throughout the book, we call out critical thinking questions to support your efforts to think critically.

As you read this book and other sources of scientific knowledge, begin to think critically about the theory and research they present. Give careful thought to the credibility of the claims made. Let's look first at theory. It is important to remember that although theorists may try to put checks on their biases, they write from their own cultural frame of reference, from a particular location in the social structure of their society, and from life experiences. So, when taking a critical look at a theory, it is important to remember that theories are generally created by people of privileged backgrounds who operate in seats of power. The bulk of theories still used today were authored by White, middle- to upper-class Western European men and men in the United States with academic appointments. Therefore, as we work in a highly diversified world, we need to be attentive to the possibilities of biases related to race, gender, culture, religion, sexual orientation, abilities/disabilities, and social class—as well as professional or occupational orientation. One particular concern is that such biases can lead us to think of disadvantaged members of society or of members of minority groups as pathological or deficient.

Social and behavioral science scholars disagree about the criteria for evaluating theory and research. However, I recommend the criteria presented in Exhibit 1.7 because they are consistent with the multidimensional approach of this book and with the value base of the social work profession. (The five criteria for evaluating theory presented in Exhibit 1.7 are also used in Chapter 2 to evaluate eight theoretical perspectives relevant to social work.) There is agreement in the social and behavioral sciences that theory should be evaluated for coherence and conceptual clarity as well as for testability and evidence of empirical support. The criterion of comprehensiveness is specifically related to the multidimensional approach of this book. We do not expect all theories to be multidimensional, but critical analysis of a theory should help us identify deterministic and unidimensional thinking where they exist. The criterion of consistency with emphasis on diversity and power arrangements examines the utility of the theory for a profession that places high value on social justice, and the criterion of usefulness for practice is essential for a profession.

Just as theory may be biased toward the experiences of members of dominant groups, so too may

Exhibit 1.7   Criteria for Evaluating Theory and Research

Criteria for Evaluating Theory

Coherence and conceptual clarity. Are the concepts clearly defined and consistently used? Is the theory free of logical inconsistencies? Is it stated in the simplest possible way, without oversimplifying?

Testability and evidence of empirical support. Can the concepts and propositions be expressed in language that makes them observable and accessible to corroboration or refutation by persons other than the theoretician? Is there evidence of empirical support for the theory?

Comprehensiveness. Does the theory include multiple dimensions of persons, environments, and time? What is included and what is excluded? What dimension(s) is (are) emphasized? Does the theory account for things that other theories have overlooked or been unable to account for?

Consistency with social work's emphasis on diversity and power arrangements. Can the theory help us understand diversity? How inclusive is it? Does it avoid pathologizing members of minority groups? Does it assist in understanding power arrangements and systems of oppression?

Usefulness for social work practice. Does the theory assist in the understanding of person–environment transactions over time? Can principles of action be derived from the theory? At what levels of practice can the theory be used? Can the theory be used in practice in a way that is consistent with the NASW Code of Ethics?

Criteria for Evaluating Research

Corroboration. Are the research findings corroborated by other researchers? Are a variety of research methods used in corroborating research? Do the findings fit logically with accepted theory and other research findings?

Multidimensionality. Does the research include multiple dimensions of persons, environments, and time? If not, do the researchers acknowledge the omissions, connect the research to larger programs of research that include omitted dimensions, or recommend further research to include omitted dimensions?

Definition of terms. Are major variables defined and measured in such a way as to avoid bias against members of minority groups?

Limitation of sample. Does the researcher make sufficient effort to include diversity in the sample? Are minority groups represented in sufficient numbers to show the variability within them? When demographic groups are compared, are they equivalent on important variables? Does the researcher specify the limitations of the sample for generalizing to specific groups?

Influence of setting. Does the researcher specify attributes of the setting of the research, acknowledge the possible contribution of the setting to research outcomes, and present the findings of similar research across a range of settings?

Influence of the researcher. Does the researcher specify his or her attributes and role in the observed situations? Does the researcher specify his or her possible contributions to research outcomes?

Social distance. Does the researcher attempt to minimize errors that could occur because of literacy, language, and cultural differences between the researcher and respondents?

Specification of inferences. Does the researcher specify how inferences are made, based on the data? What biases, if any, do you identify in the inferences?

Suitability of measures. Does the researcher use measures that seem suited to, and sensitive to, the situation being researched?

research be biased. The results may be misleading, and the interpretation of results may lead to false conclusions about members of minority groups. Bias can occur at all stages of the research process.

• Funding sources and other vested interests have a strong influence on which problems are selected for research attention. As I write this, there is much controversy about how gun violence research was frozen in the United States in 1996 when Congress, under pressure from the National Rifle Association, passed legislation that banned funding by the Centers for Disease Control for research that could be used to advocate or promote gun control (American Psychological Association, 2013).

- Bias can occur in the definition of variables for study. For example, using "offenses cleared by arrests" as the definition of crime, rather than using a definition such as "self-reported crime involvement," may lead to an overestimation of crime among minority groups of color, because those are the people who are most often arrested for their crimes (Ritzer, 2013a).

- Bias can occur in choosing the sample to be studied. Because there are fewer of them, members of minority groups may not be included in sufficient numbers to demonstrate the variability within a particular minority group. Or a biased sample of minorities may be used (e.g., it is not uncommon to make Black/White comparisons on a sample that includes middle-class Whites and low-income Blacks). Recent analysis of articles in the major behavioral science journals indicates that most of the samples are drawn almost exclusively from Western, educated, industrialized, and democratic (WEIRD) societies (Henrich, Heine, & Norenzayan, 2010). This same analysis concludes that these research participants are different from most other people of the world in important ways. We need to keep this in mind as we review available empirical research.

- Bias can occur in data collection. The validity and reliability of most standardized measuring instruments have been evaluated by using them with White, non-Hispanic male respondents, and their cultural relevance with people of color, women, impoverished persons, or members of other groups is questionable. Language and literacy difficulties may arise with both written survey instruments and interviews. Some groups may be reluctant to participate in research because they don't trust the motives of the researchers.

- Bias can occur in interpretation of the data, because empirical research typically fails to produce uncontestable results (Firestein, 2012).

As with theory evaluation, there is no universally agreed-upon set of criteria for evaluating research. I recommend the nine criteria presented in Exhibit 1.7 for considering the credibility of a research report. These criteria can be applied to either quantitative or qualitative research. Many research reports would be strengthened if their authors were to attend to these criteria.

Critical Thinking Questions 1.5

If I drew a line on the floor with objective reality at one end and subjective reality at the other end, where would you place yourself on the line to demonstrate your own understanding of human behavior?

Objective Reality _____ Subjective Reality

And, if I drew another line with determinism at one end and voluntarism at the other end, where would you place yourself on this line?

Determinism _____ Voluntarism

And, if I drew a third line with harmony, unity, and social cohesion on one end and conflict, domination, coercion, and exploitation at the other end, where would you place yourself on this line to demonstrate your theory about what happens in human social interaction?

Harmony, Unity, _____ Conflict, Domination, Social Cohesion   Coercion, Exploitation

A WORD OF CAUTION_____

In this book, Part I includes two stage-setting chapters that introduce the framework for the book and provide a foundation for thinking critically about the discussions of theory and research presented in Parts II and III. Part II comprises four chapters that analyze the multiple dimensions of persons—one chapter each on the biological person, the psychological person (or the self), the psychosocial person (or the self in relationship), and the spiritual person. The eight chapters of Part III discuss the environmental dimensions: the physical environment, culture, social structure and social institutions, families, small groups, formal organizations, communities, and social movements.

Presenting personal and environmental dimensions separately is a risky approach. I do not wish to reinforce any tendency to think about human behavior in a way that camouflages the inseparability of person and environment. I have taken this approach, however, for two reasons. First, the personal and environmental dimensions have, for the most part, been studied separately, often by different disciplines. Second, I want to introduce some dimensions of persons and environments not typically covered in social work textbooks and provide updated knowledge about all the dimensions. Third, I want to ensure that collective behavior receives the attention I think it deserves. However, it is important to remember that no single dimension of human behavior can be understood without attention to other dimensions. Thus, frequent references to other dimensions throughout Parts II and III should help develop an understanding of the unity of persons, environments, and time.

Implications for Social Work Practice

The multidimensional approach outlined in this chapter suggests several principles for social work assessment and intervention, for both prevention and remediation services.

- In the assessment process, collect information about all the critical dimensions of the changing configuration of person and environment.
- In the assessment process, attempt to see the situation from a variety of perspectives. Use multiple data sources, including the person(s), significant others, and direct observations.
- Allow people to tell their own stories and pay attention to how they describe the pattern and flow of their person–environment configurations.
- Use the multidimensional database of information about critical dimensions of the situation to develop a dynamic picture of the person–environment configuration.
- Link intervention strategies to the dimensions of the assessment.
- In general, expect more effective outcomes from interventions that are multidimensional, because the situation itself is multidimensional.
- Pay particular attention to the impact of diversity and inequality on the unique stories and situations that you encounter.
- Allow the unique stories of people and situations to direct the choice of theory and research to be used.
- Use scientific knowledge to suggest tentative hypotheses to be explored in the unique situation.

Key Terms

assumptions	deductive reasoning	empirical research
biopsychosocial approach	determinism	globalization
concepts	dimension	heterogeneity
critical thinking	diversity	hypotheses

interpretist perspective
linear time
multidetermined behavior
multidimensional
objective reality
positivist perspective

postpositivism
privilege
propositions
qualitative methods of research
quantitative methods of research
science

subjective reality
theory
time orientation
voluntarism

Active Learning

1. We have used multiple dimensions of person, environment, and time to think about Manisha's story. If you were the social worker at the refugee resettlement agency that sponsored her family's resettlement, you would bring your own unfolding person–environment–time story to that encounter. With the graphic in Exhibit 1.1 as your guide, write your own multidimensional story. What personal dimensions are important? What environmental dimensions? What time dimensions? What might happen when these two stories encounter each other?

2. Select a social issue that interests you, such as child abuse or youth gangs. List five things you "know" about this issue. Think about how you know what you know. How would you go about confirming or disproving your current state of knowledge on this topic?

Web Resources

No doubt, you use the Internet in many different ways and know your way around it. I hope that when you find something in this book that confuses you or intrigues you, you will use the incredibly rich resources of the Internet to do further exploration. To help you get started with this process, each chapter of this textbook contains a list of Internet resources and websites that may be useful to readers in their search for further information. Each site listing includes the address and a brief description of the contents of the site. Readers should be aware that the information contained on websites may not be truthful or reliable and should be confirmed before the site is used as a reference. Readers should also be aware that Internet addresses, or URLs, are constantly changing; therefore, the addresses listed may no longer be active or accurate. Many of the Internet sites listed in each chapter contain links to other sites containing more information on the topic. Readers may use these links for further investigation.

Information on topics not included in the Web Resources sections of each chapter can be found by using one of the many Internet search engines provided free of charge on the Internet. These search engines enable you to search using keywords or phrases, or you can use the search engines' topical listings. You should use several search engines when researching a topic, as each will retrieve different Internet sites. We list the search engines first.

Aol Search: http://search.aol.com

Ask: www.ask.com

bing: www.bing.com

Google: www.google.com

YAHOO! http://search.yahoo.com

There are several Internet sites maintained by and for social workers, some at university schools of social work and some by professional associations:

Council on Social Work Education (CSWE): www.cswe.org

CSWE is the accrediting body for academic social work programs; site contains information about accreditation, projects, and publications.

Information for Practice: http://ifp.nyu.edu

Site developed and maintained by Professor Gary Holden of New York University's School of Social Work contains links to many federal and state Internet sites as well as journals, assessment and measurement tools, and sites maintained by professional associations.

International Federation of Social Workers: www.ifsw.org

Site contains information about international conferences, policy papers on selected issues, and links to human rights groups and other social work organizations.

National Association of Social Workers (NASW): www.naswdc.org

Site contains professional development material, press room, advocacy information, and resources.

Society for Social Work and Research (SSWR): www.sswr.org

SSWR is a nonprofit organization devoted to involving social workers in research and research applications. Site contains research news, job postings, and links to social work–related websites.

Student Study Site

⑤SAGE edge™

Sharpen your skills with SAGE edge at **edge.sagepub.com/hutchisonpe5e**

SAGE edge for students provides a personalized approach to help you accomplish your coursework goals in an easy-to-use learning environment.

CHAPTER 2

Theoretical Perspectives on Human Behavior

Elizabeth D. Hutchison, Leanne Wood Charlesworth, and Cory Cummings

Key Ideas

As you read this chapter, take note of these central ideas:

1. The systems perspective sees human behavior as the outcome of reciprocal interactions of persons operating within linked social systems.

2. The conflict perspective draws attention to conflict, inequality, dominance, and oppression in social life.

3. The exchange and choice perspective focuses on the processes whereby individual and collective actors seek and exchange resources and the choices made in pursuit of those resources.

4. The social constructionist perspective focuses on how people learn, through their interactions with each other, to understand the world and their place in it.

5. The psychodynamic perspective is concerned with how internal processes such as psychological needs, drives, and emotions motivate human behavior.

6. The developmental perspective focuses on how human behavior unfolds across the life course.

7. The social behavioral perspective suggests that human behavior is learned as individuals interact with their environments.

8. The humanistic perspective emphasizes the individual's inherent value, freedom of action, and search for meaning.

CASE STUDY

Intergenerational Stresses in the McKinley Family

The hospice social worker meets three generations of McKinleys when she visits their home in an upper-midwestern city. She is there because the family has requested hospice services for Ruth McKinley, the 79-year-old mother of Stanley McKinley. Ruth has a recurrence of breast cancer that has metastasized to her lungs; she is no longer receiving aggressive treatment, and her condition is deteriorating. Upon entering the house, the social worker meets 50-year-old Stanley, his 51-year-old wife, Marcia, and their 25-year-old daughter, Bethany, who takes the social worker to a bedroom to meet her grandmother. She gives Ruth a gentle pat and introduces the social worker. Ruth smiles at Bethany and greets the social worker. Bethany leaves the room to give some privacy to the social worker and her grandmother. The social worker spends about 20 minutes with Ruth and finds her weak but interested in talking. Ruth says she knows that she is receiving hospice care because she is dying. She says she has lived a good life and is not afraid of dying. She goes on to say, however, that there are some things on her mind as she thinks about her life. She is thinking a lot about her estranged daughter who lives several states away, and she does not want to die with this "hardness between us." She also is thinking a lot about Stanley, who is unemployed, and hoping that he can find a spark in his life again. Bethany is very much on her mind, as well. She says she worries that Bethany is sacrificing too much of her young life to the needs of the family. As Ruth grows tired, the social worker ends the conversation, saying that she would like to visit with Ruth again next week so that they can talk some more about Ruth's life and the things that are on her mind.

Back in the living room, the social worker talks with Stanley, Marcia, and Bethany. She learns that Ruth moved into Stanley and Marcia's home 5 years ago after she had a stroke that left her with left-sided paralysis. At that time, Stanley and Marcia took out a second mortgage on their house to finance some remodeling to make the home more accessible for Ruth, providing her with a bedroom and bathroom downstairs. They also put in a much-needed new furnace at the same time. Bethany speaks up to say that her grandmother is the kindest person she knows and that they were all happy to rearrange their home life to make Ruth comfortable. Marcia notes that it seemed the natural thing to do, because Ruth had taken care of Bethany while Marcia worked during Bethany's early years. After Ruth came to live with them, Stanley continued to work at a print shop, and Marcia changed to the evening shift in her job as a police dispatcher. Bethany arranged her work and part-time community college studies so that she could be available to her grandmother between the time her mother left for work and her father returned from his workday. She took charge of preparing dinner for her dad and grandmother and giving Ruth a daily bath.

This arrangement worked well for 4 years. Bethany speaks fondly of the good times she and her grandmother had together as Bethany provided direct care to her grandmother, and her grandmother showered her with stories of the past and took a lively interest in her life, often giving her advice about her romantic life. Marcia breaks in to say that life has been tough for the past year, however, and her voice cracks as she says this. She recounts that they learned of the recurrence of Ruth's breast cancer 11 months ago and of the metastasis 5 months ago. For a few months, Stanley, Marcia, and Bethany juggled their schedules to get Ruth to doctor visits, chemotherapy treatments, and bone scans, until Ruth and the oncologist decided that it was time to discontinue aggressive treatment.

Then, 7 months ago, Stanley lost his job at the printing company where he had worked since getting out of the army, and he has been unsuccessful in finding new work. They were still managing financially with the help of unemployment checks until Marcia took a tumble down the stairs and injured her back and hip 4 months ago. She had surgery, which was followed by complications, and has been out of work on disability. She is expecting to go back to work next week. Bethany says she has wanted to work more to bring more money into the home, but she has also been needed at home more to fill in for Marcia. She lost one job because of too many absences and has pieced together two part-time jobs that give her a little more flexibility. She worries, however, about having no health insurance because she needs ongoing treatment for asthma and hears so many different stories about how the Affordable Care Act will affect her. Marcia says that Stanley has been a wonderful caregiver to her and his mom, but she knows that the caregiving has interfered with his job search and is wearing him down.

Stanley enters the conversation to report that they have been unable to make mortgage payments for the past 3 months, and the bank has notified him that they are at risk of facing foreclosure. He becomes despondent as he relates this. He says they have been in the house for 15 years and had always paid the mortgage on time. The

(Continued)

(Continued)

second mortgage for the remodeling is adding to the current financial pinch. He says he is in a quandary about what to do. Marcia is going back to work soon, but she is still not strong enough to provide much physical care to Ruth. In addition, Stanley is not at all optimistic that he will find a job in the near future. His former boss has now closed the printing shop because she lost some of her large clients. Stanley wonders if he should retrain for another occupation but knows that this is not a good time for him to try to do that, with his mother's deteriorating condition.

Bethany suggests that she take some time off from school and find a job working nights so that she can give her dad time to look for jobs during the day. She has graduated from community college and been accepted into a bachelor's degree program in nursing. She says she is feeling too sad about her grandmother and too worried about the family's future to do well in school anyway. Besides that, she would like to be able to spend more time with her grandmother before she dies. At this point, Marcia breaks down and cries, sobbing that she just wants to give up: "We work so hard, but nothing goes our way. I don't know where we will go if we lose the house."

As the family talks about their problems and possible solutions, the social worker recalls that she has heard something about a community program that provides counseling to people who are in jeopardy of home foreclosure. She wonders if that could help the McKinley family.

MULTIPLE PERSPECTIVES FOR A MULTIDIMENSIONAL APPROACH

As you think about the details of the unfolding story of the multigenerational McKinley family, you may discover that you have some theory or theories of your own about what is happening with them and what can and should be done to help them. If we asked you what caught your attention as you read the story, we would begin to learn something about your theory or theories of human behavior, as you have developed it or them so far. There is much information in the case material as presented, but the case may have raised questions for you as well, and left you wanting more information. What you see as gaps in the information might also tell us something about your theory or theories. Theories help us organize vast and multifaceted information. The purposes of this chapter are twofold: first, to help you identify and refine your own theory or theories of human behavior and, second, to help you think critically about commonly used formal theories of human behavior that have been developed by behavioral science scholars.

There is general agreement that contemporary social workers must use a range of theories that draw on a number of disciplines to help them understand the practice situations they encounter and to see the possibilities for change. As we have come more and more to recognize that human behavior is multidimensional, we have also recognized the need for multiple disciplines and a multitheoretical framework to understand it (Bell, 2012; Melchert, 2013). There are many theories from which to draw, general theories of human behavior as well as theories designed to understand the specific dimensions of person and environment covered in this book. There are also a number of ways of organizing existing theories into categories or perspectives. We have organized them into eight broad perspectives: the systems perspective, conflict perspective, exchange and choice perspective, social constructionist perspective, psychodynamic perspective, developmental perspective, social behavioral perspective, and humanistic perspective.

We have selected these eight perspectives for a number of reasons. Each has a wide range of applications across dimensions of human behavior and is used in empirical research. Each has been reconceptualized and extended over time to keep current with rapid knowledge development. Each paid little attention to diversity, and most paid little attention to inequality in early versions, but each has evolved over time to address both diversity and inequality. Each is European American in heritage, but in recent years, each has been influenced by thinking in other regions of the world. Some of the perspectives had interdisciplinary roots in their early versions, and each has benefited by collaboration across disciplines in more recent refinement and elaboration. Some blurring of the lines between perspectives has begun to occur. Theorists are being influenced by each other, as well as by societal changes, and have begun to borrow ideas from each other and to build new theory by combining aspects of existing theory. As you can see, theory, like other aspects of human behavior, is ever-changing.

Each of the perspectives presented in this chapter comprises a number of diverse theories. We present the "big ideas" of each perspective and not a detailed discussion of the various theories within the perspective. Although we trace the development of each perspective over time, we pay particular attention to some of the recent extensions of the perspectives that seem most useful in contemporary times. If you are interested in a more in-depth look at these theoretical perspectives, there are many resources to help you do this.

We introduce the perspectives in this chapter, and you will see variations of them throughout subsequent chapters where theory and research about specific dimensions of person and environment are explored. Margin notes are used in Chapters 3 through 14 to help you recognize ideas from the perspectives presented in this chapter. We hope that these linkages will help you in your efforts to better understand theory and how it is used in scientific inquiry.

In this chapter, in addition to presenting an overview of the big ideas, we analyze the scientific merit of the perspectives and their usefulness for social work practice. The five criteria for critical understanding of theory identified in Chapter 1 provide the framework for our discussion of the perspectives: coherence and conceptual clarity, testability and empirical support, comprehensiveness, consistency with social work's emphasis on diversity and power arrangements, and usefulness for social work practice.

SYSTEMS PERSPECTIVE

When you read the case study at the beginning of this chapter, you probably thought of it as a story about a family system—a story about Ruth, Stanley, Marcia, and Bethany McKinley—rather than "Ruth McKinley's story," even though the hospice case file reads "Ruth McKinley." You may have noted how Ruth's, Stanley's, Marcia's, and Bethany's lives are interrelated, how they influence one another's behavior, and what impact each of them has on the overall well-being of the family. You may be thinking about the changing health statuses of Ruth and Marcia and about how the family members keep adjusting their caregiving roles to accommodate changing care needs. You also may note that this family, like other families, has a **boundary** indicating who is in and who is out, and you may be wondering if the boundary around this family allows sufficient input from friends, extended family, neighbors, religious organizations, and so on. You probably have noted the influence of larger systems on this family, particularly the insecurities in the labor market and the gaps in the health care system. For example, Medicare coverage for hospice care is an important resource for the family as they cope with the end-of-life care needs of Ruth. These are some of the ideas that the systems perspective suggests for understanding what is happening in the McKinley family.

The **systems perspective** sees human behavior as the outcome of interactions within and among systems of interrelated parts. Its roots are very interdisciplinary, and there are many theoretical variations. During the 1940s and 1950s, a variety of disciplines—including mathematics, physics, engineering, biology, psychology, cultural anthropology, economics, and sociology—began looking at phenomena as the outcome of interactions within and among systems. Mathematicians and engineers used the new ideas about system **feedback mechanisms**—the processes by which information about past behaviors in a system are fed back into the system in a circular manner—to develop military and communication technologies. The development of the computer and sophisticated computer models for analyzing information has influenced continuous revision of the systems perspective. Exhibit 2.1 provides a visual representation of the systems perspective.

Social workers were attracted to the systems perspective in the 1960s, and *general systems theory* was the dominant theoretical perspective in the social work literature during the 1960s and 1970s. This approach was based primarily on the work of biologist Ludwig von Bertalanffy, who defined systems as "sets of elements standing in interrelation" (von Bertalanffy, 1969, p. 38). He proposed that any element is best understood by considering its interactions with its constituent parts as well as its interactions with larger systems of which it is a part. For example, the McKinley family is best understood by considering the interactions among the family members as well as the interactions the family has with other social systems, such as their neighborhood, the health care system, workplace systems, and educational systems. Von Bertalanffy identified two types of systems: closed systems and open systems. A *closed system* is isolated from other systems in its environment. An *open system* is in constant interaction with other systems. He emphasized that feedback mechanisms produce both stability (homeostasis) and change within and across systems. Socially and geographically isolated families and communities could be considered examples of closed systems. Internet-based social networks are examples of open systems.

In the 1980s, *ecological theory*, also known as ecosystems theory, became popular across several disciplines, including social work. This theory comes from the field of ecology, which focuses on the relationships and interactions between living organisms and their environments. Interdependence and mutual influence are emphasized. The environment exerts influence on an individual, family, or group, but individuals, families, and groups can also have an impact on external systems. Social workers who promoted the ecological perspective called for a holistic view of practice situations that considers the multiple environmental

Exhibit 2.1   Systems Perspective

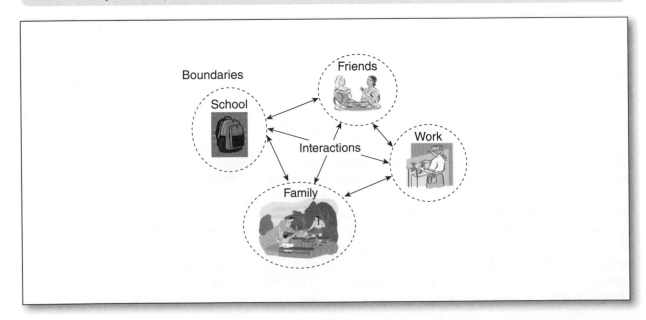

influences involved (Germain & Gitterman, 1996). The ecological perspective extended general systems theory by considering the important role of physical as well as social environments in human behavior.

Influenced by scientific inquiry in a number of disciplines, several new systems theories have emerged in the last 2 decades or so. Taken as a whole, these new theories are attempting to explain the complexity of contemporary life. One approach often used in social work is *risk and resilience theory*, which is an extension of the ecological perspective. It draws on concepts from epidemiology and public health to explain the complexity of influences on human behavior. This theory proposes risk factors and protective factors in both the person and the environment. Risk factors increase the likelihood of a harmful outcome of person and environment interactions, and protective factors support a positive outcome (see Jenson & Fraser, 2011). Proponents of the risk and resilience approach acknowledge the uncertainty of human behavior that derives from the complexity of influences on it.

Complex systems theory proposes that we are all part of numerous interacting systems that are linked through many dense interconnections (think of your social system including your Facebook, Instagram, or Twitter networks). These complex interactions produce uncertainty and unpredictability (Fuchs, 2013). Systems, including systems of human behavior theory, are always evolving toward greater complexity (Green & McDermott, 2010).

Chaos theory suggests that although it appears that the complexity of numerous interacting systems produces disorder, there is actually an underlying order that can only be discovered by analysis using complex computer models (Gleick, 2008). Chaos theory recognizes *negative feedback loops* that work like a thermostat to feed back information that the system is deviating from a steady state and needs to take corrective action as important processes that promote system stability. In addition, it proposes that complex systems produce *positive feedback loops* that feed back information

about deviation, or should we say innovation, into the steady state in such a way that the deviation reverberates throughout the system and potentially produces change, sometimes even rapid change. The change-producing feedback may come from within the system or from other systems in the environment. Small random changes in any area can lead to rapid large-scale change. Chaos theory has been recommended as a useful approach for clinical social workers and clinical psychologists as they assist clients in trying new solutions to long-standing problems (Lee, 2008) and to re-create themselves in times of transition (Bussolari & Goodell, 2009). Examples of such problems and transitions include addiction recovery and intimate partner violence.

Complex systems and chaos theories propose that it is the openness of systems that produces complexity. European social workers (see Ahmed-Mohamed, 2011; Kihlström, 2012) are drawing on another systems theory that conceptualizes the openness of systems in a very different way.

Photo 2.1 The pieces of this globe come together to form a unified whole—each part interacts and influences the other parts—but the pieces are interdependent, as suggested by the systems perspective.

© iStockphoto.com/Vipin Babu

German sociologist Niklas Luhmann (2011) has proposed a systems theory that suggests that in highly complex societies systems must find a way to reduce complexity to make life more manageable. They do this by developing cultures and structures that clearly differentiate the system from other systems. Systems are open to interaction with other systems, but they are operatively closed, meaning that system behavior is influenced only by the system's operations, its language, culture, and processes, not by the language, culture, and processes of other systems. The environment can affect the system only by causing it irritations or disruptions, but the system will have its own conditions for responding to these irritations. Luhmann argues that systems are *autopoietic*, meaning they are self-created and reproduced. As we write this in July 2013, we are thinking about the U.S. Supreme Court ruling (United States v. Windsor, 2013) regarding the Defense of Marriage Act, a ruling that found the act unconstitutional and determined that same-sex couples in recognized marriages could not be treated differently from other married couples in terms of federal benefits. Luhmann's approach would suggest that the gay rights movement and changing public opinion about same-sex marriage were irritations in the judicial system, but the system used its own language and processes to come to a decision.

Other newer systems theories take other positions on the issue of boundaries. While Luhmann argues that boundaries between systems are clear and tight, some social work scholars (see DePoy & Gilson, 2012) suggest that social workers might benefit by considering *fuzzy set theory* developed in mathematics. Fuzzy set theory proposes that membership of a set is not binary—meaning you are either a member or you are not. You may be a member to a certain degree. In fuzzy sets, objects are assigned a number from 0 to 1 to indicate the degree to which the object belongs in the set. From this perspective, I am wondering what value we would give to Ruth McKinley's estranged daughter in relation to the family system described in this story. Would you give her a value of 0 or 1, or would you say her membership lies somewhere between "member" and "not member"? Reisch and Jani (2012) suggest that social workers should consider such theories that recognize the blurring of system boundaries in complex societies. As DePoy and Gilson (2012) suggest, fuzzy set theory could be a useful way to think about issues such as group membership, including race and ethnicity; for example, where should Barack Obama fit in racial categories?

Other theories emphasize the openness of systems. *Deep ecology* has emerged with an emphasis on the notion of the total interconnectedness of all elements of the natural and physical world (Besthorn, 2012). Sociologist John Clammer (2009) suggests that deep ecology, with its addition of connections to the natural and physical worlds, can help to bridge Western and Eastern social science. The emerging *globalization theories* also emphasize the openness of systems, calling our attention to, among other things, how Stanley McKinley's job opportunities are connected to the increasingly globalized economy (Giddens, 2000).

This is how the criteria for evaluating theory apply to the systems perspective:

- *Coherence and conceptual clarity.* Although it has been popular over time, the systems perspective is often criticized as vague and somewhat ambiguous. Although consistency in use of terms has improved in recent theorizing, concepts in these theories remain highly abstract and often confusing in their generality. Chaos theory and complexity theory emerged in applied mathematics, and concepts from them are still being developed in the social sciences. Social work scholars have not yet stated or explained the concepts of these theories in the simplest and clearest way possible. An article by Mo Yee Lee (2008) made great progress in this area.

- *Testability and empirical support.* Poorly defined and highly abstract concepts are difficult to translate into measurable variables for research. Nevertheless, a long tradition of research supporting a systems perspective can be found in anthropology and sociology (see White, Klein, & Martin, 2015a, for a discussion of the use of the systems perspective to study family systems). The systems perspective has been greatly strengthened in recent years with developments in neuroscience, epidemiology, and a rapidly expanding empirical literature on ecological risk and resilience. Research methods, such as lengthy time series analyses, have been developed in the natural and social sciences for studying concepts of chaos and complexity, but these methods are still rarely used in social work. Likewise, mathematicians have developed fuzzy logic systems for analyzing membership in fuzzy sets that are beginning to be used in the social as well as natural sciences but are not yet used by social work researchers.

- *Comprehensiveness.* Clearly, the systems perspective is devoted to the ideal of comprehensiveness, or holism. It can, and has, incorporated the various dimensions of human systems as well as various dimensions of environmental systems, nonhuman as well as human. It does better than the other perspectives discussed here in accommodating rapid developments in neuroscience. Systems theorists recognize—even if they do not always make clear—the social, cultural, economic, and political environments of human behavior. They acknowledge the role of external influences and demands in creating and maintaining patterns of interaction within the system. Recent formulations have explicitly added a time dimension to accommodate both past and future influences on human behavior (see Bronfenbrenner, 2005). Certainly, chaos theory and complexity theory give implicit, if not always explicit, attention to time with their emphasis on dynamic change. Globalization theory calls attention to the impact of innovative and rapid communications on world systems.

- *Diversity and power.* Although diversity is not addressed in most systems theorizing, recent versions of the systems perspective, with their attention to complexity and continuous dynamic change, open many possibilities for diversity. Furthermore, while most systems theorists do not address the role of power in systems transactions, some can accommodate the idea of power differentials better than others. Traditional systems theories influenced by functionalist sociology assumed that social systems are held together by social consensus and shared values. The emphasis on system stability can rightly be criticized as socially conservative and oppressive to those who lack power within the system. Contemporary systems theory has begun to recognize power and oppression; conflict is seen as necessary for change in chaos theory; and some versions of globalization theory call attention to how powerful nations exploit the cultures, economies, and political arrangements of less powerful nations (McMichael, 2012).

- *Usefulness for social work practice.* The systems perspective is perhaps more useful for understanding human behavior than for directing social work interventions, but several social work practice textbooks were based on the systems perspective in the 1970s and 1980s. The risk and resilience approach is informative for both program and policy development, suggesting ways to reduce risk and increase protection. The greatest value of the systems perspective is that it can be used at any level of practice. It also has merit because it surpasses other perspectives in suggesting that we should widen the scope of assessment and intervention and expect better outcomes from multidimensional interventions. Chaos theory can be used by social workers to input information into a client system to facilitate rapid change, thereby enhancing possibilities for brief treatment; group process can be used as reverberating feedback to produce change. Social workers who work from a family systems perspective have for some time used methods such as family genograms, and other forms of feedback about the family, as information that can produce change as it reverberates through the family system. Mo Yee Lee (2008) provides a number of examples of how clinical social workers can use chaos and turbulence to help clients open to new ways of looking at and resolving problems.

CONFLICT PERSPECTIVE

As she thinks about the McKinley family, the hospice social worker is struck by Stanley and Marcia's growing sense of powerlessness to manage the trajectories of their lives. A major theme in their story, like the stories of so many other families, is lack of power in both the labor market and the housing market. Worries about access to health care are another part of the story, and one is reminded of ongoing political debates about health care funding. As we write this in July 2013, it remains to be seen what impact the federal health insurance law passed in March 2010 will have on families like the McKinleys. While the systems perspective helps us think about how interdependent the family members are, you may be thinking that they have some competing interests in relation to scarce resources of time and money. The hospice social worker knows that communications can become tense in families facing similar situations of scarce resources, and she wants to know more about how the McKinley family negotiates competing interests. She is also curious about the history of gender roles in this family and how those have been affected by Stanley's unemployment. These are some of the observations about the McKinley family suggested by the conflict perspective.

The **conflict perspective** has become popular over and over again throughout history, with roots that can be traced back to German philosopher Georg Hegel (1770–1831) and Italian philosopher Niccolo Machiavelli (1469–1527), and perhaps even further, drawing attention to conflict, dominance, and oppression in social life. The conflict perspective emphasizes conflicts that arise because of inequalities in the distribution of resources. It typically looks for sources of conflict in the economic and political arenas, and more recently in the cultural arena. Exhibit 2.2 provides a visual representation of the conflict perspective.

The roots of contemporary conflict theory are usually traced to the works of Karl Marx and his collaborator Friedrich Engels, as well as the works of Max Weber. Marx (1887/1967) and Engels (1884/1970) focused on economic structures, suggesting that the capitalist economic system is divided into capitalists and workers. Capitalists decide what is to be done and how to do it, and they own the products produced by the workers as well as the means of production. Capitalists pay workers as little as they can get away with, and they, not the workers, reap the benefits of exploiting natural resources. According to Marx, this system produces *false consciousness*: Neither capitalists nor workers are aware that the system is based on exploitation;

Exhibit 2.2   Conflict Perspective

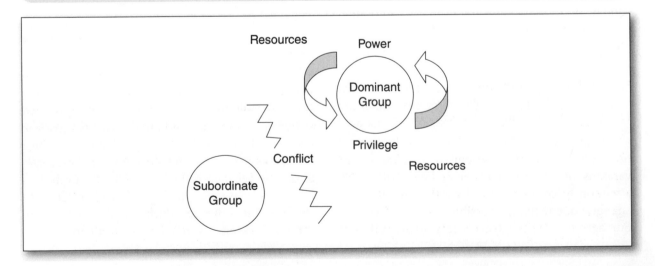

Photo 2.2   This homeless woman on a street in prosperous Beverly Hills, California, is one of many examples of unequal power in the global economy, a focus of the conflict perspective.

© Mark Ralston/AFP/Getty Images

workers think they are getting a fair day's pay, and capitalists think workers are fairly rewarded. Marx proposed, however, that workers are capable of recognizing the exploitation and achieving *class consciousness*, but capitalists are incapable of recognizing the exploitation in the system.

Weber (1904–1905/1958) rejected this singular emphasis on economics in favor of a multidimensional perspective on social class that included prestige and power derived from sources other than economics. Contemporary conflict theory tends to favor Weber's multidimensional perspective, calling attention to a confluence of social, economic, and political structures in the creation of inequality. Jürgen Habermas (1984, 1981/1987) and other **critical theorists** argue that as capitalism underwent change, people were more likely to be controlled by culture than by their work position. Our lives became dominated by

the culture industry, which is controlled by mass media. Critical theorists suggest that the culture industry plays a major role in turning workers into consumers, calling attention to the role of the advertising industry in exploiting consumers. They suggest that in the contemporary world, workers work very hard, sometimes at second and third jobs, in order to consume. They describe the exploitation of consumers as a pleasant kind of control: People spend more and more time working to be able to shop, and shopping becomes the major form of recreation. Working and shopping leave little time for reflective or revolutionary thinking. George Ritzer (2013a) recently suggested that the same might be said about the time we spend on Facebook, Twitter, and the like. But he also notes that besides informing us about what our friend ate for breakfast, social media is also used to spread the word about injustice and organize social protest, as happened during the "Arab Spring" uprisings in 2011.

Immanuel Wallerstein (2004) is a neo-Marxist who has focused on international inequality. He proposed that the capitalist world system is divided into three geographic areas with greatly different levels of power: A *core* of nations dominates the capitalist worldwide economy and exploits the natural resources and labor in other nations. The *periphery* includes nations that provide cheap raw materials and labor that are exploited to the advantage of the core. The *semiperiphery* includes nations that are newly industrializing; they benefit from the periphery but are exploited by the core.

Power relationships are a major focus of the conflict perspective. Some theorists in the conflict tradition limit their focus to the large-scale structure of power relationships, but many theorists, especially critical theorists, also look at the reactions and adaptations of individual members of nondominant groups. These theorists note that oppression of nondominant groups leads to their *alienation*, or a sense of indifference or hostility. **Critical race theory** was developed by legal scholars who wanted to draw attention to racial oppression in the law and society. They called attention to how *microaggressions*, brief, everyday exchanges that send denigrating messages and insults to people of color or members of any other minority identity group, create alienation for members of the group (Cappicci, Chadha, Bi Lin, & Snyder, 2012).

Lewis Coser (1956) proposed a *pluralistic theory of social conflict*, which recognizes that more than one social conflict is going on at all times and that individuals hold cross-cutting and overlapping memberships in status groups. Social conflict exists between economic groups, racial groups, ethnic groups, religious groups, age groups, gender groups, and so forth. Thus, it seeks to understand life experience by looking at simultaneous memberships—for example, a White, Italian American, Protestant, heterosexual, male semiskilled worker, or a Black, African American, Catholic, lesbian, female professional worker. Feminist and critical race theorists have developed a pluralistic

approach called **intersectionality theory**, which recognizes vectors of oppression and privilege, including not only gender but also class, race, global location, sexual orientation, and age (see Collins, 2012).

Although early social workers in the settlement house tradition recognized social conflict and structured inequality, and focused on eliminating oppression of immigrants, women, and children, most critics agree that social workers have not drawn consistently on the conflict perspective over time. Concepts of power and social conflict were revived in the social work literature in the 1960s. In the past 2 decades, with renewed commitment to social justice in its professional code of ethics and in its curriculum guidelines, social work has drawn more heavily on the conflict perspective to understand dynamics of *privilege*, or unearned advantage, as well as discrimination and oppression. Social workers have used the conflict perspective as a base to develop practice-oriented **empowerment theories**, which focus on processes that individuals and collectivities can use to recognize patterns of inequality and injustice and take action to increase their own power (e.g., Gutierrez, 1990, 1994; Lee, 2001; Rose, 1992, 1994; Solomon, 1976, 1987). Both in their renewed interest in domination and oppression and in their development of practice-oriented empowerment theories, social workers have been influenced by **feminist theories**, which focus on male domination of the major social institutions and present a vision of a just world based on gender equity. Feminist theories emphasize that people are socialized to see themselves through the eyes of powerful actors. Like Marx, most feminist theorists are not content to ask, "Why is it this way?" but also ask, "How can we change and improve the social world?"

Here is how the conflict perspective rates on the five criteria for evaluating social work theory:

- *Coherence and conceptual clarity.* Most concepts of the conflict perspective are straightforward—conflict, power, domination, inequality—at least at the abstract level. Like all theoretical concepts, however, they become less straightforward when we begin to define them for the purpose of measurement. Across the various versions of the conflict perspective, concepts are not consistently used. One major source of variation is whether power and privilege are to be thought of as objective material circumstances, subjectively experienced situations, or both. In general, theories in the conflict tradition are expressed in language that is relatively accessible and clear. This is especially true of many of the practice-oriented empowerment theories developed by social workers. On the other hand, most recent conflict theorizing in the critical theory tradition is stated at a high level of abstraction.

- *Testability and empirical support.* Conflict theory has developed, in the main, through attempts to codify persistent themes in history. The preferred research method is empirical research that looks at large-scale patterns of history (see McMichael, 2012; Skocpol & Williamson, 2012; Wallerstein, 2004). As with other methods of research, critics have attacked some interpretations of historical data from the conflict perspective, but the historical analyses of Theda Skocpol and Immanuel Wallerstein are some of the most influential works in contemporary sociology. In addition to historical analysis, conflict theorists have used experimental methods to study reactions to coercive power (see Zimbardo, 2007) and naturalistic inquiry to study social ranking through interaction rituals (Collins, 2004). Contemporary conflict theorists are also drawing on network analysis, which plots the relationships among people within groups, and are finding support for their propositions about power and domination. Family researchers have used conflict theory, specifically the concept of power, to study family violence (White et al., 2015b).

- *Comprehensiveness.* Traditionally, the conflict perspective focused on large-scale social institutions and social structures, such as economic and political institutions. In the contemporary era, conflict theorists integrate conflict processes at the societal level with those at the community, small-group, and family levels. They suggest that we should recognize conflict as a central process in social life at all levels. Family theorists propose a conflict theory of families (White et al., 2015b). Traditional conflict theories propose that oppression of subordinate groups leads to a sense of alienation, and recent empowerment theories give considerable attention to individual perceptions of power. The conflict perspective does not explicitly address biology, but it has been used to examine racial and social class health disparities. Most conflict theories do consider dimensions of time. They are particularly noteworthy for recommending that the behavior of members of minority groups should be put in historical context, and indeed, as discussed, empirical historical research is the method many conflict theorists prefer.

- *Diversity and power.* The conflict perspective is about inequality, power arrangements, and systems of oppression. It, more than any other perspective presented in this chapter, helps us look at group-based patterns of inequality. In that way, it also assists us in understanding diversity. Intersectionality theory, which recognizes that individuals have overlapping memberships in a variety of status groups, is particularly useful for considering human diversity. A major strength of the conflict perspective is that it discourages pathologizing members of minority groups by encouraging recognition of the historical, cultural, economic, and political context of their behavior. Empowerment theories guide practice interventions that build on the strengths of members of minority groups.

- *Usefulness for social work.* Concepts from the conflict perspective have great value for understanding power dimensions in societal, organizational, community, group, family, and dyadic relationships, as well as the power differential between social worker and client. Clearly, the conflict perspective is crucial to social work because it shines a spotlight on how domination and oppression might be affecting human behavior; it illuminates processes by which people become estranged and discouraged; and it encourages social workers to consider the meaning of their power relationships with clients, particularly nonvoluntary clients. The conflict perspective is essential to the social justice mission of social work. In recent years, social workers have been in the forefront of developing practice-oriented empowerment theories, and the conflict perspective has become as useful for recommending particular practice strategies as for assisting in the assessment process. Empowerment theories provide guidelines for working at all system levels (e.g., individual, family, small group, community, and organization), but they put particular emphasis on group work because of the opportunities presented in small groups for solidarity and mutual support. With the addition of empowerment theories, the conflict perspective can not only help us to understand how the McKinley family came to feel powerless but also help us think about how we can assist individual family members, as well as the family as a whole, to feel empowered to improve their situation. Social movement theories (see Chapter 14), which are based in the conflict perspective, have implications for the mobilization of oppressed groups, but the conflict perspective in general provides little in the way of specific policy direction.

Critical Thinking Questions 2.1

Both the systems and the conflict perspectives pay attention to the environment external to individuals. It could be argued that the hospice social worker should only be focusing on Ruth McKinley's personal needs and reactions. How would you argue in favor of that approach? How would you argue against it? To what extent do you see interactions within the family system to be important to meeting Ruth's personal needs? Explain. To what extent are conflicts external to the McKinley family influencing the well-being of the family? Explain. How might situating the McKinley family in the context of those conflicts help the social worker think about how to be helpful to the family? How would it not be helpful?

EXCHANGE AND CHOICE PERSPECTIVE

Another way to think about the McKinley family is to focus on the resources each member brings to the ongoing life of the family and each member's sense of fairness in the exchange of those resources. You might note that Ruth has diminishing resources to offer to the family, but the rest of the family seems to derive satisfaction, perhaps emotional energy, from caring for her. Marcia indicates that it is only fair that they care for her now because of the care Ruth provided to Bethany when she was a young child. Stanley's ability to provide economic resources to the family has diminished, but his contributions as caregiver have increased. Marcia has gotten satisfaction over the years from her caregiving role in the family, and her ability to bring this resource to the family has been compromised. On the other hand, the economic resources she brings into the family have become more important since Stanley became unemployed. Bethany provides economic resources as well as caregiving resources, and there is no evidence that she considers her contributions to the family to be unfair. She is weighing the long-term rewards of education against the short-term costs of adding a rigorous educational program to an already overtaxed life. This way of thinking about the McKinley family is suggested by the exchange and choice perspective.

The various streams of the **exchange and choice perspective**, which has roots in behavioral psychology, economics, anthropology, philosophy, and sociology, share the common focus on the processes whereby individual and collective actors seek and exchange resources and the choices made in pursuit of those resources. Resources may be material or nonmaterial; for example, time, money, material goods, sex, affection, loyalty, social contacts. These ideas are visually represented in Exhibit 2.3.

Social exchange theory, originally proposed by George Homans (1958), considered *social exchange*, defined as an interaction in which resources are exchanged, as the core process in

Exhibit 2.3   Exchange and Choice Perspective

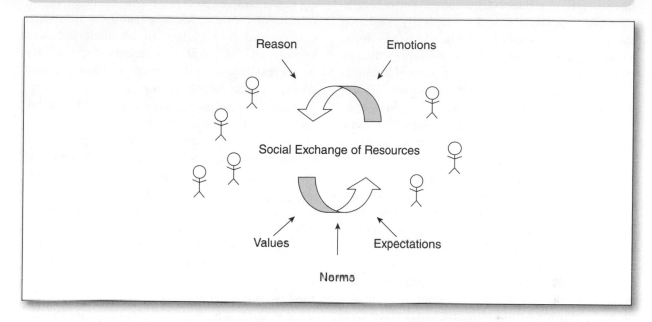

social life. Homans started with the basic premise that social exchange is based on the desire to maximize benefits and minimize costs, a basic belief that social relationships occur in a social marketplace in which people give in order to get. Homan focused on individual motivation in exchanges in dyadic relationships. He saw individuals as always calculating the rewards and costs of relationships and making choices based on those calculations.

Peter Blau (1964) developed a social exchange theory that focused on how exchange works in organizations and complex institutions. He proposed that such exchanges are governed by a norm of **reciprocity**, that receiving resources requires giving resources of relatively equal value. He suggested that such exchanges build trust over time. Blau acknowledged, however, that imbalance of exchange occurs, and, when this happens, actors with the greatest resources hold power. He suggested that the most comfortable exchanges are those in which actors have equality of resources and that trust is fragile in unequal relationships. Karen Cook and colleagues (2005) share this

concern about the fragility of trust and note the importance of "trust-nurturing bodies," like the Federal Food and Drug Administration, whose purpose is to supervise and enforce trust.

The closely related *rational choice theory* (Coleman, 1990) shares with exchange theories the view that humans are rational (weighing rewards and costs), purposive, and motivated by self-interest. But rational choice theorists are particularly interested in the group dynamics that occur when rational actors make strategic decisions. They are interested in the norms and networks formed by social exchanges and how, once created, norms and networks facilitate as well as constrain the behavior and choices of individuals. Coleman used rational choice theory to explore possible public policies that would offer incentives for actors to behave in ways that are more beneficial to others. Rational choice theory is currently popular in sociology, health promotion, and family studies.

Theorists in the rational choice tradition advanced **social network theory** (Cook, 1987). They introduced the concept of *exchange* *network*, which is a set of actors linked together, both directly and indirectly through exchange relationships. Social networks are typically presented visually, with members of the network—individuals, groups, or organizations—represented as points. Lines are drawn between pairs of points to demonstrate a relationship between them. Arrows are often used to show the flow of exchanges in a relationship. These graphic displays illuminate such issues as network size, density of relationships, strength of relationships, reciprocity of relationships, and access to power and influence. *Social capital theory* is a recent outgrowth of social network theory. Social networks provide **social capital**, both direct and indirect connections to others that are potential sources of a number of types of resources.

Traditional exchange and choice theories have been criticized on a number of grounds. Some critics have noted that exchange theory has a difficult time accounting for altruistic behavior. Others note that recent research indicates that humans are not really capable of considering all alternatives and their possible outcomes. Still other critics note that traditional exchange theory does not address why some rewards are valued more than others. We can imagine, for example, that some young adults in Bethany McKinley's position would consider it unfair to be involved in economic provider and caregiving roles in their family of origin, but she does not. What values are at play here? In response to these theoretical concerns, some behavioral scientists have proposed nonrational models of exchange and choice.

Sociologist Randall Collins (2004) introduced a form of exchange theory he calls *interaction ritual chains.* He proposes that social structures are developed by the aggregation of many exchanges over long periods of time. Rituals, or patterned sequences of behavior, develop out of these ongoing exchanges. Interaction rituals become linked or chained together by individuals who are members of multiple networks. Collins suggests that emotion, not reason, is the driving force of social exchange; emotional energy is the motive behind all exchanges. People are more likely to repeat interactions from which they take away emotional energy, and they engage in altruistic behavior because of the emotional energy they receive in the exchange. Collins proposes that physical co-presence is necessary for rituals to develop; co-presence produces common emotional mood, focused attention, and collective emotional energy. He supports this assertion by citing research indicating that the brain waves of participants in ritualized interactions become synchronized. Collins suggests that the self emerges from patterns of interaction; who we hang out with is the key to who we become.

Political scientist Deborah Stone (2012) has criticized the dominance of rational choice models of policy analysis. She refers to rational choice models as *market* models and proposes, instead, a *polis model*, which starts from the point of view of the community rather than the individual. She suggests that a theory of the political process must recognize altruism and public interest as well as self-interest. She acknowledges that reasonable people can disagree about what the public interest is and proposes that the political process involves a negotiation of ideas about that. In the political process, participants are influenced in their choices by people in their networks and by their loyalties, operating by "laws of passion," rather than "laws of reason." They form alliances to gain power. Stone argues that while the market model proposes that participants in the political process have access to accurate and complete information for making political choices, in reality, information about policy issues is "ambiguous, incomplete, often strategically shaded, and sometimes deliberately withheld" (Stone, 2012, p. 30). She argues that we cannot be effective in influencing policy if we do not understand the nonrational aspects of the policy development process.

Here is an analysis of how well the exchange and choice perspective meets the criteria for judging social work theory.

- *Coherence and conceptual clarity.* Early exchange theory contained a conceptual hole about the motivation for altruistic behavior, but recent formulations have addressed that hole. There is much consistency within each stream of the exchange and choice perspective. There is also much consistency across streams about the important role of exchange and choice in human behavior. There is a great deal of inconsistency across theories, however, about issues of rationality and self-interestedness. Although concepts are sometimes presented at a high level of abstraction, most theories in the perspective define and measure terms in a clear and consistent manner.

- *Testability and empirical support.* The exchange and choice perspective has stimulated empirical research at several levels of analysis, with mixed results. Cognitive psychologists Daniel Kahneman and Amos Tversky (1982, 1984) dealt a blow to the rational choice perspective in the 1980s. They reported research findings that individual choices and decisions are often inconsistent with assumed rationality and that, indeed, situations are often too complicated for individuals to ascertain the most rational choice. On the other hand, more than modest support for the perspective has been found in research on dyads and families (see Sutphin, 2010). Researchers across a wide range of disciplines are using statistical methods to calculate the balance of costs and benefits of particular courses of action, such as conserving natural habitats (Naidoo & Adamowicz, 2006) or prescribing antidepressant medications instead of cognitive behavioral therapy (Hollinghurst, Kessler, Peters, & Gunnell, 2005).

- *Comprehensiveness.* Although all streams of the exchange and choice perspective are interested in human interactions, the different streams focus on different dimensions in which interactions occur. The perspective has been used to study dyads, families, small groups, networks, communities, organizations, and institutions (see White et al., 2015c). In general, the exchange and choice perspective is weak in exploration of personal dimensions, but Homans (1958) was interested in human motivation, and Randall Collins (2004) has been explicit in identifying the biological mechanisms involved in the emotional energy he sees as the engine of social exchange. The exchange and choice perspective attends to time in terms of the history of past exchanges.

- *Diversity and power.* Although they were designed to look at patterns, not diversity, early exchange and choice theories provided some tools for understanding diversity in behaviors that come out of particular social exchanges. All theories in this perspective recognize power as deriving from unequal resources in the exchange process. Some versions of rational choice theory emphasize the ways in which patterns of exchange lead to social inequalities and social injustices. Although the exchange and choice perspective does not explicitly pathologize members of minority groups, those versions that fail to put social exchanges in historical, political, and economic contexts may unintentionally contribute to the pathologizing of these groups.

- *Usefulness for social work practice.* Some versions of the exchange and choice perspective serve as little more than a defense of the rationality of the marketplace of social exchange, suggesting a noninterventionist approach. In other words, if all social exchanges are based on rational choices, then who are we to interfere with this process? This stance, of course, is inconsistent with the purposes of social work. However, the perspective has also been used to analyze the service participation decision making among clients and to guide decision making about recruitment of volunteers. Social network theory, with its recent emphasis on social capital, suggests tools for enhancing the resources of individuals and groups, including networks of social service providers. Randall Collins's (2004) theory of exchange rituals suggests ways to create and reinforce altruism and group solidarity. Deborah Stone's (2012) polis model provides tools for thinking about the complexities of the policymaking process and can help social workers be more realistic about how they might influence that process.

SOCIAL CONSTRUCTIONIST PERSPECTIVE

As the hospice social worker drives back to the office, the McKinley family is on her mind. She thinks about how they are coping with a great deal of change in the external world as well as within their family system. She is interested in learning more about how they are describing and explaining these changes. For example, how do they understand their struggles in the labor market and the housing market? How much do they attribute their struggles to personal failings, and how much do they see themselves as part of a bigger story? How do their attributions affect their sense of self-worth? She thinks of Marcia's words, "nothing goes our way," and wonders whether this understanding of the world is shared by Stanley and Bethany—and, if so, how she might help them construct a different ending to the story they are telling themselves. She thinks about Ruth and her end-of-life reflections about her life and social relationships. She hopes that she can be a good listener and a partner with Ruth as she makes meaning of her life. This way of thinking about the McKinley family is consistent with the social constructionist perspective.

To understand human behavior, the **social constructionist perspective** focuses on how people construct meaning, a sense of self, and a social world through their interactions with each other. They learn, through their interactions, to classify the world and their place in it. People interact with each other and the physical world based on *shared meanings*, or shared understandings about the world. In this view, people develop their understandings of the world and themselves from social interaction, and these understandings shape their subsequent social interactions. Reality is shaped through social interaction and is continuously reshaped by ongoing social interaction. A visual representation of this way of thinking about human behavior is presented in Exhibit 2.4.

The early roots of the social constructionist perspective come from *symbolic interaction theory* developed by sociologists in the United States in the mid-20th century. This theory proposes that as humans interact, they develop symbols to which they attach meaning. Words are symbols, but so are piercings, tattoos, national flags, and fashion styles. The symbolic interactionist would be interested in how the McKinley family came to attach particular meaning to the word *family*. For the symbolic interactionist, society is constructed by human beings engaging in symbolic interaction. Through interaction, humans consciously and deliberately create their personal and collective histories. You may recall that the social exchange theorists are also concerned with social interaction, but their focus is on social interaction as an exchange of resources rather than on how social interaction produces meaning, a sense of self, and social life (society), which is the focus of the interactionist (Blumer, 1998).

To the social constructionist, there is no singular objective reality, no true reality that exists "out there" in the world. There are, instead, the shared subjective realities created as people interact in different contexts. Constructionists emphasize the existence of multiple social and cultural realities. Both persons and environments are dynamic processes, not static structures. The sociopolitical environment and history of any situation play an important role in understanding human behavior because of the way they have shaped meaning over time. The social constructionist would, for example, call attention to how Stanley's understanding of himself as a worker is being influenced by current economic uncertainties.

The importance of subjective rather than objective reality has been summed up by the words of W. I. Thomas (Thomas & Thomas, 1928): "If men define situations as real, they are real in their consequences" (p. 128). Actually, social constructionists disagree about whether there is, in fact, some objective reality out there. Radical social constructionists believe there is not. They believe there is no reality beyond our personal experiences. Most *postmodern theorists* fall in this category, arguing that there are no universals, including no universal truth, reality, or morality (Dybicz, 2011; Lyotard, 1984). The postmodernists accept that the world is "messy" and see no need to impose

Exhibit 2.4   Social Constructionist Perspective

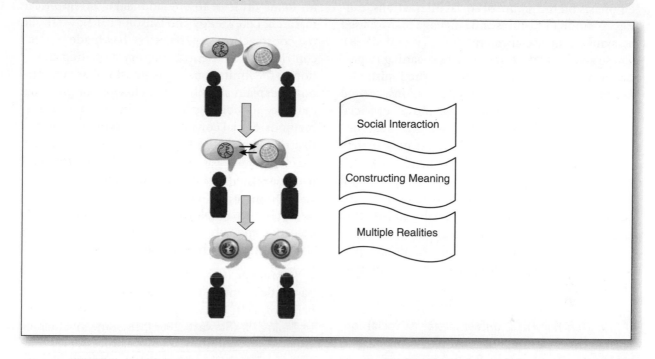

order on it. More moderate social constructionists believe there are "real objects" in the world, but those objects are never known objectively; rather, they are only known through the subjective interpretations of individuals and collectivities (Williams, 2006).

Social constructionists also disagree about how constraining the environment is. Some see individual actors in social interactions as essentially free, active, and creative (Gergen, 1985). Others suggest that individual actors are always performing for their social audiences, based on their understanding of community standards for human behavior (Berger & Luckmann, 1966; Goffman, 1959). Although this idea has been around for a while, it is taking on new meaning in the current world of proliferating communication technology, which provides us with many modalities for performing for our audiences, for engaging in what Goffman (1959) refers to as *impression management*. The dominant position is probably the one represented by Schutz's (1932/1967) *phenomenological sociology*. While arguing that people shape social reality,

Schutz also suggests that individuals and groups are constrained by the preexisting social and cultural arrangements constructed by their predecessors.

The social constructionist perspective sees human understanding, or human consciousness, as both the product and the driving force of social interaction. Some social constructionists focus on individual consciousness, particularly on the human capacity to interpret social interactions and to have an inner conversation with oneself about them. They see the self as developing from the interpretation of social interaction. Cooley introduces the concept of the *looking-glass self*, which can be explained as "I am what I think you think I am." The looking-glass self has three components: (1) I imagine how I appear to others, (2) I imagine their judgment of me, and (3) I develop some feeling about myself that is a result of imagining their judgments of me. George Herbert Mead (1959) suggests that one has a self only when one is in community and that the self develops based on our interpretation of the *generalized other*, which is the attitude of the entire community.

Other social constructionists put greater emphasis on the nature of social interactions, calling attention to gestures and language that are used as symbols in social interaction (Charon, 1998). These symbols take on particular meaning in particular situations. These social constructionists also see social problems as social constructions, created through claims making, labeling, and other social processes. Social workers have used the social constructionist approach to understand how society has constructed the meaning of phenomena such as parental incapability (Ben-David, 2011) and homelessness (Cronley, 2010) over time, as well as the processes by which these socially constructed definitions become internalized.

This is how the social constructionist perspective measures against the criteria for judging theories.

- *Coherence and conceptual clarity.* Social constructionism, both the original phenomenological and symbolic interactional concepts as well as the contemporary postmodern conceptualizations, is often criticized as vague and unclear. Over the past few decades, a great diversity of theorizing has been done within this broad theoretical perspective, and there is much fragmentation of ideas. That situation is consistent, however, with postmodernist understanding of multiple realities. Sociologists in the conflict and rational choice traditions have begun to incorporate social constructionist ideas, particularly those related to meaning making, which has further blurred the boundaries of this perspective but also attests to the usefulness of that concept. One challenge to the consistency of the social constructionist perspective is that, in its most radical form, it denies the one-absolute-truth, objective approach to reality while arguing that it is absolutely true that reality is subjective. There is inconsistency among the various streams of the perspective about how constraining history is on human interaction and how free humans are to reconstruct their social interaction.

- *Testability and empirical support.* Because of the vagueness of its concepts, the social constructionist perspective has been criticized for being difficult to operationalize for empirical research. Like DePoy and Gilson (2012), we think the constructionist perspective has made a great contribution to scientific inquiry by calling attention to the limitations of positivist research methods to explain all of human behavior, for pointing out the possibilities for bias in those research methods. Social constructionists propose alternative research methodology that focuses more on narrative and storytelling. Social constructionism has stimulated a trend in the behavioral sciences to use a mix of quantitative and qualitative research methodologies to accommodate both objective and subjective reality. This is providing a richer picture of human behavior.

- *Comprehensiveness.* Social constructionism pays little attention to the role of biology in human behavior, with the exception of a few constructivist biologists (Stewart, 2001). In some versions of social constructionism, cognitive processes are central, and the social construction of emotions is considered in others. With the emphasis on meaning making, social constructionism is open to the role of religion and spirituality in human behavior. With its emphasis on social interaction, the social constructionist perspective is strong in attention to the social environment. It has been criticized, however, for failing to pay sufficient attention to the macro world of social institutions and social structure. It has been criticized for focusing on meaning making and interpretation processes at the micro level, but it is important to acknowledge that it has also been used to propose the culture-framing perspective on social movements. Time, and the role of history, is respected in the social constructionist perspective, with many authors drawing attention to the historical era in which behavior is constructed.

- *Diversity and power.* With its emphasis on multiple social realities, the social constructionist perspective is strong in its ability to accommodate diversity. It has been criticized, however, for failure to provide the theoretical tools necessary for the analysis of power relationships. Some critics have suggested that many contemporary postmodern versions of social constructionism, by ignoring power while focusing on multiple voices and multiple meanings in the construction of reality, reduce oppression to mere difference (Williams, 2006). These critics suggest that this reduction of oppression to difference masks the fact that some actors have greater power than others to privilege their own constructions of reality and to disadvantage the constructions of other actors. This criticism cannot be leveled at all versions of social constructionism, however. Social work scholars have been attracted to those versions of the social constructionist perspective that have incorporated pieces of the conflict tradition (see Freeman & Couchonnal, 2006), particularly the early work of Michel Foucault (1969) on the relationship between power and knowledge. They propose that in contemporary society, minority or "local" knowledge is denied credibility in majority-dominated social arenas and suggest that social work practitioners can bring credibility to minority viewpoints by allowing oppressed individuals and groups to tell their own stories. Most theorizing about empowerment integrates conflict and social constructionist thinking.

• *Usefulness for social work practice.* Social constructionism gives new meaning to the old social work adage, "Begin where the client is." In the social constructionist perspective, the social work relationship begins with developing an understanding of how the client views the situation and what the client would like to have happen. The current strong interest in solution-focused and narrative and storytelling therapies is based on the social constructionist perspective. Solution-focused approaches attempt to help clients construct solutions rather than solve problems (Greene & Lee, 2011). They are based on the assumption that clients want to change and are capable of envisioning the change they would like to see. Narrative therapy starts with the assumption that we all tell ourselves stories about our lives, developing dominant story lines and forgetting material that does not fit into them. A goal of therapy is to help clients see more realities in their story lines, with other possible interpretations of events (Walsh, 2014). The social worker should engage the client in thinking about the social, cultural, and historical environments in which his or her version of reality was constructed, which, for members of oppressed groups, may lead to empowerment through *restorying*, or revision of the story line (Greene & Cohen, 2005). Joseph Walsh (2014) suggests that narrative therapy can be particularly helpful to hospice patients who are reflecting on their life stories. That is, indeed, the approach of the hospice social worker who is working with Ruth McKinley and her family. At the level of groups and organizations, the social constructionist perspective recommends getting discordant groups to engage in sincere discussion of their disparate constructions of reality and to negotiate lines of action acceptable to all (Riera, 2005).

Critical Thinking Questions 2.2

Both the exchange and choice and the social constructionist perspectives focus on social interactions. What do you see as the main difference in these two perspectives? What resources, both material and nonmaterial, do you seeing being exchanged in the McKinley family? What resources must be secured by interactions with people and systems outside the family? How might the hospice social worker help the family to increase their social capital? What shared meanings do you think the McKinley family members hold? If you were their social worker, how would the meanings you hold about the social world be similar to and different from theirs? In what contexts have you developed your sense of self and your understandings of the social world?

PSYCHODYNAMIC PERSPECTIVE

Both Stanley and Marcia McKinley's despondence and loss of hope are apparent in their first meeting with the hospice social worker—and easy to understand. Think about the losses they have faced in the past year: loss of job (Stanley), loss of income (Stanley and Marcia), loss of valued roles (provider for Stanley and caregiver for Marcia), and loss of health (Marcia). They also face the impending loss of Ruth, the last surviving parent for them, and the possible loss of their home. This rapid accumulation of loss would challenge, even overwhelm, the adaptive capacities of most any human. Bethany is thinking of dropping out of school, a decision that will involve loss of a dream, at least temporarily. In the midst of all that loss, we also note the deep attachment that all four family members—Ruth, Stanley, Marcia, and Bethany—have for each other. This suggests that early nurturing environments supported the development of secure attachments. As we explore the McKinley family's situation from the psychodynamic perspective, these and other ideas emerge.

The **psychodynamic perspective** is concerned with how internal processes such as needs, drives, and emotions motivate human behavior. The perspective has evolved over the years, moving from the classical psychodynamic emphasis on innate drives and unconscious processes toward greater emphasis on the adaptive capacities of individuals and their interactions with the environment. The origins of all psychodynamic theories are in the work of Sigmund Freud. More recent formulations of the perspective include ego psychology, object relations, self psychology, and relational-cultural theories. We elaborate on these more recent developments later. Exhibit 2.5 presents a visual representation of the psychodynamic perspective.

To trace the evolution of the psychodynamic perspective, it is essential to begin with its Freudian roots. Sigmund Freud looked at the human personality from a number of interrelated points of view; the most notable are his drive or instinct theory, topographical theory, structural theory, and psychosexual stage theory, summarized shortly. Freud revised each of these approaches to human personality over time, and different followers of Freud have attended to different aspects of his theoretical works, further revising each of them over time.

Exhibit 2.5 Psychodynamic Perspective

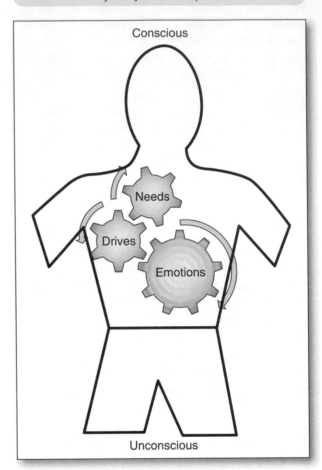

- *Drive or instinct theory.* This theory proposes that human behavior is motivated by two basic instincts: *thanatos*, or the drive for aggression or destruction, and *eros*, or the drive for life (through sexual gratification). Revisions of drive theory have suggested that human behavior is also motivated by drives for mastery (see Goldstein, 1996) and for connectedness (Borden, 2009).

- *Topographical theory of the mind.* Topographical theory proposes three states of mind: conscious mental activities of which we are fully aware; preconscious thoughts and feelings that can be easily brought to mind; and unconscious thoughts, feelings, and desires of which we are not aware but which have a powerful influence on our behavior. Although all psychodynamic theorists believe in the unconscious, the different versions of the theory put different emphases on the importance of the unconscious in human behavior.

- *Structural model of the mind.* This model proposes that personality is structured around three parts: the *id*, which is unconscious and strives for satisfaction of basic instincts; the *super-ego*, which is made up of conscience and ideals and is the censor of the id; and the *ego*, which is the rational part of personality that mediates between the id and the superego. Freud and his early followers were most interested in the id and the pathologies that emanate from it, but later followers have focused primarily on ego strengths and the drive for adaptation. Both ego psychology and self psychology are part of this later tradition.

- *Psychosexual stage theory.* This theory proposes a five-stage model of child development, based on sexual instincts: the oral phase (birth to about 18 months), when the search for pleasure is centered in the mouth; the anal phase (from about 18 months to 3 years), when the search for pleasure is centered in the anus; the phallic phase (ages 3 to 6), when the search for pleasure is centered in the genitals; the latency phase (ages 6 to 8), when erotic urges are repressed; and the genital phase (adolescence onward), when the search for pleasure is centered in the genitals and sexual intimacy. Freud asserted that there was no further personality development in adulthood. Recent revisions of psychodynamic theory, starting with the work of Erik Erikson (1963), have challenged that idea. Although they still give primacy to the childhood years, they suggest that personality continues to develop over the life course. Recent theories also put less emphasis on sexual instincts in stage development.

Let's turn now to some revisions of Freudian theory. *Ego psychology* gives primary attention to the rational part of the mind and the human capacity for adaptation. It recognizes conscious as well as unconscious attempts to cope and the importance of both past and present experiences. Defense mechanisms, unconscious processes that keep intolerable threats from conscious awareness, play an important role in ego psychology (see Goldstein, 2001). *Object relations theory* studies how people develop attitudes toward others in the context of early nurturing relationships and how those attitudes affect the view of the self as well as social relationships. In this tradition, John Bowlby's attachment theory has become the basis for a psychobiological theory of attachment (Barnekow & Kraemer, 2005). *Self psychology* focuses on the individual need to organize the personality into a cohesive sense of self and to build relationships that support it (see Goldstein, 2001). *Relational-cultural theory*, also known as relational feminist theory, proposes that the basic human drive is for relationships with others. The self is understood to develop and mature through emotional connectedness in mutually empathic relationships, rather than through a process of separation and independence as proposed by traditional object relations theory. Human connectedness is emphasized, human diversity acknowledged, and human difference normalized rather than pathologized (Borden, 2009; Freedberg, 2007).

In recent years, social workers who practice from a psychodynamic perspective have drawn on both biological research and propositions from conflict theorists to extend the psychodynamic perspective. Joan Berzoff (2011) writes about why psychodynamically oriented social work practice with "vulnerable, oppressed, and at-risk clients" must be informed by biological research, particularly neuroscience research, concepts of power and privilege, and critical race theory with its emphasis on intersectionality (p. 132). She also analyzes the contribution that traditional psychodynamic theories can make to understanding discrimination, scapegoating, and oppression. You will read more about the psychodynamic perspective in Chapter 4.

Here are the criteria for evaluating theories as applied to the psychodynamic perspective.

- *Coherence and conceptual clarity.* Criticisms that the psychodynamic perspective lacks logical consistency are directed primarily at Freud's original concepts and propositions, which were not entirely consistent because they evolved over time. Ego psychology and object relations theorists strengthened the logical consistency of the psychodynamic perspective by expanding and clarifying definitions of major concepts. Theories in the psychodynamic perspective are also criticized for the vague and abstract nature of their concepts but perhaps no more than most other theoretical perspectives.

• *Testability and empirical support.* Much empirical work has been based on the psychodynamic perspective, and research in other disciplines provides some support for some of the propositions of the perspective. Recent long-term longitudinal studies support the importance of childhood experiences but also indicate that personality continues to develop throughout life. There is growing evidence of the supremely important role that attachment plays in shaping development over the life course. Research by cognitive psychologists indicates that much of human behavior is based on activity that is outside of consciousness; although they do not use this language, it appears that they are suggesting both preconscious and unconscious activity (Kahneman, 2011). Neuroscience research is indicating the important role of emotion in human behavior, demonstrating the brain mechanisms involved in emotion and suggesting that both genetics and life experiences shape the emotional brain (Davidson & Begley, 2012). Early life experiences are important in this process, but the brain is plastic and can be changed by ongoing life experiences and mental activity.

• *Comprehensiveness.* Early psychodynamic theories were primarily concerned with internal psychological processes. Strong attention is paid to emotions, and in recent formulations, cognitions are also acknowledged. Although Freud assumed that biology determines behavior, he developed his theory several decades before neurological science began to uncover the biological base of emotions. Recently, however, psychodynamic theorists have begun to incorporate new developments in neurological sciences about early brain development into their formulations (see, e.g., Berzoff, 2011). With the exception of Carl Jung, early psychodynamic theorists were not interested in the spiritual aspects of human behavior, typically viewing them as irrational defenses against anxiety. Recently, psychodynamically oriented social workers have attempted to integrate spirituality into their practice, often drawing on Eastern psychological theories (see Nagi, 2007). As for environments, most psychodynamic theory conceptualizes them as sources of conflicts with which the individual must struggle. Relational-cultural theory, with its emphasis on supporting the growth of relationships and community, takes exception to that view. Overall, however, environments beyond the family or other close interpersonal relationships are ignored. This has led to criticisms of "mother blaming" and "family blaming" in traditional psychodynamic theories. Social, economic, political, and historical environments of human behavior are probably implied in ego psychology, but they are not explicated. As for time, the focus is on how people change across childhood. There has traditionally been little attempt to account for change after childhood or to recognize the contributions of historical time to human behavior, but this is changing.

• *Diversity and power.* Traditional psychodynamic theories search for universal laws of behavior and their applicability to unique individuals. Thus, diversity of experience at the group level has been quite neglected in this tradition until recently. Moreover, in the main, "universal" laws have been developed through analysis of European American, heterosexual, middle-class men. Feminists, as well as members of racial and ethnic minority groups, have criticized the psychodynamic bias toward thinking of people as autonomous individuals (Freedberg, 2007; Nagai, 2007). These critics suggest that viewing this standard as "normal" makes the connectedness found among many women and members of racial and ethnic minority groups seem pathological. Recently, proponents of the psychodynamic perspective have tried to correct for these biases and develop a better understanding of human diversity. Psychodynamic theories are strong in their recognition of power dynamics in parent–child relationships and in exploration of the life-worlds of children. Until recently, they have been weaker in looking at power issues in other relationships, however, including gender relationships. In the contemporary era, psychoanalytic feminists have reworked Freud's ideas to focus on patriarchy, asking the question, "Why do men work so hard to maintain patriarchy, and why do women put so little energy into challenging patriarchy?" (Lengermann & Niebrugge-Brantley, 2007). They propose that the answer to this question is found in the gender-based early child-rearing environment. African American social workers have proposed that social workers can help to empower African American clients by integrating empowerment theory and an Afrocentric perspective with the ego-strengthening aspects of ego psychology (Manning, Cornelius, & Okundaye, 2004). Relational-cultural theory was developed out of concerns about the male bias in existing psychodynamic theories. These examples illustrate the psychodynamic perspective's growing attention to issues of diversity and power.

- *Usefulness for social work practice.* Most versions of the psychodynamic perspective have included clinical theory as well as human behavior theory. Differences of opinion about principles of practice reflect the theoretical evolution that has occurred. Practice principles common to all versions of the psychodynamic perspective include the centrality of the professional–client relationship, the curative value of expressing emotional conflicts and understanding past events, and the goals of self-awareness and self-control. In contrast to the classical psychodynamic approach, recent formulations include directive as well as nondirective intervention, short-term as well as long-term intervention, and environmental manipulations—such as locating counseling regarding possible mortgage foreclosure for the McKinley family—as well as intrapsychic manipulations such as

emotional catharsis. Ego psychology has also been used to develop principles for prevention activities in addition to principles of remediation (Goldstein, 1996). In general, however, the psychodynamic perspective does not suggest practice principles at the level of communities, organizations, and social institutions. Thus, from this perspective, it would not help you to think about how to influence public policy related to housing, income security, or access to health care.

DEVELOPMENTAL PERSPECTIVE

Another way to think about the McKinley family is to view their situation in terms of the developmental tasks they face. You might note that Ruth McKinley is in late adulthood and engaged in a review of her life journey, attempting to make peace with the life she has lived. You might also note that Stanley and Marcia assumed caregiving responsibilities for Ruth 5 years ago while also continuing to provide support to Bethany as she moved into young adulthood. At the current time, their struggles to stay employed and hold onto their house are situations that were once thought to be "off time," or atypical, for individuals in middle adulthood but have become more common for the current cohort of midlife adults. Bethany assumed a caregiving role with Ruth as she emerged into adulthood, and that also may seem off time. We can think about where she stands with the developmental markers typically associated with young adulthood: education/work, intimate relationship, leaving home, and starting career. These observations are consistent with the central ideas of the developmental perspective.

The focus of the **developmental perspective**, perhaps the most widely used of the perspectives presented in this chapter, is on how human behavior unfolds across the life course, how people change and stay the same over time. Human development is seen to occur in clearly defined stages based on a complex interaction of biological, psychological, and social processes. Each new stage involves new tasks and brings changes in social

Photo 2.3 Families are composed of people in different life stages, occupying different statuses and playing different roles, as suggested by the developmental perspective.

© Brand X Pictures/Thinkstock

roles and statuses. A visual representation of these ideas is presented in Exhibit 2.6.

Although there are a great number of developmental theories, they can be categorized into two streams of theorizing, one based in psychology and one based in sociology. *Life span* or *life cycle theory*, based in psychology, focuses on the inner life during age-related stages. The study of life span development is rooted in Freud's (1905/1953) theory of psychosexual stages of childhood development, but Erikson (1963) has been the most influential developmental theorist to date because his model of development includes adult, as well as child, stages of development. Erikson (1963) proposed an *epigenetic model of human development*, in which the psychological unfolding of personality takes place in sequences influenced by biological, psychological, and social forces. Healthy development depends on the mastery of life tasks at the appropriate time in the sequence. Although life

span theorists tend to agree with this epigenetic principle, there is also growing agreement that the stages are experienced in a more flexible way than Erikson proposed, with cultural, economic, and personal circumstances leading to some differences in timing and sequencing (Sollod, Wilson, & Monte, 2009). For example, Bethany McKinley is thinking of postponing school and career development to be a support to her extended family in a stressful period in the life of the family. Stanley McKinley is faced with a need to rethink his occupational career at the age of 50.

Erikson divided the life cycle into eight stages, each with a special psychosocial crisis:

Stage 1 (birth to 1 year): basic trust versus mistrust

Stage 2 (ages 2 to 3): autonomy versus shame, doubt

Stage 3 (ages 3 to 5): initiative versus guilt

Stage 4 (ages 6 to 12): industry versus inferiority

Exhibit 2.6   Developmental Perspective

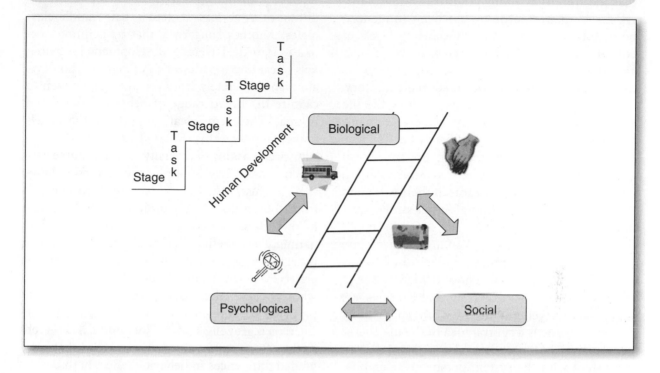

Stage 5 (ages 12 to 18 or so): identity versus role confusion

Stage 6 (early to late 20s): intimacy versus isolation

Stage 7 (late 20s to 50s): generativity versus stagnation

Stage 8 (late adulthood): integrity versus despair

Early life span theorists, including Erikson, saw their models of development as universal, applying equally well to all groups of people. This idea has been the target of much criticism, with suggestions that the traditional models are based on the experiences of European American, heterosexual, middle-class men and do not apply well to members of other groups. This criticism has led to a number of life cycle models for specific groups, such as women (Borysenko, 1996), gay and lesbian persons (e.g., Troiden, 1989), and African Americans (Cross, Parham, & Black, 1991). Life span theories have also been criticized for failing to deal with historical time and the cohort effects on human behavior that arise when groups of persons born in the same historical time share cultural influences and historical events at the same period in their lives.

These criticisms have helped to stimulate development of the *life course perspective* in sociology. This relatively new perspective conceptualizes the life course as a social, rather than psychological, phenomenon that is nonetheless unique for each individual, with some common life course markers, or transitions, related to shared social and historical contexts (George, 1993). Glen Elder Jr. (1998) and Tamara Hareven (2000) have been major forces in the development of the life course perspective. In its current state, there are six major themes in this perspective: interplay of human lives and historical time; biological, psychological, and social timing of human lives; linked or interdependent lives; human capacity for choice making; diversity in life course trajectories; and developmental risk and protection. As you may recall, the life course perspective is the conceptual framework for the companion volume to this book.

The life course perspective would suggest that the timing of young adult transition markers for Bethany McKinley has been influenced by historical trends toward increasing levels of education and delayed marriage. It would also call attention to the impact of the global economic disruptions on Stanley's occupational trajectory. This perspective would emphasize how the life course trajectories of Stanley, Marcia, Bethany, and Ruth are intertwined and how what happens in one generation reverberates up and down the extended family line. For example, Stanley, Marcia, and Bethany reorganized their work and family lives to care for Ruth after her stroke. Give some thought to how their life journeys might have been different if Ruth had not required care at that time. Or imagine what decision Bethany might be making about school if Marcia was in stronger health. This notion that families are linked across generations by both opportunity and misfortune is a central idea of the life course perspective, but you may also recognize it as consistent with the system perspective's emphasis on interdependence. The evolving life course model respects the idea of role transition that is so central to the developmental perspective, but it also recognizes the multiplicity of interacting factors that contribute to diversity in the timing and experience of these transitions.

Here is how the criteria for evaluating theories apply to the developmental perspective.

- *Coherence and conceptual clarity.* Classical developmental theory's notion of life stages is internally consistent and conceptually clear. Theorists have been able to build on each other's work in a coherent manner. Still in its early stages, the life course perspective has developed some coherence and beginning clarity about the major concepts. When viewing these two developmental streams together, contradictions appear in terms of universality versus diversity in life span/life course development.

- *Testability and empirical support.* Many of Erikson's ideas have been employed and verified in empirical research, but until recently, much of developmental research has been based on European American, heterosexual, middle-class males. Another concern is that by defining normal as statistical average, developmental research fails to capture the lifeworlds of groups who deviate even moderately from the average, or even to capture the broad range of behavior considered normal. Thus, empirical support for the developmental perspective is based to some extent on statistical masking of diversity. The life course perspective has offered a glimpse of diversity, however, because it has been developed, in general, from the results of longitudinal research, which follows the same people over an extended period of time. The benefit of longitudinal research is that it clarifies whether differences between age groups are really based on developmental differences or whether they reflect cohort effects from living in particular cultures at particular historical times. There is a growing body of longitudinal research in the life course tradition that suggests that age-graded differences in behavior reflect both developmental factors and historical trends (see Elder & Giele, 2009).

- *Comprehensiveness.* The developmental perspective, when both theoretical streams are taken together, gets relatively high marks for comprehensiveness. Both the life span and the life course streams recognize human behavior as an outcome of complex interactions of biological, psychological, and social factors, although most theorists in both streams pay little attention to the spiritual dimension. The traditional life span approach pays too little attention to the political, economic, and cultural environments of human behavior; the life course perspective pays too little attention to psychological factors. Both approaches attend to the dimension of time, in terms of linear time, but the life course perspective attends to time in a more comprehensive manner, by emphasizing the role of historical time in human behavior. Indeed, the developmental perspective is the only one of the eight perspectives discussed here that makes time a primary focus.

• *Diversity and power.* The early life span models were looking for universal stages of human development and did not attend to issues of diversity. More recent life span models have paid more attention to diversity, and diversity of pathways through life is a major theme in the life course perspective. Likewise, the traditional life span approach did not take account of power relationships, with the possible exception of power dynamics in the parent–child relationship. Moreover, traditional life span models are based on the average European American, middle-class, heterosexual male and ignore the worlds of members of nondominant groups. Newer models of life span development have attempted to correct for that failure. Daniel Levinson's (1996) study of women's lives is noteworthy in that regard; it includes a sample of women diversified by race and social class and acknowledges the impact of gender power differentials on women's development. The life course perspective recognizes patterns of advantage and disadvantage in life course trajectories, and life course researchers have done considerable work on the accumulation of advantage and disadvantage over the life course (see Seabrook & Avison, 2012).

• *Usefulness for social work practice.* Erikson's theory has often been used for assessment purposes in social work practice, and in a positive sense, the theory can aid indirectly in the identification of potential personal and social developmental resources. Traditional life span theories should be applied, however, only with recognition of the ethnocentrism expressed in them. Although it is harder to extrapolate practice principles from the more complex, still-emerging life course perspective, it seems more promising for understanding diverse persons in diverse environments. It suggests that individuals must always be assessed within familial, cultural, and historical contexts. Overall, the developmental perspective can be viewed as optimistic. Most people face difficult transitions, life crises, and developmental or other challenges at some point, and many people have been reassured to hear that their struggle is

"typical." Because the developmental perspective sees individuals as having the possibility to rework their inner experiences, as well as their family relationships, clients may be assisted in finding new strategies for getting their lives back on course. For example, Stanley McKinley could explore untapped talents and interests that might be used to get his occupational career moving again.

Critical Thinking Questions 2.3

Both the psychodynamic and developmental perspectives provide stage theories of human behavior, but they put different emphases on the importance of childhood experiences. The psychodynamic perspective sees emotion as holding a central place in human behavior. What emotions do you experience as you read the story of the McKinley family? How do you think these emotions are related to your childhood experiences? How do you think those emotions might be helpful for work with the McKinley family? How might they not be helpful? According to the developmental perspective, Bethany McKinley is in the phase of young adulthood. You are either in that phase or have already passed through it. How is Bethany's experience with young adulthood similar to yours? Different from yours? What biases do you have about the choices Bethany is making?

SOCIAL BEHAVIORAL PERSPECTIVE

The hospice social worker observed Bethany McKinley's warm and gentle interaction with her grandmother, Ruth. She wasn't surprised later to hear Bethany describe Ruth as kind. She imagined that Ruth modeled kind behavior as she cared for Bethany when she was a young child. She also observed that Stanley, Marcia, and Bethany seemed to reinforce kind behavior in each other. She noticed how Stanley and Bethany put their arms around Marcia when she began to cry. The social worker was also struck by statements by both Stanley and Marcia that seem to indicate that they have lost confidence in their ability to make things happen in their lives. She understood how recent events could have undermined their confidence, but she was curious whether she had simply caught them on a down day or if, indeed, they no longer have expectations of being able to improve their situation. Viewing the McKinley family from a social behavioral perspective can lead to such assessment and questions.

Theories in the **social behavioral perspective**, sometimes called the social learning perspective, suggest that human behavior is learned as individuals interact with their environments. There are disagreements among the different streams of social behavioral theory, however, about the processes by which behavior is learned. Over time, three major versions of behavioral theory have been presented, proposing different mechanisms by which learning occurs. The general themes of the social behavioral perspective are represented visually in Exhibit 2.7.

Classical conditioning theory, also known as respondent conditioning, sees behavior as learned through association, when a naturally occurring stimulus (unconditioned stimulus) is paired with a neutral stimulus (conditioned stimulus). This approach is usually traced to a classic experiment by Russian physiologist Ivan Pavlov, who showed, first, that dogs naturally salivate (unconditioned response) to meat powder on the tongue (unconditioned stimulus). Then, a ringing bell (conditioned stimulus) was paired with the meat powder a number of times. Eventually, the dog salivated (conditioned response) to the ringing of the bell (conditioned stimulus). In other words, an initially neutral stimulus comes to produce a particular behavioral response after it is repeatedly paired

Photo 2.4 Classical conditioning is traced to an experiment Russian physiologist Ivan Pavlov performed with dogs.

© Time & Life Pictures/Getty Images

Exhibit 2.7 Social Behavioral Perspective

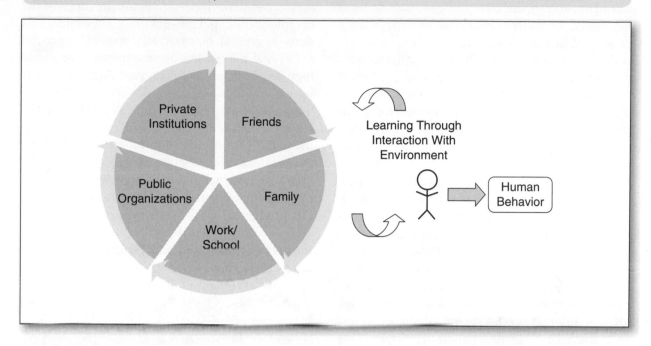

with another stimulus of significance. Classical conditioning plays a role in understanding many problems that social work clients experience. For example, a woman with an alcohol abuse problem may experience urges to drink when in a location where she often engaged in drinking alcohol before getting sober. Anxiety disorders are also often conditioned; for example, a humiliating experience with public speaking may lead to a deep-seated and long-lasting fear of it, which can result in anxiety attacks in situations where the person has to speak publicly. This approach looks for antecedents of behavior—stimuli that precede behavior—as the mechanism for learning.

Operant conditioning theory, sometimes known as instrumental conditioning, sees behavior as the result of reinforcement. It is built on the work of two American psychologists, John B. Watson and B. F. Skinner. In operant conditioning, behavior is learned as it is strengthened or weakened by the reinforcement (rewards and punishments) it receives or, in other words, by the consequences of the behavior. Behaviors are strengthened when

they are followed by positive consequences and weakened when they are followed by negative consequences. A classic experiment demonstrated that if a pigeon is given a food pellet each time it touches a lever, over time the pigeon learns to touch the lever to receive a food pellet. This approach looks for consequences—what comes after the behavior—as the mechanism for learning behavior. We all use operant conditioning as we go about our daily lives. We use positive reinforcers, such as smiles or praise, to reward behaviors we find pleasing, in hopes of strengthening those behaviors. Negative reinforcers are also used regularly in social life to stop or avoid unpleasant behavior. For example, an adolescent girl cleans her room to avoid parental complaints. Avoiding the complaints reinforces the room-cleaning behavior.

Cognitive social learning theory, also known as cognitive behavioral theory or social cognitive theory, with Albert Bandura as its chief contemporary proponent, suggests that behavior is also learned by imitation, observation, beliefs, and expectations. In this view, the "learner" is not passively manipulated by elements of the environment but can use cognitive processes to learn behaviors. Cognitive-behavioral therapy (CBT), developed in the 1960s, focuses on helping people to better understand the thoughts and emotions that lead to problematic behavior and to develop new ways of thinking and behaving. Observing and imitating models is a pervasive method for learning human behavior. Bandura (1977a, 1986) proposes that human behavior is also driven by beliefs and expectations. He suggests that **self-efficacy** (a sense of personal competence) and **efficacy expectation** (an expectation that one can personally accomplish a goal) play an important role in motivation and human behavior. Bandura (2001, 2002) has extended his theory of self-efficacy to propose three models of **agency** (the capacity to intentionally make things happen): *personal agency* of the individual actor, *proxy agency,* in which people reach goals by influencing others to act on their behalf, and *collective agency,* in which people act cooperatively to reach a goal.

Although the different streams of social behavioral theorizing disagree about the mechanisms by which behavioral learning occurs, there is agreement that all human problems can be defined in terms of undesirable behaviors. Furthermore, all behaviors can be defined, measured, and changed.

This is how the social behavioral perspective rates on the criteria for evaluating theories.

• *Coherence and conceptual clarity.* Although there are disagreements about the mechanisms of learning among the various streams of the social behavioral perspective, within each stream, ideas are logically developed in a consistent manner. The social behavioral perspective gets high marks for conceptual clarity; concepts are very clearly defined in each of the streams.

• *Testability and empirical support.* Social behavioral concepts are easily measured for empirical investigation because theorizing has been based, in very large part, on laboratory research. This characteristic is also a drawback of the social behavioral perspective, however, because laboratory experiments by design eliminate much of the complexity of person–environment configurations. In general, however, all streams of the social behavioral perspective have attained a relatively high degree of empirical support. Neuroscientists have found that CBT has a powerful effect on the brain activity involved in depression (Davidson & Begley, 2012). On the other hand, recent research in Sweden (Werbart, Levin, Andersson, & Sandell, 2013) found that CBT produced no better results than psychodynamic or integrative therapy in outpatient psychiatric care. Davidson and Begley (2012) suggest that the skill level of the CBT therapist for targeting specific neural circuits is an important variable, but understanding of this is in the early stages.

• *Comprehensiveness.* Overall, the social behavioral perspective sacrifices multidimensional understanding to gain logical consistency and testability. Little attention was paid to biology in early theorizing, but in his later work, Bandura (2001, 2002) recognized the role of biology in human behavior. Even so, biological research provides some of the best evidence for social behavioral theory. Besides the research on CBT already noted, research on neurophysiology and the immune system indicate that classical conditioning plays a role in physiological functioning (Farmer, 2009). Cognition and emotion are not included in theories of classical and operant conditioning, but they do receive attention in social cognitive theory. Spiritual factors are considered unmeasurable and irrelevant in classical and operant conditioning theories. For this reason, social behaviorism is sometimes seen as dehumanizing. Although environment plays a large role in the social behavioral perspective, the view of the environment is quite limited in classical and operant conditioning. Typically, the social behavioral perspective searches for the one environmental factor, or contingency, that has reinforced one specific behavior. The identified contingency is usually in the micro system (such as the family) or sometimes in the meso system (e.g., a school classroom), but these systems are not typically put in social, economic, political, or historical contexts. One exception is Bandura's social cognitive theory, which acknowledges broad systemic influences on the development of gender roles. Time is important in this perspective only in terms of the juxtaposition of stimuli and reinforcement. The social behaviorist is careful to analyze antecedents and consequences of behavior.

• *Diversity and power*. The social behavioral perspective receives low marks in terms of both diversity and power issues. Very little attention has been paid to recognizing diversity in human behaviors, and it is assumed that the same mechanisms of learning work equally well for all groups. Likewise, the social behavioral perspective attends little to issues of power and oppression. Operant behavioral theory recommends rewards over punishment, but it does not account for the coercion and oppression inherent in power relationships at every system level. It is quite possible, therefore, for the professional behavior modifier to be in service to oppressive forces. On the other hand, behavioral methods can be used to serve social work values. Bandura (1986) writes specifically about power as related to gender roles. He and other theorists note that persons in nondominant positions are particularly vulnerable to **learned helplessness** in which a person's prior experience with environmental forces has led to low self-efficacy and expectations of efficacy, a point also made by some feminist theorists. You may find the concepts of self-efficacy and learned helplessness particularly useful in thinking about both Stanley and Marcia McKinley's situations. Both have experienced some setbacks that may be leading them to expect less of themselves.

• *Usefulness for social work practice*. A major strength of the social behavioral perspective is the ease with which principles of behavior modification can be extrapolated, and it is probably a rare person who has not used social behavioral principles of action at some point. Social workers and psychologists have used social behavioral methods primarily to modify undesirable behavior of individuals. For example, systematic desensitization techniques are used to diminish or eradicate anxiety symptoms. Parent training programs often teach parents how to make more effective use of reinforcements to strengthen positive behaviors and weaken negative behaviors in their children. Social workers often model how to enact new behaviors for their clients. Dialectical behavior therapy teaches adaptive coping related to emotion regulation, distress tolerance, cognitive distortions, and interpersonal communication (Walsh, 2014). However, although the potential exists, behavioral methods have not been used effectively to produce social reform. Richard Stuart (1989) reminds us that behavior modification was once a "social movement" that appealed to young social reformers who were more interested in changing social conditions that produce atypical behaviors than in changing systems for managing atypical behavior. Skinner's *Walden Two* (1948) was the impetus for attempts by these young reformers to build nonpunitive communities, which represented significant modification of social conditions (see Kinkade, 1973; Wheeler, 1973). Indeed, Bandura's (2002) conceptualization of proxy agency and collective agency has implications for social reform.

HUMANISTIC PERSPECTIVE

Consistent with the social work code of ethics, the hospice social worker who is making contact with the McKinley family believes in the dignity and worth of all humans. Her experiences as a hospice social worker have reinforced her belief that each person is unique, and even though she has worked with more than 100 hospice patients, she expects Ruth McKinley's story to be in some ways unlike any other story she has heard. She is eager to hear more about how Ruth sees her situation and whether there are any things she would like to change in the limited time she has left. The social worker takes note of strengths she sees in the McKinley family, their love and kindness toward each other and their courage in the face of an accumulation of stress. She wants to hear more about how Stanley, Marcia, and Bethany are thinking about their relationships with Ruth and whether there are any changes they would like to make in that relationship during Ruth's final days. Her thoughts and planned course of action reflect the humanistic perspective.

The humanistic perspective is often called the "third force" of psychology, because it was developed in reaction to the determinism found in early versions of both the psychodynamic (behavior as intrapsychically determined) and behavioral (behavior as externally determined) perspectives (Sollod et al., 2009). We are using the term **humanistic perspective** to include humanistic psychology and existential psychology, both of which emphasize the individual's freedom of action and search for meaning. We also extend the term to include the growing movement of positive psychology and the capabilities approach. The main ideas of the humanistic perspective are presented visually in Exhibit 2.8.

Perhaps the most influential contributions to humanistic psychology were made by Carl Rogers (1951) and Abraham Maslow (1962). Abraham Maslow (1962) was drawn to understand "peak experiences," or intense mystical moments of feeling connected to other people, nature, or a divine being. Maslow found peak experiences to occur often among self-actualizing people, or people who were expressing their innate potentials. Maslow developed a theory of a **hierarchy of needs**, which suggests that higher needs cannot emerge in full motivational force until lower needs have been at least partially satisfied. Physiological needs are at the bottom of the hierarchy, and the need for self-actualization is at the top:

1. *Physiological needs*: hunger, thirst, sex

2. *Safety needs*: avoidance of pain and anxiety; desire for security

3. *Belongingness and love needs*: affection, intimacy

Exhibit 2.8 Humanistic Perspective

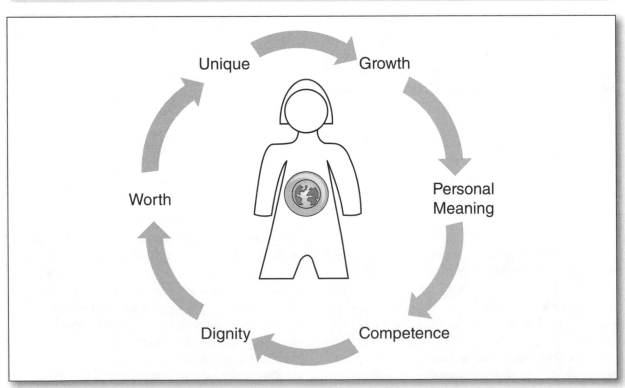

4. *Esteem needs*: self-respect, adequacy, mastery

5. *Self-actualization*: to be fully what one can be; altruism, beauty, creativity, justice

Maslow is considered one of the founders of *transpersonal psychology*, which he labeled as the "fourth force" of psychology. We include transpersonal psychology under the umbrella of the humanistic perspective, but it is not discussed here because it receives considerable attention in Chapter 6, The Spiritual Person.

Carl Rogers (1951) was interested in the capacity of humans to change in therapeutic relationships. He began his professional career at the Rochester Child Guidance Center, where he worked with social workers who had been trained at the Philadelphia School of Social Work. He has acknowledged the influence of Otto Rank, Jessie Taft, and the social workers at the Rochester agency on his thinking about the importance of responding to client feelings (Hart, 1970). He came to believe that humans have vast internal resources for self-understanding and self-directed behavior. He emphasized, therefore, the dignity and worth of each individual and presented the ideal interpersonal conditions under which people come to use their internal resources to become "more fully functioning." These have become known as the core conditions of the therapeutic process: empathy, warmth, and genuineness.

Existential psychology, which developed out of the chaos and despair in Europe during and after World War II, presented four primary themes (Krill, 1996):

1. Each person is unique and has value.

2. Suffering is a necessary part of human growth.

3. Personal growth results from staying in the immediate moment.

4. Personal growth takes a sense of commitment.

It is the emphasis on the necessity for suffering that sets existentialism apart from humanism.

Maslow is said to have coined the term *positive psychology* when he used it as a chapter title in his 1954 book, *Motivation and Personality*. As we know it today, **positive psychology** is a relatively recent branch of psychology that undertakes the scientific study of people's strengths and virtues and promotes optimal functioning of individuals and communities. Proponents of positive psychology argue that psychology has paid too much attention to human pathology and not enough to human strengths and virtues. Martin Seligman (1998, 2002), one of the authors of the concept of "learned helplessness," has been at the forefront of positive psychology, contributing the important concept of "learned optimism." Positive psychologists argue that prevention of mental illness is best accomplished by promoting human strength and competence. They have identified a set of human strengths that promote well-being and buffer against mental illness, including optimism, courage, hope, perseverance, honesty, a work ethic, and interpersonal skills (Snyder & Lopez, 2007). The positive psychology approach is drawing on both Western and Eastern worldviews. A large focus on hope is rooted in Western thinking (McKnight, Snyder, & Lopez, 2007); whereas emphasis on balance, compassion, and harmony comes more from Eastern thinking (Pedrotti, Snyder, & Lopez, 2007).

In Chapter 1, we describe the capabilities approach to social justice, which can be classified with the humanistic perspective. The *capabilities approach* was proposed by welfare economist and political philosopher Amartya Sen (1999). Like other humanistic thinkers, Sen focuses on human agency or people's ability to pursue and realize goals that they value. He and collaborator Martha Nussbaum (2001) see humans as active, creative, and able to act on behalf of their aspirations. In contrast to earlier humanistic theorists, however, the capabilities approach puts individuals in a wider context and focuses on the idea that social arrangements should aim to support and expand people's capabilities. As suggested in Chapter 1, Nussbaum lists 10 core capabilities that all people in all societies must have to be able to pursue and realize valued goals. Sen argues, instead, that no such list can be arbitrarily delineated because of the great diversity of people and environments in the world. He recognizes the intersectionalities of diversity that exist in social life, that one person can belong to many different groups. He thinks that individuals should be left to decide which capabilities they choose to enhance or neglect.

This is how the humanistic perspective rates on the criteria for evaluating theories.

• *Coherence and conceptual clarity.* Theories in the humanistic perspective are often criticized for being vague and highly abstract, with concepts such as "being" and "phenomenal self." The language of transpersonal theories is particularly abstract, with discussion of self-transcendence and higher states of consciousness. Indeed, theorists in the humanistic perspective, in general, have not been afraid to sacrifice coherence to gain what they see as a more complete understanding of human behavior. The positive psychology movement is working to bring greater consistency and coherence to humanistic concepts, and Nussbaum's core capabilities are quite explicit.

• *Testability and empirical support.* As might be expected, empirically minded scholars have not been attracted to the humanistic perspective, and consequently until recently there was little empirical literature to support the perspective. A notable exception is the clinical side of Rogers's theory. Rogers began a rigorous program of empirical investigation of the therapeutic process, and such research has provided strong empirical support for his conceptualization of the necessary conditions for the therapeutic relationship: warmth, empathy, and genuineness (Sollod et al., 2009). Recent research across several disciplines has demonstrated that a high level of practitioner empathy is associated with positive client outcomes (Gerdes & Segal, 2011). The positive psychology movement is focusing, with much success, on producing empirical support for the role of human strengths and virtues in human well-being. Some researchers have suggested that neuroscience research is calling the notion of free will (human agency) into question, arguing that it provides clear evidence that human behavior is

determined by the gene-environment interactions that shape the brain (Kurzweil, 2012). Other neuroscientists provide evidence that humans have the power to "live our lives and train our brains" in ways that shift emotions, thoughts, and behaviors (Davidson & Begley, 2012, p. 225). That is a high endorsement for some of the tenets of the humanistic perspective.

• *Comprehensiveness.* The internal life of the individual is the focus of the humanistic perspective, and it is strong in consideration of both psychological and spiritual dimensions of the person. With its emphasis on a search for meaning, the humanistic perspective is the only perspective presented in this chapter to explicitly recognize the role of spirituality in human behavior. (Other theories of spirituality are discussed in Chapter 6.) In addition, Maslow recognizes the importance of satisfaction of basic biological needs. Most theorists in the humanistic tradition give limited attention to the environments of human behavior. A dehumanizing world is implicit in the works of Maslow and Rogers, but neither theorist focuses explicitly on the environments of human behavior, nor do they acknowledge that some environments are more dehumanizing than others. The positive psychology movement has begun to examine positive environments that can promote human strengths and virtues, including school, work, and community environments (Snyder & Lopez, 2007). The capabilities perspective calls for social institutions to support and expand people's capabilities.

• *Diversity and power.* The humanistic perspective, with its almost singular consideration of an internal frame of reference, devotes more attention to individual differences than to differences between groups. The one exception is Sen's capabilities perspective, which emphasizes the great diversity of human capabilities and values. In general, far too little attention is given in the humanistic tradition to the processes by which institutional oppression influences the **phenomenal self**—the individual's subjectively felt and interpreted experience of "who I am." Like the social constructionist perspective, however, the humanistic perspective is sometimes quite strong in giving voice to experiences of members of non-dominant groups. With the emphasis on the phenomenal self, members of nondominant groups are more likely to have preferential input into the telling of their own stories. The social worker's intention to hear and honor the stories of each member of the McKinley family may be a novel experience for each family member, and the social worker may, indeed, hear very different stories from what she expects to hear. Rogers developed his respect for the personal self, and consequently his client-centered approach to therapy, when he realized that his perceptions of the worlds of his low-income clients in the Child Guidance Clinic were very different from their own perceptions.

• *Usefulness for social work.* If the social constructionist perspective gives new meaning to the old social work adage "Begin where the client is," it is social work's historical involvement in the development of the humanistic perspective that gave original meaning to the adage. It is limited in terms of providing specific interventions, but it is consistent with social work's value of the dignity and worth of the individual. The humanistic perspective suggests that social workers begin by developing an understanding of how the client views the situation, and with its emphasis on the individual drive for growth and competence, it recommends a "strengths" rather than "pathology" approach to practice. George Vaillant (2002), a research psychiatrist, suggests that this attention to strengths is what distinguishes social workers from other helping professionals. From this perspective, then, we might note that the strong commitment to helping one another displayed by the McKinley family is one of several strengths that could be the basis for successful intervention. At the organizational level, the humanistic perspective has been used by organizational theorists, such as Douglas McGregor (1960), to prescribe administrative actions that focus on employee well-being as the best route to organizational efficiency and effectiveness. Positive psychology is popular in clinical work and is beginning to propose guidelines for developing positive environments in schools, workplaces, and communities.

> ## Critical Thinking Questions 2.4
>
> Both cognitive social learning theory and theories in the humanistic perspective emphasize the important role of human agency, the capacity to intentionally make things happen, in human behavior. Other theories in the social behavioral perspective and most of the other perspectives discussed here put less emphasis on human agency. Now that you have examined eight theoretical perspectives, how much agency do you think humans have over their behavior, in general? Explain. How much agency do you think members of the McKinley family have? Explain.

THE MERITS OF MULTIPLE PERSPECTIVES

You can see that each of these perspectives puts a different lens on the unfolding story of the McKinley family. Although they all are seeking to understand human behavior, different phenomena are emphasized. You can also see that each of the eight perspectives has been used to guide social work practice over time. It was suggested in Chapter 1 that each situation can be examined from several perspectives and that using a variety of perspectives brings more dimensions of the situation into view. Cognitive psychologists have provided convincing evidence that all of us, whether new or experienced social workers, have biases that predispose us to do too little thinking, rather than too much, about the practice situations we confront. We are particularly prone to ignore information that is contrary to our hypotheses about situations. Consequently, we tend to end our search for understanding prematurely. One step we can take to prevent this premature closure is to think about practice situations from multiple theoretical perspectives. Exhibit 2.9 overviews the big ideas of the eight perspectives presented in this chapter and cues you to where you

Exhibit 2.9 Big Ideas of Eight Theoretical Perspectives as Used Throughout the Book

Perspective	Big Ideas	Found in Later Chapters
Systems	• Systems are made up of interrelated members that constitute a linked whole. • Each part of the system impacts all other parts and the system as a whole. • All systems are subsystems of other larger systems. • Systems maintain boundaries that give them their identities. • The dynamic interactions within, between, and among systems produce both stability and change, sometimes even rapid dramatic change.	Chapter 3 Chapter 4 Chapter 5 Chapter 6 Chapter 7 Chapter 8 Chapter 9 Chapter 10 Chapter 11 Chapter 12 Chapter 13 Chapter 14
Conflict	• All social systems have inequalities in the distribution of valued resources. • Power is unequally divided, and powerful social groups impose their will on subordinate groups. • Conflict and the potential for conflict underlie unequal social relationships. • Members of subordinate groups often become alienated from society. • Social change may occur when subordinate groups recognize patterns of inequality and injustice and take action to increase their own power.	Chapter 3 Chapter 4 Chapter 6 Chapter 7 Chapter 8 Chapter 9 Chapter 10 Chapter 11 Chapter 12 Chapter 13 Chapter 14
Exchange and choice	• Individual and collective actors engage in social exchange of material and nonmaterial resources and make choices in pursuit of those resources. • Choices in social exchange are based on self-interest as well as community interest. • Choices in social exchange are based on both reason and emotion and on values, norms, and expectations. • Social exchange operates on a norm of reciprocity, but exchange relationships are often unbalanced. • Power comes from unequal resources in exchange.	Chapter 3 Chapter 8 Chapter 9 Chapter 10 Chapter 11 Chapter 12 Chapter 13 Chapter 14
Social constructionist	• People construct meaning, a sense of self, and a social world through their interactions with each other. • Social reality is created when people, in social interaction, develop shared meaning, a common understanding of their world. • There is no singular objective reality but rather the multiple realities that are created in different contexts. • Social interaction is grounded in language customs, as well as cultural and historical contexts. • People can modify meanings in the process of interaction.	Chapter 3 Chapter 4 Chapter 5 Chapter 7 Chapter 8 Chapter 10 Chapter 11 Chapter 12 Chapter 13 Chapter 14

Perspective	Big Ideas	Found in Later Chapters
Psychodynamic	• Emotions have a central place in human behavior. • Unconscious, as well as conscious, mental activity serves as the motivating force in human behavior. • Early childhood experiences are central in the patterning of an individual's emotions and, therefore, central to problems throughout life. • Individuals may become overwhelmed by internal or external demands. • Individuals frequently use ego defense mechanisms to avoid becoming overwhelmed by internal or external demands.	Chapter 4 Chapter 5 Chapter 6 Chapter 7 Chapter 8 Chapter 10 Chapter 11 Chapter 14
Developmental	• Human development occurs in clearly defined, age-graded stages. • Each stage of life is qualitatively different from all other stages. • Each stage builds on earlier stages. • Human development is a complex interaction of biological, psychological, and social factors. • Moving from one stage to the next involves new tasks and changes in statuses and roles.	Chapter 3 Chapter 4 Chapter 5 Chapter 6 Chapter 7 Chapter 10 Chapter 11 Chapter 14
Social behavioral	• Human behavior is learned when individuals interact with the environment. • Human behavior is learned through different mechanisms of learning, including association of environmental stimuli, reinforcement, imitation, and personal expectations and meaning. • All human problems can be formulated as undesirable behavior. • All behavior can be defined and changed.	Chapter 4 Chapter 6 Chapter 7 Chapter 8 Chapter 11
Humanistic	• Each person is unique and has value. • Each person is responsible for the choices he or she makes within the limits of freedom. • People always have the capacity to change themselves, even to make radical change. • Human behavior can be understood only from the vantage point of the internal frame of reference of the person. • Human behavior is driven by a desire for growth, personal meaning, and competence and by a need to experience a bond with others.	Chapter 4 Chapter 5 Chapter 6 Chapter 7 Chapter 8 Chapter 10 Chapter 11 Chapter 12 Chapter 13

can find these ideas reflected in theory and research in Chapters 3 through 14. As noted earlier, margin notes in those chapters call out places where ideas from the eight perspectives are used.

A number of behavioral science disciplines offer a variety of ways of thinking about changing person–environment configurations, ways that have been worked out over time to assist in understanding human behavior. They are tools that can help us make sense of the situations we encounter. We do not mean to suggest that all eight of the perspectives discussed in this chapter will be equally useful, or even useful at all, in all situations. But each of these perspectives will be useful in some situations that you encounter as a social worker. As a competent professional, you must view the quest for adequate breadth and depth in your knowledge base as an ongoing, lifelong challenge and responsibility. We hope that over time you will begin to use these multiple perspectives in an integrated fashion so that you can see the many dimensions—the contradictions as well as the consistencies—in stories like the McKinley family's. We encourage you to be flexible and reflective in your thinking and your "doing" throughout your career. We remind you, again, to use general knowledge such as that provided by theoretical perspectives only to generate hypotheses to be tested in specific situations, not as facts inherent in every situation.

Critical Thinking Questions 2.5

At the beginning of the chapter, we wondered what got your attention when you read the story of the McKinley family. As you read about the eight theoretical perspectives, did you see any ideas that addressed the things that caught your attention about the story? If so, what were they? Were there things that caught your attention that did not seem to be addressed by any of the perspectives? If so, what were they? Which perspectives seemed more closely aligned with what caught your attention upon first reading the story? Which perspectives provided you with useful new ways to think about the story?

Implications for Social Work Practice

The eight perspectives on human behavior discussed in this chapter suggest a variety of principles for social work assessment and intervention.

- In assessment, consider any recent system changes that may be affecting the client system. Assist families and groups to renegotiate unsatisfactory system boundaries. Develop networks of support for persons experiencing challenging life transitions.
- In assessment, consider power arrangements and forces of oppression, and the alienation that emanates from them. Assist in the development of advocacy efforts to challenge patterns of dominance, when possible. Be aware of the power dynamics in your relationships with clients; when working with nonvoluntary clients, speak directly about the limits and uses of your power.
- In assessment, consider the patterns of exchange in the social support networks of individual clients, families, and organizations, using network maps where useful. Assist individuals, families, and organizations to renegotiate unsatisfactory patterns of exchange, when possible. Recognize the role of both reason and emotion in the policymaking process.
- Begin your work by understanding how clients view their situations. Engage clients in thinking about the environments in which these constructions of self and situations have developed. When working in situations characterized by differences in belief systems, assist members to engage in sincere discussions and to negotiate lines of action.
- Assist clients in expressing emotional conflicts and in understanding how these are related to past events, when appropriate. Help them develop self-awareness and self-control, where needed. Assist clients in locating and using needed environmental resources.
- In assessment, consider the familial, cultural, and historical contexts in the timing and experience of developmental transitions. Recognize human development as unique and lifelong.
- In assessment, consider the variety of processes by which behavior is learned. Be sensitive to the possibility of learned helplessness when clients lack motivation for change. Consider issues of social justice and fairness before engaging in behavior modification.
- Be aware of the potential for significant differences between your assessment of the situation and the client's own assessment; value self-determination. Focus on strengths rather than pathology; recognize the possibility of learned hopefulness as well as learned helplessness.

agency
boundary
chaos theory
classical conditioning theory
cognitive social learning theory
conflict perspective
critical race theory
critical theorists
developmental perspective
efficacy expectation

empowerment theories
exchange and choice perspective
feedback mechanism
feminist theories
hierarchy of needs
humanistic perspective
intersectionality theory
learned helplessness
operant conditioning theory
phenomenal self

positive psychology
psychodynamic perspective
reciprocity
self-efficacy
social behavioral perspective
social capital
social constructionist perspective
social exchange theory
social network theory
systems perspective

Active Learning

1. Reread the case study of the intergenerational stresses in the McKinley family. Next, review the big ideas of the eight theoretical perspectives as presented in Exhibit 2.9. Choose three specific big ideas that you think are most helpful in thinking about the McKinley family. For example, you might choose this big idea from the systems perspective: Each part of the system affects all other parts and the system as a whole. You might also choose this big idea from the humanistic perspective: Human behavior is driven by a desire for growth, personal meaning, and competence and by a need to experience a bond with others. Likewise, you might choose another specific idea from any of the perspectives. The point is to choose the three big ideas that you find most useful. Now, in a small group, compare notes with three or four classmates about which big ideas were chosen. Discuss why these particular choices, and not others, were made by each of your classmates.

2. Break into eight small groups, with each group assigned one of the theoretical perspectives described in the chapter. Each group's task is to briefly summarize the assigned theoretical perspective and then explain the group's interpretation of the perspective's usefulness when applied to the McKinley family or another case scenario.

3. Choose a story that interests you in a current edition of a daily newspaper. Read the story carefully and then think about which of the eight theoretical perspectives discussed in this chapter is most reflected in the story.

Web Resources

Conflict Theory(ies) of Deviance:
www.umsl.edu/~keelr/200/conflict.html

Site presented by Robert O. Keel at the University of Missouri at St. Louis contains information on the basic premises of conflict theory as well as specific information on radical conflict theory and pluralistic conflict theory.

International Humanistic Psychology Association: http://ihpaworld.org

Site maintained by the International Humanistic Psychology Association contains links to events, capacity-building training projects, professional collaboration and development, research, dialogues and networking, and publications and resources.

Personality Theories: webspace.ship.edu/cgboer/perscontents.html

Site maintained by C. George Boeree at the Psychology Department of Shippensburg University provides an electronic textbook on theories of personality, including the theories of Sigmund Freud, Erik Erikson, Carl Jung, B. F. Skinner, Albert Bandura, Abraham Maslow, Carl Rogers, Jean Piaget, and Buddhist psychology.

Sociological Theories and Perspectives: www.sociosite.net/topics/theory.php

Site maintained at the University of Amsterdam contains general information on sociological theory and specific information on a number of theories, including chaos theory, interaction theory, conflict theory, network theory, and rational choice theory.

William Alanson White Institute: www.wawhite.org

Site contains contemporary psychoanalysis journal articles, training programs, and a psychoanalysis-in-action blog.

Student Study Site

$SAGE edge™

Sharpen your skills with SAGE edge at **edge.sagepub.com/hutchisonpe5e**

SAGE edge for students provides a personalized approach to help you accomplish your coursework goals in an easy-to-use learning environment.

PART II

The Multiple Dimensions of Person

The multiple dimensions of person, environment, and time have unity; they are inseparable and embedded. That is the way I think about them and the way I am encouraging you to think about them. However, you will be better able to think about the unity of the three aspects of human behavior when you have developed a clearer understanding of the different dimensions encompassed by each one. A review of theory and research about the different dimensions will help you to sharpen your thinking about what is involved in the changing configurations of persons and environments.

The purpose of the four chapters in Part II is to provide you with an up-to-date understanding of theory and research about the dimensions of person. It begins with a chapter on the biological dimension and ends with one on the spiritual dimension. Because so much has been written about the psychological dimension, it is covered in two chapters: the first one about the basic elements of a person's psychology and the second one about the processes a person uses to maintain psychological balance in a changing environment.

With a state-of-the-art knowledge base about the multiple dimensions of persons, you will be prepared to consider the interactions between persons and environments, which is the subject of Part III. And then you will be able to think more comprehensively and more clearly about the ways configurations of persons and environments change across the life course. The discussion of the life course in the companion volume to this book, *The Changing Life Course*, attempts to put the dimensions of persons and environments back together and help you think about their embeddedness across time.

CHAPTER 3

The Biological Person

Stephen French Gilson

Chapter Outline

Acknowledgments: The author wishes to thank Elizabeth DePoy and Elizabeth Hutchison for their helpful comments, insights, and suggestions for this chapter.

Key Ideas

As you read this chapter, take note of these central ideas:

1. A central tenet in this chapter is the view of body and surroundings as a continuous environment that spans from proximal (most interior) to distal (or moving outward from the organic matter of the corpus).

2. Biological functioning is the result of complex transactions between interior (proximal) and exterior (distal) systems. No biological system operates in isolation.

3. The nervous system is responsible for processing and integrating incoming information, and it influences and directs reactions to that information. It is divided into three major subsystems: the central nervous system, peripheral nervous system, and autonomic nervous system.

4. The endocrine system plays a crucial role in growth, metabolism, development, learning, and memory.

5. The immune system is made up of organs and cells that work together to defend the body against disease. Autoimmune diseases occur when the immune system mistakenly targets parts of the interior (proximal) environment.

6. The cardiovascular system is made up of the heart and the blood circulatory system. The circulatory system supplies cells of the body with the food and oxygen they need for functioning.

7. The musculoskeletal system supports and protects the body and its organs and provides motion and postural stability. The contraction and relaxation of muscles attached to the skeleton is the basis for voluntary movements.

8. The reproductive system is composed of visible and interior structures that are different for males and females.

CASE STUDY 3.1

Cheryl's Brain Injury

Cheryl grew up in rural Idaho in a large extended family and enlisted as a private in the army just after she finished her 3rd year in high school. After basic training, she was first deployed to Iraq and subsequently to Afghanistan for active combat duty. Traveling en route to Ghorak base in southern Afghanistan, Cheryl's Humvee contacted an explosive device, causing Cheryl to sustain a closed head injury and multiple fractures. She was in a coma for 3 weeks.

Over a 6-month period, all of Cheryl's external bodily injuries, including the fractures, healed, and she was able to walk and talk with no apparent residual impairments. Cognitively and socially, however, Cheryl experienced change. Although able to read, she could not retain what she had just read a minute ago. She did not easily recall her previous knowledge of math and was not able to compute basic calculations such as addition and subtraction without the use of a mechanical calculator. She was slow in penmanship, taking at least 5 minutes to write her own name. Unlike her social behavior prior to the accident, Cheryl was often blunt in her comments, even to the point of becoming confrontational with friends without provocation.

Because of her observable recovery, everyone expected Cheryl to return to active duty, but 2 years after the accident, her family knows that she is not going to return to military service. Cheryl's ex-boyfriend, Sean, is about to get engaged to another woman, but Cheryl thinks that she is still dating Sean and that he will soon marry her. People who knew Cheryl before the accident cannot understand why her personality has changed so markedly, and they even say, "She's a completely different person!"

CASE STUDY 3.2

A Diabetes Diagnosis for Bess

Bess, a 52-year-old Franco-American woman who lives in rural Maine, was enjoying her empty nest just before the social worker met her. The youngest of her three children had married 6 months earlier, and although Bess was proud of what she had accomplished as a single mother, she was now ready to get on with her life. Her first order of business was to get her body back into shape, so she started on a high-carbohydrate, low-fat diet that she had read about in a magazine. Drinking the recommended eight glasses of water or more each day was easy, because it seemed that she was always thirsty. But Bess was losing more weight than she thought possible on a diet, and she was always cheating! Bess had thought that she would have to get more exercise to lose weight, but even walking to and from her car at the grocery store tired her out.

One morning, Bess did not arrive at the country store where she worked. Because it was very unusual for her not to call and also not to answer her phone, a co-worker went to her house. When there was no response to the knocking, the co-worker and one of Bess's neighbors opened the door to Bess's house and walked in. They found Bess sitting on her couch, still in her nightclothes, which were drenched with perspiration. Bess was very confused, unable to answer simple questions with correct responses. Paramedics transported Bess to the local community hospital.

In the emergency room, after some blood work, a doctor diagnosed her with diabetes mellitus (diabetes). Because diabetes is common among middle-aged and older people in this poor rural town, a social worker had already established an educational support group for persons with diabetes that Bess now attends.

CASE STUDY 3.3

Melissa's HIV Diagnosis

Melissa's "perfect life" has just fallen apart. As a young urban professional who grew up in a middle-class suburb in New York, Melissa had always dreamed of a big wedding at her parents' country club, and her dreams were about to come true. All the plans had been made, invitations sent out, bridesmaids' dresses bought and measured, and her

(Continued)

(Continued)

wedding dress selected. All that remained was finalizing the menu and approving the flower arrangements. Because Melissa and her fiancé planned to have children soon after their marriage, she went to her physician for a physical exam 2 months before her wedding. As the doctor does with all of her patients, she asked if Melissa had ever been tested for HIV. Melissa said no and gave her permission for an HIV test to be run with all the other routine blood work.

One week after her physical, the doctor's office called and asked Melissa to return for more blood work because of what was thought to be an inaccuracy in the report. Melissa went back to the office for more blood tests. Another week passed, but Melissa did not think again about the tests because she was immersed in wedding plans. Her physician called her at home at 8:00 one morning and asked her to come to her office after work that day. Because she was distracted by the wedding plans and a busy schedule at work, Melissa did not think anything of the doctor's request.

When she arrived at the doctor's office, she was immediately taken to the doctor's private office. The doctor came in, sat down, and told Melissa that two separate blood tests had confirmed that she was HIV-positive. Melissa spent over 3 hours with her physician that evening, and soon thereafter she began to attend an HIV support group.

Melissa has never used illicit drugs, and she has only had two sexual partners. She and her fiancé had decided not to have unprotected intercourse until they were ready for children, and because they used condoms, he was not a prime suspect for passing along the infection. Melissa remembered that the man with whom she was involved prior to meeting her fiancé would not talk about his past. She has not seen this former lover for the past 3 years since she moved away from New York.

CASE STUDY 3.4

Lifestyle Changes for Thomas

Thomas is a 30-year-old man who lives with his parents, both of whom are obese, as are his two older sisters. Thomas loves his mom's cooking, but some time ago he realized that its high-fat and high-sodium content was contributing to his parents' obesity and high blood pressure.

In contrast, Thomas takes pride in watching his diet (when he isn't eating at home) and is pretty smug about being the only one in the family who is not obese. Being called "the thin man" is, to Thomas, a compliment. He also boasts about being in great physical shape and exercises to the point of being dizzy.

After one of his dizziness episodes, a friend told him that he should get his blood pressure checked. Out of curiosity, the next time Thomas stopped at his local drug store, he decided to use a self-monitoring machine to check his blood pressure. To his astonishment, the reading came back 200/105, which is quite high. Thomas now seeks a social worker's help to adopt some major lifestyle changes.

CASE STUDY 3.5

Mary and Her Diagnosis of Multiple Sclerosis (MS)

Mary's "follow-up" appointment with her family practitioner was the week following her 43rd birthday. Mary's grandparents, both maternal and paternal, emigrated from Denmark. Mary's mother was raised in Brush, Colorado, and her father in Buffalo, Wyoming. Having grown up on a small ranch in rural Colorado, it seemed natural for her to eventually settle in the area near her family. In addition to working as a teacher at the local high school, she spent her time tending the garden, taking care of the chickens, and raising goats, a small herd of Belted Galloway cows, and her horses. She learned to ride before she ever attended grammar school. Although she enjoyed all types of equitation, her primary loves were barrel racing and team roping.

Over the past 5 years she began to experience several "physical symptoms" that made it difficult for her to always feel confident or even safe when she was riding, whether at her home barn practicing or competing in an event.

When she met with her physician, she described experiencing several seemingly unrelated symptoms. These included periods of intense ankle and knee discomfort, episodic vision difficulties, digestive and gastrointestinal distress, fevers, chest pains including shortness of breath and rapid heart rate, and periods of fatigue and exhaustion, among several other episodic conditions and symptoms. She regularly sought treatment for these illnesses, often being prescribed medications and a variety of treatment regimens.

Because Mary often talked about these symptoms and conditions, which seemed to vary in duration and intensity and were frequently nonspecific, she commonly referred to herself as a hypochondriac. Linked to this self-doubt was her feeling that her primary-care physician dismissed her experiences of pain and discomfort. Her physician did not refer her to outside consultation, and she set her own appointments with condition-specific health providers, such as her optometrist for her vision difficulties.

Finally, following 2 weeks of feeling constant exhaustion, regular heart palpitations when riding, and falling off her horse during a barrel racing completion, Mary's best friend convinced her to seek a medical evaluation from a neurologist. At this appointment, in addition to a general physical evaluation, Mary was referred for a comprehensive diagnostic workup. As a result of these tests, when combined with her medical history and symptom presentation, Mary was given a diagnosis of multiple sclerosis (MS).

CASE STUDY 3.6

Juan and Belinda's Reproductive Health

Juan and Belinda, now both 17 years old, grew up in the same neighbourhood of a southwestern city in the United States and attend the same church, St. Joseph's Catholic Church. They do not attend the same school, however. Belinda has received all of her education at the schools at St. Joseph's; Juan attended John F. Kennedy Elementary School and John Marshall Junior High and now attends Cesar Chavez High School. Since seventh grade, Juan has met Belinda after school and walked her home.

They both live in small, well-kept homes in a section of the community that is largely Spanish speaking with very strong influences from the wide variety of countries of origin represented by community residents: Mexico, Honduras, El Salvador, and Nicaragua, among others. The Catholic Church here is a dominant exterior (distal) environmental force in shaping community social, political, economic, and personal values and behaviors.

Both Juan's and Belinda's parents immigrated to the United States from Mexico, seeking to improve the opportunities for their families. Juan's mother found a job as a housekeeper at a local hotel, where she now manages the housekeeping staff. His father began as a day laborer and construction worker, eventually moving up to become foreman of the largest construction company in the area. He anticipates beginning his own construction company within the next year. Belinda's mother is a skilled seamstress and was able to start her own tailoring

(Continued)

(Continued)

business shortly after immigrating. Belinda's father, with a background in diesel mechanics, was able to find work at a large trucking company where he continues to work today.

Like many teenagers, Juan and Belinda face the difficulties of sorting out the complexities and intricacies of their relationship. They feel very much in love, knowing in their hearts that they want to get married and raise a family. At 17, they are at the crossroads of intimacy, because they face conflicts about their sexuality with limited information and strong prohibitions against premarital sex. Following many of the teachings of their church and the urgings of their parents, Juan and Belinda have avoided much physical contact except for kissing and holding each other.

Like many communities in the United States, their community struggled with the question of just what information should be given to students about physical health and sexuality. Their community decided to limit the amount and type of information to the basics of female and male sexual anatomy and physiology. The result of this decision for Juan and Belinda was that they learned very little about sexual response and behavior, conception, pregnancy, childbirth, contraception, safe sex practices, and other areas that are critical in today's world. The decision by the school board was based on a belief that it was the family's responsibility to provide this information to their children. The school social worker at Cesar Chavez High School is aware of the moral conflicts that arise for youth in this community that in part result from limited sex education.

AN INTEGRATIVE APPROACH FOR UNDERSTANDING THE INTERSECTION OF INTERIOR (PROXIMAL) BIOLOGICAL HEALTH AND ILLNESS AND EXTERIOR (DISTAL) ENVIRONMENTAL FACTORS _____

As we think about the stories of Cheryl, Bess, Melissa, Thomas, Mary, and Juan and Belinda, we can see that biology is an important dimension of their behavior. But despite growing agreement about the importance of biology in influencing human behavior and thus the need for social workers to be well informed in this arena, the profession is struggling to articulate exactly what social workers need to know about human biology. Although there are a variety of ways to think about our bodies, the approach presented here locates understandings of the body within theories of environment. Consistent with contemporary theory in which the distinction between the body and its exterior is not clear, a central tenet of this chapter is the view that the body and surroundings are a continuous environment that spans from *proximal* (most interior) to *distal* (or moving outward from the organic matter of the corpus). Thus environment is defined as the entire set of conditions under which one operates (DePoy & Gilson, 2012). For instructive purposes, however, the lexicon of interior or proximal and exterior or distal environment is used. Interior (proximal) is concerned with the description and explanation of embodied organic conditions, such as internal organ systems, genetics, interior psychological structures, processes, and so forth. Exterior (distal) environments are characterized as nonorganic conditions that are not contained within the body (DePoy & Gilson, 2012). This may be different from the ways you have thought about human biology, but it is consistent with the growing evidence of the interconnectedness of elements of the natural and physical world.

Because social workers deal with people, and people constitute the corpus of human biology, social workers encounter biology and its reciprocal influence with exterior (distal) environmental conditions such as poverty, addictions, violence, and child abuse each time they interact with individuals. For instructive purposes, we distinguish interior (proximal) from exterior (distal) environments on the basis of corporeality, or material that relates to the body (DePoy & Gilson, 2012). However, the division between corporeal and noncorporeal is not clear. Consider for example a knee replacement. While it is not organic in composition, it is located beneath the skin and functions as integral to body stability and movement. But is it interior (proximal) or exterior (distal)? What about eyeglasses, prostheses, or even clothes that preserve body temperature? What about speech? Although articulated by an individual, sound is created by air vibrations and received by another.

Returning to the cases of Cheryl, Bess, Melissa, Thomas, Mary, and Juan and Belinda, their interior (proximal) environments are the initial reason they are seeking social work assistance. To be efficacious in meeting professional goals, social workers must have a working knowledge of the body's systems and the ways these systems interact with one another and with other interior (proximal) and exterior (distal) environmental dimensions. Social workers also must be sufficiently informed about interior (proximal) environment theory and knowledge to be able to discuss details of biological functioning with clients when indicated (Johnson, 2004; Tangenberg & Kemp, 2002).

While the knowledge of biological structures and their function is foundational to understanding the interior (proximal) environment, this knowledge in isolation does not serve social workers, because professional decision making and activity require a complex mastery of the interactions of interior (proximal) and exterior (distal) environments. Moreover, understanding of how the interior (proximal) environment contributes to human behavior (what people do and do not do and how they do what they do), appearance, and experience (DePoy & Gilson, 2004) is critical for informed social work practice as exemplified by each of the chapter-opening case studies.

Approaching social work practice from well-accepted explanatory models requires depth of knowledge not only of interior parts but also of their complex, context-embedded interaction.

Consistent with post-postmodern thinking, which co-locates multiple fields of knowledge adjacent to and informing one another (DePoy & Gilson, 2007), social work's growing interest in human biology is essential for framing efficacious responses that consider the interstices of mind–body interactions.

Systems perspective

Systems frameworks describe and explain human phenomena as sets of interrelated parts. There are many variations and applications of systems approaches ranging from those that look at embodied or interior systems, to those that examine human systems composed of both humans and their surroundings, and even extending to systems that do not contain embodied elements (DePoy & Gilson, 2007). At this point, there is a well-developed theory, supported by rigorously conducted empirical evidence, of the complex relationships among the health of diverse embodied systems (DePoy & Gilson, 2007; Weitz, 2013).

In March 2001, the National Institutes of Health sponsored a classic conference entitled Vital Connections: The Science of Mind–Body Interactions (MacArthur Network on Mind–Body Interactions, 2001). This event spearheaded an important agenda influencing new theory and knowledge linking interior (proximal) and exterior (distal) systems and environments. Renowned scholars reported on several topics focusing on the interaction of exterior (distal) and interior (proximal) environments that continue to receive intense research scrutiny—for example, the neurobiology of human emotions, early care and brain development, the biology of social interactions, socioeconomic status (SES) and health, neuroendocrinology of stress, and the role of sleep in health and cognition. Scholarship at this conference revealed further evidence of the critical connections between exterior (distal) environmental conditions and embodied phenomena, which were previously thought to be only tangentially related to one another. Throughout the 3-day conference, presenters theorized about the "integrative mechanisms" that link social and psychological phenomena to the brain and the rest of the body.

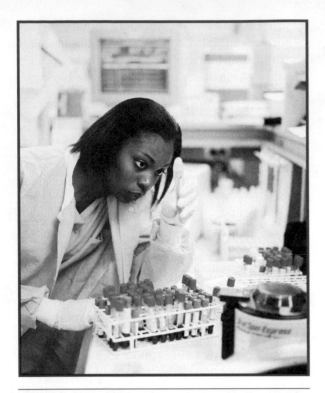

Photo 3.1 A medical researcher examines data to test a hypothesis.

© AbleStock.com/Thinkstock

Although these attempts to understand mind–body connections have led to many important theories about health and illness, they may also be misinterpreted. Social workers therefore are advised to heed the warning of a number of medical researchers and social critics against explaining behavior and emotion through a purely medicalized lens (see Conrad, 2007; Lane, 2007; Watters, 2010). Such a reductionist perspective may undermine our ability to consider the full range of environmental influences on embodied phenomena. Moreover, as defined, medicalization is a process that serves to pathologize typical daily experience and serve it up for medical intervention.

On the flip side of this caution, overattribution of physical experiences to psychological and social conditions fails to consider the interior (proximal) environmental causes of illness. We cannot separate health and illness from exterior (distal) social, political, cultural, technological, economic, and aesthetic environmental conditions (DePoy & Gilson, 2012; Saleebey, 2012). Thus comprehensive analysis of embodied integrity is warranted and requires knowledge of all biological systems, exterior (distal) environment conditions, and their reciprocation. While the efficiency of a single explanatory framework is seductive, such thinking may limit our ability to expansively identify the broad nature of problems and needs and constrain a range of appropriate interventions to resolve problems (DePoy & Gilson, 2004, 2011).

The constructivist perspective suggests that human phenomena are pluralistic in meaning. For example, rather than being a singular, scientifically supported entity, through the lens of social construction, a disabling medical condition such as paralysis or low vision is defined in large part by its meaning from interior (proximal) views as well as from political, social, cultural, technological, aesthetic, and economic exterior (distal) environments (DePoy & Gilson, 2004; Gilson & DePoy, 2000, 2002). Thus, using a social constructionist perspective, the experience of having atypical low vision can be understood in terms of shared cultural understandings of the "expected roles" for persons with atypical vision or in terms of actions or inactions of political institutions to promote or impede this subpopulation's access to physical, social, technological, and virtual environments. We may automatically assume that someone with atypical low vision is in need of professional intervention, but that person may in effect have his or her life well organized and function well in all chosen living and working environments. Thus, rather than being explained by the biological condition itself, limitation associated with an atypical biological condition may be a function of the exterior (distal) environment; the characteristics of the task; personal attitude; and available resources such as technology, assistance from family, friends, or employees, accessible transportation, and welcoming, fully accessible communities (DePoy & Gilson, 2011).

> Social constructionist perspective

As an example, although social workers do not make medical diagnoses for embodied conditions in the scope of their practice, the social work administrator who is developing or operating a shelter, a food kitchen, or an advocacy center may integrate medical and mental health services with employment, housing, financial, and companionship services (Colby, Dulmus, & Sowers, 2012; Strier, 2013) within the larger considerations of the meaning of those services to the users and community context. Miller, Pollack, and Williams (2011) have recommended a social model of practice that promotes healthy communities as well as working with individuals, families, and groups to help them identify and advocate for their own health needs if they so choose. DePoy and Gilson (2004, 2011) have built on this model by proposing *legitimate communities*, defined as those that practice acceptance of ideas and appreciate and respond to the full range of human diversity.

Critical Thinking Questions 3.1

Which theoretical perspective (perspectives) from Chapter 2 is (are) the best fit with the way of thinking of human biology suggested in the previous section? How important is biology in your own life story? In what ways is it important or not important? How do you think of the relationship between your body and other aspects of your environment?

A LOOK AT SIX INTERIOR (PROXIMAL) ENVIRONMENT SYSTEMS

Now we turn to six biological systems: the nervous system, the endocrine system, the immune system, the cardiovascular system, the musculoskeletal system, and the reproductive system. All the other biological systems (such as the digestive system, the respiratory system, and the urinary system) also warrant our attention, but with the limitations of space, we have chosen these six because they are commonly involved in many of the biologically based issues social workers encounter and thus can serve as a model for thinking about other systems as well.

As you read the descriptions of these six interior (proximal) environment systems, keep in mind their connectedness with each other as well as with all environmental conditions. As we emphasize throughout, just as human behavior is a complex transaction of person and environment, biological functioning is the result of complex interactions among all biological systems and the environments in which they function. No one system operates in isolation from other systems.

Systems perspective

Nervous System

In the first case study, Cheryl is considered to have a **brain injury (BI)**, or what is commonly termed a *traumatic brain injury* (TBI), defined as an insult to the brain caused by an external physical force that may result in a diminished or altered state of consciousness (Brain Injury Association of America, 2013). Included here are what might be classified as mild brain injuries or concussions. Traumatic brain injuries include head injuries that result from falls, automobile accidents, infections and viruses, insufficient oxygen, and poisoning. Explosions caused by land mines and improvised explosive devices have been identified as one of the primary causes of TBI in military personnel.

According to the Centers for Disease Control and Prevention (CDC; 2013a), approximately 1.7 million people sustain traumatic brain injury in the United States each year, accruing $76.5 billion yearly in hospital and injury-related costs (direct medical costs and indirect costs such as lost economic productivity) (CDC, 2013a). It is estimated that 2% of the population in the United States, or 5.3 million people, live with the atypical results of traumatic brain injuries. For children and young adults, TBI is the type of injury most often associated with deaths due to unintended injuries. It is estimated that one in four adults with TBI is unable to return to work within 1 year after the injury.

Although it has similar symptoms, *acquired brain injury* (ABI) is a different classification of brain injury. It does not result from traumatic injury to the head; is not hereditary, congenital, or degenerative; and it occurs after birth. Included in this category are oxygen deprivation (anoxia), aneurysms, infections to the brain, and stroke (Brain Injury Association of America, 2013).

Each type of BI may provoke specific atypical issues and behaviors for the person. However, brain injury in general can affect cognitive, physical, and psychological skills. Atypical cognitive function may present as atypical language and communication, information processing, memory, and perception. Cheryl's atypical writing is an example, as well as a reflection of atypical fine motor skill. Atypical physical functioning often occurs, such as walking differently or not at all (problems with ambulation) and changes in balance and coordination, strength, and endurance. Atypical psychological changes may come from two different sources. They may be *primary*, or directly related to the BI; these include irritability and judgment errors. Or they may be *reactive* to the adjustments required to live with the atypical function caused by BI and its consequences, typically resulting in a diagnosis of depression and changes in self-esteem. Cheryl's difficulty in recognizing that Sean is not going to marry her and her misjudgments in other social situations are symptoms of the psychological consequences of her BI.

The **nervous system** provides the structure and processes for communicating sensory, perceptual, and autonomically generated information throughout the body. Three major subsystems compose the nervous system:

1. Central nervous system (CNS): the brain and the spinal cord

2. Peripheral nervous system (PNS): spinal and cranial nerves

3. Autonomic nervous system (ANS): nerves controlling cardiovascular, gastrointestinal, genitourinary, and respiratory systems

The brain sends signals to the spinal cord, which in turn relays the message to specific parts of the body by way of the PNS. Messages from the PNS to the brain travel back by way of a similar pathway (Carter, 2009; Society for Neuroscience, 2012). Note that Cheryl's brain injury affects only a part of her nervous system—in fact, only part of the CNS. Damage to other parts of the nervous system can have significant atypical effects, but here we focus on her brain injury because it is so closely linked with behavioral changes.

The human brain, which constitutes only about 2% of one's total body weight, may contain as many as 10 million neurons. Its three major internal regions are referred to as the forebrain, midbrain, and hindbrain. Viewed from the side (see Exhibit 3.1), the largest structure visible is the *cerebral cortex*, part of the forebrain. The cerebral cortex is the seat of higher mental functions, including thinking, planning, and problem solving. This area of the brain is more highly developed in humans than in any other animal. It is divided into two hemispheres—left and right—that are interconnected by nerve fibers. The hemispheres are thought to be specialized, one side for language and the other for processing of spatial information such as maps and pictures. Each hemisphere controls the opposite side of the body, so that damage to one side of the brain may cause numbness or paralysis of the arm and leg on the opposite side.

The cerebral cortex has four lobes, depicted in Exhibit 3.1. As Exhibit 3.2 explains, functions such as vision, hearing, and speech are distributed in specific regions, with some lobes being associated with more than one function. The frontal lobe is the largest, making up nearly one third of the surface of the cerebral cortex. Lesions of any one of the lobes can have a dramatic impact on the functions of that lobe (Carter, 2009; Society for Neuroscience, 2012). Other forebrain structures process information from the sensory and perceptual organs and structures and send it to the cortex, or receive orders from cortical centers and relay them on down through central nervous system structures to central and peripheral structures throughout the body.

Exhibit 3.1 Selected Areas of the Brain

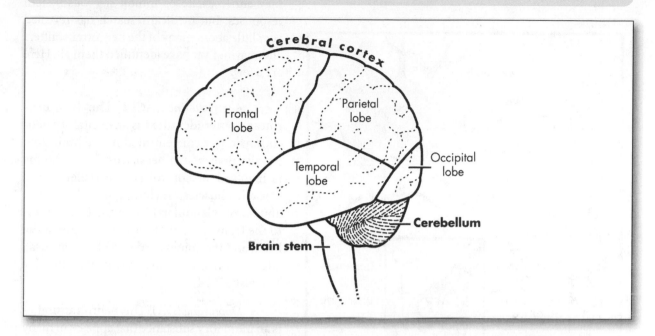

Cerebral cortex

Frontal lobe

Parietal lobe

Temporal lobe

Occipital lobe

Cerebellum

Brain stem

Exhibit 3.2 Regions of the Cerebral Cortex

Brain Region	Function
Frontal lobe	Motor behavior
	Expressive language
	Social functioning
	Concentration and ability to attend
	Reasoning and thinking
	Orientation to time, place, and person
Temporal lobe	Language
	Memory
	Emotions
Parietal lobe	Intellectual processing
	Integration of sensory information
Left parietal lobe	Verbal processing
Right parietal lobe	Visual/spatial processing
Occipital lobe	Vision

Also in the forebrain are centers for memory and emotion, as well as control of essential functions such as hunger, thirst, and biological sex drive.

The midbrain is a small area, but it contains important centers for sleep and pain as well as relay centers for sensory information and control of movement.

In Exhibit 3.1, part of the hindbrain, including the cerebellum, can also be seen. The *cerebellum* controls complex motor programming, including maintenance of muscle tone and posture. Other hindbrain structures are essential to the regulation of basic physiological functions, including breathing, heart rate, and blood pressure. The brain stem connects the cerebral cortex to the spinal cord.

The basic working unit of all the nervous systems is the **neuron**, or nerve cell. The human body has a great diversity of neuronal types, but all consist of a cell body with a nucleus and a conduction fiber, an **axon**. Extending from the cell body are *dendrites*, which conduct impulses to the neurons from the axons of other nerve cells. Exhibit 3.3 shows how neurons are linked by axons and dendrites.

Exhibit 3.3   Features of a Typical Neuron

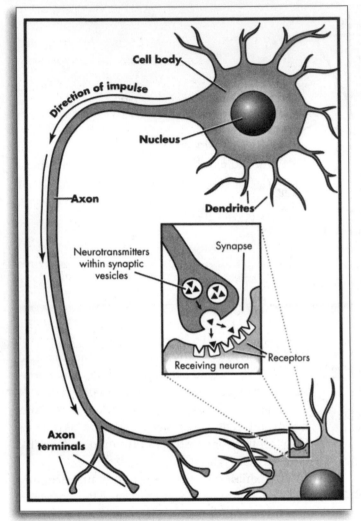

what neurotransmitters do. Essentially, they may either excite or inhibit nervous system responses. But medical research has revealed very little about many of the neurotransmitters and may not yet have identified them all. Here are a few.

• *Acetylcholine (ACh).* The first neurotransmitter identified is an excitatory neurotransmitter concentrated in the brainstem but also present in other places. Acetylcholine is involved in control of the skeleton and smooth muscles, including the heartbeat, and some glandular functions. It is critical to the transmission of messages between the brain and the spinal cord and affects arousal, attention, memory, and motivation (Bentley & Walsh, 2014).

• *Dopamine (DA).* This neurotransmitter is an inhibitory substance that appears in many parts of the body and plays a role in regulation of motor behavior, the endocrine system, and the pleasure centers of the brain. Dopamine influences emotional behavior and cognition. Dopamine abnormalities in the limbic system are thought to be involved in schizophrenia. Researchers are identifying a number of subtypes of dopamine (Bentley & Walsh, 2014).

• *Norepinephrine (NE).* This neurotransmitter is an excitatory transmitter located in the sympathetic nerves of the peripheral and central nervous systems. It is also secreted by the adrenal glands in response to stress. It influences emotional behavior and alertness and plays a role in the regulation of anxiety and tensions (Bentley & Walsh, 2014).

• *Serotonin.* Present in blood cells, the lining of the digestive tract, and a tract from the midbrain to all brain regions, serotonin is an inhibitory transmitter. It is involved in sensory processes, muscular activity, thinking, regulation of states of consciousness, mood, depression, anxiety, appetite, sleep, and sexual behavior. Several subtypes have been identified in recent years (Bentley & Walsh, 2014).

The connection between each axon and dendrite is actually a gap called a **synapse**. Synapses use chemical and electrical **neurotransmitters** to communicate. As the inset box in Exhibit 3.3 shows, nerve impulses travel from the cell body to the ends of the axons, where they trigger the release of neurotransmitters. The adjacent dendrite of another neuron has receptors distinctly shaped to fit particular types of neurotransmitters. When the neurotransmitter fits into a slot, the message is passed along.

Although neurotransmitters are the focus of much current research, scientists have not yet articulated all that positivist research reveals about

- *Amino acids.* Some types of these molecules, found in proteins, are distributed throughout the brain and other body tissues. One amino acid, gamma aminobutyric acid (GABA), is thought to play a critical role in inhibiting the firing of impulses of some cells. Thus, GABA is believed to be instrumental in many functions of the CNS, such as locomotor activity, cardiovascular reactions, pituitary function, and anxiety diagnoses (Bentley & Walsh, 2014).

- *Peptides.* Amino acids that are joined together have only recently been studied as neurotransmitters. Opioids, many of which are peptides, play an important role in activities ranging from moderating pain to causing sleepiness. Endorphins help to minimize pain and enhance adaptive behavior (Society for Neuroscience, 2012).

Biologically, behavior is affected not only by the levels of a neurotransmitter but also by the balance between two or more neurotransmitters. Psychotropic medications impact behaviors and symptoms associated with diagnoses of mental illness by affecting the levels of specific neurotransmitters and altering the balance among them. Social workers approaching their work from a medical diagnostic perspective would be well advised to keep current on medical research about the effects of neurotransmitters on human behavior when working with people referred for medications evaluation and when following up with individuals who have been placed on medication treatment regimens (Bentley & Walsh, 2014).

For Cheryl, as for many people living with traumatic brain injury, her skills, abilities, and changes may be affected by a variety of interior (proximal) and exterior (distal) environment circumstances—including which parts of the brain were injured, her achievements prior to injury, her social and psychological supports, and the training and education she is offered following her accident. Tremendous advances are being made in rehabilitation following brain injuries (Gordon et al., 2006). The better social workers understand brain functions and brain plasticity, the more they can communicate with medical personnel in a well-informed manner. We may be able to help with adjustment or adaptation to changes as well as the recovery of functions. Cheryl could benefit from cognitive retraining, support in finding and maintaining employment, family counseling, and individual counseling to help her end her relationship with Sean. A key to recovery for many people who have experienced similar trauma is an opportunity to interact with peers and other individuals with similar experiences. Such peer networks may provide the individual with access to new skills and a key link to exterior (distal) environment social support. A social worker working with Cheryl may fill several roles: case manager, advocate, counselor, resource coordinator, and referral source.

Endocrine System

Remember Bess, the middle-aged woman diagnosed with diabetes? If you had first met her in a nonhospital setting, you might have interpreted her behaviors quite differently. Because of the recent rural health initiative in Bess's town, which has a number of residents who have relocated from French Canada, it was not unusual to hear women speaking in both French and English about their diets and exercise, and initially you may have been quite pleased for Bess's success. If Bess had told you she was tired, you might have suggested she slow down and get more rest or perhaps that she include vitamins in her diet. Sitting in the morning in her nightclothes on her couch and missing work might suggest alcohol or other drug use. Confusion, switching back and forth between speaking French and English in the same sentence, and inability to answer simple questions could signal stroke, dementia, or a mental illness such as schizophrenia. But only a thorough medical assessment of her interior (proximal) environment revealed the primary and immediate cause of Bess's behaviors: a physical health condition traceable to a malfunction in the endocrine system.

The **endocrine system** plays a crucial role in our growth, metabolism, development, learning, and memory. It is made up of *glands* that secrete hormones into the blood system; those hormones bind to receptors in target organs, much as neurotransmitters do in the brain, and affect the metabolism or function of those organs (Rosenzweig, Breedlove, & Watson, 2010). Distinguishing differences between hormones and neurotransmitters are often the distance of travel from the point of release to the target, as well as the route of travel. Hormones travel long distances through the bloodstream; neurotransmitters travel shorter distances from cell to cell, across the synaptic cleft.

Endocrine glands include the pineal, pituitary, thyroid, parathyroid, pancreas, and adrenal. Endocrine cells are also found in some organs that have primarily a nonendocrine function: the hypothalamus, liver, thymus, heart, kidney, stomach, duodenum, testes, and ovaries. Exhibit 3.4 lists some of the better-known glands and organs, the hormones they produce, and their effects on other body structures.

The most basic form of hormonal communication is from an endocrine cell through the blood system to a target cell. A more complex form of hormonal communication is directly from an endocrine gland to a target endocrine gland.

The endocrine system regulates the secretion of hormones through

Systems perspective

a **feedback control mechanism**. Output consists of hormones released from an endocrine gland; input consists of hormones taken into a target tissue or organ. The system is self-regulating. Similar to neurotransmitters, hormones have specific receptors, so that the hormone released from one gland has a specific target tissue or organ (Mader & Windelspecht, 2012).

A good example of a feedback loop is presented in Exhibit 3.5. The hypothalamus secretes the gonadotropin-releasing hormone (GnRH), which binds to receptors in the anterior pituitary and stimulates the secretion of the luteinizing hormone

Exhibit 3.4 Selected Endocrine Glands and Their Effects Within the Corpus

Gland	Hormone	Effect
Pituitary	Adrenocorticotropic (ACTH) Growth (GH, somatotropic) Vasopressin Prolactin	• Stimulates adrenal cortex • Stimulates cell division, protein synthesis, and bone growth • Stimulates water reabsorption by kidneys • Stimulates milk production in mammary glands
Testes	Androgens (testosterone)	• Stimulates development of sex organs, skin, muscles, bones, and sperm • Stimulates development and maintenance of secondary male sex characteristics
Ovaries	Estrogen and progesterone	• Stimulates development of sex organs, skin, muscles, bones, and uterine lining • Stimulates development and maintenance of secondary female sex characteristics
Adrenal	Epinephrine Adrenal cortical steroids	• Stimulates fight-or-flight reactions in heart and other muscles • Raises blood glucose levels • Stimulates sex characteristics
Pancreas	Insulin Glucagon	• Targets liver, muscles, adipose tissues • Lowers blood glucose levels • Promotes formation of glycogen, proteins, and fats
Thymus	Thymosins	• Triggers development of T lymphocytes, which orchestrate immune system response
Pineal	Melatonin	• Maintains circadian rhythms (daily cycles of activity)
Thyroid	Thyroxin	• Plays role in growth and development • Stimulates metabolic rate of all organs

Exhibit 3.5   An Example of a Feedback Loop

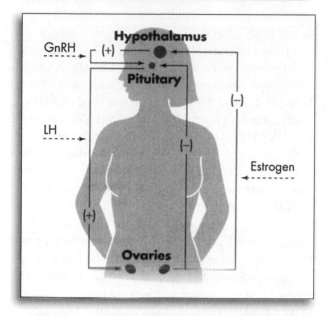

(LH). LH binds to receptors in the ovaries to stimulate the production of estrogen. Estrogen has a negative effect on the secretion of LH and GnRH at both the pituitary and hypothalamus, thus completing the loop. Loops like these allow the body to finely control the secretion of hormones.

Another good way to understand the feedback control mechanism is to observe the results when it malfunctions. Consider what has happened to Bess, who has been diagnosed with the most common illness caused by hormonal imbalance: **diabetes mellitus**. Insulin deficiency or resistance to insulin's effects is the basis of diabetes. Insulin and glucagon, which are released by the pancreas, regulate the metabolism of carbohydrates, the source of cell energy. These two substances are essential for the maintenance of blood glucose levels (blood sugar). High blood glucose levels stimulate the release of insulin, which in turn helps to decrease blood sugar by promoting the uptake of glucose by tissues. Low blood sugar stimulates the release of glucagon, which in turn stimulates the liver to release glucose, raising blood sugar. In people with insulin deficiency, muscle cells are deprived of glucose. As an alternative, those muscle cells tap fat and protein reserves in muscle tissue

as an energy source. The results include wasting of muscles, weakness, weight loss, and *metabolic acidosis,* a chemical imbalance in the blood. The increase in blood acidity suppresses higher nervous system functions, leading to coma. Suppression of the respiratory centers in the brain leads to death (Kapit, Macey, & Meisami, 2000).

Epidemiologists report a dramatic increase in the incidence of diabetes worldwide in recent years (De Fronzo, Ferrannini, Keen, & Zimmet, 2004). There are currently 25.8 million persons (8.3% of the population) in the United States who have diabetes. There are 18.8 million persons who have been diagnosed with diabetes, with an estimated 7 million having undiagnosed diabetes (National Institute of Diabetes & Digestive & Kidney Diseases [NIDDK], 2011). Nearly 800,000 new cases of diabetes are diagnosed each year, or 2,200 per day. The number of persons who have been diagnosed with diabetes has shown a steady increase over the past 15 years. It is estimated that $1 out of every $5 spent on health care in the United States is spent on diabetes and its consequences; the total cost of diagnosed diabetes in the United States in 2012 was estimated to be $245 billion (American Diabetes Association, 2013). Juvenile-onset diabetes (type 1) is found in children and young adults; risk factors may be autoimmune, genetic, or environmental. Non-Hispanic Whites are at greater risk of developing type 1 diabetes than other racial and ethnic groups. No known way to prevent type 1 diabetes exists. Maturity-onset diabetes (type 2), non-insulin-dependent diabetes mellitus, most commonly arises in people older than age 40 who are also obese. Type 2 diabetes is associated with older age, obesity, family history of diabetes, history of gestational diabetes, impaired glucose metabolism, physical inactivity, and particular races or ethnicities. Compared with non-Hispanic White adults, the risk of diabetes is 18% higher among Asian Americans, 66% higher among Hispanics/Latinos, and 77% higher among non-Hispanic Blacks (NIDDK, 2011).

For Bess, as for many people with symptoms indicating the presence of a medical condition, a crucial role for the social worker is to facilitate access to and comprehension of information about the symptoms and the diagnosed condition. Social workers can also aid in the translation of this information, so clients such as Bess, whose first language is French and who might not understand medical jargon, can grasp what is happening to them. The social worker may also help Bess begin to examine the lifestyle changes that may be suggested by this diagnosis. What might it mean in terms of diet, exercise, home and work responsibilities, and so forth? Bess may need assistance in working with her insurance company as she plans how her care will be financed. She may also need counseling as she works to adjust to life with this new medical diagnosis.

Critical Thinking Questions 3.2

How important is it for Cheryl and Bess to be well informed about their medical conditions? Explain. How would you advise them about possible sources of information for their specific conditions? How should their social workers go about becoming better informed about their medical conditions?

Immune System

Melissa is far from alone in testing positive for HIV. The Centers for Disease Control and Prevention (CDC; 2013b) estimates that approximately 49,273 people in the United States were newly infected with HIV in 2011 (the most recent year that such diagnostic data were recorded). At the end of 2010, about 1.1 million Americans were living with the **human immunodeficiency virus (HIV)**, the virus that causes **acquired immunodeficiency syndrome (AIDS)**. According to the CDC, 16% of those individuals did not know they were infected. It is estimated that the cumulative number of AIDS diagnoses through 2011 in the United States and dependent areas was 1,155,792; the estimated number of people newly diagnosed with AIDS in 2011 was 32,052. Of these diagnoses,

24,088 were among adult and adolescent males, 7,949 were among adult and adolescent females, and 15 were among children younger than 13 years of age (CDC, 2013b).

It is estimated that, in 2012, 35.3 million people were living with HIV worldwide, 2.3 million people were newly infected, and somewhere between 1.7 and 2.4 million people died of AIDS-related illness (Joint United Nations Programme on HIV/AIDS [UNAIDS], 2013). The good news is that new infections of HIV were reduced 34% from 2000 to 2012, and the number of AIDS-related deaths declined 6% in the same period (UNAIDS, 2013).

Persons of all ages and racial and ethnic groups are affected. The cumulative estimates of the number of AIDS cases from the beginning of the epidemic through 2011 include 486,282 cases of AIDS among Blacks/African Americans; 435,613 cases among Whites (not Hispanic); 202,182 cases among Hispanics/Latinos; 9,054 cases among Asians; 3,787 cases among American Indians/Alaska Natives; and 901 cases among Native Hawaiians/Other Pacific Islanders. Among people identified as or who identify as multiple races, 17,804 cases were estimated (CDC, 2013c).

HIV/AIDS is a relatively new disease, and early in its history, it was assumed to be terminal. The introduction of highly active antiretroviral therapy (HAART), which became widespread in the United States in 1996, altered the perception of AIDS. It came to be seen as a chronic instead of terminal disease. The reality is that, although some are living longer with the disease, others are still dying young. The CDC (2013b) in 2011 estimated that the average number of deaths of persons with AIDS in the United States and dependent areas was 17,489 per year from 1999 to 2008. As a result, the estimated number of persons 13 years and older living with AIDS more than doubled from 1996 (219,318) to 2008 (479,161). The cumulative estimated number of deaths in the United States and dependent areas through 2010 was 636,048 (CDC, 2013c).

The Centers for Disease Control and Prevention (2013b) reports six common transmission categories for HIV: male-to-male sexual contact, injection drug use, male-to-male sexual contact *and* injection drug use, heterosexual contact, mother-to-child (perinatal) transmission, and other (includes blood transfusions and unknown causes). According to the CDC (2013c), 84% of women who acquire HIV do so through heterosexual contact, a group to which Melissa now belongs. Although HIV is more easily transmitted from men to women, it can be transmitted from women to men as well. Heterosexual transmission occurs mainly through vaginal intercourse.

Once a person is infected with HIV, the disease-fighting immune system gradually weakens. This weakened immune system lets other diseases begin to attack the body. Over the next few years, Melissa will learn a great deal about how her body does or does not protect itself against disease and infection. The **immune system** is made up of organs and cells that are commonly thought of as working together to defend the body against disease (Sarafino & Smith, 2010; Świątczak, 2012). When operating in an optimal manner, the immune system is able to distinguish our own cells and organs from foreign elements (Sarafino & Smith, 2010). When the body recognizes something as exterior or foreign, the immune system mobilizes body resources and attacks. Remember that we cautioned you about the arbitrary distinction between exterior (distal) and interior (proximal) environments? Here is a good example: The foreign substance (which may be organic in composition and thus fit the definition of interior [proximal] environment) that can trigger an immune response may be a tissue or organ transplant or, more commonly, an antigen. **Antigens** include bacteria, fungi, protozoa, and viruses.

Sometimes, however, the immune system is mistakenly directed at parts of the body it was designed to protect, resulting in an **autoimmune disease**. Examples include rheumatoid arthritis, rheumatic fever, and lupus erythematosus. With rheumatoid arthritis, the immune system is directed against tissues and bones at the joints. In rheumatic fever, the immune system targets the muscles of the heart. With lupus erythematosus,

the immune system affects various parts of the interior environment, including the skin and kidneys (Sarafino & Smith, 2010).

Organs of the immune system are located throughout the body. They have primary involvement in the development of **lymphocytes**, or white blood cells (Sarafino & Smith, 2010). The main lymphatic organs include the following:

- *Bone marrow.* The largest organ in the body, it is the soft tissue in the core of bones. There are two types of bone marrow, red and yellow. Yellow bone marrow stores fat, which the body consumes only as a last resort in cases of extreme starvation. At birth, all bone marrow is red, but as the body ages, more and more red bone marrow is converted to yellow. In adults, red bone marrow is found in the sternum, ribs, vertebrae, skull, and long bones. The bone marrow produces both red (erythrocytes) and white (leukocytes and lymphocytes) blood cells.

- *Lymph nodes.* Small oval or round spongy masses distributed throughout the body (Sarafino & Smith, 2010). Lymph nodes are connected by a network of lymphatic vessels that contain a clear fluid called *lymph*, whose job is to bathe cells and remove bacteria and certain proteins. As the lymph passes through a lymph node, it is purified of infectious organisms. These vessels ultimately empty into the bloodstream.

- *Spleen.* An organ in the upper left quadrant of the abdomen. The spleen functions much like a very large lymph node, except that instead of lymph, blood passes through it. The spleen filters out antigens and removes ineffective or worn-out red blood cells from the body (Sarafino & Smith, 2010). An injured spleen can be removed, but the person becomes more susceptible to certain infections (Mader & Windelspecht, 2012).

- *Thymus.* Located along the trachea in the chest behind the sternum, the thymus secretes *thymosins*, hormones believed to trigger the development of T cells. *T cells*, white blood cells that mature in the thymus, have the task of slowing down, fighting, and attacking antigens (Mader & Windelspecht, 2012).

The immune system's response to antigens occurs in both specific and nonspecific ways. **Nonspecific immunity** is more general. "Scavenger" cells, or phagocytes, circulate in the blood and lymph, being attracted by biochemical signals to congregate at the site of a wound and ingest antigens (Parham, 2009; Sarafino & Smith, 2010; Sompayrac, 2012). This process, known as *phagocytosis*, is quite effective but has two limitations: (1) Certain bacteria and most viruses can survive after they have been engulfed, and (2) because our bodies are under constant attack and our phagocytes are constantly busy, a major assault on the immune system can easily overwhelm the nonspecific response. Thus, specific immunity is essential (Parham, 2009; Sarafino & Smith, 2010; Sompayrac, 2012).

Specific immunity, or acquired immunity, involves the lymphocytes. They not only respond to an infection but also develop a *memory* of that infection and allow the body to make rapid defense against it in subsequent exposure. Certain lymphocytes produce **antibodies**, protein molecules designed to attach to the surface of specific invaders. The antibodies recruit other protein substances that puncture the membrane of invading microorganisms, causing the invaders to explode. The antibodies are assisted in this battle by T cells, which destroy foreign cells directly and orchestrate the immune response. Following the *primary response*, the antibodies remain in the circulatory system at significant levels until they are no longer needed. With reexposure to the same antigen, a *secondary immune response* occurs, characterized by a more rapid rise in antibody levels—over a period of hours rather than days. This rapid response is possible because, during initial exposure to the antigen, memory cells were created. *Memory T cells* store the information needed to produce specific antibodies. They also have very long lives (Parham, 2009; Sarafino & Smith, 2010; Sompayrac, 2012).

The immune system becomes increasingly effective throughout childhood and declines in effectiveness in older adulthood. Infants are born with relatively little immune defense, but their immune system gradually becomes more efficient

and complex. Thus, as the child develops, the incidence of serious illness declines. During adolescence and most of adulthood, the immune system, for most people, functions at a high level of effectiveness. As we age, although the numbers of lymphocytes and antibodies circulating in the lymph and blood do not decrease, their potency diminishes.

Developmental perspective

The functioning of the immune system can be hampered by a diet low in vitamins A, E, and C and high in fats and cholesterol, and by excess weight (Parham, 2009; Sarafino & Smith, 2010; Sompayrac, 2012). There are also far more serious problems that can occur with the immune system, such as HIV, that are life threatening. HIV, like other viruses, infects "normal" cells and "hijacks" their genetic machinery. These infected cells in essence become factories that make copies of the HIV, which then go on to infect other cells. The hijacked cells are destroyed. A favorite target of HIV is the T cells that tell other cells when to start fighting off infections. HIV thus weakens the immune system and makes it increasingly difficult for the body to fight off other diseases and infections. Most of us host organisms such as fungi, viruses, and parasites that live inside us without causing disease. However, for people with HIV, because of the low T cell count, these same organisms can cause serious infection. When such a disease occurs or when the individual's number of T cells drops below a certain level, the person with HIV is considered to have AIDS (Cressey & Lallemant, 2007).

Melissa's life may undergo significant changes as symptoms of HIV infection begin to emerge. For example, Melissa may be at increased risk for repeated serious yeast infections of the vagina, and she may also be at increased risk for cancer of the cervix and pelvic inflammatory disease. Both men and women are vulnerable to opportunistic diseases and infections such as Kaposi's sarcoma, cytomegalovirus (CMV), AIDS retinopathy, pneumocystis carinii pneumonia (PCP), mycobacterium tuberculosis, and Candida albicans (thrush); atypical functioning such as AIDS dementia, loss of memory, loss of judgment, and depression; and other symptoms such as gastrointestinal dysfunction/distress, joint pain, anemia, and low platelet counts. (Details on these conditions can be found in medical sources.) The social worker may help to educate Melissa about these increased risks. In order to protect her health and the health of others, Melissa will most likely be advised to take special precautions. She can be supported in staying well by getting early treatment, adopting a healthy lifestyle, and remaining informed about new treatments (Voronin & Phogat, 2010).

The social worker also may have a role to play in working with Melissa as she tells her family and fiancé about her diagnosis. Melissa and her fiancé may need advice about how to practice safe sex. The social worker should also be available to work with Melissa, her fiancé, and her family as they adjust to her diagnosis and the grief they may feel, an experience frequently associated with a diagnosis of HIV. The social worker may explore reactions and responses of Melissa, her fiancé, and her parents to this health crisis.

Because of the tremendous costs for medications, particularly the new HAART, the social worker may link Melissa to sources of financial support. This aid will become increasingly critical if she gets sicker, her income declines, or her medical expenses increase. Given advances in medical diagnostics and therapeutics, recent estimates indicate that the lifetime costs of health care associated with HIV may be more than $385,200 per person diagnosed in adulthood (Schackman et al., 2006). Treatment with HAART is not a cure, but it allows the person with HIV to fight off other infections and increase life expectancy (Maggiolo & Leone, 2010; Pokorná, Machala, Rezáčová, & Konvalinka, 2009). However, side effects of some of the drugs are just as debilitating as the effects of AIDS.

In addition to providing Melissa with information about her immune system, HIV, AIDS, and other health issues, the social worker can advise Melissa about the protections guaranteed to her under the Americans with Disabilities Act of 1990 and the Amendments Act of 2008. Melissa has joined an HIV support group, but the social worker may also offer to provide her with or refer her to counseling. The social worker may also have a role to play on behalf of all people with HIV/AIDS, working to address prevention and public health in part by providing HIV/AIDS education to business groups, schools, civic and volunteer associations, and neighborhood groups and by influencing policy to support public health HIV prevention initiatives.

Cardiovascular System

Thomas, from Case Study 3.4, is one of many people living with one or more types of *cardiovascular disease* (CVD), disease of the heart and blood vessels. The most common types of CVD are coronary disease, hypertension, and stroke. CVD is the most common cause of death in this country, responsible for one in three deaths, with one death every 40 seconds (American Heart Association, 2013a). Stroke is the fourth leading cause of death, having declined significantly since the 1970s, due in large part to improvement in both prevention and treatment. It is the leading cause of long-term disability (American Heart Association, 2013a).

In 2011, 6.6% of U.S. adults age 18 and older reported being told by a health professional that they had coronary disease, 25.5% had been told they had hypertension, and 2.7% reported a history of stroke (Schiller, Lucas, & Peregoy, 2012). Men were twice as likely as women to have coronary disease, but the prevalence of hypertension and stroke was about the same for men and women. American Indian or Alaska Natives were more likely than other racial and ethnic groups to have some type of CVD, and Hispanic or Latino adults were less likely than White and African American adults to have CVD. The highest prevalence occurred in adults reporting two or more races (Schiller et al., 2012). As educational and income level increased, the prevalence of CVD decreased (Schiller et al., 2012).

Thomas's cardiovascular diagnosis is **high blood pressure (hypertension)**, defined as a systolic blood pressure equal to or greater than ($\geq$) 140 mm Hg and/or a diastolic blood pressure $\geq$ 90 mm Hg (his was 200/105). Blacks, Puerto Ricans, Cubans, and Mexican Americans are all more likely to suffer from high blood pressure than are Whites, and African Americans have the highest rates of high blood pressure in the world (American Heart Association, 2013b). An estimated 6.4 million Blacks have high blood pressure, with more frequent and severe effects than in other population subgroups. Blacks also develop high blood pressure earlier in life (American Heart Association, 2013b).

In 2013, it was estimated that one in three adults in the United States had high blood pressure, with 81.5% of those individuals aware of their condition and 52.5% having it under control (American Heart Association, 2013c). In 90% to 95% of the cases of individuals with high blood pressure, the cause is unknown. The death rate from high blood pressure has steadily increased by 17.1% from 1999 to 2009, but with the rising population of older adults, the actual number of deaths rose by 43.6%. The death rate per 100,000 population from high blood pressure in 2009 was 17.0 for White males, 51.6 for Black males, 14.4 for White females, and 38.3 for Black females (American Heart Association, 2013c).

The cost of cardiovascular disease and stroke in 2010 was estimated to be about $444 billion, including health care expenses and lost productivity, with these costs expected to rise (Centers for Disease Control and Prevention, 2011). According to the American Heart Association (2013c), the estimated combined direct and indirect cost associated with high blood pressure for 2006 was $51 billion.

To better understand cardiovascular disease, it is first important to gain insight into the functioning of the **cardiovascular system**, which is composed of the heart and the blood circulatory system (Kapit et al., 2000; Mader & Windelspecht, 2012). The heart's walls are made up of specialized muscle. As the muscle shortens and squeezes the hollow cavities of the heart, blood is forced in the directions permitted by the opening or closing of valves. Blood vessels continually carry blood from the heart to the rest of the body's tissues and then return the blood to the heart. Exhibit 3.6 shows the direction of the blood's flow through the heart.

Exhibit 3.6   The Direction of Blood Flow Through the Heart

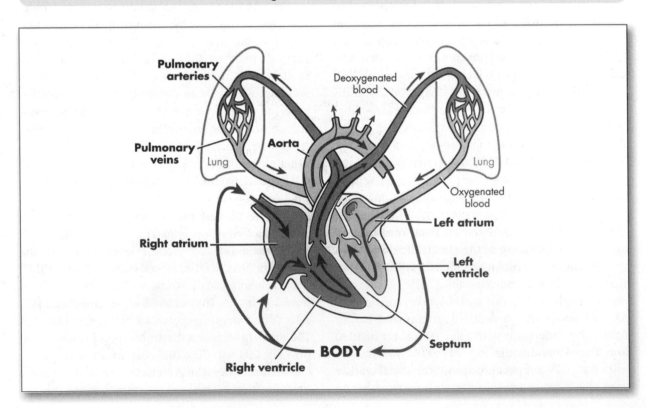

There are three types of blood vessels:

1. *Arteries*. These have thick walls containing elastic and muscular tissues. The elastic tissues allow the arteries to expand and accommodate the increase in blood volume that occurs after each heartbeat. Arterioles are small arteries that branch into smaller vessels called capillaries.

2. *Capillaries*. A critical part of this closed circulation system, they allow the exchange of nutrients and waste material with the body's cells. Oxygen and nutrients transfer out of a capillary into the tissue fluid in surrounding cells and absorb carbon dioxide and other wastes from the cells.

3. *Veins*. These take blood from the capillaries and return it to the heart. Some of the major veins in the arms and legs have valves allowing the blood to flow only toward the heart when they are open and block any backward flow when they are closed (Kapit et al., 2000; Mader & Windelspecht, 2012).

The heart has two sides (right and left), separated by the septum. Each side is divided into an upper and a lower chamber. The two upper, thin-walled chambers are called **atria**. The atria are smaller than the two lower, thick-walled chambers, called **ventricles**. Valves within the heart direct the flow of blood from chamber to chamber and, when closed, prevent its backward flow (Kapit et al., 2000; Mader & Windelspecht, 2012).

As Exhibit 3.6 shows, the right side of the heart pumps blood to the lungs, and the left side pumps blood to the tissues of the body. Blood from body tissues that is low in oxygen and high in carbon dioxide (deoxygenated blood) enters the right atrium. The right atrium then sends blood through a valve to the right ventricle. The right ventricle then sends the blood through another valve and the pulmonary arteries into the lungs. In the lungs, the blood gives up carbon dioxide and takes up oxygen. Pulmonary veins then carry blood that is high in oxygen (oxygenated) from the lungs to the left atrium. From the left atrium, blood is sent through a valve to the left ventricle. The blood is then sent through a valve into the

aorta for distribution around the body (Kapit et al., 2000; Mader & Windelspecht, 2012).

Contraction and relaxation of the heart moves the blood from the ventricles to the lungs and to the body. The right and left sides of the heart contract together—first the two atria, then the two ventricles. The heart contracts ("beats") about 70 times per minute when the body is at rest. The contraction and relaxation cycle is called the cardiac cycle. The sound of the heartbeat, as heard through a stethoscope, is caused by the opening and closing of the heart valves.

Although the heart will beat independently of any nervous system stimulation, regulation of the heart is primarily the responsibility of the ANS. *Parasympathetic activities* of the nervous system, which tend to be thought of as normal or routine activities, slow the heart rate. *Sympathetic activities*, associated with stress, increase the heart rate. As blood is pumped from the aorta into the arteries, their elastic walls swell, followed by an immediate recoiling. The alternating expansion and recoiling of the arterial wall is the pulse. The normal pulse rate at rest for children ages 6 to 15 is 70 to 100 beats per minute; for adults age 18 and older, the normal pulse rate at rest is 60 to 100 beats per minute (Cleveland Clinic, 2014).

Blood pressure is the measure of the pressure of the blood against the wall of a blood vessel. A *sphygmomanometer* is used to measure blood pressure. The cuff of the sphygmomanometer is placed around the upper arm over an artery. A pressure gauge is used to measure the *systolic blood pressure*, the highest arterial pressure, which results from ejection of blood from the aorta. *Diastolic blood pressure*, the lowest arterial pressure, occurs while the ventricles of the heart are relaxing. Medically desired and healthy blood pressure for a young adult is 120 mm of mercury systole over 80 mm of mercury diastole, or 120/80 (Kapit et al., 2000; Mader & Windelspecht, 2012).

Blood pressure accounts for the movement of blood from the heart to the body by way of arteries and arterioles, but skeletal muscle contraction moves the blood through the venous system. As skeletal muscles contract, they push against the thin or weak walls of the veins, causing the blood to move past valves. Once past the valve, the blood cannot return, forcing it to move toward the heart.

High blood pressure has been called the silent killer, because many people like Thomas have it without noticeable symptoms. It is the leading cause of strokes and is a major risk factor for heart attacks and kidney failure.

Conflict perspective

Suddenly faced with startling information, such as a dramatic change in what was believed to be good health, Thomas might experience a range of responses, including but not limited to denial, questioning, self-reflection, self-critique, and even anger. The social worker can play many critical roles with Thomas. Perceptions of exterior (distal) conditions such as daily hassles and stressful life events place him at increased risk for having a stroke or dying as a result of his high blood pressure (Paradies, 2006). Social workers are uniquely positioned to see the links between external environment issues—such as vocational and educational opportunities, economics and income, housing, and criminal victimization—and interior (proximal) environment health issues.

On an individual level, being better informed about the cardiovascular system and its care can help Thomas maximize the benefits of medical examination and treatment. The social worker can participate in medical care by helping Thomas learn the essential elements of effective health practice, including what it means to have high blood pressure, what causes high blood pressure, and how to lower the risks of high blood pressure. If medication is prescribed, the social worker can support the medication regimen and Thomas's decision about how to follow it.

The social worker also can process with Thomas a strategy for identifying and deciding on his preferred lifestyle changes to help lower his blood pressure. These may include examination of sources of stress and patterns of coping, diet, how much exercise he gets on a regular basis, and his social and economic external environmental conditions.

Because high blood pressure has been shown to run in families, the social worker can also work with Thomas's family to discuss lifestyle factors that might contribute to high blood pressure, such as exposure to stress, cigarette/tobacco use, a diet high in cholesterol, physical inactivity, and excess weight.

The social worker may also work with community organizations, community centers, and religious organizations to advance policy and public health practices to support education and prevention programs as well as a physician and health care provider referral program. Given the ubiquity of smartphone use, the social worker might recommend that Thomas use contemporary technologies such as free smartphone apps for monitoring blood pressure and fitness activity.

Systems perspective

Critical Thinking Questions 3.3

Melissa and Thomas are both in the young adulthood period. What impact could their health conditions have on their young adult development? What are the implications for the later phases of their life journeys?

Musculoskeletal System

After a number of years with a variety of physical symptoms, Mary from Case Study 3.5 was diagnosed with multiple sclerosis (MS). The symptoms and presentation of multiple sclerosis vary depending on the location of the affected nerve fibers. Symptoms can include weak or stiff muscles, in one or more limbs, often with painful muscle spasms; tingling, pain, and/or numbness in the arms, legs, trunk of the body, or face; vision problems such as complete loss of central vision (usually in one eye), blurred or double vision, or pain in the eye; lack of coordination, clumsiness, unsteady gait, and difficulty staying balanced when walking; dizziness; slurred speech; fatigue; and bladder control problems. Subsequent symptoms often include fatigue, mental or physical; changes in mood; difficulty concentrating or effectively attending to multiple tasks; and difficulty making decisions, planning, or prioritizing (Mayo Foundation for Medical Education and Research, 2012; National Institute of Neurological Disorders and Stroke, 2013).

It is quite common for people in the beginning stages of multiple sclerosis to experience periods of symptom expression followed by complete or partial remission of the symptoms. For some individuals this symptom presentation is followed by long periods of partial or apparent full recovery. This unpredictability is also exhibited in how the disease affects the range of people with the diagnosis. Some individuals may have a mild course of the disease, with little functional impairment, while others may have a steadily worsening constellation of symptoms, with increasing severity of functional impairment. MS is often considered one of the most common functionally impairing neurological diseases of young adults. Although MS can affect children and adults age 60 and older, it most often occurs in individuals ages 20 to 40 years old (Mayo Foundation for Medical Education and Research, 2012; National Institute of Neurological Disorders and Stroke, 2013).

Multiple sclerosis (MS) is a neuroinflammatory disease that affects myelin. Myelin is an insulating layer or membrane (called the myelin sheath) that wraps around nerve fibers (axons) of the brain and spinal cord. The role of the myelin sheath is to enable nerve impulses to transmit quickly and efficiently along a nerve fiber. The rapid transmission of nerve impulses allows individuals to function in a more typical fashion. MS is also considered an autoimmune disorder (a condition in which the immune system mistakenly attacks and destroys healthy body tissue), where the immune system attacks the myelin, resulting in lesions. These lesions then slow or halt the nerve impulse, leading to neurological signs and symptoms associated with MS.

The prevalence of people diagnosed with MS in the United States currently ranges from 250,000 to 350,000. It appears that the rate of the disease or at least the diagnosis of MS has steadily increased during the 20th century and the first part of the 21st century. It is suggested that approximately 200 individuals are diagnosed with MS each week (National Institute of Neurological Disorders and Stroke, 2013).

About twice as many women are diagnosed with MS as men. MS seems to be more common in colder climates than more temperate climates. Caucasians (particularly those of northern European decent) seem to be more at risk for diagnosis than other ethnic groups, but people of African and Hispanic ancestry also develop the disease. Asian American populations and Native Americans of North and South America have relatively low rates of MS (National Institute of Neurological Disorders and Stroke, 2013; National Multiple Sclerosis Society, n.d.).

As suggested earlier, for Mary, as well as for many people who have received a diagnosis of multiple sclerosis, the symptom presentation may vary in severity and functional limitation. During an acute phase or exacerbation, which may also be called a relapse, flare-up, or attack, there is a sudden worsening of symptoms that lasts for at least 24 hours (National Institute of Neurological Disorders and Stroke, 2013). A social worker working with Mary should acquire a solid and complete knowledge of MS and how it may differentially affect individuals. It is critical that the social worker not assume that because Mary has MS she needs services but rather to be available to meet Mary's needs as they arise.

Among the range of symptoms of MS is dysfunction in the **musculoskeletal system**, which supports and protects the body and provides motion. The contraction and relaxation of muscles attached to the skeleton is the basis for all voluntary movements. Over 600 skeletal muscles in the body account for about 40% of body weight (Mader & Windelspecht, 2012). When a muscle contracts, it shortens; it can only pull, not push. Therefore, for us to be able to extend and to flex at a joint, muscles work in "antagonistic" pairs. As an example, when the hamstring group in the back of the leg contracts, the quadriceps in the front relax; this allows the leg to bend at the knee. When the quadriceps contract, the hamstring relaxes, allowing the leg to extend.

The contraction of a muscle occurs as a result of an electrical impulse passed to the muscle by a controlling nerve that releases acetylcholine. When a single stimulus is given to a muscle, it responds with a twitch, a contraction lasting only a fraction of a second. But when there are repeated stimulations close together, the muscle cannot fully relax between impulses. As a result, each contraction benefits from the previous contraction, giving a combined contraction that is greater than an individual twitch. When stimulation is sufficiently rapid, the twitches cease to be jerky and fuse into a smooth contraction/movement called *tetanus*. However, tetanus that continues eventually produces muscle fatigue due to depletion of energy reserves.

Skeletal muscles exhibit tone when some muscles are always contracted. Tone is critical if we are to maintain body posture. If all the muscle fibers in the neck, trunk, and legs were to relax, our bodies would collapse. Nerve fibers embedded in the muscles emit impulses that communicate to the CNS the state of particular muscles. This communication allows the CNS to coordinate the contraction of muscles (Kapit et al., 2000; Mader & Windelspecht, 2012). In its entirety, the musculoskeletal system both supports the body and allows it to move. The skeleton, particularly the large heavy bones of the legs, supports the body against the pull of gravity and protects soft body parts. Most essential, the skull protects the brain, the rib cage protects the heart and lungs, and the vertebrae protect and support the spinal cord.

Bones serve as sites for the attachment of muscles. It may not seem so, but bone is a very active tissue, supplied with nerves and blood vessels. Throughout life, bone cells repair, remold, and rejuvenate in response to stresses, strains, and fractures (Kapit et al., 2000). A typical long bone, such as the arm or leg bone, has a cavity surrounded by a dense area. The dense area contains compact bone; the cavernous area contains blood vessels and nerves surrounded by spongy bone. Far from being weak, spongy bone is designed for strength. It is the site of red marrow, the specialized tissue that produces red and white blood cells. The cavity of a long bone also contains yellow marrow, which is a fat-storage tissue (Kapit et al., 2000; Mader & Windelspecht, 2012).

Most bones begin as cartilage. In long bones, growth and calcification

| Developmental perspective |

(hardening) begin in early childhood and continue through adolescence. Growth hormones and thyroid hormones stimulate bone growth during childhood. Androgens, which are responsible for the adolescent growth spurt, stimulate bone growth during puberty. In late adolescence, androgens terminate bone growth.

Bones are joined together at joints. Long bones and their corresponding joints are what permit flexible body movement (Mader & Windelspecht, 2012). Joints are classified according to the amount of movement they permit. Bones of the cranium, which are sutured together, are examples of immovable joints. Joints between the vertebrae are slightly movable. Freely movable joints, which connect two bones separated by a cavity, are called *synovial joints*. Synovial joints may be hinge joints (knee and elbow) or ball-and-socket joints (attachment of the femur to the hipbone). Exhibit 3.7 shows the structure of the knee joint. Synovial joints are prone to arthritis because the bones gradually lose their protective covering and grate against each other as they move (Mader & Windelspecht, 2012).

The bones in a joint are held together by *ligaments*, while *tendons* connect muscle to bone. The ends of the bone are capped by cartilage, which gives added strength and support to the joint. Friction between tendons and ligaments and between tendons and bones is eased by fluid-filled sacs called *bursae*. Inflammation of the bursae is called bursitis.

Because of the commonly held perspective that individual independence is most desirable, it is not unusual for social workers and other health care professionals to discourage a person with a medical explanation for atypical function from using exterior (distal) environmental modifications and resources when they are not essential, even though they may be quite useful. These may include ramps, elevators, and electrically operated doors or

Exhibit 3.7   Structure of the Knee Joint

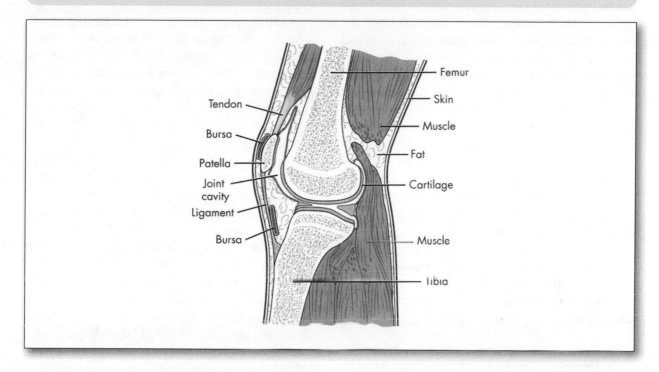

assistive devices. **Assistive devices** are those products designated by the medical community to help an impaired person to communicate, see, hear, or maneuver. Examples used by individuals with atypical activity include manual wheelchairs, motorized wheelchairs, motorized scooters, and other aids that enhance mobility; hearing aids, telephone communication devices, listening devices, visual and audible signal systems, and other products that enhance the ability to hear; and voice-synthesized computer modules, optical scanners, talking software, and other communication devices. In suggesting technological devices, the social worker should be attentive to stigma that accompanies the term *assistive* and the medicalized appearance of many products named assistive technology.

Those who believe that working to "overcome" challenges is a helpful approach in adjusting to or working with atypical function may be well meaning. But implicit within this belief system is the impression that being labeled as "disabled" ascribes deficiency that makes an individual less than whole, less than competent, and less than capable.

While the most commonly held perspective of disability is one of medical deficiency, contemporary disability studies challenge this belief. DePoy and Gilson have theorized disability as disjuncture or an ill fit between body and context (DePoy & Gilson, 2011). Thus, using this perspective, the diagnosed body is not the sole locus for intervention. Social work addresses policy change, exclusion or lack of access, or other conditions that limit a person's progress toward meeting his or her desired goal.

In working with Mary, the social worker has many options or none. Mary may make a decision to follow up with ongoing health care services or stop after the initial workup and diagnosis. Since there is no single test to diagnose MS, Mary may have been subjected to a wide range of tests to rule out or to confirm the diagnosis. In addition to providing a complete medical history and undergoing a physical examination and full neurological evaluation, Mary may have an MRI scan of the head and spine to look for the characteristic lesions of MS. An additional common medical procedure ordered when MS is suspected is a lumbar puncture (sometimes called a spinal tap) to obtain a sample of cerebrospinal fluid. Once the social worker is aware of the many procedures and processes Mary may have experienced, the social worker is then able to serve as a knowledgeable and informed resource and referral agent. He or she may work with other rehabilitation professionals, such as physical therapists and occupational therapists, in identifying useful adaptions and modifications in Mary's work, recreation, and home environments. The social worker might provide counseling but also could refer Mary to a wide range of community groups ranging from yoga classes to MS peer support groups. Should Mary choose to acquire new technology to support any limitation connected with MS, the social worker may also intervene with insurance companies reluctant to purchase the needed technological equipment.

Reproductive System

Juan and Belinda are at an age when an understanding of reproduction and sexuality is critical. In the United States, as in many countries around the globe, the typical age for first experience of sexual intercourse is approximately 17. However, individuals tend not to marry until they reach their mid-20s (Guttmacher Institute, 2013). According to the Centers for Disease Control and Prevention (2012a), 47.4% of high school students surveyed in 2011 reported having had sexual intercourse during their life. Nearly 34% reported having had sexual intercourse in the previous 3 months, with 39.8% reporting that they did not use a condom the last time they had sex and 76.7% reporting that they did not use birth control pills or Depo-Provera to prevent pregnancy the last time they had sexual intercourse. According to the Centers for Disease Control and Prevention (2012b), in 2011 44.3% of White high school students reported having sexual intercourse during their life; the percentage among Black students was 60% and 48.6% among Hispanic students. Less than 2% of adolescents have had sex by the time they are 12; the percentage rises to 16% by age 15, 33% by age 16, and 48% by age 17 (Guttmacher Institute, 2013).

Contraception use has been increasing among sexually active teens in the United States. From 2006 to 2010, an estimated 78% of sexually active females and 85% of sexually active males used contraception during their first experience with sexual intercourse. For females, this is an increase from 48% in 1982 (Guttmacher Institute, 2013). This is an encouraging trend, but sexually active U.S. teens still lag behind sexually active teens in other wealthy countries in contraceptive use. This contributes to a higher incidence of teen pregnancy and sexually transmitted infections (STIs) in the United States than in other wealthy countries. Annually, about 750,000 females aged 15 to 19 become pregnant in the United States, with 82% of teen pregnancies unintended, 59% ending in birth, and 26% ending in abortion (Guttmacher Institute, 2013). Two thirds of all teen pregnancies occur in teens aged 18 to 19 years old. The highest teen pregnancy rates occur in Black and Hispanic women (117 and 107 per 1,000 women aged 15 to 19, respectively); White adolescent women have a rate of 43 per 1,000 (Guttmacher Institute, 2013). The teen pregnancy rate in the United States has declined steadily from 117 pregnancies per 1,000 women aged 15 to 19 in 1990 to 68 per 1,000 in 2008 (Guttmacher Institute, 2013). Among Black teenagers aged 15 to 19, the pregnancy rate fell by 48%, compared with the overall decline of 42% (Guttmacher Institute, 2013). The teen abortion rate declined by 59% from 1988 to 2008 (Guttmacher Institute, 2012). The Guttmacher Institute (2013) estimates nearly 19 million new STIs each year, with nearly half occurring among youth and young adults ages 15 to 24, even though this group is only about 25% of the sexually active population.

Adolescents consider parents, peers, and the media to be important sources of information about sexual health, but there is also strong evidence that comprehensive sex education programs help young people to delay sexual activity and to use responsible protection once beginning to engage in sexual activity (Guttmacher Institute, 2012). From 2006 to 2008, 93% of teens had received formal education about STIs, 89% had received formal education about HIV, and 84% had received formal education about abstinence. About one third of teens had not received formal education about contraception (Guttmacher Institute, 2012). The great majority, 87%, of school districts have sex education policies that promote abstinence as the most effective method to avoid pregnancy, HIV, and other STDs. A 2007 study found that federally funded abstinence-only education programs had no beneficial effect on teen sexual behavior (Boonstra, 2010), and in 2010, Congress eliminated the two federal programs that had funded abstinence-only education, the Adolescent Family Life (AFL) Prevention Program and the Community-Based Abstinence Education (CBAE) Program. However, 37 states require that sex education include information on abstinence, with 26 states requiring that abstinence be stressed and 11 states mandating that abstinence be included in the instruction (Guttmacher Institute, 2012). Twenty states and the District of Columbia require that public schools teach both sex and HIV education, only one state mandates that sex education be taught alone, and 13 states require HIV education alone (Guttmacher Institute, 2012).

If adolescents are to make responsible decisions about their sexuality, they would be wise to develop an understanding of the structures and functions of the reproductive system. For some individuals, this information may come from the home; for others, from schools, community activity centers, websites, and social networking interactions; and for others, from family planning centers where social workers may work. The discussion that follows focuses on the interior (proximal) environmental aspects of heterosexual sexuality and reproduction, but before beginning this discussion we raise several important points.

First, recent theory and research have advanced concepts suggesting that gender and sexuality are multifaceted. Some theorists identify ways in which culture influences gender definitions, attitudes about sexuality, and sexual behaviors (Caron, 2011). Second, many contemporary definitions of gender, and thus of sexuality, move beyond the binary of male and female to the assertion that experience itself is a major element in ascribing gender. Moreover, experience does not have to be consistent with one's biology (Davies, 2006). Third, according to some contemporary approaches, rather than being a biological phenomenon, gender is considered by some to be a function of comfort as a member of a particular gendered group (Siragusa, 2001).

Finally, although many may typically think of gender as male or female, more recently the number of biologically described genders has expanded to five (heterosexual male, heterosexual female, homosexual male, homosexual female, and transsexual) (Davies, 2006) and six (McDermott, 1997): feminine, masculine, androgynous, transsexual, cross-dresser, and culturally specific genders (DePoy & Gilson, 2007). It is possible for a person to be a chromosomal male with female genitals and vice versa. Chromosomal, genetic, anatomical, and hormonal aspects of sex are sometimes not aligned (Rudacille, 2005).

Let us now return to our discussion of the interior environment of heterosexual sexuality and gender. In humans, the reproductive system comprises internal and external structures. After conception, the sex-determining chromosome produced by the father unites with the mother's egg, and it is this configuration that determines the child's sex. At birth, boys and girls are distinguished by the presence of specific genitalia.

As Exhibit 3.8 shows, the external male organs are the penis and scrotum. Internal organs consist of the testes, the tubes and ducts that serve to transfer the sperm through the reproductive system, and the organs that help nourish and activate sperm and neutralize some of the acidity that sperm encounter in the vagina. The penis functions as a conduit for both urine and semen.

Externally, one can view the shaft and the glans (often referred to as the head or tip) of the penis. The shaft contains three cylinders. The two largest are called the corpa cavernosa (singular: *corpus cavernosum*). During sexual arousal, these become engorged with blood and stiffen. The corpus spongiosum, the third cylinder, contains the urethra. It

Exhibit 3.8   The Male Reproductive System

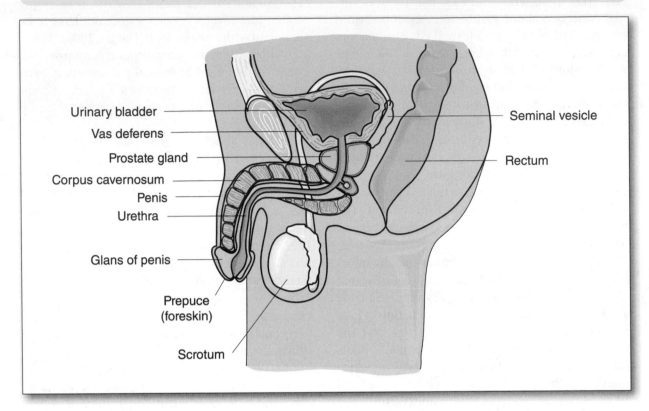

enlarges at the tip of the penis to form a structure called the glans. The ridge that separates the glans from the shaft of the penis is called the corona. The frenulum is the sensitive strip of tissue connecting the underside of the glans to the shaft. At the base of the penis is the root, which extends into the pelvis.

Three glands are part of the feedback loop that maintains a constant level of male hormones in the bloodstream. The primary functions of the **testes**, or male gonads, are to produce sperm (mature germ cells that fertilize the female egg) and to secrete male hormones called *androgens*. *Testosterone* is one of the most important hormones in that it stimulates the development of the sex organs in the male fetus and the later development of secondary sex characteristics such as facial hair, male muscle mass, and a deep voice. The two other glands in the feedback loop are the hypothalamus and the pituitary gland. Both secrete hormones that serve a regulatory function, primarily maintaining a constant testosterone level in the blood.

Before we move forward, let's pause to briefly review heredity and genetics. For humans, chromosomes come in pairs, one member from the father and one from the mother, which are transferred at fertilization. Each individual has 22 pairs of uniquely shaped autosomal chromosomes (not sex chromosomes) plus 1 pair of sex chromosomes (XX or XY), for a total of 23 chromosome pairs. In the early stages of their development, sperm cells are called spermatocytes. Each contains 46 chromosomes, including both an X and a Y chromosome that determine sex. The X chromosome (female) is larger than the Y (male) chromosome. As the spermatocytes mature and divide, chromosomes are reduced by half, and only one (either the X or Y) sex-determining chromosome is retained. The mature sperm cell is called the spermatozoan. This cell fertilizes the female egg (ovum), which contains only X chromosomes. Thus, the spermatozoan is the determining factor for the child's sex. (Females have two X chromosomes, and males have one X and one Y chromosome.) Chromosomes are threadlike bodies found in the nucleus of a cell that contain the DNA molecule, with each DNA molecule being composed of many genes, or individual segments or subunits of DNA. Any gene that appears at a specific site on a chromosome is called an allele (one member of a pair). Genes carry the code or set of instructions for a specific trait (characteristic). These traits make up the physical, biochemical, and physiologic makeup of every cell in the body.

Robinson (2010) notes that "when genes are passed on, some are assertive and dominant while others are shy and recessive" (Kindle location 376). More commonly we refer to genes as either dominant or recessive. A *dominant gene* is one that expresses its effect in the cell regardless of whether its allele on the matching chromosome is the same or different from the dominant gene (a gene in one strand of DNA that is stronger than the corresponding gene in another strand of DNA), whereas a *recessive gene* is a gene in one strand of DNA that is weaker than the corresponding gene in another strand of DNA, the effect of which is not evident unless its paired allele on the matching chromosome is also recessive. Recessive genes can be passed on to offspring. When the matching genes for a trait are different, the alleles are heterozygous. When the genes for a trait are the same (both dominant or both recessive), the alleles are homozygous. Any trait carried on a sex chromosome is sex linked. Most sex-linked traits are carried on the X chromosome. Sex-linked traits appear almost exclusively in males, and most of these traits are recessive. Robinson (2010) reminds us that "some traits are truly X-linked (such as hemophilia) or Y-linked (such as hairy ears). Other traits are expressed differently in males and females even though the genes that control the traits are located on nonsex chromosomes" (Kindle location 2039).

Of particular interest for professions such as social work is Bonduriansky's (2012) observation that contemporary discussions of heredity have moved away from a "hard heredity" model associated with classical Mendelian genetics. In its place "the model of heredity now emerging is pluralistic, or 'inclusive' or 'extended,' in that it combines genetic and non-genetic mechanisms of inheritance. The pluralistic model therefore recognizes the reality of both hard and soft inheritance, and the potential for a range of intermediate phenomena" (Bonduriansky, 2012, p. 334). Mendelian genetics, or hard heredity, would assert a model of heredity whereby the characteristics of the offspring (child) are determined at the point of conception, "of a set of factors whose nature is unaffected by the environment or phenotype of the parents" (Bonduriansky, 2012, p. 330). Before discussing genetics and social work, we return to the reproductive system.

Before ejaculation, the sperm pass through a number of tubes and glands, beginning with a testis, proceeding through a maze of ducts, and then to an epididymis, which is the convergence of the ducts and serves as the storage facility for sperm in a testicle. Each epididymis empties into the vas deferens, which brings the mature sperm to the seminal vesicles, small glands that lie behind the bladder. In these glands, a nourishing and activating fluid combines with the sperm before the mixture is carried through the urethra to the outside of the penis. The *prostate gland*, through which the urethra passes, produces and introduces the milky fluid that preserves the sperm and neutralizes the alkalinity found in the female reproductive system. Cowper's glands also make their contribution to the seminal fluid before it leaves the male.

However, even if there is early ejaculation and the Cowper's glands do not have time to secrete fluid, viable sperm exist in the ejaculate and can fertilize the female egg. Early withdrawal of the penis from a woman's vagina therefore does not prevent the passage of some viable sperm cells. It is also important to know that sperm only compose about 1% of the ejaculate (3 to 5 milliliters of fluid total), but this small percentage contains from 200 million to 400 million sperm. The number of sperm decreases with frequent ejaculation and advancing age.

Exhibit 3.9 shows the external female sex organs. They include the pudendum, also called the vulva, which consists of the mons veneris, the fatty tissue below the abdomen that becomes covered

Exhibit 3.9   The Female External Sex Organs

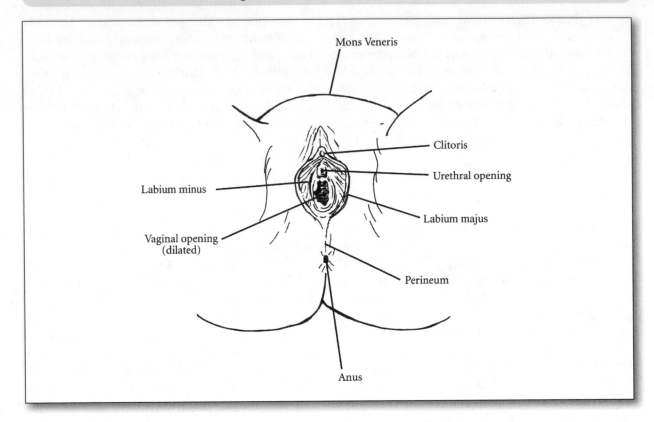

Mons Veneris

Clitoris

Urethral opening

Labium minus

Labium majus

Vaginal opening
(dilated)

Perineum

Anus

with hair after puberty; the labia majora and minora; the clitoris; and the vaginal opening. Unlike the male, the female has a physical separation between excretion and reproductive organs. Urine passes from the bladder through the urethra to the urethral opening, where it is expelled from the body. The urethra is located immediately in front of the vaginal opening and is unconnected to it.

The labia majora, large folds of skin, contain nerve endings that are responsive to stimulation and protect the inner genitalia. Labia minora join the prepuce hood at the top that covers the clitoris. These structures, when stimulated, engorge with blood and darken, indicating sexual arousal. Resembling the male penis and developing from the same embryonic tissue, the clitoris is about 1 inch long and ¼ inch wide. However, unlike the penis, the clitoris is not directly involved in reproduction but serves primarily to produce sexual pleasure. The

vestibule located inside the labia minora contains openings to the urethra and the vagina. It is also a site for arousal because it is rich in nerve endings sensitive to stimulation.

Internal structures of the female reproductive system, shown in Exhibit 3.10, include the vagina, ovaries, fallopian tubes, cervical canal (cervix), and uterus. The vagina connects with the external sexual structures. Composed of three layers and shaped cylindrically, the vagina both receives the penis during intercourse and functions as the birth canal through which the child passes from the uterus to the world outside the mother. Because of its multiple functions, the vagina has the flexibility to expand and contract and to change its climate from dry to lubricated. The cervix is the lower end of the uterus and protrudes into the vagina. It maintains the chemical balance of the vagina through its secretions.

Exhibit 3.10   The Female Internal Sex Organs

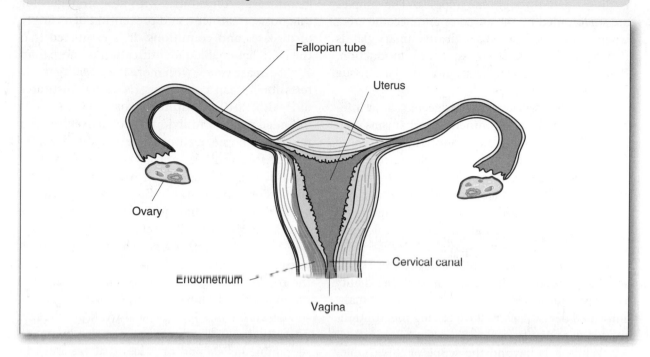

The **uterus**, also called the womb, serves as the pear-shaped home for the unborn child for the 9 months between implantation and birth. The innermost of its three layers, the endometrium, is the tissue that builds to protect and nourish the developing fetus. If pregnancy does not occur, the endometrium is shed monthly through the process of menstruation. If pregnancy does occur, the well-muscled middle layer of the uterus produces the strong contractions necessary at birth to move the fetus out of the uterus, into the vaginal canal, and then into the world. The external layer protects the uterus within the body.

The fallopian tubes connect the ovaries to the uterus and serve as a conduit for the ova (egg cells) from the ovaries to the uterus. Located on either side of the uterus, the ovaries have two major functions: the production of ova and the production of the female sex hormones, progesterone and estrogen.

Until recently it was believed that females were born with the total number of ova they would ever possess. However, several recent studies have strongly suggested that women may make new eggs throughout their reproductive years (Dell'Amore, 2012). This finding could prove to have profound implications not only in terms of overall fertility health but also in terms of our response to issues of women's health, aging, osteoporosis, muscle loss, menopause, and postmenopause (Dell'Amore, 2012).

Estrogen facilitates sexual maturation and regulates the menstrual cycle in premenopausal women. The benefits of estrogen in postmeno-pausal women, who can only obtain it from taking a supplement, are debatable. Some argue that estrogen maintains cognitive function and cardiac well-being in older women. However, estrogen supplements (also called hormone replacement therapy [HRT]) have been associated with increasing breast and uterine cancer risk, among other problems. Progesterone, though less discussed in the popular media, is critically important in preparing the uterus for pregnancy. It also is a regulator of the menstrual cycle.

Women's breasts are considered to be secondary sex characteristics because they do not have a direct function in reproduction. Mammary glands contained in the breast produce milk that is discharged through the nipples. The nipples are surrounded by the aureoles and become erect when stimulated. The size of the mammary glands is incidental to breast size and milk production. Rather, breast size is a function of the fatty tissue within the breast.

The social worker knowledgeable about interior (proximal) environment mechanisms can clarify the specifics of male and female sexuality for Juan and Belinda. In the school setting or a local community agency or on virtual sites, youth may talk about their feelings for each other and ask questions regarding sexual and emotional intimacy. It is not unusual for youth to hold misconceptions about heterosexual and other types of sexuality and the biological aspects of sexual intimacy. Accurate information about sexuality could provide a basis for Juan and Belinda to make informed decisions about exercising their options related to sexuality.

While it is beyond the scope of this chapter to discuss sexual activity among diverse genders and sexual orientations, we urge you to consider this important area and the implications for social work practice.

However, as promised, let's briefly return to the topic of genetics. In 1990, the National Institutes of Health and the Department of Energy joined forces with international partners to sequence the *human genome*, the complete set of DNA in the human body, in the Human Genome Project (HGP). Since its inception in 1990, this work has progressed exponentially. In April 2003, researchers announced that they had mapped the complete human genome (National Human Genome Research Institute, 2013). The initial primary goals of the HGP were "(i) to identify all genes of the human genome (initially estimated to be 100,000); (ii) to sequence the approximately 3 billion nucleotides (segments) of the human genome; (iii) to develop databases to store this information; (iv) to develop tools for data analysis; (v) to address ethical, legal, and social issues; and (vi) to sequence a number of 'model organisms'" (Gannett, 2008).

This knowledge has provided researchers and health care professionals with new strategies for diagnosis, treatment, and prevention of a variety of diseases and conditions. It is estimated that the HGP has enabled identification of more than 1,800 disease genes, with more than 2,000 genetic tests for human conditions (National Institutes of Health, 2010). Continued work on the HGP is intended to allow individualized analysis of each person's genome, leading to personalized strategies of intervention, prevention, and "preemptive medicine" (National Institutes of Health, 2010). For social workers, the National Institutes of Health (2010) has also identified that "the increasing ability to connect DNA variation with non-medical conditions, such as intelligence and personality traits, will challenge society, making the role of ethical, legal and social implications research more important than ever" (p. 2).

Given the mission of social work to celebrate diversity, it is incumbent on social workers to reexamine beliefs and practices that are and will be reshaped by the advancement of the HGP and genetic medicine intervention. For example, teasing apart the right to choose to have a child versus abortion as eugenics should be a major ethical debate engaged by social work. Questions such as which interior traits should be eliminated and how are critical bioethical concerns. Moreover, the intersection of economic disparity and unequal access to genetic medicine is a policy and praxis issue to be engaged within our profession.

Critical Thinking Questions 3.4

What are the available sources of information about the reproductive system in contemporary societies? What sources of information have you used to learn about the reproductive system? At what age did you begin to gather information about the reproductive system? How did you sort out accurate from inaccurate information? How would you like your little sister or brother to learn about the reproductive system?

EXTERIOR (DISTAL) SOCIOECONOMIC ENVIRONMENT AND INTERIOR (PROXIMAL) HEALTH ENVIRONMENT _____

Public health experts have long noted the association of poor health outcomes, in all body systems, with low income, low education, unsanitary housing, inadequate health care, unstable employment, and unsafe physical environments (Engels, 1892; Speybroeck et al., 2010). Until recently, however, researchers have made little attempt to understand the reasons behind this empirically supported connection of SES and health.

But by the mid-1990s, researchers in several countries began to try to understand how health is related to SES. In the United States, that research effort became much more focused in 1997, when the MacArthur Foundation established the Research Network on Socioeconomic Status and Health. This network is interdisciplinary, including scholars from the fields of biostatistics, epidemiology, economics, medicine, neuroscience, psychoneuroimmunology, psychology, and sociology. Beginning in 2000, there was a big jump in research on health inequalities related to SES, oppression, and discrimination in the United States (Adler & Stewart, 2010a).

The relationship between SES and health is turning out to involve complex interactions of interior (proximal) and exterior (distal) environments, and researchers are finding some surprises. For example, immigrants to the United States have a longer life expectancy than native-born persons, and this difference increased from 1979 to 2003 (Singh & Hiatt, 2006). This increase may be at least partially explained by U.S. immigration policies, which have been favoring immigrant populations with skill sets well suited for contemporary global capitalism.

In February 2010, the *Annals of the New York Academy of Sciences* presented a special volume, "The Biology of Disadvantage: Socioeconomic Status and Health." In that volume, Nancy Adler and Judith Stewart (2010b) reviewed research on socioeconomic status and health. They note that

in the United States about twice as many Blacks and Hispanics report being in poor or fair health as Whites and that adults living in poverty are about five times as likely as adults with the highest incomes to report poor or fair health. Their review of the research indicates several mechanisms by which "socioeconomic status gets under the skin" (p. 11), including these:

Conflict perspective

- *Differential access to health care.* Adler and Stewart (2010b) note that health insurance alone does not guarantee access to health care. Other important access issues include "travel time, transportation availability and cost, scheduling flexibility, sense of self-efficacy and control" (p. 12). In addition, they note that health promotion is more important than disease treatment for overall health and longevity.

- *Environmental exposures.* People with lower SES have greater exposure to such environmental hazards as air, water, and noise pollution; hazardous waste; and toxins than people with higher SES. These environmental factors have received limited research to date.

- *Health behaviors.* People with lower incomes are more likely than people with higher incomes to be engaged in several types of risky health behaviors, including smoking, physical inactivity, and unhealthy diet. There is some evidence that these behaviors are used as coping strategies in the face of stress.

- *Exposures to stress.* Chronic stress has been linked to such adverse health outcomes as hypertension, susceptibility to infection, buildup of fat in blood vessels and the abdomen, and brain cell atrophy. It has also been linked to premature aging at the cellular level, indicated by reduced length of telomeres.

- *Neighborhood and community.* Individuals living in low-income neighborhoods have been found to have poorer health than individuals living in middle- or high-income neighborhoods, whether or not they themselves are poor.

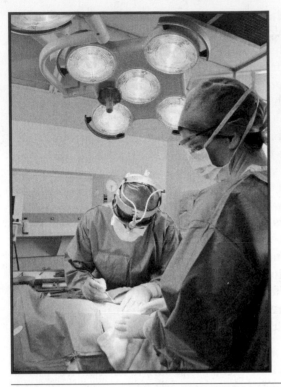
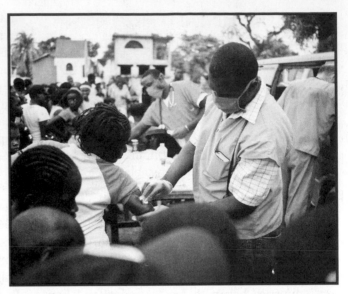

Photos 3.2a & 3.2b Biological health and illness greatly impact human behavior. Here, contrast how medical care is delivered in two very different situations, one in a high-tech operating room in the United States and the other in a temporary clinic in Haiti.

© Jupiterimages/Polka Dot/Thinkstock; © Fred Dufour/AFP/Getty Images

The research so far supports the notion that the health care system alone cannot offset the effects of other external environment forces on health. Therefore, an important social work domain is public health research and practice. One study found that governmental policies aimed at reducing social inequalities result in lowered infant mortality rates and increased life expectancy at birth (Navarro et al., 2006).

An additional critical factor in health status (positive and negative) involves health literacy. The Institute of Medicine defines health literacy as "the degree to which individuals have the capacity to obtain, process, and understand the basic health information and services needed to make appropriate health decisions" (National Network of Libraries of Medicine, 2013, para. 1). Health literacy involves much more than simply translating health information into multiple languages. It also involves consideration of reading and listening skills; analytic and decision-making skills; and the freedom to be able to engage in dialogue, questioning, and critical evaluation of health information and health care options.

Critical Thinking Questions 3.5

What could be some reasons why the incidence of heart attack, cancer, homicide, and infant mortality increases as the level of societal inequality increases? What are the implications of these statistics for public health policies?

This discussion of the interior (proximal) biological person suggests several principles for social work assessment and intervention:

- Develop a working knowledge of the body's interior (proximal) environmental systems, their interconnectedness, and the ways they interact with other dimensions of human behavior.
- In assessments and interventions, recognize that interior (proximal) environmental conditions of health and illness are influenced by the exterior (distal) environmental social, political, cultural, and economic context.
- Recognize that the exterior (distal) environmental meanings attached to health and illness may influence not only the physical experience but also the values and socioemotional response assigned to health and illness.
- In assessment and intervention activities, look for the ways behavior affects biological functions and the ways biological functions affect behavior.
- In assessment and interventions, evaluate the influence of health status on cognitive performance, emotional comfort, and overall well-being.
- In assessment and intervention, consider the ways in which one person's interior (proximal) environment health status is affecting other people in the person's exterior (distal) environment.
- Where appropriate, incorporate multiple social work roles into practice related to the health of the biological system, including the roles of researcher, clinician, educator, case manager, service coordinator, prevention specialist, and policy advocate.

Key Terms

acquired immunodeficiency syndrome (AIDS)
antibodies
antigens
assistive devices
atria
autoimmune disease
axon
blood pressure
brain injury (BI)

cardiovascular system
diabetes mellitus
endocrine system
feedback control mechanism
high blood pressure (hypertension)
human immunodeficiency virus (HIV)
immune system
lymphocytes

musculoskeletal system
nervous system
neuron
neurotransmitters
nonspecific immunity
specific immunity
synapse
testes
uterus
ventricles

Active Learning

1. You have been asked by the local public middle school to teach youth about the experience of living with one of the following conditions: brain injury, diabetes, HIV, high blood pressure, or multiple sclerosis. Locate literature and web resources on your chosen topic, select the material you wish to present, and prepare a presentation in lay terms that will be accessible to the youth audience.

2. Working in small groups, prepare two arguments, one supporting and one opposing sex education in public schools. Give some consideration to content that should or should not be included in sex education programs in public schools and the ages at which such education should occur. Provide evidence for your arguments.

American Diabetes Association: www .diabetes.org

Site contains basic diabetes information as well as specific information on type 1 diabetes, type 2 diabetes, community resources, and healthy living.

American Heart Association: www .americanheart.org

Site contains information on diseases and conditions, healthy lifestyles, and health news and a heart and stroke encyclopedia.

Centers for Disease Control and Prevention (CDC) Division of HIV/AIDS Prevention: www.cdc.gov/hiv

Site contains basic science information on HIV/AIDS, basic statistics, fact sheets, and links to other resource sites.

Guttmacher Institute: www.guttmacher.org

Site presented by the Guttmacher Institute (formerly the Alan Guttmacher Institute)—a nonprofit organization that focuses on sexual and reproductive health research, policy analysis, and public education—contains information on abortion, law and public policy, pregnancy and birth, pregnancy and disease prevention and contraception, sexual behavior, sexually transmitted infections and HIV, and sexuality and youth.

MacArthur Research Network on SES & Health: www.macses.ucsf.edu

Site has overviews of questions of interest to four working groups: a social environment group, a psychosocial group, an allostatic load (physiological wear and tear on the body resulting from chronic stress) group, and a developmental group.

Multiple Sclerosis Association of America (MSAA): www.mymsaa.org

Site contains news and helpful information for managing multiple sclerosis.

National Center for Health Statistics: www .cdc.gov/nchs

Site contains FastStats on a wide range of health topics as well as news releases and a publication listing.

Neuroscience for Kids: http://faculty .washington.edu/chudler/neurok.html

Site maintained by faculty at the University of Washington presents basic neuroscience information on the brain, spinal cord, peripheral nervous system, neurons, and sensory system, including the effects of drugs on the nervous system and neurological and mental disorders.

Student Study Site

$SAGE edge™

Sharpen your skills with SAGE edge at **edge.sagepub.com/hutchisonpe5e**

SAGE edge for students provides a personalized approach to help you accomplish your coursework goals in an easy-to-use learning environment.

CHAPTER 4

The Psychological Person

Cognition, Emotion, and Self

Joseph Walsh

Chapter Outline

Opening Questions

- How is human behavior influenced by cognitions and emotions?
- How do humans develop a sense of self?

Key Ideas

As you read this chapter, take note of these central ideas:

1. Cognition and emotion are different but interrelated internal processes, and the nature of their relationship has long been debated.

2. Cognition includes the conscious thinking processes of taking in relevant information from the environment, synthesizing that information, and formulating a plan of action based on that synthesis. Cognitive theory in social work practice asserts that thinking, not emotion, should be the primary focus of intervention.

3. Moral development is related to cognitive development, because it proceeds from stages of egocentrism through abstract principles of justice and caring. Stages of moral development differ among men and women and people of different cultures.

4. Emotions can be understood as feeling states characterized by appraisals of a stimulus, changes in bodily sensations, and displays of expressive gestures.

5. The symptoms of psychological problems may be primarily cognitive or emotional, but both cognition and emotion influence the development of problems.

6. The self may be conceptualized as a soul, unfolding potentials, an organizing activity, a cognitive structure, a shared symbolic activity, or the flow of experience.

CASE STUDY

The Pre-med Student

Dan Lee was a 24-year-old single Chinese American male undergraduate student working toward admission into medical school. He came to the university counseling center to get help with his feelings of anxiety, tension, sadness, and anger related to that task and also for some ongoing interpersonal conflicts. Dan was having difficulty concentrating on his studies and was in danger of failing a course he needed to pass in order to stay on track for medical school. He was specifically preoccupied with perceived personal slights from several friends, his sister, and his mother. Dan told the social worker that he needed help learning how to get these significant others to behave more responsibly toward him so that he could focus more intensively on his own work. Dan reported that he also had been diagnosed several years ago with an auditory processing disorder, which meant he was slow to process other people's verbal communications at times and prepare his reponses to them.

Dan is the older of two children (his sister was 22) born to a couple who had grown up in Taiwan and moved to the United States before the children were born. His father was a surgeon and his mother a homemaker, and they had divorced when Dan was 7. He and his sister had lived with their mother since then and only had occasional contact with their father. Dan had internalized the values of his family and culture; he understood that he needed to assume primary responsibility for the well-being of his mother and sister while also achieving high social status for himself. He also exhibited the cultural value of obedience to authority and saw himself as the family's primary authority figure, being the only male member. While a student at the diverse university, Dan maintained cultural ties through his membership in a church that served the Chinese American community.

Dan tried hard to be a good son and brother but held a firm position that others should always accede to his directives. He believed he was always "right" in decisions he made about his mother and sister (regarding where they lived, how his mother spent her time, and what kinds of friends and career choices his sister should make). Regarding his friends, who were mostly limited to casual contacts at school and at his volunteer job at a community health center, Dan felt that whenever there was a conflict or misunderstanding it was always "their fault." He felt disrespected at these times and became so preoccupied with these "unjust sleights" that he couldn't concentrate on much else for days afterward. Dan gave one example of a friend who had arrived more than 20 minutes late on two occasions for scheduled social outings. The second time he demanded that the friend apologize for being irresponsible and insensitive, and when the friend did not do so to Dan's satisfaction, the relationship ended. These kinds of relationship disruptions were common in his life. Dan's family and friends often did not accept his admonitions, and he wanted to learn from the social worker how to better help these other people see that he was always "rational" and "correct" in his thinking. Dan had warmer feelings toward his peers at church, all of whom were Asian Americans. He spent most of his Sunday afternoons there, participating in social events and singing in the choir. Dan was also in regular contact with an ex-girlfriend, mostly by e-mail but occasionally by phone. He had broken up with her 6 months ago, and while she hoped they would resume a romantic relationship, Dan did not think this would happen.

Spencer, the social worker, was a U.S.-born Caucasian male, several years older than Dan, who had some understanding of the Chinese value system in which the client was raised. He liked Dan, appreciating his intelligence, his motivation to get help, and his ability to articulate his concerns, but he also observed that Dan demonstrated a striking rigidity in his attitudes toward others. Still, he initally validated Dan's perspective on the presenting issues. Spencer easily engaged Dan in substantive conversations each time they met, reflecting back to Dan the difficulty of his competing demands and desire to help his familiy lead safe and productive lives. Before long, however, Dan began challenging Spencer's nondirective feedback. "I want to know what you think I should do here." "How can I approach my sister so she won't be so defensive about my input?" "I tell my mother she shouldn't speak to my dad so often, but she keeps doing so anyway. How can I get her to stop?"

Dan was having difficulty balancing his desires for personal development with his need to care for two adult family members in the manner he felt appropriate. He seemed to have internalized conditions of worth related to his family responsibility and, due to having begun doing so at such a young age, had become quite rigid in his approach to helping the family. Dan's defensive posture involved distorting the motives of others as oppositional rather than expressions of their own personal inclinations. Further, he never seemed to be able to relax and have fun, except when at church. In recognizing Dan's rigidity as a defense, Spencer helped him reflect on the possibility that the behaviors of others toward him might not be intentionally oppositional but reflective of differences of opinion and that perhaps Dan could feel good about his well-meaning efforts while recognizing that one's influence over others cannot be absolute.

(Continued)

Spencer was patient in his responses to Dan: "It's a difficult situation you are in, and you're trying your hardest to do the best for your family, and it's frustrating that you can't find ways to help them understand your concern." "It hurts you to see other people move in directions you believe are not good for them." "You feel strongly that certain people should do what you suggest even though they disagree." Still, despite these empathic responses that Spencer believed reflected positive regard, Dan became increasingly frustrated with the social worker. "I thought you were a professional. I thought you were trained to help people. Why can't you come up with some new ideas for me to try?"

Dan's emotions were not always evident beneath his rigid exterior. The primary feelings he expressed to the social worker were anxiety, anger, sadness, and frustration. Over time Dan continued to function with his rigid perspective. He tried to consider his situation from the points of view of others, but he always came back to the position that he was "rational" and others were "irrational." He occasionally accused the social worker of being incompetent for not answering his questions concretely enough. Spencer himself became frustrated with his inability to help Dan broaden his perspective on interpersonal differences and Dan's inability to distinguish disagreement from disrespect. During the course of their year of working together, Spencer employed the following interventions, which alternately focused on Dan's thinking and emotions: cognitive therapy (restructuring), behavioral change, and psychodynamic therapy (so that Dan might become more aware of the range of his feelings and how the sources of his anger might be based in his family history and early upbringing). While Dan noted little progress for several months, Spencer was encouraged by the fact that he continued coming in faithfully, week after week.

COGNITION AND EMOTION

Dan's problems at college reflect his personal **psychology**, which can be defined as his mind and his mental processes. His story illustrates the impact on social functioning of a person's particular patterns of cognition and emotion. **Cognition** can be defined as our conscious or preconscious thinking processes—the mental activities of which we are aware or can become aware with reflection. Cognition includes taking in relevant information from the environment, synthesizing that information, and formulating a plan of action based on that synthesis (Ronen & Freeman, 2007). *Beliefs*, key elements of our cognition, are ideas we hold to be true. Our assessment of any idea as true or false is based on the synthesis of information. Erroneous beliefs, which may result from misinterpretations of perceptions or from conclusions based on insufficient evidence, frequently contribute to social dysfunction.

Emotion is a difficult concept to define but can be understood as a feeling state characterized by our appraisal of a stimulus, changes in bodily sensations, and displays of expressive gestures (Mulligan & Scherer, 2012). The term *emotion* is often used interchangeably in the study of psychology with the term **affect**, but the latter refers only to the physiological manifestations of feelings. Affect may be the result of *drives* (innate compulsions to gratify basic needs), which generate both conscious and **unconscious** feelings (those of which we are not aware but that influence our behavior). In contrast, emotion is always consciously experienced. Likewise, emotion is not the same as **mood**, a feeling disposition that is more stable than emotion, usually less intense, and less tied to a specific situation.

The evolution of psychological thought since the late 1800s has consisted largely of a debate about cognition and emotion—their origins, the nature of their influence on behavior, and their influence on each other. The only point of agreement seems to be that cognition and emotion are complex and interactive.

THEORIES OF COGNITION

Theories of cognition, which emerged in the 1950s, assume that conscious thinking is the basis for almost all behavior and emotions. Emotions are defined within these theories as the physiological responses that follow our cognitive evaluations of input. In other words, thoughts produce emotions.

Cognitive Theory

Jean Piaget's cognitive development theory is the most influential theory of cognition in social work and psychology (Lightfoot, Lalonde, & Chandler, 2004). In his system, our capacity for reasoning develops in stages, from infancy through adolescence and early adulthood. Piaget saw the four stages presented in Exhibit 4.1 as sequential and interdependent, evolving from activity without thought, to thought with less emphasis on activity—from doing, to doing knowingly, and finally to conceptualizing. He saw normal physical and neurological development as necessary for cognitive development.

Developmental perspective

A central concept in Piaget's theory is that of the **schema** (plural *schemata*), defined as an internalized representation of the world or an ingrained and systematic pattern of thought, action, and problem solving. Our schemata develop through *social learning* (watching and absorbing the experiences of others) or *direct learning* (our own experiences). Both of these processes may involve **assimilation** (responding to experiences based on existing schemata) or **accommodation** (changing schemata when new situations cannot be incorporated within an existing one). As children, we are motivated to develop schemata as a means of maintaining psychological *equilibrium*, or balance. Any experience that we cannot assimilate creates anxiety, but if our schemata are adjusted to accommodate the new experience, the desired state of equilibrium will be restored. From this perspective, you might interpret Dan's difficulties with his college peers as an inability to achieve equilibrium by assimilating new interactional experience within his existing schemata. Dan was accustomed to functioning within a relatively small group of family and friends from his own cultural background, where roles were clearly defined. He could not easily adjust to the challenge of managing relationships among a much larger and more diverse student population, where the members' motivations and worldviews were difficult to comprehend.

Exhibit 4.1 Piaget's Stages of Cognitive Operations

Stage	Description
Sensorimotor stage (birth to 2 years)	The infant is egocentric; he or she gradually learns to coordinate sensory and motor activities and develops a beginning sense of objects existing apart from the self.
Preoperational stage (2 to 7 years)	The child remains primarily egocentric but discovers rules (regularities) that can be applied to new incoming information. The child tends to overgeneralize rules, however, and thus makes many cognitive errors.
Concrete operations stage (7 to 11 years)	The child can solve concrete problems through the application of logical problem-solving strategies.
Formal operations stage (11 to adulthood)	The person becomes able to solve real and hypothetical problems using abstract concepts.

Another of Piaget's central ideas is that cognitive development unfolds sequentially. Infants are unable to differentiate between "self" and the external world; the primary task in early cognitive development is the gradual reduction of such egocentricity, or self-centeredness. The child gradually learns to perform **cognitive operations**—to use abstract thoughts and ideas that are not tied to situational sensory and motor information. Piaget's four stages of normal cognitive development are summarized in Exhibit 4.1.

Information Processing Theory

> Social behavioral perspective; systems perspective

Cognitive theory has been very influential, but, as you might guess, it leaves many aspects of cognitive functioning unexplained. Whereas Piaget sought to explain how cognition develops, **information processing theory** offers details about how our cognitive processes are organized (Logan, 2000). This theory makes a clear distinction between the thinker and the external environment; each is an independent, objective entity in the processing of inputs and outputs. We receive stimulation from the outside and code it with sensory receptors in the nervous system. The information is first represented in some set of brain activities and is then integrated (by accommodation or assimilation) and stored for purposes of present and future adaptation to the environment. All of us develop increasingly sophisticated problem-solving processes through the evolution of our cognitive patterns, which enable us to draw attention to particular inputs as significant. It should be noted that Dan's auditory processing deficit did not affect the nature of his cognitions. Information processing is a *sensory theory* in that it depicts information as flowing passively from the external world inward through the senses to the mind. It views the mind as having distinct parts—including the sensory register, short-term memory, and long-term memory—that make unique contributions to thinking in a specific sequence. Interestingly, information processing theory has become important in designing computer systems. In contrast, a *motor theory* such as Piaget's sees the mind as playing an active role in processing—not merely recording but actually constructing the nature of the input it receives. In Dan's case, information processing theory would suggest that he lacks the schemata adequate for adapting to his novel interpersonal situations. Cognitive theory would suggest that Dan's cognitive biases were making his adjustment difficult.

Social Learning Theory

According to *social learning theory*, we are motivated by nature to experience pleasure and avoid pain. Social learning theorists acknowledge that thoughts and emotions exist but understand them as behaviors in need of

> Social behavioral perspective; developmental perspective

explaining rather than as primary motivating factors. Social workers should be aware that there are many ways in which adults may learn, even in the context of social learning theory (Kunkel, Hummert, & Dennis, 2006). People continue to experience cognitive development in adulthood, with age- and experience-related changes in memory, cognition, and the brain. The basic principles of social learning theory continue to apply, however.

Social learning theory relies to a great extent on social behavioral principles of conditioning, which assert that behavior is shaped by its reinforcing or punishing consequences (operant conditioning) and antecedents (classical conditioning). Albert Bandura (1977b) added the principle of vicarious learning, or *modeling*, which puts forth that behavior is also acquired by witnessing how the actions of others are reinforced.

Social learning theorists, unlike other social behavioral theorists, assert that thinking takes place between the occurrence of a stimulus and our response. They call this thought process **cognitive mediation**. The unique patterns we learn for evaluating environmental stimuli explain why each of us may adopt very different behaviors in response to the same stimulus—for example, why Dan's reaction to the behavior of his peers is very different from how many of them might react to each other.

Photo 4.1 Information processing theory would suggest that the information these children are receiving from the computer flows through their senses to their minds, which operate much like computers.

© Creatas Images/Thinkstock

Bandura takes this idea a step further and asserts that we engage in self-observations and make self-judgments about our competence and mastery. We then act on the basis of these self-judgments. Bandura (2001) criticizes information processing theory for its passive view of human agency, arguing that it omits important features of what it means to be human, including subjective consciousness, deliberative action, and the capacity for self-reflection. For example, Dan may have made some negative self-judgments about his competence to complete his pre-med studies that are affecting his functioning.

Theory of Multiple Intelligences

Howard Gardner's (1999, 2006) theory of **multiple intelligences** constitutes a major step forward in our understanding of how people come to possess different types of cognitive skills and how the same person is able to effectively use cognition and emotion in some areas of life but not others. In this theory, intelligence is defined as a "biopsychosocial potential to process information that can be activated in a cultural setting to solve problems or create products that are of value in a culture" (Gardner, 1999, p. 23). Intelligence includes the following:

- The ability to solve problems one encounters in life
- The ability to generate new problems to solve
- The ability to make something or offer a service that is valued within one's culture

In this theory, the brain is understood not as a single cognitive system but as a central unit of

Exhibit 4.2   Gardner's Eight Intelligences

Linguistic intelligence. The capacity to use language to express what is on your mind and to understand other people. Linguistic intelligence includes listening, speaking, reading, and writing skills.

Logical/mathematical intelligence. The capacity for mathematical calculation, logical thinking, problem solving, deductive and inductive reasoning, and the discernment of patterns and relationships. Gardner suggests that this is the type of intelligence addressed by Piaget's model of cognitive development, but he does not think Piaget's model fits other types of intelligence.

Visual-spatial intelligence. The ability to represent the spatial world internally in your mind. Visual-spatial intelligence involves visual discrimination, recognition, projection, mental imagery, spatial reasoning, and image manipulation.

Bodily kinesthetic intelligence. The capacity to use your whole body or parts of your body to solve a problem, make something, or put on some kind of production. Gardner suggests that our tradition of separating body and mind is unfortunate because the mind can be trained to use the body properly and the body trained to respond to the expressive powers of the mind. He notes that some learners rely on tactile and kinesthetic processes, not just visual and auditory processes.

Musical intelligence. The capacity to think in musical images, to be able to hear patterns, recognize them, remember them, and perhaps manipulate them.

Intrapersonal intelligence. The capacity to understand yourself, to know who you are, what you can do, what you want to do, how you react to things, which things to avoid, which things to gravitate toward, and where to go if you need help. Gardner says we are drawn to people who have a good understanding of themselves because those people tend not to make mistakes. They are aware of their range of emotions and can find outlets for expressing feelings and thoughts. They are motivated to pursue goals and live by an ethical value system.

Interpersonal intelligence. The ability to understand and communicate with others, to note differences in moods, temperaments, motivations, and skills. Interpersonal intelligence includes the ability to form and maintain relationships and assume various roles within groups and the ability to adapt behavior to different environments. It also includes the ability to perceive diverse perspectives on social and political issues. Gardner suggests that individuals with this intelligence express an interest in interpersonally oriented careers, such as teaching, social work, and politics.

Naturalist intelligence. The ability to recognize and categorize objects and processes in nature. Naturalist intelligence leads to talent in caring for, taming, and interacting with the natural environment, including living creatures. Gardner suggests that naturalist intelligence can also be brought to bear to discriminate among artificial items such as sneakers, cars, and toys.

SOURCE: Based on Gardner, 1999, 2006.

Systems perspective

neurological functioning that houses relatively separate cognitive faculties. During its evolution, the brain has developed separate organs, or modules, as information-processing devices. Thus, all of us have a unique blend of intelligences derived from these modules. Gardner has delineated eight intelligences, which are described in Exhibit 4.2, although in his ongoing research he is considering additional possibilities. Some proponents of multiple intelligence have proposed spiritual or religious intelligence as a possible additional type,

and Gardner (2006) has acknowledged that such an "existential" intelligence may be a useful construct. You may be interested to note that in one study, social work educators rated intrapersonal, interpersonal, and linguistic intelligences as the most important for social work practice, and the same educators rated bodily kinesthetic, musical, and spatial intelligences as important for culturally sensitive practice (Matto, Berry-Edwards, Hutchison, Bryant, & Waldbillig, 2006).

Two intelligences, the *linguistic* (related to spoken and written language) and the *logical-mathematical* (analytic), are most consistent with traditional notions of intelligence.

The theory of multiple inteliigences is rather new and has not yet been empirically validated by research (Waterhouse, 2010). Still, it has proven useful in understanding a

Humanistic perspective

person's range of strengths and can even serve as a guide for social work practitioners in deciding on interventions that will maximize client motivation and participation (for example, art therapy for persons with strong visual-spatial intelligence) (Booth & O'Brien, 2008). One of the most positive implications of the theory of multiple intelligences is that it helps us see strengths in ourselves that lie outside the mainstream. For example, Dan has a strong logico-mathmatical intelligence that contributes to his ability to master difficult physiological concepts. He may benefit from help, however, in further development of his intrapersonal and interpersonal domains, especially outside his cultural group.

Critical Thinking Questions 4.1

Why do you think social work educators rated intrapersonal, interpersonal, and linguistic intelligences as the most important for social work practice? Would you agree with that? Why or why not? Why do you think the same educators rated bodily kinesthetic, musical, and spatial intelligences as important for culturally sensitive practice? Would you agree with that? Why or why not? Shouldn't all social work practice be culturally sensitive?

Theories of Moral Reasoning

Developmental perspective

Morality is our sensitivity to, and perceptions of, what is right and wrong. It develops from our acquired principles of justice and ways of caring for others. Theories of moral reasoning are similar to those of cognitive development in that a sequential process is involved.

Familiarity with these theories can help social workers understand how clients make decisions and develop preferences for action in various situations. Both of these issues are important in our efforts to develop goals with clients. The best-known theories of moral reasoning are those of Lawrence Kohlberg and Carol Gilligan. In reviewing these theories, it is important to keep in mind that they are based on studies of men and women in the United States. It is likely that moral development unfolds differently in other cultures, although more research is needed to investigate these differences (Gardiner & Kosmitzki, 2011).

Kohlberg (1969) formulated six stages of moral development, divided into three levels, which begin in childhood and unfold through adolescence and young adulthood (see Exhibit 4.3). His perspective is based on an individualistic notion of justice. The first two stages represent **preconventional morality** in which the child's primary motivation is to avoid immediate punishment and receive immediate rewards. **Conventional morality** emphasizes adherence to social rules. A person at this level of morality might be very troubled, as Dan is, by circumstances that make him or her different from other people. Many people never move beyond this level to **postconventional morality**, which is characterized by a concern with moral principles transcending those of their own society.

One limitation of Kohlberg's theory is that it does not take into account

Conflict perspective

gender differences (his subjects were all male). In fact, he claims that women do not advance through all six stages as often as men. Addressing this issue, Gilligan (1982, 1988) notes that boys tend to emphasize independence, autonomy, and the rights of others in their moral thinking, using a *justice-oriented* approach. Girls, on the other hand, develop an ethic of *care* and *interdependence* that grows out of a concern for the needs of others rather than the value of independence. To account for this difference, Gilligan proposed the three stages of moral development listed in Exhibit 4.4. Her stages place greater emphasis than Kohlberg does on the ethic

Exhibit 4.3 Kohlberg's Levels and Stages of Moral Development

Stage	Description
Preconventional level	
Stage 1: Heteronomous morality	Accepting what the world says is right
Stage 2: Instrumental purpose	Defining the good as whatever is agreeable to the self and those in the immediate environment
Conventional level	
Stage 3: Interpersonal experiences	Seeking conformity and consistency in moral action with significant others
Stage 4: The societal point of view	Seeking conformity and consistency with what one perceives to be the opinions of the larger community
Postconventional level	
Stage 5: Ethics	Observing individual and group (societal) rights
Stage 6: Conscience and logic	Seeking to apply universal principles of right and wrong

Exhibit 4.4 Gilligan's Three Stages of Moral Development

Stage	Description
Survival orientation	Egocentric concerns of emotional and physical survival are primary.
Conventional care	The person defines as right those actions that please significant others.
Integrated care	A person's right actions take into account the needs of others as well as the self.

of care and are meant to more accurately describe the moral development of females. We see in the next chapter how Gilligan's work has influenced feminist psychology.

The research findings on gender differences in moral reasoning are inconsistent. Some research indicates that boys do tend to emphasize justice principles, whereas girls emphasize caring, but these differences are not great (see, e.g., Malti, Gasser, & Buchmann, 2009). Other researchers find no differences in the ways males and females reason about moral dilemmas (e.g., Donleavey, 2008; Hauser, Cushman, Young, Mikhail, & Jin, 2007). It is possible that gender differences in moral reasoning, when they do occur, are related to power differences and differences in the typical ethical dilemmas faced by males and females. In one revealing study, a sample of men and women were asked to respond to a set of hypothetical scenarios in which they needed to assume positions of limited power as well as take on caregiving roles (Galotti, 1989). Under these conditions, the moral responses of men and women were similar. Researchers have also found evidence that culture may have a greater influence on moral reasoning than gender does, with Anglo Americans putting less emphasis on an ethic of care than members of other ethnic groups (Gardiner & Kosmitzki, 2011).

Both Kohlberg's and Gilligan's stages of moral reasoning, like Piaget's cognitive theory, assume an increasing ability to think abstractly as the person progresses through adolescence. The theories can also be seen as complementary, especially considering that both authors articulated respect for each other's work (Jorgensen, 2006). With his great concern about individual achievement, along with a desire to care for his sister and mother, Dan seems to fall into Kohlberg's stage of conventional morality and Gilligan's stage of conventional care.

Gardiner and Kosmitzki (2011) argue that moral development may not follow a universal script across cultures and suggest that the ecological system in which early social interactions occur shapes moral thought and behavior. For understanding moral reasoning across cultures, they recommend a social constructionist theory of moral development proposed by Neff and Helwig (2002) and Haan (1991), who suggest that moral reasoning comes from the understanding of the interdependence of self and others that develops through social interactions. They propose that the most mature moral reasoner is the one who makes moral decisions that balance the person's own needs and desires with those of others affected by the issue at hand. Haan found that people who are able to control their own emotions in order to think about possible solutions engage in higher levels of moral action than people who are not able to control their emotions. In this view, moral reasoning would take different forms in different cultures, based on different definitions of needs and desires. Even so, research has tended to support the idea that moral development unfolds in stages across cultures (Gibbs, Basinger, Grime, & Snarey, 2007).

Theories of Cognition in Social Work Practice

When theories of cognition first emerged, they represented a reaction against psychodynamic theories, which focused on the influence of unconscious thought. Many practitioners had come to believe that although some mental processes may be categorized as unconscious, they have only a minor influence on behavior. Rather, conscious thinking is the basis for almost all behavior and emotions (Walsh, 2014).

As we have seen, Piaget's cognitive theory postulates that we develop mental schemata, or general information-processing rules that become enduring, from past experiences. Schemata are the basis for the ways we screen, discriminate, and code stimuli; categorize and evaluate experiences; and make judgments. Cognition is viewed as active—our minds do not merely receive and process external stimuli but are active in constructing the reality we seek to apprehend. We are "rational" to the extent that our schemata, the basis for our perceptions, accommodate available environmental evidence and our decisions do not rely solely on preconceived notions about the external world. From the perspective of cognitive theory, the sources of our problems may involve accurate assessments of the environment (for which problem-solving interventions may be provided), cognitive *deficits* (lacking information about a situation) or cognitive misperceptions, or *distortions* (Murphy, 2004).

So long as our cognitive style helps us to achieve our goals, it is considered healthy. However, thinking patterns can become distorted, featuring patterns of bias that dismiss relevant environmental information from judgment, which can lead in turn to the maladaptive emotional responses described in Exhibit 4.5. These *cognitive distortions* are habits of thought that lead us at times to distort input from the environment and experience psychological distress (A. T. Beck, 1976; J. S. Beck, 2005).

As a social worker, you could use cognitive theory to surmise that Dan is distressed because he subjectively assesses some of his life situations in a distorted manner. For example, *arbitrary inferences* may lead him to conclude that because other students do not share his perspectives on how they should behave, they do not respect his point of view. Because he concludes this, he may also conclude that he will continue to feel isolated from his peers, and this thought produces his emotional response of sadness.

To adjust his emotions and mood, Dan needs to learn to evaluate his external environment differently. He needs to consider changing some of the

Exhibit 4.5 Common Cognitive Distortions

Cognitive Error	Description
Absolute thinking	Viewing experiences as all good or all bad and failing to understand that experiences can be a mixture of both
Overgeneralization	Assuming that deficiencies in one area of life necessarily imply deficiencies in other areas
Selective abstraction	Focusing only on the negative aspects of a situation and consequently overlooking its positive aspects
Arbitrary inference	Reaching a negative conclusion about a situation with insufficient evidence
Magnification	Creating large problems out of small ones
Minimization	Making large problems small and thus not dealing adequately with them
Personalization	Accepting blame for negative events without sufficient evidence

beliefs, expectations, and meanings he attaches to events, because they are not objectively true. He might conclude, for example, that people possess honest differences of opinion and that some of his peers appreciate him more than he assumes. He may even notice that their opinions are consistent with his more than he realizes. Cognitive theorists would make Dan's thinking the primary target of change activity, assuming that cognitive change will in turn produce changes in his emotional states.

Cognitive theory is a highly rational approach to human behavior. Even though the theory assumes that some of a person's beliefs are irrational and distorted, it also assumes that human beings have great potential to correct these beliefs in light of contradictory evidence. In clinical assessment, the social worker must assess the client's schemata and identify the source of his or her difficulties as being rooted in cognitive deficits, distortions, or accurate assessment of a situation. During intervention, the social worker helps the client adjust his or her cognitive process to better facilitate the attainment of goals. As a result, the client will also experience more positive emotions. It is important to emphasize that clients are not encouraged to rationalize all of their problems as involving faulty assumptions, as many challenges people face are due to oppressive external circumstances. Still, Dan's belief that his family, former girlfriend, and peers do not value his feedback is an arbitrary inference.

To help him overcome this distortion, the social worker could review the available evidence of that conclusion, helping Dan to understand that his significant others may often give consideration to his points of view even though they do not always accede to them.

Social learning theory takes the tendency in cognitive theory to de-emphasize innate drives and unconscious thinking even further. Some practitioners in the social learning tradition make no attempt to understand internal processes at all and avoid making any inferences about them. Social workers who practice from the behavioral approach conceptualize thoughts and emotions as behaviors subject to *reinforcement contingencies* (Thyer, 2005). That is, we tend to behave in ways that produce rewards (material or emotional) for us. Thus, behaviors can be modified through the application of specific action-oriented methods, such as those listed in Exhibit 4.6. If Dan feels socially isolated due to his lack of skills at engaging in casual conversation, the social worker would first help him understand that improved social skills might help him feel more connected to his peers. Through behavioral rehearsal Dan could learn through step-by-step modeling and role-playing how to informally interact with his classmates more effectively. His positive reinforcers might include the sense of interpersonal connection, a new sense of efficacy, and reduced anxiety.

Exhibit 4.6 Four Behavioral Change Strategies

Strategy	Description
Desensitization	Confronting a difficult challenge through a step-by-step process of approach and anxiety control
Shaping	Differentially reinforcing approximations of a desired but difficult behavior so as to help the person eventually master the behavior
Behavioral rehearsal	Role-playing a desired behavior after seeing it modeled appropriately and then applying the skill to real-life situations
Extinction	Eliminating a behavior by reinforcing alternative behaviors

The combination of assessing and intervening with a person's thought processes, and then helping the client to identify and develop reinforcers for new ways of thinking and behaving, is known as *cognitive-behavioral therapy* (CBT). Most cognitive practitioners use cognitive-behavioral methods because it is important to help the client experience rewards for any changes he or she risks.

The more we learn about cognition, however, the more complex it becomes. For example, psychologist and economist Daniel Kahneman (2011) suggests that people place too much confidence in the rationality of their judgment. In fact, his research concludes that we all have built-in cognitive biases. One of these is that we are more driven to avoid pain than to experience pleasure, but more problematic is our "optimistic bias," which generates a false sense that we have substantial control of our lives. This bias may be adaptive in an evolutionary sense, but as a result we fail to comprehend and take complexity into account in assessing past and present events, and our understanding of the world consists of small, not necessarily representative sets of observations. One implication of this bias is that we tend to be overconfident in our judgments; our "rational" minds generally do not account for the role of chance in events and thus falsely assume that future events will mirror past ones. Kahneman's work provides a reminder that there is much to be learned about the nature of cognition and the potential for people to act "rationally."

> **Critical Thinking Questions 4.2**
>
> How important do you think conscious thinking is in human behavior in general and for Dan Lee in particular? What do you think of Daniel Kahneman's thesis that we place too much confidence in the rationality of our judgments?

THEORIES OF EMOTION

Emotion is physiologically programmed into the human brain (see Chapter 3). Its expression is primarily mediated by the hypothalamus, whereas the experience of emotion is a limbic function. But emotion also involves a cognitive labeling of these programmed feelings, which is at least partially a learned process. That is, some emotional experience is an interpretation and not merely given by our physiological state. For example, two students might feel anxious walking into the classroom on the first day of a semester. The anxiety would be a normal reaction to entering a new and unfamiliar situation. However, one student might interpret the anxiety as a heightened alertness that will serve her well in adjusting to the new students and professor, whereas the other student might interpret the same emotion as evidence that she is not prepared to manage the course material. The first student may become excited, but the second student becomes distressed.

Many theorists distinguish between primary and secondary emotions (Parkinson, Fischer, & Manstead, 2005). **Primary emotions** may have evolved as specific reactions with survival value for the human species. They mobilize us, focus our attention, and signal our state of mind to others. There is no consensus on what the primary emotions are, but they are usually limited to anger, fear, sadness, joy, and anticipation (Panksepp, 2008). **Secondary emotions** are more variable among people and are socially acquired. They evolved as humans developed more sophisticated means of learning, controlling, and managing emotions to promote flexible cohesion in social groups. Secondary emotions may result from combinations of primary emotions (Plutchik, 2005), and their greater numbers also imply that our processes of

perception, though largely unconscious, are significant in labeling them. These emotions include (but are not limited to) envy, jealousy, anxiety, guilt, shame, relief, hope, depression, pride, love, gratitude, and compassion (Lazarus, 2007).

The autonomic nervous system is key to our processing of emotion (Bentley & Walsh, 2014). This system consists of nerve tracts running from the base of the brain, through the spinal cord, and into the internal organs of the body. It is concerned with maintaining the body's physical homeostasis. Tracts from one branch of this system, the sympathetic division, produce physiological changes that help make us more alert and active. These changes are sustained by the release of hormones from the

> Systems perspective

Photo 4.2   Here a boy experiences joy from the kiss of his mother.

endocrine glands into the bloodstream. Parasympathetic system nerve tracts produce opposite, or calming, effects in the body. The two systems work together to maintain an appropriate level of physical arousal.

Still, psychologists have debated for more than a century the sources of emotion. Theories range from those that emphasize physiology to those that emphasize the psychological or the purely social context, and they give variable weight to the role of cognition.

Physiological Theories of Emotion

A theory of emotion developed more than a century ago by the psychologist William James (1890) speculated that our bodies produce automatic physiological reactions to any stimulus. We notice these reactions and then attempt through cognition to make sense of them. This "making sense" involves labeling the emotion. Thus, emotion follows cognition, which itself follows the physiological reaction to a stimulus. The original theory stated that a distinct emotion arises from each physiological reaction.

A few decades later, another theory (Cannon, 1924) argued that physiological arousal and the experience of emotion are unrelated. Our physiological responses to a stimulus are nonspecific and only prepare us for a general *fight-or-flight response* (to confront or avoid the stimulus). This response in itself has nothing to do with the experience of emotion because any particular physiological activity may give rise to different emotional states and may not even involve our emotions at all. Thus, a separate process of perception produces our feeling of emotion. Emotion derives from the associations we make based on prior attempts to understand the sensation of arousal.

Physiology-based theories of emotion lost favor in the mid-20th century, but recent brain research is once again suggesting a strong link between physiological processes and emotion. This **differential emotions theory** (Magai, 2001) asserts that emotions originate in our neurophysiology and that our personalities are organized around "affective biases." All of us possess the primary emotions of happiness, sadness, fear, anger, and interest/excitement. These emotions are instinctual, hardwired into our brains, and the source of our motivations. When our emotions are activated, they have a pervasive influence on our cognition and behavior. A key theme in this theory is that emotions influence cognition, a principle opposite to that stressed in cognitive theory.

For example, Dan has a persistent bias toward sadness, which may reflect some personal or material losses that occurred long before he started college. His episodes of sadness produce the temporary physical responses of a slowing down and decreased general effort. The sadness thus allows Dan time to reevaluate his needs and regain energy for more focused attempts to reach more achievable goals. It is also a signal for others to provide Dan with support. (You can certainly recall times when the sadness of another person prompted your own empathic response.) Of course, it is likely that "appearing sad" may have been more functional for Dan in his home community, where he was more consistently around people who knew and took an interest in him. In contrast, the emotion of anger tends to increase a person's energy and motivate behavior intended to overcome frustration. Furthermore, it signals others to respond with avoidance, compliance, or submission so that the person may resolve the problem. Dan becomes angry rather frequently, and his sullen demeanor clearly encourages his peers, but not necessarily his family, to give him space.

Researchers have speculated for decades about the precise locations of emotional processing in the brain. Much has been learned about structures that participate in this process, and it is clear that

> Social constructionist perspective

many areas of the brain have a role (Farmer, 2009). Furthermore, it is now widely accepted that cultural patterns shape the ways in which environmental input is coded in the brain (Kagan, 2007).

As suggested in Chapter 3, the brain may be conceived as having three sections: hindbrain, midbrain, and forebrain. The *hindbrain* is the oldest of these and is sometimes called the reptilian brain. It consists of the brain stem and cerebellum and is responsible for involuntary life support functions. The *midbrain* is located just above the brain stem. It represents a second level of brain evolution, more advanced than the hindbrain. It includes the limbic system, a group of cell structures and the center of activities that create emotions. The *forebrain* is more focused on the external environment and on "rational" functions. It is the center of emotion, memory, reasoning, abstract thought, and judgment, and it integrates diverse brain activities. All of these sections have a role in the processing of emotion that researchers are only beginning to understand in depth.

The physiology of emotion begins in the *thalamus*, a major integrating center of the brain. Located in the forebrain, the thalamus is the site that receives and relays sensory information from the body and from the environment to other parts of the brain. Any perceived environmental event travels first to the thalamus and then to the sensory cortex (for thought), the basal ganglia (for movement), and the hypothalamus (for feeling). The *amygdala*, part of the limbic system, is key in the production of emotional states. There are in fact two routes to the amygdala from the thalamus. Sensations that produce primary emotions described earlier may travel there directly from the thalamus, bypassing any cognitive apparatus, to produce an immediate reaction that is central to survival. Other inputs first travel through the cortex, where they are cognitively evaluated prior to moving on to the limbic system and amygdala to be processed as the secondary emotions.

Culture and the characteristics of the individual may influence the processing of stimulation because the cognitive structures (schemata) that interpret this stimulation may, through feedback loops to the thalamus, actually shape the neural pathways that will be followed by future stimuli. In other words, neural schemata tend to become rigid patterns of information processing, shaping subsequent patterns for making sense of the external world.

Systems perspective

Richard Davidson's research has focused on the neurological processes underlying emotion, and he perceives the interactions between the prefrontal cortex and amygdala as significant in this regard (Davidson & Begley, 2012). Through brain imaging research he has found that the greater the number of connections between the amygdala and prefrontal cortex, the better we tend to be at managing our emotions. As one example, activity in the left prefrontal cortex is higher in persons who are more resilient to negative emotions, and from this Davidson infers that the left prefrontal cortex sends inhibitory messages to the amygdala.

Davidson claims that we all have different *emotional styles*, composed of combinations of six components, that determine how we react to experiences in our lives and how likely we are to have particular moods (see Exhibit 4.7). The interrelation between the prefrontal cortex and amygdala plays a major role in determining these emotional styles. People with fewer connections tend to be less effective emotional regulators, making them more irritable, quick-tempered, and less able to manage their emotions in a healthy way. Davidson further cites research suggesting that genes associated with emotional styles can gradually change their expression based on our environments, behaviors, and life experiences.

Psychological Theories of Emotion

Perhaps the most contentious debates about the role of cognition in emotion have taken place among psychological theorists. As Exhibit 4.8 shows, some psychologists have considered emotion as primary, and others have considered cognition as primary. Psychological theories in the social behavioral perspective, somewhat like physiology-based theories, assume an automatic, programmed response that is then interpreted as emotion, perhaps first consciously but eventually (through habit) unconsciously.

Exhibit 4.7   Davidson's Six Components of Emotional Style

Resilience. How quickly we recover from negative emotions.

Outlook. The duration of our positive emotions.

Context. The degree to which we modulate our emotional responses in a manner appropriate to the context (for example, not directly taking out our work-related anger on the boss).

Social intuition. Our sensitivity to social cues, including all verbal and nonverbal expressions, that reflect our ability to understand and empathize with other people's emotional worlds.

Self-awareness. The extent to which we are aware of emotional signals within our own bodies and minds. The more aware we are of our emotions, the better we will manage them.

Attention. The extent to which we can focus our attention on one thing at a time rather than becoming easily distracted.

Psychoanalytic Theory

Freud's landmark work, *The Interpretation of Dreams*, first published in 1899, signaled the arrival of **psychoanalytic theory**. Freud's theories became prominent in the United States by the early 1900s, immediately influencing the young profession of social work, and were a dominant force through the 1950s. Psychoanalytic thinking continues to be influential in social work today, through the theories of ego psychology, self psychology, object relations, and relational theory, among others.

The basis of psychoanalytic theory is the primacy of internal drives and unconscious mental activity in human behavior. Sexual and aggressive drives are not "feelings" in themselves, but they motivate behavior that will presumably gratify our impulses. We experience positive emotions when our drives are gratified and negative emotions when they are frustrated. Our

| Psychodynamic perspective |

Exhibit 4.8   Psychological Views of the Source of Emotion

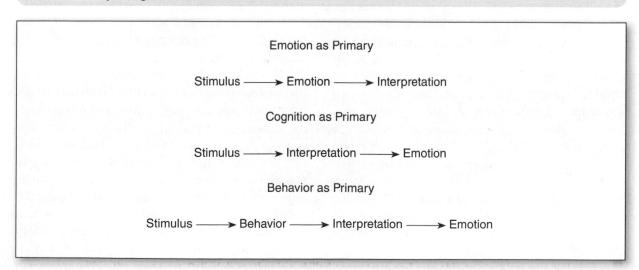

SOURCE: Adapted from Ellsworth, 1991.

conscious mental functioning takes place within the **ego**, that part of the personality responsible for negotiating between internal drives and the outside world. It is here that cognition occurs, but it is influenced by those unconscious impulses that are focused on drive satisfaction.

In psychoanalytic thought, then, conscious thinking is a product of the drives from which our emotions also spring. By nature, we are pleasure seekers and "feelers," not thinkers. Thoughts are our means of deciding how to gratify our drives. Defense mechanisms (see Chapter 5) result from our need to indirectly manage drives when we become frustrated, as we frequently do in the social world, where we must negotiate acceptable behaviors with others. The need to manage drives also contributes to the development of our unconscious mental processes. According to psychoanalytic theory, personal growth cannot be achieved by attending only to conscious processes. We need to explore all of our thoughts and feelings to understand our essential drives. Change requires that we uncover unconscious material and the accompanying feelings that are repressed, or kept out of consciousness.

Let us grant, for example, that Dan has a normal, healthy drive for pleasure. He may also be angry with his father for breaking up the family, providing it with limited resources and leaving him in a responsible position at such a young age. This anger might be repressed into unconsciousness, however, because Dan is also emulating his father professionally and may believe, due to his cultural background, that it is not permissible for a child to be angry with a parent. Dan's unconscious anger, having been turned inward at himself, may be contributing to his frustrations and inability to experience joy. An analytical social worker might suspect from Dan's presentation that he experiences this anger but is not aware of it. The social worker might try to help Dan uncover the feeling by having him reflect on his family history in detail, in a safe clinical environment. With the insights that might result from this reflection, Dan's anger may become conscious, and he can then take direct measures to work through it.

Ego Psychology

Ego psychology, which emerged in the 1930s (Goldstein, 2009), shifted

Psychodynamic perspective

to a more balanced perspective on the influences of cognition and emotion in social functioning. As an adaptation of psychoanalytic theory, it signaled a reaction against Freud's heavy emphasis on drives and highlighted the ego's role in promoting healthy social functioning. Ego psychology represents an effort to build a holistic psychology of normal development. It was a major social work practice theory throughout much of the 20th century because of its attention to the environment as well as the person, and it continues to be taught in many schools of social work.

In ego psychology, the ego is conceived of as present from birth and not as derived from the need to reconcile drives within the constraints of social living, as psychoanalytic theory would say. The ego is the source of our attention, concentration, learning, memory, will, and perception. Both past and present experiences are relevant in influencing social functioning. The influence of the drives on emotions and thoughts is not dismissed, but the autonomy of the ego, and thus conscious thought processes, receives greater emphasis than in psychoanalytic theory. The ego moderates internal conflicts, which may relate to drive frustration, but it also mediates the interactions of a healthy person with stressful environmental conditions.

If we experience sadness, then, it is possible that we are having internal conflicts related to drive frustration. It is also possible that we are experiencing person–environment conflicts in which our coping efforts are not effective; the negative emotion may result from a frustration of our ability to manage an environmental stressor and thus may arise from cognitive activities. Dan may be experiencing both types of conflict. His anger at the lack of adequate nurturance in his early family history may have been turned inward and produced a moderate depression. At the same time, the mismatch between his personal needs for mastery and the demands of the academic environment may also be contributing to his negative feelings.

Attribution Theory: A Cognitive Perspective

Social behavioral perspective

Attribution theory was the first of the psychological theories of emotion to give primacy to cognition as a producer of emotions (Schacter & Singer, 1962). **Attribution theory** holds that our experience of emotion is based on conscious evaluations we make about physiological sensations in particular social settings. We respond to situations as we understand them cognitively, which leads directly to our experience of a particular emotion. For example, Dan has often experienced anxiety, but he interprets it differently in dealing with his family (frustration due to their lack of perceived loyalty) and his fellow students (being ridiculed). Attribution theory also notes that the social setting determines the type of emotion experienced; the physiological response determines the strength of the reaction. In other words, the nature of the social setting is key to the process of emotional experience.

Richard Lazarus (2001) has proposed a three-part psychological theory of emotion based on appraisals of situations. He suggests that emotion develops when we assess a situation as somehow relevant to a personal value or life concern. First, we make an unconscious appraisal of whether a situation constitutes a threat. This appraisal is followed by coping responses, which may be cognitive, physiological, or both and may be conscious or unconscious. Once these coping mechanisms are in place, we reappraise the situation and label our associated emotion. This process implies that our feelings originate with an automatic evaluative judgment. We decide whether there is a threat, take immediate coping action to deal with it, and then take a closer look to see exactly what was involved in the situation. At the end of this process, we experience a specific secondary emotion.

A major life concern for Dan is feeling secure in his interpersonal environments. He feels secure in familiar environments (such as his hometown, at his church, and with his family) but feels threatened in unfamiliar places. When he walks into a new classroom, he experiences anxiety. The feeling seems to Dan to be automatic, because his need for security is threatened in the situation. His means of coping is to ignore the other students, neither speaking to nor making eye contact with them, and to sit in a relatively isolated area of the room. Dan then makes at least a partly conscious appraisal that the room is occupied with strangers who are judging him in negative ways. Dan labels his emotion as resentment because he concludes that his classmates are incorrectly perceiving him as socially inferior.

Critical Thinking Questions 4.3

We have just looked at three types of theories of emotion: physiological theories, psychological theories, and attribution theory. What did you find most interesting about these different ways of thinking about emotion? Which ideas did you find most appealing? Most convincing? Explain.

Theory of Emotional Intelligence

Emotional intelligence is a person's ability to process information about

Systems perspective

emotions accurately and effectively and, consequently, to regulate emotions in an optimal manner (Goleman, 2005). It includes self-control, zest and persistence, and the ability to motivate oneself, understand and regulate one's own emotions, and read and deal effectively with other people's feelings. This is a relatively new concept in psychology. The idea of integrating the emotional and intellectual systems was considered contradictory for many years. Emotions deal with narrow informational content and specific events that are seen as changeable and unique. The intellect is related to patterns and regularities, but recently psychologists have determined that emotional stimulation is necessary for activating certain schematic thought patterns.

Emotional intelligence involves recognizing and regulating emotions in ourselves and other people. It requires emotional sensitivity, or the ability to evaluate emotions within a variety of social circumstances. A person who is angry but knows that certain expressions of anger will be counterproductive in a particular situation, and as a result constrains his or her expressions of anger, is emotionally intelligent. On the other hand, a person with this same knowledge who behaves angrily in spite of this awareness is emotionally unintelligent.

People are not necessarily equally emotionally intelligent about themselves and other people. We may be more emotionally intelligent about other people than we are about ourselves, or vice versa. The first possibility helps to explain why some people, social workers included, seem to be better at giving advice to others than to themselves.

Emotional intelligence requires an integration of intellectual and emotional abilities. Recognizing and regulating emotions requires emotional self-awareness and empathy, but it also necessitates the intellectual ability to calculate the implications of behavioral alternatives. To understand how and why we feel as we do, and other people feel as they do, demands emotional awareness and intellectual reasoning. Emotional intelligence is more important to excellence in many aspects of life than pure intellect because it includes intellect plus other capacities.

There is no necessary relationship between emotional intelligence and emotional intensity. Emotional intelligence includes the capacity to regulate and use emotions, which may in fact favor a type of detachment not typical of emotionally expressive people. As we have already seen, Dan generally lacks emotional self-awareness, and he displays a flat emotional style with most people.

Social Theories of Emotion

Social theories of emotion also take the view that perception, or the interpretation of a situation, precedes emotion. These interpretations are learned, and as such they become automatic (unconscious or preconscious) over time. Social theories emphasize the purpose of emotion, which is to sustain shared interpersonal norms and social cohesion. Two social theories are considered here.

James Averill's (2012) social constructionist theory states that emotions can be understood as socially constructed, transitory roles. They are socially constructed because they originate in our appraisals of situations, transitory in that they are time limited, and roles because they include a range of socially acceptable actions that may be performed in a certain context. We organize and interpret our physiological reactions to stimuli with regard to the social norms involved in the situations where these reactions occur. Emotions permit us, in response to these stimuli, to step out of the conventional social roles to which people not experiencing the emotion are held. For example, in our culture, we generally would not say that we wish to harm someone unless we were feeling anger. We would generally not lash out verbally at a friend or spouse unless we felt frustrated. We would generally not withdraw from certain personal responsibilities and ask others for comfort unless we felt sad. Because of the social functions of emotions, we often experience them as passions, or feelings not under our control. Experiencing passion permits unconventional behavior because we assume that we are somehow not "ourselves," not able to control what we do at that moment. Our society has adopted this mode of thinking about emotions because it allows us to distance ourselves from some of our actions. Emotions are thus legitimized social roles or permissible behaviors for persons in particular emotional states.

George Herbert Mead (1934), the originator of symbolic interaction theory, took a somewhat different view. He suggested that emotions develop as symbols for communication. He believed that humans are by nature more

> Social constructionist perspective

sensitive to visual than to verbal cues. Emotional expressions are thus particularly powerful in that they are apprehended visually rather than verbally. Our emotional expression is a signal about how we are inclined to act in a situation, and others can adjust their own behavior in response to our perceived inclinations. Dan's lack of eye contact and physical distancing from others are manifestations of his anxiety. Other persons, in response, may choose either to offer him support or, more likely in a classroom or lab setting, to avoid him if they interpret his expressions as a desire for distance. Dan was accustomed to people noticing his sadness at home, and responding to it by reaching out to him, but in the faster-paced, more impersonal context of the university culture, this was not happening. One reason he may be continuing contact with his ex-girlfriend is that, despite their differences, she perceives and affirms his sadness.

Theories of Emotion in Social Work Practice

The preceding theories are useful in assessment and intervention with clients because they enhance the social worker's understanding of the origins of emotional experiences and describe how negative emotional states may emerge and influence behavior. The social worker can help the client develop more positive emotional responses by providing insight or corrective experiences. What follows, however, is a theory that is even more precise in identifying the processes of emotional experience.

L. S. Greenberg (2011) has offered an emotion-focused practice theory, similar to psychoanalytic theory, that may be helpful in social work interventions. Greenberg asserts that all primary emotions—those that originate as biologically based rapid responses—are adaptive. Every primary emotion we experience has the purpose of helping us adjust our relationship with an environmental situation to enhance coping. Secondary emotions emerge from these primary emotions as a result of cognitive mediation. From this perspective, problems in social functioning may occur in one of four scenarios, summarized in Exhibit 4.9.

From this perspective, it is the unconscious or **preconscious** (mental activity that is out of awareness but can be brought into awareness with prompting) appraisal of situations in relation to our needs that creates emotions. Furthermore, as George Herbert Mead (1934) pointed out, we experience our emotions as images, not as verbal thoughts. Emotions are difficult to apprehend cognitively, and in our attempts to do so, we may mistake their essence. The bad feelings that trouble us come not from those primary emotional responses, which, if experienced directly, would tend to dissipate, but from defensive distortions of those responses. We tend to appraise situations accurately with our primary emotions, but our frustration in achieving affective goals can produce distortions. Thus, in contrast to

Psychodynamic perspective

Exhibit 4.9   Four Sources of Emotion-Based Problems in Social Functioning

1. A primary emotion may not achieve its aim of changing our relationship with the environment to facilitate adaptation.

2. We may, prior to awareness of a primary emotion, deny, distort, avoid, or repress it and thus become unable to constructively address our person–environment challenge.

3. We may develop cognitive distortions, or irrational "meaning construction" processes, that produce negative secondary emotions.

4. We may regulate our appropriate emotional experiences poorly, by either minimizing or not maintaining control over them.

the assumptions of cognitive theory, distortions of thought may be the *result* of emotional phenomena rather than their cause.

Consider Dan's distress as an example. Perhaps he accurately perceives wariness in others (due to his standoffish demeanor). His need to be in control is threatened by this appraisal, and the intensity of his reaction to this frustration becomes problematic, making it hard for him to concentrate on his studies. His emotional patterns, resulting from Source 3 and Source 4 in emotion-focused theory, evoke his tendencies at times to become confrontational almost to the point of verbal abuse.

Personal reality, then, may be as much a product of emotion as cognition. In any situation, the meanings we construct may automatically determine our conscious responses. It is when we directly experience primary emotions that we are functioning in an adaptive manner.

In emotion-focused practice, the social worker would attempt to activate the person's primary emotional reactions, making them more available to awareness within the safety of the social worker–client relationship and making secondary emotional reactions amenable to reflection and change when necessary. Emotional reactions, cognitive appraisals, and action tendencies may then be identified more clearly by the client. Affective needs can be identified, and a new sense of self may emerge along with an improved capacity for self-direction.

From this perspective, a social worker could help Dan understand that he carries much anger at his family because of their long-term lack of adequate support for his emotional development. Dan could be encouraged within the safety of the social worker–client relationship to experience and ventilate that anger and gain insight into his pattern. Once Dan can consciously identify and experience that negative emotion, he may be less incapacitated by the depression, which is a secondary emotion resulting from his suppression of anger. He might then have more energy to devote to his own social and academic goals and to develop new ways of interacting with others in the university setting.

COGNITIVE/EMOTIONAL "DISORDERS"

As social workers, we are reluctant to label people as having cognitive or emotional "disorders." Instead, we conceptualize problems in social functioning as mismatches in the fit between person and environment. Still, in our study of the psychological person, we can consider how problems are manifested in the client's cognitive and emotional patterns.

Many social workers are employed in mental health agencies and use the *Diagnostic and Statistical Manual of Mental Disorders* (DSM-5; American Psychiatric Association [APA], 2013) to make diagnoses as part of a comprehensive client assessment (see Chapter 5 for details). The *DSM* has been the standard resource for clinical diagnosis in the United States for more than half a century. The purpose of the manual is to provide clear descriptions of diagnostic categories so that practitioners of all disciplines can diagnose, communicate about, and treat people with mental and emotional disorders. The *DSM* includes 20 chapters of disorders that address, among others, neurodevelopmental (such as autism spectrum disorder), schizophrenia spectrum, bipolar, depressive, anxiety, obsessive-compulsive, trauma, dissociative, eating, elimination, sleep-wake, disruptive, substance-related, neurocognitive (such as Alzheimer's disease), personality, and paraphilic disorders, as well as sexual dysfunctions and gender dysphoria.

It is important to recognize that the *DSM* provides a medical perspective on human functioning. There is tension between the social work profession's person-in-environment perspective and the requirement in many settings that social workers use the *DSM* to "diagnose" mental, emotional, or behavioral disorders in clients (Corcoran & Walsh, 2010). This is discussed further in Chapter 5.

With this brief introduction, we can consider four examples of disorders selected from the *DSM* to illustrate how either cognitive or emotional characteristics may predominate in a client's symptom profile, even though both aspects of the psychological person are always present.

- Two disorders that feature cognitive symptoms are obsessive-compulsive disorder and anorexia nervosa. Obsessive-compulsive disorder is characterized by persistent thoughts that are experienced as intrusive, inappropriate, unwelcome, and distressful. The thoughts are more than excessive worries about real problems, and the person is unable to ignore or suppress them. In anorexia nervosa, an eating disorder, the person becomes obsessive about food, thinking about it almost constantly. The person refuses to maintain a reasonable body weight because of distorted beliefs about physical appearance and the effects of food on the body.

- Two disorders that feature emotional symptoms are persistent depressive disorder (PDD) and agoraphobia. PDD, a mood disorder, is characterized by a lengthy period of depression. It features the emotion of sadness, which tends to persist regardless of external events. Agoraphobia is an anxiety disorder characterized by fear. The person is afraid to be in situations (such as crowds) or places (such as large open areas) from which escape might be difficult or embarrassing. The person must restrict his or her range of social mobility out of fear of being overwhelmed by anxiety for reasons that are not consciously clear.

As a social worker, you might note that Dan displays symptoms of obsessive-compulsive disorder. He experiences persistent and unwanted ideas and thoughts that significantly intrude on his desire to do or think of other things. He does not, however, experience compulsions or illogical impulses to perform certain behaviors (such as repeatedly checking to see if his apartment door is locked). You might thus conclude that Dan's problems are primarily cognitive. However, Dan's cognitive patterns have contributed to, and been affected by, his development of negative emotions. His difficulties at school sustain his chronic anxiety, and his distorted beliefs about the attitudes of others contribute to his sadness at being isolated from them. It is rarely the case that only cognitive factors or only emotional factors are behind a client's problems.

Critical Thinking Questions 4.4

Some research suggests that emotional intelligence is more important to career success than intelligence measured as IQ. Does that make sense to you? Why or why not? How can we enhance our own emotional intelligence? How could you help Dan enhance his emotional intelligence? How helpful do you think it would be for Dan's social worker to make a clinical diagnosis using the *DSM-5*?

THE SELF

It remains for us to integrate elements of cognition and emotion into a cohesive notion of the self. This is a difficult task—one that may, in fact, be impossible to achieve. All of us possess a sense of self, but it is difficult to articulate. How would you define *self*? Most of us tend to think of it as incorporating an essence that is more or less enduring. But beyond that, what would you say? Thinkers from the fields of philosophy, theology, sociology, psychology, and social work have struggled to identify the essence of the **self**, and they offer us a range of perspectives: the self as a soul, an unfolding of innate potentials, an organizing activity, a cognitive structure, a process of shared symbolic activity, or a flow of experience. Cultural psychologists suggest that all of these perspectives assume an independent self, but in many cultures of the world, the self is an interdependent one that cannot be detached from the context of human relationships (Markus & Kitayama, 2009).

The Self as a Soul

Understanding the self as a soul appeals to those who see their essence as constant throughout life and perhaps transcending their physical being (Gray, 2010). It is certainly true that most of us experience ourselves as more than just bodies; as an "entity" that is consistent

Humanistic perspective

across time. This idea is based on certain spiritual traditions (see Chapter 6), and though widely shared, it does not easily lend itself to examination in terms of changing configurations of person and environment. If the self as soul is constant, and apart from the material environment, it may not be substantively influenced by interactions with that environment. Still, the idea of a soul has merit within social work (and other professions). The contrasting notion of physicalism asserts that there will eventually be a complete explanation of human beings in terms of the atoms and molecules in their bodies. Without a spiritual framework, the value of human life may be reduced to the value that society places on certain kinds of people.

The Self as Unfolding Potentials

Humanistic perspective

According to person-centered theory, every human being is a unique biological organism, born with inherent, organically based potentials and ideally striving to lead a life in which the sense of "self" is consistent with those potentials (Rogers, 1986). Put another way, all of us are born with a genetic blueprint to which specific substance is added as our lives progress, depending on social and environmental circumstances. Our core tendency is to actualize our inherent potentials, which Rogers terms the striving toward self-actualization. Further, all potentials serve the maintenance and enhancement of life.

The actualizing tendency is not consciously known to a person until the self-concept emerges. Thus, many of us often find it difficult to appreciate our actualizing tendencies on the intuitive grounds of our experiences. Further, this is a conscious, fluid, and unfolding self, one that is experienced and defined differently throughout life. In fact, it resembles the concept of self presented by narrative theory (described shortly). Our inherent potentials are genetically determined, but our self-concept is socially determined and based in part on our experience of approval or disapproval from others.

The Self as Organizing Activity

The concept of self as an organizing activity incorporates the notions of action, initiative, and organization. We certainly experience ourselves as capable of initiating

Psychodynamic perspective

action, and the sense of organization emerges as we synthesize our activities and experiences. Psychoanalytic theory and ego psychology are consistent with these ideas, as they conceptualize the ego as the organizer of drives and mediator of internal and external conflicts. Your "ego," which incorporates cognitive and emotional elements, is largely (but not completely) your conception of "who you are." It is the "you" who thinks, feels, and acts in a reasonably consistent manner. It is everything you do to reflect, plan, and act in ways that allow you to "fit in" more or less adequately with the environments in which you live. More formally, the ego is the part of one's personality that is responsible for negotiating between internal needs and the demands of social living. It is where cognition occurs, but unconscious mental processes also influence conscious thinking. The ego organizes the drives in response to external restrictions on their satisfaction and is responsible for defensive functions, judgment, rational thinking, and reality awareness.

The ego is largely, although not entirely, conscious, whereas the other portions of the mind—including the id (the source of drives) and the superego (our sense of ideal behavior)—remain outside awareness and thus cannot be apprehended as part of our sense of self. Healthy human behavior is enhanced by bringing unconscious mental activity into conscious awareness, so we can have more choices and solve problems more rationally.

The Self as Cognitive Structure

The self as a cognitive structure is accepted as at least part of most accounts of the self. All of us are in touch (to varying degrees) with our conscious thinking processes and may come to accept them as representing our essence. This cognitive self includes self-representations that develop within our schemata. The self as thinker implies that action and emotion originate in thought.

Within cognitive theory there are no assumed innate drives or motivations that propel us to act in particular ways. We develop patterns of thinking and behavior through habit, but these patterns can be adjusted as we acquire new information. Recall that these schemata are our internalized representation of the world, or patterns of thought, action, and problem solving. They are the necessary biases with which we view the world, based on our early learning. Flexible schemata are desirable, but all schemata tend to be somewhat rigid. Our assumptions and related strategies are not "correct" or "incorrect" as much as they are "functional" or "nonfunctional" for our ability to achieve our goals. Schemata can change, but not always easily.

Humanistic perspective

This self may be consistent with the view of reality as a human construction. As thinkers, our sense of self evolves as we actively participate in processing stimuli and define our realities in accordance with our perceptions. The cognitive self is thus interactional and dynamic, not static.

The Self as Shared Symbolic Experience

Social constructionist perspective

The self can be understood as the product of symbols that we negotiate and share with other people in our culture. The theory of **symbolic interactionism** seeks a resolution to the idea that person and environment are separate (Blumer, 1998; Denzin, 2001; Mead, 1934). It stresses that we develop a sense of meaning in the world through interaction with our physical and social environments, which include other people but also all manifestations of cultural life. The mind represents our capacity to respond subjectively to external stimuli through conceptualizing, defining, symbolizing, valuing, and reflecting. Through social interaction, interpretation of symbols (objects and ideas with shared cultural meanings), and the filtering processes of the mind, we acquire meaning about the world and ourselves.

The sense of self develops from our perceptions of how others perceive us. It is a role-taking process at odds with the psychoanalytic view that the self involves internal drives. Symbolic interactionism suggests that we define ourselves through the attitudes and behavior of others toward us and ultimately from the standards of our society. Our sense of self changes with the changing expectations of others about how we should behave, think, and feel. The medium through which these processes occur is language. Words are symbols, and language is a product of the shared understandings of people within a culture. Thus, social interaction involves an ongoing negotiation of the meanings of words among persons. Consciousness and the sense of self become possible through language as we learn to talk to ourselves, or think, using these symbols.

Communicators must share an understanding of the cultural norms and rules governing conduct for their interaction to proceed coherently. Symbolic interactionism suggests that socialization is a highly dynamic process that continues throughout life and consists of the creation of new meanings, understandings, and definitions of situations through social interaction (Handel, Cahill, & Elkin, 2007). We change as we bring structure to ambiguous social situations to solve problems.

This concept of self includes both the *I* and the *me* (Vryan, Adler, & Adler, 2003). The *I* is the conscious self—what we are aware of in self-reflection and what actively processes information and solves problems. This self emerges as we become objects of our own thoughts. It develops through the influence of *significant others*—persons who have immediate influence on our self-definitions. The *me*, on the other hand, incorporates thoughts, feelings, and attitudes internalized over time and beneath the level of ready awareness. The *me* is influenced by *generalized others*—the types of people whose expectations have come to guide our behavior over time.

By guidance and example, an individual may become involved in a community of supportive individuals whose role expectations strengthen the self-concept. The sense of self as competent in specific situations may improve, and the sense of having a substantial role as a member of a social group may also develop. Dan's sense of himself as needing to be a high achiever may have originated in messages he received from his family, relatives, neighbors, teachers, and peers early in life. Those significant others may have acted toward him in ways that encouraged him to assume dominant roles. Still, interacting with the people around him today (generalized others) who have more flexible expectations for Dan might influence him to enact different behaviors and eventually achieve greater social competence. If these alternative social actions became prevalent in his life, Dan's *me* would experience change as well. He might come to think of himself as more of an "equal" peer rather than one who is always smarter.

The Self as a Flow of Experience

The concept of self as an ongoing process of experience is incorporated in the philosophy and practice

Humanistic perspective

theory of *existentialism* (Burston & Frie, 2006; Krill, 1996). People who assume the existential viewpoint hold that there is no standard or "correct" human nature; we are all unique and unable to be categorized. What we are is a subjective and ever-changing notion. The

Photo 4.3 Some see the self as an ongoing process of experience. The play and exploration of these schoolgirls in Bhutan contribute to their developing self-concepts.

© Rob Howard/Corbis

self is never any "thing" at a single point in time, because we are defined by the process of becoming, a process for which there is no end point. The self is always in process. Our essence is defined by our freedom to make choices and our need to discover or create meaning (sometimes called *will* or *drive*) for ourselves. The self unfolds as we make commitments to ideals outside ourselves (Frankl, 1988).

Existential philosophy is often seen as a pessimistic view of reality because it emphasizes human loneliness, but it does remind us of our uniqueness and the idea that we can always make choices about the directions our lives will take. However negatively Dan sees the world, for example, he need not necessarily maintain that perspective. He can and will always make choices that will make him a different person—that is, a different self. If Dan can recognize this (it won't happen quickly), he can perhaps make those choices that will enable him to define himself differently.

The self as a flow of experience is also consistent with **narrative theory**, a relatively new approach to social work practice. Its major premise is that all of us are engaged in an ongoing process of constructing a life story, or personal narrative, that determines our understanding of ourselves and our positions in the world (Herman, 2003). Narrative theory holds that human development is inherently fluid, that there are no developmental "milestones" we should experience to maximize our chances for a satisfying life. Instead, it is the stories we learn to tell about ourselves and about others that create our psychological and social realities. These life narratives are co-constructed with the narratives of significant people in our family, community, and culture. According to narrative theory, all personal experience is fundamentally ambiguous, and we arrange our lives into stories to give our lives coherence and meaning. These stories do not merely reflect our lives—they shape them! As we develop a dominant "story line" (and self-concept), our new experiences are filtered in or out depending on whether they are consistent with the ongoing life narrative. Many problems in living are related to life narratives that exclude certain possibilities for future action.

A value of narrative practice is that of empowering clients, helping them to gain greater control over their lives. Narrative theory is unique in its conceptualization of problems as, at least in part, by-products of cultural practices that are oppressive to the development of functional life narratives. In this sense, it is a "therapy of advocacy." While some argue that narrative interventions may not be well suited for client problems related to basic needs such as food, shelter, safety, and physical health, they are certainly suitable for issues related to self-concept, interpersonal relationships, and personal growth. From this perspective, we might want to help Dan understand that his sense of self has been strongly influenced by certain cultural traditions that demand he function as a head of household. Understanding the arbitrary nature of this assumption may be an important step toward Dan's becoming able to focus on his broader range of strengths and thereby achieve more of his personal goals.

These theories of the self represent only a partial overview. Many people believe that the self can only be defined in relation to others, and while this theme has been addressed here, it receives more attention in the next chapter.

Critical Thinking Questions 4.5

How do you define the self? You just read about six ways of thinking about self. Which of these ways makes the most sense to you? Which one comes closest to the way you think about your self? How important is culture in influencing the nature of the self? Does religion or spirituality play a role in the development of self? If so, how?

Implications for Social Work Practice

The study of the psychological person as a thinking and feeling being and as a self has many implications for social work practice:

- Be alert to the possibility that practice interventions may need to focus on any of several systems, including family, small groups, organizations, and communities. The person's transactions with all of these systems affect psychological functioning.

- During assessment, remember that developmental theories have limited applicability to members of diverse populations and be open to interpersonal differences with regard to patterns of thinking, feeling, and morality.
- Where appropriate, help individual clients to develop a stronger sense of competence through both ego-supportive and ego-modifying interventions.
- Where appropriate, help individual clients to enhance problem-solving skills through techniques directed at both cognitive reorganization and behavioral change.
- Where appropriate, help individual clients strengthen their sense of self by bringing balance to emotional and cognitive experiences.
- Help clients consider their strengths in terms of the unique sets of intelligences they may have and show how these intelligences may help them address their challenges in unique ways.
- Where appropriate, encourage clients to become involved in small-group experiences that assist them to understand and change their thoughts, emotions, and behaviors.
- Help clients assess their transactions with formal organizations and the effects of these transactions on their psychological functioning.
- Help clients assess and make necessary changes in their transactions with the community.

Key Terms

accommodation (cognitive)
affect
assimilation (cognitive)
attribution theory
cognition
cognitive mediation
cognitive operations
conventional morality
differential emotions theory
ego

ego psychology
emotion
emotional intelligence
information processing theory
mood
multiple intelligences
narrative theory
postconventional morality
preconscious
preconventional morality

primary emotions
psychoanalytic theory
psychology
schema (schemata)
secondary emotions
self
symbolic interactionism
unconscious

Active Learning

1. Reread the case study at the beginning of this chapter. As you read, what do you see as the driving force of Dan's behavior as he struggles with earning admission to medical school? Is it cognition? Is it emotion? What patterns of thinking and feeling might Dan have developed from his cultural background? What theories presented in the chapter are most helpful to you in thinking about this, and why?

2. Howard Gardner has proposed a theory of multiple intelligences and suggests that each profession must decide which intelligences are most important to its work. Working in small groups, discuss which of Gardner's eight intelligences are most important for doing social work. Are some intelligences more important in some social work settings than in others? Develop a list of criteria for admission to your social work program based on multiple intelligences.

3. What is your own perspective on the nature of the self? How does this affect your work with clients when you consider their potential for change?

Association for Behavioral and Cognitive Therapies: www.abct.org

ABCT is a multidisciplinary organization committed to the advancement of scientific approaches to the understanding and improvement of human functioning through the investigation and application of behavioral, cognitive, and other evidence-based principles to the assessment, prevention, and treatment of human problems and the enhancement of health and well-being.

Association for Moral Education: www.amenetwork.org

AME was founded in 1976 to provide an inter-disciplinary forum for professionals interested in the moral dimensions of educational theory and practice. The association is dedicated to fostering communication, cooperation, training, curriculum development, and research that links moral theory with educational practice. It supports self-reflective educational practices that value the worth and dignity of each individual as a moral agent in a pluralistic society.

Emotional intelligence, social intelligence, ecological intelligence: http://danielgoleman .info/topics/emotional-intelligence

This is the website and blog of Daniel Goleman, author of *Emotional Intelligence: Why It Can Matter More Than IQ* and *Social Intelligence: The New Science of Human Relationships*.

Howard Gardner: http://howardgardner.com

The website of Howard Gardner of Harvard Graduate School of Education includes information about his and others' research on multiple intelligences.

Narrative Therapy Centre of Toronto: www .narrativetherapycentre.com

Site contains information on narrative therapy, events and training, articles and books, and links to other websites on narrative therapy.

Piaget's developmental theory: www .learningandteaching.info/learning/piaget.htm

Site maintained by James Atherton of the United Kingdom, overviews Jean Piaget's key ideas and developmental stages.

University of Wisconsin Lab for Affective Neuroscience: http://psyphz.psych.wisc .edu/web

The Laboratory for Affective Neuroscience is engaged in a broad program of research on the brain mechanisms that underlie emotion and emotion regulation in normal individuals throughout the life course and in individuals with various psychiatric disorders.

$SAGE edge™

Sharpen your skills with SAGE edge at **edge.sagepub.com/hutchisonpe5e**

SAGE edge for students provides a personalized approach to help you accomplish your coursework goals in an easy-to-use learning environment.

CHAPTER 5

The Psychosocial Person

Relationships, Stress, and Coping

Joseph Walsh

Chapter Outline

Key Ideas

As you read this chapter, take note of these central ideas:

1. Understanding the nature of a person's relationship patterns is important for evaluating his or her susceptibility to stress and potential for coping and adaptation. A variety of psychological (e.g., relational and feminist) and social (e.g., social identity development) theories are useful toward this end.

2. The quality of one's relationships with primary caregivers in infancy and childhood affects neurological development and has lasting effects on the capacity for mental and physical health in later life.

3. Stress, an event that taxes adaptive resources, may be biological, psychological, or social in origin; psychological stress can be categorized as harm, threat, or challenge.

4. Traumatic stress refers to events that are so overwhelming that almost anyone would be affected—events such as natural and technological disasters, war, and physical assault.

5. Our efforts to master the demands of stress are known as coping.

6. All people rely on social supports as means of dealing with stress.

7. Classification of human behavior as normal or abnormal differs among the helping professions.

CASE STUDY

Dan's Coping Strategies

To summarize more specifically how Dan (whom you met in Chapter 4) was functioning, and how Spencer tried to help him, we begin this chapter with a discussion of the intervention process.

Dan's goal was to be able to focus on his studies so that he could perform well academically and achieve admission to medical school. He was an intelligent student who had done well through most of his academic career, but for the past year he had been preoccupied with obsessional thoughts about not being able to resolve personal "slights" from his mother, younger sister, and university peers. (He felt comfortable among his Chinese American friends, who included the people in his church congregation and a former girlfriend who lived back home, an hour away.) When Dan experienced "rejection" from his family or peers, he became angry, and later sad, thinking that if those persons only understood the "rationality" of his admonitions and advice, they would see his point of view and admit that they were "wrong" in their perceptions of an interpersonal issue. Further, Dan would only feel vindicated if they apologized for their behaviors with him.

Spencer, while validating Dan's feelings, believed that his goals were unrealistic. He hoped Dan would eventually come to perceive that his influence over others was limited, that people might respect him even as they did not always agree with his advice, and, most basically, that people have different ideas regarding what is best for them. He shared his concerns with Dan, who was willing to consider other ways of assessing situations despite feeling skeptical of the utility of this process. Spencer used some psychodynamic and cognitive interventions during their year of working together, but he experienced most success with a series of behavioral interventions.

Spencer helped Dan to use relaxation techniques and to consider the environments in which he was best able to focus on his studies. They determined, for example, that Dan was best able to concentrate during the middle of the day and when there were people around him. They set up a schedule of study in the medical library, where Dan could sit at a table with other students (whom he did not necessarily know). Spencer rehearsed deep-breathing activities with Dan, which helped calm his anxieties, and he further suggested that Dan study after a physical workout, when his body was calmer (Dan enjoyed swimming). Spencer also suggested that physical activity might help him release some of his anger after an interpersonal conflict.

Dan never articulated openly that his ideas about the appropriate behavior of others were anything but "correct," but over time he reported fewer conflicts with his sister, mother, and peers, and his study habits and grades improved to the point that he was admitted to medical school. After a year-long weekly intervention Dan finally decided to terminate because of his busy medical school schedule. During their final session together, he said to Spencer, "I don't know how much I've gotten out of this, but I know you tried to help, and I appreciate that."

Reviewing the intervention with his supervisor, Spencer regretted that he had felt such frustration with Dan, but he felt he had been able to contain those feelings. Further, despite Dan's ongoing misgivings about the quality of the intervention, he had continued meeting with Spencer for a full year and eventually demonstrated behaviors evident of improvement. It seemed that Dan had reached a higher level of adaptability even though it wasn't as apparent to him.

THE SELF IN RELATIONSHIPS

In this chapter, we focus on how the psychological person manages challenges to social functioning, particularly stress. We look at the common processes by which we all try to cope with the stresses we experience in life. As Dan understood, but had trouble managing, the ability to form, sustain, and use significant relationships with other people is a key to the process of successful coping and adaptation. With this theme in mind, we begin by considering several theories that address the issue of how we exist in the context of relationships, including the relational, feminist, and social identity theories, and evidence demonstrating the importance of early nurturing in the ability to build relationships throughout life.

Relational Theory

In recent years, an integration of the psychoanalytic and interpersonal theoretical perspectives (which focus on relationships as the driving force of personality development) has come to be called **relational theory** (Borden, 2009). In relational theory the basic human tendency (or drive) is for relationships with others, and our personalities are structured through ongoing interactions with others in the social environment. In this theory there is a strong value of recognizing and supporting diversity in human experience, avoiding the pathologizing of differences, and enlarging traditional conceptions of gender and identity.

Relational theory assumes that all patterns of behavior are learned in the give-and-take of relational life and are adaptive ways of negotiating

Photo 5.1   Relationships with significant others are resources for coping with stress.

© iStockphoto.com/paul kline

experience in the context of our need to elicit care from, and provide care for, others. Serious relationship problems are seen as self-perpetuating because we all have a tendency to preserve continuity in our interpersonal worlds. What is new is threatening because it lies beyond the bounds of our experience in which we recognize ourselves as cohesive beings.

For social work practice, the relational perspective enriches the concept of empathy by adding the notion of mutuality between the social worker and client. The ability to participate in a mutual relationship through empathic communication contributes to the client's growth. Contrary to traditional analytic notions, the relational social worker expresses a range of thoughts and feelings "in the moment" with the client to facilitate their mutual connection (Freedberg, 2007). Intervention focuses on here-and-now situations in the client's life, including those involving the social worker and client. Current social work literature reflects diverse views regarding the degree to which practitioners should self-disclose with their clients, but the general consensus calls for the worker to maintain a neutral, objective persona (Walsh, 2000). In relational theory, however, the more the worker expends energy on keeping parts of herself or himself out of the process, the more rigid and less genuine he or she will be with the client. Relational theorists encourage the social worker's natural, authentic manner of engagement, the strategic use of self-disclosure, and the encouragement of the client to regularly comment on the intervention process. The social worker also tries to avoid relegating the two parties into dominant and subordinate roles.

Psychodynamic perspective;
humanistic perspective

To expand on these points, relational theory incorporates a major focus on the intersubjective basis of self-development (Perlman & Brandell, 2011). There is a mutual recognition of the self and the other as people with unique experiences and differences, and each person influences the other in conscious and unconscious ways. This does not imply a neglect of appropriate boundaries, however, as the social worker must maintain a clear sense of self while engaged in the emotional and cognitive integration necessary for empathy to be effective. The intervention process features many *enactments*, or discussions about the ways the social worker and client are relating to one another. Through this process the client gradually becomes able to recognize other people's uniqueness, developing capacities for sensitivity and a tolerance of difference. The client is freed from the "pull" of problematic relationship patterns.

Despite its limitations with regard to empirical validation, the assumptions of relational theory are consistent with the findings of the American Psychological Association (APA) on the significance of the worker/client relationship. The APA has systematically evaluated the significance of the practitioner/client relationship in determining intervention effectiveness and concluded that several relationship variables used in practice were *demonstrably* effective (the alliance in individual and family therapy; cohesion in group therapy; empathy; and collecting client feedback), and others were *probably* effective (attention to goal consensus, collaboration, and positive regard) (Norcross & Wampold, 2011). Three other relationship elements (congruence/genuineness, repairing alliance ruptures, and managing countertransference) were deemed *promising*. Another review concluded that the quality of the worker/client relationship, in combination with the resources of the client (extratherapeutic variables), accounts for a majority of the variance in intervention outcomes (Miller, Duncan, & Hubble, 2005).

Attachment Theory

Psychodynamic perspective

To understand how we develop our initial relationship patterns, it may be useful to consider one model of parent–child attachment here (Shorey & Snyder, 2006). All children seek proximity to their parents, and they develop attachment styles suited to the types of parenting they encounter. Ainsworth and her colleagues (Ainsworth, Blehar, & Waters, 1978) identified three infant attachment styles—secure, anxious-ambivalent, and avoidant types. A fourth attachment style has been identified more recently—the disorganized type (Madigan, Moran, & Pederson, 2006).

Securely attached infants act somewhat distressed when their parent figures leave but greet them eagerly and warmly upon return. Parents of secure infants are sensitive and accepting. Securely attached children are unconcerned about security needs and are thus free to direct their energies toward nonattachment-related activities in the environment. Infants who are not securely attached must direct their attention to maintaining their attachments to inconsistent, unavailable, or rejecting parents, rather than engaging in exploratory behaviors. Because these children are only able to maintain proximity to the parents by behaving as if the parents are not needed, the children may learn not to express needs for closeness or attention.

Anxious-ambivalently attached infants, in contrast, are distraught when their parent figures leave. Upon their parent's return, these infants continue to be distressed even as they want to be comforted and held. These children employ "hyperactivation" strategies. Their parents, while not overtly rejecting, are often unpredictable and inconsistent in their responses. Fearing potential caregiver abandonment, the children maximize their efforts to maintain close parental attachments and become hypervigilant for threat cues and any signs of rejection.

Avoidantly attached infants seem to be relatively undisturbed both when their parent figures leave and when they return. These children want to maintain proximity to their parent figures, but this attachment style enables the children to maintain a sense of proximity to parents who otherwise may reject them. Avoidant children thus suppress expressions of overt distress and, rather than risk further rejection in the face of attachment figure unavailability, may give up on their proximity-seeking efforts.

The *disorganized attachment* style is characterized by chaotic and conflicted behaviors. These children exhibit simultaneous approach and avoidance behaviors. Disorganized infants seem incapable of applying any consistent strategy to bond with their parents. Their conflicted and disorganized behaviors reflect their best attempts at gaining some sense of security from parents who are perceived as frightening. When afraid and needing reassurance, these children have no options but to seek support from a caregiver who is frightening. The parents may be either hostile or fearful and unable to hide their apprehension from their children. In either case, the child's anxiety and distress are not lessened, and one source of stress is merely traded for another.

Although children with disorganized attachments typically do not attain senses of being cared for, the avoidant and anxious-ambivalent children do experience some success in fulfilling their needs for care.

If you are concerned that your own early relationships might have been problematic, don't worry. Relational theorists do not assert that caregivers need to be perfect (whatever that might be), only that they communicate a sense of caring and permit the child to develop a sense of self (Winnicott, 1975). Even if early attachments are problematic, a person's ability to develop trusting relationships can always be improved, sometimes with therapy.

Cultural psychologists argue that most Western psychological theories assume an independent, autonomous self as the ideal self-in-relationship (see Markus & Kitayama, 2009). They suggest that in many cultures of the world, including Asian, African, Latin American, and southern European cultures, the ideal self is an interdependent self that recognizes that one's behavior is influenced, even determined, by the perceived thoughts, expectations, and feelings of others in the relationship. Markus and Kitayama (2003) note that in U.S. coverage of the Olympics, athletes are typically asked about how they personally feel about their efforts and their success. In contrast, in Japanese coverage, athletes are typically asked, "Who helped you achieve?" This idea of an interdependent self is consistent with relational theory, as well as feminist perspectives on relationships.

Impact of Early Nurturing on Development

We have been looking at theories that deem relationships to be important throughout our lives.

Psychodynamic perspective; developmental perspective

Turning to both human and animal research, we can find physiological evidence that, as suggested by relational and attachment theory, the quality of our early relationships is crucial to our lifelong capacity to engage in healthy relationships and even to enjoy basic physical health.

A large body of research is devoted to studying the links between early life experiences and physical and mental health risks (e.g., Lally, 2011) This work demonstrates that negative early life experiences such as child abuse, family strife, poverty, and emotional neglect correlate with later health problems ranging from depression to drug abuse and heart disease. Relational elements of our early environments appear to permanently alter the development of central nervous system structures that govern our autonomic, cognitive, behavioral, and emotional responses to stress (Farmer, 2009). These findings tend to support the lifelong significance of specific relationship interactions.

Animal models are common in this research, tracing the physiological aspects of rat and monkey stress responses all the way to the level of gene expression (Kempes, Gulickx, van Daalen, Louwerse, & Sterck, 2008; Novak, Fan, O'Dowd, & George, 2013). It has been found that highly groomed young rats (pups) develop more receptors in their brains for the substances that inhibit the production of corticotrophin-releasing hormone (CRH), the master regulator of the stress response. As a result of the tactile stimulation they received from mothers, the pups' brains develop in a way that lowers their stress response—not only while being groomed but throughout life. When the rats are switched at birth to different mothers, the pups' brain development matched the behavior of the mothers who reared them, not their biological mothers. Furthermore, high-licking and high-grooming (nurturing) mother rats change their behavior significantly when given a substance that stimulates the hormonal effects of chronic stress, raising their CRH and lowering oxytocin, a hormone related to the equanimity many human mothers feel after giving birth. That is, under the influence of these stress hormones, the high-nurturing mothers behaved like the low-nurturing mothers, and their offspring grew up to have the same stress responses.

Some of you may be familiar with the tradition of research on the nurturing practices of rhesus monkeys. Research continues in this area (Asher, Michopoulos, Reding, Wilson, & Toufexis, 2013). In some of these experiments, monkeys are separated from their mothers at age intervals of 1 week, 1 month, 3 months, and 6 months and raised in a group of other monkeys that includes a different mother. The infants who are separated later (3 or 6 months) exhibit normal behavior in the new setting. Those separated earlier, however, show a variety of abnormalities. The monkeys separated at 1 month initially exhibit a profound depression and refuse to eat. Once they recover, they show a deep need for attachments with other monkeys and also show great anxiety during social separation whenever they feel threatened. The monkeys separated at 1 week showed no interest in social contact with other monkeys, and this behavior did not change

as they grew older. Autopsies of these monkeys showed changes in brain development. The timing of separation from the primary caregiver seems to be significant to their later development. These findings in monkeys may have a sad counterpart in human children who are separated at early ages from their mothers.

Although much of this research is being conducted on rats, monkeys, and other animals, it has clear implications for human development. The concept of **neural plasticity**, which refers to the capacity of the nervous system to be modified by experience, is significant here (Bryck & Fisher, 2012). Humans may have a window of opportunity, or a critical period for altering neurological development, but this window varies, depending on the area of the nervous system. Even through the second decade of life, for example, neurotransmitter and synapse changes are influenced by internal biology, but perhaps by external signals as well. In other words, the brain is not a static organ.

Much research currently under way explores the relationship between the processes of attachment and specific neurological development in young persons (Diamond & Fagundes, 2010). Persistent stress in an infant or toddler results in an overdevelopment of areas of the brain that process anxiety and fear, and the underdevelopment of other areas of the brain, particularly the cortex. Of particular concern to one leading researcher (Schore, 2002) is the impact of the absence of nurturance on the orbitofrontal cortex (OFC) of the brain. Chronic levels of stress contribute to fewer neural connections between the prefrontal cortex and the amygdala, a process significant to psychosocial functioning. The OFC is particularly active in such processes as our concentration, judgment, and ability to observe and control internal subjective states. Further, the frontal cortex is central to our emotional regulation capacity and our experience of empathy. The amygdala, part of the limbic system (as discussed in the previous chapter), is attributed with interpreting incoming stimuli and information and storing this information in our implicit (automatic) memory. The amygdala assesses threat and triggers our immediate responses to it (the fight, flight, or freeze behaviors). A reduction in neural connections between these two areas suggests that the frontal cortex is not optimally able to regulate the processing of fear, resulting in exaggerated fear responses.

Stress can clearly affect brain development, but there is evidence that the first few years of life are not all-important, given the role of resilience influences (Korosi & Baram, 2010). A study of 2,600 undergraduate students found that even in late adolescence and early adulthood, satisfying social relationships were associated with greater autonomic activity and restorative behaviors when confronting acute stress (Cacioppo, Bernston, Sheridan, & McClintock, 2000).

In summary, research indicates that secure attachments play a critical role in shaping the systems that underlie our reactivity to stressful situations. When infants begin to form specific attachments to adults, the presence of warm and responsive caregivers begins to buffer or prevent elevations in stress hormones, even in situations that distress the infant. In contrast, insecure relationships are associated with higher CRH levels in potentially threatening situations. Secure emotional relationships with adults appear to be at least as critical as individual differences in temperament in determining stress reactivity and regulation (Eagle & Wolitzky, 2009).

Still, there is much to be learned in this area. Many people subjected to serious early life traumas become effective, high-functioning adolescents and adults. Infants and children are resilient and have many strengths that can help them overcome these early life stresses. Researchers are challenged to determine whether interventions such as foster care can remedy the physical, emotional, and social problems seen in children who have experienced poor nurturing and early problems with separation.

We now consider several social influences on one's sense of attachment to persons outside the family.

Critical Thinking Questions 5.1

Imagine that you were the social worker working with Dan Lee. How would you respond to Dan's statement: "I don't know how much I've gotten out of this, but I know you tried to help and I appreciate that"? What thoughts and emotions would you have on hearing this evaluation? What would you say to Dan in response to the evaluation? What guidance can you draw from relational theory? What are the policy implications of research on the impact of early nurturing on development?

Feminist Theories of Relationships

The term *feminism* does not refer to any single body of thought. It refers to a wide-ranging system of ideas about human experience developed from a woman-centered perspective. Feminist theories may be classified as liberal, radical, Marxist, socialist, existential, postmodern, multicultural, or ecofeminist (Lengermann & Niebrugge-Brantley, 2007). Among the psychological theories are psychoanalytic feminism (Angers, 2008) and gender feminism (Marecek, Kimmel, Crawford, & Hare-Mustin, 2003). We focus on these latter two as we consider how feminism has deepened our capacity for understanding human behavior and interaction. All of these theorists begin from the position that women and men approach relationships differently and that patriarchal societies consider male attributes to be superior.

Psychoanalytic feminists assert that women's ways of acting are rooted deeply in women's unique ways of thinking. These differences may be biological, but they are

Psychodynamic perspective

certainly influenced by cultural and psychosocial conditions. Feminine behavior features gentleness, modesty, humility, supportiveness, empathy, compassion, tenderness, nurturance, intuitiveness, sensitivity, and unselfishness. Masculine behavior is characterized by strength of will, ambition, courage, independence, assertiveness, hardiness, rationality, and emotional control. Psychoanalytic feminists assert that these differences are largely rooted in early childhood relationships. Because women are the primary caretakers in our society, young girls tend to develop and enjoy an ongoing relationship with their mothers that promotes their valuing of relatedness as well as other feminine behaviors. For young boys, on the other hand, the mother is eventually perceived as fundamentally different, particularly as they face social pressures to begin fulfilling male roles. The need to separate from the mother figure has long-range implications for boys: They tend to lose what could otherwise become a learned capacity for intimacy and relatedness.

Gender feminists tend to be concerned with values of separateness (for men) and connectedness (for women) and how these lead to a different morality for women. Carol Gilligan (1982; see also the section on theories of moral reasoning in Chapter 4 of this book) is a leading thinker in this area. She elucidated a process by which women develop an ethic of care rather than an ethic of justice, based on the value they place on relationships. Gender feminists believe that these female ethics are equal to male ethics, although they have tended in patriarchal societies to be considered inferior. Gilligan asserts that all of humanity would be best served if both ethics could be valued equally. Other gender feminists go further, however, arguing for the superiority of women's ethics. For example, Noddings (2002, 2005) asserts that war will never be discarded in favor of the sustained pursuit of peace until the female ethic of caring, aimed at unification, replaces the male ethic of strenuous striving, aimed at dividing people.

All psychological feminist theories promote the value of relationships and the importance of reciprocal interpersonal supports. Dan was raised to be achievement- and task-oriented. These are admirable characteristics, but they represent male perspectives. Dan's inclinations for interpersonal experience may have been discouraged, which was harmful to his overall development.

Social Identity Theory

Social identity theory is a stage theory of socialization that articulates the process by which we come to identify with some social groups and develop a sense of difference from others (Hornsey, 2008; Nesdale, 2004). This is especially important to consider because the population in the United States and many other countries is becoming increasingly diverse. During the past decade, Hispanic and Asian populations have increased by 43% in the United States, compared with total population growth of 9.7% (U.S. Census Bureau, 2013a). It is estimated that by 2050 Latinos will make up 25%, and Asians 8%, of the nation's population.

Social identity development can be an affirming process that provides us with a lifelong sense of belonging and support. I might feel good to have membership with a Roman Catholic or Irish American community. Because social identity can be exclusionary, however, it can also give rise to prejudice and oppression. I may believe that my race is more intelligent than another or that persons of my cultural background are entitled to more social benefits than those of another.

Social identity development proceeds in five stages. These stages are not truly distinct or sequential, however; people often experience several stages simultaneously.

1. *Naïveté.* During early childhood, we have no social consciousness. We are not aware of particular codes of behavior for members of our group or any other social group. Our parents or other primary caregivers are our most significant influences, and we accept that socialization without question. As young children, we do, however, begin to distinguish between ourselves and other groups of people. We may not feel completely comfortable with the racial, ethnic, or religious differences we observe, but neither do we feel fearful, superior, or inferior. Children at this stage are mainly curious about differences.

2. *Acceptance.* Older children and young adolescents learn the distinct ideologies and belief systems of their own and other social groups. During this stage, we learn that the world's institutions and authority figures have rules that encourage certain behaviors and prohibit others, and we internalize these dominant cultural beliefs and make them a part of our everyday lives. Those questions that emerged during the stage of naïveté are submerged. We come to believe that the way our group does things is normal, makes more sense, and is better. We regard the cultures of people who are different from us as strange, marginal, and perhaps inferior. We may passively accept these differences or actively do so by joining organizations that highlight our own identity and (perhaps) devalue others.

3. *Resistance.* In adolescence, or even later, we become aware of the harmful effects of acting on social differences. We have new experiences with members of other social groups that challenge our prior assumptions. We begin to reevaluate those assumptions and investigate our own role in perpetuating harmful differences. We may feel anger at others within our own social group who foster these irrational differences. We begin to move toward a new definition of social identity that is broader than our previous definition. We may work to end our newly perceived patterns of collusion and oppression.

4. *Redefinition.* Redefinition is a process of creating a new social identity that preserves our pride in our origins while perceiving differences with others as positive representations of diversity. We may isolate from some members of our social group and shift toward interactions with others who share our level of awareness. We see all groups as being rich in strengths and values. We may reclaim our own group heritage but broaden our definition of that heritage as one of many varieties of constructive living.

5. *Internalization.* In the final stage of social identity development, we become comfortable with our revised identity and are able to incorporate it into all aspects of our life. We act unconsciously, without external controls. Life continues as an ongoing process of discovering vestiges of our old biases, but now we test our integrated new identities in wider contexts than our limited reference group. Our appreciation of the plight of all oppressed people, and our enhanced empathy for others, is a part of this process. For many people, the internalization stage is an ongoing challenge rather than an end state.

For all ethnic groups, higher levels of ethnic identity are associated with higher levels of self-esteem, purpose in life, and self-confidence (Rogers-Sirin & Gupta, 2012). Further, ethnic identity is associated with lower levels of depression among White, African American, and Asian youth. Social identity theory is sometimes used, however, to explain a process by which those who most strongly identify with their groups may come to hold less favorable attitudes about dissimilar groups (Negy, Shreve, Jensen, & Uddin, 2003). One study showed that the more Caucasian and Hispanic persons embraced their identity, the more negative views they held toward people who did not belong to their respective ethnic groups. Interestingly, this trend was not found among African American persons.

Another theory, *multicultural theory*, has arisen to propose more positively that affirmations toward one's group, particularly with regard to ethnicity, should correspond with higher levels of acceptance toward dissimilar groups. Ethnic identity is defined as a sense of belonging to an ethnic group and the part of one's thinking, perceptions, feelings, and behavior that is due to group membership (Smith, Smith, Levine, Dumas, & Prinz, 2009). This sense of belonging is supported by shared heritage, values, traditions, and often languages. Two dimensions of ethnic identity include *identity achievement*, the developmental process of exploring and committing to one's identity, and *affirmation and belonging*, the sense of pride and emotional attachment an adolescent feels for his or her ethnic group (Greene, Way, & Pahl, 2006). The importance of race and ethnicity to a person's identity, sometimes referred to as centrality (Charmaraman & Grossman, 2010), represents a relatively stable perception of the significance one attributes to his or her racial and ethnic background. Those who face greater racial adversity attribute higher centrality to racial aspects of their identities, and studies have shown that adolescents of color report higher racial-ethnic centrality than do White youth. In the United States, ethnic identity, in fact, tends to be strongest among African American persons, followed by Asians and multiethnic adolescents.

Critical Thinking Questions 5.2

Give some thought to social identity theory. With what social groups do you identify? How did you come to identify with these groups? How might your social identities affect your social work practice?

THE CONCEPT OF STRESS

One of the main benefits of good nurturing is, as you have seen, the way it strengthens our ability to cope with stress. **Stress** can be defined as any event in which environmental or internal demands tax our adaptive resources. Stress may be biological (a disturbance in bodily systems), psychological (cognitive and emotional factors involved in the evaluation of a threat), and even social (the disruption of a social unit). Dan experienced psychological stress, of course, as evidenced by his negative feelings resulting from marginalization and perceived rejection, but he also experienced other types of stress. He experienced biological stress because, in an effort to attend all his classes and study every day, he did not give his body adequate rest. As a result, he was susceptible to colds, which kept him in bed for several days each month and compounded his worries about managing coursework. Dan also experienced social stress, because he was functioning in a social system that he perceived to be threatening, and he had few positive relationships there.

Three Categories of Psychological Stress

Psychological stress, about which we are primarily concerned in this chapter, can be broken down into three categories (Lazarus, 2007).

1. *Harm.* A damaging event that has already occurred. Dan minimized interactions with his classmates during much of the semester, which may have led them to decide that he is aloof and that they should not try to approach him socially. Dan has to accept that this rejection happened and that some harm has been done to him as a result, although he can learn from the experience and try to change in the future.

2. *Threat.* A perceived potential for harm that has not yet happened. This is probably the most common form of psychological stress. We feel stress because we are apprehensive about the possibility of the negative event. Dan felt threatened when he walked into a classroom during the first semester because he had failed once before and, further, anticipated rejection from his classmates. We can be proactive in managing threats to ensure that they do not in fact occur and result in harm to us.

3. *Challenge.* An event we appraise as an opportunity rather than an occasion for alarm. We are mobilized to struggle against the obstacle, as with a threat, but our attitude is quite different. Faced with a threat, we are likely to act defensively to protect ourselves. Our defensiveness sends a negative message to the environment: We don't want to change; we want to be left alone. In a state of challenge, however, we are excited, expansive, and confident about the task to be undertaken. The challenge may be an exciting and productive experience for us. Because Dan has overcome several setbacks in his drive to become a physician, he may feel more excited and motivated than before when resuming the program. He might be more aware of his resilience and feel more confident.

Photo 5.2 This woman is experiencing psychological stress; she is challenged by the task at hand but feels equal to the task.

© Jupiterimages/Pixland/Thinkstock

Stress has been measured in several ways (Aldwin & Yancura, 2004; Lazarus, 2007). One of the earliest attempts to measure stress consisted of a list of *life events*, uncommon events that bring about some change in our lives—experiencing the death of a loved one, getting married, becoming a parent, and so forth. The use of life events to measure stress is based on the assumption that major changes, even positive ones, disrupt our behavioral patterns.

More recently, stress has also been measured as **daily hassles**, common occurrences that are taxing—standing in line waiting, misplacing or losing things, dealing with troublesome co-workers, worrying about money, and many more. It is thought that an accumulation of daily hassles takes a greater toll on our coping capacities than do relatively rare life events.

Sociologists and community psychologists also study stress by measuring **role strain**—problems experienced in the performance of specific roles, such as romantic partner, caregiver, or worker. Research on caregiver burden is one example of measuring stress as role strain (Gordon, Pruchno, Wilson-Genderson, Murphy, & Rose, 2012).

Social workers should be aware that as increasing emphasis is placed on the deleterious effects of stress on the immune system, our attention and energies are diverted from the possibility of changing societal conditions that create stress and toward the management of ourselves as persons who respond to stress (Becker, 2005). For example, it is well documented that the experience of discrimination creates stress for many African Americans (Anderson, 2013). With the influence of the medical model, we should not be surprised when we are offered individual or biomedical solutions to such different social problems as discrimination, working motherhood, poverty, and road rage. It may be that the appeal of the stress concept is based on its diverting attention away from the environmental causes of stress. This is why social workers should always be alert to the social nature of stress.

Stress and Crisis

A **crisis** is a major upset in our psychological equilibrium due to some harm, threat, or challenge with which we cannot cope (James & Gilliland, 2013). The crisis poses an obstacle to achieving a personal goal, but we cannot overcome the obstacle through our usual methods of problem solving. We temporarily lack either the necessary knowledge for coping or the ability to focus on the problem, because we feel overwhelmed. A crisis episode often results when we face a serious stressor with which we have had no prior experience. It may be biological (major illness), interpersonal (the sudden loss of a loved one), or environmental (unemployment or a natural disaster such as a flood or fire). We can regard anxiety, guilt, shame, sadness, envy, jealousy, and disgust as stress emotions (Zyskinsa & Heszen, 2009). They are the emotions most likely to emerge in a person who is experiencing crisis.

Crisis episodes occur in three stages:

1. Our level of tension increases sharply.

2. We try and fail to cope with the stress, which further increases our tension and contributes to our sense of being overwhelmed. We are particularly receptive to receiving help from others at this time.

3. The crisis episode ends, either negatively (unhealthy coping) or positively (successful management of the crisis).

Crises can be classified into three types (Lantz & Walsh, 2007). *Developmental* crises occur when events in the normal flow of life create dramatic changes that produce extreme responses. Examples of such events include going off to college, college graduation, the birth of one's child, a midlife career change, and retirement from work. People may experience these types of crises if they have difficulty negotiating the typical challenges outlined by Erikson (1968) and Gitterman (2009). *Situational* crises refer to uncommon and extraordinary events that a person has no way of forecasting or controlling. Examples include physical injuries, sexual assault, loss of a job, major illness, and the death of a loved one. *Existential* crises are characterized by escalating inner conflicts related to issues of purpose in life, responsibility, independence, freedom, and commitment. Examples include remorse over past life choices, a feeling that one's life has no meaning, and a questioning of one's basic values or spiritual beliefs.

Dan's poor midterm grades during his first semester of taking courses that would help him qualify for medical school illustrate some of these points. First, he was overwhelmed by the negative emotions of anger and sadness. Then, he occasionally retreated to church and his hometown, where he received much-needed support from his friends, mother, and sister. Finally, as the situation stabilized, Dan concluded that he could try to change some of his behaviors to relieve his academic-related stress.

Traumatic Stress

Although a single event may pose a crisis for one person but not another, some stressors are so severe that they are almost universally experienced as crises. The stress is so overwhelming that almost anyone would be affected. The term **traumatic stress** is used to refer to events that involve actual or threatened severe injury or death, of oneself or significant others (American Psychiatric Association, 2013). Three types of traumatic stress have been identified: natural (such as flood, tornado, earthquake) and technological (such as nuclear) disasters; war and related problems (such as concentration camps); and individual trauma (such as being raped, assaulted, or tortured) (Aldwin, 2007). People respond to traumatic stress with helplessness, terror, and horror. Many trauma survivors experience a set of symptoms known as *post-traumatic stress disorder* (American Psychiatric Association, 2013). These symptoms include persistent reliving of the traumatic event, persistent avoidance of stimuli associated with the traumatic event, and a persistently high state of arousal. The symptoms of post-traumatic stress disorder (which we discuss in more detail later) may occur as soon as 1 week after the event, or even years later.

Some occupations—particularly those of emergency workers such as police officers, firefighters, disaster relief workers, and military personnel in war settings—involve regular exposure to traumatic events that most people do not experience in a lifetime. The literature about the stress faced by emergency workers refers to these traumatic events as *critical incidents* and the reaction to them as *critical incident stress* (Prichard, 2004). Emergency workers, particularly police officers and firefighters, may experience threats to their own lives and the lives of their colleagues, as well as encounter mass casualties. Emergency workers may also experience *compassion stress*, a feeling of deep sympathy and sorrow for another who is stricken by misfortune, accompanied by a strong desire to alleviate the pain (Adams, Boscarino, & Figley, 2006). Any professionals who work regularly with trauma survivors are susceptible to compassion stress. Many social workers fall into this category.

Vulnerability to Stress

Systems perspective

Many social work practitioners and researchers use a biopsychosocial *risk and resilience* framework for understanding how people experience and manage stress (Scholz, Blumer, & Brand, 2012). Although the biological and psychological levels relate to the individual, the social aspect of the framework captures the positive or adverse effects on the family, community, and wider social culture. The processes within each level interact, prompting risks for stress and impaired coping and the propensity toward *resilience*, or the ability to function adaptively despite stressful life circumstances. *Risks* can be understood as hazards occurring at the individual or environmental level that increase the likelihood of impairment. *Protective mechanisms* involve the personal, familial, community, and institutional resources that cultivate individuals' aptitudes and abilities while diminishing the possibility of problem behaviors. These protective influences may counterbalance or buffer against risk and are sometimes the converse of risk. For instance, at the individual level, poor physical health presents risks while good health is protective. The biopsychosocial framework provides a theoretical basis for social workers to conceptualize human behavior at several levels and can assist them in identifying and bolstering strengths as well as reducing risks. The framework offers a balanced view of systems in considering risks and strengths, as well as recognizing the complexity of individuals and the systems in which they are nested.

Individual factors encompass the biological and psychological realms. Within biology these include genes, temperament, physical health, developmental stage, and intelligence. At the psychological level it is useful to examine one's self-efficacy, self-esteem, and coping strategies. Social mechanisms include the family and household, the experience of traumatic events, the neighborhood, and societal conditions, including poverty, ethnicity, and access to health care.

Within the risk and resilience perspective, social workers can complete comprehensive assessments to determine the nature of their clients' problems. Knowledge of the risk and resilience influences helps social workers focus interventions onto the relevant areas of the client's life. Finally, the strengths perspective encourages social workers to build on the client's areas of real or potential resilience in recovering from, or adapting to, mental disorders and in so doing helps the client develop a greater sense of self-efficacy.

Critical Thinking Questions 5.3

Why do you think we easily get diverted from thinking about societal conditions that create stress and come, instead, to focus on helping individuals cope with stress? How does such an approach fit with social work's commitment to social justice?

COPING AND ADAPTATION

Our efforts to master the demands of stress are referred to as **coping**. Coping includes the thoughts, feelings, and actions that constitute these efforts. One method of coping is **adaptation**, which may involve adjustments in our biological responses, perceptions, or lifestyle.

Biological Coping

The traditional biological view of stress and coping, developed in the 1950s, emphasizes the body's attempts to maintain physical equilibrium, or **homeostasis**, which is a steady state of functioning (Selye, 1991). Stress is considered the result of any demand on the body (specifically, the nervous and hormonal systems) during perceived emergencies to prepare for fight (confrontation) or flight (escape). A stressor may be any biological process, emotion, or thought.

In this view, the body's response to a stressor is called the **general adaptation syndrome**. It occurs in three stages:

1. *Alarm.* The body first becomes aware of a threat.

2. *Resistance.* The body attempts to restore homeostasis.

3. *Exhaustion.* The body terminates coping efforts because of its inability to physically sustain the state of disequilibrium.

The general adaptation syndrome is explained in Exhibit 5.1.

In this context, *resistance* has a different meaning than is generally used in social work: an active,

positive response of the body in which endorphins and specialized cells of the immune system fight off stress and infection. Our immune systems are constructed for adaptation to stress, but the cumulative wear and tear of multiple stress episodes can gradually deplete our body's resources. Common outcomes of chronic stress include stomach and intestinal disorders, high blood pressure, heart problems, and emotional problems. If only to preserve healthy physical functioning, we must combat and prevent stress.

This traditional view of biological coping with stress came from research that focused on males, either male rodents or human males. Since 1995, the federal government has required federally funded researchers to include a broad representation of both men and women in their study samples. Consequently, recent research on stress has included female as well as male participants, and gender differences in responses to stress have been found.

Recent research (Cardoso, Ellenbogen, Serravalle, & Linnen, 2013; Taylor & Stanton, 2007) suggests that females of many species, including humans, respond to stress with "tend-and-befriend" rather than the "fight-or-flight" behavior described in the general adaptation syndrome. Under stressful conditions, females have been found to protect and nurture their offspring and to seek social contact. The researchers suggest a possible biological basis for this gender difference in the coping response. More specifically, they note a large role for the hormone oxytocin, which plays a role in childbirth but also is secreted in both males and females in response to stress. High levels of oxytocin in animals are associated with calmness and increased sociability. Although males as well as females secrete oxytocin in response to stress, there is evidence that male hormones reduce the effects of oxytocin. This is thought to, in part, explain the gender differences in response to stress.

Psychological Coping

The psychological aspect of managing stress can be viewed in two ways. Some theorists consider

Exhibit 5.1 The General Adaptation Syndrome

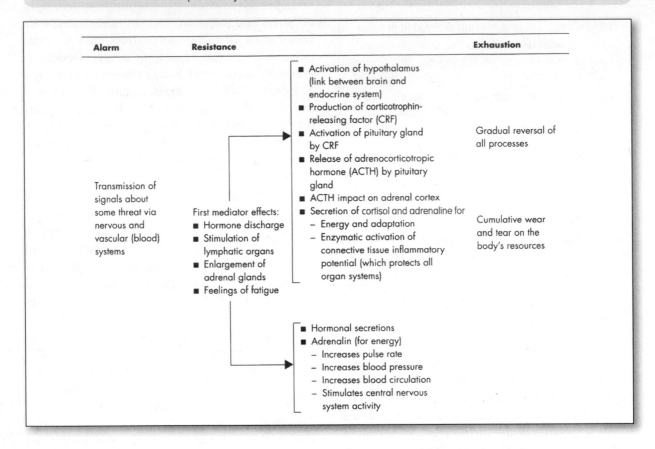

Alarm	Resistance		Exhaustion

Transmission of signals about some threat via nervous and vascular (blood) systems

First mediator effects:
- Hormone discharge
- Stimulation of lymphatic organs
- Enlargement of adrenal glands
- Feelings of fatigue

- Activation of hypothalamus (link between brain and endocrine system)
- Production of corticotrophin-releasing factor (CRF)
- Activation of pituitary gland by CRF
- Release of adrenocorticotropic hormone (ACTH) by pituitary gland
- ACTH impact on adrenal cortex
- Secretion of cortisol and adrenaline for
  - Energy and adaptation
  - Enzymatic activation of connective tissue inflammatory potential (which protects all organ systems)

- Hormonal secretions
- Adrenalin (for energy)
  - Increases pulse rate
  - Increases blood pressure
  - Increases blood circulation
  - Stimulates central nervous system activity

Gradual reversal of all processes

Cumulative wear and tear on the body's resources

coping ability to be a stable personality characteristic, or **trait**; others see it instead as a transient **state**—a process that changes over time, depending on the context (Lau, Eley, & Stevenson, 2006).

Those who consider coping to be a *trait* see it as an acquired defensive style. **Defense mechanisms** are unconscious, automatic responses that enable us to minimize perceived threats or keep them out of our awareness entirely. Exhibit 5.2 lists the common defense mechanisms identified by ego psychology (discussed in Chapter 4). Some defense mechanisms are considered healthier, or more adaptive, than others. Dan's denial of his need for intimacy, for example, did not help him meet his goal of developing relationships with peers. But

Psychodynamic perspective

through the defense of sublimation (channeling the need for intimacy into alternative and socially acceptable outlets), he has been an effective and nurturing tutor for numerous high school science students.

Those who see coping as a *state*, or process, observe that our coping strategies change in different situations. After all, our perceptions of threats, and what we focus on in a situation, change. The context also has an impact on our perceived and actual abilities to apply effective coping mechanisms. From this perspective, Dan's use of denial of responsibility for relationship problems would be adaptive at some times and maladaptive at others. Perhaps his denial of needing support from classmates during

Systems perspective

Exhibit 5.2 Common Defense Mechanisms

Defense Mechanism	Definition	Example
Developmentally Earlier		
Acting out	Direct expression of impulses to avoid tension that would result from their postponement.	An adolescent steals money from her mother to buy alcohol and gets into constant arguments with her older sister who tries to monitor her behavior.
Denial	Negating an important aspect of reality that one may actually perceive.	A woman with anorexia acknowledges her actual weight and strict dieting practices but firmly believes she is maintaining good self-care by dieting.
Projection	Attributing unacceptable thoughts and feelings to others.	A man does not want to be angry with his girlfriend, so when he is upset with her, he avoids owning that emotion by assuming she is angry at him.
Regression	Resuming behaviors associated with an earlier developmental stage or level of functioning in order to avoid present anxiety. The behavior may or may not help to resolve the anxiety.	A young man throws a temper tantrum as a means of discharging his frustration when he cannot master a task on his computer. The startled computer technician, who had been reluctant to attend to the situation, now comes forth to provide assistance.
Splitting	The tendency to see the good and bad aspects of the self or others as separate; to see the self and others as alternately "all good" or "all bad."	A primary school child "hates" his teacher when reprimanded and "loves" his teacher for praise and behaves accordingly.
Developmentally Later		
Displacement	Shifting feelings about one person or situation onto another.	A student's anger at her professor, who is threatening as an authority figure, is transposed into anger at her boyfriend, a safer target.
Intellectualization	Avoiding unacceptable emotions by thinking or talking about them rather than experiencing them directly.	A person talks to her counselor about the fact that she is sad but shows no emotional evidence of sadness, which makes it harder for her to understand its effects on her life.
Isolation of affect	Consciously experiencing an emotion in a "safe" context rather than the threatening context in which it was first unconsciously experienced.	A person does not experience sadness at the funeral of a family member but the following week weeps uncontrollably at the death of a pet hamster.
Rationalization	Using convincing reasons to justify ideas, feelings, or actions so as to avoid recognizing true motives.	A student copes with the guilt normally associated with cheating on an exam by reasoning that he was too ill the previous week to prepare as well as he wanted.
Reaction formation	Replacing an unwanted unconscious impulse with its opposite in conscious behavior.	A person cannot bear to be angry with his boss, so after a conflict he convinces himself that the boss is worthy of loyalty and demonstrates this by volunteering to work overtime.

(Continued)

Exhibit 5.2 (Continued)

Defense Mechanism	Definition	Example
Repression	Keeping unwanted thoughts and feelings entirely out of awareness.	A son may begin to generate an impulse of hatred for his father, but because the impulse would be consciously unacceptable, he represses the hatred and does not become aware of it.
Somatization	Converting intolerable impulses into somatic symptoms.	A person who is unable to express his negative emotions develops frequent stomachaches as a result.
Undoing	Nullifying an undesired impulse with an act of reparation.	A man who feels guilty about having lustful thoughts about a co-worker tries to make amends to his wife by purchasing a special gift for her.
Most "Mature" Defenses		
Sublimation	Converting an impulse from a socially unacceptable aim to a socially acceptable one.	An angry, aggressive young man becomes a star on his school's debate team.
Humor	The expression of painful or socially unacceptable feelings without discomforting the person who is being humorous or (often) the recipient.	An employee manages her discomfort at being in a supervisory meeting by making self-deprecating jokes.

SOURCE: Adapted from Schamess & Shilkret, 2011; Goldstein, 1995.

the first academic semester helped him focus on his studies, which would help him achieve his goal of receiving an education. During the summer, however, when classes are out of session, he might become aware that his avoidance of relationships has prevented him from attaining interpersonal goals. His efforts to cope with loneliness might also change when he can afford more energy to confront the issue.

The trait and state approaches can usefully be combined. We can think of coping as a general pattern of managing stress that allows flexibility across diverse contexts. This perspective is consistent with the idea that cognitive schemata develop through the dual processes of assimilation and accommodation, described in Chapter 4.

Coping Styles

Another way to look at coping is based on how the person responds to crisis. Coping efforts may be problem focused or emotion focused (Sideridis, 2006). The function of **problem-focused coping** is to change the situation by acting on the environment. This method tends to dominate whenever we view situations as controllable by action. For example, Dan was concerned about his professors' insensitivity to his learning disability (auditory processing disorder). When he took action to educate them about it and explain more clearly how he learns best in a classroom setting, he was using problem-focused coping. In contrast, the function of **emotion-focused coping** is to change either the way the stressful situation is attended to (by vigilance or avoidance) or the meaning to oneself of what is happening. The external situation does not change, but our behaviors or attitudes change with respect to it, and we may thus effectively manage the stressor. When we view stressful conditions as unchangeable, emotion-focused coping may dominate. If Dan learns that one of his professors has no empathy for students with learning disabilities, he might avoid taking that professor's courses in the future or decide that getting a good grade in that course is not as important as being exposed to the course material.

U.S. culture tends to venerate problem-focused coping and the independently functioning self and to distrust emotion-focused coping and what may be called relational coping. **Relational coping** takes into account actions that maximize the survival of others—such as our families, children, and friends—as well as ourselves (Zunkel, 2002). Feminist theorists propose that women are more likely than men to employ the relational coping strategies of negotiation and forbearance, and some research (Taylor & Stanton, 2007) gives credence to the idea that women are more likely than men to use relational coping. As social workers, we must be careful not to assume that one type of coping is superior to another. Power imbalances and social forces such as racism and sexism affect the coping strategies of individuals (Lippa, 2005). We need to give clients credit for the extraordinary coping efforts they may make in hostile environments.

Richard Lazarus (1999) has identified some particular behaviors typical of each coping style:

- *Problem-focused coping:* confrontation, problem solving
- *Emotion-focused coping:* distancing, escape or avoidance, positive reappraisal
- *Problem- or emotion-focused coping (depending on context):* self-control, search for social support, acceptance of responsibility

Lazarus emphasizes that all of us use any or several of these mechanisms at different times. None of them is any person's sole means of managing stress.

Using Lazarus's model, we might note that Dan used many problem-focused coping strategies to manage stressors at the university, even though he was mostly ineffective because of the specific strategies he used. For example, he directly confronted his peers, teachers, family members, and social worker, and he also tried with limited success to control his moods through force of will.

I probably don't need to tell you that college students face many predictable stressors when attending to the demands of academic work. A few years ago, I wanted to learn more about how students use both problem- and emotion-focused coping strategies in response to stress. I surveyed social work students in several Human Behavior in the Social Environment courses at a large urban university, at the beginning of an academic year, about their anticipated stressors and the ways they might cope with them. The results of this informal survey are outlined in Exhibit 5.3. The students chose problem- and emotion-focused coping strategies almost equally—a healthy mix (although they may not have been forthcoming about some socially "unacceptable" strategies).

Given our discussion in Chapter 1 of conceptions of the self, it may be interesting to review a stress/coping model that focuses on the *tripartite* self. Hardie (2005) proposes that the self includes three domains, the relational (experiencing the self most fully in relationships), individual (a strong sense of independence, autonomy, and separateness), and collective (a preference for social group memberships), and that the relative strength of a person's domains will guide his or her preferences for coping styles. Those with a well-developed self in all three domains will possess a full range of coping options, and those with a more limited self-experience will have fewer. A person with a sense of self that encompasses three domains will also experience more sources of stress, but Hardie's model suggests that when a source of stress matches one's developed self-domain, coping will be most effective. That is, if a highly relational person experiences relational stress (such as a conflict with a friend), he or she will be inclined to address the issue in an effective manner. Dan, on the other hand, has a stronger sense of an "independent" self than others, so when he experiences interpersonal conflict, his range of available coping strategies is limited due to the mismatch. And while Dan is attached to persons from his cultural group, he has a limited sense of a broader collective self and thus tends to have limited judgment or skill in how to deal with conflict with representatives of other social groups (including his school peers).

Exhibit 5.3 Coping Styles Among Social Work Students

Problem-Focused Coping

Confrontation
- Learn to say no.

Problem Solving
- Exercise.
- Work with other students.
- Talk with professors.
- Go to the beach (for relaxation).
- Manage time.
- Undertake self-care.
- Reserve time for oneself.
- Stay ahead.
- Use relaxation techniques.
- Walk.
- Clean the house.
- Carry own lunch (save money).
- Aim for good nutrition.
- Take breaks.
- Look for "free" social activities.
- Pursue art interest.
- Organize tasks.
- Carefully budget finances.
- Plan for a job search.

Self-Control
- Bear down and "gut it out."
- Take on a job.

Search for Social Support
- Talk.
- Network with others.
- Demand support from others.
- Reserve time with family.

Emotion-Focused Coping

Distancing
- Deny that problem exists.
- Procrastinate.

Escape or Avoidance
- Drink.
- Smoke.
- Drink too much caffeine.
- Overeat, undereat.
- Give up.
- Vent on others.
- Curse other drivers.
- Neglect others.
- Watch too much television.
- Neglect other important concerns.
- Use charge cards.

Positive Reappraisal
- Think of money produced by job.
- Maintain perpective.
- Maintain flexibility.
- Reframe frustrations as growth opportunities.

Self-Control
- Push too hard.
- Study all night.

Search for Social Support
- Seek intimacy.
- Engage in sex.
- Participate in therapy.

Acceptance of Responsibility
- Cry.

Coping and Traumatic Stress

People exhibit some similarities between the way they cope with traumatic stress (described earlier) and the way they cope with everyday stress. However, coping with traumatic stress differs from coping with everyday stress in several ways (Aldwin & Yancura, 2004).

- Because people tend to have much less control in traumatic situations, their primary emotion-focused coping strategy is emotional numbing, or the constriction of emotional expression. They also make greater use of the defense mechanism of denial.
- Confiding in others takes on greater importance.
- The process of coping tends to take a much longer time, months or even years.
- A search for meaning takes on greater importance, and transformation in personal identity is more common.

Although there is evidence of long-term negative consequences of traumatic stress, trauma survivors sometimes report positive outcomes as well. Studies have found that 34% of Holocaust survivors and 50% of rape survivors report positive personal changes following their experiences with traumatic stress (Koss & Figueredo, 2004). A majority of children who experience such atrocities as war, natural disasters, community violence, physical abuse, catastrophic illness, and traumatic injury also recover, demonstrating their resilience (Husain, 2012; Le Brocque, Hendrikz, & Kenardy, 2010).

However, many trauma survivors experience a set of symptoms known as **post-traumatic stress disorder (PTSD)** (American Psychiatric Association, 2013). These symptoms include the following:

- *Exposure to actual or threatened death, serious injury, or sexual violence* either directly, by witnessing it, or by learning about it
- *Persistent reliving of the traumatic event:* intrusive, distressing recollections of the event; distressing dreams of the event; a sense of reliving the event; intense distress when exposed to cues of the event
- *Persistent avoidance of stimuli associated with the traumatic event:* avoidance of thoughts or feelings connected to the event; avoidance of places, activities, and people connected to the event; inability to recall aspects of the trauma; loss of interest in activities; feeling detached from others; emotional numbing; no sense of a future
- *Negative alterations in cognition or mood* after the event, such as memory problems, negative emotions, and distorted beliefs about the event (such as self-blame)
- *Persistent high state of arousal:* difficulty sleeping, irritability, difficulty concentrating, excessive attention to stimuli, exaggerated startle response

Symptoms of post-traumatic stress disorder have been noted as soon as 1 week following the traumatic event or as long as 20 years after (Middleton & Craig, 2012). It is important to understand that the initial symptoms of post-traumatic stress are normal and expectable and that PTSD should only be considered a disorder if those symptoms do not remit over time and result in serious, long-term limitations in social functioning. Complete recovery from symptoms occurs in 30% of cases, mild symptoms continue over time in 40%, moderate symptoms continue in 20%, and symptoms persist or get worse in about 10% (Becker, 2004). Children and older adults have the most trouble coping with traumatic events. A strong system of social support helps to prevent or to foster recovery from post-traumatic stress disorder. Besides providing support, social workers may be helpful by encouraging the person to discuss the traumatic event and by providing education about support groups.

> ### Critical Thinking Questions 5.4
>
> What biases do you have about how people should cope with discrimination based on race, ethnicity, gender, sexual orientation, and so on? How might the coping strategy need to change in different situations, such as receiving service in a restaurant, being interviewed for a job, or dealing with an unthinking comment from a classmate?

Social Support

In coping with the demands of daily life, our social supports—the people we rely on to enrich our lives—can be invaluable. **Social support** can be defined as the interpersonal interactions and relationships that provide us with assistance or feelings of attachment to persons we perceive as caring (Hobfoll, 1996). Three types of social support resources are available (Walsh, 2000):

1. *Material support:* food, clothing, shelter, and other concrete items

2. *Emotional support:* interpersonal support

3. *Instrumental support:* services provided by casual contacts such as grocers, hairstylists, and landlords

Some authors add "social integration" support to the mix, which refers to a person's sense of belonging. That is, simply belonging to a group, and having a role and contribution to offer, may be an important dimension of support (Wethington, Moen, Glasgow, & Pillemer, 2000). This is consistent with the "main effect" hypothesis of support, discussed shortly.

Systems perspective

Our **social network** includes not just our social support but all the people with whom we regularly interact and the patterns of interaction that result from exchanging resources with them (Moren-Cross & Lin, 2006). Network relationships often occur in *clusters* (distinct categories such as nuclear family, extended family, friends, neighbors, community relations, school, work, church, recreational groups, and professional associations). Network relationships are not synonymous with support; they may be negative or positive. But the scope of the network does tend to indicate our potential for obtaining social support. Having supportive others in a variety of clusters indicates that we are supported in many areas of our lives, rather than being limited to relatively few sources. Our **personal network** includes those from the social network who, in our view, provide us with our most essential supports (Bidart & Lavenu, 2005).

Exhibit 5.4 displays Dan's social network. He is supported emotionally as well as materially by his family members, with whom he keeps in regular contact, although the relationship with his father is strained. Dan particularly looks to his sister for understanding and emotional support, while at the same time being critical of her failure to be adequately supportive of him. Dan does not see his grandmother except for the trips he takes to China every 3 or 4 years, but he feels a special closeness to her and writes to her regularly. Dan has had an on-again, off-again relationship with his girlfriend Christine, who lives 1 hour away in his hometown and keeps in touch with him primarily by e-mail. Their communications are civil, and Dan seems to enjoy giving her advice when she needs to make certain decisions about her jobs and daily living activities. Dan has instrumental relationships with his landlord and several other tenants in his apartment building, and one neighbor is a friend with whom he has lunch or dinner every few weeks. Dan is further instrumentally connected with several other students because they represent consistency in his life and are casually friendly and supportive. This is also true of two peers with whom he performs volunteer work in the medical center lab. It is apparent from Dan's social network that he receives most of his emotional support from peers at the church where he attends services and social activities every Sunday.

In total, Dan has 19 people in his social support system, representing seven clusters. He identifies 9 of these people as personal, or primary, supports. It is noteworthy that 7 of his network members provide only instrumental support, which is important but the most limited type. Because people in the general population tend to identify about 25 network members (Uchino, Holt-Lunstad, Smith, & Bloor, 2004), we can see that Dan's support system, on which he relies to cope with stress, may not be adequate to meet his needs at this time in his life. The social worker might explore with Dan his school, neighborhood, and work clusters for the possibility of developing more active or meaningful supports.

Dan is not alone in having an inadequate support network. McPherson, Smith-Lovin, and

Exhibit 5.4   Dan's Social Network

Network Cluster	Network Member*	Type of Support
Family of origin	Mother*	Material and emotional
	Father*	Material and emotional
	Sister*	Emotional
Extended family	Grandmother (Taiwan)*	Emotional
Intimate friends	Christine (girlfriend)*	Emotional
Neighborhood	Landlord	Instrumental
	Alan	Instrumental, emotional
	Perry	Instrumental
	Jason	Instrumental
School	Lucy	Intrumental
	Joan	Instrumental
	Spencer*	Emotional
Work	Thomas	Instrumental
	Laura	Instrumental
Church	Chen*	Emotional
	Michelle*	Emotional
	Garrett*	Emotional
	Ming	Emotional
	Russell	Emotional

* = Identified as close personal support.

Brashears (2006) found that 43.6% of their 2004 sample reported having either no one or only one person with whom they discuss important matters in their lives, in contrast to an average of three such persons reported in a 1985 sample. These findings raise several important questions for further exploration: Is it possible that people today have larger but less intimate networks? How is the level of intimate exchange affected by time spent in electronic communication? Do the trends in the United States toward increased time spent at work and in commuting have a negative impact on social support networks?

Virtual Support

I don't need to tell you, of course, that much social support is now provided through connective technologies that allow people to be "in contact" without being physically present with one another. Facebook, Skype, e-mail, blogging, tweets, and texts put people in touch with one another instantaneously, regardless of where they are or what they are doing. While there is much to be admired about these developments, and they clearly allow us to be in touch with significant others we might never otherwise see, they also create the potential for us to reduce the frequency of, and even our desire for, face-to-face contacts and thus redefine the nature of relationships, support, and intimacy. The number of people with whom people physically interact has fallen in recent years. Dan, like many of his peers, spent several hours per day on the Internet communicating with others; in his case it was primarily through e-mail. Spencer believed this was a mixed blessing for his client, because while it did help Dan feel connected to his support system, it prevented any efforts he might otherwise expend for intimate interaction with people whose lives physically intersected with his own. Turkle (2011), among others, is concerned about the unpredictable ways social technology may alter the nature of our relationships. As one disconcerting yet very real example of this process, she writes at length about the coming use of robots to provide people with major interpersonal support, existing as their full-time companions.

How Social Support Aids Coping

The experience of stress creates a physiological state of emotional arousal, which reduces the efficiency of cognitive functions (Caplan & Caplan, 2000). When we experience stress, we become less effective at focusing our attention and scanning the environment for relevant information. We cannot access the memories that normally bring meaning to our perceptions, judgment, planning, and integration of feedback from others. These memory impairments reduce our ability to maintain a consistent sense of identity.

Social support helps in these situations by acting as an "auxiliary ego." Our social support—particularly our personal network—compensates for our perceptual deficits, reminds us of our sense of self, and monitors the adequacy of our functioning. Here are 10 characteristics of effective support (Caplan, 1990; Caplan & Caplan, 2000):

1. Nurtures and promotes an ordered worldview

2. Promotes hope

3. Promotes timely withdrawal and initiative

4. Provides guidance

5. Provides a communication channel with the social world

6. Affirms one's personal identity

7. Provides material help

8. Contains distress through reassurance and affirmation

9. Ensures adequate rest

10. Mobilizes other personal supports

Some of these support systems are formal (service organizations), and some are informal (such as friends and neighbors). Religion, which attends to the spiritual realm, also plays a distinctive support role (Caplan, 1990). This topic is explored in Chapter 6.

Systems perspective

Two schools of thought have emerged around the question of how we internalize social support (Bal, Crombez, & Oost, 2003; Cohen, Gottlieb, & Underwood, 2001).

1. *Main effect model.* Support is seen as related to our overall sense of well-being. Social networks provide us with regular positive experiences, and within the network a set of stable roles (expectations for our behavior) enables us to enjoy stability of mood, predictability in life situations, and recognition of self-worth. We simply don't experience many potential stressors as such, because with our built-in sense of support, we do not perceive situations as threats.

2. *Buffering model.* Support is seen as a factor that intervenes between a stressful event and our reaction. Recognizing our supports helps us to diminish or prevent a stress response. We recognize a potential stressor, but our perception that we have resources available redefines the potential for harm or reduces the stress reaction by influencing our cognitive, emotional, and physiological processes.

Most research on social support focuses on its buffering effects, in part because these effects are

Social constructionist
perspective; psychodynamic
perspective

more accessible to measurement. Social support as a main effect is difficult to isolate because it is influenced by, and may be an outcome of, our psychological development and ability to form attachments. The main effect model has its roots in sociology, particularly symbolic interaction theory, in which our sense of self is said to be shaped by behavioral expectations acquired through our interactions with others. The buffering model, more a product of ego psychology, conceptualizes social support as an external source of emotional, informational, and instrumental aid.

Perceived support is consistently linked to positive mental health, which is typically explained as resulting from objectively supportive actions that buffer stress. Yet this explanation does not fully account for the often-observed main effects between support and mental health. *Relational regulation theory* hypothesizes that main effects occur when people regulate their affect, thoughts, and actions through ordinary, yet affectively consequential, conversations and shared activities, rather than through conversations about how to cope with stress (Lakey & Orehek, 2011). This form of regulation is primarily relational in that the types of people and social interactions that help recipients are mostly a matter of personal taste. Dan reports that he receives emotional support from nine people, but he is not necessarily drawn to these people to the same degree, which is partly why he does not experience adequate social support.

How Social Workers Evaluate Social Support

There is no consensus about how social workers can evaluate a client's level of social support. The simplest procedure is to ask for the client's subjective perceptions of support from family and friends (Procidano & Smith, 1997). One of the most complex procedures uses eight indicators of social support: available listening, task appreciation, task challenge, emotional support, emotional challenge, reality confirmation, tangible assistance, and personal assistance (Richman, Rosenfeld, & Hardy, 1993). One particularly useful model includes three social support indicators (Uchino, 2009):

1. *Listing of social network resources.* The client lists all the people with whom he or she regularly interacts.

2. *Accounts of supportive behavior.* The client identifies specific episodes of receiving support from others in the recent past.

3. *Perceptions of support.* The client subjectively assesses the adequacy of the support received from various sources.

In assessing a client's social supports from this perspective, the social worker first asks the client to list all persons with whom he or she has interacted in the past 1 or 2 weeks. Next, the social worker asks the client to draw from that list the persons he or she perceives to be supportive in significant ways (significance is intended to be open to the client's interpretation). The client is asked to describe specific recent acts of support provided by those significant others. Finally, the social worker asks the client to evaluate the adequacy of the support received from specific sources and in general. On the basis of this assessment, the social worker can identify both subjective and objective support indicators with the client and target underused clusters for the development of additional social support.

NORMAL AND ABNORMAL COPING _____

Normality is characterized by conformity with our community and culture. We can be deviant from some social norms, so long as our deviance does not impair our reasoning, judgment, intellectual capacity, and ability to make personal and social adaptations (Bartholomew, 2000). Most people readily assess the coping behaviors they observe in others as "normal" or "abnormal." But what does "normal" mean? We all apply different criteria. The standards we use to classify coping thoughts and feelings as normal or abnormal are important, however, because they have implications for how we view ourselves and how we behave toward those different from us (Francis, 2013). For example, Dan was concerned that other students at the university perceived him as abnormal because of his ethnicity and social isolation. Most likely, other students did not notice him much at all. It is interesting that, in Dan's view, his physical appearance and demeanor revealed him as abnormal. However, he was one of many Asian American students at the university, and his feelings were not as evident to others as he thought.

Social workers struggle just as much to define *normal* and *abnormal* as anybody else, but their definitions may have greater consequences. Misidentifying someone as normal may forestall needed interventions; misidentifying someone as abnormal may create a stigma or become a self-fulfilling prophecy. To avoid such problems, social workers may profitably consider how four disciplines define normal.

The Medical (Psychiatric) Perspective

One definition from psychiatry, a branch of medicine, states that we are normal when we are in harmony with ourselves and our environment. Significant abnormality in perceived thinking, behavior, and mood may even classify as a mental disorder. In fact, the current definition of *mental disorder* used by the American Psychiatric Association (2013), which is intended to help psychiatrists and many other professionals distinguish between normality and abnormality, is a "syndrome characterized by clinically significant disturbance in an individual's cognition, emotion regulation, or behavior that reflects a dysfunction in the psychological, biological, or developmental processes underlying mental functioning" (p. 20). Such a disorder usually represents significant distress in social or occupational functioning. This represents a medical perspective, only one of many possible perspectives on human behavior, although it is a powerful, socially sanctioned one. The medical definition focuses on underlying disturbances *within* the person and is sometimes referred to as the *disease model* of abnormality. This model implies that the abnormal person must experience changes within the self (rather than create environmental change) in order to be considered "normal" again.

In summary, the medical model of abnormality focuses on underlying disturbances within the person. An assessment of the disturbance results in a diagnosis based on a cluster of observable symptoms. Interventions, or treatments, focus on changing the individual. The abnormal person must experience internal, personal changes (rather than induce environmental change) in order to be considered normal again. Exhibit 5.5 summarizes the format for diagnosing mental disorders as developed by psychiatry in the United States and published in the *Diagnostic and Statistical Manual of Mental Disorders* (American Psychiatric Association, 2013). Many people in the helping professions are required to follow this format in mental health treatment facilities, including social workers.

Psychological Perspectives

One major difference between psychiatry and psychology is that psychiatry tends to emphasize biological and somatic interventions to return the person to a state of normalcy, whereas psychology emphasizes various cognitive, behavioral, or reflective interventions. That is, through their own decisions and determination, and sometimes with the help of a professional, the person can change certain problematic (abnormal) characteristics into more agreeable, functional (normal) ones.

Psychological theory is quite broad in scope, but some theories are distinc-

Developmental perspective

tive in that they postulate that people normally progress through a sequence of life stages. The time context thus becomes important. Each new stage of personality development builds on previous stages, and any unsuccessful transitions can result in abnormal behavior—that is, a deviant pattern of coping with threats and challenges. An

Exhibit 5.5   *DSM-5* Classification of Mental Disorders

- Record the mental disorder, beginning with the problem most responsible for the current evaluation. Many diagnoses also contain subtypes or specifiers (for example, "mild," "moderate," and "severe") for added diagnostic clarity.
- When uncertain if a diagnosis is correct, the social worker should use the "provisional" qualifier, which means he or she may need additional time or information to be confident about the choice.
- More than one diagnosis can be used for a client, and medical diagnoses should also be included if they are significant to the client's overall condition. Social workers cannot make medical diagnoses, of course, but they can be included if they are noted in a client's history or the client reports their existence.
- If a person no longer meets criteria for a disorder that may be relevant to his or her current condition, the qualifier "past history" can be used, although this would not be the primary diagnosis. For example, if a woman seeks help for depression while she is pregnant, it may be important to note if she had an eating disorder history.
- Social and environmental problems that are a focus of clinical attention may also be included as part of the diagnosis. A chapter in the *DSM* titled "Other Conditions That May Be a Focus of Clinical Attention" includes a list of conditions (popularly known as "V-codes") that are not considered formal diagnoses but can be used for that descriptive purpose.

unsuccessful struggle through one stage implies that the person will experience difficulties in mastering subsequent stages.

One life stage view of normality well known in social work is that of Erik Erikson (1968), who proposed eight stages of normal *psychosocial* development (see Exhibit 5.6). Dan, at age 24, is struggling with the developmental stage of young adulthood, in which the major issue is intimacy versus isolation. Challenges in young adulthood include developing a capacity for interpersonal intimacy as opposed to feeling socially empty or isolated within the family unit. According to Erikson's theory,

Dan's current difficulties would be related to his lack of success in negotiating one or more of the five preceding developmental phases or challenges, and reviewing this would be an important part of his intervention.

From this perspective, Dan's experience of stress would not be seen as abnormal, but his inability to make coping choices that promote positive personal adaptation would signal psychological abnormality. For example, at the university, he was having difficulty with relationship development and support seeking. He avoided social situations such as study groups, recreational activities, and

Exhibit 5.6   Erikson's Stages of Psychosocial Development

Life Stage	Psychosocial Challenge	Significant Others
Infancy	Trust versus mistrust	Maternal persons
Early childhood	Autonomy versus shame and doubt	Parental persons
Play age	Initiative versus guilt	Family
School age	Industry versus inferiority	Neighborhood
Adolescence	Identity versus identity diffusion	Peers
Young adulthood	Intimacy versus isolation	Partners
Adulthood	Generativity versus self-absorption	Household
Mature age	Integrity versus disgust and despair	Humanity

university organizations in which he might learn more about what kinds of people he likes, what interests he might share with them, and what insecurities they might share as well. From a stage theory perspective, Dan's means of coping with the challenges of intimacy versus isolation might be seen as maladaptive, or abnormal.

The Sociological Approach: Deviance

Social constructionist perspective

The field of sociology offers a variety of approaches to the study of abnormality, or deviance, one of which is derived from symbolic interactionism. It states that those who cannot constrain their behaviors within role limitations that are acceptable to others become labeled as deviant. Thus, *deviance* is a negative label assigned when one is considered by a majority of significant others to be in violation of the prescribed social order (Curra, 2011). Put more simply, we are unable to grasp the perspective from which the deviant person thinks and acts; the person's behavior does not make sense to us. We conclude that our inability to understand the other person's perspective is due to that person's shortcomings rather than to our own rigidity, and we label the behavior as deviant. The deviance label may be mitigated if the individual accepts that he or she should think or behave otherwise and tries to conform to the social order. (It should be emphasized, however, that sociologists are increasingly using the term *positive deviance* to describe those persons whose outstanding skills and characteristics make them "outliers" in a constructive sense.)

From this viewpoint, Dan would be perceived as abnormal, or deviant, only by those who had sufficient knowledge of his thoughts and feelings to form an opinion about his allegiance to their ideas of appropriate social behavior. He might also be considered abnormal by peers who had little understanding of his Asian American cultural background. Those who knew Dan well might

understand the basis for his negative thoughts and emotions and, in that context, continue to view him as normal in his coping efforts. However, it is significant that Dan was trying to avoid intimacy with his university classmates and work peers so that he would not become well known to them. Because he still views himself as somewhat deviant, he wants to avoid being seen as deviant (or abnormal) by others, which in his view would lead to their rejection of him. This circular reasoning poorly serves Dan's efforts to cope with stress in ways that promote his personal goals.

The Social Work Perspective: Social Functioning

The profession of social work is characterized by the consideration of systems and the reciprocal impact of persons and their environments (the bio-psycho-social-spiritual perspective) on human behavior. Social workers tend not to classify individuals as abnormal. Instead, they consider the person-in-environment as an ongoing process that facilitates or blocks one's ability to experience satisfactory social functioning. In fact, in social work, the term *normalization* refers to helping clients realize that their thoughts and feelings are shared by many other individuals in similar circumstances (Hepworth, Rooney, Rooney, & Strom-Gottfried, 2013).

Three types of situations are most likely to produce problems in social functioning: stressful life transitions, relationship difficulties, and environmental unresponsiveness (Gitterman, 2009). Note that all three are related to transitory interactions of the person with other persons or the environment and do not rely on evaluating the client as normal or abnormal.

Social work's **person-in-environment (PIE) classification system** formally organizes the assessment of individuals' ability to cope with stress around the four factors

Systems perspective

shown in Exhibit 5.7: social functioning problems, environmental problems, mental health problems,

Exhibit 5.7   The Person-in-Environment (PIE) Classification System

Factor I: Social Functioning Problems

A. Social role in which each problem is identified
   1. Family (parent, spouse, child, sibling, other, significant other)
   2. Other interpersonal (lover, friend, neighbor, member, other)
   3. Occupational (worker/paid, worker/home, worker/volunteer, student, other)

B. Type of problem in social role

1. Power	4. Dependency	7. Victimization
2. Ambivalence	5. Loss	8. Mixed
3. Responsibility	6. Isolation	9. Other

C. Severity of problem

1. No problem	4. High severity
2. Low severity	5. Very high severity
3. Moderate severity	6. Catastrophic

D. Duration of problem

1. More than five years	4. Two to four weeks
2. One to five years	5. Two weeks or less
3. Six months to one year	

E. Ability of client to cope with problem

1. Outstanding coping skills	4. Somewhat inadequate
2. Above average	5. Inadequate
3. Adequate	6. No coping skills

Factor II: Environmental Problems

A. Social system where each problem is identified

1. Economic/basic need	4. Health, safety, social services
2. Education/training	5. Voluntary association
3. Judicial/legal	6. Affectional support

B. Specific type of problem within each social system

C. Severity of problem

D. Duration of problem

Factor III: Mental Health Problems

A. Clinical syndromes (Axis I of DSM)

B. Personality and developmental disorders (Axis II of DSM)

Factor IV: Physical Health Problems

A. Disease diagnosed by a physician

B. Other health problems reported by client and others

and physical health problems. Such a broad classification scheme helps ensure that Dan's range of needs will be addressed. James Karls and Maura O'Keefe (2008), the authors of the PIE system, state that it "underlines the importance of conceptualizing a person in an interactive context" and that "pathological and psychological limitations are accounted for but are not accorded extraordinary attention" (p. x). Thus, the system avoids labeling a client as abnormal. At the same time, however, it offers no way to assess the client's strengths and resources.

With the exception of its neglect of strengths and resources, the PIE assessment system is appropriate for social work because it was specifically developed to promote a holistic biopsychosocial perspective on human behavior. For example, at a mental health center that subscribed to psychiatry's *DSM* classification system, Dan might be given an Axis I diagnosis of adjustment disorder or dysthymic disorder, and his auditory processing disorder might also be diagnosed. With the PIE system, the social worker would, in addition to addressing mental and physical health concerns, assess Dan's overall social and occupational functioning, as well

as any specific environmental problems. For example, Dan's problems with the student role that might be highlighted on PIE Factor I include his isolation, the high severity of his impairment and its 6-month to a year's duration, and the inadequacy of his coping skills. His environmental stressors on Factor II might include a deficiency in affectional support, of high severity, with a duration of 6 months to a year. Assessment with PIE provides Dan and the social worker with more avenues for intervention, which might include personal, interpersonal, and environmental systems.

Critical Thinking Questions 5.5

How important is virtual support to you? Which types of virtual support are the most meaningful to you? What have you observed about how social technology is affecting the way people give and receive social support? What do you see as the contributions of the medical, psychological, sociological, and social work perspectives on normal and abnormal coping? What do you see as the downsides of each of these perspectives?

Implications for Social Work Practice

Theory and research about the psychosocial person have a number of implications for social work practice, including the following:

- Always assess the nature, range, and intensity of a client's interpersonal relationships.
- Help clients identify their sources of stress and patterns of coping. Recognize the possibility of particular vulnerabilities to stress and the social and environmental conditions that give rise to stress.
- Help clients assess the effectiveness of particular coping strategies for specific situations.
- Use the risk and resilience framework to understand the nature of a client's resources, assets, and limitations.
- Where appropriate, help clients develop a stronger sense of competence in problem solving and coping. Identify specific problems and related skill-building needs, teach and rehearse skills, and implement graduated applications to real-life situations.
- Where appropriate, use case management activities focused on developing a client's social supports through linkages with potentially supportive others in a variety of social network clusters.

- Recognize families as possible sources of stress as well as support.
- Recognize the benefits that psychoeducational groups, therapy groups, and mutual-aid groups may have for helping clients cope with stress.
- Where appropriate, take the roles of mediator and advocate to attempt to influence organizations to be more responsive to the needs of staff and clients. Where appropriate, take the roles of planner and administrator to introduce flexibility into organizational policies and procedures so that agency–environment transactions become mutually responsive.
- For clients who experience stress related to inadequate community ties, link them to an array of formal and informal organizations that provide them with a greater sense of belonging in their communities.
- When working with persons in crisis, attempt to alleviate distress and facilitate a return to the previous level of functioning.
- Assess with clients the meaning of hazardous events, precipitating factors of hazardous events, and potential and actual support systems. When working with persons in crisis, use a here-and-now orientation and use tasks to enhance support systems. Help clients to connect current stress with patterns of past functioning and to initiate improved coping methods. As the crisis phase terminates, review with the client the tasks accomplished, including new coping skills and social supports developed.

Key Terms

adaptation
coping
crisis
daily hassles
defense mechanisms
emotion-focused coping
general adaptation syndrome
homeostasis
neural plasticity

personal network
person-in-environment (PIE) classification system
post-traumatic stress disorder (PTSD)
problem-focused coping
relational coping
relational theory
role strain

social identity theory
social network
social support
state
stress
trait
traumatic stress

Active Learning

1. You have been introduced to four ways of conceptualizing normal and abnormal coping: mental disorder, psychosocial development, deviance, and social functioning. Which of these ways of thinking about normality and abnormality are the most helpful to you in thinking about Dan's situation? For what reasons?

2. Think of your own social support network. List all persons you have interacted with in the past month. Next, circle those persons on the list whom you perceive to be supportive in significant ways. Describe specific recent acts of support provided by these significant others. Finally, evaluate the adequacy of the support you receive from specific sources and in general. What can you do to increase the support you receive from your social network?

3. Consider several recent situations in which you have used problem-focused or emotion-focused coping strategies. What was different about the situations in which you used one rather than the other? Were the coping strategies successful? Why or why not? How does the tripartite conceptual framework help you to understand your choice of strategy?

American Psychiatric Association *DSM-5* Implementation and Support: www.dsm5.org/Pages/Default.aspx

Site includes information on implementation of the manual, answers frequently asked questions, lists *DSM-5* corrections, and provides a mechanism for submitting questions and feedback regarding implementation of the manual. Links are provided to educational webinars about the *DSM-5* and trainings being conducted throughout the United States and abroad.

Institute of Contemporary Psychotherapy and Psychoanalysis: www.icpeast.org

Site contains information on conferences, training, and links to other resources on contemporary self and relational psychologies.

Jean Baker Miller Training Institute (JBMTI): www.jbmti.org

The JBMTI at the Wellesley Centers for Women is the home of relational-cultural theory (RCT), which posits that people grow through and toward relationships throughout the life span and that culture powerfully impacts relationship. JBMTI is dedicated to understanding the complexities of human connections as well as exploring the personal and social factors that can lead to chronic disconnection.

MEDLINEplus: Stress: www.nlm.nih.gov/medlineplus/stress.html

Site presented by the National Institute of Mental Health presents links to the latest news about stress research, coping, disease management, specific conditions, and stress in children, seniors, teenagers, and women.

MIT Initiative on Technology and Self: http://web.mit.edu/sturkle/techself/welcome.html

The goal of the MIT Initiative on Technology and Self is to be a center for research and reflection on the subjective side of technology and to raise the level of public discourse on the social and psychological dimensions of technological change. The initiative features seminars, work groups, conferences, research, and publications.

National Center for Post-traumatic Stress Disorder: www.ptsd.va.gov

Site presented by the National Center for PTSD, a program of the U.S. Department of Veterans Affairs, contains facts about PTSD, information about how to manage the traumatic stress of terrorism, and recent research.

Student Study Site

$SAGE edge™

Sharpen your skills with SAGE edge at **edge.sagepub.com/hutchisonpe5e**

SAGE edge for students provides a personalized approach to help you accomplish your coursework goals in an easy-to-use learning environment.

CHAPTER 6

The Spiritual Person

Michael J. Sheridan

Chapter Outline

CASE STUDY 6.1

Caroline's Challenging Questions

Caroline, who grew up in a large, close-knit family from North Carolina, is in her first year of college at a university in another state where she is encountering all kinds of new experiences. A devout Christian, Caroline is a member of a Baptist church back home, where her family has attended for generations. She was very involved in her home church, singing in the choir and actively engaged in several youth programs. Most of her high school friends attended her church, so she was more than a little uncomfortable when she learned that her roommate, Ruth, was Jewish. Caroline has met a number of other students who are from different faiths or who say that they don't belong to a church at all. This has been a new and challenging experience for her.

At first she tried to stay away from anyone who wasn't Christian but struggled with this because so many of her non-Christian classmates seemed like nice people and she really wanted to have friends. All sorts of questions began to emerge in her mind, like "How can they not believe in Jesus Christ?" and "What *do* they believe?" and "What will happen to them in the afterlife if they are not saved?" These questions only grew as she took a comparative religions class where she learned about faiths that she had never heard of before. In one class exercise, she was paired with a student from Turkey who said she was Muslim. At first, Caroline was anxious about talking with her, but as they moved through the exercise, she began to feel that they were more alike than different. They both were from very religious families, their faith was important to them personally, and they both were struggling with all the different perspectives they were encountering in college. Later that day, Caroline realized that if she had been born in Turkey, she would probably be a Muslim too. This thought both intrigued and unsettled her. More and more she is asking herself, "What *do* I really believe and why?"

CASE STUDY 6.2

Naomi's Health Crisis

Naomi is a 42-year-old mother of three children who are 10, 7, and 3 years old. Naomi discovered a lump in her breast a couple of weeks ago, and she and her husband, David, have been anxiously awaiting news regarding test results. When the diagnosis of cancer finally comes, they are both stunned and frightened but pull themselves together for the sake of the children. Naomi begins the long journey of doctors, surgery, chemotherapy, and radiation treatments while simultaneously trying to maintain family life and a part-time job as best she can. David takes on new duties as a more active parent and homemaker while still going to his full-time job. He struggles with his own fears and anger about what is happening, initially not sharing these with Naomi because he is determined to be her "rock."

Naomi and David are members of Temple Shalom, a local Reform Jewish congregation, which they joined after their first child was born. When they were growing up, Naomi's family were members of a Reform congregation, while David's family expressed their Jewish heritage in more secular and cultural terms, gathering annually for a Passover Seder but not attending services except occasionally on Yom Kippur. Naomi had not regularly attended services after her bat mitzvah, but both she and David decided that they wanted to be part of a spiritual community for their children. They had heard good things about the temple in their neighborhood and decided to explore it. They liked its open, welcoming atmosphere; its liberal viewpoints on social issues; and its active engagement in social action in the community. They both enjoy the weekly connection with other adults and are happy with the religious classes their children attend. Recently, Naomi and David have been engaged in weekly Shabbat Torah study sessions, to deepen their understanding of Jewish sacred texts.

Now that Naomi is facing this health crisis, both she and David are feeling a bit lost and are searching for answers. Although friends have been supportive, both of their families live far away, and their short visits and phone calls only provide minimal comfort. One night, when they both can't sleep, Naomi and David begin to share their doubts and fears with one another, even admitting that they feel angry with God and wondering if there is such a thing as God at all. Naomi finally suggests, "I think it would help to talk with Rabbi Shapiro and some of the people we've met at Temple Shalom." David agrees and adds that they should also explore the Jewish Healing Network that was described in the bulletin the previous week.

Matthew's Faith Journey

Matthew will be 70 next month—a fact that is hard for him to believe. He's been a widower for 5 years now since his wife, Betty, died of a sudden heart attack. The first few years following her death were rough, but Matthew made it through with the help of his sons and their families and members of his Catholic parish, which he has been attending for 40 years. His faith has always been very important to him, even though he has struggled with periods of doubt and confusion—the latest following Betty's death. At one point when he was younger, he considered leaving the church, when disagreements about doctrine and rumblings about the new priest were causing uproar in the congregation. He even visited several other denominations to see if they were a better fit for him. But after much reflection and conversation with Betty, Matthew decided to stick with his commitment to the Catholic faith and his parish, saying, "No church is perfect, and this is where I truly belong."

For the past couple of years, he has been actively involved with the outreach activities of the church, working on the Food Bank and Affordable Housing committees. Recently, he has been a member of the Interfaith Dialogue Program, which promotes respect and mutual understanding across religious and cultural perspectives. Matthew finds the panel discussions, conferences, and interfaith community projects both challenging and invigorating. He's particularly looking forward to an upcoming conference on the role of interfaith dialogue in advancing world peace. He's also been involved with the National Religious Partnership for the Environment (NRPE), a Judeo-Christian association composed of many faiths that focuses on environmental stewardship. As a result of all of these activities, Matthew has also been reading a number of books on different religions and is struck by the similar themes reflected in the teachings of very diverse traditions. He is beginning to feel a new sense of purpose for his life, which both surprises and delights him as he heads into his 70s. Some of his friends have asked him if his involvement with the Interfaith Dialogue Program is making him question his own religion, but Matthew says, "No, quite the opposite. I feel more deeply connected to my faith as I understand more about other religions. It's not that I think mine is right and theirs is wrong, but I appreciate and respect other religions, while still knowing that mine is right for me."

Trudy's Search for the Sacred

Trudy is a 35-year-old single woman living in Berkeley, California—which is a long way from the little town in Arkansas where she lived until she left home at 18. She's moved several times since then, searching for a new home that feels right to her. She thinks she may have finally found it. A new job in a health food store, a small but comfortable and affordable apartment, a great yoga class, and a welcoming Buddhist Sangha (community) of like-minded people all make her feel like she's finally found what she's been looking for.

Trudy's early years were not easy. Her father was an alcoholic who flew into rages when drunk, which happened more often as the years went by. It was not an unusual event for someone in her family to be physically hurt during these episodes. Trudy, her mother, and her two sisters were afraid of her father and "walked around on eggshells" most of the time to avoid triggering his angry spells. Trudy found refuge in the woods in back of her house and in books, which she devoured as they took her to places beyond her current reality. She could stay curled up in a nook of her favorite tree for hours, transporting herself to somewhere else—anywhere else. She promised herself she would leave as soon as she finished high school.

Life since then has not been easy either. Trudy was briefly married in her 20s to a man who also had a hard time controlling his anger and began to drink more and more as problems in the marriage started to emerge. Trudy even found herself turning to alcohol as a way of numbing her pain, which really scared her. With the support of some friends, she finally left the marriage and was off again, searching for a new home. After a couple of other relationships that didn't work out, Trudy decided to avoid men and increasingly became isolated from all social ties. But in her new home in Berkeley, she finds that she likes the people who attend her Sangha and likes even more the fact that they don't share a lot of personal information, focusing more on spiritual practices. She loves the group meditation and the dharma talks and has made a commitment to increased periods of solitary meditation when she is at home. Trudy is now rising at 4:00 a.m. to meditate for 3 hours before work, and she meditates an additional 2 hours most evenings. Her reading is now totally focused on books about spirituality, which support her quest to rise above personal concerns and ego to become an enlightened being. Although Trudy was not exposed to a particular religious tradition during childhood, her spiritual development is now her highest priority.

CASE STUDY 6.5

Leon's Two Worlds

Leon is a 23-year-old man who is feeling torn in two. He is the oldest son in a family with five kids and the mainstay of his mother's life. Regina became a widow 8 years ago when her husband, Rodney, was killed in an accident at the mill yard where he worked. Since then, she's leaned heavily on Leon for help with his brothers and sisters and as a major contributor to the family's finances. He is also the one she confides in the most, sharing things with him that she once shared with her husband. The whole family also relies heavily on their African Methodist Episcopal (AME) church for both social support and spiritual nurturance.

Leon has grown up in the church and loves the fellowship and the joyous feeling that comes over him as he sings and worships on Sundays. But it is also a place that increasingly troubles him, as he has finally admitted to himself that he is gay. He has denied this for years, trying hard to follow church teachings about homosexuality being a sin and something that can be overcome with the help of God. He has prayed and prayed to God to change him, but this has not worked. Leon is now battling despair, as he fears that he will always be caught between his love for his faith and his church and a longing to be who he truly is. The idea of telling his mother about his sexual orientation seems unthinkable, but he's not sure how long he can go on living a lie. He knows he will have to leave the church if it ever becomes known that he is gay. That possibility also seems unthinkable. He has been feeling more and more depressed, to the point where his mother keeps asking him what's wrong. He's even had thoughts of suicide, which frightens him. In his nightly prayers to God he asks, "Why must I lose you to be who I am?"

Jean-Joseph's Serving the Spirits

Jean-Joseph is a 50-year-old man, originally from Haiti, who came with his family to the United States 10 years ago. He and his family were adherents of the Roman Catholic faith in Haiti and now attend a Catholic church near their new home. Jean-Joseph's family are also believers in Vodoun (known by most Westerners as Voodoo), which is widely practiced in Haiti and often integrated with belief in Catholicism. Most Roman Catholics who are active in this spiritual tradition refer to it as "serving the spirits." Although this belief system holds that there is only one God, Bondje, who created the universe, he is considered to be too far away for a personal relationship with humans. Instead, believers in Vodoun center on *Loa*, or spirits of ancestors and animals, natural forces, and good and evil spirits. Family Loa are spirits who are seen to protect their "children"—the Haitian people—from misfortune. Jean-Joseph and his family regularly participate in rituals to feed the Loa food and drink and offer them other gifts.

Recently, a Loa visited Jean-Joseph in a dream, telling him that his youngest son was ill and needed healing. His son Emmanuel had indeed been listless for days, not wanting to eat or play, and his parents were very worried about him. Jean-Joseph decided that they needed to take him to a *Mambo*, a Vodoun priestess, who could mediate between the human and spirit worlds to diagnose and treat Emmanuel's illness. The Mambo agreed to perform a healing ceremony, which was held at a *hounfour*, or Vodoun temple, around a *poteau-mitan*, a center pole where the spirits can communicate with people. A *veve*, or pattern of cornmeal unique to the Loa who was the focus of the ceremony, was created on the floor, and an altar was decorated with candles, pictures of Christian saints, and other symbolic items. A goat was also sacrificed for the ceremony. The Mambo and her assistants began to chant and dance, accompanied by the shaking of rattles and beating of drums. Finally, the Mambo was possessed by the Loa and fell down. The Loa then spoke through the Mambo and told the family how to treat the distressed spirit that was causing Emmanuel's illness. After the ceremony, the Mambo gave Jean-Joseph an herbal remedy to give to his son and instructions on how to continue feeding the spirit of the Loa until Emmanuel was healed. The family also prayed to the Christian God and Catholic saints to bring healing to Emmanuel.

Beth's Framework for Living

Beth grew up as the only child of parents who were very clear about not wanting their child to be "brainwashed by religion." Beth's mother, Sarah, had been the daughter of a Presbyterian minister but had not spoken to her father for several years before he died over conflicts about her leaving the church. Beth's father, Sam, was raised by two union organizer parents who had not been involved with any particular religious faith throughout their lives. Both Sarah and Sam felt strongly that everyone needed a strong code of personal ethics, and they felt confident they could give Beth a solid "framework for living" that didn't involve religion. Instead they taught Beth to be honest and fair and to "always walk a mile in someone else's shoes" before she judged anyone. Beth didn't think much about religion during her growing-up years except when it came up in school or when she became aware that a few of her friends' families were very religious. She tended to feel more comfortable with kids from more secular families like hers, but she didn't let this stop her from making friends with kids from more religious families as well. As Beth grew older she relied more and more on her parents' "framework for living" to help her navigate challenges, like when some of her friends wanted her to go shoplifting with them or when other friends cheated on an exam. In both cases, she didn't go along with her friends, but she didn't tell on them either—telling herself that she didn't really know what it was like to "walk in their shoes" and she shouldn't judge them. She had many long talks with her father about the importance of having personal integrity and caring about social injustices that others faced. She also loved to hear him tell stories of his parents' union organizing days when they "fought the system" and sometimes won. So when it came time to choose her major in college she chose political science, and when she graduated she became a union organizer for the SEIU (Services Employees International Union). Her first job was as a field organizer in West Virginia, focused on organizing nursing home, home care, hospital, and other social service employees. The hours were long and the work was tough, but she felt she was living from a place of integrity and making the world a better place. She recently became close friends with Karen, another field organizer, who shared with Beth that her commitment to workers' rights was grounded in her deep Catholic faith—something Beth found surprising as she hadn't thought of religious people as being very concerned about the struggles ordinary people face. She began to wonder if she needed to rethink her views about "all those religious people." Was it time to walk a bit in *their* shoes?

THE SPIRITUAL DIMENSION

Systems perspective

All of the stories presented in the seven case studies could be viewed through many different lenses. Social work's biopsychosocial framework would be helpful in understanding many facets of these cases. Knowledge of the biological components of health certainly would be useful in understanding the circumstances of Naomi's health crisis and Jean-Joseph's attempts at healing his son's illness. Psychological perspectives would shed light on Caroline's discomfort with encountering different beliefs, Matthew's deepening faith perspective, Trudy's search for a home and a different sense of self, Leon's despair at being torn between his faith and his sexual identity, and Beth's views about religious people. Social theories of family dynamics, ethnicity and culture, social movements, socioeconomic class, and social institutions would yield invaluable information about all of the people in these cases, providing a wider frame for understanding their individual lives. This use of multiple perspectives to understand human behavior is consistent with social work's focus on changing configurations of person and environment.

However, the biopsychosocial framework omits an important dimension of human existence: spirituality. This omission seems antithetical to social work's commitment to holistic practice. What would be gained if we added a spiritual lens in our attempt to understand Caroline's challenging questions, Naomi's health crisis, Matthew's faith journey, Trudy's search for the sacred, Leon's two worlds, Jean-Joseph's serving of the spirits, and Beth's framework for living? And how would this perspective help you as a social worker provide holistic and effective service in working with them? Keep these questions and all of the stories in mind as you read the rest of the chapter.

The Meaning of Spirituality

The concept of spirituality is often confused with religion, and writers in social work and related fields point to a number of attempts to delineate these terms and distinguish them from one another (Carroll, 1998; Wuthnow, 2003; Zinnbauer et al., 1997). Canda and Furman (2010) provide a detailed discussion of how the two terms are understood in social work and related fields, including medicine, nursing, and psychology. They also report findings from a series of national studies they have conducted in the United States, the United Kingdom, Norway, and New Zealand, which show relative consistency across countries. Specifically, the top six descriptors of *spirituality* across geographic locales were "meaning, personal, purpose, values, belief, and ethics." Similar congruence was found for the term *religion*, where the top six descriptors selected in all of the countries were "belief, ritual, community, values, prayer, and scripture" (p. 67). Drawing from these studies and additional research in the helping professions, Canda and Furman propose the following definitions for these two concepts.

Spirituality is "a process of human life and development

- focusing on the search for a sense of meaning, purpose, morality, and well-being;
- in relationship with oneself, other people, other beings, the universe, and ultimate reality however understood (e.g., in animistic, atheistic, nontheistic, polytheistic, theistic, or other ways);
- orienting around centrally significant priorities; and
- engaging a sense of transcendence (experienced as deeply profound, sacred, or transpersonal)" (p. 75).

Religion is "an institutionalized (i.e., systematic and organized) pattern of values, beliefs, symbols, behaviors, and experiences that involves

- spirituality;
- a community of adherents;
- transmission of traditions over time; and
- community support functions (e.g., organizational structure, material assistance, emotional support, or political advocacy) that are directly or indirectly related to spirituality" (p. 76).

Thus, the term *spirituality* is generally used in the social work literature to mean a broader concept than religion in that spiritual expression may or may not involve a particular religious faith or religious institution. But some writers have pointed out that for persons affiliated with certain faith perspectives, the two terms cannot be separated from one another, or *religion* is considered to be the broader construct, subsuming spirituality (Pals, 1996; Praglin, 2004). Others propose that the separation of the two terms in social work has resulted in discrimination against particular religious worldviews, especially those of evangelical or conservative faiths (Hodge, 2002; Ressler & Hodge, 2003). Clearly, there is a need for continued exploration and dialogue about definitional issues. Regardless of how the scholarly definition of these terms evolves, it is important as social workers to always inquire about and honor the client's definition of spirituality and religion and use the term that is most acceptable and relevant for that person, family, or community.

For the sake of clarity, it should be noted that when the term *spirituality* is used in the current chapter, it is meant to convey spirituality as the broader concept, inclusive of both religious and nonreligious expressions. Occasionally, the two terms are used together in the same sentence (e.g., "gathering religious or spiritual information"). In this case, the reader should recognize that both are included in order to be applicable regardless of whether persons identify themselves as primarily religious, primarily spiritual, both religious and spiritual, or neither.

Regardless of the precise words used to capture the meaning of spirituality, the term brings to mind many related themes. Exhibit 6.1 lists 20 symbolic themes of spirituality identified by Patrick O'Brien (1992). Which themes do you think are most applicable to the seven case studies presented at the beginning of this chapter?

Spirituality in the United States and Globally

The current spiritual landscape in the United States reveals both common threads and a colorful array of unique patterns. A number of Gallup polls have

Exhibit 6.1   Symbolic Themes of Spirituality

1. Morality, ethics, justice, and right effort
2. The nature and meaning of self and the intention and purpose of human existence
3. Interconnection; wholeness; alignment; and integration of persons, place, time, and events
4. Creativity, inspiration, and intuition
5. Altruistic service for the benefit of others
6. The mystery and wonder woven into nature, the universe, and the unknown
7. Sociocultural-historical traditions, rituals, and myths
8. Virtues (such as compassion, universal love, peace, patience, forgiveness, hope, honesty, trust, faith)
9. Mystical, altered states of consciousness
10. Sexuality
11. Openness, willingness, surrender, and receptivity
12. The power of choice, freedom, and responsibility
13. Special wisdom or revealed knowledge
14. Prayer, meditation, and quiet contemplation
15. Answers to pain, suffering, and death
16. Identity and relation to the metaphysical grounds of existence, ultimate reality, and life force
17. The relationship of cause and effect regarding prosperity or poverty
18. Beliefs or experiences related to intangible reality or the unobstructed universe
19. The path to enlightenment or salvation
20. Sensitive awareness of the earth and the nonhuman world

SOURCE: Adapted from O'Brien, 1992.

consistently reported that over 90% of people in the United States say they believe in God or a universal spirit, 78% report that religion is either "very important" or "fairly important" in their life, and 40% report attending religious services on a weekly basis (Newport, 2011, 2013). These statistics indicate a strong thread of spirituality in the United States. However, expressions of both religious and nonreligious spirituality have become increasingly diverse, making the United States likely the most religiously diverse country in the world today, with more than 1,500 different religious groups (Parrillo, 2009; Pew Forum on Religion & Public Life, 2008).

This diversity is due, in part, to ongoing schisms and divisions among many of the organized religions historically present within the United States. For example, the number of Christian denominations alone grew from 20 to more than 900 from 1800 to 1988 (Melton, 1993). In addition, there has been a significant rise in other spiritual traditions with each new influx of immigrants from other parts of the world. They have brought not only faiths recognized as major religions (e.g., Islam, Buddhism, Confucianism, Hinduism) but also various forms of spiritualism, folk healing, and shamanism (e.g., Santeria, *espiritismo*,

Photo 6.1 Spirituality is understood and expressed differently by individuals but is generally associated with a person's search for meaning.

© Sergio Pitamitz/Corbis

Vodoun, *curanderismo*, *santiguando*, *krou khmer*, and *mudang*). This trend is further augmented by a growing interest in Eastern and Middle Eastern religions (e.g., Islam, Buddhism, and Hinduism) and earth-based spiritualities (e.g., neo-paganism, goddess worship, and deep ecology). There has also been a revived or more visible involvement in traditional spiritual paths within Indigenous communities, as increasing numbers of Native Americans or First Nations peoples explore their tribal traditions or combine these traditions with faith in Christianity. Many of these "new" religions are among the fastest growing in the United States, although their overall numbers are still relatively small. Exhibit 6.2 shows the self-identification of the U.S. adult population by religious tradition in 1990, 2001, and 2008.

It should be noted that estimates of members of any particular religious group vary widely depending on the source, data collection methods, and definition of "adherents" (e.g., self-identified, formal membership, or regular participant). For example, in the United States, figures for adherents of Islam range from 1 million to 8 million; adherents of Judaism from 1 million to 5 million; adherents of Buddhism from 1 million to 5 million; and adherents of neo-paganism from 10,000 to 770,000 (Canda & Furman, 2010; Parrillo, 2009).

As tempting as it is to make overarching statements based on statistics concerning belief in God and religious identification—for example, that the U.S. population is highly religious—we must be cautious in drawing specific conclusions, as the picture changes depending on the particular

Exhibit 6.2 Self-Identification of U.S. Adult Population by Religious Tradition, 1990, 2001, 2008

Religious Tradition	1990 Estimate	1990 Percentage of U.S. Population	2001 Estimate	2001 Percentage of U.S. Population	2008 Estimate	2008 Percentage of U.S. Population
Christianity	151,225,000	86.2	159,514,000	76.7	173,402,000	76.0
Jewish	3,137,000	1.8	2,837,000	1.4	2,680,000	1.2
Eastern Religions	687,000	0.4	2,020,000	1.0	1,961,000	0.9
Muslim	527,000	0.3	1,104,000	0.5	1,349,000	0.9
No Religion	14,331,000	8.2	29,481,000	14.1	34,169,000	15.0

SOURCE: Kosmin & Keysar, 2009.

indicator. During generally the same time period, 1990 to 2001, the percentage of U.S. adults who regularly attended religious services decreased from 49% to 36%, reflecting a worldwide trend among industrialized countries (Reeves, 1998). More recent data drawn from Gallup reveal only 40% reporting that they attend religious services on a weekly basis (Newport, 2013). Furthermore, recent data from the Pew Research Center's Religion & Public Life Project (2012) reveal that one fifth of adults (46 million) report being unaffiliated, making them a substantial category second only to Christians in the United States. This percentage is even higher among younger adults, with almost one third of people younger than 30 stating that they are not affiliated with any religion. However, unaffiliated may not mean that spirituality is not important to this group of adults. Among unaffiliated Americans, 68% say they believe in God, 58% say they feel a deep connection with nature and the earth, 37% identify as "spiritual" but not "religious," and 21% report praying every day. Additionally, most of the religiously unaffiliated think that "churches and other institutions benefit society by strengthening community bonds and aiding the poor" (Pew Research Center's Religion & Public Life Project, 2012, para. 4).

Moreover, there appears to be increasing fluidity in religious affiliation. Data on changes from one major religious tradition to another (e.g., from Protestantism to Catholicism or from Judaism to no religion) show that 28% of U.S. adults have changed their affiliation from that of their childhood. When changes within affiliations are examined (e.g., from Baptist to Methodist), an even larger percentage (44%) of American adults report shifts in religious affiliation. The two affiliations showing the greatest net gains are the unaffiliated, increasing from 7.3% to 16.1%, and nondenominational Protestantism, increasing from 1.5% to 4.5% (Pew Forum on Religion & Public Life, 2008).

Groups that show a net loss due to changes in affiliation include Baptists, Methodists, and other Protestant groups, which show decreases ranging from less than 1% to 3.7%. Judaism also shows a small loss due to changing affiliations (0.2%). But the group that has experienced the greatest decrease is the Catholic Church, with 31.4% reporting being raised as Catholic but only 23.9% identifying as Catholic today, a net loss of 7.5% (Pew Forum on Religion & Public Life, 2008). It should be noted, however, that the overall proportion of the U.S. population that is Catholic is roughly the same as it was in the early 1970s. This can be explained in part by the number of converts, but the greatest contributor to replacing those who have left the Catholic Church has been immigrants coming into the United States who are adherents of this faith.

Overall, it is noteworthy that the percentage of respondents moving from "some" religious affiliation to "none" (12.7%) is greater than that of people moving from "none" to "some" religious affiliation (3.9%) (Pew Forum on Religion & Public Life, 2008). All of this suggests that the current phenomenon of "religion switching" may be a reflection of deeper cultural changes within our society, perhaps in part explained by what Roof (1993) calls the "generation of seekers," referring to the substantial baby boomer cohort in the United States.

These figures concerning shifts and declines in organized religious affiliation or identification emerge at a time when people in the United States are expressing an unprecedented interest in spirituality in general. In 1994, an estimated 58% of the U.S. population said they felt the need to experience spiritual growth in their lives; by 2001, this percentage was 80% (Gallup, 2002; Gallup & Lindsay, 1999). It is apparent that this interest in spiritual growth may or may not be expressed within traditional religious institutions and is increasingly focused on a spirituality that is more subjective, experiential, and personalized (Roof, 1993, 1999). This reflects Ulrich Beck's (1992) understanding of spirituality as attending to the development of positive human qualities—such as generosity, gratitude, a capacity for awe and wonder, an appreciation of the interconnectedness among all beings, and deeper awareness and insight—as much as or even more than a search for any divine form of transcendence.

It is important to consider all of these data within the context of global statistics (see Exhibit 6.3). Although adherents of Christianity remain the highest proportion of the population in the United States, worldwide they compose only 31.5% of all religious adherents, with the remainder being composed of those who self-identify with some other perspective, including Islam (23.2%), unaffiliated (16.3%), Hinduism (15%), Buddhism (7.1%), folk religions (5.9%), and Judaism and other religions

(less than 1% each) (Pew Research Center's Religion & Public Life Project, 2010).

It is important to understand the impact of globalization on religious or spiritual diversity both within and outside of the United States. *Globalization* is used here to refer to "the worldwide diffusion of practices, expansion of relations across continents, reorganization of social life on a global scale, and a growth of a shared global consciousness" (Lechner, 2005, as quoted in Swatos, 2005, p. 320). Simply put, it is our growing sense of the world being "a single place" (Robertson, 1992). As with other aspects of human life, globalization is also increasing our awareness of the many religious and spiritual traditions in the world and the role they play in various conflicts, both between and within countries.

Lester Kurtz (2012) posits three factors—modernism, multiculturalism, and modern technologies of warfare—significant to understanding religious conflict today. First, *modernism*, based on scientific, industrial, and technological revolutions, has had an ongoing contentious relationship with religious perspectives and institutions since the beginning of the 17th

> Conflict perspective

century, when church authorities charged Galileo with heresy for stating that the earth revolved around the sun. Present-day examples include debates regarding evolution versus creationism and intelligent design; the question of when life begins and ends; the ethics of stem cell research and genetic manipulation; the proper codes of behavior, especially sexual behavior; the rightful roles of women in society; the correct way to raise children; and the appropriate place of religion in the political sphere. Thus, this tension between science and religion continues during our current postmodern times as scientific and secular thought compete with religious traditions and doctrine as the authority for "truth" and moral guidelines for contemporary life.

Second, *multiculturalism* increasingly requires us to recognize myriad worldviews and ways of life, within the United States and globally. This pluralistic reality stands in contrast to unilateral belief systems, both religious and cultural, that have historically

Exhibit 6.3 World Religions, 2010

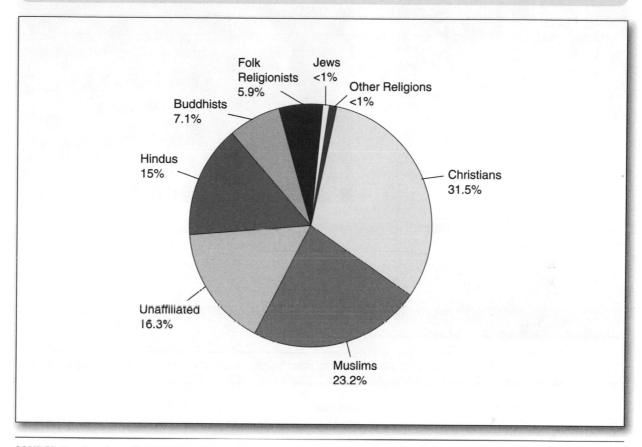

Folk Religionists 5.9%
Jews <1%
Other Religions <1%
Buddhists 7.1%
Hindus 15%
Christians 31.5%
Unaffiliated 16.3%
Muslims 23.2%

SOURCE: Pew-Templeton Global Religious Futures Project, 2014.

NOTE: Folk religionists include followers of African traditional religions, Chinese folk religions, Native American religions, and Australian aboriginal religions.

provided what Peter Berger (1969) calls a "sacred canopy," or the security and certainty of one view of the universe, one answer to profound and mundane questions, and one approach to organizing individual and collective life. Such a unified perspective is difficult to maintain as individuals and whole cultures are increasingly exposed to a religious and spiritual "marketplace" of diverse belief systems and practices, which often challenge the basic tenets previously held as absolute (Warner, 1993).

The potential for conflict is inherent in both modernism and multiculturalism, conflict that becomes especially deadly when combined with the third aspect of globalization—the dispersion

of *modern technologies of warfare.* Violent conflict, often intertwined with religious issues, has been part of human history for thousands of years. But in the current period of globalization, the cost of such conflict has grown unimaginably high in that our arsenal now includes nuclear, biological, and chemical weapons of mass destruction as opposed to stones, clubs, and other primitive weapons. As Lester Kurtz (2012) succinctly states, "Given the destructive capabilities of modern weaponry and the consequent necessity for peaceful coexistence, the potential for religious traditions to promote either chaos or community becomes a crucial factor in the global village" (pp. 279–280).

Photos 6.2a & 6.2b   Religion involves the patterning of spiritual beliefs and practices into social institutions; different cultures focus their beliefs around different central figures.

© iStockphoto.com/Robert Young; © iStockphoto.com/Bryan Busovicki

In light of this complex and ever-changing picture, social workers gain very little real understanding of a person by simply knowing his or her primary religious affiliation. First, religious affiliation may or may not hold great significance for the person, and identification with a religion alone does not indicate depth of involvement. Second, belief, practice, and involvement can be quite varied, even among adherents of the same spiritual tradition or among members of the same family, kinship group, or faith community—even if they all self-identify as Methodist or Muslim or Wiccan. Third, some people feel connected to multiple spiritual perspectives simultaneously, such as a combination of Judaism and Buddhism or traditional Indigenous spiritual beliefs and Christianity. Fourth, the meaning of religious or spiritual affiliation may change across the life course; a person may feel more or less connected to a particular tradition at different points in his or her life. And finally, the meaning of a person's religious or spiritual affiliation must be understood within his or her broader historical, sociopolitical, and cultural context in order for its full significance to be realized. It is important to understand the range of spiritual influences (both religious and nonreligious) that may contribute to anyone's life story and the larger collective realities that impact that story at any particular point in time.

Critical Thinking Questions 6.1

At the beginning of the chapter, you read about the spiritual and religious beliefs of seven people. With which of the stories were you most comfortable? For what reasons? With which of the stories were you least comfortable? For what reasons? How

TRANSPERSONAL THEORIES OF HUMAN DEVELOPMENT

Psychodynamic perspective

The idea that spirituality is an important dimension of human behavior is not a new one in social work or in other helping professions. Although Sigmund Freud (1928) asserted that all religious and spiritual beliefs were either illusions or projections of unconscious wishes, many other early behavioral science theorists viewed the role of spirituality differently.

Developmental perspective

Notably, Carl Jung, a student of Freud's, differed with his former teacher and mentor in regard to the topic of spirituality. Jung's (1933) theory of personality includes physical, mental, and spiritual selves, which all strive for unity and wholeness within each person. In Jung's (1959/1969) view, an important *archetype* (a universal unconscious idea) is "the Spirit" (p. 214). Jung further proposed that the evolution of consciousness and the struggle to find a spiritual outlook on life were the primary developmental tasks in midlife. If this task is successfully accomplished, the result is *individuation*, which Jung defined as "the moment when the finite mind realizes it is rooted in the infinite" (as quoted in Keutzer, 1982, p. 76).

Robert Assagioli (1965, 1973) also emphasized the spiritual dimension in his approach known as *psychosynthesis*. His understanding of the human psyche included the constructs of "higher unconscious" or "superconscious" as the source of creativity and spirituality. In Assagioli's view, some psychological disturbances are best understood as crises of spiritual awakening rather than symptoms of psychopathology. In such cases, the responsibility of the therapist is to facilitate the client's exploration of spiritual possibilities while dealing with the difficulties such awakenings can engender. As Assagioli (1989) defined it, "'spiritual' refers not only to experiences traditionally considered religious but to *all* the states of awareness, all the human functions and activities which have as their common denominator the possession of *values* higher than average" (p. 30, italics in original).

A third major contributor to early formulations on spirituality and human behavior was Abraham Maslow, founding father of humanistic psychology. Maslow (1971) described spirituality as an innate and key element in human nature. In his study of optimally functioning people, he characterized people at the top of his hierarchy as "transcendent self-actualizers" and described them as having (among other traits) a more holistic view of life; a natural tendency toward cooperative action; a tendency to be motivated by truth, goodness, and unity; a greater appreciation for peak experiences; an ability to go beyond their ego self to higher levels of identity; and more awareness of the sacredness of every person and every living thing. Maslow later came to believe that even this definition was not adequate to explain the highest levels of human potential. Near the end of his life, he predicted the emergence of a more expansive understanding of human behavior: "a still 'higher' Fourth Psychology; transpersonal, trans-human, centered in the cosmos, rather than in human needs and interests, going beyond humanness, identity, self-actualization, and the like" (as quoted in Wittine, 1987, p. 53).

Humanistic perspective

Describing this evolution of forces within psychology, Au-Deane Cowley (1993, 1996) delineates four major therapeutic approaches that have emerged over the past century, each developed in response to our understanding of human behavior and human needs at the time.

1. **First force therapies** are based on dynamic theories of human behavior. The prime concern of these therapies is dealing with repression and resolving instinctual conflicts by developing insight.

Psychodynamic perspective

2. **Second force therapies** evolved from behavioral theories. These therapies focus on learned habits and seek to remove symptoms through various processes of direct learning.

3. **Third force therapies** are rooted in existential/ humanistic/experiential theories. They help the person deal with existential despair and seek the actualization of the person's potential through techniques grounded in immediate experiencing.

4. **Fourth force therapies**, based on transpersonal theories, specifically target the spiritual dimension. They focus on helping the person let go of ego attachments—identifications with the mind, body, and social roles—and transcend the self through various spiritually based practices. (Cowley, 1996)

The fourth force builds on the previous three forces and thus incorporates existing knowledge concerning human behavior within its framework. What differentiates the fourth force—the **transpersonal approach**—from other theoretical orientations is the premise that some states of human consciousness and potential go beyond our traditional views of health and normality. These states explicitly address the spiritual dimension of human existence (Cowley & Derezotes, 1994).

The term *transpersonal* literally means "beyond" or "through" the "persona" or "mask" (Wittine, 1987). When applied to theories of human behavior, transpersonal means going beyond identity tied to the individual body, ego, or social roles to include spiritual experience or higher levels of consciousness. The self is experienced as in unity with all others. A major focus of transpersonal theory is on "humanity's highest potential" (Lajoie & Shapiro, 1992, p. 91). Increasingly recognized is the relevance of a transpersonal orientation to the realm of everyday life as well, including the "lower end" of human functioning. Thus, transpersonal practice approaches must "include the whole—not just the high end of human experience but the very personal

realm of ordinary consciousness as well" (Cortright, 1997, p. 13). Several branches of transpersonal thought are currently recognized, including Jungian psychology; depth or archetypal psychology; spiritual psychology; positive psychology; psychosynthesis; and approaches based on the writings of Abraham Maslow, Stanislav Grof, Ken Wilber, Michael Washburn, Frances Vaughan, Roger Walsh, Jorge Ferrer, and Charles Tart, among others. A major objective of all transpersonal theories is to integrate spirituality within a larger framework of human behavior. One key application of transpersonal theory is as a conceptual underpinning for theories that address spiritual development.

Two theorists who have developed comprehensive perspectives on spiritual development are James Fowler and Ken Wilber. Although these two theorists are not the only contributors to this area, they have produced two of the best-known approaches in the field today. The following sections give an overview of these two theories of spiritual development, providing key concepts and discussion of their respective models. Along the way, we consider the people you read about in the case studies at the beginning of this chapter and see how these two perspectives enhance our understanding of their current life situations and spiritual journeys.

Fowler's Stages of Faith Development

James Fowler's (1981, 1995) theory of faith development grew out of

359 in-depth interviews conducted from 1972 to 1981 in Boston, Chicago, and Toronto. The sample was overwhelmingly White (97.8%), largely Christian (over 85%), evenly divided by gender, and widely distributed in terms of age (3.5 years to 84 years). Each semistructured interview consisted of more than 30 questions about life-shaping experiences and relationships, present values and commitments, and religion. After the responses were analyzed, interviewees were placed in one of

six **faith stages**. Fowler found a generally positive relationship between age and stage development; as age increased, so did the tendency for persons to be in higher stages. However, only a minority of persons revealed characteristics of Stages 5 or 6, regardless of age.

To Fowler (1996), **faith** is broader than religious faith, creed, or belief. It can, in fact, be expressed even by people who do not believe in God. Instead, faith is viewed as a universal aspect of human existence,

> an integral, centering process, underlying the formation of beliefs, values, and meanings that (1) gives coherence and direction to people's lives, (2) links them in shared trusts and loyalties with others, (3) grounds their personal stances and communal loyalties in a sense of relatedness to a larger frame of reference, and (4) enables them to face and deal with the limited conditions of life, relying upon that which has the quality of ultimacy in their lives. (p. 56)

Thus, Fowler's definition of faith is more aligned with the definition of spirituality given at the beginning of this chapter and is clearly distinguished from more specific notions of particular beliefs or religious traditions.

Another important concept in Fowler's theory is the **ultimate environment** (also known as the ultimate reality or simply the ultimate)—the highest level of reality. Faith is not only your internal image of the ultimate environment but also your relationship with that image. Your view of the ultimate environment—as personal or impersonal, trustworthy or not dependable, capable of dialogue or silent, purposeful or based on chance—and your relationship with it is an evolving, dynamic process strongly influenced by your experiences throughout the life course. Thus, Fowler's *faith* is best understood as a verb, or a way of being, versus a noun, or a thing that is unchangeable.

Fowler's stages of faith development should not be viewed as goals to be achieved or as steps necessary for "salvation." Rather, they help us understand a person's values, beliefs, and sense of meaning and help us better appreciate the tasks, tensions, and challenges at various points in life. They also reveal increasing capacity in terms of cognitive functioning; moral reasoning; perspective taking; critical reflection and dialectical thought; understanding of symbols, myths, and rituals; deeper faith commitments; and openness to and acceptance of difference. Here is a brief description of Fowler's faith stages.

Pre-stage: primal faith (infancy). If consistent nurturance is experienced, the infant develops a sense of trust and safety about the universe and the divine. Negative experiences produce images of the ultimate as untrustworthy, punitive, or arbitrary.

Stage 1: intuitive-projective faith (early childhood, beginning about age 2). The young child's new tools of speech and symbols give rise to fluid and magical thoughts, based on intuition and imagination. Faith is fantasy filled and imitative and can be powerfully influenced by examples, actions, stories of significant others, and familial and cultural taboos.

Stage 2: mythic-literal faith (middle childhood, beginning about age 6, and beyond). The child begins to take on stories, beliefs, and practices that symbolize belonging to his or her community. There is a high degree of conformity to community beliefs and practices. The ability to participate in concrete operational thinking allows distinction between fantasy and reality. There is increased capacity to take the perspective of others, and ideas about reciprocity and fairness become central.

Stage 3: synthetic-conventional faith (adolescence and beyond). For many adolescents, the capacity for abstract thinking and manipulation of concepts affects the process of developing faith as well as overall identity. Authority is perceived as external and is found in traditional authority figures, but there is an increased influence of peers, school and work associates, the media, and popular culture. Beliefs and values are often deeply felt but not critically examined or systematically reflected on. Symbols are not perceived as literally as in Stage 2.

Stage 4: individuative-reflective faith (young adulthood and beyond). Beginning in young adulthood, many people experience an increased responsibility for their own commitments, lifestyles, beliefs, and attitudes. Previously held creeds, symbols, and stories are demythologized through critical analysis. The ultimate becomes more explicit and personally meaningful, and symbols are reshaped into more powerful conceptualizations.

Stage 5: conjunctive faith (midlife and beyond). A minority of adults begin in midlife to rework the past and become open to voices of the "deeper self." They develop the capacity for "both/and" versus "either/or" thinking and come to tolerate ambiguity and paradox, taking into account and looking for balance in such polarities as independence and connection and determinism and free will. They recognize that there are many truths and engage in critical examination of their own beliefs, myths, and prejudices. They expand their definition of community and their sense of connection and responsibility to others.

Stage 6: universalizing faith (midlife and beyond). A very small minority of adults develop the capacity to truly embrace paradox. They develop an enlarged awareness of justice and injustice. The vision of truth is expanded to recognize partial truths. Symbols, myths, and rituals are appreciated and cherished at a deeper level. Divisions within the human family are felt with vivid pain because of the recognition of the possibility of the inclusive union of all beings. They lead selfless lives of service and action for justice aimed at the transformation of humankind.

Now let us consider the stories revealed in the seven case studies through the lens of Fowler's faith stages, based on both his early research and later theoretical refinements. In Fowler's model, our early experiences set the stage for later faith development. Given what we know about the seven people described in the case studies, it is probably safe to assume that most of them were able to develop at least a "good enough" fund of basic trust and mutuality during the *Pre-stage: primal faith* for later development of a relationship with the ultimate. A possible exception to this is Trudy, whose early years were marked by parental substance abuse and violence. It would be important

to know when these problems first appeared within her family and how much they interfered with her initial bonding with her mother and father, as these factors would be influential in both her ability to trust and her internal sense of the ultimate as she moves through her life.

None of the seven case studies tells us much about the development of early images of the ultimate environment during *Stage 1: intuitive-projective faith*. However, we can speculate that these images were probably drawn from each person's particular faith affiliation. For Caroline, Matthew, and Leon, these initial conceptions of the divine would have been grounded within their particular Christian denominations, while Naomi would have developed her sense of the ultimate as it was reflected in her Jewish faith. Caroline's partner in the comparative religions class exercise would most likely have developed her sense of the divine based on examples, modes, actions, and stories that she experienced in her family's belief in Islam. Jean-Joseph's sense of the ultimate would have been influenced by a combination of Catholic symbols, narratives, and rituals and the spiritual beliefs and practices of Vodoun. Trudy and Beth were not raised in any particular religious tradition but found meaning and purpose in other ways. Trudy found solace in nature and Beth found significance through social justice activities. It would be important to talk with both of them about how their early experiences affected their sense of what they held to be most important in their lives and to not assume their lack of exposure to organized religion meant they had no early images or experiences with the ultimate, as spirituality is experienced and expressed through both religious and nonreligious means. In working with all seven people, we would want to understand how this process of image making was handled by their families and others in their lives and how much support they were given for their own intuition and imagination during this time.

If Fowler had interviewed any of the seven during middle childhood, he more than likely would have seen many of the aspects of *Stage 2: mythic-literal faith* reflected in this group. It would be important to understand the role of their childhood spiritual communities in shaping each person's sense of the world and his or her place in it. It would be particularly useful to explore the stories and narratives they remember from that time, especially as they transmitted values, attitudes, and norms for behavior. For example, discussing with Leon what he understood as his church's core principles relative to sin and redemption would be invaluable in comprehending his current struggle. It would also be important to understand the messages Caroline received regarding her own religion as the only true faith. For Naomi and Jean-Joseph, it would be key to talk about how their communities handled being believers of a nondominant (or "other") religion, in a culture where Christianity is the dominant faith and is generally seen as "the norm." For Beth, it might mean understanding the meaning of the stories she heard about her grandparents' experiences as union organizers. For all seven people, it would be vital to explore what helped create a sense of order and meaning at this stage of life and what provided a sense of guidance and belonging.

The events that occur during adolescence generally have a significant effect on faith development during *Stage 3: synthetic-conventional faith*, as this is the point where people are heavily engaged in the process of identity development, including spiritual identity. It is also a time when the person's world is greatly expanded, bringing diverse and complex ideas and experiences regarding all of life. Adolescents must make coherent meaning from all the different messages they receive from family, school, work, media, and the larger sociocultural realm. A person's faith understanding can help synthesize various values and viewpoints and provide a basis for forming a stable identity and worldview. There is a tendency to construct one's faith through conforming to a set of values and beliefs that are most familiar and to defer to whatever authority is most meaningful. As the two people most recently in this life stage, both Caroline and Leon illustrate the strong impetus to form a faith identity that provides a solid sense of self and a feeling of belonging to a particular group. For both of them, the faith of their families and their home churches were highly instrumental in this process. As another young person at this stage of life, Beth is also in the midst of developing an identity. For her this identity is composed of attributes of personal integrity and commitment to actions grounded in the socially conscious, ethical framework of her family. For all of them, entry into the next stage of life brought questions regarding the beliefs and values of these key social institutions and an urge to explore beyond what they had previously known.

If we look at Caroline's, Leon's, and Beth's lives as they move into *Stage 4: individuative-reflective faith*, we see young people grappling with key questions about themselves and their belief systems. Caroline's experiences at college have opened the door to considering different worldviews, which she handles with an approach-avoidance strategy. On the one hand, she is troubled by her experience with others who believe and practice differently from the way she does, but on the other hand, she is increasingly curious about these differences. For Leon, the struggle is more difficult, as he is attempting to live with values, attitudes, and beliefs that tell him a core aspect of his identity is unacceptable. Beth is being challenged to reconsider whether she has misperceptions or even biases about people who are religious and the possible positive role religion might play in societal change. For all of these young adults, the task ahead is to construct a unique, individual self (identity) and outlook (**ideology**) from previously held conventional beliefs and develop an approach to faith that is both personal and workable. It is important to recognize that this task does not exclude Beth as a nonreligious person, as "faith" in Fowler's (1996) terms involves developing "an integral, centering process, underlying the formation of beliefs, values, and meanings" for living one's life—whether or not this is found through a particular religious orientation (p. 56). Thus, the process at this point for all three young people requires a level of critical reflection and a capacity to struggle with conflicts and tensions that were not yet fully developed in the previous stage. As a social worker, you would want to facilitate this process while being mindful of the social work principles of self-determination and empowerment.

Naomi and David provide another example of *individuative-reflective faith*, even though they are considerably older than Caroline, Leon, and Beth. When they were in their late teens and early 20s, their identity formation led them to a more secular worldview, as Naomi lessened her involvement with her faith and David continued to base his identity and outlook on more humanistic understandings of self and the world. But the creation of a family caused them both to reconsider the role of Judaism in their lives as they realized their desire for a spiritual community. As their children grew, their involvement with their temple has provided the personal and workable framework characteristic of this phase. That framework is now being challenged by Naomi's illness and is leading both her and David to a deeper reflection of their faith. Social work with this couple would involve supporting this reflection, as well as exploring with them possible supports they could receive from their rabbi and larger faith community in dealing with Naomi's health crisis.

According to Lownsdale (1997), only 1 in 6 adults reflects characteristics of *Stage 5: conjunctive faith*. Of our seven life stories, only Matthew's provides glimpses of this faith stage. Although there is not much information about Matthew's internal reflection on the paradoxes of life (a key criterion of *conjunctive faith*), we do know that he was able to work through the loss of his wife, and other losses that inevitably come with aging, to embrace a new chapter in his life. As a social worker, you might find it useful to explore with Matthew his understanding of life's paradoxes (such as God being both personal and abstract and life being both rational and mysterious) and talk with him about any previously unrealized parts of himself that are now emerging. What is apparent in Matthew's story is his enthusiastic willingness to acknowledge and honor multiple faith perspectives, while being open to new depths within his own spirituality. We also see him engaging in service for others and concern for the natural world. All of these activities

suggest a perspective that goes beyond egocentric and ethnocentric views to a more **worldcentric** (identification with the entire global human family) and **ecocentric** (identification with the whole ecosphere, of which humans are only one part) way of being in the world. As a result of these commitments, he is experiencing a renewed sense of purpose, meaning, and connection in his life. All of these are characteristic of persons of *conjunctive faith*, which brings a broader social consciousness, a passion for social justice, and a wider and deeper understanding of the sacred.

It is clear that none of the seven people reflects the self-sacrificial life of Fowler's *Stage 6: universalizing faith*. Persons at this stage are exceedingly rare, perhaps two to three individuals per thousand (Lownsdale, 1997). Given the exceptional nature of such persons, it is not surprising that the seven case studies do not reveal examples of this faith stage. Some might point to Trudy's total immersion in spiritual practices as evidence of this stage, but another perspective on her development is offered later in this chapter during discussion of the second theorist, Ken Wilber, and his integral theory of consciousness.

Finally, we must address Jean-Joseph's spiritual path, which includes a syncretism (combination) of Catholicism and Vodoun, or "serving the spirits." If a social worker embedded in dominant Western culture assessed his faith development solely from the standpoint of this context, he or she might determine that Jean-Joseph falls within an early stage, either *mythic-literal* or perhaps even *intuitive-projective*. This determination would no doubt lead to a conclusion that this 50-year-old man is an example of underdeveloped faith and may lead to interventions aimed at helping him give up his "primitive and immature" beliefs and practices for a worldview seen as more appropriate for mature adults. If this was the stance taken by a practitioner, he or she would be showing ethnocentric and religiocentric bias, as well as cultural insensitivity. Viewed within his sociocultural context, Jean-Joseph is exhibiting a faith stage that could be more accurately determined to be at least *synthetic-conventional*, given its congruence with the spiritual beliefs and practices of his Haitian culture. Upon further exploration with him—with an open mind, respect, and humility for the limits of one's knowledge about his religion—a social worker may discover that Jean-Joseph displays characteristics of higher stages of faith development. This highlights the need for social workers to constantly be aware of their own lack of knowledge and their internalized biases when working with religious and spiritual traditions unfamiliar to them, in order to engage in culturally sensitive service respectful of those traditions (Weaver, 2011).

Wilber's Integral Theory of Consciousness

Developmental perspective

Ken Wilber first published his transpersonal theory of development in 1977 in *The Spectrum of Consciousness* but has continued to develop and refine his model in numerous writings. His work reflects a unique integration of biology, history, psychology, sociology, philosophy, and religion. It is rooted in both conventional Western knowledge and contemplative-mystical traditions of Eastern religions and other spiritual perspectives. Wilber (2006) currently refers to his approach as an "integral theory of consciousness." He identifies it as "integral" because it explores human development across **four quadrants** or vantage points (interior-individual, exterior-individual, interior-collective, and exterior-collective) and through *three levels of consciousness* (pre-personal, personal, and transpersonal). He posits that human development must be understood through the lenses of subjective awareness of *personal meaning and sense of self* (the interior of individuals), objective knowledge of the *physical body and observable behaviors* (the external part of individuals), intersubjective understanding of *sociocultural values and shared meanings* (the interior of collectives), and interobjective knowledge of *institutional structures and systemic forces* (the external part of collectives). Within each quadrant, the three levels of consciousness unfold in a way that reflects the unique properties of that particular quadrant (see Exhibit 6.4). According to Wilber, integrated knowledge of these areas is

---

Exhibit 6.4 Wilber's Integral Theory: Four Quadrants and Three Levels of Consciousness

	Interior	Exterior
Individual	*Upper Left Quadrant* (Individual Interior) "I" INTENTIONAL (Personal meaning and sense of self) *subjective truthfulness*	*Upper Right Quadrant* (Individual Exterior) "IT" BEHAVIORAL (Physical body and observable behaviors) *objective truth*
Collective	*Lower Left Quadrant* (Collective Interior) "WE" CULTURAL (Culture and shared values) *intersubjective justness*	*Lower Right Quadrant* (Collective Exterior) "ITS" SOCIAL (Institutions, systems, nature) *intersubjective functional fit*

SOURCE: Wilber, 1996, 2006.

required for an accurate and complete understanding of human behavior.

Wilber sees the ultimate goal of human development (at the individual and collective levels) as evolving to a higher, nondual level of consciousness well integrated into personal and societal functioning. This requires movement through the three stages of spiritual development, marked by increasingly complex, comprehensive, and inclusive understandings of spirituality and expanded consciousness about reality. We look closer at Wilber's description of transpersonal levels within the *interior of individuals*, as this is a major contribution of his model to theories of spiritual development. But first we need to review some key concepts underpinning integral theory.

As already noted, Wilber (1995, 2000a, 2000b, 2006) agrees with other transpersonal theorists that consciousness spans from pre-personal to personal to transpersonal. This

> Systems perspective

overall spectrum is reflected in the world's major spiritual traditions and is referred to as the "great chain of being" (matter to body to mind to soul to spirit). Wilber points out that because this process is not strictly linear, it is best understood as a "great nest of being" in that it is really a series of enfolding and unfolding spheres or spirals. In other words, spirit transcends but includes soul, which transcends but includes mind, which transcends but includes body, which transcends but includes matter. This process of incorporation is rooted in the concept of a *holon*, or "that which, being a *whole* in one context, is simultaneously a *part* in another" (Wilber, 1995, p. 18, italics in original). Thus, Wilber refers to his spectrum of consciousness as a *holarchy* (rather than a hierarchy), because it reflects an ordering of holons (or increasing levels of complexity and wholeness) throughout the developmental process. It may be helpful to visualize this as a set of Russian nesting dolls, with each larger doll both including and going beyond the smaller ones. With each larger level (or doll), one expands his or her awareness of reality and develops a larger repertoire of individual and social functioning.

There are five major components relative to the development of interior individual consciousness in Wilber's theory. The following gives an overview of each of these components, leading to a more detailed discussion of the higher or transpersonal levels of consciousness.

1. The term **levels** (or waves) **of consciousness** refers to various developmental milestones that unfold within the human psyche. As our discussion of holarchy suggests, this is not a strictly linear process. Rather, it involves "all sorts of regressions, spirals, temporary leaps forward, peak experiences, and so on" (Wilber, 1996, p. 148). A person does not have to master all the competencies of one level to move on to the next; in fact, most people at any given level will often respond about 50% from that level, 25% from the level above and 25% from the level below. However, levels cannot be skipped over, as each level incorporates the capacities of earlier levels. Drawing from various cross-cultural sources, Wilber posits several major levels of consciousness, all of which are *potentials*—but not *givens*—at the onset of development. We consider these in more detail following introduction of the other major components.

2. Multiple **lines** (or streams) **of consciousness** flow through the basic levels of consciousness. Wilber (2000a) identifies the following developmental lines as areas for which we have empirical evidence: "morals, affects, self-identity, psychosexuality, ideas of the good, role taking, socio-emotional capacity, creativity, altruism, several lines that can be called 'spiritual' (care, openness, concern, religious faith, meditative stages), joy, communicative competence, modes of space and time, death-seizure, needs, worldviews, logico-mathematical competence, kinesthetic skills, gender identity, and empathy" (p. 28). He proposes that these lines or streams are relatively independent of one another in that they can develop at different rates within the same individual. Thus, a person can be at a relatively high level of development in some lines (such as cognition), medium in others (such as morals), and low in still others (such as spirituality). Thus, although most *individual* lines

unfold sequentially, *overall development* does not and can be a relatively uneven process.

3. Wilber also includes in his model **states of consciousness**, which include both ordinary (e.g., waking, sleeping, dreaming) and nonordinary experiences (e.g., peak experiences, religious experiences, altered states, and meditative or contemplative states). He points out that research has shown that a person at virtually any *level* of consciousness can have an altered *state* of consciousness, including a peak or spiritual experience. Whatever the actual experience, individuals can only interpret these experiences at their current level of consciousness and may have to grow and develop further to really accommodate the full depth or meaning of the experience. In order for these *temporary* experiences or states to become *permanent* aspects of a person's level of consciousness, they must become fully realized through continual development.

4. Wilber proposes that levels, lines, and states of consciousness are all navigated by the self or **self-system**. He posits at least two parts to the self: (a) an observing self (an inner subject or watcher) and (b) an observed self (the object that is watched and can be known in some way). As a person negotiates each unfolding *level* and various *lines* of consciousness and integrates experiences from various *states* of consciousness, he or she moves from a narrower to a deeper and wider sense of self and self-identity.

5. At each point of development, the self goes through a **fulcrum**, or switch point. Specifically, each time the self moves to a different level on the developmental spiral, it goes through a three-step process. First, the self becomes comfortable and eventually identifies with the basic functioning of that level. Second, new experiences begin to challenge the way of being at this level, and the self begins to differentiate or "disidentify" with it. Third, the self begins to move toward and identify with the next level while integrating the functioning of the previous basic structure into the sense of self. If the person is able to negotiate

these fulcrum points successfully, development is largely nonproblematic. However, disturbances at different fulcrum points tend to produce various pathologies.

As noted earlier, Wilber's spectrum of consciousness can be further categorized into the three phases of development: the pre-personal (pre-egoic) phase, the personal (egoic) phase, and the transpersonal (transegoic) phase. The six levels of consciousness at the pre-personal and personal phases in Wilber's theory are very similar to the first five of Fowler's faith stages and are not presented in detail here. (See Wilber [1995, 1996, 1997a, 1997b] for a detailed discussion of these levels.) A review of the levels of pre-personal and personal phases of consciousness should sound familiar to students of conventional approaches to human development. In contrast, the levels of the transpersonal phase (and the language used to describe them) are most likely unfamiliar to those not well versed in contemplative Eastern ideas about human development. However, this synthesis of both conventional and contemplative approaches and the inclusion of higher-order levels of development is Wilber's primary contribution to our attempts to understand human behavior.

As one moves into the transpersonal or transegoic phase, the world and life in general are perceived in more holistic and interconnected terms. There is movement from an egocentric and ethnocentric perspective to a worldcentric and ecocentric grasp of the complete interdependence of all things in the cosmos. There is also the realization that the self is more than a body, mind, and culture-bound social roles and awareness of a self that exists beyond time-space limits or ego boundaries. This realization facilitates a growing awareness of how all beings are unified within a singular or nondual ultimate reality. As people move further into the transpersonal or transegoic phase, they retain all the capacities developed during previous levels and incorporate these functions into expanded consciousness experienced at higher, transpersonal levels. The three transpersonal levels are described shortly. As you read through each one, focus on what the descriptions say about a person's *level of consciousness* at each level. In other words, what is the person perceiving or what is he or she aware of beyond the ordinary states of reality (waking, sleeping, dreaming) common to most people?

1. *Level 7 (psychic)* is characterized by a continuing evolution of consciousness as the observing self develops more and more depth. Wilber refers to this evolving inner sense as the *witness*, because it represents an awareness that moves beyond ordinary reality (sensorimotor, rational, existential) into the transpersonal (beyond ego) levels. A distinguishing spiritual experience at this level is a strong interconnectedness of self with nature. For example, a person may temporarily become one with a mountain or bird or tree. This type of experience is not psychotic fusion—the person is still very clear about his or her own personal boundaries—but it is a strong awareness of communion with the natural world. At this point, one's higher self becomes a *world soul* and experiences *nature mysticism*. Because of this powerful experience of connection and identification, there is a natural deepening of compassion for all living things, including nature itself.

2. *Level 8 (subtle)* is characterized by an awareness of more subtle processes than are commonly experienced in gross, ordinary states of waking consciousness. Examples of such processes are interior light and sounds; awareness of transpersonal archetypes; and extreme states of bliss, love, and compassion. At this point, even nature is transcended, yet it is understood as a manifest expression of the ultimate. One's sense of connection and identification is extended to communion with a deity, or union with God, by whatever name. Thus, consciousness at this level is not just nature mysticism—union with the natural world—but gives way to *deity mysticism*—union with the divine. This level of consciousness can be experienced in many forms, often rooted in the person's personal or cultural history. For example, a Christian may feel union with Christ, while a Buddhist might experience connection with the Buddha.

3. *Level 9 (causal)* transcends all distinctions between subject and object (even self and God). The witness is experienced as pure consciousness and pure awareness, prior to the manifestation of anything. Thus, this level is said to be timeless, spaceless, and objectless. As Wilber (1996) describes it, "Space, time, objects—all of those merely parade by. But you are the Witness, the pure Seer that is itself pure Emptiness, pure Freedom, pure Openness, the great Emptiness through which the entire parade passes, never touching you, never tempting you, never hurting you, never consoling you" (p. 224). This level is pure *formless mysticism*, in that all objects, even God as a perceived form, vanish into pure consciousness. This level of consciousness is sometimes referred to as "full Enlightenment, ultimate release, pure nirvana" (Wilber, 1996, p. 226). But it is still not the final story.

Wilber also proposes a *Level 10 (nondual)*, which is characterized by disidentification with even the witness. The interior sense of *being* a witness disappears, and the witness turns out to be everything that is witnessed. At this level, emptiness becomes pure consciousness itself. There is no sense of two, there is only one (hence the name *nondual*). Essentially, the person's awareness has moved beyond nature, deity, and formless mysticism to *nondual mysticism*. Furthermore, it is not really a level among other levels but is rather the condition or reality of *all* levels. It is simultaneously the source, the process, and the realization of consciousness. Wilber does not depict the nondual as a separate level in his illustration of the structures of consciousness because it represents the ground or origin of all other levels—the paper on which the figure is drawn.

With this model, Wilber is proposing that the personal phase of development, with its achievement of strong ego development and self-actualization, is not the highest potential of human existence, although a necessary point along the way. Rather, the ultimate goal of human development is the transpersonal or transegoic phase—beyond ego or self to self-transcendence and unity with the ultimate reality. The capacity for attaining the highest levels of consciousness is seen as innate within each human being, although Wilber acknowledges that very few people reach the higher transpersonal levels.

As for the characteristic pathologies, or problems in development at each level, all the disorders or conditions that Wilber identifies at the lower phases of development are well recognized within conventional diagnostic approaches (albeit with different labels). It is again at the transpersonal phase that Wilber (2000a) strikes new ground, by including what he calls psychic disorders and subtle or causal pathologies. Examples of such problems in living include unsought spiritual awakenings, psychic inflation, split life goals, integration-identification failure, pseudo nirvana, and failure to differentiate or integrate. Likewise, the treatment modalities that Wilber identifies at the pre-personal and personal phases are well-known to most social workers. However, the approaches Wilber proposes for transpersonal phase disorders—nature mysticism, deity mysticism, and formless mysticism—are largely unknown (and sound a bit strange) to the majority of helping professionals. But they have been used in non-Western cultures for centuries. Furthermore, they are becoming more widely accepted in the United States as effective, complementary treatment approaches (e.g., prayer and meditation, yoga, visualization and spiritual imagery, focusing, dreamwork, dis-identification techniques, bodywork, acupuncture, journaling, intuition techniques). Wilber (1996, 2000a) stresses that practitioners should be able to correctly identify the level of development in order to provide the most appropriate treatment. If not correctly identified, there is the probability of what Wilber (1995, 2000b) calls the "pre/trans fallacy," which occurs when a problem at a transpersonal level (such as a spiritual awakening) may be treated as if it were a pre-personal or personal disorder (a psychotic episode or existential crisis) or vice versa.

Let's revisit Trudy's story to better understand what Wilber is talking about here. Trudy is currently focusing most of her time and energy toward developing her spiritual self in order to achieve enlightenment. She is meditating 5 hours a day, is engaged with a daily yoga practice, and limits her reading and interpersonal contacts to those she identifies as spiritual. Given that most transpersonal theorists and spiritual leaders would agree that engagement in some type of spiritual practice is necessary for spiritual growth, one might characterize Trudy's behavior as that of a disciplined, spiritual seeker. But there is evidence in her story that Trudy is caught up in **spiritual bypassing**, a term first coined by John Welwood (2000), which he describes as "the tendency to use spiritual practice to bypass or avoid dealing with certain personal or emotional 'unfinished business'" (p. 11). He states that persons struggling with life's developmental challenges are particularly susceptible to spiritual bypassing, as they attempt to *find themselves by giving themselves up*—or prematurely trying to move beyond their ego to self-transcendence, ignoring their personal and emotional needs. This attempt to create a new "spiritual" identity in order to avoid the pain of working through unresolved psycho-social issues does not work and frequently causes additional problems. As Trudy's social worker, you would want to do a thorough assessment, taking into account the substantial unresolved trauma and losses in her life. To ignore these issues and focus only on supporting her quest for enlightenment would be to commit Wilber's "pre/trans fallacy." As a responsible and ethical social worker, you would help her address these unresolved issues at the personal, and perhaps even pre-personal, level while maintaining respect for her spiritual perspective. You would also help her discern the appropriate role of her spiritual practices in support of her overall growth and development. Consulting with a spiritual teacher or a transpersonal practitioner, with Trudy's permission, also might be helpful in this case.

Likewise, if a practitioner identifies a client's spiritual practices as signs of a serious problem simply because they are unfamiliar or seem "strange," he or she would be moving to the other side of the "pre/trans fallacy"—treating potentially spiritual or transpersonal experiences as if they were psychological disorders. The potential for this type of error is evident in the case of Jean-Joseph and his family. If this family sought help from conventional health care services, while also following traditional spiritually based healing processes, as a social worker your task would be to help the family and the medical professionals find a way to work together. This is not always an easy task, as is poignantly illustrated in Anne Fadiman's (1998) book, *The Spirit Catches You and You Fall Down*, which tells the tragic story of a Hmong child with epilepsy who becomes brain-dead because of the failure of professionals to understand unfamiliar spiritual worldviews and negotiate cultural differences. This true account highlights the critical need for social workers to develop the knowledge, values, and skills of spiritually sensitive practice in order to serve clients from diverse spiritual traditions.

Summary and Critique of Fowler's and Wilber's Theories

Both Fowler's and Wilber's models of individual spiritual development reflect fourth force theory in that they incorporate the first three forces (dynamic, behavior, and existential/humanistic/experiential theories). In fact, Fowler and Wilber use many of the same theorists (e.g., Piaget, Kohlberg, Maslow) as foundations for their own work, and both are delineating higher and more transcendent levels of human development than have been previously proposed by Western theories. In later writings, both theorists also offer additional conceptual formulations at the larger sociocultural levels (Fowler, 1996; Wilber, 2000b).

The major difference between the two models in terms of individual development is that Wilber provides more substance and specification than Fowler does about what transpersonal levels of development look like and how they evolve. Wilber also provides more detailed descriptions of the potential pitfalls of spiritual development than Fowler, who provides only a general overview of the possible dangers or deficits of development at each of his faith stages. However, Fowler provides more specification about the content and process of spiritual development at the pre-personal and personal phases. In terms of their utility for social work practice, we could say that Fowler's model is more *descriptive* and Wilber's is more *prescriptive*. Both theories have been critiqued in a number of areas. An overview of these critiques is presented next.

First, as developmental models, Fowler's and Wilber's models are open

> Conflict perspective

to the criticisms of all developmental perspectives, including charges of dominant-group bias. Such perspectives do not pay enough attention to social, economic, political, and historical factors and the role of power dynamics and oppression in human development. Developmental perspectives are also said to convey the idea that there is only one right way to proceed down the developmental path and thus display an ethnocentrism often rooted in middle-class, heterosexual, Anglo-Saxon male life experience.

Both Fowler and Wilber might counter by pointing out that familial, cultural, and historical contexts are considered in their models. Wilber, in particular, would highlight the extensive use of cross-cultural knowledge in the development of his theory and point to the cessation of ethnocentrism as a major characteristic of his later stages of consciousness. He would also stress the integral nature of his more current theoretical developments, which pay equal attention to *exterior* impacts on spiritual development as to *interior* aspects (Wilber, 2000b, 2001, 2006). Both theorists would also support the notion of many paths in spiritual development, although they would say that these many paths have common features in their evolution.

A second critique of both theories is their relative lack of attention to the spiritual capacities and potentialities of children, focusing more on the emergence of spiritual issues in adulthood. This is due to the assertion that higher levels of cognitive functioning (capacity for formal operations and abstract thought) are necessary to fully experience and incorporate spiritual experience. A number of writers have contested this assertion, proposing that childhood is a unique time of enhanced, not diminished, spiritual awareness (Coles, 1990; Hay, Nye, & Murphy, 1996; Levine, 1999). They base this viewpoint on in-depth interviews with children ranging in age from 6 to 11 (Hay & Nye, 2006), which often revealed a richness and depth regarding spirituality that is generally not expected of people of this age, including a variety of spiritual experiences and epiphanies such as archetypical mythical dreams; visionary experiences; profound insights about self-identity, life, and death; and heightened capacities for compassion for all living things. Results from a national survey of seasoned social workers who work with children and adolescents reveal that practitioners generally see the relevance of religion and spirituality in the lives of children and that they encounter youth who present spiritual issues in practice (Kvarfordt & Sheridan, 2007).

Wilber (2000a) concedes that children can have a variety of spiritual experiences, including peak experiences that provide glimpses of the transpersonal realm, but he states that these incidents are experienced and incorporated within the child's pre-personal or personal stage of development. Regardless of the particular developmental level, there clearly is a need for further exploration of children's spirituality in order to understand their unique spiritual experiences, developmental processes, and needs. Similarly, there is also a need to revisit assumptions about the spiritual experiences and capacities of adults who have lower cognitive functioning, either congenitally or as a result of injury.

A third critique concerns empirical investigation of the theories. Although Fowler's model was developed through an inductive research process and Wilber's formulations are grounded in a synthesis of many lines of research and philosophical analysis, there is an ongoing need for empirical verification of both models. Empirical exploration of Fowler's faith stages has provided both support and critique for his framework (see Slee, 1996; Streib, 2005, for reviews of this work). Similarly, there have been more than 150 articles published on Integral Theory over the past decade

(Esbjörn-Hargens, 2010), providing both support and challenge to some of the theory's key tenets. The fact that findings are not conclusive regarding Fowler's and Wilber's theories is understandable, given the difficulties of empirical investigation in such an abstract realm. It is difficult enough to operationalize and measure such concepts as formal operational cognition or self-esteem; the challenge of investigating faith development or transcendence is even more daunting. Nonetheless, strategies from both positivist and constructivist research approaches are currently available to study interior states and subjective experiences of meaning as well as biophysical manifestations of different states of consciousness. (See Chapter 1 for a review of positivist and constructivist research approaches.) As is true for all theories of human behavior, transpersonal models such as Fowler's and Wilber's need to be specifically tested and refined through the research process. This research also must be replicated with different groups (defined by sex and gender, age, race, ethnicity, socioeconomic status, geopolitical membership, and the like) in order to explore the universality of the models.

In conclusion, both Fowler and Wilber provide perspectives beyond our traditional biopsychosocial framework that allow us to better understand human development and functioning, and they suggest a direction for working with people from diverse spiritual perspectives. Their theories are major contributions to human behavior theory. However, we also need viable practice theories and practice models that explicitly address the spiritual dimension. There have been promising developments in this area. Examples include Smith's (1995) transegoic model for dealing with death and other losses; Cowley's (1999) transpersonal approach for working with couples and families; Hickson and Phelps's (1998) model for facilitating women's spirituality; and Clark's (2007) model for working with spirituality, culture, and diverse worldviews. There are also practice models that directly integrate spirituality within biopsychosocial approaches. Examples are Almaas's (1995, 1996) diamond approach, which incorporates object relations and body sensing within Sufism, and Grof's (2003; Grof & Bennett, 1992) holotropic breathwork model, which combines bodywork and altered states of consciousness to address unresolved psychological issues from earlier points in development. Finally, Cortright (1997) provides a good overview of how a transpersonal orientation can be generally incorporated within psychoanalytic and existential therapies, and Mikulas (2002) offers a practice approach that integrates a transpersonal perspective with behavioral approaches. All of these developments reflect a synthesis of transpersonal with earlier therapeutic modalities (first, second, and third force therapies). As with human behavior theories of spiritual development, these practice theories and models also must be tested and continually refined to determine their utility and applicability for a wide range of client situations.

Critical Thinking Questions 6.2

Fowler and Wilber both think of spirituality in terms of development to higher levels of faith or consciousness over time. Do you think this is a helpful way to think about spirituality? Explain. Is it a helpful way to think about your own spiritual life? Explain. Do you see any cultural biases in either of the theories? Explain.

THE ROLE OF SPIRITUALITY IN SOCIAL WORK

Canda and Furman (2010) outline five broad historical phases that trace the development of linkages between spirituality and social work in the United States. An overview of these phases is presented next.

1. *Indigenous precolonial period.* This period includes the thousands of years when Indigenous cultures in North America employed a variety of spiritually based approaches to healing and mutual support. These practices, discussed in greater detail later in the chapter, focused beyond

human welfare to include the well-being of other living beings and the earth itself. Many of these traditional ways continue into the present, both outside of and within social work (Baskin, 2006; Brave Heart, 2001; Bucko & Iron Cloud, 2008).

2. *Sectarian origins.* This phase began with the colonial period and lasted through the first 20 years of the 20th century. Early human services, institutions, and social welfare policy were significantly influenced by Judeo-Christian worldviews on charity, communal responsibility, and social justice (Leiby, 1985; Lowenberg, 1988; Popple & Leighninger, 2005). At this time, there were also competing explanations of human behavior: on the one hand, an emphasis on distinguishing individual moral blame or merit (e.g., the worthy versus unworthy poor) and on the other hand, a focus on social reform and social justice (e.g., Jewish communal service and Christian social gospel). Human service providers typically had a strong spiritual foundation for their work but offered service through nonsectarian means (e.g., Jane Addams and the settlement house movement). Indigenous, African American, and Spanish and French Catholic spiritual perspectives also contributed to the evolution of social work during this time frame (Martin & Martin, 2002; Van Hook, Hugen, & Aguilar, 2001).

3. *Professionalization and secularization.* Beginning in the 1920s and continuing through the 1970s, social work began to distance itself from its early sectarian roots. This movement mirrored a shift within the larger society, which began to replace moral explanations of human problems with a scientific, rational understanding of human behavior. The social work profession increasingly relied on scientific empiricism and secular humanism as the major foundations for its values, ethics, and practice approaches (Imre, 1984; Siporin, 1986). This period also witnessed social work's reliance on a variety of emerging psychological and sociological theories (such as psychoanalytic, behavioral, and social functionalism), which did not recognize the spiritual dimension as significant either for understanding human

behavior or as a focus for practice. However, several religiously affiliated agencies continued to provide social services (e.g., Catholic Social Services, Jewish Family Services, Lutheran Social Services, the Salvation Army). Nonsectarian spiritual influences were also felt, including principles of 12-step programs; humanistic, existential, and Jungian thought; and ideas about human development drawn from Eastern religions (Robbins, Chatterjee, & Canda, 2012).

4. *Resurgence of interest in spirituality.* A renewed interest in the spiritual dimension began in the 1980s (Canda, 1997; Russel, 1998). Indicators of this new phase within the profession included a marked increase in the number of publications and presentations on the topic; the development of a national Society for Spirituality and Social Work (SSSW); and the first national conference on spirituality and social work, held in 1994. As part of this substantial activity, there was infusion of new and diverse perspectives on spirituality that influenced the profession, including Buddhism, Confucianism, Hinduism, Shamanism, Taoism, and transpersonal theory. This period differed from the earlier sectarian period in that it emphasized the need to address spirituality in a way that recognizes the value of diverse spiritual traditions and respects client self-determination (Canda, 1988; Sheridan, Bullis, Adcock, Berlin, & Miller, 1992). This trend toward reexamination and reintegration of spirituality within the profession corresponded with increased interest within the larger culture (Gallup & Lindsay, 1999).

5. *Transcending boundaries.* From 1995 to the present, the profession has witnessed an elaboration and expansion of prior trends. This includes the reintroduction of references to religion and spirituality in the Council on Social Work Education's (CSWE) 1995 Curriculum Policy Statement and 2000 Educational Policy and Accreditation Standards after an absence of more than 20 years. The first international conference of the SSSW was held in 2000, with other national and international conferences increasingly including presentations on spirituality (e.g., National Association of Social Workers [NASW], CSWE's Annual Program Meeting, International Federation of Social Workers [IFSW], International Association of Schools of Social Work [IASSW]). The Canadian Society for Spirituality and Social Work was established in 2002 and cohosts conferences with the U.S. SSSW. A recent development has been the establishment of CSWE's Religion & Spirituality Clearinghouse in 2011, which provides curricular resources for social work educators. New postmodern perspectives on spirituality have also entered the arena, including feminist, ecophilosophical, postcolonial, and expanded transpersonal frameworks, which have broadened the focus of spirituality to include all peoples, all nations, all beings, and the planet itself, with special concern for marginalized and oppressed groups (Besthorn, 2001; Canda, 2005; Coates, 2003). There also has been exponential growth in empirical work during this period, including more than 50 studies of social work practitioners, faculty, and students (see Sheridan, 2004 and 2009, for reviews of this literature) and growing numbers of studies relative to direct practice with social work clients (see, for example, Beitel et al., 2007; Brown, Carney, Parrish, & Klem, 2013; Nelson-Becker, 2006). There also have been developments in integrating spirituality and macro practice (see, for example, Hugen & Venema, 2009; Rogers, 2009; Sheridan, 2013). Clearly, the focus has shifted from *whether* the topic should be included in the profession to *how* to integrate spirituality within social work practice in an ethical, effective, and spiritually sensitive manner (Canda & Furman, 2010; Canda, Nakashima, & Furman, 2004; Sheridan, 2009; Van Hook, Hugen, & Aguilar, 2001).

Regarding social work education, two major rationales have been proposed for including content on spirituality within undergraduate and graduate studies. Studies of social work educators (Sheridan, Wilmer, & Atcheson, 1994) and students (Sheridan & Amato-von Hemert, 1999) reveal general endorsement of these two rationales, as reflected in the following statements:

- Religious and spiritual beliefs and practices are part of multicultural diversity. Social workers should have knowledge and skills in this area in order to work effectively with diverse client groups (90% of educators "strongly agree/agree"; 93% of students "strongly agree/agree").
- There is another dimension of human existence beyond the biopsychosocial framework that can be used to understand human behavior. Social work education should expand this framework to include the spiritual dimension (61% of educators "strongly agree/agree"; 72% of students "strongly agree/agree").

A number of publications address the relevance of spirituality for the profession in these two domains, and the range of this literature has become extensive. Thus, the following sections provide examples of writings that examine the role of spirituality relative to human diversity or the human condition. Readers are encouraged to use these as a starting place for further exploration.

Spirituality and Human Diversity

Conflict perspective

Commitment to issues of human diversity and to oppressed populations is a hallmark of the social work profession. At various times in history, some branches of organized religion have played a negative or impeding role in the attainment of social justice for various groups. Examples include the use of religious texts, policies, and practices to deny the full human rights of persons of color; women; and gay, lesbian, bisexual, and transgendered persons. At the same time, organized religion has a rich heritage of involvement in myriad social justice causes and movements, including the civil rights movement, the peace movement, the women's movement, the gay rights movement, abolition of the death penalty, the antipoverty movement, and the deep ecology movement.

It is beyond the scope of this chapter to do an overall analysis of the role of religion in the struggle for social and economic justice. However, the following sections provide examples of the impact of both religious and nonreligious spirituality in the lives of oppressed groups as defined by race and ethnicity, sex and gender, sexual orientation, and other forms of human diversity.

Race and Ethnicity

Spirituality expressed in both religious and nonreligious forms has been pivotal in the lives of many persons of color and other marginalized ethnic groups. This brief discussion of spirituality and race/ethnicity emphasizes common experiences and themes in order to provide a general overview. However, remember that a great deal of diversity exists within these groups and that every person's story is unique.

1. *African Americans.* In a survey conducted by the Pew Research Center's Forum on Religion & Public Life (Sahgal & Smith, 2009), African Americans emerged as notably more religious than the general U.S. population based on a number of indicators. They have the highest percentage of religiously affiliated adults of all racial/ethnic groups (87%), and nearly 8 in 10 (79%) say that religion is very important in their lives, compared with 56% of all U.S. adults. Even the majority (72%) of African Americans who are not affiliated with any particular faith report that religion plays at least a somewhat important role in their lives, and almost half (45%) of this group say that it is very important. Furthermore, 53% report attending religious services at least once a week, 76% pray daily, and 88% declare that they are absolutely certain about the existence of God. Data from this survey show the majority of African Americans identifying as Protestant (78%), followed by Catholic (5%), and Jehovah's Witness (1%). Four percent reported some other type of affiliation, and 12% identify as "unaffiliated." African Americans account for about one fourth of adherents to Islam in the United States (Pew Forum, 2008), including membership in Sunni Islam or other mainstream Islamic denominations, the Nation of Islam, or smaller Black Muslim sects (Haddad, 1997). Black churches, in particular, have historically been a safe haven for African Americans facing racism

and oppression, as well as an important source of social support, race consciousness and inspiration, leadership training, human services, and empowerment and social change (Franklin, 1994; Logan, 2001; Taylor, Chatters, & Levin, 2004). The legacy of slavery and the integrated heritage of African and African American spiritual values have emphasized collective unity and the connection of all beings (Nobles, 1980). Afrocentric spirituality stresses the interdependence among God, community, family, and the individual. Its central virtues include beneficence to the community, forbearance through tragedy, wisdom applied to action, creative improvisation, forgiveness of wrongs and oppression, and social justice (Paris, 1995). *Kwanzaa* is an important nonsectarian Afrocentric spiritual tradition developed by Maulana Karenga in the 1960s as a mechanism for celebrating and supporting African and African American strengths and empowerment. Seven principles represent the core values of Kwanzaa: *umoja* (unity), *kujichagulia* (self-determination), *ujima* (collective work and responsibility), *ujamaa* (collective economics), *nia* (purpose), *kuumba* (creativity), and *imani* (faith) (Karenga, 1995). Many writers stress the importance of paying attention to the role of spirituality in its various forms when working with African American clients, families, and communities (see, for example, Banerjee & Canda, 2009; Bennett, Sheridan, & Richardson, 2014; Freeman, 2006; Stewart, Koeske, & Pringle, 2007).

2. *Latino(a) Americans.* This category includes people with ties to 26 countries in North, South, and Central America; the Caribbean; and Europe (Spain). Thus, the categorizing of these peoples under a reductionist label such as Latino(a) or Hispanic denies the considerable diversity within this population. Keeping this in mind, the majority (58%) of Latino(a) Americans are Roman Catholic, but there is also a large and growing number (23%) of Protestants among this group. Almost 5% report other religious affiliations, including Muslim and Jewish, and 14% are unaffiliated (Pew Forum, 2008). In addition, many Latino(a) people follow beliefs and practices that represent a blending of Christian, African, and Indigenous spiritual traditions (Castex, 1994; Canda & Furman, 2010). Latino(a) American spirituality has been strongly affected by factors related to colonialism (Costas, 1991). This history includes military, political, economic, cultural, and religious conquest, forcing many Indigenous peoples to take on the Catholicism of their conquerors. Many traditional places of worship, spiritual texts, beliefs, and practices were destroyed, repressed, or blended with Catholic traditions (Canda & Furman, 2010). Today, Christian Latino(a) faith has several central features: a personal relationship with God that encompasses love and reverence as well as fear and dread; an emphasis on both faith and ritual behavior; belief in the holiness of Jesus Christ as savior, king, and infant God; special reverence shown to Mary as the mother of God; recognition of saints as models of behavior and as benefactors; significance of sacred objects as both symbols of faith and transmitters of luck or magic; and special events and celebrations, such as saints' feast days, Holy Week, Christmas Eve, feasts of the Virgin, and life passages (e.g., baptisms, first communions, confirmations, coming-of-age ceremonies, weddings, and funerals) (Aguilar, 2001; Ramirez, 1985). In addition to mainstream religions, a number of African and Indigenous spiritual healing traditions continue to be practiced by some Latino(a) groups today, including curanderismo, santiguando, espiritismo, Santeria, and Vodoun (Delgado, 1988; Paulino, 1995; Torrez, 1984). Social workers need to understand the importance of both religious institutions and folk healing traditions when working with Latino(a) populations. These various expressions of spirituality serve as important sources for social support, coping strategies, means of healing, socialization and maintenance of culture, and resources for human services and social justice efforts (Aranda, 2008; Burke, Chauvin, & Miranti, 2005; Faver & Trachte, 2005; Paulino, 1998).

3. *Asian Americans and Pacific Islanders.* This population represents many cultures, including

Chinese, Filipino, Japanese, Korean, Asian Indian, Vietnamese, Hawaiian, Cambodian, Laotian, Thai, Hmong, Pakistani, Samoan, Guamanian, and Indonesian (Healey, 2012). These different peoples are affiliated with a wide range of spiritual traditions, including Hinduism, Buddhism, Islam, Confucianism, Sikhism, Zoroastrianism, Jainism, Shinto, Taoism, and Christianity (Tweed, 1997). In the United States, 27% of this group is Protestant, 17% Catholic, 14% Hindu, 9% Buddhist, and 4% Muslim. Approximately 6% report other religious affiliations, and 23% are unaffiliated (Pew Forum, 2008). There is much diversity within these various religious traditions as well, making it particularly difficult to discuss common elements of spiritual beliefs or practices. However, several themes can be discerned: the connection among and the divinity of all beings; the need to transcend suffering and the material world; the importance of displaying compassion, selflessness, and cooperation; the honoring of ancestors; a disciplined approach to life and spiritual development; and a holistic understanding of existence (Canda & Furman, 1999; Chung, 2001; Singh, 2001). Both religious institutions and traditional practices have been helpful to a variety of Asian and Pacific Islander immigrants and refugees and their descendants. For example, many southeast Asian refugee communities have established Buddhist temples and mutual assistance associations, which provide social, physical, mental, and spiritual resources (Canda & Phaobtong, 1992; Morreale, 1998; Timberlake & Cook, 1984), and the Korean church has been an essential provider of social services and community development efforts (Boddie, Hong, Im, & Chung, 2011; Choi & Tirrito, 1999). Some Asian Americans and Pacific Islanders also use Indigenous healers, such as the Cambodian krou khmer, the Korean mudang, the Hmong spirit medium, and the Hawaiian kahuna (Canda & Furman, 1999; Canda, Shin, & Canda, 1993; Hurdle, 2002). As with other groups, there is an emerging literature stressing the importance of attending to spirituality in practice with clients from this large and diverse cultural population (Canda, 2001; Chung,

2001; Diwan, Jonnalagadda, & Balaswamy, 2004; Hodge, 2004; Hurdle, 2002; Leung & Chan, 2010; Singh, 2001; Tan, 2006). In addition, several writers have proposed incorporating concepts and practices from Asian spiritual traditions into mainstream social work practice, including meditation (Keefe, 1996; Logan, 1997), Zen-oriented practice (Brandon, 1976), body-mind-spirit integration approaches (Leung, Chan, Ng, & Lee, 2009), and yoga (Fukuyama & Sevig, 1999).

4. *Native Americans.* Native Americans, or First Nations peoples, originally numbered in the millions and were members of hundreds of distinct tribes or nations, each with its own language, heritage, and spiritual traditions (Healey, 2012). As part of the effort to "humanize and civilize" Native Americans, Congress regularly appropriated funds for Christian missionary efforts beginning in 1819 (U.S. Commission on Human Rights, 1998). American Indian boarding schools were a major component of these efforts, where children were forbidden to wear their native attire, eat their native foods, speak their native language, or practice their traditional religion and were often severely punished for failure to adhere to these prohibitions (Haig-Brown, 1988; Snipp, 1998). Through a long history of resistance and renewal, however, Indigenous spiritual traditions have persisted and currently are being restored and revitalized (Swift, 1998). Various expressions of Native American spirituality have several common themes: the inseparability of spirituality from the rest of life; connection to and responsibility for the earth and all her creatures; the sacredness of all things, including animals, plants, minerals, and natural forces; the values of balance, harmony, and connectedness; the importance of extended family and community; and the use of myth, ritual, and storytelling as spiritual practices (Duran & Duran, 1995; Matheson, 1996; Yellow Bird, 1995). Many of these values are of increasing appeal to non-Indigenous people, producing great concern among Native American people regarding appropriation of their customs, ceremonies, rituals, and healing practices (Kasee,

1995; LaDue, 1994). This cross-tradition borrowing of spiritual practices requires sensitivity, respect, competence, and permission in such matters (Canda & Yellow Bird, 1996). Social workers also should become informed regarding ongoing efforts to protect Native American cultural and religious freedoms, including issues related to sacred lands, free exercise of religion in correctional and educational institutions, repatriation of human remains and sacred objects held in museums and scientific institutions, and protection of sacred and cultural knowledge from exploitation and appropriation (Harvard Pluralism Project, 2005). Many service providers also call for sensitivity and awareness of the effects of historical trauma on Native Americans and recommend the integration of traditional practices for more effective service delivery (Brave Heart, 2001; Burke et al., 2005; Chong, Fortier, & Morris, 2009; Limb & Hodge, 2008; Skye, 2002; Weaver, 2011). In addition, Indigenous worldviews and spiritual practices have application to social work in general (Canda, 1983; Voss, Douville, Little Soldier, & Twiss, 1999).

It is important to remember the experience of other groups that have been more extensively assimilated into the dominant culture of the United States (e.g., Irish, Italian, and Jewish Americans). Many of these groups also have histories of discrimination and religious intolerance, the effects of which are felt by succeeding generations. Since the terrorist attacks of September 11, 2001, we in the United States have witnessed increased discrimination and oppressive acts against Muslim Americans, especially those of Middle Eastern descent (Crabtree, Husain, & Spalek, 2008; Pew Research Center, 2009). Given this atmosphere and the growing Muslim population within the United States, it is imperative that social workers develop sensitivity and competence in working with Muslim clients (Carolan, Bagherinia, Juhari, Himelright, & Mouton-Sanders, 2000; Hodge, 2005a). Indeed, social workers must be sensitive to the particular history and spiritual traditions of all racial and ethnic groups.

Photo 6.3 Native American dance is a cultural and highly spiritual form of expression.

© iStockphoto.com/Juan Monino

Sex and Gender

Women are more likely than men to report that they are religious, church-affiliated, and frequent users of prayer; are certain in their belief of God; feel close to God; hold a positive view of their church; and are more religiously engaged (Pew Forum, 2008). Women also are the majority of members in most religious bodies in the United States and play important roles in the life of many religious communities (Braude, 1997).

However, in several denominations, women's participation has been significantly restricted, prohibiting them from holding leadership positions or performing certain religious rites and ceremonies (Burke et al., 2005; Holm & Bowker, 1994; Reilly, 1995). In addition, women members of traditional Judeo-Christian and Islamic faiths generally experience conceptualizations and symbols of the divine as masculine, suggesting that men are closer to (and thus more like) God than women (Reuther, 1983). In response to this, some scholars are calling for increased ordination of women and more women in leadership positions in order to create a more woman-affirming environment within religious institutions (Roberts & Yamane, 2012).

Although most women who belong to mainstream denominations report being generally satisfied with their affiliations (Corbett, 1997), some struggle with the patriarchal aspects of their faith. One study conducted in-depth interviews of 61 women ages 18 to 71 who were affiliated with Catholic, United Methodist, Unitarian Universalist, or Jewish congregations (Ozorak, 1996). Most (93%) perceived gender inequality within their religions. Sixteen percent viewed these inequalities as appropriate, and thus accepted them; 8% left their faith in reaction to this issue and others. The remainder coped by using behavioral strategies (e.g., requesting equal treatment; requesting gender-inclusive language; substituting feminine words, images, or interpretations; participating in feminist activities), cognitive strategies (e.g., focusing on positive aspects of the religion, comparing their faith favorably to others, emphasizing signs of positive change), or a combination of both behavioral and cognitive mechanisms.

Christian and Jewish feminist theologians have made efforts to emphasize the feminine heritage of conventional faiths, and some Christian and Jewish denominations have increased opportunities for women in both lay leadership roles and clerical positions (Canda & Furman, 2010). There also has been a movement toward alternative women's spiritualities. Some women have become involved in spiritual support groups or explored other religious traditions, such as Buddhism (Carnes & Craig, 1998; Holm & Bowker, 1994). Others have pursued feminist-identified theology, such as Goddess worship (Manning, 2010), Wicca (Starhawk, 1979; Warwick, 1995), Jewish feminism (Breitman, 1995), or Christian womanist spirituality (Jackson, 2002). These spiritual traditions emphasize the feminine aspect of the divine; the sacredness of women's bodies, rhythms, and life cycles; the power and creativity of women's spirituality; a connection to earth-centered practices; and the care of all people and the planet (Kidd, 1996; Martin, 1993; Ochshorn & Cole, 1995; Warwick, 1995). Some men are also turning to alternative spiritual traditions to overcome religious experiences and conceptions of God and masculinity they feel have been detrimental to them (Kivel, 1991; Warwick, 1995).

Sexual Orientation

Nonheterosexual persons are often linked together as the LGBT community (lesbian, gay, bisexual, and transgendered persons). It should be noted, however, that transgendered persons may identify themselves as heterosexual, bisexual, or homosexual; therefore, transgendered status is a matter of sex and gender, not sexual orientation. However, as a group, transgendered persons have much in common with gay men, lesbians, and bisexual persons when it comes to experiences with oppression and thus are included with these groups in this discussion of spirituality.

As an oppressed population, LGBT persons have suffered greatly at the hands of some groups affiliated with organized religion. Some egregious examples are the pronouncement by certain religious leaders that AIDS is a "punishment for the sins" of LGBT persons and the picketing of funerals of victims of antigay hate crimes by religiously identified individuals. More pervasively, many LGBT members of various faiths have had to struggle with religious teachings that tell them their feelings and behaviors are immoral or sinful. A growing body of literature reveals the serious impacts of religious rejection and abuse experienced by many LGBT persons, resulting in spiritual loss, depression, internalized shame, substance abuse, and thoughts of suicide (e.g., Barton, 2010; Hansen & Lambert, 2011; Super & Jacobson, 2011). Other studies show LGBT persons remaining connected to their faith despite negative experiences and relying on spirituality as an important source of coping and support (e.g., Bozard & Sanders, 2011; Yarhouse & Carr, 2012). In particular, involvement in gay-affirming congregations has been shown to provide significant benefits to LGBT persons facing conflict between their sexual and religious identities (Sherry, Adelman, Whilde, & Quick, 2010).

Every major religious and spiritual tradition has LGBT adherents. Furthermore, there are religious rationales within Christianity, Islam, Judaism, Buddhism, Confucianism, and Taoism for tolerance of nonheterosexual orientations, even though historically these religions have privileged heterosexuality (Ellison & Plaskow, 2007). There are also associations within every major religion that go beyond tolerance to work for full inclusion of LGBT persons. Examples include the following: Affirmation—United Methodists for Lesbian, Gay, Bisexual & Transgender Concerns; Association of Welcoming & Affirming Baptists; Integrity (Episcopal); Dignity USA (Catholic); Lutherans Concerned; More Light Presbyterians; United Church of Christ Coalition for Lesbian, Bisexual, Gay and Transgender Concerns; World Congress of Gay, Lesbian, Bisexual, and Transgender Jews: Keshet Ga'avah; Al-Fatiah (Muslim); Gay Buddhist Fellowship; the Gay and Lesbian Vaishnava Association (Hindu); and Seventh Day Adventist Kinship. There are also denominations that generally identify themselves as "open and gay affirming," including Metropolitan Community Church, Society of Friends (Quakers), United Church of Christ, Unitarian Universalism, and Reform and Reconstructionist branches of Judaism.

LGBT persons who grow up in less tolerant religious communities experience considerable tension between their faith and their sexuality. They, and others close to them, must decide how to respond to this tension. Canda and Furman (2010) identify four alternative ideological responses that are evident within Christianity but are also applicable to other faiths. The first three refer to the faith's stance on nonheterosexual orientation, and the fourth refers to a possible stance that LGBT persons or LGBT allies may take regarding organized religion:

1. Condemn homosexuality and homosexual persons.

2. Accept homosexual persons but reject homosexual behavior.

3. Affirm and accept LGBT persons at every level.

4. Reject the faith's position relative to LGBT persons and depart from the faith.

These four responses have implications for both LGBT persons and social work practitioners. For LGBT persons, involvement with religious institutions characteristic of the first response exacerbates both the direct and internalized oppression that most experience as a result of living in a society that privileges heterosexual orientation and views any other sexual expression as deviant or "less than." At the other end of the spectrum, involvement with congregations that display the third response of affirmation and acceptance would allow the LGBT person to honor both his or her sexual identity and faith commitments. The middle position of accepting the person but rejecting the behavior would most likely maintain the tension and internal conflict that an LGBT person experiences when an important part of his or her identity is "not welcome at the table." The final reaction, leaving one's faith, is unsatisfactory for many LGBT persons who want to be involved with communal religious experiences and desire a spiritual community welcoming of their whole self. For others, it represents a choice that is self-affirming and liberating.

Regarding social work practitioners, Canda and Furman (2010) point out that the first response is clearly antithetical to social work values and ethics, while the third position is congruent with ethical standards of practice. The second response brings up questions concerning how this stance will affect the practitioner's work with LGBT clients. It is challenging enough to affirm a positive self-identity and possess confidence and self-assurance as an LGBT person in a heterosexist and homophobic society without experiencing negative attitudes from one's social worker. If the practitioner cannot transmit the level of empathy and respect for LGBT persons and their sexual orientation required by the NASW Code of Ethics, referral to another practitioner is warranted. Furthermore, the practitioner needs to engage in a process of reflection and self-examination in order to be able to move toward a more positive and ethical response to LGBT clients. Social workers who themselves have left a faith tradition (the fourth response) due to disagreement with teachings on sexual orientation, or any other issue, also need to be vigilant that they are not transmitting negative and disrespectful attitudes toward religious clients, whether they are LGBT or heterosexual.

It also is important to respect the unique spiritual journeys that individual LGBT persons may take. If you were working with Leon as he struggles with the conflict between his church and his sexual identity, it would be important to work collaboratively with him to discern what option was best for him, providing him information about alternatives while maintaining respect for his self-determination. As Barret and Barzan (1996) point out, regardless of the individual decisions LGBT persons make regarding religion, the process of self-acceptance is a spiritual journey unto itself.

Other Aspects of Diversity

The issues and implications relative to spirituality that pertain to race and ethnicity, sex and gender, and sexual orientation apply to other forms of human diversity as well. For example, some religious teachings have interpreted disability as a punishment for the sins of the person or family (Miles, 1995; Niemann, 2005) or as a means for nondisabled persons to acquire spiritual status through expressions of pity and charity (Fitzgerald, 1997). Conversely, spirituality has been noted as both a significant means of coping and a vehicle toward positive self-definition for persons with disabilities (Fitzgerald, 1997; Hurst, 2007; Niemann, 2005; Parish, Magana, & Cassiman, 2008; Swinton, 2012).

Spirituality and age is another area that has been widely addressed. Both religious and nonreligious forms of spirituality are important sources of social support for older persons and a pathway for coping, ongoing development, and successful aging (Burke et al., 2005; Hedberg, Brulin, & Alex, 2009; Lee, 2011). In addition, spirituality is viewed as an essential foundation for healthy development among young people (Hay & Nye, 2006; Myers,

1997; Roehlkepartain, King, Wagener, & Benson, 2006). Research has shown spirituality to be a significant protective factor against substance abuse, premature sexual activity, and delinquency for children and adolescents (Holder et al., 2000; Johnson, Jang, Larsen, & De Li, 2001; Miller, Davies, & Greenwald, 2000; Smith & Denton, 2005). Other research highlights the potential for the religious or spiritual abuse and neglect of youth (Bottoms, Nielsen, Murray, & Filipas, 2003; Kvarfordt, 2010). As our understanding of the interaction between religious and nonreligious spirituality and other forms of human diversity increases, social work will be in a better position to work sensitively, competently, and ethically with many diverse groups and communities.

Critical Thinking Questions 6.3

With globalization, we have more regular contact with people of diverse religious and spiritual beliefs. How much religious and spiritual diversity do you come in contact with in your everyday life? How comfortable are you with honoring different religious and spiritual beliefs? How have you seen religious and spiritual beliefs used to discriminate against some groups of people? How have you seen religious and spiritual beliefs used to promote social justice?

Spirituality and the Human Experience

Social workers deal with every aspect of the human experience. They simultaneously focus on solving problems in living while supporting optimal human functioning and quality of life. The literature regarding spirituality in these two areas is immense, with significant development in social work, psychology, nursing, medicine, rehabilitation counseling, pastoral counseling, marital and family counseling, and other helping disciplines. The following discussion highlights examples of this continually evolving knowledge base. Similar to the previous discussion of spirituality and diversity, this brief overview will serve readers as an entry point to this expanding literature.

Problems in Living

It is difficult to find an area related to problems in living in which spirituality is not being explored. For example, much has been written about the link between spirituality and mental health. Various indicators of spirituality—such as religious commitment, involvement in spiritual or religious practices, and level of religiosity or spirituality—have been shown to have an inverse relationship with depression, anxiety, hopelessness, suicide, and other mental health problems while showing a positive relationship with self-esteem, self-efficacy, hope, optimism, life satisfaction, and general well-being (Koenig, 2005; Mueller, Plevak, & Rummans, 2001; Pargament, 1997).

Similar influences are found between spirituality and physical health, with spirituality linked to a variety of better health outcomes (Ellison & Levin, 1998; Koenig, King, & Carson, 2012; Matthews et al., 1998). Various propositions have been investigated to explain the exact mechanisms of this relationship. Findings suggest that religion and spirituality benefit physical health through their support of health-promoting behaviors and discouragement of risk behaviors, while others indicate possible biological processes that mediate the negative impacts of stress and support healthy immune functioning (Koenig, 1999; Mueller et al., 2001; Ray, 2004; Segerstrom & Miller, 2004). Specific spiritual practices, such as mindfulness-based stress-reduction techniques, have shown positive outcomes in several areas, including chronic pain, anxiety disorders, recurrent depression, psoriasis, and general psychological well-being (Grossman, Niemann, Schmidt, & Walach, 2004; Williams, Teasdale, Segal, & Kabat-Zinn, 2007), as well as benefits to the immune system (Davidson et al., 2003).

For both mental and physical health problems, religion and spirituality have been noted as major means of coping (Koenig, 2005; Koenig, Larson, & Larson, 2001; Koenig et al., 2012; Pargament, 1997).

In an extensive review of the social and behavioral science literature, Oakley Ray (2004) cites spirituality as one of four key factors significantly linked to positive coping, along with knowledge, inner resources, and social support. The specific benefits of spiritually based coping include relieving stress, retaining a sense of control, maintaining hope, and providing a sense of meaning and purpose in life (Koenig, 2001, 2005).

Higher levels of social support through religious and spiritual networks also play a significant role in positive coping with health issues (Ellison & Levin, 1998; Perry, 1998; Reese & Kaplan, 2000). Both religious and nonreligious forms of spirituality have proven helpful to persons coping with caregiving demands related to health problems of family members (Bennett, Sheridan, & Richardson, 2014; Koenig, 2005; Vickrey et al., 2007). Similar effects are noted for coping with poverty (Greeff & Fillis, 2009; Parish et al., 2008) and homelessness (Ferguson, Wu, Dryness, & Spruijt-Metz, 2007; Lindsey, Kurtz, Jarvis, Williams, & Nackerud, 2000).

Still another body of scholarship explores spirituality and substance abuse. Both religiosity and spirituality have been noted as protective factors in this area for both adults and children (Hodge, Cardenas, & Montoya, 2001; Smith & Denton, 2005; Wills, Yaeger, & Sandy, 2003). In addition, the spiritual dimension as a key factor in recovery from substance abuse has long been recognized in self-help groups such as Alcoholics Anonymous, Narcotics Anonymous, and other treatment approaches (Hsu, Grow, Marlatt, Galanter, & Kaskutas, 2008; Streifel & Servaty-Seib, 2009).

There is also a growing literature addressing the role of spirituality in understanding and dealing with the effects of various types of trauma—including physical and sexual abuse and assault (Bowland, Biswas, Kyriakakis, & Edmond, 2011; Robinson, 2000; Walker, Reid, O'Neill, & Brown, 2009); domestic and community violence (Benavides, 2012; Garbarino & Bedard, 1997; Parappully, Rosenbaum, van den Daele, & Nzewi, 2002); serious injury and natural disasters (Ashkanani, 2009; Johnstone, Yoon, Rupright, & Reid-Arndt, 2009; Tausch et al., 2011); incarceration (O'Brien, 2001;

Redman, 2008; Sheridan, 1995); and ethnic trauma, war, displacement, and terrorism (Drescher et al., 2009; Markovitzky & Mosek, 2005; Meisenhelder & Marcum, 2009; Schuster et al., 2001). Certain spiritually oriented interventions, such as the use of ceremony and ritual, appear to have particular utility in helping persons recover from trauma and loss (Cairns, 2005; Galambos, 2001; Lubin & Johnson, 1998).

Finally, nowhere has spirituality been viewed as more relevant than in the area of death and dying. Religious and spiritual issues often arise at the end of life, and thus practitioners need to be able to deal with these issues effectively (Cox, 2000; MacKinlay, 2006; Morgan, 2002; Nelson-Becker, 2006). Spiritual sensitivity is also needed in working with those grieving the loss of loved ones (Angell, Dennis, & Dumain, 1998; Golsworthy & Coyle, 1999; Winston, 2006) or facing divorce or other kinds of loss (Coholic, 2011; Marsh, 2005; Nathanson, 1995).

Individual and Collective Well-Being

Spirituality also has a role to play in regard to the second major focus of social work: supporting and enhancing optimal human functioning and quality of life. This role is evident at all levels of human systems, including the individual, family, community, organizational, and societal spheres. The following discussion identifies key points of this influence on well-being at both the individual and collective levels.

At the individual level, interest in wellness, holistic health, and the mind–body connection has exploded in recent years, as evidenced by increasing numbers of workshops and retreats, weekly groups, self-help books, and media reports on the topic. Furthermore, there has been a marked increase in the use of complementary and alternative medicine (CAM), sometimes referred to as "integrative medicine," which includes "an array of health care approaches with a history of use or origins outside of mainstream medicine" (National Center for Complementary and Alternative Medicine [NCCAM], n.d.). These approaches, which

often are grounded in spiritual traditions and a holistic understanding of the human condition, include homeopathy and naturopathic medicine; acupuncture; massage therapy; mindfulness or transcendental meditation; movement therapies; relaxation techniques; spinal manipulation; Tai chi and Qi gong; yoga; healing touch; hypnotherapy; and Ayurvedic and traditional Chinese medicine (NCCAM, n.d.).

More than 1,200 research projects have been funded by NCCAM, which is the lead agency under the National Institutes of Health (NIH) charged with investigating the efficacy of these approaches for both physical and mental health. Many of these studies have found positive effects of various CAM modalities, while also identifying approaches that are ineffective. Regardless of the scientific results, Americans are increasingly using CAM processes and products. Findings from a 2007 national survey reveal that approximately 50% of Americans used some form of alternative or complementary medicine (Barnes, Bloom, & Nahin, 2008), compared with 34% in 1990 (Williamson & Wyandt, 2001). There is a rise in the use of CAM by physical health and mental health practitioners as well. In a study of social work practitioners, over 75% of the sample reported either direct use or referral to mind–body techniques or community health alternatives in work with their clients (Henderson, 2000).

In related research, investigations are uncovering the specific mechanisms of the mind–body connection. In a meta-analysis of 30 years of research, findings show clear linkages between psychological stress and lowered immune system functioning, the major biological system that defends the body against disease (Segerstrom & Miller, 2004). In another review of 100 years of research, Oakley Ray (2004) reports mounting evidence that stressors affecting the brain are harmful to the body at both a cellular and molecular level, and they diminish a person's health and quality of life. In addition, intriguing results are coming out of research on the "neurobiology of consciousness." Several studies have shown demonstrable links between subjective experiences reported during meditation and noted alterations in brain function (e.g., EEG patterns, gamma activity, phase synchrony), as well as evidence of neuroplasticity (transformations of the brain) in long-term meditators (Lutz, Dunne, & Davidson, 2007). Taken together, these investigations suggest that many of our core mental and emotional processes not only are pivotal in maintaining optimal health but also affect our capacity for personal happiness and compassion for others. Results from the consciousness studies suggest that positive workings of the mind are trainable skills through practices such as meditation. This possibility has significant implications for both individual and communal well-being.

As a result of this research, a growing number of articles in the professional literature also promote the use of wellness or mind–body approaches for both clients and practitioners. Examples include the development of specialized wellness programs (Clark, 2002; Kissman & Maurer, 2002; Neufeld & Knipemann, 2001; Plasse, 2001; Scott et al., 2001), the use of stress management and relaxation techniques (Finger & Arnold, 2002; McBee, Westreich, & Likourezos, 2004; Payne, 2000), and the use of mindfulness meditation and yoga (Bell, 2009; Brantley, Doucett, & Lindell, 2008; Lee, Ng, Leung, & Chan, 2009; Vohra-Gupta, Russell, & Lo, 2007; Wisniewski, 2008). Many of these approaches are rooted in spiritual traditions, especially Eastern traditions.

There also has been a great deal of recent development concerning spirituality and work. Much of this literature focuses on the search for "right livelihood," or the conscious choice of work consistent with one's spiritual values and supportive of ongoing spiritual growth (Fox, 1994; Neal, 2000; Sinetar, 2011). Other writers exploring the role of spirituality in the workplace discuss such issues as use of power, management style, workplace environment, and integrating spiritual values with overall work goals (Natale & Neher, 1997; Roberson, 2004; Smith, 2006). The social work enterprise itself has been the subject of such interest. Examples include Canda and Furman's (2010) identification of principles for spiritually sensitive administration of human service organizations and Chamiec-Chase's (2009) focus on measuring social workers' integration of spirituality in the workplace.

The connection between spirituality and creativity is another area being addressed by a variety of writers. Much of this writing emphasizes the potential that linking spirituality and creativity has for healing as well as nurturing self-expression and optimal development. Examples include use of the visual arts (Coholic, 2011; Farrelly-Hansen, 2009); journaling, poetry, and creative writing (Cameron, 1992; Wright, 2005); music and sound (Campbell, 1997; Goldman, 1996); and movement and dance, drama, and other performing arts (Pearson, 1996; Wuthnow, 2001). Engaging in the creative process seems to facilitate spiritual growth and well-being by encouraging the person to go beyond ego limitations, surrender to process, and tap into spiritual sources of strength and self-expression (Fukuyama & Sevig, 1999; Mayo, 2009).

Spirituality is also emerging as an important factor in the optimal functioning of various human collectives. In social work with couples and families, paying attention to the spiritual dimension of family life is viewed as important not only for the religiously affiliated but for the nonaffiliated as well (Dosser, Smith, Markowski, & Cain, 2001; Duba & Watts, 2009; Walsh, 2009a). It has been identified as an important component in working with couples and families relative to a wide range of issues, including discord (Cowley, 1999; Derezotes, 2001; Hunler & Gencoz, 2005), challenges of adoption and parenting (Belanger, Copeland, & Cheung, 2009; Evans, Boustead, & Owens, 2008), health issues (Cattich & Knudson-Martin, 2009), death and loss (Walsh, 2009b), and building on family strengths and resilience (Anderson, 2009; Bell-Toliver & Wilkerson, 2011; Gale, 2009; Hames & Godwin, 2008).

The literature also notes the role of spirituality in community-based and social change initiatives. Examples include community health promotion programs (Brown, Jemmott, Mitchell, & Walton, 1998; Clark, 2002), collective action and social justice efforts (Hill & Donaldson, 2012; Hutchison, 2012; Perry & Rolland, 2009; Tripses & Scroggs,

2009), services to rural communities (Furman & Chandy, 1994; Johnson, 1997), and other types of community-focused practice (Garland, Myers, & Wolfer, 2008; Obst & Tham, 2009; Pargament, 2008; Tangenberg, 2008). Social workers are also becoming acquainted with the newly emerging "spiritual activism" movement, which goes beyond a focus on political and economic forces as primary mechanisms for social change to incorporate a spiritual framework for activism. Emerging principles of this new model include such themes as "recognition of interdependence," "acceptance of not knowing," "openness to suffering," and "outer change requiring inner work" (Sheridan, 2014). This more holistic approach is viewed as having greater potential for achieving liberation and social justice than previous efforts embedded in a conflict perspective.

Attention to religious and spiritual resources is also being identified in organizational practice. President Obama announced the reconfigured White House Office of Faith-Based and Neighborhood Partnerships on the 17th day of his first administration, while also stressing the importance of such partnerships remaining consistent with constitutional principles and American values:

> The goal of this office will not be to favor one religious group over another—or even religious groups over secular groups. It will simply be to work on behalf of those organizations that want to work on behalf of our communities, and to do so without blurring the line that our founders wisely drew between church and state. This work is important, because whether it's a secular group advising families facing foreclosure or faith-based groups providing job-training to those who need work, few are closer to what's happening on our streets and in our neighborhoods than these organizations. People trust them. Communities rely on them. And we will help them. (Office of Faith-Based and Neighborhood Partnerships, 2009, para. 1)

The proliferation of congregational and faith-based social services, which began with the George W. Bush administration in 2001, is being closely followed and evaluated by social work scholars. Some note positive opportunities and outcomes as a result of this trend, while others point to negative and unanticipated consequences (Belcher, Fandetti, & Cole, 2004; Boddie & Cnaan, 2006; Netting, O'Connor, & Singletary, 2007; Thomas, 2009). NASW's (2001) response to the federal faith-based initiative remains cautious, stressing the need for services to be delivered in a way that makes them clearly voluntary and emphasizing the central role and responsibility of government in providing social services. Although acknowledging and supporting the role that religious social service providers play in providing essential services, NASW also has emphasized that social work "must not allow the vital series of faith-based groups to become co-opted by the government as mere government-funded religion" (NASW, 2006, para. 5). Although faith-based organizations clearly have an important role to play in the provision of social services, there is a need for ongoing research on the impact of these organizations for both clients and social workers employed in such agencies.

At the larger policy and societal levels, both conservative and progressive religious perspectives have a significant voice in a host of issues that impact the well-being of individuals, families, and communities. The Pew Forum on Religion & Public Life (n.d.) has identified four arenas where religion plays a role in public life, often creating controversy and debate due to differing visions of the common good:

1. Religion and politics (e.g., the influence of religion and religious organizations on political behavior, including political campaigns and voting)

2. Religion and the law (e.g., church–state controversies, such as legal battles over the Ten Commandments and public displays of nativity scenes, the Pledge of Allegiance, suicide, the death penalty, and school vouchers)

3. Religion and domestic policy (e.g., issues such as abortion; gay rights, including marriage and adoption; stem cell research, genetic engineering, and cloning; and faith-based initiatives)

4. Religion and world affairs (e.g., the appropriate role for religion in foreign policy, international initiatives, and climate change and environmental issues)

Social workers should keep abreast of these issues, particularly as they impact the client populations they serve.

Finally, spirituality is being increasingly identified as a needed force in nurturing and sustaining life beyond the circle of the human family to include all living beings and our planet that is home to all. Growing numbers of religious congregations, both conservative and progressive, are identifying "stewardship of the planet" as part of their commitment to God's creation (National Religious Partnership for the Environment, 2014). Many writers are pointing to the critical link between our capacity to view all of nature as sacred and the mounting issues of environmental degradation, climate change, and ecojustice for vulnerable and marginalized populations (Berry, 2009; Coates, 2003, 2007; Dylan & Coates, 2012; Jenkins, 2008). This spiritually grounded perspective challenges us to redefine the meaning of community and reenvision our rightful place in the "sacred hoop" of life.

In sum, spirituality in both its religious and nonreligious forms holds much potential for promoting well-being and quality of life at all levels of the human experience, as well as for helping the profession address the problems and possibilities inherent in the human condition.

Critical Thinking Questions 6.4

A study of social work practitioners in 2000 found that more than 75% of the sample reported either direct use of mind–body techniques or referral to community health practitioners who use complementary and alternative medicine (CAM). What CAM practices do you use in your own life? What CAM practices do you expect to incorporate into your own practice? To what types of CAM practitioners do you expect to make referrals?

Spiritual Assessment

Given the important role of spirituality in understanding both human diversity and human experience, it has become evident that gathering information about a client's religious or spiritual history and assessing spiritual development and current interests are as important as learning about biopsychosocial factors. Assessment needs to go beyond the surface features of faith affiliation (such as Protestant, Catholic, Jewish, or Muslim) to include deeper facets of a person's spiritual life (Sheridan, 2002). For example, talking with Caroline about where she is in her unfolding spiritual development would be helpful in supporting her exploration of different faith perspectives. Asking Matthew what brings him meaning, purpose, and connection right now would be valuable in assisting him in the next chapter of his life. And in working with Leon, it would be useful to know what aspects of his current religious affiliation are the most important and meaningful to him as he struggles with the conflicts regarding his faith and his sexual identity. None of this knowledge would be gleaned by a simple response to "What is your current religious affiliation?"

Social workers also need to assess both the positive and negative aspects of clients' religious or spiritual beliefs and practices (Canda & Furman, 2010; Joseph, 1988; Lewandowski & Canda, 1995; Sheridan & Bullis, 1991). For example, Naomi and David's understanding of the meaning of illness may be either helpful or harmful in dealing with Naomi's health crisis; Trudy's current spiritual practices may be supportive or detrimental to her physical, emotional, and social well-being; and Jean-Joseph's synthesis of Catholic and Vodoun beliefs and practices may be very positive for his personal and family life but may be problematic in his interactions with the wider social environment. Assessing the role and impact of all of these factors would be important areas for exploration in developing a spiritually sensitive relationship with any of these individuals.

A growing number of assessment instruments and approaches are available to help social workers.

These include brief screening tools, which can provide an initial assessment of the relevance of religion or spirituality in clients' lives. Examples include the HOPE (Anandarajah & Hight, 2001), the FICA (Puchalski & Romer, 2000), the MIMBRA (Canda & Furman, 2010), and the Brief RCOPE (Pargament, Koenig, & Perez, 2000). There are also several more comprehensive assessment tools that focus on religious/spiritual history and current life circumstances. For example, Bullis (1996) developed a spiritual history that includes questions about individuals, their parents or guardians, and their spouses or significant others. Canda and Furman (2010) provide a discussion guide for a detailed spiritual assessment, which covers spiritual group membership and participation; spiritual beliefs, activities, experiences, and feelings; moral and value issues; spiritual development; spiritual sources of support and transformation; spiritual well-being; and extrinsic/intrinsic styles of spiritual propensity.

There are also examples of more implicit assessment approaches, which do not directly include a reference to "religion" or "spirituality" but are composed of open-ended questions that tap into spiritual themes, such as those identified by Titone (1991) and Canda and Furman (2010). (See Exhibit 6.5 for examples of these kinds of questions.) A number of other creative, nonverbal strategies for gathering such information have also been developed, including the use of spiritual timelines (Bullis, 1996); spiritual lifemaps, genograms, ecomaps, and ecograms (Hodge, 2005b); and spiritual trees (Raines, 1997). Finally, Lewandowski and Canda (1995) and Canda and Furman (2010) provide questions for assessing the helpful or harmful impacts of participating in spiritual groups or organizations (e.g., satisfaction with leadership style, methods of recruitment, response to members leaving the group).

Assessment must also be able to distinguish between a religious/spiritual problem and a mental disorder. Peteet, Lu, and Narrow's 2011 book *Religious and Spiritual Issues in Psychiatric Diagnosis* provides guidance in this area. Spiritual problems

---

Exhibit 6.5   Examples of Questions for Implicit Spiritual Assessment

1. What nourishes you spiritually—for example, music, nature, intimacy, witnessing heroism, meditation, creative expression, sharing another's joy?

2. What is the difference between shame and guilt? What are healthy and unhealthy shame and guilt?

3. What do you mean when you say your spirits are low? Is that different from being sad or depressed?

4. What is an incident in your life that precipitated a change in your belief about the meaning of life?

5. What helps you maintain a sense of hope when there is no immediate apparent basis for it?

6. Do you need forgiveness from yourself or someone else?

7. What currently brings a sense of meaning and purpose to your life?

8. Where do you go to find a sense of deep inspiration or peace?

9. For what are you most grateful?

10. What are your most cherished ideals?

11. In what way is it important or meaningful for you to be in this world (or in this situation)?

12. What are the deepest questions your situation raises for you?

SOURCE: Canda & Furman, 2010; Titone, 1991.

may include distress due to mystical experiences, near-death experiences, spiritual emergence/ emergency, or separation from a spiritual teacher (Turner, Lukoff, Barnhouse, & Lu, 1995). This framework would be helpful in understanding any extraordinary or mystical experiences that Trudy, Jean-Joseph, or any of the other people in the case studies might share with you. Accurate assessment of such an occurrence can help determine whether the experience needs to be integrated and used as a stimulus for personal growth or whether it should be recognized as a sign of mental instability.

Assessment is just one component of spiritually sensitive social work practice. The field is accumulating a number of publications that provide more comprehensive discussion of spiritually sensitive practice (see, for example, Bullis, 1996; Canda & Furman, 2010; Derezotes, 2006; Frame, 2003; Mijares & Khalsa, 2005; Pargament, 2007; Scales et al., 2002; Sheridan, 2002).

Critical Thinking Questions 6.5

How comfortable are you in discussing religious and spiritual themes with others? Which of the questions in Exhibit 6.5 would you be comfortable asking a client? Which would you be comfortable answering?

Implications for Social Work Practice

Spiritually sensitive social work practice involves gaining knowledge and skills in the areas discussed in this chapter, always keeping in mind that this approach must be grounded within the values and ethics of the profession. The following practice principles are offered as guidelines for effective and ethical social work practice in this area.

- Maintain clarity about your role as a spiritually sensitive practitioner, making a distinction between being a social worker who includes a focus on the spiritual dimension as part of holistic practice and being a religious leader or spiritual director.
- Be respectful of different religious or spiritual paths and be willing to learn about the role and meaning of various beliefs, practices, and experiences for various client systems (individuals, families, groups, communities).
- Critically examine your own values, beliefs, and biases concerning religion and spirituality and be willing to work through any unresolved or negative feelings or experiences in this area that may adversely affect your work with clients.
- Inform yourself about both the positive and negative role of religion and spirituality in the fight for social justice by various groups and be sensitive to this history in working with members of oppressed and marginalized populations.
- Develop a working knowledge of the beliefs and practices frequently encountered in your work with clients, especially those of newly arriving immigrants/refugees or nondominant groups (for example, Buddhist beliefs of southeast Asian refugees, spiritual traditions of First Nations peoples).
- Conduct comprehensive spiritual assessments with clients at all levels and use this information in service planning and delivery.
- Acquire the knowledge and skills necessary to employ spiritually based intervention techniques appropriately, ethically, and effectively.
- Seek information about the various religious and spiritual organizations, services, and leaders pertinent to your practice and develop good working relationships with these resources for purposes of referral and collaboration.
- Engage in ongoing self-reflection about what brings purpose, meaning, and connection in your own life and make disciplined efforts toward your own spiritual development, however you define this process.

ecocentric
faith
faith stages
first force therapies
four quadrants
fourth force therapies
fulcrum

ideology (personal)
levels of consciousness
lines of consciousness
religion
second force therapies
self-system
spiritual bypassing

spirituality
states of consciousness
third force therapies
transpersonal approach
ultimate environment
worldcentric

Active Learning

1. Consider any of the case studies presented at the beginning of the chapter. Using either Fowler's stages of faith development or Wilber's integral theory of consciousness as the conceptual framework, construct a timeline of the person's spiritual development. Trace the overall growth patterns through the different stages, including any ups and downs, as well as plateau periods. Identify the significant points or transitions you consider pivotal to the person's spiritual development.

   - How would this information help you to better understand the person's story and overall development? How would this information help you work with him or her as a social worker at various points in his or her life?
   - What would your own spiritual timeline look like, including patterns throughout various stages and significant points or transitions that were particularly significant for your own growth and development?

2. Select a partner for this exercise. This chapter provides a brief overview of the spiritual diversity in the United States. Given both your knowledge and experiences with different spiritual traditions, both religious and nonreligious, address the following questions. Take a few moments to reflect on each question before answering it. Partners should take turns answering the questions.

   - To which spiritual perspectives do you have the most positive reactions (e.g., are in the most agreement with, feel an appreciation or attraction toward, are the most comfortable with, find it easiest to keep an open mind and heart about)? What is it about you that contributes to these reactions (e.g., previous knowledge, personal experiences, messages from family or larger culture)?
   - To which perspective do you have the most negative reactions (e.g., are in the most disagreement with, feel a repulsion or fear about, are the most uncomfortable with, find it most difficult to keep an open mind and heart about)? What is it about you that contributes to these reactions (e.g., previous knowledge, personal experiences, messages from family or larger culture)?
   - What impact(s) might your reactions (both positive and negative) have on work with clients (especially with those who may hold different spiritual perspectives from yourself)? What personal and professional "work" on yourself is suggested by your positive and/or negative reactions?

3. Select a partner for this exercise. Together select one of the open-ended questions listed in Exhibit 6.5 to consider as it applies to your own lives. After a few moments of quiet reflection, write your response to the question, allowing yourself to write freely without concern for the proper mechanics of writing (e.g., spelling, grammar). Then sit with what you've written, reading it over with fresh eyes. When you're ready, share this experience with your partner, sharing as much or as little of what you've written as you feel comfortable with. Then talk together about the following questions:

- What was the experience like of answering this question and then reading the response to yourself (e.g., easy, difficult, exciting, anxiety-producing, confirming)?
- Are there previous times in your life when you considered this question? Did you share your thoughts about it with others? If so, what was that like? What is it like to do that now with your partner?
- Can you see yourself asking this kind of a question with a client? What do you think that experience might be like for both the client and yourself?

Web Resources

Adherents.com: www.adherents.com

Site not affiliated with any religious, political, educational, or commercial organization. Contains a comprehensive collection of more than 41,000 statistics on religious adherents, geography citations, and links to other major sites on diverse religious and spiritual traditions.

Association of Religion Data Archives: www.thearda.com

Site sponsored by the Lilly Endowment, the John Templeton Foundation, and Pennsylvania State University. Provides more than 350 data files on U.S. and international religions using online features for generating national profiles, maps, overviews of church memberships, denominational heritage trees, tables, charts, and other summary reports.

Canadian Society for Spirituality and Social Work: http://stu.ca/~spirituality

Site includes information about the activities of this society, links to other websites, and other resources.

Pew Research Religion & Public Life Project: http://pewforum.org

Site sponsored by the larger Pew Research Center. Functions as both a clearinghouse for research and other publications related to issues at the intersection of religion and public affairs and also a virtual town hall for discussion of related topics.

Religious Tolerance: www.religioustolerance.org

Site presented by the Ontario Consultants on Religious Tolerance, an agency that promotes religious tolerance as a human right. Contains comparative descriptions of world religions and diverse spiritual paths from Asatru to Zoroastrianism and links to other related sites.

Society for Spirituality and Social Work: http://societyforspiritualityandsocialwork.com

Site includes information about joining the U.S. Society for Spirituality and Social Work, a selected bibliography, and other resources.

Virtual Religion Index: www.virtualreligion.net/vri

Site presented by the Religion Department at Rutgers University. Contains analysis and highlights of religion-related websites and provides links to major sites for specific religious groups and topics.

⑤SAGE edge™

Sharpen your skills with SAGE edge at **edge.sagepub.com/hutchisonpe5e**

SAGE edge for students provides a personalized approach to help you accomplish your coursework goals in an easy-to-use learning environment.

PART III

The Multiple Dimensions of Environment

Social workers have always recognized the important role the environment plays in human behavior and, equally important, have always understood the environment as multidimensional. The social work literature has not been consistent in identifying the significant dimensions of environment, however. Although all dimensions of environment are intertwined and inseparable, social scientists have developed specialized literature on several specific dimensions. Both the environment and the study of it become more complex with each new era of technological development, making our efforts to understand the environment ever more challenging.

The purpose of the eight chapters in Part III is to provide you with an up-to-date understanding of the multidisciplinary theory and research about dimensions of environment. It begins with Chapter 7 on an important dimension often overlooked in the social work literature, the physical environment. Next comes Chapter 8, which reviews our historical attempts to understand culture and presents a contemporary framework to help us become more competent social workers in a multicultural world. Chapter 9 explores the macro environment, focusing on contemporary trends in social structure and social institutions, placing U.S. trends in a global context. Chapters 10 and 11 cover the smaller-scale configurations of families and small groups. Part III ends with Chapters 12, 13, and 14 on the moderate-size configurations of formal organizations, communities, and social movements. In Part II, you learned about the multiple dimensions of persons. When you put that together with the knowledge gained about multiple dimensions of environments, you will be better prepared to understand the situations you encounter in social work practice. This prepares you well to think about the changing configurations of persons and environments across the life course—the subject of the companion volume to this book, *The Changing Life Course*.

CHAPTER 7

The Physical Environment

Elizabeth D. Hutchison

Chapter Outline

Key Ideas

As you read this chapter, take note of these central ideas:

1. To better understand the relationship between the physical environment and human behavior, social workers can draw on multidisciplinary research from the behavioral sciences and design disciplines.

2. Four broad categories of theories about human behavior and the physical environment are stimulation theories, control theories, behavior settings theories, and ecocritical theories.

3. Researchers have found a strong human preference for elements of the natural environment and positive outcomes of time spent in the natural environment, but overstimulation of features of the natural environment can be hazardous to human well-being.

4. Information and communication technologies are reshaping human behavior and social life.

5. Built environments may promote health and healing.

6. Humans form bonds of attachment with physical places as well as with other humans.

7. A recent recognition that built physical environments can be disabling has led to legislation to protect the civil rights of persons with disabilities.

CASE STUDY

Ben Watson's Changing Experience With the Physical Environment

Author's Note: Ben Watson narrates his own story.

I finished my final semester in the Bachelor's of Architecture Program, and a couple of friends and I decided to spend a few days doing some rock climbing before graduation. I already had a job lined up with a small architecture firm down in North Carolina. Things were looking good.

It doesn't take but a minute to change things forever. I fell 500 feet and knew, as soon as I came to, that something was very wrong. My legs were numb, I couldn't move them, and I had terrific pain in my back. My friends knew not to move me, and one stayed with me while the other went for help.

I don't remember much about the rescue, the trip to the nearest hospital, or the medivac to the closest trauma center. In my early days at the trauma hospital, I saw lots of medical people, but I vividly remember the doc who told me that I had an incomplete spinal cord injury, that I would have some sensation below my lesion but no movement. I didn't really believe it. Movement was what I was all about. I spent 5 months in the hospital and rehabilitation center, and I gradually began to understand that my legs were not going to move. I was depressed, I was angry (furious really), and for 1 week I wanted to give up. My parents and my brothers pulled me through. They showered me with love but were firm when I tried to refuse rehabilitation treatments. Oh yeah, some of my friends were terrific also. When things get rough, you learn who your real friends are. I also appreciated a chance to talk with the rehab social worker about my grief over this unbelievable turn in my life. It was good to talk with him because he wasn't dealing with his own grief about my situation the way my family and friends were.

I left rehab with my new partner, a sophisticated titanium wheelchair, and went home to live with my parents. They rearranged the house so that I could have the first-floor bedroom and bath. I appreciated the assistance from my parents and brothers, and my friends made heroic efforts to get me out of the house. As we did so, I began to learn the importance of the word *access*. The first time my friends took me out, we wanted to go to a bar; after all that's what 20-something guys do. My friends called around to find a nearby bar that would be accessible to me and my wheelchair. That turned out to be tougher than they thought. Did you ever notice how many bars require dealing with stairs? Finally, they were assured that one bar was accessible—well, actually, nobody wanted to say their place wasn't accessible, given the law and all, plus most folks haven't given any thought to what that really means. So, my friends had to run through a set of questions about stairs, ramps, size of doors, etc., to make their own determination about accessibility. One question they didn't think to ask was whether there were stairs leading to the bathroom. So, we went out drinking, but I was afraid to drink or eat because I couldn't get to the bathroom.

After several months at home, I began to get restless and wanted to get on with my life. After my accident, the architecture firm down in North Carolina had told my parents that they would still be interested in having me work for them when I was strong enough. So, I began to talk with my parents about making the move to North Carolina. They understood that I needed to get on with my life, but they worried about me moving 350 miles away. I was still dependent on them for a lot of personal care, but I was gradually learning to do more for myself.

I knew from my interviews that the architecture firm was accessible by wheelchair—it was in a relatively new building with a ground-level entrance, a spacious elevator, wide doors, and accessible bathrooms. With some trepidation my dad drove me down to look for housing. There were plenty of new apartment complexes, but we found that everybody, not just people with disabilities, wants ground-floor apartments with the open architectural features that make wheelchair mobility so much easier. After a lot of calls, we found a one-bedroom apartment that I could afford. I immediately loved the location in a part of the city where there was a lot happening on the streets, with shops, restaurants, and a movie theater. The apartment was attractive, convenient, and accessible, but most important it was mine. I was finally beginning to feel like an adult. I would have my privacy, but the open floor plan would allow me to have friends over without feeling cramped. And I loved the abundance of windows that would allow for good natural lighting from the sun. I couldn't afford to get my own car with hand controls yet, but the apartment luckily was only a short cab ride from my office.

My father and brothers helped me make the move, and my grandmother came for a visit to add some charming decorating touches. I hired a personal assistant to help me get ready in the mornings—well, actually, my parents paid him for the first few months, until I could get my finances worked out.

Given my profession, it is good that I still have excellent function of my upper body, particularly my hands. My colleagues at work turned out to be good friends as well as good colleagues. And I never paid much attention to issues of accessibility in my design studios at school, but I have become the local expert on accessible design.

(Continued)

I learned a lot about accessible design from some of my own frustrating experiences. I have been lucky to develop a close set of friends, and we have an active life. My friends and I have learned where the streets are that don't have curb cuts, which bars and restaurants are truly accessible, where the "accessible" entry is really some dark-alley back entrance, and to watch out for retail doorways blocked by displays of goods.

My friends and I travel, and I find some airline personnel handle me and my wheelchair well while some are disastrous—imagine being rolled over on the ramp, with an audience no less. The natural environment was always an important part of my life—it provides beauty and serenity—and my friends and I could write a book about all the wonderful hiking trails that are wheelchair accessible. In the past year, however, I have become deeply concerned about the damage I see humans doing to the natural environment and have been considering how I might join forces with other folks concerned about our human responsibility to care for the natural environment. As I have researched this on the Internet, I have also been learning about issues of environmental justice—how some communities are suffering more than others from the health consequences of industrial and agricultural practices that put toxins into the soil, water, and air. That gives me something else to think about. I hope you'll think about it, too.

HUMAN BEHAVIOR AND THE PHYSICAL ENVIRONMENT

As with most stories we hear as social workers, Ben Watson's is a multidimensional story of person and environment interactions over time. It presents issues of life course development, family and friend relationships, physical disability, a struggle for emotional well-being, and interactions with formal organizations. And, of course, a supremely important dimension of this unfolding story is the physical environment. Ben's story reminds us that all human behavior occurs in a physical context, and it also reminds us of the impact that human behavior has on the physical environment.

Jane Addams, founder of the U.S. settlement house movement, recognized a robust relationship between the physical environment and public health. She was concerned about urban overcrowding, sanitation, and factory inspection, and she ran for and was elected to be neighborhood sanitation inspector in 1895 (Addams, 1910). Throughout most of its history, however, the social work profession has paid little attention to the physical

Systems perspective

environment; its person and environment construct considered the social environment but ignored the physical environment. In the 1970s, Carel Germain proposed an ecological model of social work, which she and colleague Alex Gitterman called the life model (see Gitterman & Germain, 2008). This model recognized the physical environment as an important dimension of the person and environment construct (see Germain, 1981). In recent years, some social work scholars, like scholars in other behavioral science disciplines, have begun to pay attention to robust findings about the relationship between human well-being and the physical environment (see Gray, Coates, & Hetherington, 2013).

The relationship between human behavior and the physical environment is a multidisciplinary study that includes contributions from the social, behavioral, and health sciences of psychology, sociology, geography, anthropology, neuroscience, and public health, as well as from the design disciplines of architecture, landscape architecture, interior design, and urban and regional planning. This chapter gives you some ways of thinking about the relationship between human behavior and the physical environment as you begin to consider the role it plays in the stories of the individuals and collectivities you encounter in practice. When thinking about human interactions with the physical environment, it is important to consider both the natural and the built environments; both of these aspects of the physical environment are examined in this chapter.

Four broad categories of theory about human behavior and the physical environment are introduced in this chapter: stimulation theories, control theories, behavior settings theories, and ecocritical theories. Each of these categories of theory, and the research they have stimulated, provides useful possibilities for social workers to consider as they participate in person–environment assessments and consider possibilities for intervention at multiple levels of person and environment interactions. The ecocritical perspective is raising interesting and important new questions about the social work profession's responsibilities to the natural environment. Exhibit 7.1 presents the key ideas and important concepts of these four types of theories.

Stimulation Theories

Have you thought about how you would react to the abundance of sunlight in Ben Watson's new apartment or the activity on his street? That question is consistent with **stimulation theories**, which focus on the physical environment as a source of sensory information essential for human well-being. The stimulation may be light, color, heat, texture, or scent, or it may be buildings, streets, and parks. Stimulation theorists propose that patterns of stimulation influence thinking, feelings, social interaction, and health.

Stimulation varies by amount—intensity, frequency, duration, number of sources—and by type. Stimulation theories based on theories of psychophysiological arousal assume that moderate levels of stimulation are optimal for human behavior (Gifford, 2007). Thus, both *stimulus overload* (too much stimulation) and *restricted environmental stimulation* (once called *stimulus deprivation*) have a negative effect on human behavior. Theorists

interested in the behavioral and health effects of stimulus overload have built on Han Selye's work regarding stress (see Chapter 5).

Some stimulation theories focus on the direct, concrete effect of stimulation on behavior; others focus on the meanings people construct regarding particular stimuli. In fact, people respond to both the concrete and the symbolic aspects of their physical environments. A

Social behavioral perspective; social constructionist perspective

doorway too narrow to accommodate a wheelchair has a concrete effect on the behavior of a person in a wheelchair; it will also have a symbolic effect, perhaps contributing to the person's feelings of exclusion and stigma. You probably will have a very different emotional reaction to a loud bang depending on whether it occurs during a street riot or at a New Year's Eve party; your understanding of the meaning of the noise has a strong influence on your reaction. In this case, your response is primarily symbolic. Stimulation theories alert social workers to consider the quality and intensity of sensory stimulation in the environments where their clients live and work.

Environmental design scholars have begun to incorporate recent advances in neuroscience research to understand how people's brains respond to different types of stimulation in physical environments (see Eberhard, 2008). Their goal is to use this knowledge to design environments that support brain development and functioning for the general population as well as for groups with special needs, such as premature newborns and persons with Alzheimer's disease (Zeisel, 2006, 2009). Neuroscientists are also working with architects and environmental psychologists to learn what aspects of the physical environment stimulate emotional and physical healing (Sternberg, 2009).

Control Theories

The ability to gain control over his physical environment is a central theme of Ben Watson's story. In that way, the story is a good demonstration of

Exhibit 7.1 Four Categories of Theories About the Relationship Between the Physical Environment and Human Behavior

Theories	Key Ideas	Important Concepts
Stimulation theories	The physical environment is a source of sensory information essential for human well-being. Patterns of stimulation influence thinking, emotions, social interaction, and health.	Stimulus overload Restricted environmental stimulation
Control theories	Humans desire control over their physical environments. Some person–environment configurations provide more control over the physical environment than others.	Privacy Personal space Territoriality Crowding
Behavior settings theories	Consistent, uniform patterns of behavior occur in particular settings. Behaviors of different persons in the same setting are more similar than the behaviors of the same person in different settings.	Behavior settings Programs Staffing
Ecocritical theories	All elements of nature and the physical world are interconnected. Humans have no more value than other forms of nature. Nondominant groups bear the burdens of environmental hazards.	Deep ecology Ecofeminism Environmental sustainability

Psychodynamic perspective; social behavioral perspective

the ideas found in control theories. **Control theories** focus on the issue of how much control we have over our physical environments and the attempts we make to gain control (Gifford, 2007). Four concepts are central to the work of control theorists: privacy, personal space, territoriality, and crowding. Personal space and territoriality are *boundary regulating mechanisms* that we use to gain greater control over our physical environments.

Privacy

Pychodynamic perspective

Altman (1975, p. 18) defines **privacy** as "selective control of access to the self or to one's group." This definition contains two important elements: Privacy involves control over information about oneself as well as control over interactions with others. Virginia Kupritz (2003)

has extended Altman's work by making a distinction between speech or conversational privacy (being able to hold conversations without being overheard) and visual privacy (being free of unwanted observation). Contemporary innovations in communication technologies have introduced new concerns about having control over information with respect to oneself and one's group and about how to balance, among other things, national security with rights to privacy. Privacy is a frequent topic of articles in the journal *Computers in Human Behavior* (see, for example, Mohamed & Ahmad, 2012).

Some of us require more privacy than others, and some situations stimulate privacy needs more than other situations. Ben Watson was accustomed to sharing a house with his university pals and didn't mind the lack of privacy that came with that situation. He felt differently about lack of privacy in his parents' home after rehab and was eager for a more private living situation, even though his privacy in some areas would be compromised by his need for a personal care assistant.

It appears that people in different cultures use space differently to create privacy. Susan Kent (1991) theorizes that the use of partitions, such as walls or screens, to create private spaces increases as societies become more complex. She particularly notes the strong emphasis that

European American culture places on partitioned space, both at home and at work (see Duvall-Early & Benedict, 1992). More recent research supports this idea; for example, college students in the United States have been found to desire more privacy in their residence halls than Turkish students (Kay & Weber, 2003). The situation appears to be different when it comes to privacy in online communications, however. For example, researchers have found college students in China and Japan to be more concerned about privacy in online communications than college students in the United States (Lowry, Cao, & Everard, 2011; Maynard & Taylor, 1996).

Researchers have examined the physical attributes of workplace offices that satisfy the privacy needs of the U.S. workforce. In recent decades employers have limited personal space of employees, using open-plan cubicles, based on the belief that such open-plan arrangements will facilitate communication among employees, as well as on a desire to cut costs. The consistent finding is that employees are not satisfied with the level of privacy in open-plan arrangements (see Lee, 2010). There is also evidence that employees tend to communicate less when they feel they cannot control the privacy of communications (Kupritz, 2003). Personal space and territoriality are two mechanisms for securing privacy.

Personal Space

Personal space, also known as interpersonal distance, is the physical distance we choose to maintain in interpersonal relationships. Robert Sommer (1969) has defined it as "an area with invisible boundaries surrounding a person's body

into which intruders may not come" (p. 26). More recent formulations (Gifford, 2007) emphasize that personal space is not stable but contracts and expands with changing interpersonal circumstances and variations in physical settings. The distance you desire when talking with your best friend is likely to be different from the distance you prefer when talking with a stranger, or even with a known authority figure like your social work professor. The desired distance for any of these interpersonal situations is likely to expand in small spaces (Sinha & Mukherjee, 1996). We will want to recognize our own personal space requirements in different work situations and be sensitive to the personal space requirements of our co-workers and clients.

Variations in personal space are also thought to be related to age, gender, attachment style, previous victimization, mental health, and culture. Personal space requirements have been found to increase with age until early adulthood (Gifford, 2007). One research proj-

ect found that, in shopping malls in the United States and Turkey, adolescents interacting with other adolescents kept the largest interpersonal distance of any age group (Ozdemir, 2008). Males have often been found to require greater personal space than females, and research indicates that the largest interpersonal distances are kept in male-male pairs, followed by female-female pairs, with the smallest interpersonal distances kept in male-female pairs (Ozdemir, 2008). There is evidence that adults with insecure attachment style require a larger personal space than children and adults with secure attachments (Kaitz, Bar-Haim, Lehrer, & Grossman, 2004). Physically abused children have been found to keep significantly larger personal space than nonabused children, suggesting that personal space provides a protective function for these children (Vranic, 2003). A study of combat veterans in Croatia found that veterans diagnosed with PTSD preferred significantly larger interpersonal distance than veterans without PTSD (Bogovic, Mihanovic,

Photo 7.1 Personal space and territoriality are two mechanisms for securing privacy.

© Chris Barrett/Hedrick Blessing/Arcaid/Corbis

Jokic-Begic, & Svagelj, 2013). Both groups of veterans maintained greater interpersonal distance when approached by a man than when approached by a woman. The veterans with PTSD required greater distance when they were approached from behind while the veterans without PTSD required greater distance when approached from the front. Individuals diagnosed with schizophrenia have also been found to require more personal space than people without such a diagnosis (Nechamkin, Salganik, Modai, & Ponizovsky, 2003).

In *The Hidden Dimension*, Edward Hall (1966) reported field research indicating that members of contact-oriented, collectivist cultures (e.g., Latin, Asian, Arab) prefer closer interpersonal distances than members of noncontact-oriented,

individualist cultures (e.g., northern European, North American). More recent research has supported this suggestion; for example, pairs in Turkish malls have been observed to interact more closely than pairs in U.S. malls (Ozdemir, 2008), but within-culture differences in interpersonal distance preferences have also been noted (Evans, Lepore, & Allen, 2000). There is some evidence that people require less personal space when interacting with people they consider to be like themselves in some important category (Novelli, Drury, & Reicher, 2010).

Sommer (2002) has updated his discussion of personal space by raising questions about how personal space is affected by digital technology. Perhaps you have been interested, as I have been, with how people define their personal space while talking on their cell phones. It seems that we are still negotiating the appropriate interpersonal distance while using our cell phones, but I have been surprised to sit very close to strangers in public spaces who are using cell phones to "break up" with a partner or to try to straighten out a credit problem. Sommer also raises questions about the impact of the computer on personal space, noting that at work people sometimes communicate by e-mail with co-workers who are sitting beside them in the same office. Other researchers have examined how much personal space people need when using automatic teller machines and other technology where private information is stored and found that people report larger desired space than the space actually provided (Shu & Li, 2007). Researchers are also investigating how personal space applies to virtual worlds such as Second Life and computer games and finding that people tend to keep and protect a space around their avatars in much the same way they do in the "real" world (see Amaoka, Laga, Yoshie, & Nakajima, 2011). Developers of artificial intelligence systems are concerned about *active personal space* (APS) in human-robot interactions; they want to program service robots in such a way that they do not invade the personal space of humans (Banik, Gupta, Habib, & Mousumi, 2013).

Critical Thinking Questions 7.1

Have you given much thought to your need for private space? Do you have sufficient privacy in your home and work environments to feel some sense of control over who has access to you and your interpersonal interactions? Do the clients at your field agency have private space? What have you observed about how people deal with privacy issues when using cell phones? When using social media of various types?

Territoriality

Personal space is a concept about individual behavior and the use of space to control the interpersonal environment. **Territoriality** refers primarily to the behavior of individuals and small groups as they seek control over physical space (Taylor, 1988), but recently, the concept has also been used to refer to attempts to control objects, roles, and relationships (Brown, Lawrence, & Robinson, 2005). For example, Robert Gifford (2007) defined territoriality as "a pattern of behavior and attitudes held by an individual or group, based on perceived, attempted, or actual ownership or control of a definable physical space, object, or idea" (p. 166). Territoriality leads us to mark, or personalize, our territory to signify our "ownership" and to engage in a variety of behaviors to protect it from invasion. The study of animal territoriality has a longer history than the study of human territorial behavior. For humans, there is much evidence that males are more territorial than females, but there is also some contradictory evidence (Kaya & Burgess, 2007; Kaya & Weber, 2003). For example, in crowded living conditions in Nigerian university residence halls, female students appeared to use more territorial strategies to cope while male students used more withdrawal strategies (Amole, 2005). By their midteens, many youth want some territory of their own, as is sometimes demonstrated with graffiti, tagging, and gang behavior (Pickering, Kintrea, & Bannister, 2012).

Irwin Altman (1975) classifies our territories as primary, secondary, and public. A **primary territory** is one that evokes feelings of ownership that we control on a relatively permanent basis and that is vital to our daily lives. For most of us, our primary territory would include our home and place of work. **Secondary territories** are less important to us than primary territories, and control of them does not seem as essential to us; examples might be our favorite table at Starbucks, our favorite cardio machine at the gym, or our favorite seat in the classroom (Costa, 2012). **Public territories** are open to anyone in the community, and we generally make no attempt to control access to them—places such as public parks, public beaches, sidewalks, and stores. For people who are homeless and lack access to typical primary territories, however, public territories may serve as primary territories.

Much of the literature on territoriality draws on the functionalist sociological tradition, emphasizing the positive value of territorial behavior to provide order to the social world and a sense of security to individuals (Taylor, 1988). We know, however, that territorial behavior can also be the source of conflict, domination, and oppression. Recently, it has been suggested that globalization is reducing territoriality among nation-states (Kythreotis, 2012). And, indeed, globalization does blur national boundaries, but ongoing national conversations about "securing our borders" are prime examples of territorial behaviors, and wars are still being fought to protect both geographical boundaries and ideas.

> Systems perspective; conflict perspective

Crowding

Crowding has sometimes been used interchangeably with *density*, but environmental psychologists make important distinctions between these terms. **Density** is the ratio of persons per unit area of a space. Crowding is the subjective feeling of having too many people around. **Crowding** is not always correlated with density; the feeling of being crowded seems to be influenced by an interaction of personal, social, and cultural as well as physical factors. For example, in one study the perception of crowding was associated with density among older adults living

> Social constructionist perspective

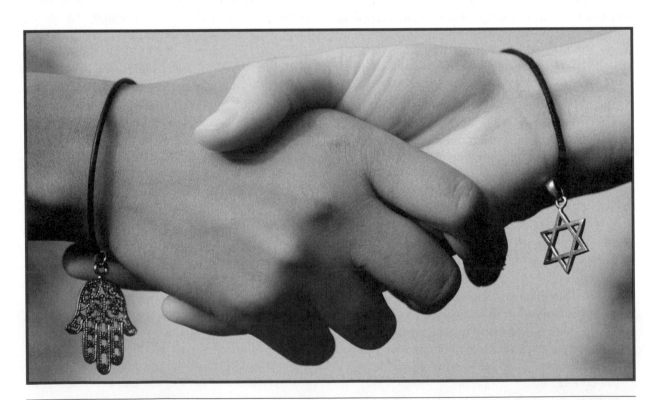

Photo 7.2 Both geographical boundaries and shared ideas provide a sense of security to individuals, and both can become a source of conflict.

© Sebastien Desarmaux/Godong/Corbis

with extended families in India, but perceived social support in high-density environments buffered the perception of crowding and decreased personal space requirements (Sinha & Nayyar, 2000). Researchers (Evans et al., 2000) have compared different ethnic groups that live in high-density housing in the United States. They found that Latin American and Asian American residents tolerate more density before feeling crowded than Anglo Americans and African Americans. These researchers also found, however, that all four ethnic groups experienced similar psychological distress from crowding. Another research team found that Middle Eastern respondents were less likely to perceive high-density retail situations as crowded than their North American counterparts (Pons, Laroche, & Mourali, 2006).

Research has also found gender differences in response to crowding. Women living in crowded homes are more likely to be depressed while men living in crowded homes demonstrate higher levels of withdrawal and violence (Regoeczi, 2008). In crowded elementary school classrooms, girls' academic achievement and boys' classroom behavior are adversely affected (Maxwell, 2003).

Crowding has been found to have an adverse effect on child development (Evans & Saegert, 2000) and to be associated with elevated blood pressure and neuroendocrine hormone activity (Gifford, 2007), poor compliance with mental health care (Menezes Scazufca, Rodrigues, & Mann, 2000), increased incidence of tuberculosis (Baker, Das, Venugopal, & Howden-Chapman, 2008; Wanyeki et al., 2006), and aggressive behavior in prison inmates (Lawrence & Andrews, 2004).

Behavior Settings Theories

Social behavioral perspective; systems perspective

Would you expect to observe the same behaviors if you were observing Ben Watson in different settings—for example, his parents' home, his apartment, running errands in his neighborhood, at work, at a party with friends, or on an outing in the natural environment? My guess is that you would not. A third major category of theories about the relationship between human behavior and the physical environment is **behavior settings theories**. According to these theories, consistent, uniform patterns of behavior occur in particular places, or **behavior settings**. Behavior is *always* tied to a specific place, and the setting may have a more powerful influence on behavior than characteristics of the individual (Scott, 2005).

Behavior settings theory was developed by Roger Barker (1968), who, unexpectedly, found that observations of different persons in the same setting were more similar than observations of the same person in different settings. For example, your behavior at a musical festival is more similar to the behavior of other festival attendees than it is to your own behavior in the classroom or at the grocery store. Barker suggested that **programs**—consistent, prescribed patterns of behavior—develop and are maintained in many specific settings. For example, when you enter a grocery store, you grab a cart, travel down aisles collecting items and putting them in the cart, and take the cart to a checkout counter where you wait while store employees tabulate the cost of the items and bag them. Imagine how surprised you would be if you went into the grocery store to find everybody kicking soccer balls! Behavioral programs are created conjointly by individuals and their inanimate surroundings, and behavior settings are distinctive in their physical-spatial features as well as their social rules.

In recent years, behavior settings theory has been extended to explain behavior in settings other than physical behavior settings, more specifically to explain behavior in *virtual behavior settings* such as chat rooms and blogs (Blanchard, 2004; Stokols & Montero, 2002). This line of inquiry is interested in how interaction in such virtual behavior settings is integrated, or not, with the place-based settings in which it occurs, such as home, workplace, or Internet café.

Behavior settings as conceptualized by Barker had a static quality, but Allan Wicker (2012) has more recently written about the changing nature— the life histories—of behavior settings. Some settings disappear, and some become radically altered. The high school prom my neighbor attended in 2009 was a different setting, with a very different behavioral program, from the high school prom I attended in 1963. And, these days, that trip to the grocery store often involves getting your own reusable grocery bags from the car before entering the store (or making a trip back to the car to get them when you are almost at the store door). It may also include running your own items through a scanner and bagging them yourself. Wicker (2012) also argues that behavioral scientists must pay attention to the larger contexts of settings, which often belong to networks that include a number of other settings.

Community psychologist Edward Seidman (2012) argues that focusing on the setting, rather than the individual, as the location for change opens the way for a wealth of interventions. Behavior settings theory has implications for social work assessment and intervention. It suggests that patterns of behavior are specific to a setting and, therefore, that we must assess settings as well as individuals when problematic behavior occurs. Behavior settings theory also suggests that the place where we first learn a new skill helps re-create the state necessary to retrieve and enact the skill. When assisting clients in skill development, we should pay particular attention to the discontinuities between the settings where the skills are being "learned" and the settings where those skills must be used.

Another key concept in behavior settings theory is the level of **staffing** (Barker, 1968; Brown, Shepherd, Wituk, & Meissen, 2007). Different behavior settings attract different numbers of participants, or staff. It is important to have a good fit between the number of participants and the behavioral program for the setting. Overstaffing occurs when there are too many participants for the behavioral program of a given setting; understaffing occurs when there are too few participants. A growing body of research also suggests that larger settings tend to exclude more people from action, and smaller settings put pressure on more people

to perform. The issue of appropriate staffing, in terms of number of participants, for particular behavioral programs in particular behavior settings has great relevance for the planning of social work programs. Indeed, behavior settings theory and the issue of optimal staffing have been used to understand the benefits of member participation in consumer-run mental health organizations (Brown et al., 2007).

Ecocritical Theories

In Chapter 2, we wrote about ecological theory in the systems perspective, a theory that focuses on

Systems perspective; conflict perspective

the relationships and interactions between living organisms and their environments. This theory emphasizes the interdependence and mutual influence of organisms and their environments. In the past 2 decades, ecological theory has been extended in several disciplines to take a more critical view of human interactions with the natural environment. For the purpose of this discussion, I will call the theories in this tradition **ecocritical theories**, because they call attention to the ways that human behavior degrades and destroys the natural world, the unequal burden of environmental degradation on different groups, and ethical obligations that humans have to nonhuman elements of the natural environment. Given space limitations, this discussion will touch on two such theories developed in the last quarter of the 20th century: deep ecology and ecofeminism.

Deep ecology is both a theory and a social movement. In simplest terms, deep ecology suggests that social work should focus on "person *with* environment," rather than "person *and* environment" (Besthorn, 2012). It emphasizes the total interconnectedness of all elements of the natural and physical world and the inseparability of human well-being and the well-being of planet Earth. It argues for the intrinsic value of all life forms, for the value of ecological diversity, and for the responsibility of humans to respect the rest of nature and live in ways that have minimal impact on the well-being of other life forms. It calls attention to the way that current human interactions with the natural environment are *unsustainable*, leading to global warming, atmospheric pollution, and other forms of environmental degradation that put the long-term survival of all elements of nature at risk. What distinguishes deep ecology from other theories discussed in this book is that it is *ecocentric* (earth centered) rather than *anthropocentric* (human centered). It insists on a nonhierarchical form of justice, in which humans do not control or have dominance over nature. Humans have no more value than other forms of nature. Deep ecologists note that some cultures have long held the view that ethical decision making must respect the interests of the natural world. Fred Besthorn (2012) has been a strong voice recommending that deep ecology is the theory that social workers should use to think about human environment interactions.

Ecofeminism, also both a theory and a social movement, took shape about the same time as deep ecology, in the 1970s, but its roots go back much further. Although there are different strains of **ecofeminism**, the approach is best described as a feminist approach to environmental ethics. Ecofeminists see the oppression of women and the domination of nature as interconnected. They suggest that nature and women, as well as other groups such as children and people of color, have been conceptualized as separate and inferior in order to legitimate dominance over them by an elite male-dominant social order (Gaard, 2011). More than the deep ecologists, they call attention to the ways that women and other nondominant groups bear the burdens of environmental hazards such as toxic waste. Susan Mann (2011) argues that the intersection of feminism and environmentalism is not new, noting that throughout the Progressive Era in the United States, women played important roles in both wildlife conservation and activism to promote clean air, water, and food for people living in urban centers. As noted earlier, Jane Addams was such a woman.

Critical Thinking Questions 7.2

What have you observed about the impact of the physical environment on your behavior and the behavior of others? How well do stimulation theories, control theories, or behavior settings theories account for the influence of the physical environment on your behavior and the behavior of other people you know? What do you think of the deep ecology argument that humans have no more value than other forms of nature?

THE NATURAL ENVIRONMENT

If I asked you to engage in a relaxation exercise by picturing yourself in your favorite place, where would that be? Research shows that places in the **natural environment**—that part of the environment made up of all living and nonliving things naturally occurring—are among people's favorite places (White, Pahl, Ashbullby, Herbert, & Depledge, 2013). This is, of course, not true for all people, but it appears to be true for the majority of people in all cultures (Wolsko & Hoyt, 2012). Most of the research on the relationship between human behavior and the natural environment has been in the stimulation theory tradition—looking for ways in which aspects of the natural environment affect our thinking, feeling, social interaction, and health. At a time of great international concern about the damage being done to the natural environment by human endeavors, ecocritical theorists are calling for humans to rethink their relationship with the natural environment.

Benefits and Costs of Human Interaction With the Natural Environment

Do you find that you feel refreshed from being in the natural environment—walking along the beach, hiking in the mountains, or even walking in your neighborhood? As it has for many people, the natural environment has always been a place of serenity for Ben Watson. There is a long tradition of research into the benefits of the natural environment for human behavior. In recent years, this research has been based on two theories developed by environmental psychologists. *Attention restoration theory* (ART) proposes that interacting with nature restores depleted cognitive resources (Kaplan & Berman, 2010). *Psychophysiological stress recovery theory* (PSRT) is interested in how interacting with nature helps people to recover emotionally and physiologically (Ulrich et al., 1991).

In general, this research finds many positive outcomes of time spent in the natural environment and suggests that you should consider the benefits of interacting with nature for both you and your clients.

Exhibit 7.2   Benefits of Time Spent in the Natural Environment (Based on Stimulation Theory Research)

- Engaging children's interest
- Stimulating children's imagination
- Stimulating activity and physical fitness
- Increasing productivity
- Enhancing creativity
- Providing intellectual stimulation
- Aiding recovery from mental fatigue
- Improving concentration
- Increasing working memory
- Enhancing group cohesiveness and community cooperation
- Fostering tranquility and serenity
- Fostering a sense of oneness or wholeness
- Fostering a sense of control
- Fostering recovery from surgery
- Lowering heart rate, blood pressure, and muscle tension
- Improving emotional states, such as calmness, relaxation, and vitality
- Contributing to cognitive and emotional improvements in persons diagnosed with major depressive disorder (MDD)
- Reducing psychophysiological stress
- Decreasing vulnerability to illness

These benefits are summarized in Exhibit 7.2, but because of the extensive research in this area only a few of the recent findings are reported here.

There are consistent findings from research using a variety of methods that interaction with natural environments can restore depleted emotional and cognitive resources (see White et al., 2013, for a review of these findings). Our interaction with nature can help to recharge our attentional capacities (Felsten, 2009), reduce psychophysiological stress (Kjellgren & Buhrkall, 2010), and enhance emotional states (Bowler, Buyung-Ali, Knight, & Pullin, 2010). This finding of benefit from interaction with the natural environment has been found even when controlling for individual characteristics, alone or with a group, types of activities, and length of interaction. It is not clear which aspects of the natural environment provide benefit, but research indicates that environments with water have the greatest positive effect (Barton & Pretty, 2010; Karmanov & Hamel, 2008). Interactions with woodlands and mountains have also been found to have a positive effect (White et al., 2013), and there is considerable evidence that interactions with domestic and companion animals have emotional and physiological benefits for humans (Anderson, 2008). There is some evidence that late adolescents derive less benefit from time spent in nature than other age groups, and middle-aged people derive the greatest benefit (White et al., 2013).

A preponderance of the research has investigated the effects of interaction with nature in populations in good health, but recently researchers have been interested in whether nature has similar benefits for people with specific health concerns. Berman and colleagues (2012) studied the benefits of walking in nature, versus walking in an urban setting, for a group of people diagnosed with major depressive disorder (MDD). Participants were found to have improvements in memory span and positive emotion after both types of walks, but the improvements were significantly greater after the nature walks, and the effect sizes were larger than those found in populations without MDD. Kjellgren and Buhrkall (2010) studied a group of people identified as suffering from high stress and burnout and found improvements in stress level and energy after interaction with the natural environment. Walking in outdoor green spaces has been found to improve attention among children and adolescents with attention deficit disorder (ADD) (Taylor & Kuo, 2009).

Researchers have found synergistic effects between nature and physical activity, with moderate-intensity exercise in natural environments associated with the most positive effects (White et al., 2013). Thompson Coon et al. (2011) found that exercising in natural environments, compared with exercising indoors, was associated with greater revitalization and greater reduction in tension, confusion, anger, and depression. Research with individuals involved in both community gardening and backyard gardening indicates benefits that include a sense of tranquility, sense of control, and improved physical health (Shepard, 2013).

There is some evidence that you do not have to be active in the natural environment to derive benefits from it. Views of nature have been found to have positive benefits for cognitive and emotional functioning and to promote recovery from stress and surgery. Office workers have been found to experience less anger and stress when art posters with nature paintings are present (Byoung-Suk, Ulrich, Walker, & Tassinary, 2008). Indoor plants have also been found to be associated with improved attention in office settings (Raanaas, Evensen, Rich, Sjostrom, & Patil, 2011). Researchers have begun to explore whether views of nature are as beneficial as time spent in nature. In a study of participants identified as suffering from stress and burnout, Kjellgren and Buhrkall (2010) investigated the similarities and differences in reactions to 30 minutes of relaxation in a natural environment versus 30 minutes of relaxation while viewing a slide show of photographs of the same natural environment. They found that pulse and diastolic blood pressure were lower after relaxation in both the natural environment and the simulated natural environment. They also found that the two types of relaxation situations were equally efficient in stress reduction.

However, relaxation in the natural environment produced greater improvement in energy, sense of well-being, and tranquility than relaxation in the simulated natural environment.

The findings just discussed are not surprising, given the distinctive place accorded to the natural environment in the cultural artifacts—music, art, literature—of all societies. Sociobiologists propose that humans have a genetically based need to affiliate with nature; they call it **biophilia** (Simaika & Samways, 2010; Wilson, 2007). They argue that humans have a 2-million-year history of evolving in natural environments and have only lived in cities for a small fraction of that time, and that therefore we are much better adapted to natural environments than built environments. On the other hand, Karmanov and Hamel (2008) suggest that physical environments, both natural and built, accumulate meanings over time, and their research suggests that these meanings can be changed through storytelling about the environments in which people find themselves. It is important to note that access to nature is not equally shared by all groups.

The growing evidence of the psychophysiological benefits of time spent in nature is beginning to influence health policy and practice. Perhaps the best example of the use of this research to inform policy is a statement put out by the Faculty of Public Health, the standard-setting body for specialists in public health in the United Kingdom. This statement called for more use of walks in parks to treat mental illness, for general practitioners to consider providing advice about physical activity in the natural environment, for local authorities to provide more accessible green spaces, for full governmental support for programs to support physical activity in green spaces, and for major funding for research investigating the potential role of green space in preventing mental and physical ill health and reducing health inequalities (Faculty of Public Health, 2010). There is a growing call for **ecotherapy**, exposure to nature and the outdoors as a component of psychotherapy, as a major agenda for mental health promotion and treatment (see

Social constructionist perspective

Photo 7.3 The physical environment (both natural and human-made) impacts our behavior. Researchers have found a strong preference for elements of the natural environment and positive outcomes of time spent in nature.

© iStockphoto.com/Xavi Arnau

Buzzell & Chalquist, 2009; Wolsko & Hoyt, 2012). Proponents of ecotherapy propose such interventions as inquiring about clients' relationships with the natural environment, assigning a walk in the park as homework, use of plants and photos of natural settings in therapist offices, and developing forest experiences for adolescents (Hayward, Miller, & Shaw, 2013; Wolsko & Hoyt, 2012). The combination of green spaces with physical exercise has been found to be a particularly potent program for mood elevation in people experiencing symptoms of depression and anxiety (Mackay & Neill, 2010). This research indicates that the degree of perceived "greenness" of the environment has a greater influence than the intensity of the exercise on symptom relief, with the greater benefits coming from enhanced perception of greenness.

Ecotherapy includes time spent with domestic and companion animals.

Ben Watson made special note of the ample sunlight in his apartment. Design innovations for older adults, particularly those with Alzheimer's disease, are emphasizing the benefit of natural over artificial light (Brawley, 2006, 2009). However, the relationship between sunlight and human behavior is curvilinear, with benefit coming from increasing amounts until a certain optimum point is reached, after which increasing amounts damage rather than benefit. Excessive sunlight can have negative impacts, such as glare and overheating, and inadequate sunlight has been identified as a contributor to depression, sometimes referred to as seasonal affective disorder (SAD), in some persons (Kurlanski & Ibay, 2012). Sunlight penetration in indoor spaces is related to feelings of relaxation, with patches of sunlight as the optimum situation, and both too little and too much penetration decreasing the feeling of relaxation (Brawley, 2009).

Although the natural environment can be a positive force, it also has the potential to damage cognitive, emotional, social, and physical well-being. The relationship between sunlight and human behavior provides a clue. Too little sun causes harm, but so does too much sun. Water is a favorite environmental feature for many people, but too little water causes drought and too much water causes flooding. The natural environment provides sensory stimulation in an uncontrolled strength, and the patterns of stimulation are quite unstable. Extremely stimulating natural events are known as natural disasters, including such events as hurricanes, tornadoes, floods, earthquakes, volcanic eruptions, landslides, avalanches, tsunamis, and forest fires. Natural disasters are cataclysmic events—a class of stressors with great force, sudden onset, excessive demands on human coping, and large scope. There is growing concern that climate change is leading to more frequent natural disasters (Datar, Liu, Linnemayr, & Stecher, 2013). Natural disasters have immediate effects on health and mortality, but they also have indirect long-term effects because they lead to disruptions in shelter, food supplies, income, and access to health care. Social workers play active roles in providing services to communities that have experienced natural disasters.

Environmental/Ecological Justice

Conflict perspective

Ben Watson says that he has become concerned about the damage he sees humans doing to the natural environment and about how some communities are suffering more than others from the health consequences of industrial and agricultural practices that put toxins into the soil, water, and air. Some social workers have also become concerned about these issues as indicated by recently published books, such as *Environmental Social Work* (Gray et al., 2013) and

Green Social Work: From Environmental Crises to Environmental Justice (Dominelli, 2012). The concerns raised by Ben Watson and the authors of these books are at the heart of two social movements—the environmental justice movement and the ecological justice movement. These movements share a concern about the ways in which human activities are exhausting natural resources and polluting air, water, and land. But they differ in one important way: The environmental justice movement is concerned about human rights in relation to degradation of the natural environment while the ecological justice movement is concerned about the rights of nature to be protected from human activity (Besthorn, 2013).

Environmental justice is thought to occur when all groups of people have equal share of the harmful environmental effects of policies and operations of business and governments. In the United States, there is considerable evidence that the toxic load of pollution from pesticides, fertilizers, and factories is generally heaviest in poor communities of color (Perkins, 2012), and considerable research establishes that such pollution is a risk factor for cancer and respiratory diseases. There is also clear evidence that hazardous waste facilities are more likely to be located in poor and minority communities. One research team found that brownfields—properties that are no longer operational because of the presence of hazardous substances—are much more likely to be located in poor and minority communities than in areas of higher socioeconomic status. They also found that brownfields are cleaned up much more slowly when they are located in communities with larger minority populations (Eckerd & Keeler, 2012). Internationally, wealthy nations are exploiting the natural resources of poor nations, exacerbating the poverty in those nations. The degradation of the world ecosystems is growing significantly worse, and the burdens of that degradation go increasingly to the most marginalized populations, poor people, people of color, older people, women, and children (Hetherington & Boddy, 2013). Social justice and environmental justice become more and more tightly entwined; in many communities it is not possible to promote social justice without working on issues of environmental justice. That is certainly true in the Coachella Valley of California where I live. At a recent community forum I attended in the eastern end of the valley, which is populated primarily by undocumented farm workers, community members reported that their greatest concerns are the lack of access to potable (drinkable) water, high levels of pesticides in the soil and groundwater, sewage sitting on top of the ground, and the impact of a nearby toxic waste treatment facility on soil, water, and air quality. If those are the community concerns, social workers should be collaborating with other community agencies to address those concerns. (You may know Coachella, California, as home to the huge music festival. The festival site sits in proximity to the conditions just described.)

As suggested earlier, the *ecological justice movement* approaches environmental issues from the standpoint of the rights of nature, not the rights of humans. Adherents argue for humanity in service to nature rather than nature in service to humanity. Besthorn (2013) gives two examples of national governments pursuing policies to promote ecological justice. In September 2008, Ecuador ratified a new constitution, becoming the first nation in the world to recognize the rights of nature and natural systems. In April 2011, the Bolivian National Congress passed legislation that emphasized that all human activities must align with the rights of the natural world. The thrust of the 2013 book *Environmental Social Work* is that social workers need to move beyond anthropocentric environmental justice to value ecological justice. They call for social work to reconsider its person and environment construct to develop a better balance between human and nature needs. Scientists in a number of disciplines are interested in understanding how people perceive their relationships with the natural environment and what motivates them to be concerned about protecting it (see Scannell & Gifford, 2013). The track record of environment policy implementation is not good, and there are grave concerns about the pace of environmental degradation. Indeed, in August 2013, Ecuador abandoned its conservation plan for the Amazon rainforest, blaming the international community

for failure to provide economic support for the plan (Watts, 2013).

> ### Critical Thinking Questions 7.3
>
> What have you observed about how time spent in nature affects your emotions, cognitions, and behavior? How might social workers incorporate ecotherapy into their practice in different settings? Have you seen examples of this being done? How do you think social workers should be involved with environmental or ecological justice, if at all?

THE BUILT ENVIRONMENT

It is the uncontrollable quality of the natural environment that humans try to overcome in constructing the **built environment**—the portion of the physical environment attributable to human effort. The built environment includes tools, structures, buildings, and technologies of various sorts designed and built by humans to create comfort and controllability and to extend their abilities to meet goals. The built environment is produced by human behavior, and what humans build has a great effect on human behavior. Winston Churchill is often quoted as saying, "We shape our dwellings, and afterwards our dwellings shape us" (Mardy, n.d.). This is true for all aspects of the built environment, whether dwellings or technologies.

For several decades, environmental psychologists have been studying the impact of the built environment on such factors as mood, problem solving, productivity, and violent behavior. They have examined physical designs that encourage social interaction, **sociopetal spaces**, and designs that discourage social interaction, **sociofugal spaces**. Researchers have studied design features of such institutional settings as psychiatric hospitals, state schools for persons with cognitive disabilities, college dormitories, and correctional facilities. Exhibit 7.3 summarizes some of the key results of this line of inquiry. Late-20th-century

Therapeutic Design Features	Positive Behaviors
Tables with chairs instead of shoulder-to-shoulder and back-to-back seating Large spaces broken into smaller spaces Flowers and magazines placed on tables	Increase in both brief and sustained interaction
Special activity centers with partitions Sleeping dormitories divided into two bedrooms with table and chairs Long hallways broken up Sound baffles added to high ceilings Improved lighting, bright colors, and large signs added	Increase in social interaction Decrease in passive and inactive behavior
Painted walls replacing bars Carpeted floors Conventional furniture with fabric upholstery Visually interesting public areas Private rooms with outside windows Solarium with exercise equipment	Decrease in violent behavior in correctional facilities
Open sleeping wards and dayroom turned into personal living spaces and a lounge	Increase in social interaction
Places for personal belongings provided Personalized decorations	Decrease in stereotypical behavior Increase in alert, purposive behavior
Institutional furniture replaced with noninstitutional furniture Rugs, lamps, and draperies added Control over lighting	Decrease in intrusive behaviors Increase in use of personal space

developments in biomedical science, particularly new understandings of the brain and the immune system, have allowed more sophisticated analysis of how the built environment affects physical and mental health and can be a source of healing. In the past 2 decades, researchers have also been interested in how information, communication, and other assistive technologies are affecting human behavior.

Technology

Ben Watson is in a partnership with his sophisticated titanium wheelchair. As I am working on this book, I am in partnership with my computer, which allows me to search for information (with soothing music in the background), put my thoughts into digital format that with time will be shared with you, and check my e-mail to see how contributing authors are progressing with their chapters. And, aided by my computer, in a few minutes I will take a break, view some photos of our recent family vacation, and check in to see what my Facebook friends have been doing lately. Since they first appeared on the earth, humans have used their cognitive capacities to build tools to manipulate and control the environment. Humans are not the only animals that have developed tools, but, to date, humans are the only animals to develop the types of complex tools resulting in rapid changes in our individual and collective behaviors. For the purposes of this discussion, **technology** is defined as the tools, machines, instruments, and devices developed and used by humans to enhance their lives. There are many types of technologies; examples include construction technology, industrial technology, information technology, communication technology, weapon technology, and medical technology. There is clear evidence that the pace of technological development is speeding up, as you may have noticed as your cell phone becomes obsolete very quickly these days.

Across time, and certainly since the industrial revolution, there have been proponents and critics of technological development. Proponents have had confidence that technology will benefit society. The most optimistic have believed that technology will allow humans to master all problems and control the future. Critics have argued that technology can limit our freedoms and have negative effects on our psychological health. And recently, the ecological justice movement has emphasized the ways in which new technologies destroy the natural environment. As with earlier technological revolutions, the rapid developments in information and communication technologies we are currently experiencing have both proponents and critics. Recent work by Ray Kurzweil and Sherry Turkle highlight some of the arguments on both sides.

Ray Kurzweil is an author, inventor, futurist, and director of engineering at Google. Among other things, he has invented an image scanner, a reading machine that allows people with visual impairments to have computer text read out loud, and a music synthesizer. He is, as you might guess, a great proponent of technology. In his 2012 book, *How to Create a Mind: The Secret of Human Thought Revealed*, Kurzweil enthusiastically reports that advancements in neurological science technologies are allowing us to understand our brains in more and more precise detail. This growing understanding will soon allow us to fix our brains when needed and vastly expand the powers of our own intelligence. He joyfully reminds us of the capacities of computers to route e-mails, produce an electrocardiogram, fly and land airplanes, and play games. He revels in the story of how the IBM computer Watson obtained a higher score on the game of *Jeopardy* than the best two human players in the world, answering questions based on 200 million pages of information in 3 seconds! He tells of work under way to develop a new version of Watson that will read vast amounts of medical literature and become a master diagnostician. He reminds us that we have artificial intelligence all around us with the

Photo 7.4 Spanish entrepreneur Victor Rosich displays some of the old mobile phones purchased by his company Mobileswap, which recovers old phones through a network of distributors and sells them in Asian and African markets.

© TONI GARRIGA/epa/Corbis

digital brain that stores old memories, e-mail, text messaging, and Siri on the iPhone. He predicts that Google self-driving cars will have fewer accidents than human-driven cars. Kurzweil argues that we build these tools to extend our own reach and are producing and will continue to produce very powerful abilities. He predicts that humans will sooner or later create an artificial neocortex that has the range and flexibility of the human neocortex. He says that the machines of the future will appear to be conscious and come to be accepted as "conscious persons" (p. 209).

Sherry Turkle has a joint doctorate in sociology and personality psychology and is a clinical psychologist. She is professor of social studies and science and technology at the Massachusetts Institute of Technology. In her 2011 book *Alone Together: Why We Expect More From Technology and Less From Each Other*, Turkle reports on her research in two areas: human interaction with robots and human interaction with communication technologies. While she finds some benefit of both types of human interactions, she is not optimistic about the way these technologies are reshaping human emotional life.

The first half of the book is based on her research with human interaction with *sociable robots*, a type of robot that has a body, can sense its environment and respond to it, has some understanding of humans, and can communicate and interact with humans. R2-D2 and WALL-E are part of our science fiction genre, but sociable robots are a part of our current world, as well as a part of tomorrow's story. Turkle reminds us of our succession of attempts to build the perfect sociable robot, Zhu Zhu robot pet hamsters, Furby robot toys, and My Real Baby robot. She also reports on the current state of development of robot companions being used to break the isolation of children and older adults. She notes that enthusiasm for robots is especially strong in Japan, where robot companions are used routinely in elder care facilities. Turkle acknowledges that robots can provide comfort and break isolation, but her own sensibilities coincide with those of a child in one of her studies who commented, "Don't we have people to

do that?" She found that both children and older adults suggest that robots can be more dependable than people, and she worries that humans are not present enough to each other. She also worries that interactions with robots can become preferable to human-human interaction because robots are less complex than people. She wonders if her concerns are peculiarly American, noting that the enthusiasm for robots in Japan makes sense in a culture where it is commonplace to think of inanimate objects as having a life force. Reminiscent of Kurzweil's suggestion that we will come to think of machines as "conscious persons," Turkle (2011) finds that her research participants describe the robots with which they interact as "alive enough to love and mourn" (p. 29). She suggests that this raises new questions about what makes a person and what makes a relationship.

Turkle is equally unenthusiastic about our thoroughly networked lives, which she describes as "always wirelessly connected" and "living full-time on the net" (pp. 151–152). She notes that communication technologies allow us to live in multiple worlds at the same time, so that we may be sitting together but using our smartphones to be somewhere else. She tells one story of attending a memorial service where attendees were using the memorial service program to hide their cell phones while they texted during the service. She suggests that our communication devices create new freedoms and pleasures but also create compulsions to use them: I *must* check my e-mail first thing in the morning; I have 150 text messages that *must* be answered. She notes that we get anxious when we leave our cell phone at home—or worse, when we lose it. Turkle (2011) also writes about the part of human life lived in virtual space, creating virtual selves in Second Life, playing computer games, and interacting on social networking sites, suggesting that "we have moved from multi-tasking to multi-lifing" (p. 160), sometimes creating new selves to share in virtual environments. She is concerned about what is happening to human societies as people live in a "continual world of partial attention" (p. 160) and concludes that we have to find a way to live with the seductive technologies we have created and make them work to support our values and goals.

Ray Kurzweil emphasizes that we develop technologies to extend our capabilities. This is especially true in the rapidly expanding field of assistive technology. **Assistive technology** is technology developed and used to assist individuals with disabilities to perform functions that might otherwise be difficult or impossible. A tremendous variety of assistive technology is available today, including technology to assist with mobility, visual, hearing, and cognitive impairment; computer accessibility technology; and personal emergency response systems. Assistive technology can be as low-tech as colorful Post-it notes to serve as visual reminders for students who struggle with attention and organization or as high-tech as assistive robots for people with mobility impairments. Exhibit 7.4 provides a variety of examples of contemporary assistive technology but is not an exhaustive list of the rich array of available technologies. Unfortunately, the great majority of these technologies are quite expensive and beyond the reach of most people.

Healing Environments

By many accounts, Roger Ulrich (1984) was the first researcher to measure the effects of the physical environment on physical health of hospital patients. He studied patients who had undergone gallbladder

Exhibit 7.4   Current and Near-Future Examples of Assistive Technology for Persons With Disabilities

Assistive Technology Device(s)	Functions
iPads	iPads can be used to record lectures, upload books, provide easier Internet access, take pictures, use social media, and allow easy ways to operate other devices.
Voice recognition software and hardware	Voice recognition provides the ability to use personal computers by voice only. A voice-activated device can now be plugged into the wall to access the Internet via Wi-Fi to control devices such as lights, Internet, TV, phone, and thermostat by using the voice only—no buttons to push.
Infrared technology to control environment and surroundings	Infrared (IR) technology allows a PC to be used remotely to control another device. IR receivers can now be attached to most any device.
Wheelchairs	Technology has vastly improved mobility with advances in wheelchair capabilities and ease of operation.
Computer eyeglasses	Google's Glass allows those with arm, hand, or finger impairments to wear a smartphone and operate it by voice in order to take pictures, use the phone, and search the net, all by voice command.
Robot suits/exoskeletons	Soon a "wearable robot suit" that attaches to legs and torso to allow a person with paraplegia to walk may be as common as wheelchairs.
Brain/computer interface technologies	Interfacing brain signals with technology allows robotic arms to assist or replace nonfunctional limbs.
Adaptive sports equipment	Technology now allows those with body impairments to enjoy athletic activities such as skiing (sit skis, special chairs) and rafting (special chairs), increased body movement capabilities (bionic limbs, exoskeletons to allow movement and retrain limb function), and accessible playgrounds (wheelchair-friendly surfaces, better-designed play equipment, ramps and larger swing chairs).
Medical devices and prosthetics	Hearing aids, prostheses, and pacemakers, to name just a few, have vastly improved with technological advances.

surgery and had different views out their hospital room windows. One group had views of a brown brick wall, and the other group had views of a small stand of trees. The patients who had views of the trees left the hospital almost a day sooner than the patients with views of a brick wall. They also required less pain medication, received fewer negative comments from the nurses, and had slightly fewer postoperative complications.

The idea that nature is important to healing is not new; indeed, it has been around for thousands of years (Sternberg, 2009). There is a long tradition in architecture that proposes a connection among nature, architecture, and health (Joye, 2007). In the 19th century, hospitals were built with large windows, even skylights, and often in beautiful natural settings (Joye, 2007; Sternberg, 2009). Clinics and hospitals were particularly designed to take advantage of natural light because it was thought that sunlight could heal. Some public health scholars argue, however, that as medical technology became more sophisticated, design of hospital space began to focus more on care of the equipment than on care of the patient (Maller, Townsend, Pryor, Brown, & Ledger, 2005; Sternberg, 2009). These public health scholars are calling attention to biomedical research that links physical environments and human health.

Based on his early research, Roger Ulrich, a behavioral scientist, has collaborated with architects, environmental psychologists, and public and private agencies and foundations to develop a field called **evidence-based design**, which uses physiological and health outcome measures to evaluate the health benefits of hospital design features (Ulrich, 2006; Center for Health Design, 2008). Following on the earlier work of Ulrich, researchers use such measures as length of stay; amount of pain medication; rates of health complications; and patient satisfaction, stress, and mood to evaluate design innovations. By 2006, 700 rigorous studies had been identified (Ulrich, 2006), and the Center for Health Design had been established to engage in ongoing hospital design innovations and evaluations. Two foci of this research are discussed here: noise and sunlight.

A great deal of international research has focused on hospital noise as an impediment to healing. This research consistently finds that hospital noise has continued to increase over the past 50 years and exceeds the guidelines recommended by the World Health Organization (Eggerston, 2012). Hospital noise comes from a variety of sources, for example, staff conversations, roommates, overhead paging, moving of bed rails, and medical equipment alarms. The problem is exacerbated in hospitals that have hard, sound-reflecting floors and ceilings. It is also intensified in multibed rooms because of the activity of caring for multiple patients. Noise has been associated with high blood pressure and elevated heart rates; sleep loss; slower recovery from heart attack; and negative physiological responses such as apnea and fluctuations in blood pressure and oxygen saturation in infants in neonatal intensive care (Brown, 2009; Eggerston, 2012; Ulrich, 2006). Preterm infants exposed to prolonged high levels of noise are at risk for hearing loss, impaired brain development, and speech and language problems (Brown, 2009). Excessive noise also contributes to staff fatigue (Eggerston, 2012). A number of design innovations have been found to be effective in reducing hospital noise. These include single-bed rooms, replacing overhead paging with a noiseless system, covering neonatal incubators with blankets, and installing high-performance sound-absorbing ceiling tiles and floor carpets (Brown, 2009; Ulrich, 2006). These innovations have been found to be related to improved health outcomes and fewer rehospitalizations for patients as well as to improved staff satisfaction and home sleep quality (Sternberg, 2009).

There is also growing evidence that 19th-century hospital designers were accurate in their belief that sunlight can heal. Beauchemin and Hays (1998) found that patients recovering from heart attacks in sunny hospital rooms had significantly shorter hospital stays than patients recovering in rooms without natural light. Another research team studied patients recovering from spinal surgery in one hospital and compared the experiences of patients in sunny rooms with the experiences of patients in rooms without sunlight. Patients in sunny rooms took 22% less

Photo 7.5 A long tradition in architecture proposes a connection among nature, architecture, and healing.

© iStockphoto.com/Lisa F. Young

pain medication and had 21% less medication costs than similar patients recovering in rooms without sunlight (Walch, Day, & Kang, 2005). The patients in the sunny rooms also reported less stress than patients in the rooms without sunlight. Hospital rooms with morning sunlight have also been found to reduce the hospital stay of patients with unipolar and bipolar depression (Benedetti, Colombo, Barbini, Campori, & Smeraldi, 2001).

Roger Ulrich and Craig Zimring (2005) have reviewed the large array of evidence-based design research and proposed a list of hospital design changes that have been found to promote healing. These are overviewed in Exhibit 7.5. Ulrich (2006) reports that these design upgrades would increase initial construction cost by 5.4%, but those costs would be recaptured in only 1 year.

Critical Thinking Questions 7.4

Do you consider yourself a proponent or a critic of rapid advancements in information and communication technologies? Are you as optimistic as Ray Kurzweil? Why or why not? Are you as pessimistic as Sherry Turkle? Why or why not? Have you seen any evidence of evidence-based design in your visits to health care facilities?

Urban Design and Health

Prior to the early 20th century in the United States, public health experts focused on what they called "the urban penalty" for health and mortality. As city size increased, so did the death rate. Infectious diseases, such as tuberculosis, measles, small pox, and

SOURCE: Based on Ulrich & Zimring, 2005.

influenza, were the main cause of the urban penalty. Such diseases spread quickly in high-density environments. By the 1920s, improved sanitation and other public health measures had eliminated the urban penalty in the United States and other wealthy nations, but it still exists in very large cities in poorer nations and in the poorest sections of cities in wealthy nations. The biggest threats to urban populations in the United States today are violent crime and pollution, the latter of which contributes to high rates of asthma (Sternberg, 2009).

In recent years, some public health officials have begun to suggest an increasing rural and suburban penalty and an urban advantage (see Vlahov, Galea, & Freudenberg, 2005). In 2007, New York City was declared the healthiest location in the United States. Life expectancy increased by 6.2 years from 1990 to 2007, compared with 2.5 years for the rest of the country (Sternberg, 2009). In her book *The End of the Suburbs*, Leah Gallagher (2013) provides evidence that, while a majority of people still live in the suburbs, the United States is experiencing a population shift from the suburbs

to cities—people moving to the city because they want access to city amenities and to spend less time in their cars. Considerable research has focused in recent years on urban sprawl and design features of suburban built environments that contribute to decreased physical activity. The researchers note the long distances suburban dwellers need to travel to work and to amenities, requiring more time spent in the car. These researchers have been particularly interested in whether suburban built environments contribute to obesity and the related health problems of cardiovascular disease and diabetes. The evidence is mixed on this question. Some researchers have found that urban sprawl is associated with overweight and obesity (Garden & Jalaludin, 2009; Slater et al., 2010). A Canadian study found an association between urban sprawl and coronary heart disease in women (Griffin et al., 2013). Others have found no significant relationship between urban sprawl and obesity (Seliske, Pickett, & Janssen, 2012), and some suggest that any connection between urban sprawl and obesity can be explained by a selection process whereby more sedentary people choose more sprawling locations to live (Cao, Mokhtarian, & Handy, 2009). The research indicates that urban sprawl may have a more negative effect on the health of adults than it does on the health of children and youth.

In response to concerns about negative health effects of urban sprawl as well as concerns about harm to the environment caused by automobile use, the *new urbanist designers* are designing suburban towns with several features known to contribute to walkability. These features include houses with front porches; neighborhood spots for congregation; sidewalks; short blocks; good lighting; amenities accessible by foot; public transportation; mixed-used areas, including residences, businesses, offices, and recreation centers; and bike paths, tennis courts, parks, and golf courses (Stevens & Brown, 2011). The hope is that these design features will contribute to resident activity and health. Researchers have found these design features to be associated with more physical activity in the neighborhood, and one research team found that the relationship holds when controlling for preexisting preferences for activity level, the selection issue noted earlier (Stevens & Brown, 2011).

Lopez and Hynes (2006) enter this conversation with a more complicated story. They report that although it is true that obesity is associated with urban sprawl, inner-city populations have higher rates of obesity and inactivity than suburban dwellers. They suggest that different aspects of the physical environment are contributing to ill health for inner-city residents and making their neighborhoods unwalkable. Inner-city neighborhoods have some of the design features recommended by the new urbanist designers, features such as sidewalks, short blocks, and public transportation, but they have a set of barriers to walking that do not exist in suburbs, barriers such as hazardous waste sites, abandoned buildings, decaying sidewalks, disappearing tree canopies, and dilapidated school playgrounds and parks. For example, one study found that low-income neighborhoods are four times as likely as high-income neighborhoods to have hazardous waste facilities, power plants, and polluting industrial plants, and low-income minority neighborhoods are 20 times as likely as high-income neighborhoods to have these facilities (Faber & Krieg, 2005, cited in Lopez & Hynes, 2006). Public health officials also warn that with the new types of infectious diseases whose spread is fueled by global warming, dense cities contribute to contagion (Sternberg, 2009).

PLACE ATTACHMENT

Have you ever been strongly attached to a specific place—a beloved home, a particular beach or mountain spot, or a house of worship? **Place attachment**—the process in which people and groups form bonds with places—is the subject of a growing literature (Lewicka, 2011). Recent research on place attachment conceptualizes it as a multidimensional phenomenon involving person, place, and psychological processes of attachment (Scannell & Gifford, 2010a). In terms of

Social constructionist perspective, psychodynamic perspective, social behavioral perspective

person, researchers explore how place attachment occurs at both the individual and group levels. At the individual level, place attachment develops out of personally important experiences. At the group level, attachment develops out of symbolic meanings shared by a group. In the context of place attachment, *place* is defined as a "space that has been given meaning through personal, group, or cultural processes" (Low & Altman, 1992, p. 5). In terms of the *psychological processes of attachment*, place attachment is usually discussed in terms of emotional bonding (see Morgan, 2010), but an interplay of emotions, cognitions, and behaviors and actions appears to be what forges the people-place bond (Scannell & Gifford, 2010a).

When a strong place attachment develops, it has been suggested that the place has become an important part of the self, that we can't think of who we are without some reference to the place (Rollero & Piccoli, 2010). When a particular place becomes an important part of our self-identity, this merger of place and self is known as **place identity**. Place attachment and place identity have been found to occur at several levels, including home, workplace, community, municipality, region, country, and continent (Lewicka, 2011). We run into the concept of place attachment again in Chapter 13 when we discuss community as a dimension of environment. Place identity can develop where there is strong negative, as well as positive, place attachment, resulting in negative views of the self.

Much of the research on place attachment has focused on the social aspects of the attachment, suggesting that we become attached to places because of the satisfying social relationships we experience in those places. Some researchers have begun to examine attachment to physical places, particularly to places in the natural environment. They are particularly interested in how attachment to places in nature affects behavior toward the natural environment. One research team (Scannell & Gifford, 2010b) found that attachment to the natural aspects of place contributes to pro-environmental behavior, but attachment to the social aspects of place, which they called civic place attachment, does not. Another research team (Cheng & Monroe, 2012) found that children's connection to nature was the single best predictor of interest in engaging in nature-friendly behaviors. And another team (Collado, Staats, & Corraliza, 2013) found that experiences in nature increased children's attachment to nature, ecological beliefs, and willingness to engage in nature-friendly behavior.

Researchers have been interested in the distress and grief people experience when a place of attachment and identity is lost, particularly in situations of forced relocation (Scannell & Gifford, 2010a). We should pay particular attention to issues of place attachment and place identity when we work with immigrant and refugee families and families displaced by disaster. We should also consider the long-term consequences of early experiences, such as homelessness or frequent movement between foster homes, in which no stable place of attachment forms or that result in a negative place attachment.

HOMELESSNESS

As suggested, place attachment can be quite problematic for people without homes. In January 2012, a new definition of *homeless* was implemented by the U.S. Department of Housing and Urban Development (HUD; 2011) to delineate who is eligible for HUD-funded homeless assistance. This new definition includes the four broad categories presented in Exhibit 7.6. In general, people are homeless because they cannot find housing they can afford; there is a real scarcity of affordable housing. HUD defines housing affordability as spending no more than 30% of monthly income on housing, but according to the National Alliance to End Homelessness (NAEH; 2013a) about 12 million households in the United States pay more than 50% of their annual incomes for housing.

It is a challenge to count the exact number of homeless people, and no recent estimates of the number of homeless persons worldwide are available. In the United States, HUD requires that each community do a point-in-time count on a single night in January every other year. According to the count in January 2012, 633,782 people experience homelessness on any given night in the United States. About 38% of these are people in families and 62% are individuals. For many people, homelessness is a short-lived experience, and only about 16% of those homeless on a given night are chronically homeless (NAEH, 2013b). More than half, 62.7%, of homeless persons are male, and 37.2% are female, but 79.3% of homeless persons in families are female. About equal proportions are White, Non-Hispanic (39.5%) and Black or African American (38.1%). The remainder are of other ethnicities. That means, of course, that Black or African American persons are greatly overrepresented in the homeless population, because they make up only about 13% of the total U.S. population. By age group, 22.1% of the homeless population is younger than age 18; 23.8% is 18 to 30; 35.8% is 31 to 50; 15.5% is 51 to 61; and 2.9% is 62 and older.

NAEH has special concern about four groups of homeless persons: families, youth, veterans,

---

Exhibit 7.6 Categories in the U.S. Department of Housing and Urban Development Definition of *Homeless*

1. People who are living in a place not meant for human habitation, in emergency shelter, in transitional housing, or are exiting an institution where they have temporarily resided for up to 90 days.

2. People who are losing their primary nighttime residence, which may include a motel or hotel or a doubled-up situation, within 14 days and lack resources or support networks to remain in housing.

3. Families with children or unaccompanied youth who are unstably housed and likely to continue in that state.

4. People who are fleeing or attempting to flee domestic violence, have no other residence, and lack the resources or support networks to obtain other permanent housing.

SOURCE: U.S. Department of Housing and Urban Development, 2011.

and those who are chronically homeless (NAEH, 2013a). The reason for family homelessness is usually an unforeseen financial crisis such as a medical emergency or death in the family. Most homeless families are able to bounce back from homelessness with little public assistance, but they may need rent assistance, help finding permanent housing, or job assistance. Family conflict such as divorce, or neglect or abuse, is the most common reason youth become homeless. There is special concern about LGBTQ youth who become homeless because of family abuse or rejection. About 13% of homeless persons are veterans, who are often homeless because of war-related disabilities. Those counted among the chronic homeless either are homeless long-term or experience repeated bouts of homelessness. They often live in shelters and consume a large portion of the available homeless services. They are more likely than other homeless persons to have severe physical and mental health challenges.

The cost of homelessness can be quite high. When they become hospitalized, homeless people require, on average, 4 more days in the hospital than nonhomeless people. Homeless people are increasingly spending time in jail or prison, often for violating regulations against loitering, sleeping in cars, or begging. Emergency shelter is a costly way to house people. Research suggests that providing chronically homeless persons with permanent supportive housing is less costly than current arrangements when medical, correctional, and shelter costs are considered (NAEH, 2013c).

ACCESSIBLE ENVIRONMENTS FOR PERSONS WITH DISABILITIES

In recent years, we have been reminded that environments, particularly built environments, can be disabling because of their inaccessibility to many persons, including most people with mobility and visual disabilities. Ben Watson provides us with several examples of how the physical environment curtailed his activity at times, and he is now in a professional position to try to minimize the barriers people with disabilities experience in the

world. The *social model of disability* emphasizes the barriers people with impairments face as they interact with the physical and social world, arguing that disability is a result of the relationship between the individual and the environment (see Martin, 2013).

This way of thinking about disability was the impetus for development

Conflict perspective

of the Disabled People's International (2013) in 1981, a network of national organizations that promotes the rights of people with disabilities worldwide. In the United States, the social model of disability led to legislation at all levels of government during the 1970s and 1980s, most notably two pieces of federal legislation. The Rehabilitation Act of 1973 (Pub. L. No. 93-112) was the first federal act to recognize the need for civil rights protection for persons with disabilities. It required all organizations receiving federal assistance to have an affirmative action plan to ensure accessibility of employment to persons with disabilities. The Americans with Disabilities Act of 1990 (ADA) (Pub. L. No. 101-336) extended the civil rights of persons with disabilities to the private sector. It seeks to end discrimination against persons with disabilities and promote their full participation in society. The social model of disability was also the driving force behind the United Nations Convention on the Rights of Persons with Disabilities that entered into force in May 2008 (United Nations Enable, 2013).

The five titles of the ADA seek to eliminate environmental barriers to the full participation of persons with disabilities. You will want to be aware of the legal rights of your clients with disabilities. Ben Watson has discovered that, in spite of the law, he still encounters many physical barriers to his full participation in society.

- Title I addresses discrimination in the workplace. It requires reasonable accommodations, including architectural modification, for disabled workers.
- Title II requires that all public services, programs, and facilities, including public transportation, be accessible to persons with disabilities.
- Title III requires all public accommodations and services operated by private organizations to be

Photo 7.6 The kitchen in the Michael Ciravolo Jr. Wheelchair Suite, dedicated specifically by the Hotel Delmonico in New York City to accommodate people with disabilities.

© Diane L. Cohen/Getty Images

accessible to persons with disabilities. It specifically lists 12 categories of accommodations: hotels and places of lodging; restaurants; movies and theaters; auditoriums and places of public gathering; stores and banks; health care service providers, hospitals, and pharmacies; terminals for public transportation; museums and libraries; parks and zoos; schools; senior centers and social service centers; and places of recreation.

- Title IV requires all intrastate and interstate phone companies to develop telecommunication relay services and devices for persons with speech or hearing impairments to allow them to communicate in a manner similar to that of persons without impairments.
- Title V covers technical guidelines for enforcing the ADA.

Under industrial capitalism, wages are the primary source of livelihood. People who cannot earn wages, therefore, tend to be poor. Around the world, people with disabilities are less likely than other people to be employed. In 2012, the unemployment rate in the United States for people with disabilities was 13.4%, compared with 7.9% for people without a disability (U.S. Bureau of Labor Statistics, 2013a). People with disabilities who lobbied for passage of the ADA argued that government was spending vast sums of money for what they called "dependency programs" but was failing to make the investments required to make environments accessible so that people with disabilities could become employed (Roulstone, 2004).

Social workers need to keep in mind the high prevalence of disabilities among older persons, the fastest growing group in the United States. More accessible environments may be an important way to buffer the expected deleterious effects of a large elderly population. As the baby boomers age, they will benefit from the earlier activism of the disability community. Exhibit 7.7 lists some of the elements of environmental design that improve accessibility for persons with disabilities. It is important to remember, however, that rapid developments in assistive technology are likely to alter current guidelines about what is optimal environmental design. For example, the minimum space requirements in the ADA's guidelines for wheelchairs are already too tight for the new styles of motorized wheelchairs.

Critical Thinking Questions 7.5

Which do you think are the healthiest type of communities in which to live: rural, small town, suburban, or urban? What do you think are the costs and benefits of living in each of these types of communities? How much thought have you given to what makes an accessible environment for people with the type of mobility disability that Ben Watson has? How easy would it be for Ben to visit your home, your favorite restaurant, or your classroom?

Exhibit 7.7 Elements of Accessible Environments for Persons With Disabilities

- Create some close-in parking spaces widened to 8 feet to accommodate unloading of wheelchairs (1 accessible space for every 25 spaces).
- Create curb cuts or ramping for curbs, with 12 inches of slope for every inch of drop in the curb.
- Make ramps at least 3 feet wide to accommodate wheelchairs and provide a 5-by-5-foot square area at the top of ramps to entrances to allow space for door opening.
- Remove high-pile carpeting, low-density carpeting, and plush carpeting, at least in the path of travel. Put nonslip material on slippery floors.
- Avoid phone-in security systems in entrances (barrier for persons who are deaf).
- Make all doorways at least 32 inches wide (36 is better).
- Use automatic doors or doors that take no more than 5 pounds of force to open.
- Use door levers instead of doorknobs.
- Create aisles that are at least 3 feet wide (wider is better). Keep the path of travel clear.
- Connect different levels in buildings with ramps (for small level changes) or a wheelchair-accessible elevator.
- Place public phones no higher than 48 inches (35 to 42 is optimal). Place other things that need to be reached at this optimal height.
- Provide brightly lit foyers and areas with directories to assist persons with low vision. Use 3-inch-high lettering in directories.
- Install Braille signs about 5 feet off the ground.
- Make restroom stalls at least 3 feet deep by 4 feet wide (5 feet by 5 feet is optimal).
- Install toilets that are 17 to 19 inches in height. Provide grab bars at toilets.
- Hang restroom sinks with no vanity underneath, so that persons in wheelchairs can pull up to them.
- Avoid low seats and provide arm supports and backrests on chairs.
- Apply nonslip finish to tubs and showers. Install grab bars in tubs and showers.
- Use both visual and audible emergency warning systems.

SOURCE: Based on Brawley, 2006; Johnson, 1992.

Implications for Social Work Practice

This discussion of the relationship between human behavior and the physical environment suggests several practice principles:

- Assess the physical environment of your social service setting. Do clients find it accessible, legible, and comfortable? Do they find that it provides adequate privacy and control? Does it provide optimal quality and intensity of sensory stimulation? If it is a residential setting, does it promote social interaction?

- Routinely evaluate the physical environments of clients, particularly those settings where problem behaviors occur. Check your evaluation against clients' perceptions. If you have no opportunity to see these environments, have clients evaluate them for you. Provide space on the intake form for assessing the physical environments of clients.
- Know the physical environments of the organizations to which you refer clients. Assist referral agencies and clients in planning how to overcome any existing environmental barriers. Maximize opportunities for client input into design of their built environments.
- Be alert to the meanings that particular environments hold for clients. Recognize that people have attachments to places as well as to other people.
- When assisting clients to learn new skills, pay attention to the discontinuities between the setting where the skills are learned and the settings where they will be used.
- When planning group activities, ensure the best possible fit between the spatial needs of the activity and the physical environment where the activity will occur.
- Keep the benefits of the natural environment in mind when planning both prevention and remediation programs. When possible, help clients gain access to elements of the natural environment, and where appropriate, help them plan activities in the natural environment.
- Recognize any issues of environmental justice impacting the communities where you work.
- Assess the uses that clients make of information and communication technologies, considering both the benefits and the costs of their use of such technologies.
- Become familiar with new developments in assistive technologies for persons with disabilities and with the resources for financing them.
- Become familiar with technology for adapting environments to make them more accessible.

Key Terms

assistive technology
behavior settings
behavior settings theories
biophilia
built environment
control theories
crowding
deep ecology
density
ecocritical theories

ecofeminism
ecotherapy
evidence-based design
natural environment
personal space
place attachment
place identity
primary territory
privacy
programs

public territory
secondary territory
sociofugal spaces
sociopetal spaces
staffing
stimulation theories
technology
territoriality

Active Learning

1. Take a walking tour of your neighborhood. Do you see any signs of stimulus overload or restricted environmental stimulation in the physical environment? What signs do you see of people engaging in territorial behavior? Do you see any behavior settings in which specific programs are enacted? How well do people seem to be caring for the natural environment? Are there features of the natural environment that seem particularly appealing to you? Are there places in the neighborhood to which you have a strong attachment bond? Do you note any of the design features to improve accessibility for persons with disabilities noted in Exhibit 7.7? What effects do you think the physical environment of the neighborhood might have on children, adolescents, and elderly adults?

2. Sitting with a small group of classmates, make a list of all the communication technology devices you make use of. Make another list of the uses you have made of these devices in the last 2 days. Discuss your relationship to these devices: how attached you are to them, how big a part of your life they are, and how you feel when you don't have access to them. How do you see these devices making your life better? What, if any, are their ill effects on your life? Finally, make a list of the benefits these devices provide to society. Make another list of the downside of these devices for society. What have you heard other people say about the benefits and downside of these technological devices?

3. Sitting with a small group of classmates, imagine that Ben Watson is visiting your community for the weekend. Your group would like to take him out to dinner. Working together, develop a list of questions that you will want to ask of restaurant managers about their accessibility for Ben to dine there. Now, each of you get out your cell phone and call one of your favorite restaurants and go through your list of questions. What did you learn?

Web Resources

Academy of Neuroscience for Architecture: www.anfarch.org

Site maintained by the Academy of Neuroscience for Architecture contains information about the academy and its projects, upcoming workshops on neuroscience and specific design environments, and links to neuroscience and architecture organizations.

American Association of People with Disabilities: www.aapd.com

Site maintained by the American Association of People with Disabilities, a national nonprofit cross-disability organization, contains information on benefits, information on disability rights, news, and links to other disability-related sites.

Center for Health Design: www.healthdesign .org

Site maintained by the Center for Health Design, a research and advocacy organization committed to using architectural design to transform health care settings into healing environments.

Environmental Justice in Waste Programs: www.epa.gov/oswer/ej

Site maintained by the U.S. Environmental Protection Agency contains basic information about environmental justice, action plans, contacts, publications, and laws and regulations.

Job Accommodation Network: askjan.org

Site maintained by the Job Accommodation Network of the Office of Disability Employment Policy of the U.S. Department of Labor contains ADA statutes, regulations, guidelines, technical sheets, and other assistance documents.

National Alliance to End Homelessness: www .endhomelessness.org

Site maintained by the National Alliance to End Homelessness contains basic facts about homelessness; facts and policy issues related to homeless families, chronic homelessness, rural homelessness, homeless youth, homeless veterans, domestic violence, and health care; and suggested solutions for ending homelessness.

Student Study Site

$SAGE edge™

Sharpen your skills with SAGE edge at **edge.sagepub.com/hutchisonpe5e**

SAGE edge for students provides a personalized approach to help you accomplish your coursework goals in an easy-to-use learning environment.

Culture

Linwood Cousins

Chapter Outline

Key Ideas

As you read this chapter, take note of these central ideas:

1. In contemporary society, culture refers to a people's ethos (how people feel about the world around them) and worldview (how people perceive the world around them), all of which is encoded in how people construct and employ meanings that guide their perceptions and behavior in multiple contexts.

2. The meaning-making activities of people include what is called material culture—music, dance, art, language, clothing, literature, stories and narratives, architecture and shelter and so forth—all of which is in constant motion.

3. Features of life such as ethnic customs, traditions, values, beliefs, and notions of common sense are not static entities, but neither are they changing very rapidly.

4. Our understandings of others are always based on the understandings we have constructed both about ourselves and about how the world does and should operate. We can easily misunderstand others by using our own categories and rankings to order such realities.

5. A practice orientation is a contemporary approach to understanding culture by thinking of human action as a product, producer, and transformer of history and social structures.

6. Members of nondominant groups may respond to the dominant culture with different processes, including assimilation, accommodation, acculturation, and bicultural socialization.

7. A multidimensional understanding of culture is necessary to grasp the increasing complexity of the construction and employment of meaning regarding identities and the distribution of resources, remembering that both identities and resources are based in political, social, and economic structures and processes.

CASE STUDY

Stan and Tina at Community High School

Community High School in Newark, New Jersey, has approximately 1,300 students, the majority of whom are Black (African American, Afro-Caribbean, and West African). Most of the students live in the community of Village Park, which has a total population of approximately 58,000 people, also predominantly Black. Village Park has a distinct social history and identity as well as distinct physical boundaries that distinguish it from less prosperous communities and schools in Newark.

Village Park evolved from a middle- and working-class Jewish community that centered on its academic institutions, such as Community High. The school generated a national reputation for academic excellence as measured by the number of graduates who went on to become doctors, lawyers, scientists, professors, and the like. But after the Newark riots of the late 1960s, Jews and other Whites started moving out. By the early 1970s, upwardly mobile middle- and working-class Black families had become the majority in Village Park. The same process has occurred in other communities, but what's interesting about Village Park is that its Black residents, like the Jewish residents who preceded them, continued to believe in the ethic of upward mobility through schooling at Community High.

Since the mid-1980s, however, Village Park and Community High have undergone another transformation. Slumps in the economy and ongoing patterns of racial discrimination in employment have reduced the income base of the community's families. Many families who were able to maintain a middle-class income moved to the suburbs as crime and economic blight encroached on the community. Increasingly, Village Park was taken over by renters and absentee landlords, along with the social problems—drug abuse, crime, school dropout—that accompany economically driven social despair.

By 1993, the population profile of Newark reflected an ethnic mix that was simultaneously Black and multi-ethnic. In the 1990s, the majority of Newark's residents were African American, but the city had a considerable population of other ethnic groups: Hispanics (e.g., Puerto Ricans, Colombians, Mexicans, Dominicans), Italians, Portuguese, Africans (from Nigeria, Sierra Leone, Liberia, Ghana, and other countries), Polish, and small groups of others. At the same time, the governing bodies of the city, the school system, and Community High in particular were predominantly composed of Black people. By 2010 little had changed. With an estimated population of 277,540 in 2011 (latest population estimates by the U.S. Census Bureau [2013b]), Newark remains an ethnically diverse urban community.

The intermingling of such history and traditions has had an interesting impact on the students at Community High. Like many urban high schools all over the nation, Community High has suffered disproportionate levels of dropouts, low attendance, and violence. Yet a few parents, teachers, school staff, and community officials have tried hard to rekindle the spirit of academic excellence and social competence that are the school's tradition.

In this context, many of the students resist traditional definitions of academic success but value success nonetheless. Consider the behaviors of Stan and Tina, both students at Community High. Stan is the more troubled and academically marginal of the two students. He is 17 years old, lives with his girlfriend who has recently had a baby, and has made a living selling drugs (which he is trying to discontinue). Stan was arrested (and released) for selling drugs some time ago. He was also under questioning for the drug-related murder of his cousin, because the police wanted him to identify the perpetrator. However, Stan has considerable social prestige at school and is academically successful when he attends school and is focused. Stan's mother—who has hammered into his head the importance of education—is a clerical supervisor, his stepfather works in a meat factory, and his biological father sells drugs. Stan has three brothers, and his mother and biological father were never married.

Among his male and female peers, Stan is considered the epitome of urban maleness and style. He is an innovator. He mixes and matches the square-toe motorcycle boots normally associated with White bikers with the brand-name shirts and jeans commonly associated with urban, rap-oriented young people of color. At the same time, Stan is respected by teachers and administrators because he understands and observes the rules of conduct preferred in the classroom and because he can do his work at a level reflecting high intelligence. Before the end of his senior year, Stan visited Howard University in Washington, DC, and was smitten by the idea that young Black men and women were participating in university life. He said he will try very hard to go to that school after he graduates, but the odds are against him.

(Continued)

(Continued)

Tina is also 17 years old, but she is more academically successful than Stan. She ranks in the top 25 of her senior class and has been accepted into the premed program of a historically Black university. Tina talks about the lower academic performance of some of her Black peers. She sees it as a manifestation of the social distractions that seem to preoccupy Black youths—being popular and cool. On the other hand, Tina sees her successful academic performance, level of motivation, and assertive style of interacting in the classroom as part of being Black, too—taking care of business and trying to make it in this world. Tina is an only child. Her father is an engineer, and her stepmother is a restaurant manager. Tina has never known her biological mother, and she was raised primarily by her father until about 6 years ago. They moved to Village Park from Brooklyn, New York, around that time. Tina's is the kind of family that is likely to leave Village Park, not for the suburbs but for a more productive and less hostile urban community. Tina has been raised in a community that, despite its ills, centers on Black identity and culture.

Like Stan, Tina is an innovator. She adopted modes of language, demeanor, and clothing that are seen by some as decidedly mainstream in their origins. In reality, Tina mixes the aesthetics of Black and mainstream White culture as well as the contemporary urban flavor that textures the lives of many youths today. Perhaps the results are most apparent in the way Tina mixes and matches hip-hop-influenced clothing, attitudes, and hairstyles with mainstream clothing styles and the mannerisms associated with the norms and standards of professional, middle-class occupations.

However, anyone who would approach Tina as an ally of "the system"—defining the system as the White establishment—would meet with disappointment. They would discover that in Tina's view, and perhaps in Stan's, there is nothing generally wrong with Black people and their behavior. But there is something wrong with Black individuals who do things that are not in their own best interest and consequently not in the best interest of the Black community.

Furthermore, they would hear Tina, Stan, and other students at Community High describe academic success and failure not just in terms of students' actions. They would hear these students indict uninterested and complacent teachers and staff and schools that do not understand "how to educate Black people."

SOURCE: Based on an ethnographic study of culture, race, and class during the 1992–1993 academic year in Cousins (1994). See Fordham (1996) and Ogbu (2003) for similar studies of Black high school students that confirm the persistence of the characteristics described here.

THE CHALLENGE OF DEFINING CULTURE

The case of Tina and Stan has been selected because it makes a point we often miss in the United States in general and in social work and human services in particular: Culture is right under our noses and therefore often concealed from our awareness. Like Tina and Stan, you are actually immersed in many different cultures, including U.S. culture, family culture, school (university) culture, digital culture, consumer culture, peer culture, gender culture, entertainment culture, and more. For example, you may be involved in a work culture, a religious or spiritual culture, or some identity culture such as LGBT culture. You are continually learning the **norms**, the culturally defined standards or rules of conduct, of these different cultures.

When we think of culture, however, we are more likely to think of immigrants and non-Americans as the real examples of culture because they represent peoples who appear to be more different from us than perhaps they are. Indeed, it is much easier to think of Tina and Stan as more like you (or people you know) and me than perhaps they are. As such, the case example highlights not only race and ethnicity but also social class, power relations, gender, popular culture, and other significant features of interactions between people and environments. Consequently, I ask you to pay attention to the subtleties of the case example as you read the presentation of the evolution and variation in the definitions of culture, including its history as a concept. If you conclude that we should not be as confident about some concepts and ideas as we are, then you get one of the main points of this chapter and of the move in social work toward evidence-based practice. In our everyday lives, we think we know what we see, but our life experiences lead us to see some things and not others. It is incredibly hard for us to take a detached viewpoint about our person–environment interactions.

The U.S. Census Bureau (2013b) tells us that there are now more than 7 billion people in the world. More than 313 million of them live in the United States. The United States is the third most populated country, behind China (just over 1.3 billion) and India (just over 1.2 billion), with the smallest population being in Montserrat, a small Caribbean island of 5,189 people. The U.S. population includes 199 million White (non-Hispanic) people of various ancestries, just over 46 million Hispanics/Latinos, just over 37 million African Americans/Blacks, more than 13 million Asians, and over 3 million American Indians and Alaskan Natives, with Native Hawaiian and other Pacific Islanders and other peoples constituting the rest (U.S. Census Bureau, 2013b). Finally, approximately 40 million of the U.S. population is foreign born (U.S. Census Bureau, 2013c).

Much diversity is concealed in this numerical portrait, but it is a good place to begin our discussion of the diverse society we live in. Given this scenario, how should we as social workers interpret the multifaceted contexts of Tina's and Stan's lives? Economics, race/ethnicity, traditions and customs, gender, political processes, immigration, popular culture, psychology, academic processes, technology, and a host of other factors are all involved. All this and more must be considered in our discussion of culture.

More than 40 years ago, Peter Berger and Thomas Luckmann (1966) stated the following: "Society is a human product. Society is an objective reality. Man is a social product" (p. 61). If you replace *society* with *culture*, you get the following: Culture is a human product, culture is an objective reality, and man (or humankind) is a cultural product. These restatements suggest the enormous span of human behavior we try to make intelligible through the concept of culture.

> Social constructionist perspective

In this chapter, you will learn how the concept of culture evolved and how it applies to the puzzle of human diversity so dominant in public discussions today about our multicultural society. Understanding culture as a concept and a process can help you interpret changes in what people believe and value within families, and it can help you deal with communities with large immigrant populations.

But let me caution you: Defining culture is a complex and arbitrary game. It is a word we use all the time but have trouble defining (Gardiner & Kosmitzki, 2011; Griswold, 2008). Long ago, Alfred Kroeber and Clyde Kluckhohn (1963, 1952/1978), two renowned anthropologists, cataloged more than 100 definitions of culture (see Exhibit 8.1). Definitions and discussions of culture tend to reflect the theoretical perspectives and purposes of the definers.

Like other views of culture, the one presented here has its biases. In keeping with the emphases in this book, a view of culture is presented that exposes not only social differences or human variation but also the cultural bases of various forms of inequality. This chapter looks at the ways in which variations in human behavior have led to subjugation and have become the basis of, among other things, racial, ethnic, economic, and gender oppression and inequality.

Exhibit 8.1   Categorical Definitions of Culture

Enumeration of Social Content

- That complex whole that includes knowledge, belief, art, morals, law, custom, and any other capabilities and habits acquired by humans as members of society; the sum total of human achievement

Social Heritage/Tradition

- The learned repertory of thoughts and actions exhibited by members of a social group, independently of genetic heredity from one generation to the next
- The sum total and organization of social heritages that have acquired social meaning because of racial temperament and the historical life of the group

Rule or Way of Life

- The sum total of ways of doing and thinking, past and present, of a social group
- The distinctive way of life of a group of people; their complete design for living

Psychological and Social Adjustment and Learning

- The total equipment of technique—mechanical, mental, and moral—by use of which the people of a given period try to attain their ends
- The sum total of the material and intellectual equipment whereby people satisfy their biological and social needs and adapt themselves to their environment
- Learned modes of behavior that are socially transmitted from one generation to another within a particular society and that may be diffused from one society to another

Ideas and Values

- An organized group of ideas, habits, and conditioned emotional responses shared by members of a society
- Acquired or cultivated behavior and thought of individuals; the material and social values of any group of people

Patterning and Symbols

- A system of interrelated and interdependent habit patterns of response
- Organization of conventional understandings, manifest in act and artifact, that, persisting through tradition, characterizes a human group
- Semiotics—those webs of public meaning that people have spun and by which they are suspended
- A distinct order or class of phenomena—namely, those things and events dependent on the exercise of a mental ability peculiar to the human species—that we have termed symboling; or material objects (such as tools, utensils, ornaments, amulets), acts, beliefs, and attitudes that function in contexts characterized by symboling

SOURCE: Adapted from Kroeber & Kluckhohn, 1952/1978, pp. 40–79.

A Preliminary Definition of Culture

Culture as we have come to know it today is rooted in definitions based on behavioral and material inventions and accomplishments. The late-19th-century German intellectual tradition, for example, distinguished between peoples who had or did not have art, science, knowledge, and social refinement (Stocking, 1968). These aspects of culture were thought to free humans from the control of nature and give them control *over* nature. The word *culture* also derives from the Latin verb *colere*—to cultivate. Note that this sense of the concept is associated with tilling the soil and our agricultural origins (Wagner, 1981)—another way of controlling nature.

But is culture simply the opposite of nature? According to Raymond Williams (1983), "Culture is one of the two or three most complicated words in the English language" (p. 87), partly because of its intricate historical development in several European languages but also because it is used as a concept that sometimes has quite different meanings in several incompatible systems of thought. For example, early German intellectual traditions merged with English traditions to define culture as general processes of intellectual, spiritual, and aesthetic development. A modified version of this usage is found in the contemporary field of arts and humanities, which describes culture in terms of music, literature, painting, sculpture, and the like. By contrast, U.S. tradition has produced the use of culture as we know it in contemporary social sciences to describe a particular way of life of a people, a period of time, or humanity in general. But even in this tradition, anthropologists have used the concept to refer to the material production of a people, the "stuff" we create, whereas historians and other scholars have used it to refer to symbolic systems such as language, stories, and rituals. Currently, and with the rise of postmodern theorizing, these uses of the concept overlap considerably.

A more useful definition for a multidimensional, postmodern approach to human behavior sees culture as "a set of common understandings, manifest in act and artifact. It is in two places at once: inside somebody's head as understandings and in the external environment as act and artifact. If it isn't truly present in both spheres, it is only incomplete culture" (Bohannan, 1995, p. 47). **Culture**, in other words, includes both behavior (act or actions) and the material outcomes of that behavior (artifacts, or the things we construct from the material and technological world around us—such as houses, clothing, cars, nuclear weapons, jets, the Internet, smartphones, texting, laptops, and the like). It both constrains and is constrained by nature, biology, social conditions,

Systems perspective; psychodynamic perspective

and other realities of human existence. But at the same time, it is "inside our heads," or part of our thoughts, perceptions, and feelings. It is expressed through our emotions and thought processes, our motivations, intentions, and meanings as we live out our lives.

It is through culture that we construct meanings associated with the social and material world. Art, shelter, transportation, guns, cell phones, computers, the Internet, music, food, and clothing are material examples. The meanings we give these products influence how we use them. For example, some women's clothing is considered provocative, texting while in a meeting with others or while driving may be considered offensive or unsafe, and pork for some people is considered "polluted." Think of the different meanings that guns have for gun rights and gun control advocacy groups. In interaction with the social world and things around us, we construct religion, race and ethnicity, family and kinship, gender roles, and complex modern organizations and institutions.

Here's an example from U.S. history of how human beings construct meaning in a cultural context. Slaves of African descent tended to interpret their plight and quest for freedom in terms of Judeo-Christian religious beliefs, which were pressed on them by their slaveholders but which were also adapted for better fit with their oppressive situations. They likened their suffering to that of the crucifixion and resurrection of Jesus Christ. Just like the biblical "children of Israel" (the Jews) who had to make it to the Promised Land, so it was that slaves had to find freedom in the promised land of northern cities in the United States and Canada. The association of the plight of Christians and Jews in the Bible with racial oppression lives on today in the lives of many African Americans.

You may encounter clients who believe that their social, economic, and psychological difficulties are the result of God's will, or issues of spirituality, rather than of the biopsychosocial causes we study and apply as social workers. How would you apply a multidimensional approach to human behavior in this context? Should a social work assessment include the various meanings people construct about their circumstances? Applying a cultural perspective that considers these questions will help you find more empowering interpretations and solutions to issues you face as a social worker, especially when working with members of oppressed communities.

Here is another example. Disability in our culture seems to be about its opposite: being normal, competent, and "properly human" (Jenkins, 1998, p. 2). It is also about the "assumption or desirability of equality"—that is, sameness or similarity (Ingstad & Whyte, 1995, pp. 7–8). We may think that physical, emotional, or cognitive disabilities are purely biological or psychological and therefore real in a scientific sense. But deciding what is normal is embedded in culture. For example, a recent study documents differences in perceptions of Latino and Anglo mothers about the positive impact of having a child with an intellectual disability (Blacher,

Begum, Marcoulides, & Baker, 2013). Across time periods, Latino mothers reported more positive impact than Anglo mothers. Thus, like race and gender, what disabilities mean to the person possessing them and to those looking on and judging is a matter of the meanings individuals assign to differing abilities (Snyder & Mitchell, 2001; Thomson, 1996). These meanings play out in social, economic, and political relations that determine the distribution of resources and generate various types of inequality.

What are your emotional responses to seeing a child in a wheelchair? How do you suppose that child feels? Can you imagine the sexual attractiveness of people whose legs dangle freely below them as they walk with metal crutches? Do you suppose they see themselves as sexual beings? What are the bodily images we hold for being "handsome" or "beautiful"? Do they correspond with the images that others hold? The point is that if the culturally diverse people who reside in the United States see life in various ways, we must expect no less regarding those with different types and levels of ability. Here again, we as social workers must use a multidimensional conceptualization of culture to guide our actions.

The examples about African Americans and disability occur in a historical context. But history is about more than dates, names, inventions, and records of events. Rather, history is an ongoing story about the connections among ideas, communities, peoples, nations, and social transformations within the constraints of the natural world (Huynh-Nhu et al., 2008; McHale, Updegraff, Ji-Yeon, & Cansler, 2009). Think about how the historical plight of Native Americans, Asian Americans, or Hispanic Americans in the United States influences how they perceive their lives today. Think about the historical development of the language and ideas associated with disability: "crippled," "handicapped," "disabled," "differently abled," and so on.

Now consider the history of social work. It is about more than mere dates and events. Think of the people involved in social work, such as Mary Richmond, a leader in the early charity movement,

Photo 8.1 These dancers take part in a cultural festival to increase awareness of their traditions.

© AP Photo/Sean Thompson

and Jane Addams, a leader in the early settlement house movement. Think about the philosophy and social practices they espoused in working with the disadvantaged people of their time. What do you know about the ethnic identity, socioeconomic status, gender, and living conditions of these social work pioneers? What about the dominant thinking and political, social, and economic trends of their time? What do you know about what may have influenced their very different conceptions of social work and how those influences connect to the ideas and practices of contemporary social work? Now, think about Ida B. Wells-Barnett, former slave, contemporary of Jane Addams, and founder of an African American settlement house. How much do you know about her achievements (Carlton-LaNey, 2001)? Why have her achievements received less attention in the social work literature than those of Mary Richmond? This line of thought reveals a lot about U.S. culture and how it has interacted with the development of social work.

To sum up, culture includes multiple levels of traditions, values, and beliefs, as well as social, biological, and natural acts. It includes material culture and how, for example, the appeal and meaning of hip-hop music to youth and young adults differs from its appeal and meaning to older adults. The same could be said about clothing styles, the types of literature or art you enjoy, or even the type of house you decide to live in and its location. These processes are driven by the meanings we give to and take from them. These meanings are fortified or changed in relations between people, as history unfolds. Culture so defined is therefore not limited to the elite. It affects all of us.

Among those affected by culture are the students and staff at Community High School. Culture affects the social and academic process of schooling by influencing what curriculum is delivered, how, and by whom. A cultural interpretation would reveal competition and *strain*, or unequal power relations, in this process. For example, many Village Park residents and Community High students have cultural frames of reference that give

Conflict perspective

adversarial meanings to requirements that students act "studiously and behave a certain way" in class. These community members and students, whose schools and housing are still racially segregated, do not necessarily dismiss education and classroom rules, but they may see education and some of its rules as part of a system of mainstream institutions that have been oppressive and insensitive toward Blacks. They see schools as dismissing their norms and points of view, and the power to change things eludes them. When a White teacher at Community High asks Black students like Stan and Tina to stop talking out of turn in class, these students hear more than an impartial and benign request. Of course, any adolescent student might resent being told to stop talking by an adult authority figure. However, the interpretation of that request by Black students is likely to reflect their understanding about what it means to be "put down" or "dissed" in front of one's peers by an "outsider" who represents the dominant White society and does not respect the Black community.

These are complex issues, but they are part of the everyday problems social workers encounter. Further examination of what culture is and how its meaning has varied over time helps in our quest for multidimensional knowledge and skills.

TRADITIONAL UNDERSTANDINGS OF CULTURE AND VARIATION IN HUMAN BEHAVIOR

Ideas about culture have changed over time, in step with intellectual, social, economic, and political trends. Understanding these changes is integral to understanding current definitions of culture. As you learned earlier, the concept of culture has a lengthy history. But for our purposes, we summarize some of the ideas and concepts that have become a part of our understanding of culture today. Exhibit 8.2 provides an overview of the evolution of culture as a concept since the 18th century.

Some of the influential ideas that have remained with us from the past come from the Enlightenment and Romantic intellectual traditions, dating back to

Exhibit 8.2   Ideas and Processes Influencing the Evolution of Culture as a Concept

Time Period	Ideas and Human Processes
18th and 19th centuries: Enlightenment and Romanticism	• Rankings of logic, reason, art, technology • Culture seizing nature • Psychic unity of humankind
19th and 20th centuries: variation in human behavior and development	• Cultural relativism • Culture as patterns and structures • Culture and personality • Symbols as vehicles of culture
Contemporary understandings: integration and synthesis of processes of human development and variation since the 1950s	• Cultural psychology (cognitive psychology and anthropology) • Meaning, ecology, and culture • Political and economic systems and culture • Culture as private and public • Physical environment, biology, and culture • Ideology, history, common sense, tradition as cultural systems

the 18th century. A result of Enlightenment thinking in the early 18th century was that cultures and civilizations could be ranked according to their developed logic, reason, and technology (or mastery and use of the physical environment). Africans and Native Americans, for example, were seen as less civilized and less valuable than Europeans because their technology was not on the same scale as some European countries. Can you think of situations that demonstrate Enlightenment biases today? Is this the same framework that justifies interpreting the actions of Tina and Stan as less developed, less mature, and less rational than the actions of more mainstream students?

Conflict perspective

Another set of ideas comes from a Romantic orientation dating from the late 18th century. This orientation suggests that all people and their cultures are relatively equal in value. Differences in culture reflect different frameworks of meaning and understanding and thus result in different lifestyles and ways of living (Benedict, 1946, 1934/1989; Shweder, 1984/1995). From this tradition comes the idea of **cultural relativism** that frames contemporary multiculturalism. For example, at some point you may have been asked which is superior, Islam or Christianity, Black culture or White culture, African culture or European culture, or being a Republican, Democrat, or Independent. These religions, cultures, and political identities differ in content and meaning, but is one better than the other? If so, what is the standard of measure, and in whose interest is it developed and enforced?

Some today dismiss cultural relativism as "politically correct" thinking, but it does have practical value. For instance, as a social worker, you could contrast the behavior of Tina and Stan with that of successful White students to identify differences between them. How will doing so help Tina, Stan, or the successful White students—or any other students, for that matter? In the context of the conflict between the United States and some Middle Eastern societies regarding the 9/11 (September 11, 2001) strikes in the United States, one may question the value and moral tenets of Islam compared with Christianity or Eastern culture compared with Western. Perhaps it is more productive to measure each of these against some mutually relevant standard, such as how well the students will be able to succeed in their own communities or how well a religion or culture serves humanity. The point here is not that we should apply different standards to different people. Rather, in social work at least, to start where individuals are, to understand their points of view and the context of their lives, has been an effective method of helping them gain control of their lives.

In the United States today, we still see conflicts between Enlightenment thinking and the cultural relativism of Romanticism. Romanticism is reflected by those who call for respect for diversity in our multicultural society. But Enlightenment thinking, with its emphasis on ranking cultures, continues to have a great influence on our everyday understanding of culture. Again, consider recent public debates over crime, welfare, health insurance, Islam, and other issues that associate historical and contemporary social problems with people's race or ethnicity, religion, and socioeconomic status. Some social scientists and the popular media frequently express mainstream, Enlightenment-oriented values, attitudes, and morals in examining these issues, assigning more value to some things than to others (Lakoff, 2006; O'Reilly, 2007).

Another outcome of Enlightenment thinking is **biological determinism**—the attempt to differentiate social behavior largely on the basis of biological and genetic endowment. One form of biological determinism is based on racial identity. For example, a person's intellectual performance is associated by some people with brown skin and other physical differences believed to be related to race. *Race*, however, is a social construction based on biological differences in appearance. No relationship between differences in racial identity and differences in cognitive and intellectual capacities has been proved as biologically based. There is no verifiable evidence that the fundamental composition and functioning of the brain differs between Blacks and Whites, Asians and Hispanics, or whatever so-called racial groups you can identify and compare (Mukhopadhyay, Henze, & Moses, 2007; Mullings, 2005). Yet many still believe that race makes people inherently different. Such false associations are a vestige of Enlightenment thinking.

As a social work student, you can recognize the maligned power and influence of such tendencies. Thinking in terms of natural, ordained, and inevitable differences based on race reinforces the social tendency to think in terms of "we-ness" and "they-ness," which often has unfortunate effects (Jandt, 2010). It leads to what has come to be called **othering**, or labeling people who fall outside of your own group as abnormal, inferior, or marginal. In your personal and professional lives, pay attention to the images and thoughts you use to make sense of the economic, social, and behavioral difficulties of Black people or other ethnic groups. Pay attention to the characterizations of English-speaking and non-English-speaking immigrants or of documented and undocumented immigrants.

Critical Thinking Questions 8.1

Which cultures are you a part of? What are three important norms of each of those cultures? Are there any conflicts in norms across the different cultures in which you participate? Explain. What examples have you seen recently of Enlightenment thinking about culture? What examples have you seen of a Romantic orientation to culture?

CONTEMPORARY/POSTMODERN UNDERSTANDINGS OF CULTURE AND VARIATION IN HUMAN BEHAVIOR

Twentieth- and twenty-first-century scholars of culture inherited both advances and limitations in thought from scholars of previous centuries. With these challenges in mind, anthropologist Franz Boas (1940/1948) encouraged us to understand cultural differences as environmental differences interacting with the accidents of history. Boas's ideas, along with those developed by others, have led to the basic axioms about culture found in Exhibit 8.3 (Kottak, 1994, 2008).

Before we go further, it is important to note that many contemporary culture scholars suggest that environmental differences interacting with

> Social constructionist perspective; social behavioral perspective

Exhibit 8.3   Basic Axioms About Culture

- Culture is learned through social interaction.
- A society may have customary practices, but not all members have the same knowledge of them or attach the same significance to them.
- Culture seizes nature. That is, humans seek to control nature (in the form of climate, oceans, and rivers, for example) and shape it according to their own needs and interests.
- Culture is patterned, culture is symbolic, and culture is both adaptive and maladaptive.

accidents of history have produced three major types of cultures in recent centuries (see Gotham, 2013; Griswold, 2013). They suggest the name *traditional culture*, or *premodern culture*, to describe preindustrial societies based on subsistence agriculture. They argue that this type of culture was markedly different from *modern culture*, which arose with the 18th-century Enlightenment and is characterized by rationality, industrialization, urbanization, and capitalism. **Postmodernism** is the term many people use to describe contemporary culture. They suggest that global electronic communications are the foundation of postmodern culture, exposing people in advanced capitalist societies to media images that span place and time and allow them to splice together cultural elements from these different times and places (Griswold, 2013). Exhibit 8.4 presents the primary characteristics usually attributed to these three types of culture. While culture scholars who make these distinctions often present these three types as a historical timeline, running from traditional to modern to postmodern culture, traits of all three types of culture can in fact be found in advanced capitalist societies today and often become the source of contemporary culture wars within societies. Furthermore, many nonindustrial and newly industrializing societies can be characterized as either traditional or modern cultures.

Let's return now to Boas's axioms (Exhibit 8.3). Why are these axioms important for social workers? Three things come to mind if we are going to

work effectively and sensitively with people like Stan and Tina and communities whose norms vary from mainstream norms.

1. We must be able to understand how mainstream beliefs, customs, traditions, values, social institutions, and technology composing "normal" social behavior fit into the lives of our clients, especially those whose behaviors and traditions are considered "abnormal."

2. We must recognize that beliefs, customs, values, traditions, and social institutions vary in degrees of complexity from one society to another. People have a tendency to consider cultures other than their own to be aberrations from a universal norm or standard that all people should meet. For example, human service norms and standards in Canada differ from U.S. norms and standards. Two questions evolve from this point: Which norms and values are accepted as universal, and what criteria are these norms based on? Are these universals adaptive, or functional, under all social, economic, political, and environmental conditions?

3. Finally, we must pay attention to the development of emotional and cognitive frameworks as elements of society and culture. We must avoid the trap of confounding emotional and cognitive capacities with hierarchies of race, ethnicity, gender, and other ways of ranking humankind.

A few additional concepts help round out our discussion of past and present conceptions of culture.

- *Ideology.* **Ideology** is a set of shared beliefs about the way things are and should work. Problems of inequality and discrimination arise when social, economic, and political structures are influenced by ideologies that determine the distribution of power and resources (i.e., laws, rules, and regulations), which results in the exploitation and subjugation of people. Institutionalized gender bias, for example, is the systematic incorporation into the culture's structures of ideologies that directly and indirectly

> Conflict perspective

Exhibit 8.4 Characteristics of Traditional, Modern, and Postmodern Culture

Characteristic	Traditional Culture	Modern Culture	Postmodern Culture
Role of rationality	Positive value for irrational aspects of life; religious traditions superior to reason	Supreme value of rationality; rational control of nature	Questions the limits of rationality
Status	Status based on bloodline; hierarchy as natural order; patriarchy	Status based on achievement; egalitarianism	Emphasis on difference, not power
Source of authority	Religious authority	Nation-state; science	Globalization; national authority breaks down
Stability and change	Stability and order valued; order based on religion	Progress valued	Unpredictability and chaos
Unit of value	Communal values	Individualism	Diversity: multiplicity of perspectives and voices
Life structure	Agrarian, subsistence agriculture	Industrialization, urbanization, capitalism, commodity fetishism, specialization of function	Electronic communications, simulation, mass consumption

support the subordination of women (most typically) or men. These subordinating elements are built into the everyday, taken-for-granted way the culture's members live their lives.

Social constructionist perspective; psychodynamic perspective

• *Ethnocentrism.* Through cross-cultural comparisons, anthropologists have demonstrated that Western culture is not universal. They have exposed our tendency to elevate our own ethnic group and its social and cultural processes over others, a tendency known as **ethnocentrism**. For instance, theories of personality development are based on Western ideals of individuality and reliance on objective science rather than Eastern ideals of collective identity and reliance on subjective processes such as spirituality (Kottak, 2008). In addition, most of the existing behavioral science research is based on samples from Western industrialized cultures, and researchers often present their findings about human behavior as universally applicable. In reality, the samples for these studies are very different in many ways from most of the world's people, including some groups in the United States, and presenting the behavior of these research participants as universal elevates the culture from which they are drawn over other cultures of the world (Henrich, Heine, & Norenzayan, 2010).

• *Cultural symbols.* A **symbol** is something, verbal or nonverbal, that comes to stand for something else. The letters *d-o-g* have come to stand for the animal we call *dog*; golden arches forming a large *M* stand for McDonald's restaurants or hamburgers; and water in baptism rites stands for something sacred and holy, which moves a person from one state of being to another (Kottak, 2008). But as Conrad Kottak (1996) points out, "Water is not intrinsically holier than milk, blood or other liquids. A natural thing has been arbitrarily associated with a particular meaning for Catholics" and other religious groups (p. 26). Race, ethnicity, and gender are symbols that can be thought of in this way as well. For instance, beyond biological differences, what comes to mind when you think of a girl or woman? What about a boy or man? How do the images, thoughts, and feelings you possess about gender influence how you interact with boys and girls and men and women? Gendered thinking undoubtedly influences your assessment of persons, even those you have not actually met. In short, symbols shape perception, or the way a person sees, feels, and thinks about the world, and they communicate a host of feelings, thoughts, beliefs, and values that people use to make sense of their daily lives (Wilkin, 2009). They are vehicles of culture that facilitate social action. The role of symbols in culture raises questions that social workers face all the time: Do we really know what's going on inside people's heads—what they mean and intend when, for example, they use concepts such as "discipline," "being on time," "budgeting," or "love"? The idea that symbols express meaning within a culture is part of many recent models of practice in social work and psychology. For example, social constructionists focus on how narratives and stories can bring about emotional and behavioral changes in clinical social work practice.

- *Worldview and ethos.* A **worldview** is an idea of reality, a "concept of nature, of self, of society" (Geertz, 1973, p. 126). **Ethos** is the "tone, character, and quality of [people's] life, its moral and aesthetic style and mood; it is the underlying attitude toward themselves and their world that life reflects" (Geertz, 1973, p. 126). Worldview is associated with the cognitive domain, what we think about things; ethos is associated more with the emotional or affective and stylistic dimensions of behavior—how we feel about things (Ortner, 1984). Like Stan and Tina, recent Hispanic/Latino and African immigrants are adept at using symbols such as clothing, language, and music to convey specific feelings and perceptions that express their worldview and ethos. Exhibit 8.5 compares some additional symbols that convey differences in worldview and ethos.

- *Cultural innovation.* Culture is not static; it is adapted, modified, and changed through interactions over time. This process is known as

cultural innovation. For example, Stan and Tina were described earlier as innovators. Both restyle mainstream clothing to fit with their sense of meaning and with the values of their peers and their community. In addition, in the classroom and with peers, Stan and Tina can switch between Standard English and Black English. The mode of language they use depends on the social and political message or identity they want to convey to listeners. We see economic cultural innovation with immigrants, both recent and in the past. Many focus on and successfully exploit areas of the U.S. economy that are relatively underused by native populations—for example, engineering; computer science; and for better or worse, farm work, lawn care, and maintenance.

- *Cultural conflict.* The symbols we use are arbitrary. They can mean one thing to you and something different to others. Therefore, **cultural conflict** over meanings can easily arise. For example, jeans that hang low on

| Conflict perspective |

the hips of adolescents and young adults generally signify an ethos of hipness, toughness, and coolness. This is the style, mood, and perspective of a particular generation. (Some of us who are professionals, or soon will be, have a similar need to fit in with the particular ethos and worldview that is important to us and to the people with whom we interact. We are likely to choose an entirely different style of clothing.) However, the clothing, music, and language of politically and economically disadvantaged Black and Hispanic/Latino adolescents convey a different symbolic meaning to law enforcers, school officials, parents, and even social workers. In today's sociopolitical climate, these authority figures are likely to perceive low-slung jeans not only as a sign of hip-hop culture but also as a sign of drug and gang culture or a form of social rebellion, decadence, or incivility. What one culture considers "cool" may be "uncool" to another cultural group.

In sum, culture is both public and private. It has emotional and cognitive components, but these play out in public in our social actions. Symbols

Exhibit 8.5 Sociocultural Creations

Ask yourself what judgments you make and meanings you attribute in the following areas:

Music:
Classical versus jazz
Rhythm and blues versus bluegrass
Celtic versus rock and roll

Food:
Hamburger versus eel
Ants versus hot dogs
Kangaroo tail versus squid
Pigs' feet versus horse

Household/Domestic Activities:
Parents and children sleeping in separate beds and/or separate rooms versus sleeping in the open

Sexual intercourse in private versus public

Bathing in private versus public

Breast-feeding in private versus public

Families living, eating, and sleeping in one large room versus separate rooms

Eating with fingers and hands versus forks, spoons, and knives

are a way of communicating private meaning through public or social action. Furthermore, people's actions express their worldview (how they think about the world) and their ethos (how they feel about the world)—just as Tina and Stan do when they alternate between Black and mainstream styles.

These concepts have great relevance to social work. For example, arguments accompanying welfare reform legislation in the United States in the 1990s represented shifting meanings regarding poverty, single parenting, and work. During the 1960s, it was considered society's moral duty to combat poverty by assisting the poor. Today, poverty does not just mean a lack of financial resources for the necessities of life; to many people, it symbolizes laziness, the demise of family values, and other characteristics that shade into immorality. Thus, to help people who are poor is now often purported to hurt them by consigning them to dependency and immoral behavior (Cousins, 2013).

As social workers, we depend on the NASW Code of Ethics for professional guidance in negotiating these shifts. But what is the source of the values and beliefs that guide our personal lives? And what happens when what we believe and value differs from our clients' beliefs and values? These questions raise the issue of how we form and act on meanings derived from our private cultural leanings that are part of our professional lives. Exhibit 8.6 demonstrates several cultural conflicts that may arise as our personal social habits confront the principles, values, and ethics of professional social workers.

Critical Thinking Questions 8.2

When you think of your day-to-day life, do you think you live in a traditional, modern, or postmodern culture? Explain. What do you see as the benefits and costs of each of these types of culture? What is an example of a cultural conflict you have observed or been a part of? What meanings were involved in the conflict? Give examples of what is "cool" in a culture important in your life.

A POSTMODERN, HOLISTIC APPLICATION OF CULTURE _____

The discussion to this point has attempted to assist social workers in expanding their understanding of the multidimensional nature of human behavior by examining what culture is and how thinking about culture has evolved. What follows is a discussion of how to apply a multidimensional concept of culture.

To increase our understanding of culture and human behavior, we might ask how it is that Tina's and Stan's ways of living are different from our own. We can apply the same question to immigrants and other groups that differ from the mainstream norm. We need to recognize that their lives may be based on values, beliefs, and rationalizations that we don't fully understand. We could try to understand them, but would we succeed by applying our own cultural frame of reference, our own worldview and ethos? If we limit our quest to our own terms, to our authority and power as social workers to define who they are, what do we achieve? We are likely to

---

Exhibit 8.6 Customary Social Habits Interacting With Social Work Principles, Values, and Ethics on a Continuum

---

What are your beliefs about the following interactions with clients and colleagues?

Continuum

Most Professional (Formal) .... *Least Professional (Informal)*

Greetings by handshake .... hugging .... kissing

Use of last name/title .... first name .... nickname
(Mr., Ms., Dr.)

Authority by credentials .... age, experience, ... religion/politics
(BSW, MSW, etc.)   gender, marital status

Sharing no personal .... pertinent information .... open-ended,
information   mutual sharing

Confidentiality .... sharing with professionals/ .... sharing with friends/
                                     family   community members

---

learn more about ourselves and our standards than about people like Stan and Tina. The most we can learn about these students by looking at them from our own frame of reference is how they compare with us. The comparison, however, is in our terms, not theirs. For example, we may well say that Stan is at greater than average risk of failing socially and academically. But he might say that he is more successful than most at negotiating the oppressive structures of school and society.

Ask yourself what would happen if we as social workers compared the views and feelings of clients regarding their lives and problems with our own views and feelings. What would we have to give up, and what would we and our clients gain? We need a multidimensional perspective of cultural diversity and human behavior to ground our professional actions in this way. But what should a multidimensional approach to a culture analysis consist of, and what would it be trying to explain? These are important questions for social workers.

A Practice Orientation

Forty or more years ago, the problems of Village Park and Community High School would have been explained largely in terms of a culture of poverty. The term **culture of poverty** was originally used to bring attention to the way of life developed by poor people to adapt to the difficult circumstances of their lives. Proponents of this theoretical orientation twisted it to suggest that Black schools and communities were impoverished because of Black people's own beliefs, values, traditions, morals, and frames of reference. Mainstream culture's racism and discrimination were not considered to be decisive factors. That Black people faced *redlining*, a practice that forced them to buy or rent homes only in Black communities, was not considered to be a factor. That Black people were working in low-income jobs despite qualifications for better ones was likewise not considered to be a factor. That major colleges and universities were denying admission to qualified Black applicants was not considered to be a factor either. The list could go

on. The culture-of-poverty orientation was used to argue both for and against publicly financed social programs. From time to time, some of my students even today use a culture-of-poverty line of reasoning to explain people on welfare, poor single parents, and other problems of inner cities.

Contemporary and postmodern culture scholars (anthropologists, sociologists, psychologists, political scientists, social workers, and economists) have also adopted some of the tenets of past theorizing. However, they have taken the better parts of it to develop what has come to be called postmodern and **practice orientations** (Berger & Luckmann, 1966; Bourdieu, 1977; Giddens, 1979; Ortner, 1989, 1996, 2006; Sahlins, 1981). *Practice* as used here is different from its use in social work. This theoretical orientation seeks to explain what people do as thinking, intentionally acting persons who face the impact of history and the restraints of structures embedded in our society and culture. It asks how social systems shape, guide, and direct people's values, beliefs, and behavior. But it also asks how people, as human actors or agents, perpetuate or shape social systems. The underlying issues, in sum, are about understanding two things:

1. How, through culture, human beings construct meaning, intentionality, and public behavior

2. How human beings produce systemic cultural change or adapt to and maintain the culture

The hope of the practice orientation is that—by reflection on history, structure, and agency—we can develop a deeper understanding of inequalities based on race, ethnicity and social class, and gender relations, among other sociocultural processes.

The issue of poverty offers one example of how the practice orientation can be applied. The practice orientation would not blame poverty's prevalence and influence in Tina and Stan's community solely on the failings of individuals. Rather, it would seek to identify the structural factors—such as low-income jobs, housing segregation, and racism—that impede

Social constructionist perspective; conflict perspective

upward mobility. It would also seek to understand how poor African Americans perceive and contribute to their conditions; how nonpoor, non-Black Americans perceive and contribute to the conditions of poor African Americans; and how all of these perceptions and actions shape the lives and influence the upward mobility of poor African Americans. Thus, this perspective would ask, are poor African Americans as different in values, beliefs, and attitudes as other people think they are? Is there a "culture" of poverty, or do people in dire circumstances adapt their values and beliefs to the demands of survival? These are matters of considerable importance and complexity.

Other examples of the types of questions fruitfully addressed through the practice orientation apply to Stan's situation: How have Stan's family and community influenced his behavior in general and his response to racism and classism in school in particular? How have Stan's own responses contributed to his subordination as a Black youth, thereby leaving certain oppressive structures in society unchanged? Likewise, how have the values and beliefs encoded through the rules and regulations in public schools like Community High served to perpetuate or reproduce various forms of structural or systemic subjugation? What are the symbolic meanings of school and education, and what role do they play in Stan's behavior? From our position as educated Americans with many mainstream values, we would tend to see schools as intrinsically good because they are largely about academic growth rather than social and cultural relations. But is this the whole, multidimensional picture?

The same types of questions apply to social work. How have the values, beliefs, and practices of the profession helped to maintain the profession and society as they are? When we label a person or group as having a social problem or dysfunction, are we perpetuating or reproducing subjugation of the person or group? For better or worse, when social science categorizes human functioning, it does just that. When we label the people we have failed to help as resistant, unmotivated, and pathological, are we carelessly overlooking the ineffectiveness of our modes of understanding and intervention?

Are we blaming the victim and reproducing his or her victimization? These and other questions are important for all of us to ponder.

History, social structure, and human agency are the key elements in a practice orientation. This chapter has tried to demonstrate how some life events reflect the intertwined influences of history, social structure, and human agency. These kinds of interactions sometimes reflect social strain and sometimes social solidarity. Sometimes they reflect a conflict between the objective and the subjective nature of what we do and believe. In any case, the relationship between human action and social systems is never simple in a political world.

> Systems perspective

History, Social Structure, and Human Agency

History is made by people, but it is made within the constraints of the social, economic, political, physical, and biological systems in which people are living. History includes, but is not totally defined by, chains of events and experiences to which people simply react. To understand human diversity, especially as it relates to oppression, exploitation, and subjugation, we must listen to the memories of both official and unofficial observers. We must hear those voices that are represented in the official records and those that are not. We must listen to clients as much as to social workers.

Social Structure refers to the ordered forms and systems of human behavior in public life (e.g., capitalism, kinship, public education). It also includes cognitive, emotional, and behavioral frameworks that are mapped onto who we are as people. Structure influences how we construct ourselves—that is, what we make of ourselves based on what things mean to us. We carry forth meanings, values, and beliefs through social, economic, and political practices in our everyday, personal lives and the institutions in which we participate. We reproduce structures when we assume the rightness of our values, beliefs, and meaning and see no need to change them. When this process dominates, **cultural hegemony** results—the dominance of a particular way of seeing the world. Most observers of culture in the United States would agree that it is based on the hegemony of a European American, or Anglo, worldview. People in many other parts of the world have observed the hegemony of the U.S. worldview. As the artist Diego Rivera said in 1931 and Mike Davis (2000) reiterates in his book on Latino influences on U.S. cities, "When you say 'America' you refer to the territory stretching between the icecaps of the two poles. So to hell with your barriers and frontier guards!" (p. ix). As the quote implies, those whose cultures are overtaken by another culture often resent the hegemony, which they see as cultural imperialism. Chapter 9 deals with trends and patterns in contemporary social institutions and social structures, at the national and global levels.

Human agency asserts that people are not simply puppets, the pawns of history and structure; people are also active participants, capable of exercising their will to shape

Humanistic perspective

their lives. Thus, although racism is structured into society, it is not so completely dominant over Tina and Stan that they have no room for meaningful self-expression in their social and political lives.

Human agency helps to counteract cultural hegemony as well. Consider the influence of African American urban youth culture. Rap music and clothing styles that originated with Black teens like Tina and Stan have become popular with White, middle-class young people. This is a way individuals and groups exercise agency by constructing culture. They invest the world with their own subjective order, meaning, and value. They rely on their frame of mind or worldview to consciously and unconsciously make choices and take action. They construct social and political identities that help them resist and contest cultural hegemony.

However, no individual or group is a fully free agent. All are constrained by external factors such as climate, disease, natural resources, and population size and growth—although we may be able to modify these constraints through technology (Turkle, 2011). Examples of technologies that modify facts of biology and nature are medicines, agricultural breakthroughs, climate-controlled homes, telecommunications, transportation, and synthetic products that replace the use of wood in furniture and related items.

A contemporary example of the interface of culture and technology is the cell or mobile phone. Scholars are still not sure of its impact, but they have begun to identify the aesthetic or fashion value of the phone on the one hand—the styles and colors and what they mean to and convey about the owner (Goggin, 2008). Its practical function, on the other hand, points to enhanced communication, as well as invasiveness and annoyance due to its ubiquity. Add to this the role of the camera in the phone in documenting personal events such as family reunions, and misconduct of, say, the police against citizens. But to raise prior questions, does the technology shape us—our culture—or does our culture shape the technology? How has cell phone technology shaped social work, for example? Is a practitioner assisted by the phone as a security device, or is the practitioner's workload unnecessarily extended by being available relatively endlessly? If core practices of social work change as a result of this technology, what does that mean for clients?

Sherry Turkle (2011) talks about how simulation of human interactions through computers and robotics—computers and machines replacing live individuals—may on the one hand provide reassurance and emotional safety to individuals who are insecure with people. On the other hand, do interactions through robotics distance people and perhaps limit opportunities to experience empathy, anger, frustration, and other rich emotions from interaction with another individual versus a machine? Contemporary communication technologies allow us to be connected to a wide network of people across time and place. They also allow us to be fragmented in our attention—to be both present and not present in a given situation. And they raise new cultural questions, such as, Does receipt of a text message demand an immediate reply? and Is it okay to break up by text message? Neil Postman (1993) says this is a bargain struck by every society and culture in which technology gives and technology takes away. Every society and culture must negotiate with technology.

In sum, human agents are "skilled and intense strategizers" (Ortner, 1996, p. 20). We are constantly stretching the process by which we live and define ourselves. But we do so within the constraints of structures or forces that can never wholly contain us. Human agency is a major source of hope and motivation for social workers who encounter people, organizations, and systems that seem unable to break away from the constraints of daily life.

Cultural Maintenance, Change, and Adaptation

Tina's and Stan's experiences with mainstream schooling provide a good example of how cultural structures are maintained, how they change, and how they adapt. School systems are centered on the norms, values, and beliefs preferred by those who have had the power to decide what is or is not appropriate to learn and use in our lives. Some things we learn in school fit well with the needs of industry. Other things we learn fit well with the needs of our social and political institutions. These include the values and workings of family and community life and of local, state, and national governing bodies. From the outside looking in, schools look like benign or innocent institutions that are simply about academics and education. Yet which academic subjects are taught, how they are taught, who teaches them, and how they are to be learned involve an assertion of someone's values and beliefs, whether right or wrong, whether shared by many or by few. Exhibit 8.7 lists some of the factors involved in the cultural construction of schooling. As you can see, schooling's influence extends far beyond reading, writing, and arithmetic.

Even in the face of evidence that schools do not work for many of us, they persist. Education is strongly correlated with economic and social

Exhibit 8.7 Sociocultural Factors in the Construction of Education and Schooling

Politics and Law

Legislation, laws, and regulations regarding attendance and social behavior; educational content; segregation/desegregation; school funding

Family

Socialization regarding gender roles and relations; sex; discipline; health/hygiene/nutrition; recreation; emotional support and development

Religion

Prayer; holidays; family and personal morality and ethics

Social Structure and Economics

Status, opportunities, and rewards associated with knowledge, grades, and credentials; individual versus collective achievement; appropriate versus inappropriate behavior and social skills; media, market, and popular cultural trends and factors

Community

Ethnic representation and attitudes; economic resources and stability; levels of crime success. Therefore, ineffective schools play a role in the persistent poverty we have faced in this country. In addition, if you examine how girls are treated in schools, you will discover correlations with women's subjugation in other domains as well. The experiences of immigrants in schools also raise issues regarding cultural processes in schools and beyond.

Culture provides stability to social life, but it changes over time. It does not change rapidly, however. First, we look at some ideas about how culture produces stability, and then we turn to how culture changes over time through immigration and processes of negotiating multicultural community life.

Common Sense, Custom, and Tradition

Over time, the ways in which families, schools, cities, and governments do things in the United States have come to seem natural to us. They seem to fit with the common sense, customs, and traditions of most people who live here.

Keep in mind, however, that **common sense** is a cultural system. It is what people have come to believe everyone in a community or society should know and understand as a matter of ordinary, taken-for-granted social competence. It is based on a set of assumptions that are so unself-conscious that they seem natural, transparent, and an undeniable part of the structure of the world (Geertz, 1983; Swidler, 1986). For example, rain is wet, fire burns, and, as I hear more and more in the general population, as well as from many Community High students, "One can't make it without an education!" In addition, "Common sense tells you that you gotta speak English to make it in America" is something you might overhear a citizen of Charlotte, North Carolina, say about the Mexicans who have recently come to the city.

Yet not everyone—especially not members of oppressed, subjugated, or immigrant groups within a society—is likely to share these common schemes of meaning and understanding. Thus, common sense becomes self-serving for those in a position of power to determine what it is and who has it. We believe common sense tells us what actions are

appropriate in school or in any number of other contexts. But, as a part of culture, common sense is subject to historically defined standards of judgment related to maleness and femaleness, parenting, poverty, work, education, and psychosocial functioning, among other categories of social being. For better or worse, common sense helps to maintain cultures and societies as they are.

We need to approach customs and traditions with the same caution with which we approach common sense. **Customs**, or cultural practices, come into being and persist as solutions to problems of living (Goodenough, 1996). **Tradition** is a process of handing down from one generation to another particular cultural beliefs and practices. In particular, it is a process of ratifying particular beliefs and practices by connecting them to selected social, economic, and political practices. When this is done well, traditions become so taken for granted that they seem "natural" parts of life, as if they have always been here and as if we cannot live without them (Hobsbawm, 1983; Swidler, 1986; Williams, 1977). Some customs and traditions are routine; others, such as special ceremonies, are extraordinary. They are not necessarily followed by everyone in the culture, but they seem necessary and ordained, and they stabilize the culture. They are, in a sense, collective memories of the group. They reflect meanings at a particular moment in time and serve as guides for the present and future (Chung, 2006; McHale et al., 2009).

Customs and traditions are selective, however. They leave out the experiences, memories, and voices of some group members while highlighting and including others. African American students generally do not experience schooling as reflecting their customs and traditions. In many cases, Latino or Hispanic immigrants in Charlotte, North Carolina, will not, either. Stan, Tina, and their peers often raised this point in their classes at Community High, and several residents of Village Park have been raising similar issues for many years. Latino/Hispanic families express similar concerns.

To reflect Village Park residents' customs and traditions, Community High would have to respect and understand the use of Nonstandard English as students are learning Standard English. Literature and history classes would make salient connections between European traditions and customs and those of West Africans, Afro-Caribbeans, and contemporary African Americans. In addition, processes for including a student's family in schooling would include kinship bonds not based on legalized blood ties or the rules of state foster care systems. What would a school social worker have to learn to assist schools and immigrant families in having a more successful experience in school?

Customs and traditions, moreover, play a role in the strain that characterizes shifts from old patterns and styles of living to new ones in schools and other institutions in society. To survive, groups of people have to bend their customs and traditions without letting them lose their essence. Nondominant ethnic, gender, religious, and other groups in the United States often have to assimilate or accommodate their host culture if they are to share in economic and political power. In fact, the general survival of the customs and traditions of nondominant groups requires adaptability.

Customs and traditions are parts of a cultural process that are changing ever so subtly and slowly but at times abruptly. Sometimes groups disagree about these changes, and some members deny that they are occurring because they believe they should still do things the old way. Social workers have to understand a group's need to hold on to old ways. They do this to protect their worldview about what life means and who they are as a people.

Photo 8.2 These mothers from different cultural backgrounds may have some different traditions and customs regarding child rearing, but they find their toddlers have much in common.

© iStockphoto.com

Immigration

It would be foolish to deny that the United States is a nation of immigrants (Parrillo, 2009). Immigration to this land began with the gradual migration of prehistoric peoples and picked up speed when Columbus and other Europeans arrived from across the Atlantic Ocean. It continued with the involuntary arrival of Africans and the voluntary and semivoluntary arrivals of various European ethnic groups. Later came Asian peoples and others. Forceful extension of the nation's borders and political influence incorporated Hispanics and Pacific Islanders. There have been many subsequent waves of immigration, with a great influx late in the 20th century and continuing today. Now, more than ever, people are coming to the United States from all over the world. Today, we define cultural diversity as a relatively new issue. But the nation's fabric has long included a rich diversity of cultures (Hing, 2004).

Although diversity has been a feature of life in the United States for centuries, immigration is an especially prominent feature of society today. According to U.S. Census estimates, 40 million foreign-born residents now reside in the United States (U.S. Census Bureau, 2013d). They represent approximately 12.9% of the total U.S. population of just over 313 million, or about one in eight residents. They are mostly from Latin America (53%; about 37% born in Central America). They are agents of what the media have called the "browning" of the United States. The 2010 census data indicate that 28% of all foreign-born U.S. residents were born in Asia, 12% in Europe, and 7% in other regions of the world. Seventy percent of these immigrants live in the Northeast and Midwest, and they have a median age of around 41.4 years; two of three are high school graduates and one in four have earned a bachelor's degree (U.S. Census Bureau, 2013c, 2013d).

Population profiles of immigrants are complex and do not capture the dynamic complexity within and between groups based on, for example, region, language, and cultural traditions (Migration Policy Institute, 2013; Pew Research Hispanic Center, 2013). Whether they come from Mexico, South America, or Central America, Hispanics and other immigrant groups bring with them their own cultural traditions and languages, which influence their worldview, ethos, and social, economic, and political beliefs and values.

Although many immigrants realize their dream of economic opportunity, many, but not all, encounter resistance from the native born. Let us consider the case of immigrants from Latin American countries (Central and South America and the Caribbean). This group recently surpassed African Americans as the largest minority in the United States and is therefore the group social workers are increasingly likely to encounter. New York City, Los Angeles, Chicago, San Antonio, Houston, and other southwestern cities are traditional sites for the settlement of Hispanic/Latino immigrants. However, they are also settling in increasing numbers in growing metropolitan areas such as Charlotte, North Carolina, where I formerly resided. Charlotte is centered in a metropolitan region of more than a million residents. Prior to the financial crisis of 2007–2010, it had a vibrant economy and was the second largest banking center in the nation (home to Bank of America). People came to Charlotte because economic opportunities abounded.

Like other Americans, Hispanic/Latino immigrants come to Charlotte to get a piece of the economic pie. However, Hispanic/Latino immigrants face a unique set of circumstances. One often hears complaints in Charlotte about "foreigners taking our jobs." African Americans and Latinos/Hispanics face social conflicts over lifestyles in the low-income neighborhoods they share. Social service and law enforcement agencies scramble for Spanish-language workers and interpreters. Banks decry the fact that many new Spanish-language residents don't trust banks and consequently don't open checking and savings accounts.

Current legislative debates about immigration policy reflect people's differing views of immigration and what it means to them. This situation can be thought of from different perspectives. Is immigration, or are immigrants, inherently a problem? Or are they perceived as a problem because of what they mean in the economic, political, and social context of these cities? Who should be more concerned about losing cultural ground, Hispanic/Latino immigrants or long-term U.S. residents? Notions of common sense, tradition, and custom apply in this situation. An understanding of cultural processes also helps social workers interpret the issues they encounter in practice.

Processes of Cultural Change

In multicultural societies, cultural change can be understood in terms of four processes: assimilation, accommodation, acculturation, and bicultural socialization. These processes describe the individual's or group's response to the dominant culture and may have implications for clients' well-being.

- *Assimilation.* **Assimilation** is the process in which the cultural uniqueness of the minority group is abandoned, and its members try to blend invisibly into the dominant culture (Kottak, 2008). Some culture scholars have noted a prevailing assimilation ideology that asserts the ideal of Anglo conformity (Gordon, 1964). In keeping with this view, some people have argued that the root of the problems faced by African Americans and by economically marginal immigrants is that they have not assimilated successfully. This argument is oversimplified. First, to the extent that discrimination is based on obvious features such as skin color or lack of facility with Standard English, the ability to assimilate is limited. Second, capitalist economies and societies arbitrarily select different group characteristics as desirable at different times. Historically, we have done this in part through immigration policies that admit some groups but not others. For example, the Chinese Exclusion Act of 1882, which was not repealed until 1943, suspended the right of people from China to immigrate to the United States. Many minorities, especially first-generation immigrants, often resist giving up parts of their ethnic identity in order to protect their sense of meaning and purpose in life.

- *Accommodation.* This process is more common than assimilation in multicultural, multiethnic society in the United States. **Accommodation** is the process of partial or selective cultural change. Nondominant groups follow the norms, rules, and standards of the dominant culture only in specific circumstances and contexts. When Punjabi Sikh children attended school in Stockton, California, in the 1980s, they generally followed the rules of the school (Gibson, 1988). They did not, however, remove their head coverings, socialize with peers of both sexes as is normal in mainstream U.S. society, or live by U.S. cultural standards at home. Some of the Muslim students at Community High could be compared to the Punjabis. Black Muslim girls at Community High, for example, refuse to remove their head coverings or customary long gowns to attend school, even though the school asks them to do so. Similar stories continue to turn up in local and national newspapers about students whose Islamic religious attire conflicts with school norms and rules, especially in light of the conflict between the United States and terrorists who claim an Islamic background. Increasingly, Latino/Hispanic immigrants and native citizens are refusing to give up Spanish in many settings, even though they can and will speak English when necessary.

- *Acculturation.* **Acculturation** is a mutual sharing of culture (Kottak & Kozaitis, 2008). Although cultural groups remain distinct, certain elements of their culture change, and they exchange and blend preferences in foods, music, dance, clothing, and the like. As cities and towns grow in diversity, Mexican, Vietnamese, Asian, Indian, and other cuisines are becoming more common in the United States. At the same time, these diverse cultural groups are incorporating parts of regional cultures into their lives.

- *Bicultural socialization.* The process of **bicultural socialization** involves a nonmajority group or member mastering both the dominant culture and his or her own (Robbins, Chatterjee, & Canda, 2012). Bicultural socialization is necessary in societies that have relatively fixed notions about how a person should live and interact in school, work, court, financial institutions, and the like. A person who has achieved bicultural socialization has, in a sense, a dual identity. Mainstream economic, political, and social success (or "crossing over") requires nonmajority musicians, athletes, intellectuals and scholars, news anchors, bankers, and a host of others to master this process of cultural change and adaptation.

Social workers who conduct a multidimensional cultural analysis should seek to uncover the processes by which culture is being maintained, changed, and adapted in the lives of the individuals and groups with whom they work. We must also be alert to the fact that the process of cultural change is not always voluntary, or a free and open exchange of culture. We must also pay attention to the political, social, and economic practices that undergird institutional norms and values. If these processes are harmful and oppressive for some people, we have a professional obligation, through our code of ethics, to facilitate change.

Women, people of color, immigrants, and poor people have historically not had a significant say in how cultural change proceeds. But having a limited voice does not eliminate one's voice altogether. Predominantly

Conflict perspective

Black schools and institutions sometimes seek to preserve and strengthen elements of African American culture. Organizations dominated by women and feminists, such as NOW (National Organization of Women), give women a voice in a male-dominated culture. Other examples of different cultures being expressed include the aisles of ethnic foods in many grocery stores, ethnic and "world" music in music stores, a significant presence of Black literature in bookstores, and the influence of Latino/Hispanic/Chicano culture on the social, economic, and political life in cities such as Los Angeles and Houston.

As social workers, we must comprehend the process of cultural change affecting our clients and act in accord with such knowledge. We cannot accept only the dominant notions about the meaning of the actions of people of color and poor people. We cannot look only to mainstream culture and traditions of knowledge to determine

the actions we take with nonmajority people. If we do, we are merely reproducing inequality and subjugation and limiting our effectiveness as human service providers.

Critical Thinking Questions 8.3

How much human agency do you think you have to take charge of your life? Do all people have the same level of human agency? What factors make a difference in how much human agency people have? What cultural changes have you witnessed? What do you think are the forces driving those cultural changes? What forces are opposing them?

Diversity

The *practice orientation* is a model for conceptualizing, organizing, and analyzing cultural processes. It helps us to explore different meanings for things we take for granted. It is especially useful for interpreting variation in the social environment. Such variables as race, ethnicity, social class, gender, and family are important symbols in the U.S. psyche and express a host of feelings, beliefs, thoughts, and values about the world around us. Lakoff (2004) demonstrates the use of symbols in the form of metaphors in a discussion of the 2000 and 2004 U.S. presidential elections and their aftermath. He says that metaphors work powerfully by framing how we see the world. He describes how the term *permission slip*—as in the United States does not need to "ask for a permission slip" (p. 11) from the United Nations to act against rogue nations such as Iraq—was used in President G. W. Bush's 2004 State of the Union address to justify war against Iraq. The use of *permission slip* in this context frames the metaphor of an adult–child relationship and suggests that, as an adult nation, the United States has the authority to act like a grown-up and make independent decisions. The concepts that follow have been similarly employed as symbols—indeed, as metaphors—across centuries and continents to generate meaning and power in society. Let's examine them.

Race

Race is first and foremost a system of social identity. It has been constructed over many years through cultural, social, economic, and political relations. Social and cultural meanings have been mapped onto physical or biological aspects of human variation such as skin color, hair texture, and facial characteristics. Race has become a fundamental principle of social organization, even though it has no validity as a biological category (Mullings, 2005; Winant, 2004). The physical or biological characteristics—*phenotypes*—we associate with race are in fact variations resulting from human adaptation to different geographic environments over thousands of years. Some phenotypes have been publicly categorized as European (White), African (Black), Asian, Latino/Hispanic, or Native American (to see a visual representation of this, go to www.understandingrace.org/home.html). However, the physical attributes of each group have no intrinsic or natural relationship to emotional, cognitive, or social capacities. **Racism** is the term for thinking and acting as if the phenotype (or as we like to say, the "genes") and these other capacities are related and imply inferiority or superiority.

The meanings and uses of race shift, depending on the social, economic, and political context. In one context, for example, being Black or African American is an asset, whereas in another it is a deficit. Even among Black students and communities, these meanings shift. This variability is a result of the social, political, and economic advantages or disadvantages associated with a Black racial identity at a particular moment in time. Race relations and identity issues in the 1960s were somewhat different from what they were in 2014 because the social, economic, and political climates were very different.

Consider the issue of racial identity among Community High students. Today's Black students experience less conflict among themselves about "acting White" than did the Black students who attended Community High 2 decades ago (Cousins, 2008; Fordham, 1996; Fordham & Ogbu, 1986). *Acting White* is the term used to identify behavior that fits with the norms of speech, demeanor, dress, and so on that are preferred and valued by mainstream European American society. "White" norms are perceived to be at play in school activities such as doing homework, carrying books, and speaking in Standard English when answering questions in the classroom. Today, as 2 decades ago, Black students who do "act White" possess "cultural capital" and are therefore likely to receive more social, economic, and political acceptance within the larger society. They will also be given more privilege and prestige than those who act in accord with what is perceived as distinctly "Black" behavior. These judgments are made by both Blacks and non-Blacks. In addition, the demands of survival require adaptability. Therefore, many families of Black students at Community High and the Black residents of that community are allowing a greater range of flexibility in defining "Black" behavior.

Stan and Tina offer examples of the current blurring of distinctions between behaviors that have historically been defined as Black and those defined as White. Both students borrow from mainstream norms as they shape their ethnic identity. Stan redefines the mainstream meaning of brand-name shirts and biker boots. Tina can speak directly and assertively in class using mainstream Standard English, but her attitude and demeanor are perceived as distinctly Black. Both of these students maintain an ethos and worldview seated in the experience of their Black community. But at the same time, they are relatively bicultural and accommodating toward mainstream standards. Such changes in meaning and practice are likely to continue in their community in predictable and unpredictable ways.

Ethnicity

Ethnicity is often associated with static traditions, customs, and values that reflect a deep and enduring cultural identity and a desire to keep that identity intact. Ethnic identity has traditionally been asserted through preferences in food, clothing, language, and religion. It is also often tied up with blood relations, geographic location, and nationality. Conflict between Bosnians and Serbs in the 1990s; in Syria, Egypt, and the Central African Republic (Congo) more recently; and the ongoing Israeli–Palestinian conflict are each in their own way matters of nationality and land against a backdrop of religious beliefs and traditions (see United Nations and the Human Rights Watch websites for more information). In the United States, ethnic conflict includes more than Black–White relations. We see conflict between Koreans and Blacks, Hispanics/Latinos and Blacks, Whites and Hispanics/Latinos, Arabs and Blacks, Arabs and Whites, and so forth.

Ethnic identity is how ethnic groups define themselves and maintain meaning for living individually and as a group. In contemporary industrial societies, ethnic identity is part of a person's social identity (which also includes occupational roles, gender roles, individual and family mobility, and family rituals—regarding meals, for instance). Ethnic identity also includes methods of solving family problems and social conflicts with schools and other institutions. The meaning of a person's identity shifts, however subtly and slowly, as a result of economic, social, and political processes interacting with individual and collective beliefs and values. Consequently, people do not end up practicing the exact particulars of what they espouse about their values, customs, traditions, and other things that make up ethnic identity (Chung, 2006; McHale et al., 2009). Think back to the process of acculturation discussed earlier.

Such a dilemma of ideal versus real ethnic identity might be thought of as the difference between upholding the spirit (intentions) versus the letter (exact meaning or interpretation) of the law. Ethnic groups in complex societies such as the United States often are better able to uphold the spirit rather than the letter of their values, customs, and beliefs. It is less a matter of truth or fact than one of process, change, and adaptation. When change and adaptation do not occur, ethnic culture may become a trap in an

Conflict perspective

inflexible society. A group that is not willing or able to adapt is left economically, socially, and politically disenfranchised (Bohannan, 1995). Societies and their institutions could be thought of as trapped as well when they do not support the kind of changes that foster equality among all peoples.

The rejection and disdain that members of some ethnic groups experience in the United States take a toll on identity (Healey, 2012). The result is that people of color or members of ethnic groups may need help to sort out their identities. Stan and Tina were able to develop relatively positive identities because they live in communities and families that celebrate and affirm being Black or African American. Likewise, Puerto Rican youth in some communities see themselves positively and tend to achieve highly in school (Flores-Gonzalez, 1999). However, those whose ethnicity is not as well supported may need help. Three steps social workers can take are to (1) teach clients about the effects of the political realities of racism, (2) teach clients how to use the strengths and resources of their own culture in rearing their children, and (3) organize ethnic communities to seek cultural democracy in dealing with institutions such as schools (Crocetti, Rubini, & Meeus, 2008).

Social Class

Social class (which includes **socioeconomic status**, or **SES**) is a dirty phrase among people in the United States, who generally believe that any class differences that may exist are of one's own making. But class differences do exist, and they document another form of cultural inequality, as well as imperfections in our capitalist economic system. Social class is a way of ascribing status, prestige, and power. It is based on education, income, and occupation. Each of these indices—how much education one has, how much money one makes or has, and what one does for a living—carries poignant meanings. These meanings are derived from subjective values and beliefs in interaction with dominant customs, traditions, and notions of common sense. Social scientists do not fully know how or why, but the meanings associated with social class get condensed into our society's fascination with lifestyles.

The terms we commonly use to categorize class status are *upper class*, *middle class*, *working class*, and *lower class* or *underclass*. We also talk in terms of jobs that are blue collar (working class), pink collar (supervisory, especially in traditionally female occupations), and white collar (managerial and professional). These categories and their meanings become infused into identities such as race and ethnicity. For instance, Stan's and Tina's identities as African Americans automatically tend to reduce their social class status to the category of lower or underclass. The income, occupation, and education of Stan's and Tina's families, however, would generally place them in the middle class.

To understand the power of class or socioeconomic status, think about the class status of your family of origin when you were living at home. Why was that status assigned? What did it mean in social terms? When did you first recognize that your social class status differed in significant ways from that of some other people? That background of experience with social class colors our values and beliefs throughout life. What do you think of today when a person is referred to as lower class? What are your thoughts about clients who are on welfare? What about disparities in health care? Do poor people and members of ethnic minority groups receive health care on par with higher-income White citizens?

> Conflict perspective

Gender

Along with race, gender has been and remains a controversial concept. Gender is what our culture symbolizes and means by maleness and femaleness. These terms are further defined through the prescribed roles of men and women, boys and girls, and husbands and wives. The physical characteristics of male and female bodies, combined with their sexual and reproductive functions, carry strong symbolic meanings. Physical differences between males and females are perceived by many as an indisputable basis for assigning different gender roles. That is, some believe that "anatomy is destiny." Cultural definition of gender in binary terms leads to widespread prejudice and discrimination against transgender and other gender-nonconforming individuals (Tebbe & Moradi, 2012). This is another example of culture in motion and of the ways in which people invest meaning into their lives and how such meanings are contested and change over time. Moreover, all of these meanings are ideological, but some become more dominant than others and influence the social and political policies of a given time period.

Natural differences translate into inequitable power and opportunity for men and women, as seen in social, economic, and political arenas. In other words, natural differences translate into differences in rank, power, and prestige. This plays out at home and at work; in churches, mosques, or synagogues; and in school and at play.

> Conflict perspective

No doubt, meanings surrounding gender involve historical processes. Gender meanings are also the product of dominant structures reinforced by traditions, customs, and our dominant notions of common sense. A thorough understanding of gender is hindered without consideration of these factors. However, gender meanings are currently in flux in our society.

At Community High, for example, aggressive behavior by boys toward girls has generated a provocative response from girls. Girls have regendered some of their social practices by adopting the aggressive language and posturing of boys as a defense against them (Cousins & Mabrey, 2007). Many of Tina's female peers have abandoned ascribed characteristics such as passivity, weakness, and inactivity (lack of agency), which are part of the traditional meanings assigned to female gender roles (Ortner, 1996). One consequence, in school and beyond, is that these girls have been defined as unladylike and "loud" (Fordham, 1993). By contrast, the aggressiveness and loudness of boys have been defined in school and beyond as "toughness" and "boys being boys"—being who they naturally are and doing what they naturally do as males. In the domain of sexual activity, strong traditions and entrenched frames of reference among school staff and some students still define the girls as the polluted or promiscuous participants in sexual liaisons. Sexual activity becomes a social problem for a boy only if the boy gets a venereal disease or the girl gets pregnant. Underlying these gender relations are traditions and customs that have shaped how girls' and boys' bodies and activities are defined. The process of girls redefining themselves in response to social and cultural forces, however,

is a good example of human agency, structure, and history in action.

Family

Family and kinship are key symbols in U.S. life. Family may be defined as a set of relationships among two or more people to carry out various social and biological functions, such as support, nurturance, sexual mating, procreation, and child rearing. Family is also an ideological construct on which we impose ideas about intimacy, love, morality, and kinship connections and obligations. Issues of contemporary versus traditional family values, structure, and change can serve as one last example of how culture works as a process, as well as how

Photo 8.3 Family life is structured by meanings, values, and beliefs that fit our desires and imaginations about what is right and appropriate.

© Comstock Images/Thinkstock

cultural change and adaptation proceed (Mason, Skolnick, & Sugarman, 2003).

We have been bombarded in recent years by scholarly and public dialogue about the demise of "family and cultural values" (Acs, Braswell, Sorensen, & Turner, 2013). Many believe this demise leads to the destruction of family life and thereby society (Gallagher, 1996; Popenoe, 1996; Whitehead, 1997). Recent debates about family life and its role in the maintenance of society at large have been fueled by both research and the opinions of influential politicians. On one side is the argument that increases in single parenting, divorce, and out-of-wedlock births are a reflection and a source of moral malaise. They reflect beliefs about misplaced or absent values and the social instability and demise of U.S. society. Families of the past have been presented as the model for families of the present and future. On the other side are arguments attempting to counter the "hysteria" about family values. John Gillis (1996), in particular, notes that neither family change nor anxiety about such change is new. In fact, "diversity, instability, and discontinuity have been part of the European experience of family at least since the late Middle Ages, and continued into the new world" (Skolnick, 1997, p. 87). In recent times, some societies, including the United States, have debated whether to expand the meaning of family to include families created by same-sex couples. The changing legal status of such families is a prime example of culture change in the making.

At the heart of these debates is a process addressed differently by different sides: If we value family coherence in the form of a stable household consisting of mother, father, and children, why do we have such a high divorce rate, an increase in single parenting, and an increase in nontraditional types of relationships? One side claims that recent trends reflect the absence of morals and virtue in our society; if we punish those who don't have morals and reward those who do, we can fix things. The other side argues

that a host of medical and economic changes—including birth control and women working outside the home—have fueled social and cultural changes. At particular issue is the disagreement between the two sides about how women fit into society and family life. In the debates about same-sex marriage, arguments have shifted over time. In the current dialogue, one side argues for equality in the right to marry and the other side argues that sacred texts prescribe that marriage is a relationship between a man and a woman. This process is related to what we stated earlier about gender, culture in motion, contested and changing meanings, and ideology in culture.

The process of family change and adaptation is complex. Much of it reflects the values we *want* our families to live by versus the values families actually *practice* (G. H. Albrecht, 2002; Erera, 2002; Stuening, 2002). Family life is structured by meanings, values, and beliefs that fit our desires and imaginations about what is right and appropriate. But family life is also constructed and lived in a world of competing and interacting meanings and material realities. People do not always do what they intend. They do construct and author their lives, so to speak, but they do so with a host of choices among very real constraints.

> Exchange and choice perspective

Social workers who want to understand and assist families have to understand the processes that create these realities. For instance, Stan and his parents intended for him to be successful in school and avoid criminal behavior. So far, however, Stan's life has not turned out that way. But his experience cannot be reduced solely to psychological, economic, or social factors outside the cultural contexts that shape his life: history, social structure, human agency, common sense, traditions, customs, and the like. All of us, and these processes, are in the embrace of constantly changing social, economic, and political realities of life in society.

Critical Thinking Questions 8.4

How important is gender in your life today (or how important was it yesterday)? What about race or ethnicity? How important has that been in your life in the past 2 days? And what about social class? How important has that been in your life in the past 2 days? What factors can make a difference in how important gender, race/ethnicity, and social class are in people's lives?

THE MEANING OF CULTURE

Social workers must not limit themselves to understanding culture only in the terms provided by other academic, scholarly, and professional traditions. We must position ourselves to understand what culture means and how it works in our own terms and in a multidimensional context. Such an understanding of culture challenges simplistic psychological analyses of individual and collective human practices that claim to adequately explain child abuse and neglect, poverty, academic failure, parent–child problems, substance abuse, school dropouts, and a host of other psychosocial and social policy issues. We want to know how our world and the worlds of our clients are constructed in all their complexity. Even though this knowledge will inevitably remain incomplete due to the motion of life and the complex world of nature impinging on us and we on it, we must try. Indeed, tools are available for just such an activity: a practice orientation and a multidimensional conceptualization of culture.

Ann Swidler's (1986) definition of culture summarizes what this chapter has tried to explain—culture as a process and as a system (Yanagisako, 2002). Culture is thus a tool kit of symbols, stories, rituals, and worldviews that people may use in varying configurations to solve different kinds of problems. Culture works by suggesting strategies of action or persistent ways of ordering or patterning action

through time, rather than only shaping ultimate ends or values toward which action is directed (Rosaldo, 1993; Swidler, 1986). Corresponding with Ortner's notion of human agents—our clients and ourselves included—as intense strategizers, Swidler's succinct description does not dismiss the challenges to maintain a coherent concept of culture that adequately explains the "mixing up" of ways people know themselves and others and the ways they develop and express meanings (Abu-Lughod, 1999; Ortner, 1999, 2006).

In the case of Community High students like Stan and Tina, who they have become and how they perform depend on a complex maze of social and psychological processes embedded in European American and African American cultures. The interaction of these processes contributes to Stan's and Tina's ethos and worldview. The extent to which these processes limit and restrain their overall academic and social success is an important issue. Neither Stan nor Tina can live outside the meaning of their blackness or their gender in the strained social world they inhabit. Their individual human agency is a factor, however, and it gives them flexibility to interpret or act on such meanings. Tina has managed to transcend culturally insensitive school processes without giving up her ethnic identity. Stan is still finding his way. Still, their interpretations of life events could serve either as motivation to succeed in terms they define or as a source of debilitating anxiety and despair. Their interpretations could also generate indignation and ethnic zealotry in the fight for equality in the mainstream United States. If they do, will Tina or Stan respond by becoming a race leader? Or will their interpretations result in a loss of self-worth and personal value, leading to a fatalistic dependence on drugs and alcohol to soften the reality of not being powerful and White? Members of immigrant groups face similar questions.

Clearly, U.S. culture and society have a role in this experience. Earlier, the concept of cultural hegemony was discussed, referring to the way dominant social, economic, and political processes subjugate those who do not comply or fit in. Cultural hegemony skews our search for problems and solutions. If a person has an interpersonal or psychologically oriented social problem, we tend to look to the individual for the cause and answer rather than also considering culture and society.

What will your interpretations be as a social worker encountering people who differ from the norm? Will you accept the fact that people experience strain and contradictions between the meanings in their heads and the social, economic, and political realities of everyday public life? Will you interpret social and economic problems as largely personal deficits? Will you misinterpret personal functioning due to a one-dimensional understanding of culture? Will your cultural understanding leave out issues of inequality in society and their role in the oppression of people of color; women; poor people; immigrants; older adults; people who are physically, mentally, or cognitively disabled; or gay and lesbian people?

In summarizing a contemporary paradox of family life, Arlene Skolnick (1997) offers us insight into a host of practice and policy issues for social work: "Americans have still not come to terms with the gap between the way we think our families ought to be and the complex, often messy realities of our lives" (p. 86). Insert *traditions*, *customs*, *values*, and so on for the word *families*, and we have a succinct formulation of the simplicity and complexity of culture as a lived process in postindustrial societies.

Critical Thinking Questions 8.5

Ann Swidler says that culture is a tool kit of symbols, stories, rituals, and worldviews people use to solve different kinds of problems. How does culture serve as a tool kit for Stan? What symbols, stories, rituals, and worldviews are in his tool kit? What problems is he trying to solve with this tool kit? How does culture serve as a tool kit for Tina? What symbols, stories, rituals, and worldviews are in her tool kit? What problems is she trying to solve with her tool kit? And how about you? How does culture serve as a tool kit for you? What symbols, stories, rituals, and worldviews are in your tool kit? What problems do you try to solve with your tool kit?

Implications for Social Work Practice

I learned how the practice orientation works when I was an ethnographer at Community High, conducting research largely to describe the students' culture from their points of view as well as mine as a researcher. As a social worker, you may be doing ethnographic inquiry without knowing it. Here are a few principles you can follow:

- Recognize the categories of knowledge—social science theories and perspectives; folk or common, everyday theories and perspectives—that you rely on to understand human behavior in the social environment.
- Embrace the traditions, customs, values, and behaviors of disparate groups identified by race, ethnicity, sexual orientation, gender, physical differences, age, nationality, and religion. Avoid approaching these groups in a cookbook, stereotyped, or one-size-fits-all fashion.
- Appreciate the tension between the force of social structure and the resiliency and intentionality of human agency in complex societies such as ours.
- Attempt to understand both personal and social acts of making meaning and realize how such acts give substance to and obscure our own lives as well as those of our clients.
- Examine culture through the lens of the practice orientation using a "strengths" and person-in-environment perspective that allows you to assess the simultaneous forces of history, social structure, and human agency and the political context in which all of these forces work themselves out in the lives of your clients.

- Use the practice orientation to frame the actions of those who resist being mainstream Americans. This perspective will help you see the creativity and hope, as well as the ugliness and pain, of their resistance.
- Pay attention to processes of cultural change, including assimilation, accommodation, acculturation, and bicultural socialization, in the lives of individuals and groups with whom you work.
- Work to ensure that members of nondominant groups have a significant say in how cultural change proceeds.

Key Terms

accommodation (cultural)	cultural relativism	othering
acculturation	culture	postmodernism
assimilation (cultural)	culture of poverty	practice orientation
bicultural socialization	customs	race
biological determinism	ethnic identity	racism
common sense	ethnocentrism	socioeconomic status (SES)
cultural conflict	ethos	symbol
cultural hegemony	ideology (cultural)	tradition
cultural innovation	norm	worldview

Active Learning

1. *The cultural construction of schooling.* Compare and contrast Stan's and Tina's experiences at Community High School with your own high school experience, considering the following themes:

   - Material and behavioral cultural symbols
   - Processes of cultural change (assimilation, accommodation, acculturation, bicultural socialization)
   - Ways in which race, ethnicity, social class, and gender play out in the school setting
   - Cultural conflict

   Next, imagine that you spend a day as a student at Community High, and Stan and Tina spend a day at your high school. How do you think you might react to the cultural symbols at Community High? How might Stan and Tina react to the cultural symbols at your high school? How do you account for these reactions?

2. *Cultural change* (adapted from an exercise in Bradshaw, Healey, & Smith, 2001). Either by telephone or face-to-face, interview an adult older than age 60 for the purpose of learning about cultural change over time.

   - Ask the respondent to reflect on his or her childhood. What favorite activities can the respondent recall from early childhood? What were the person's favorite toys? What types of clothing were worn? What values were stressed? How was family life structured? What kind of relationship did the respondent have with his or her parents? What type of discipline was used in the family? What was the nature of peer relationships?
   - Ask the respondent to think about the one most important technological change since he or she was a child (e.g., television, the Internet, medical technologies). Ask the respondent whether this innovation has been good or bad for children and for family life and to think about exactly how it has changed the lives of children and families.
   - Ask the respondent to think about the one most important change in customs and traditions of how people go about their everyday lives since he or she was a child (e.g., mothers working outside the home, smaller families). Again, ask the respondent whether this change has been good or bad for children and families and to talk about exactly how it has changed the lives of children and families.
   - Write a brief paper to summarize the thoughts of your respondent and your analysis of the responses, based on concepts from this chapter.

Critical Multicultural Pavilion: www.edchange .org/multicultural

Site maintained by Paul C. Gorski contains resources, research, awareness activities, and links to multicultural topics.

International Journal of Multicultural Education: ijme-journal.org/index.php/ijme

An open-access e-journal committed to promoting educational equity, cross-cultural understanding, and global awareness in all levels of education.

National Association for Ethnic Studies: ethnicstudies.org

Site provides an interdisciplinary forum for scholars and activists concerned about national and global dimensions of ethnicity and contains links to other relevant sites and publication lists.

Student Study Site

$SAGE edge™

Sharpen your skills with SAGE edge at **edge.sagepub.com/hutchisonpe5e**

SAGE edge for students provides a personalized approach to help you accomplish your coursework goals in an easy-to-use learning environment.

CHAPTER 9

Social Structure and Social Institutions

Global and National

Elizabeth D. Hutchison

Chapter Outline

Key Ideas

As you read this chapter, take note of these central ideas:

1. Social structure is a set of interrelated social institutions developed by human beings to support and constrain human interaction for the purpose of the survival and well-being of the society.

2. Social institutions are patterned ways of solving the problems and meeting the requirements of a particular society.

3. Social institutions are relatively stable but also changing. Most of the major global and U.S. social institutions have undergone extraordinary changes from 1970 to the present.

4. Since 1974, income inequality has grown substantially in the United States.

5. Eight key social institutions in societies around the world are the government and political institution, economic institution, educational institution, health care institution, social welfare institution, religious institution, mass media institution, and family and kinship institution. Each of these institutions plays a role in the creation and maintenance of social inequality.

6. Over time, societies have vacillated between a conservative thesis that inequality is the natural order and the radical antithesis that equality is the natural order to answer the question of whether social inequality is a good or bad thing.

CASE STUDY

Leticia Renteria's Struggle to Make It in the United States

Leticia Renteria is a 30-year-old woman who, along with her husband Marcos Vargas, is parent to three young children. She lives in the Coachella Valley of California, which is a dichotomous region hosting both extreme wealth and extreme poverty. Leticia, unfortunately, fits into the latter category. Born in the border town of Mexicali, Baja California, Mexico, Leticia grew up poor, in proximity to the United States and surrounded by American culture. As a youth, she enjoyed a renewable visitor visa, which allowed her to travel back and forth across the border to visit an aunt and several cousins (some of whom were born in the United States), who lived not far away in the Imperial and Coachella valleys of California. Leticia's experiences in the United States gave her even more understanding of the differences in opportunities between the United States and Mexico and made her yearn for those available in the United States, especially as she grew to working age. Work in Mexicali mostly consisted of very long hours at the extremely laborious maquiladoras (U.S. factories producing products for export in a free trade zone) or in various other low-paying informal occupations, such as selling *raspados* on street corners. Mexico's minimum wage remained at less than US$5.00 per day, and actual average wages for industries in which she was qualified to work with her high school–equivalent degree only rose slightly to US$8.00 to US$10.00 per day. With prices in the border region growing steadily to match U.S. prices in some areas, these wage rates simply became unfeasible for Leticia, and she soon made one of the most difficult decisions of her life: at age 19, she entered the United States legally on her visitor visa and decided to stay past her permissible time of visit—she thusly became an *undocumented immigrant*.

Leticia moved outside of the heavier border patrol enforcement zone, a zone within 60 miles of the border, to the nearby Coachella Valley, where she was able to stay with a relative for a low amount of rent. At age 20, she met Marcos. The two married within a year. Marcos is a *lawful permanent resident* of the United States, having *adjusted status* many years ago after immigrating without papers from Mexico. Marcos works year-round in a landscaping company that provides services to the lush golf courses and country clubs of the affluent part of the Coachella Valley; Leticia toils in seasonal positions in produce packing houses and landscaping crews, those positions beginning and ending based on seasonal need. In between her periods of employment, Leticia is without income altogether due to her inability to qualify for unemployment benefits because of her immigration status.

Despite their employment challenges, Leticia and Marcos were able to get together enough money to buy a used mobile home in a nearby settlement, where they pay rent for the space upon which their home sits. Leticia has mixed feelings about their home ownership—while she is excited to accomplish this version of the "American dream," she is frustrated and disappointed by the conditions of their mobile home park. The park is located in a rural area, several miles outside of the nearest city, and is not connected to water and wastewater services offered by the local municipal water district. The park's owner pipes water to the spaces from a well independently dug on the site, and the water coming from the well has recently been tested and reveals impermissibly high levels of arsenic contamination. The lack of wastewater services means that all of the homes are relying on septic systems, which unfortunately frequently fill or clog up, resulting in overflow, stench, and other problems. Moreover, not far down the street sits an illegal dump, which was created by the landowner "under the radar" without the knowledge of enforcement authorities and which now causes an unbearable stench and sometimes smoke in Leticia's settlement. To make matters worse, when Leticia is not working and Marcos has the family's only car at his work, she is stuck at home, given that the nearest public transportation stop is more than 5 miles away and the nearest grocery stores, services, and recreation are more than 10 miles away.

Over the years, Leticia and Marcos had three children together, who are now 4, 5, and 7 years old. Leticia does her best to find child care for the children with neighbors and acquaintances during the times she is able to work and continues working at night to complete the cooking, cleaning, and other tasks that Marcos and others expect her to do as a woman. All three of the children suffer from varying degrees of asthma, which Leticia believes is related to the dusty nature of their desert mobile home park, as well as the fumes and smoke that frequently come from the nearby dump. However, the community clinic where Leticia takes the children to be treated does not keep any data related to these kinds of causes and does not connect patients' health indicators to any environmental factors, so Leticia is left to rely on her own suspicions. The children receive medical care in the clinic, thanks to the state insurance program, since they are citizens of

(Continued)

the United States. Leticia cannot qualify for any such assistance, given that she remains undocumented. Leticia and Marcos hope that their children will succeed in school, but they are not really sure how the system works, and they are really intimidated by the English-speaking teachers and big buildings and campuses, so they have mostly thus far refrained from getting involved with their children's school. Leticia tries her best to access some of the few other resources in the area for her children to help them supplement their education and get their minds off other stressors. The children particularly enjoy spending time at the new Boys and Girls Club in the nearby town of Mecca when the family has the time and transportation to get there.

Despite her marriage to a *lawful permanent resident*, Leticia has not yet applied for legal immigration status because she and Marcos cannot afford the immigration and attorney fees, which would cost more than $4,000. Even with their hard work, Leticia and Marcos remain at the minimum wage rate of $8.00 per hour and are only bringing home a little more than $20,000 per year. This is far from enough to support their family of five and to cover the $50 to $100 per month they try to send to family back in Mexico. Leticia does not apply for food stamps or other cash assistance for her children (though they do qualify, since they are U.S. citizens) because she has heard that children who receive government benefits are the first ones sent to war when they turn 18 and that the children have to pay back all the benefits they received when they become adults. She just wishes that someday there will be an increase in the minimum wage, so that she and Marcos could make ends meet on their own. From everything Leticia hears on television, though, a lot of companies and politicians really don't want to see that happen. She figures that nothing ever happens unless powerful people want it to happen, so she thinks her minimum wage will never change.

Leticia finds her low wage rate doubly unjust because of all the things she has to tolerate in her workplace. As is common in landscaping and agricultural jobs, Leticia frequently encounters supervisors and co-workers who make unwelcome sexual comments to her and who sometimes even touch her in uncomfortable ways. Though these interactions would constitute illegal sexual harassment, Leticia, like most other women, never complains, for fear of losing her job, fear of immigration enforcement, and even fear of stigma among acquaintances as well as consequences in her own relationship with Marcos if he were to find out.

Early one morning, Leticia was detained by immigration authorities on her way to work, after having been originally stopped by a sheriff's deputy for a supposed violation related to a frame around her license plate. In immigration detention, she is offered the right to stay in detention and present her deportation defenses to a judge—which could take months—or the option to leave the country immediately through *voluntary departure*. Leticia has heard horror stories about deported mothers whose children get placed into the state foster care system and lose connection with their families. She tries to reach a local nun who helps in the community, to see if she can get any advice. However, even the nun isn't sure what to do or where to turn. So, even though Leticia knew that she could apply for status through her husband, she was scared to wait out the multimonth process and decided to leave voluntarily. She returned to the United States with her cousins by car with no papers only a few days later, simply telling the immigration officers at the border that she was a U.S. citizen just like her cousins. What Leticia wouldn't realize until much later, when she and Marcos finally went to apply for her status, is that her *voluntary departure* followed by her quick illegal return effectively disqualified her for any legal immigration status until she spends 10 years outside of the United States as a penalty.

—Megan Beaman

PATTERNS OF SOCIAL LIFE _____

As you read this story, you were probably aware of both the people and the environments involved. A number of people are involved in the story, and you may be observing how they are interacting with each other and what each contributes to the current situation. Although you do not want to lose sight of the personal dimensions of Leticia Renteria's story, in this chapter consider the broad patterns of social life that she and her family have encountered and continue to encounter. I want you to see the connections between the personal troubles of this family and broader social conditions.

A good way to begin to think about broad patterns of social life is to imagine that you and 100 other people have made a space journey to a new planet that has recently, thanks to technological breakthroughs, become inhabitable by humans. You are committed to beginning a new society on this new frontier. How will you work together to be successful in this endeavor? What will you need to do to ensure your survival? Now imagine that your society of 100 has grown to include more than 7 billion people, spread across six continents, with news and ideas being carried around the globe instantly through multiple media outlets, billions of dollars moving across continents with the click of a computer mouse, and products being manufactured and services being provided by a dispersed global labor force. How would you suggest that people work together to ensure the survival of this global society? One way to think about Leticia Renteria's story is to think of it as a globalization story. In Chapter 1, we defined globalization as a process by which the world's people are becoming more interconnected economically, politically, environmentally, and culturally.

Sociologists and anthropologists have given much thought to how people work together to try to ensure the survival of a society. They have identified two concepts—social structure and social institutions—as central to understanding those endeavors. Social structure

| Systems perspective |

and social institutions are among the more abstract concepts used by sociologists. In the broadest sense, social structure is another term for *society*, or simply an acknowledgment that social life is patterned, not random. It provides the framework within which individual behavior is played out in daily life. **Social structure** is a set of interrelated social institutions developed by human beings to support and constrain human interaction for the purpose of the survival and well-being of the collectivity. Certainly, we can see some supports as well as some constraints that various social institutions provide and impose on Leticia Renteria's family.

Our understanding of social institutions is complicated by the casual, everyday use of the term *institution* to cover a variety of meanings. In this book, however, we use the definition of **social institutions** as "patterned ways of solving the problems and meeting the requirements of a particular society" (Newman, 2012, p. 30). To provide stability, social institutions organize rights and duties into statuses and roles and the expected behaviors that accompany them. **Statuses** are specific social positions; **roles** are the usual behaviors of persons occupying particular statuses. Sociologists have identified a set of interrelated social institutions—such as family, religion, government, economy, and education—with each institution organizing social relations in a particular sector of social life. We see evidence of each of these institutions in the lives of Leticia Renteria and her family.

Sociological treatment of social structure and social institutions emphasizes the ways in which they persist and contribute to social stability. But often they persist despite unintended consequences and evidence that they are ineffective. In addition, although social institutions are relatively stable, they also change—whether by accident, by evolution, or by design (McMichael, 2012; Scott, 2014). Social institutions persist only when they are carried forward by actors and only when they are actively monitored.

W. Richard Scott (2014) suggests three types of processes that contribute to the stability of social institutions: regulatory processes, normative processes, and cultural-cognitive processes. Different types of processes are at work in different social institutions. *Regulatory processes* involve rules, monitoring, and enforcement through rewards and punishment. *Normative processes* involve values and norms about how things should be done. *Cultural-cognitive processes* involve beliefs about the world and how to behave in it.

Eight interrelated social institutions are discussed in this chapter: the government and political institution, economic institution, educational institution, health care institution, social welfare institution, religious institution, mass media institution, and family and kinship institution. We can see how important each of these institutions is in the current lives of Leticia Renteria and her family. Exhibit 9.1 presents these social institutions and the major functions they perform for society.

CONTEMPORARY TRENDS IN GLOBAL AND U.S. SOCIAL INSTITUTIONS _____

As suggested, social institutions are relatively stable, but they also change. They are created and modified over time as people interact in various social configurations. They have undergone great changes over time, yet they often seem so resistant to change. Usually the pace of institutional change is slow, but there are also times of transition when the pace of institutional change is quite rapid, for example, the period at the beginning of the industrial revolution. Contemporary futurists suggest that we have entered a time when the pace of technological change will continue to accelerate rapidly, and we might expect that continued rapid technological change will produce change, sometimes rapid

Exhibit 9.1 Key Social Institutions and the Functions They Perform

Social Institution	Functions Performed
Government and political institution	Making and enforcing societal rules Resolving internal and external conflicts Mobilizing collective resources to meet societal goals
Economic institution	Regulating production, distribution, and consumption of goods and services
Educational institution	Passing along formal knowledge from one generation to the next Socializing individuals
Health care institution	Promoting the general health
Social welfare institution	Allocating goods, services, and opportunities Enhancing social functioning of individuals Contributing to the social health of the society
Religious institution	Answering questions about the meaning and purpose of life Socializing individuals Maintaining social control Providing mutual support
Mass media institution	Managing the flow of information, images, and ideas
Family and kinship institution	Regulating procreation Conducting initial socialization Providing economic, emotional, and physical care of its members

change, in most if not all major social institutions (Kurzweil, 2012). As the contributing authors and I have worked on this, the fifth edition of this book, we have often been amazed at how quickly knowledge of human behavior becomes outdated in the contemporary era.

Writing about global social structure and social institutions at the beginning of the 21st century, Anthony Giddens (2000), a British social scientist, suggested that the recent pace and scope of change has produced a "runaway world." Some social scientists suggest that the pace and scope of change in the past few decades has produced several crises for global as well as U.S. social institutions, for example, a food crisis, energy crisis, climate crisis, and social inequality crisis. They propose that these combined crises are leading to a quest for new ways of organizing the global social structure and that we may now be at a turning point transitioning to yet unclear new ways of organizing social life (see McMichael, 2012). I cannot predict future trends in social structure and social institutions, but I believe it is important for social workers to think about their work in the context of contemporary trends and to imagine the possibilities for how they might help to shape future trends in such a way that they bend toward social justice.

It is increasingly difficult to understand the changes in our own society without recognizing the global context of those changes. Globalization is affecting all aspects of social life around the world. Indeed, the process of globalization has been stimulating changes in the major social institutions for several decades, but in a pronounced way for the past few decades. The discussion that follows positions trends in U.S. social institutions within a global context. Doing so illuminates how U.S. society is both different from and the same as other societies, and it aids critical thinking about the question of why we do things the way we do.

Perhaps the most important and troubling trend in contemporary life is the continued extremely high level of social inequality, both between nations and within nation-states. Although globalization has brought

Conflict perspective

some improvements in literacy, health, and living standards for many, we pay particular attention to trends in social inequality because the profession of social work has historically made a commitment to persons and groups that are disadvantaged in the distribution of resources by social institutions. To carry out this commitment, we must have a way of understanding social inequality and its influence on human behavior. Throughout this chapter, I demonstrate how social inequality is created and maintained in eight major interrelated social institutions. But first we take a closer look at inequality globally and in the United States.

There are many debates about whether globalization is leading to increased or decreased global inequality, and the answer depends on how the question is asked. McMichael (2012) argues that although a global middle class has emerged in some previously low-income countries such as Brazil, Russia, India, China, and South Africa, global inequality is deepening if China, which has both the largest population in the world and growing wealth, is removed from the calculations. He reports that 80% of the world's population lives in countries where income differentials are widening. On the other hand, the United Nations Development Programme (UNDP; 2013) reports that, in recent years, a large number of developing countries have been transformed into dynamic major economies. It notes, however, that economic growth does not automatically translate into reduced inequality. Its most recent report (UNDP, 2013) indicates that in the recent great economic growth for some developing countries, most regions of the world had declining inequality in health and education but rising income inequality. Although different data sources report different numbers, there is agreement that we are talking about comparatively huge disparities in the contemporary world. For example, the richest 1% of the world's people receives more income than the poorest half of the world's people (Sernau, 2014).

It is clear that not all regions of the world have shared equally in the benefits of globalization and that high levels of inequality exist in regions of the world experiencing recent economic growth.

During a time of massive income growth worldwide, average incomes fell in most of Sub-Saharan Africa, and much of that region is now further behind the rest of the world than in 1990 (Sernau, 2014). Twenty years ago, 93% of poor people lived in low-income countries; now 75% of the world's poorest people live in middle-income countries (McMichael, 2012). So, while available data show a slight average decline in global inequality, they also indicate that income inequality is growing between the poorest 10% and the richest 10% of the world's people.

Although most of the global inequality is due to inequality *between* countries, as you see from this discussion, the gap within nations is also staggering. Let's look at income inequality in the United States. In the period from 1947 to 1973, income inequality in the United States declined slightly. Since 1974, however, income inequality has grown substantially. The most commonly used measure of income inequality is the **Gini index**, which measures the extent to which the distribution of income within a country deviates from a perfectly equal distribution. Gini index scores

range from 0 (perfect equality) to 100 (perfect inequality). As Exhibit 9.2 shows, the Gini index in the United States grew from 39.4 in 1970 to 47.7 in 2012. Emmanuel Saez (2012) reports that the incomes of the top 1% of earners in the United States captured more than half of the overall economic growth in the country in the period from 1993 to 2010. Looking at wealth instead of income, Ritzer (2013a) reports that 80% of the wealth gained in the United States from 1983 to 2009 went to the wealthiest 5% of the population, while the poorest 60% saw a 7.5% decline in wealth.

The United States has the highest level of inequality of all the wealthy industrialized nations (Sernau, 2014). Exhibit 9.3 shows the income inequality ranking of 19 advanced industrialized countries from 2000 to 2010, based on the Gini index, moving from the country with the least inequality at the bottom (Sweden, Gini index of 23.0) to the country with the greatest inequality at the top (United States, Gini index of 45.0). The 19 countries presented in Exhibit 9.3 are used throughout this chapter to make comparisons between the United States and other wealthy

Exhibit 9.2   Gini Index of Inequality in the United States, 1970–2012

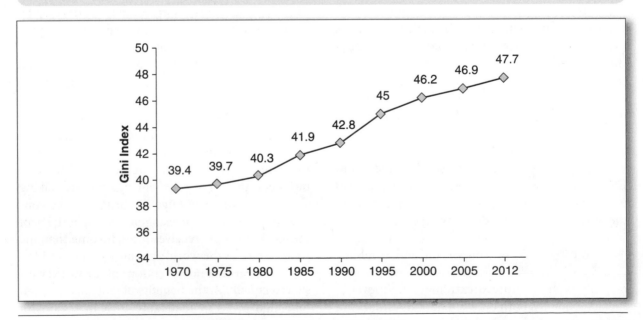

SOURCE: DeNavas-Walt, Proctor, & Hill Lee, 2006; DeNavas-Walt, Proctor, & Smith, 2013.

Most Inequality	
⬆	United States (45.0)
	United Kingdom (40.0)
	Israel (39.2)
	Japan (37.6)
	Ireland (33.9)
	France (32.7)
	Canada (32.1)
	Spain (32.0)
	Italy (31.9)
	Netherlands (30.9)
	Australia (30.3)
	Switzerland (29.6)
	Belgium (28.0)
	Germany (27.0)
	Finland (26.8)
	Austria (26.3)
	Norway (25.0)
⬇	Denmark (24.8)
	Sweden (23.0)
Least Inequality	

SOURCE: Based on Central Intelligence Agency, 2013a.

countries. I call these countries the comparison countries. Of course, the United States does not have more inequality than all countries in the world. In a general sense, highly industrialized, high-income countries have much lower levels of inequality than nonindustrial or newly industrializing countries. The rate of inequality is much lower in the United States than in many low- to middle-income countries. Overall, the highest rates of inequality can be found in some African and Latin American countries, but the rate of inequality is not consistent within these regions.

Leticia Renteria came to the United States to escape brutal poverty in Mexico. In recent years, Mexico has developed trade agreements with a number of other countries and has moved from being the world's 26th largest economy to being the 8th largest. Most of Mexico's recent industrial growth has been in the maquiladoras, and real wages in Mexico have declined by about 20% in this period of growth. A large percentage of workers, about 40% of Mexico's workforce, are poorly paid and have few employment options (Sernau, 2014). Half of Mexican families live in poverty, a rate that has not changed since the early 1980s. Half of the country's rural population earns less than $1.40 per day (McMichael, 2012). Although Leticia Renteria and Marcos Vargas are struggling for economic survival in the United States, they do not wish to return to Mexico.

Some social analysts argue that social inequality is the price of economic growth and suggest that the poorest families in the United States enjoy a much higher standard of living than poor families in other countries (Hederman & Rector, 1999). But a comparison of the United States with other advanced industrialized countries suggests that societal health is best maintained when economic growth is balanced with attention to social equality. A growing international research literature suggests that high levels of inequality are bad for the social health of a nation. Let's look at three social indicators for the 19 industrialized countries in Exhibit 9.3: childhood mortality (probability of dying before age 5), life expectancy, and secondary school enrollment. In 1960, the United States had a lower childhood mortality rate than 10 of the comparison countries listed in Exhibit 9.3. In 2012, the United States had the highest childhood mortality rate of the 19 countries (World Bank, 2013b). Likewise, all of the comparison countries have longer life expectancies than the United States (Central Intelligence Agency, 2013b). The United States does better in terms of educational equality; looking at the 25- to 34-year-old age group, the United States has higher secondary education completion rates than 12 of the comparison countries (Organisation for Economic Co-operation and Development [OECD], 2013a). These data suggest that education does not reduce economic inequality as much as sometimes suggested.

There is growing support for the idea that economic inequality is associated with a number of social ills, including low social cohesion, distrust, violence, poor health, and economic stagnation (see Fairbrother & Martin, 2013; Karlsson, Nilsson, Lyttkens, & Leeson, 2010; Stiglitz, 2012; Van de Werfhorst & Salverda, 2012). The evidence of a correlation between economic inequality and a variety of social ills is strong, but because most of the research is cross-sectional we must be cautious about concluding that economic inequality is the cause of the other social ills. Researchers are currently taking a hard look at that issue (see van de Werfhorst & Salverda, 2012).

Poverty is one measure of social inequality, but there are different approaches to measuring poverty across the world. It is estimated that in 2013 1.4 billion, or about 20%, of the world's population lived in extreme poverty on less than US$1.25 a day (Global Poverty Project, 2013). Women and children are overrepresented in the world's poor. People living in extreme poverty go to bed hungry every night, and children living in these circumstances are vulnerable to death caused by malnutrition. It is estimated that one third of all deaths in the world each year are due to poverty-related causes (Ballantine & Roberts, 2014).

Poverty rates in the United States demonstrate that social inequality is related to race and ethnicity, age, gender, family structure, and disability (DeNavas-Walt et al., 2013). The overall poverty rate in 2012 was 15.0%, up from 12.5% in 2007. Although the majority of people living below the poverty level are White, and people of color can be found in all income groups, Blacks and Hispanics are more than 2.5 times as likely as Whites to be poor. The poverty rate in 2012 was 27.2% for Blacks, 25.6% for Hispanics, 11.7% for Asians, and 9.7% for non-Hispanic Whites. The good news is that the differential between Whites and groups of color has decreased in recent years. The bad news is that the differential remains quite large. For example, in the 1940s, the median income of Black families was about 50% of that of White families; by 2005, the median income of Black families was 61% of that of non-Hispanic White families (Bradshaw, Healey,

& Smith, 2001; DeNavas-Walt et al., 2006). Unfortunately, Black families did not recover as well as White families from the 2007 recession, and in 2012, the median income of Black families was 58% of non-Hispanic White families (DeNavas-Walt et al., 2013). Foreign-born *noncitizens* have a higher poverty rate (24.9%) than foreign-born *naturalized citizens* (12.4%) (DeNavas-Walt et al., 2013). You can see from Leticia Renteria's story how lack of citizenship makes people particularly vulnerable in the labor market.

Over the past 50 years, vulnerability to poverty has shifted from older adults to children. From 1959 to 2012, the percentage of the U.S. population 65 years and older living in poverty decreased from about 35% to about 9.1% (DeNavas-Walt et al., 2006, 2013). The proportion of the population younger than age 18 living in poverty showed a smaller decrease in this same period, from about 27.0% to 21.8%. Since 1974, the poverty rate for persons younger than 18 has been higher than for those 65 and older.

Women are more likely than men to be poor in the United States as well as globally. In the United States, women's poverty rate (16.3%) is higher than men's (13.6%), and this difference continues to grow across the life course, rising to 11.0% of women 65 and older compared with 6.6% of men of the same age (DeNavas-Walt et al., 2013). Single-parent, mother-only families are more likely to live in poverty (30.9%) than two-parent families (6.3%) or single-parent father-only families (16.4%) (DeNavas-Walt et al., 2013).

The poverty rate for adults with a disability is more than twice the poverty rate for adults without a disability. In 2012, the poverty rate for people aged 18 to 64 with a disability was 28.4%, compared with 12.5% for adults of the same age without a disability (DeNavas-Walt et al., 2013).

We turn now to analysis of trends in eight major social institutions, both globally and in the United States. We look for the good news in these trends, but we also pay close attention to how social inequality and social conflict are created or maintained in each institution.

Trends in the Government and Political Institution

Systems perspective; conflict perspective

Leticia Renteria lives in fear of agents of the government, particularly immigration agents. For the most part, she sees the government as a coercive force rather than a supportive one in her life. She believes that only powerful people can influence government actions. The **government and political institution** is responsible for how decisions get made and enforced for the society as a whole. It is expected to resolve both internal and external conflicts and mobilize collective resources to meet societal goals.

Political systems around the world vary widely, from authoritarian to democratic. Authoritarian systems may have a hereditary monarchy or a dictator who seized power; sometimes democratically elected leaders become dictators. Leaders in democratic systems are elected by their citizens and are accountable to them; they must govern in the context of written documents (Ballantine & Roberts, 2014). Evidence suggests that the government institution is in transition globally, including in the United States. There is much complexity in global trends in government and politics, but the following historical factors are supremely important for beginning to understand current complexities.

1. *Colonialism.* The contemporary global political landscape must be understood in the historical context of **colonialism** (Kurtz, 2012; McMichael, 2012). Eight European countries (Belgium, Britain, France, Germany, Italy, the Netherlands, Portugal, and Spain) and Japan were involved over several centuries in setting up colonial empires, which allowed them to strengthen their own economies by exploiting the raw materials and labors of the colonized countries. Colonial governments took power away from local governance and prevented the localities from establishing stable political systems. Most of these empires came to a rather abrupt end after World War II, but they left a disorganized political legacy in their wake in much of Africa, Central and South America, and parts of Asia and the Middle East. After the colonized countries established their independence, the United States and other Western powers advanced a new institutional framework that called for free trade and transformation of the formerly colonized countries into democracies. This new institutional framework, sometimes referred to as **neocolonialism**, is promoted by such international organizations as the World Bank, the International Monetary Fund (IMF), and the World Trade Organization (WTO). These organizations, which are led by the United States and western Europe, regulate relations between countries, and this role carries much power over political and economic institutions (Loomis, 2013). The United States and western Europe also played a major role in coercing former colonies to organize into nation-states and imposed national boundaries that were inconsistent with age-old ethnic divisions. This has resulted in ongoing ethnic clashes throughout the former colonies (McMichael, 2012).

2. *International power struggles.* Across time, groups have tried to assert their will over other groups, and the struggle for power over people, ideas, and natural resources is very much a part of the contemporary geopolitical scene. Sometimes nations or transnational organizations use the hard power of military force. Other times, they use the soft power of persuasion and

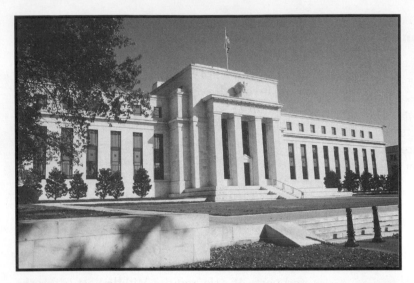

Photos 9.1a & 9.1b State, local, and federal governments are social institutions responsible for making and enforcing societal rules. Here we see the U.S. Federal Reserve building and the capitol in Sacramento, California.

© Tom Brakefield/Stockbyte/Thinkstock; © iStockphoto.com/Gene Chutka

interests around the world in a struggle known as the Cold War. The collapse of the Soviet Union in 1989 produced political instability in the former Soviet Union, and that country is no longer considered a superpower. In the meantime, after World War II, the nations of Europe began a process of unification, a process that has not always been smooth but has produced the European Union (EU). China and India are now emerging as major powers in the world. During the Cold War, the United States made extensive use of the soft power of foreign aid to encourage loyalty to its political (democracy) and economic (free market capitalism) visions. In the contemporary era, powerful countries are using foreign aid to ensure access to scarce natural resources. For example, in 2006, China made a $1.4 billion deal to develop new oil fields in Angola, which became the biggest supplier of oil to China. In this deal, China agreed to rebuild Angola's railway and bridges, roads, irrigation systems, hospitals, and schools (Brautigam, 2009). Overall, there has been a downward trajectory of international aid, and the United States lags behind most European countries with respect to the amount of its gross national product (GNP) that goes to non-military international aid, far behind the northern European countries (Karger & Stoesz, 2014).

inducement. Two bloody world wars in the 20th century left Europe weakened and wary of war as a viable solution to conflicts between nations. With the European states weakened after World War II, the United States and the Soviet Union emerged as competing superpowers. These two superpowers became competing spheres of influence, each trying to promote its political and economic

3. *Economic globalization.* Changes in the government institution are intertwined with changes in the economic institution, and these changes taken together are playing a large role in global inequality. Beginning in the 1970s, economic globalization started to present serious challenges

to nationally based democracies (Newman, 2012). For a number of centuries, political and economic life had been organized into nation-states with bureaucracies for maintaining order and mobilizing resources to meet societal needs. Starting in the 1970s, however, new information and transportation technologies made possible the development of **transnational corporations (TNCs)**, which carry on production and distribution activities in many nations. These corporations cross national lines to take advantage of cheap labor pools, lax environmental regulations, beneficial tax laws, and new consumer markets. It is hard for any nation-state to monitor or get control over TNCs, and no international government exists (Sernau, 2014). Under these circumstances, around 1970, governments began to retrench in their efforts to monitor and control the economic institution. A **neoliberal philosophy** that governments should keep their hands off the economic institution took hold, perhaps nowhere more than in the United States.

4. *Transnational centers of power.* Although no international government exists, the United States played a leadership role in the development of several transnational political and economic organizations and policies at the end of World War II. The United Nations (UN) was developed to ensure international peace and security. The World Bank was developed to promote reconstruction in war-torn nations but has, in recent years, taken on a concern for poverty. The World Bank president is appointed by the U.S. president. The International Monetary Fund (IMF) was developed to promote international monetary cooperation and a fair balance of trade. The managing director of the IMF is appointed by the United Kingdom, France, and Germany. The General Agreement on Tariffs and Trade (GATT) was designed to provide an international forum for developing freer trade across national boundaries; the World Trade Organization (WTO) was developed under GATT in 1995 to regulate the global economy according to principles of free trade. More recently, the United States, Canada, and Mexico signed the North American Free

Trade Agreement (NAFTA) in 1994. European nations joined together as the EU, adopting a common currency, a set of common legal and economic structures, and other joint endeavors. Similar organizations are in various stages of development in Latin America, Asia, and Africa. The World Bank, IMF, and WTO, all governed by unelected officials, have become very powerful in dictating how nation-states should govern. For example, when making loans, the World Bank requires that borrowing nations follow the principles of neoliberalism, including reducing their social welfare programs, privatizing their public services, and becoming more open to imports. The IMF has enforced these principles, sometimes overriding decisions made at the national level. The deliberations of the WTO are secret; members can lodge complaints, but the decision of the WTO's dispute settlement program is binding unless every member of the WTO votes to reverse it. There is much evidence that the decisions of the World Bank, IMF, and WTO have been more favorable to some nations than others (McMichael, 2012).

Countries around the world have attempted to adapt to the challenges of economic globalization by changing the way that government does business. In a period of rising doubt about the ability of nation-states to govern, many of them, including the United States, have been passing policy responsibilities down to state governments. As pressures increase on states, some devolve responsibilities to local governments. On the other hand, some states in the United States have tackled tough issues like same-sex marriage, immigration, health, and environmental policy that are not being addressed by federal policy. Growing faith across the world in the wisdom and efficiency of the economic institution led many nation-states to withdraw from direct control of activities they had hitherto controlled. They do this in several ways. The government sells enterprises that produce goods or deliver services to the private sector. This can be done at any level of government. From 1986 to 1992, monetary policies of the World Bank and IMF required former colonial countries to engage in massive privatization in exchange for rescheduling their debts (McMichael, 2012). Another approach is for the government to retain ultimate control over a program but contract with private organizations for some activities. The United States makes heavy use of contracting in many governmental sectors. And, finally, governments sometimes give up their claims to the right to regulate particular activities they have previously regulated but not controlled. It is widely noted that deregulation of financial institutions over several decades in the United States and Europe was a primary factor in the 2008 financial crisis (Jeffers, 2013).

The future of the neoliberal philosophy is not clear. For a number of decades, it served wealthy nations and wealthy individuals well. However, the 2008 global economic crisis called its principles into question and began to chip away at its primary premise that the market has its own wisdom and should not be interfered with. The wisdom of deregulation is getting another review. For some time now, poor nations and social justice advocates have engaged in growing resistance to the neoliberal philosophy and its implementation by the World Bank, IMF, and WTO. There has been much concern about the unfair advantage given to wealthy nations and the exploitation of labor and natural resources in poor nations. However, there is also much resolve by rich and powerful individuals and societies to hold on to neoliberal principles.

Economic globalization combined with war and political strife has produced mass cross-national migration. Most of this migration has occurred within regions; for example, most refugees fleeing Syria have gone to neighboring countries Turkey, Lebanon, Jordan, and Iraq (Migration Policy Centre, 2013). But there is also a trend of migration from low-wage to high-wage countries (Newman, 2012). This has led to considerable political attention to immigration issues around the globe. In the United States and Europe, immigration issues are the source of intense political debate.

As we think about the trials of Leticia Renteria and her family, we are reminded of

Exchange and choice perspective

this increased attention to immigration issues. Some observers (Teeple, 2000) have suggested that nation-states compensate for their inability to control the business processes that cross their borders by heightening their attempts to control the human movement across their borders. By controlling borders, a nation-state can get some control of the flow of labor across national boundaries.

In the United States, three issues are creating concern in the government and political institution: a sharply divided electorate, the role of money in the political process, and voter turnout. Concerning a sharply divided electorate, recent elections and attempts at legislation have been more acrimonious than at any time in recent history. There are sharp divisions about the kind of country the United States should be: regional divisions, rural/urban divisions, divisions between young and old voters, divisions between male and female voters, divisions between religious and nonreligious voters, and divisions between White and minority voters. Concerning money in the political process, *political action committees* (PACs) are private groups organized to campaign for or against candidates, ballot initiatives, or legislation. Federal legislation limits how much individuals can contribute to PACs and the role corporations and unions can play in PAC funding. However, a Supreme Court decision and subsequent federal court of appeal ruling in 2010 resulted in wealthy individuals, corporations, and unions having the right to make unlimited political expenditures as long as the contributions are independent of specific candidates or political parties. After this ruling, a new phenomenon called the *super PAC* emerged to solicit huge sums of money to be used for political spending that is, in theory, independent of specific candidates and their organizations (Ritzer, 2013a). Much money flowed into super PACs from billionaires in the 2012 presidential campaign. Comedian Stephen Colbert, with some help from comedian Jon Stewart, did much to increase public awareness of the potential

Exhibit 9.4 Average Voter Turnout (Vote to Voting-Age Population Ratio), 1945–2011, in Advanced Industrial Democracies

Italy	89.4%
Belgium	85.3%
Australia	83.9%
Denmark	83.6%
Sweden	82.6%
Austria	82.4%
Netherlands	81.7%
Norway	78.7%
Israel	78.2%
Germany	77.7%
Finland	76.7%
Spain	74.6%
Ireland	73.6%
United Kingdom	72.2%
Japan	68.9%
Canada	65.4%
France	63.7%
United States	47.5%
Switzerland	46.6%

SOURCE: International Institute for Democracy and Electoral Assistance, 2011.

impact of super PACs on the election process. The United States is next to the bottom of comparison countries in terms of voter participation. Exhibit 9.4 shows average voter turnout (the percentage of the voting-age population who voted) for the period 1945 to 2011. Most comparison countries have seen a decline in voter turnout in recent years. In the United States, there is much controversy about recently passed state voter ID laws, which conservatives say are needed to prevent voter fraud and liberals say are intended to suppress the vote of minorities of color.

What happens in the government and political institution has enormous impact on the life chances of every group in society. For example,

two important political issues play a large role in the level of inequality in a society: tax policy and minimum wage policy. European governments tax their wealthier citizens at a much higher rate than the United States and set higher minimum wages. These actions of the government impact what social workers can and cannot do to promote individual and collective well-being. Social workers cannot afford to ignore processes and trends in the political arena. In the United States, social workers must be attuned to the important role money plays in providing access to government and politics, to continuing underrepresentation of women and people of color among elected officials, and to existing and proposed barriers to access to the electoral process. They must also be aware of the possibilities of what can be accomplished by collective action.

Trends in the Economic Institution

As you read the story of Leticia Renteria and her family, their economic struggles seem paramount, and yet, both Leticia and Marcus are employed and working hard to provide for their family. The **economic institution** has primary responsibility for regulating the production, distribution, and consumption of goods and services. In a capitalistic market economy, such as the one in the United States and many parts of the world, what one is able to consume is dependent on how much one is paid for selling goods and services in the economic marketplace. Most people, if they are not independently wealthy, exchange labor for wages, which they then use for consumption. The nature of the economy has been ever changing since premodern times, but the rate of change has accelerated wildly since the beginning of the industrial revolution, particularly in recent decades under neoliberalism and economic globalization.

Economic life can be organized in many ways, and a great variety of ways have been used over time. In recent times, different approaches to organizing the economic institution around the world fall on a continuum with market capitalism at one end and a centralized or planned economy at the other end. In market capitalism, the economy operates by voluntary exchange in a free market and is not planned or controlled by a central authority. The goods and services produced by human labor are exchanged in the market and not produced for consumption by the laborer. The means of production are privately owned by one group, and another group, the workers hired through a labor market, own little besides their capacity to work. No governmental interference is thought to be needed because "the invisible hand of the market" will ensure fair production and distribution, including fair profit for some and not for others. Investment is privately controlled. In a centralized or planned economy, the government plans and controls production and distribution of goods and services. The means of production are collectively rather than privately owned, and the terms of labor are regulated by the government rather than by the market. In such economies, there is deep distrust of the exploitation of labor thought to occur in a market run by a financial elite in pursuit of their own self-interests (Ballantine & Roberts, 2014; Ritzer, 2013a).

In reality, no country in the world today practices either pure market capitalism or a pure planned (centralized) economy. The U.S. economy is thought to be a special case of capitalism in the world today, coming the closest to pure market capitalism. And, yet, there are a number of ways in which national and state governments in the United States interfere with market-based production and distribution of goods and services, including labor regulations, public education, public libraries, social security legislation, Medicare, and Medicaid. A number of countries have mixed economies where the good of the whole society is considered paramount, and private profit is less important than in pure capitalism. In these countries, collective planning is engaged in an attempt to balance societal needs with individual economic freedom. The Scandinavian and most European countries are the best examples of mixed economies. The former Soviet Union was once considered to be the best example of a planned economy, but since its fall in 1991, the region no longer holds that distinction. China is often thought to be the current best example of a pure planned economy today but, in fact, is becoming a dominant capitalist force while holding on to its highly centralized government (McMichael, 2012). There is much agreement that economic globalization is pushing all countries toward some embrace of market capitalism.

Before further discussion, some clarity is needed about what we mean by *economic globalization*. The primary ingredients are a global production system, a global labor force, and global consumers organized through a global market. Much of what we wear, eat, and use has global origins. If you look around your room, you will see many examples of economic globalization, but much of the global process will be invisible to you. A few examples, taken from the work of Philip McMichael (2012), demonstrate some of the complexity of current globalization. First, let's look at the U.S.-based athletic shoe industry. The design and marketing of the shoes are typically done at headquarters in the United States by workers earning relatively high wages. The materials are produced, dyed, cut, stitched, and assembled and then packed and transported in work sites in South Korea, Taiwan, China, Indonesia, and the Philippines, primarily by women earning low wages. The shoes are sold globally but disproportionately to consumers in wealthy advanced industrialized countries.

A second example involves the food we eat. In wealthy countries, we have become accustomed to having our favorite fruits and vegetables available year-round. We can have this because of the global food market. During the winter months, if we live in the United States, we can get grapes, apples, pears, apricots, cherries, peaches, and avocados from Chile and tomatoes, broccoli, bell peppers, cucumbers, and cantaloupe from Mexico. If we live in Japan, we might get pineapples and asparagus from Thailand; and if we live in Europe, we can buy strawberries, mangoes, and chilies grown in Kenya as well as organic fruits and vegetables from China. What do you know about the labor conditions under which the food on your table was produced? As Philip McMichael (2012) suggests, it is now "virtually impossible for consumers to recognize the impact of their consumption on people and environments elsewhere" (p. 20).

The global economy is driven by corporate desire for the bigger profits that come from cheap raw materials and cheap labor and by consumer desire for cheap and novel products. Corporations are constantly seeking cheaper labor sites to stay competitive. Much of the global economy is controlled by TNCs. TNCs have become very powerful over the past several decades; in fact, UN data indicate that TNCs account for two thirds of world trade and hold most product patents (cited in McMichael, 2012). Most TNCs are headquartered in France, Germany, Japan, the United Kingdom, or the United States.

Conflict perspective

Proponents of economic globalization argue that in time it will bring modernity and prosperity to all regions of the world. Critics argue that it is just an unsustainable pyramid scheme that must end because prosperity of victors is always paid for by the losses of latecomers or because the physical environment can no longer sustain the economic activities (Sernau, 2014). This is a good place to point out that not all peoples of the world put a high value on consumerism and chasing economic growth, values that are central to globalization. Unfortunately, however, policies of the World Bank, IMF, and WTO have made it impossible to make a living on subsistence farms and small craft enterprises. Some globalization scholars argue that economic globalization as we have known it is not sustainable because of the social disruption and environmental degradation it has wrought and that we may be seeing the beginning of a transition to a different form of capitalism that puts greater emphasis on sustainability (see McMichael, 2012). The future of globalization is not certain, but several trends can be identified at its current stage of development.

1. *Regional disparities.* Rich nations have been getting richer, a few nations have made impressive gains, most poor nations have made few gains, and the poorest nations have lost ground.

Consumers in high-income countries benefit from the cheap labor of workers in newly industrializing countries. Current regional disparities must be put into historical context. Globalization gained speed just as European colonialism collapsed, at the end of World War II. Formerly colonized countries began the global era in a compromised position created by colonial exploitation. The newly created World Bank made large loans to the former colonies to improve their infrastructures, and much of the money was used to import technology from wealthy industrialized countries. In the 1980s, a combination of factors, including recession in the United States and other wealthy Western nations, produced a debt crisis in many previously colonized countries. They began taking out new loans to pay for previous loans. The World Bank and IMF imposed austerity measures, which resulted in social service cuts, as a condition for restructuring the loans. Some countries have not been able to recover from the debt crisis, especially those facing a massive AIDS crisis. More recently, low-income countries have been severely affected by the 2008 global economic crisis, which originated in the financial systems of the wealthy countries of the world. Poor countries entered the recession in already weak fiscal positions, and there have been several negative impacts of the recession on their fragile economies: a decline of foreign aid, restricted access to credit, lost trade, and loss of remittances from family members who have migrated to wealthy countries (UNESCO, 2012). Sub-Saharan Africa has been the global region most vulnerable to these economic losses, but low-income countries in eastern Europe, Asia and the Pacific, and Latin America have also been at risk.

2. *Labor force bifurcation.* As globalization progressed, wage labor began to **bifurcate**, or divide into two branches. One branch is the *core* of relatively stable, skilled, well-paid labor. The other branch is the *periphery* of periodic or seasonal (often referred to as casual) low-wage labor. In the new global division of labor, the upper tier of jobs is found disproportionately in the wealthy advanced industrialized countries, and the lower tier of jobs

Photo 9.2 Walmart is a growing symbol of economic globalization.

© Teh Eng Koon/AFP/Getty Images

is found disproportionately in the previously colonized countries. Recently, bifurcation of labor has occurred all over the world, in advanced industrial societies as well as in poor, newly industrializing societies (McMichael, 2012). Work in the *core* is usually full time and comes with nonwage compensation such as sick leave, health insurance, and retirement benefits. Work in the *periphery* is usually part time and/or temporary, with many working

on a contract basis, and it provides few if any nonwage benefits. Use of such casual, irregular low-wage labor provides employers with a lot of flexibility as they try to stay competitive. Workers in the *periphery* often work very long hours in crowded and unsafe workplaces, and, if they are women like Leticia Renteria, they may cope with sexual harassment on the job. Women have been reported to compose 70% to 90% of the temporary workers in advanced industrial societies, but, recently, many jobs historically performed by middle-class men are being filled by contract workers who do not receive the nonwage benefits once associated with these jobs (McMichael, 2012). In the United States, the period of labor force bifurcation has been accompanied by a precipitous increase in CEO salaries and stagnation in wages of other workers. From 1978 to 2011, CEO compensation grew by more than 876% while the annual compensation of a typical private-sector worker grew by 5.4% (Mishel, 2013). This is an important contributor to growing inequality in the United States.

3. *Outsourcing.* **Outsourcing** relocates the production of goods and services from one place to another as a strategy to reduce costs. Today, when we think of globalization, we tend to think first of outsourcing, like the outsourcing of the production of athletic shoes noted earlier. Industrial products are manufactured and assembled in export zones of poor countries with low wages and few or nonexistent labor and environmental protections and then shipped to wealthier consumers around the world (Sernau, 2014). Information and communication technologies allow corporations to coordinate these outsourcing projects. Under neoliberalism, governments as well as corporations have been outsourcing service contracts. Again, information and communication technologies have allowed the

outsourcing of such activities as call centers, graphic design, computer programming, and accounting. In an interesting twist to the outsourcing trend, as wages have risen in India, India began to outsource some of work outsourced there to other countries such as the Philippines, Thailand, Poland, China, and Mexico (McMichael, 2012).

4. *Displacement.* Automation and outsourcing of work sheds stable jobs. At the beginning of the 21st century, it is estimated that 1 billion workers, or one third of the world's labor force, mostly in the Global South, were either unemployed or underemployed (Davis, 2006). Peasants in the Global South were pushed from their subsistence farms as corporate and governmental organizations pressed for monoculture, or the growing of one crop for export purposes, on agricultural land. They were pulled to low-wage, insecure work in urban export zones. As corporations and governments sought more flexibility in hiring the work force, more workers in the Global North, particularly in the United States, became involuntary part-time workers, or casual laborers working on a contract basis with no job benefits or job security (Ritzer, 2013a). In both wealthy and poor nations, people have increasingly worked "off the books" as servants to the wealthy. It is estimated that 50% of the workers in the Global South work in the shadow, also called underground, economy of illegal or undeclared work (McMichael, 2012).

5. *Labor exportation.* Migration for the purpose of finding work is not a new phenomenon, but it has become an important part of economic globalization. As many formerly colonized countries struggled to repay debt incurred during the 1980s, exporting workers became a way for countries to gain access to foreign currency. First, labor migrants in the Global South moved to other areas within their region, from the farms to the cities. When cities became overburdened, laborers began to migrate to northern regions. In 2013, the World Bank (2013c) estimated that

nearly 1 billion people, one in every seven in the world, had migrated either internally or across international borders to seek better opportunities. It further reports that remittance flows to developing countries more than quadrupled from 2000 to 2012. It suggests that labor migration and remittances from the migrants to folks back home offer a vital lifeline for many countries. For example, Indonesian villages use remittances to finance schools, roads, and housing (McMichael, 2012). Although they are struggling financially, Leticia Renteria and Marcos Vargas are committed to sending remittances back home to Mexico because they are well aware of the extreme poverty in which many of their relatives live. A majority of labor migrants are women and children, and both women and children are vulnerable to human trafficking. Human trafficking, or the trade in humans, has received increasing global attention in the past decade (World Health Organization, 2012a). Labor-related trafficking occurs in a wide range of labor sectors, including domestic servitude, hospitality services, agriculture, fishing, manufacturing, mining, and construction. Women and children may also be forced to serve as wives. Trafficking, then, is a form of modern-day slavery. Although it is difficult to find reliable data on the extent of trafficking, UNICEF (2013a) reports human trafficking in all 50 U.S. states.

6. *Limited protection by organized labor.* Since the beginning of industrial capitalism, labor unions have been the force behind governmental protection of workers' rights, fighting successfully for such protection as workplace safety, a minimum wage, a reduced workweek, and pensions. Economic globalization has seriously weakened the bargaining power of nationally based labor unions, because companies can always threaten to take their business somewhere else. In the United States, the rate of union membership, or the percentage of all workers who are union members, decreased from 20.1% in 1983 to 11.3% in 2012 (Bureau of Labor Statistics, 2013). However, labor unions are still strong in some countries. Exhibit 9.5 shows OECD

Exhibit 9.5 Rate of Union Membership in Selected Countries, 2011

Spain	15.6%
Switzerland	17.1%
Germany	18.0%
Australia	18.1%
Japan	18.1%
Netherlands	18.2%
United Kingdom	25.6%
Canada	26.8%
Austria	27.8%
Ireland	32.6%
Italy	35.6%
Belgium	50.4%
Norway	54.6%
Denmark	60.8%
Sweden	67.5%
Finland	69.0%

SOURCE: OECD, 2013b.

data on the rate of union membership in selected countries in 2011. You might notice that the five countries with the highest rate of union membership are among the seven countries with the lowest rates of inequality. In the United States, the union membership rate of public-sector workers (35.9%) is more than five times that of private-sector workers (6.6%) (OECD, 2013b). In 2012, among full-time workers, the median usual weekly earnings of union members was $943.00, compared with $742 for nonunion workers.

Social workers who participate in policy development must be informed about the serious challenges to job security in the contemporary era. They are also called on to deal with many of the social problems arising out of these changes in the economic institution—problems such as inadequate resources for family caregiving, domestic violence, substance abuse, depression, and anxiety.

Critical Thinking Questions 9.2

What have you heard about the benefits of economic globalization? What have you heard about harms from economic globalization? What do you make of the controversy about whether economic globalization is a good or bad thing? How is economic globalization affecting the government institution? How is economic globalization affecting Leticia Renteria and her family?

Trends in the Educational Institution

Leticia Renteria and Marcos Vargas know that education is important for their children, but they are not sure how to help their children succeed at school. Traditionally, the primary purpose of the **educational institution** has been to pass along formal knowledge from one generation to the next—a function that was largely performed by the family, with some help from the religious institution, until the 19th century. Formal education, schooling that includes a predetermined curriculum, has expanded dramatically around the world in the past several decades. In the process, there has been a trend toward convergence in educational curricula, especially in mathematics and science, but it is not clear whether universal curricula work equally well for the needs of different societies (Ballantine & Roberts, 2014).

The education-for-all movement is an international effort to meet the basic learning needs of all children, youth, and adults of the world. In 2000, this movement established six goals to be accomplished by 2015 (UNESCO, 2012):

Goal 1: To expand and improve comprehensive early childhood care and education (EECE), especially for the most disadvantaged children

Goal 2: To ensure that all children, particularly girls and ethnic minority children, have access to free primary education of good quality

Goal 3: To ensure that all youth and adults have access to appropriate learning and life-skills programs

Goal 4: To achieve a 50% improvement in adult literacy, especially for women

Goal 5: To achieve gender equality in education

Goal 6: To improve all aspects of the quality of education

Some progress has been made on these goals globally. There has been an expansion of early childhood care and education and improvements in gender equality in primary school education. Adult literacy increased by 12% from 1990 to 2010 (UNESCO, 2012).

However, in an era of a knowledge-based global economy, there continue to be large global gaps in opportunities for education. There is much evidence of long-term benefits of quality early childhood education, but in both low-income and wealthy nations, children from low-income families have less access to early childhood education than other children (UNESCO, 2012). Although educational participation is almost universal from the ages of 5 to 14 in affluent countries, 61 million of the world's children of primary school age, most residing in Sub-Saharan Africa or South and West Asia, are out of school. Lack of access to primary school education in low-income countries was worsened by conditions the World Bank set on debt refinancing in the late 1980s, which mandated reductions in education expenditure. The result was reduced educational levels in Asia, Latin America, and Africa and a widening gap in average years of education between rich and poor countries (McMichael, 2012). The drive for universal primary education made good progress from 1999 to 2004 but stagnated from 2008 to 2010 during the international financial crisis that started with the banking collapse in high-income countries. Both nations and families found it necessary to cut back on education spending. This happened in wealthy nations such as the United States, but the impact was greatest in low-income nations (UNESCO, 2012). In 123 low- and lower-middle-income countries, about one in five young people ages 15 to 24 have not completed

Conflict perspective

primary school (UNESCO, 2012). Sub-Saharan Africa has the world's lowest rate of secondary school enrollment, 40% in 2010. There were still 775 million adults who could not read or write in their native language in 2010; about 75% of them live in just 10 countries, 37% living in India (UNESCO, 2012). Gender disparities in educational attainment are declining across the globe, but women still make up nearly two thirds of the world's adults who lack literacy (UNESCO, 2012).

Nations around the world structure their educational systems in different ways, and we have heard a lot in this era of intensified global competition about how educational outcomes in the United States stack up against those in other high-income countries. U.S. educational historian Diane Ravitch (2013) sums up much of what I have heard from the mass media:

> In the early years of the twenty-first century, a bipartisan consensus arose about education policy in the United States. Right and left, Democrats and Republicans, the leading members of our political class and our media elite seemed to agree: Public education is broken. Our students are not learning enough. Public schools are bad and getting worse. We are being beaten by other nations with higher test scores. Our abysmal public schools threaten not only the performance of our economy but our national security, our very survival as a nation. This crisis is so profound that half measures and tweaks will not suffice. Schools must be closed and large numbers of teachers fired. Anyone who doubts this is unaware of the dimensions of the crisis or has a vested interest in defending the status quo. (p. 3)

Ravitch (2010) provides some context for this contemporary concern about the U.S. educational institution. Her historical research taught her that in almost every decade of the 20th century, critics loudly proclaimed that the public education system was in crisis. The nature of the proposed crisis shifted over time: sometimes the schools were considered too academic and not sufficiently tied to the needs of the industrial economy, and other times the schools were attacked for their lack of academic rigor. Most recently, the proposed crisis in the educational institution has focused on the achievement gap between children of different racial and ethnic groups, but contemporary criticisms also emphasize the poor performance of U.S. students on international tests. Just as the nature of the proposed crisis has shifted over time, so has the nature of the proposed solutions, with each generation of policymakers assuming they have found the "silver bullet" to "fix" the educational institution.

The story told by the mass media is often one of decline in the educational institution. For example, a 2010 *Newsweek* story indicated that "once upon a time, American students tested better than any other students in the world. Now, ranked against European schoolchildren, America does about as well as Lithuania, behind at least 10 other nations" (Thomas, Wingert, Conant, & Register, 2010, p. 24). Let's take a closer look at that story of decline. As I write this, I am looking at the most recent performance (2012) of U.S. 15-year-old students on testing by the Program for International Student Assessment (PISA). The results for the three literacy areas—math, science, and reading—are summarized in Exhibit 9.6, along with a comparison of U.S. student scores with scores of students from other high-income countries. Overall, 18 education systems had higher average scores than the United States in all three literacy areas. So, it is, indeed, true that U.S. students are not the top-ranked students in international testing. But is this a sign of decline of the U.S. educational institution? Long-term data suggest not. In fact, there has not been a time when U.S. students were first on international tests. When the first international tests were administered in the mid-1960s, U.S. students ranked at or the near the bottom of all students tested. In the 1970s, 1980s, and 1990s, U.S. students typically scored in the bottom quartile or near the international average (Ravitch, 2010). The story told by these data is that U.S. students do not stand out on international tests but are not faring worse over time, nor are they faring much better after the past 12 years of ongoing national policy experiments. National test scores tell a different story, a story of constant improvement over time. U.S. fourth and eighth grade students have made significant, even remarkable, gains in national reading and mathematics test scores since 1978 (Ravitch, 2013; Rothstein, 2011).

But what of the recent concern about the achievement gap between White and minority

Exhibit 9.6 Comparison of PISA Scores for 15-Year-Old U.S. Students With Students From Other Wealthy Countries

Literacy Area	Scores of U.S. Students Compared With Students From Other Wealthy Countries
Mathematics	• The average score for U.S. students was 481, compared with an average score of 494 for all students tested. • 9% of U.S. students scored at the proficiency level (highest level), compared with 13% of all students tested. • The U.S. average score was higher than 26 education systems, lower than 29 education systems, and about the same as 9 education systems.
Science	• The average score for U.S. students was 497, compared with an average score of 501 for all students tested. • 7% of U.S. students scored at the proficiency level, compared with 8% of all students tested. • The U.S. average score was higher than 29 education systems, lower than 21 education systems, and about the same as 14 education systems.
Reading	• The average score for U.S. students was 498, compared with an average score of 496 for all students tested. • 8% of U.S. students scored at the proficiency level, compared with 8% of all students tested. • The average score for U.S. students was higher than 34 education systems, lower than 19 education systems, and about the same as 11 education systems.

SOURCE: National Center for Education Statistics, 2013.

students of color, more specifically Black and Hispanic students? This is a more complicated question. There is, no doubt, a very substantial gap between the educational achievement of the White and Black populations in the United States, a gap that is as old as the nation, and there is strong evidence of a White–Hispanic gap as well. Paul Barton and Richard Coley (2010) of the Educational Testing Service examined the White–Black gap in educational achievement from the beginning of the 20th century to 2010. They found a large reduction in the gap in the 1970s and 1980s, when Black students made greater gains than White students. They also found that improvement in reducing the gap stagnated in the 1990s, and progress has continued to slow since that time. The gap remains large. Ravitch (2013) provides evidence that Black and Hispanic students have continued to make impressive gains since 1990, but White students have been making gains as well, slowing the pace of reduction in the gap. For example, in 1990, 83% of Black fourth graders and 67% of Hispanic fourth graders scored "below basic" in mathematics; in 2011 the percentages dropped to 34% for Black fourth graders and 28% for Hispanic fourth graders. The improvements in reading scores were not as dramatic but impressive nonetheless. The Black–White achievement gap is now smaller than the achievement gap between the poorest and most affluent students in the United States (Reardon, 2011). The income achievement gap has been growing for the past 50 years and continues to increase. Carnoy and Rothstein (2013) argue that given the high rate of inequality in the United States, it is impressive that the average scores of U.S. students on international tests are as high as they are, given the clear evidence that around the world children from low-income families do not perform as well academically as children from middle- and high-income families.

This analysis suggests that the U.S. educational institution needs some improvement, but it does not suggest an institution in a crisis of steep decline as the architects of recent policy experiments have often suggested. Since the beginning of the 21st century, two national policy experiments have created instability in the U.S. educational institution: the 2001 No Child Left Behind (NCLB) legislation passed during the George W. Bush administration and the Race to the Top policy direction of the Obama administration. The stated goals of both policies are to raise academic achievement for all students, out of concern that U.S. students are falling behind those in other wealthy nations, and to close the achievement gaps that divide low-income students and students of color from their peers.

NCLB was based on the belief that testing and school accountability would lead to significant improvement in student performance and narrow the achievement gap. The law required all states to engage in annual testing of every child in Grades 3 through 8 in reading and mathematics and to report the test scores by race, ethnicity, low income status, disability status, and limited English proficiency. All students in every group were expected to achieve proficiency on state tests by 2014. Any school that failed to meet its annual target would be labeled "in need of improvement," and punishments were to increase over time, with the eventual punishments including staff firings, school closing, state control or private management, or some other form of "restructuring." The schools most likely to be labeled as failing were schools with high proportions of students with disabilities and poor and minority students. As 2014 approached, most schools in the country were considered failing by NCLB standards, including 80% of the public schools in Massachusetts, the state with the highest test performance. Ravitch (2013) points out that 100% proficiency is an impossible goal that no country has ever achieved.

Barack Obama became president in the midst of an economic crisis in January 2009. The economic stimulus bill passed by Congress included $5 billion to be used in a competition among the states known as Race to the Top. Secretary of Education Arne Duncan established the conditions for receipt of the moneys: recipient states had to agree to adopt new Common Core standards and tests, expand charter schools, evaluate teacher effectiveness using student test scores as a major component of evaluation, and turn around their lowest-performing schools by such methods as firing staff and closing schools (and subsequently opening new privately managed charter schools). The most important piece added by Race to the Top was the wedding of teacher evaluation to value-added student test scores (Ravitch, 2010, 2013). In other words, teachers were considered effective if they could "cause" their students' test scores to go up every year. This aspect of recent educational policy is interesting, given that in this same time period, corporate CEO pay has become quite disconnected from the economic success of the corporation; teachers are responsible for student performance, but CEOs are not responsible for the bottom line of the corporation.

Both NCLB and Race to the Top greatly expanded the role of the federal government in the educational institution, but they also favored the neoliberal principles of privatization and market competition. Even though both policies have had wide support across the political spectrum, the data do not support the success of these two policy initiatives. There is increasing international evidence that the achievement gap is highly correlated with economic inequality, and school policy has limited impact. Students begin their journey through the public school system with an already existing achievement gap. Changes in the governmental and economic institutions would be the most effective way to close that gap. There is clear evidence that the most effective educational changes for reducing the achievement gap are quality early childhood education and smaller class size (Ravitch, 2010; Schweinhart, Barnett, & Belfield, 2005). Testing alone has not proven to raise student scores (Ravitch, 2013), and reliance on test-based teacher and school accountability has led to score inflation and cheating in some school systems (see Severson, 2011). When schools have been closed and replaced by new charter schools, the charter schools have not performed better than the closed schools (Gleason, Clark, Clark Tuttle, Dwoyer, & Silverberg, 2010). Wedding teacher evaluation to student test scores ignores the many variables that go into test scores, including the specific makeup of a teacher's class in a given year (Baker et al., 2010).

Diane Ravitch (2010) reminds us that the U.S. educational institution has contended with three major policy changes in the government and political institution since 1960. First, legally sanctioned racial segregation of schools came to an end. Unfortunately, the legal rulings that ended it were followed by the flight of Whites and middle-class Blacks from some urban schools, leaving behind school districts struggling with racial isolation and concentrated poverty. Second, court rulings and legislation required public schools to serve students with disabilities. This change in policy direction was long overdue but also expensive and challenging for the schools. Third, changes in federal immigration policy brought millions of non-English-speaking students into the public schools. In addition, the educational institution has needed to adjust to changes in the family institution (to be discussed shortly), growing societal inequality, and ever-changing information and communication technology. In recent years, teachers and school administrators have had to live with persistent attacks from politicians and the mass media. Another recent trend is the entry of for-profit colleges and universities at the tertiary educational level.

Around the world, citizens and leaders are concerned about whether their educational institution is responding well to globalization and the rapid pace of change in other institutions (Ballantine & Roberts, 2014). Certainly, there is a need for improvements in the U.S. educational institution, and it makes sense to look for ideas from the countries that have successful educational institutions based on two criteria: first, their students score well on international testing, and second, their students' socioeconomic status does not have a large impact on learning outcomes. Evidence suggests that the best educational outcomes occur in countries where there are universal early childhood education programs; where the teachers are well-trained, experienced, well-paid, highly respected, and given professional autonomy; where the curriculum is broad-based and rigorous; and where there are resources to address the needs of students in every school (Ravitch, 2013; Ripley, 2013; Tucker, 2011).

Photos 9.3a & 9.3b The contrast between these two classrooms—one in a well-resourced suburban school in the United states and the other on a footpath in Ahmedabad, India—demonstrates global inequality in resources for education.

© AP Photo/Michael Sohn; © Sam Panthaky/AFP/Getty Images

Leticia Renteria and Marcos Vargas value education for their children but are intimidated by the schools their children attend. The children are often aware of their parents' lack of comfort in interacting with the school. Social workers can help schools and parents become more comfortable with each other. Social workers should also become active partners in efforts at educational reform, particularly those that equalize educational opportunities, but to be

effective in these efforts, we need to be informed about trends in the educational institution. By the time you read this, the public conversation about the educational institution and ways to improve it may have shifted again. We must carefully evaluate whether what we see and hear in the mass media about circumstances in the educational institution are supported by available evidence.

Trends in the Health Care Institution

Health is an important issue for Leticia Renteria and her family. Leticia is concerned that environmental hazards are the cause of her children's asthma. She is happy that the children are able to receive health care at the community clinic and hopes to stay healthy herself since she does not qualify for health care. Health is important to this family, but health is also important to a society. Child development, adult well-being, and family stability are all affected by health. The **health care institution** is the primary one for promoting the general health of a society. At one time, health care was addressed primarily in the home, by families. Today, in wealthy countries, health care is a major social institution, and health care organizations are major employers (Ballantine & Roberts, 2014).

Unfortunately, there is much disparity in the global health care institution, both between and within countries (OECD, 2013c; World Health Organization, 2013). Global inequalities in child and adult mortality are large

Conflict perspective

and growing. They are highly influenced by factors in the economic institution and the health care institution but also by factors in the educational institution and the family institution. In 2012, globally, more than 29 million children younger than age 5 suffered from acute malnutrition or wasting. Although more children of the world survive their 5th birthday than ever before, in 2012 6.6 million children younger than age 5 died, about 18,000 per day (UNICEF, 2013b). Almost all of the children who die each year live in poor countries.

In poor countries, basic health prevention and treatment services have been slowly improving, but serious gaps remain. In 2011, 67% of the population in low-income countries had access to safe drinking water, compared with 99% of the population in high-income countries. Likewise, 37% of the population in low-income countries was using adequate sanitation methods, compared with 100% of the population in high-income countries (World Health Organization, 2013). The lowest rates of safe drinking water and adequate sanitation occurred in the African region. More than 1 billion people in the world lack sanitation facilities and must continue practices that pose serious health and environmental risks (UNICEF, 2013b). You may be as shocked as I am that Leticia Renteria and her family, living in the United States, have neither safe drinking water nor adequate sanitation. Unfortunately, they are not alone in this circumstance. The World Health Organization (2012b) identifies 17 tropical diseases referred to as "neglected" because they have not received the attention of pharmaceutical companies in the past. The people affected by these diseases typically are the poorest in the world and live in remote, rural areas; urban slums; or conflict zones. The diseases are caused by unsafe water, poor housing conditions, and poor sanitation. Recently, the Bill and Melinda Gates Foundation (2012) funded four grants totaling $68.2 million to accelerate pharmaceutical research on 10 neglected tropical diseases.

Within-country health disparities are very prominent in the United States, where deep inequalities are related to socioeconomic status, race, and ethnicity, and poverty is seen as the driving force behind the growing health disparities (Centers for Disease Control and Prevention, 2013d). Research consistently finds that life expectancy increases as personal income increases (Burtless, 2012). The infant mortality rate for non-Hispanic Blacks is more than double the rate for non-Hispanic Whites, and the rates are higher in the South and Midwest than in other parts of the country. Non-Hispanic Black adults are 50% more likely than other adults to die of heart disease or stroke before age 75. Compared with Asian and non-Hispanic White adults, the prevalence of diabetes is higher among Hispanic and non-Hispanic Black adults, as well as among adults of mixed races. The prevalence is also higher among adults with lower incomes (Centers for Disease Control and Prevention, 2013d). It is clear that race and social class critically impact health disparities in the United States. Even at the higher ends of education, there are large health gaps between African Americans and Whites (Williams, Mohammed, Leavell, & Collins, 2010).

Although much of the health disparities in the United States are related to factors in other social institutions, aspects of the health care institution play a large role. At the time this book went to press, the United States and Mexico were the only two countries of the 34 in the OECD without universal health coverage, and the United States was the only one of the comparison countries used in this chapter without such coverage (OECD, 2013c). The proportion of the population covered has grown rapidly in Mexico since health care reform in 2004, reaching nearly 90% by 2011. In 2012, 15.4%, or 48.0 million, of the population in the United States was still uninsured, but that percentage is expected to shrink after January 2014 with expanded coverage through the Affordable Care Act. The percentage covered by private health insurance was 63.9% in 2012, and the percentage covered by government health insurance was 32.6%. The uninsured rate varied by race and ethnicity in 2012: 11.1% of non-Hispanic Whites, 15.1% of Asians, 19.0% of Blacks, and 29.1% of Hispanics (any race) were uninsured (DeNavas-Walt et al., 2013).

Jeanne Ballantine and Keith Roberts (2014) suggest that the United States has both the best and the worst health care system in the industrialized world. It is one of the best in the world in terms of quality of care, trained practitioners, facilities, and medical technology. But it is the worst in terms of costs, inefficiency, equality of access, and fragmentation. As demonstrated in Exhibit 9.7, the United States spends a much greater percentage of its GDP on health care than any of the other wealthy countries covered in this chapter, but this expenditure does not pay off in terms of the most often used measure of the health of a nation, life expectancy.

The reasons why the health care institution is so costly in the United States are quite complex, but two contributing factors are discussed here. First, compared with the health care systems in other countries, the U.S. approach to financing health care is extremely complex, and the administrative cost of this complex system is greater than in the more streamlined universal systems in other industrialized countries (Reinhardt, Hussey, & Anderson, 2004). Second, the health care institution is influenced by culture. Health care in the United States reflects the aggressive, can-do spirit of the

Exhibit 9.7 Health Spending as Percentage of GDP (2010) and Life Expectancy (2011) in Wealthy Industrial Countries

Country	Percentage of Gross Domestic Product Spent	Life Expectancy
Israel	7.7	82
Australia	9.0	82
Finland	9.0	82
Japan	9.2	83
Ireland	9.2	81
Norway	9.3	81
Italy	9.5	82
Spain	9.6	82
Sweden	9.6	82
United Kingdom	9.6	80
Belgium	10.5	80
Switzerland	10.9	83
Austria	11.0	81
Denmark	11.1	79
Canada	11.4	82
Germany	11.5	81
France	11.7	82
Netherlands	12.1	81
United States	17.6	79

SOURCE: World Health Organization, 2013.

mainstream culture (Gardiner & Kosmitzki, 2011). For example, compared with European physicians, U.S. physicians recommend more routine examinations and perform many more bypass surgeries and angioplasties than European doctors. These are both examples of a more aggressive approach to treatment that could be attributed to a reimbursement system that rewards such aggressiveness as much as to a cultural bias toward aggressive treatment (Reinhardt, Hussey, & Anderson, 2002).

Societies around the world struggle with health care costs and quality, access to care, and medical technology (OECD, 2013c; Rapoport, Jacobs, & Jonsson, 2009). Most governments in Europe made a decision in the late 1800s and early 1900s to support health care as a human right and put some form of national health care system into place. It appears that they were operating out of a belief that maintaining a healthy population is necessary to maintain a strong society (Ballantine & Roberts, 2014). In the United States, health care has not been viewed as a human right, historically, and the health care system developed with less direction and made piecemeal policies over time. Medical research has been a major strength in the U.S. health care system, but the two biggest challenges in the past 3 decades have been lack of universal access to care and continuously escalating costs. Access to health care was improved with the passage of Medicare and Medicaid in the 1960s, but large numbers continue to have no health care insurance. Several attempts were made to develop federal legislation to address these problems for a number of decades, but these efforts failed because politicians had conflicting philosophical positions on the role of government in health care delivery and because of considerable opposition from private insurance companies, physicians, and pharmaceutical companies.

After a year-long contentious debate, the U.S. Congress passed the Patient Protection and Affordable Care Act and the Health Care and Education Reconciliation Act of 2010, and both bills were signed into law in March 2010. The health insurance reforms were to roll out over several years. Here are some of the key pieces of the legislation (Cockerham, 2012; U.S. Department of Health and Human Services, 2013a):

- Young adults can stay on their parents' health insurance policies until age 26.
- People with Medicare can get key preventive services for free and receive a 50% discount on drugs in the "donut hole."
- An additional 32 million people are to be covered by health insurance by 2014, and it is projected that 95% of people in the United States will be covered by the end of 2018.
- Medicaid coverage will be expanded for the poor, extending coverage to people with incomes of up to 133% of the federal poverty line.
- Almost all people will be required to have health insurance (individual mandate) or be fined.
- Employers with more than 50 employees will be required to provide health insurance for their employees or be fined.
- Health insurance companies will be unable to reject applicants because they have preexisting conditions, charge excessive rates, or cancel policies after policyholders become sick.

As this book is being prepared for production, the future of this health care reform is uncertain. Several states challenged the legality of the law, and the challenges went to the U.S. Supreme Court in 2012. The Supreme Court upheld the individual mandate provision but ruled that states could refuse to participate in the Medicaid expansion piece of the legislation. As of December 2013, half of the states have decided not to participate. Republican senators and representatives continue to challenge the health care reforms, and the House of Representatives has voted to repeal the law so many times I have lost count. Individual states were encouraged to create their own health care exchanges to assist the uninsured in getting enrolled in insurance plans, but the great majority of states decided to rely on a federal exchange rather than run their own. The rollout of the federal government exchange in October 2013 had massive technical problems that were mostly worked out by early December 2013. Proponents of the legislation argue that it will make health insurance more affordable, but the reform is off to a rough start. Early in the formulation of the policy, a public insurance option, whose intent was to keep prices down by competing with private insurance, was dropped from the plan. It was hoped that Medicaid expansion would lower the costs for many people, but the Supreme Court made that piece optional. The hopes for cost containment rest to a great extent on the willingness of currently uninsured healthy young adults to become insured and join the risk pools of insurance companies. This is key to lowering the overall costs of insurance. We continue to be a deeply divided country about the appropriate role for government in the health care institution. Stay tuned.

Like many other families, the family of Leticia Renteria may need social work assistance to navigate the very complex, quite fragmented health care system if the children's health problems worsen. Social workers need to be particularly sensitive to the situation of some immigrant families who try to integrate traditional healing traditions with Global North, technology-oriented medical practices.

Critical Thinking Questions 9.3

As this chapter was being written, there were many conflicting stories in the mass media about the performance of both the educational institution and the health care institution in the United States. How is what you have seen in the mass media about these social institutions in the past week similar to and different from what is reported in this chapter? How do you understand the strengths and limitations of these two social institutions in the United States, as compared with their counterparts in other wealthy countries? Why are these social institutions so controversial in the United States?

Trends in the Social Welfare Institution

People in the community where Leticia Renteria and her family live are very excited about the new Boys and Girls Club in the nearby town. However, Leticia Renteria has heard many stories that make

her fear the U.S. social welfare institution. Although food stamps and cash assistance programs might help bring some economic stability to the family, Leticia fears that receiving such assistance would make her children vulnerable to oppressive governmental intervention later in life. Her decision to voluntarily depart when she was faced with immigration detention was driven by fears about her children being placed in the state foster care system. Social workers working in such situations must have a good understanding of the special stressors of undocumented immigrants. We can play an important role in such communities to counter misinformation about social welfare services, such as what Leticia has heard. As social workers, we are well aware of the network of social welfare agencies and programs that could help such families; we are also aware of the gaps in the contemporary social welfare institution.

The **social welfare institution** is concerned with the fair allocation of goods, services, and opportunities to enhance social functioning of individuals and contribute to the social health of the society. The social

Systems perspective

welfare institution also engages in social control, in programs such as child protective services. The social welfare institution developed in all industrialized countries in the 19th and 20th centuries as these nations tried to cope with the alienation and disruption caused by social inequalities of industrial market capitalism (Teeple, 2000). It was an expression of altruism toward the people who did not fare well in this economic arrangement, but it also was an expression of concern that the inequalities inherent in the system could destabilize a society and undermine its social health.

The social welfare institution, like any other social institution, reflects the culture of the society. Social welfare scholars often call attention to the cultural attitudes toward social welfare in the United States compared with European countries (Karger & Stoesz, 2014). The U.S. social welfare institution has, historically, put primary emphasis on promoting independence and preventing dependence. In contrast, the European social welfare states have put more emphasis on promoting social inclusion and using the social welfare institution as an investment to protect the health of the society, which they refer to as social protection (European Commission: Employment, Social Affairs & Inclusion, 2013; Sernau, 2014). Exhibit 9.8 demonstrates that public expenditure on social welfare (including old age, survivors,

disability, health, family, unemployment, housing, and other policies), as a percentage of GDP, varies among affluent societies. It also demonstrates that public expenditures on social welfare increased in most affluent societies from 1980 to 2013. Almost all of the listed countries made a substantial increase in the percentage of GDP spent on social welfare after the 2008 financial crisis, with the United States making one of the largest increases (OECD, 2013d).

Four things are important to remember when interpreting this trend. First, countries suffered a decline in GDP during and in the aftermath of the 2008 financial crisis, as always occurs at such times (Papell & Prodan, 2011). Second, in the midst of economic decline, many countries stepped up their social welfare expenditures in some areas to cushion the blow of the crisis and stimulate the economy. Third, in the aftermath of the financial crisis, governments around the world are being encouraged to engage in austerity measures, including trimming back the social welfare institution. Fourth, even though public expenditures for social welfare have been growing as a portion of GDP, it is important to note that as wealthy societies grey, expenditures on old-age benefits are increasing at a much faster rate than those in other social welfare sectors. In many affluent countries, government expenditures for children and families have been falling, and child poverty rates have been growing while poverty rates for older adults have not (UNICEF, 2012). Given what we are learning about the long-term negative health consequences of early deprivation, cost cutting in programs serving children and their families in order to fund programs for older adults could pose serious challenges for the social welfare institution in the future. For all wealthy nations, the social welfare needs of an aging society pose a serious challenge for the social welfare institution going forward.

Social welfare policy is driven by political and economic philosophies. The United States is a diverse society, and there is much competition of ideas about what constitutes the public good and what type of social welfare institution is needed, if

Exhibit 9.8 Public Social Expenditures on Social Welfare as a Percentage of GDP in 1980 and 2013

Country	1980	2013
Israel	-------	15.8%
Canada	13.7%	18.2%
Switzerland	13.8%	19.1%
Australia	10.3%	19.5%
United States	13.2%	20.0%
Ireland	16.5%	21.6%
Japan	10.2%	22.3%*
Norway	16.9%	22.9%
United Kingdom	16.5%	23.8%
Netherlands	24.8%	24.3%
Germany	22.1%	26.2%
Spain	15.5%	27.4%
Austria	22.4%	28.3%
Italy	18.0%	28.4%
Sweden	27.1%	28.6%
Finland	18.1%	30.5%
Belgium	23.5%	30.7%
Denmark	24.8%	30.8%
France	20.8%	33.0%

SOURCE: OECD, 2013d.

*value for 2010.

at all. Although the philosophical differences are more complex than this, we can divide them into conservative and liberal views of social welfare. Conservatives believe that the public good is best served when the federal government has a minimal role in social welfare. They believe that to the extent that social welfare programs are needed, they should be run by a combination of state and local governments and the private sector. They believe that income inequality and some level of unemployment are good for the society, and any attempt by the government to stabilize the economy is harmful. Liberals believe that the government institution, particularly the federal government, should be the primary force in the social welfare institution because it is the institution most capable of promoting social justice, thereby promoting the public good. In their view, social justice is incompatible with high levels of inequality and unemployment, and the government has a role to play in minimizing the harms of market capitalism (for a fuller discussion, see Karger & Stoesz, 2014).

Social welfare policy in the United States, as in any society, varies with who holds political power at any given time and has shifted over time. From the 1930s to the 1970s, beginning with the presidency of Franklin Delano Roosevelt, the general policy direction was for the federal government to play a strong role in the social welfare institution. The Social Security Act of 1935 began a process of government protections that was expanded during the 1960s and 1970s, with the passage of Medicare, Medicaid, the Food Stamp Program, and Head Start, among other programs (Marx, 2012). In the late 1970s, the traditional liberal belief in a federally based social welfare system began to lose favor. The new liberals (neoliberals) began to assume some of the conservative philosophy, which led to a diminishing sense of public responsibility and an increasing emphasis on individual responsibility for the social well-being of the nation. Neoliberal philosophy, under the democratic administration of Bill Clinton in the 1990s, led to welfare reform that greatly curtailed supports to poor children and their families. Since the 1980s, the conservative philosophy has been in ascendancy with ongoing attempts to privatize social security (unsuccessful to date) and to otherwise limit the role of the federal government in the social welfare system. (At the same time, however, cultural conservatives have called for an increased role for the federal government in issues such as contraception, abortion, and school prayer.) With a huge federal debt caused by tax cuts, two wars, and a financial crisis, it does not appear that a liberal philosophy of social welfare will regain prominence in the near future.

The data cited in Exhibit 9.8 indicate that 14 of the 18 wealthy countries used as comparison in this chapter devote a greater percentage of their GDP to public social welfare expenditures than the United States. We must be careful in interpreting the data, however. Given ambivalence about government and a strong belief in the market, the United States has developed a mixed social welfare system made up of federal, state, and local governmental programs; private nonprofit social welfare organizations; and a growing number of private for-profit organizations. It is hard to compare this system with the European model in terms of expenditures, but it is safe to say that the welfare institution in the United States is more fragmented than the European model, and its family support policies, such as family leave, family allowances, and early childhood education and care, are much less comprehensive. Indeed, the European countries are not alone in providing more generous public support to families than is offered in the United States. Parental leave policies are a good example. In the United States, parents are offered 12 weeks of *unpaid* leave under the Family and Medical Leave Act, which exempts companies with fewer than 50 paid employees. All other wealthy countries used as comparison in this chapter as well as many low- and middle-income countries provide *paid* parental leave. For example, Venezuela offers 18 weeks of paid leave, and Pakistan, South Africa, and Mexico each offer 12 weeks of paid leave (Yost, 2012). The average number of paid weeks of parental leave for the 34 countries in the OECD is 19 (OECD, 2012).

How should we evaluate the performance of the social welfare institution? It is not a simple matter to consider how a given society's social welfare system is doing with allocating goods, services, and opportunities to enhance social functioning of individuals and contribute to the social health of the society. Let's take a look at three approaches that have been taken to that question.

Annually, the United Nations prepares the Human Development Index (HDI) to rank the social health of nations. HDI rankings are based on a composite of three variables: life expectancy, educational attainment, and income. On this index, the United States consistently scores in the top five countries of the world, based on its high GDP. As noted earlier, the United States has the lowest life expectancy of the comparison nations. It scores relatively high on educational attainment in terms of number of years of education completed, but student performance on international test scores is not stellar. When the HDI is adjusted for level of societal inequality, the U.S. position falls by 13 places (United Nations Development Programme, 2013).

In the United States, the Institute for Innovation in Social Policy (IISP) is critical of using income as such an important measure of the social health of a nation and developed the Index of Social Health (ISH) as a more comprehensive way to monitor the social well-being of U.S. society. The ISH includes the 16 indicators found in Exhibit 9.9, grouped by stage of life. The ISH is based on the premise that the social health of a nation is not revealed by any one measure but by the combined effect of a number of interacting variables. IISP has been using the ISH since 1987 to track the social health of the United States. In their research covering the years from 1970 to 2005, they found five main phases in the social health of the nation (Miringoff & Opdycke, 2008):

1970–1976: social health at a record high

1976–1983: social health declined rapidly

1983–1993: social health stagnated at low level

1993–2000: period of progress, highest score since 1978

2000–2005: social health stalled again

Exhibit 9.9   Indicators of Social Health

Children	Infant mortality
	Child abuse
	Child poverty
Youth	Teenage suicide
	Teenage drug abuse
	High school dropouts
Adults	Unemployment
	Weekly wages
	Health insurance coverage
Elderly	Poverty, age 65+
	Out-of-pocket health costs, age 65+
All ages	Homicides
	Alcohol-related traffic fatalities
	Food insecurity
	Affordable housing
	Income inequality

SOURCE: Institute for Innovation in Social Policy, 2013.

More recent data indicate that the social health of the United States increased slightly in 2006 and 2007 and then declined again during the financial crisis and its aftermath. The most recent data for 2011 showed improvement in social health over 2010 but still 7 points below the 2007 index score. The scores for 2009 to 2011 are the lowest of the past 15 years. The ISH is based on a total score of 100. Overall, the ISH declined from 64.0 to 50.2 from 1970 to 2011, a drop of 21.6% (Institute for Innovation in Social Policy, 2013).

The ISH provides a broad, multivariable measure for tracking the social health of a nation, but it has not been used for international comparisons. UNICEF (2012) suggests that child poverty, a measure included in the ISH but not in the HDI, is the best single measure for making international comparisons of the social health of nations. UNICEF proposes that since children are the future of a society, nations pay a large future price for child poverty, in terms of reduced educational achievement, reduced skills, lost productivity, increased unemployment, lower levels of health, increased welfare dependence, increased costs in the criminal justice system, and loss of social cohesion. There is, indeed, growing evidence that childhood poverty is related to most of these social conditions.

According to UNICEF's 2012 report of child poverty, the United States had the highest rate of child poverty of any of the comparison countries reported in the chapter, using a definition of relative poverty as living in a household with disposable income, when adjusted for family size, of less than 50% of the national median. Four of the countries used for comparison in this chapter—Finland, the Netherlands, Norway, and Denmark—had child poverty rates less than 7%. Six others—Sweden, Austria, Switzerland, Ireland, Germany, and France—had rates from 7% to 10%. A third group of five countries—Belgium, Australia, the United Kingdom, Canada, and Japan—had rates from 10% to 15%. Two other countries—Italy and Spain—had rates from 15% to 20%. The child poverty rate for the United States was 25.5%. Childhood poverty data were not available for Israel. UNICEF (2012) also studies the impact of social policy on child poverty rates by considering the child poverty rate before and after taxes and benefits programs. It concludes that social policy makes a considerable difference in the relative child poverty rate. For example, its data indicate that Canada and the United States begin with the same level of relative child poverty (just over 25%), but after taxes and social benefits are calculated, the rate in Canada is about half the rate of the United States. Social policy had the biggest impact on relative child poverty in Ireland, which had a more than 40% rate of relative child poverty before taxes and social benefits but a rate less than 10% after taxes and benefits. It is clear that the social health of a society is affected by decisions made in a number of social institutions, including the government and political institution, the economic institution, the educational institution, the health care institution, and the social welfare institution, as well as the family and kinship institution discussed later.

Some welfare scholars suggest a social welfare institution in transition (Karger & Stoesz, 2014). Across the Global North, countries pursued liberal social policies after World War II. As a result of the competition inherent in economic globalization, Western industrial nations have been cutting or slowing the growth of their social welfare programs since the 1970s. At the same time, demand for social services has increased as workers have tried to cope with the insecurities in the global labor market. Retrenchment of the social welfare institution in combination with increased concentration of income and wealth has produced political unrest across Europe and the United States and spurred rage across the political spectrum. In the United States, this rage produced both the very conservative Tea Party and the liberal Occupy Movement at the beginning of the 2nd decade of the 21st century. The future of the social welfare institution is uncertain.

Leticia Renteria seems to think of the social welfare institution only as a coercive institution, one that tries to control behavior rather than provide compassionate support. Indeed, the social welfare institution in the United States has always played a social control function as well as a social reform function (Hutchison, 1987). In recent times, it has moved toward greater attention to social control than to social reform (Hutchison & Charlesworth, 2000; Teeple, 2000). Social workers cannot be active participants in moving that balance back to social reform unless they clearly understand trends in the interrelated social institutions discussed in this chapter.

| Conflict perspective |

Trends in the Religious Institution

Although the Catholic Church was a very important part of the life of Leticia Renteria back in Mexico, she and Marco do not regularly attend church. However, when Leticia was frantic at being detained by immigration officials, one person she thought might be able to help her was a nun in her community. The **religious institution** is the primary one for addressing spiritual and ethical issues. It also serves important socialization, social control, and mutual support functions. Sociologists study three components of the institution: a belief system, religious rituals, and an organizational structure that provides networks of support as well as roles and statuses (Roberts & Yamane, 2012).

Although there is a long history of conflict and adaptation as the major world religions confronted each other in the same political and geographic areas, globalization has urgently increased the need for religious communities to find ways to coexist globally as well as locally. A religious belief system helps people to feel secure, and exposure to different belief systems can be unsettling and sometimes perceived as a threat to the integrity of one's own beliefs and identity. Today, however, it is almost impossible for believers in one religious tradition to be isolated from other religious traditions. We are increasingly exposed to the beliefs, rituals, and organizations of diverse religious groups, and this is not a trend that is likely to be reversed. There are few choices about how to cope with this trend. We can attempt to impose one belief system on the world and commit genocide if that doesn't work. Or we can attempt to find a unified ethical code that is consistent with all religious traditions and respectfully agree to disagree if that doesn't work, giving legal protections to all groups. In the past, both of these choices have been put into practice at one time or another.

We are living in a time of much religious strife. Serbian Orthodox Christians recently engaged in ethnic cleansing of Muslims in the former Yugoslavia. Catholics and Protestants have waged a long and often violent battle in Northern Ireland. The Ku Klux Klan in the United States has used religious arguments to vilify and sometimes persecute Jews, African Americans, and other groups. Terrorists have killed and injured thousands in the name of Islam. The United States has called on the name of God, and the language of good and evil, to justify the war on terror and the invasion of Afghanistan and Iraq. Hindus and Muslims kill each other in India. When religious differences are woven with other forms of struggle, such as social class, ethnic, or political struggle, the conflict is likely to be particularly intense (Kurtz, 2012).

On the other hand, there are also historical and current stories of peaceful coexistence of religious groups. In 1893, representatives of a wide range of religions were brought together to create the Parliament of the World's Religions. The second meeting of the parliament did not convene until a century later, in 1993 (Kurtz, 2012). It met again in 1999, 2004, and 2009. The mission of the parliament is "to cultivate harmony among the world's religious and spiritual communities and foster their engagement with the world and its other guiding institutions in order to achieve a just, peaceful and sustainable world" (Council for a Parliament of the World's Religions, 2013). Among the issues discussed and debated at the 2009 parliament were healing the earth, reconciling with Indigenous peoples, overcoming poverty in a patriarchal world, increasing social cohesion in villages and cities, sharing wisdom in search for inner peace, securing food and water for all people, and building peace in pursuit of justice. A planned 2014 parliament was cancelled because of a funding crisis (Interfaith Observer, 2012).

It is not surprising that both violence and nonviolence have been used in the name of religion. The texts of all the major world religions include what Lester Kurtz (2012) calls both a "warrior motif" and a "pacifist motif" (pp. 283–284). All major religions justify violence on occasion, but no religion justifies terrorism. All religions also include norms of mercy, compassion, and respect. In the contemporary era, Islam is sometimes characterized as a violent religion, but Christianity was seen as the most violent world religion during the Crusades and the Inquisition. All of the major world religions have proven capable of perpetrating violence in the name of religion, and all have demonstrated compassion and tolerance.

It is good to get a sense of the global religious landscape. Consider a group of 10 people that represent the distribution of world religions. Three will be Christian, two will be Muslim, two will be unaffiliated or atheists, one will be Hindu, one will be Buddhist or from another East Asian religion, and the remaining one will represent every other religion of the world (Kurtz, 2012). This landscape includes two Eastern religions (Hinduism and Buddhism) and three Western religions (Judaism, Christianity, and Islam). The Western religions are *monotheistic*, believing that there is only one God, while the Eastern religions are either *polytheistic*, believing in multiple Gods (e.g., Hinduism, some forms of Buddhism) or not believing in a deity (e.g., some forms of Buddhism). Eastern religions are less insistent on the primacy of their "truth" than the Western religions and are more likely to embrace nonviolence. Eastern religions have also tended to be less centrally organized than the Western religions.

Conflict perspective

Each of the major world religions has changed over time and place and become more diverse. Lester Kurtz suggests that we should speak of all the major world religions in the plural: Hinduisms, Buddhisms, Judaisms, Christianities, and Islams. He also argues that some of the most violent contests occur *within* these religious traditions and not *between* them, as experienced by the Christian Catholics and Protestants in Northern Ireland and the Muslim Sunnis and Shias in some Muslim countries.

Each of the major world religions, but especially the Western religions, has an internal struggle, sometimes called a culture war (Hunter, 1994), between a branch of traditionalists and a branch of modernists (Kurtz, 2012). *Traditionalists* believe that moral obligations are rigid, given, and absolute. *Modernists* believe that moral commitment is voluntary, conditional, and fluid. These two branches often engage in a struggle for the heart and soul of the religious tradition, sometimes using violence to press their case.

Although many religious peoples around the world fear that modernism and postmodernism are destroying religion, there is clear evidence that the religious institution is quite resilient. Public opinion polls consistently report that religion is important in the lives of a great majority of people in the United States, and yet, a great majority

of people also believe that religion is losing its influence (Gallup, 2013). International data indicate that people in the United States have much higher weekly attendance at religious services than Europeans; they spend more time in private devotions and more money on religious activities than residents of other advanced industrialized countries. In 2012, about 60% of the U.S. population were church members, compared with about 10% in 1776 (Gallup, 2013; Kurtz, 2012). As suggested in Chapter 6, diversity is the hallmark of the religious institution in the United States today, with about 1,500 to 2,000 religious groups represented, about half of them Christian (Kurtz, 2012; Parrillo, 2009). Indeed, the United States might be the most religiously diverse country in the world today.

Christianity remains dominant within the

Conflict perspective

United States, but there are intense culture wars between traditionalists and modernists, with the conflict centering on such issues as the definition of family, the role of women, the beginning and end of life, same-sex relationships, prayer in school, and theories of the creation of the world. Both traditionalists and modernists base their arguments on their understanding of biblical texts, but each tends to see the other as immoral. Some examples will help to clarify the competing moral precepts regarding some of these questions. Traditionalists see the push for women's rights as destructive to the traditional family and motherhood. Modernists see women's rights as necessary in a just society. Likewise, traditionalists see the gay rights movement as a particularly vicious attack on the traditional family, and modernists see it as a struggle for dignity. Traditionalists argue that school prayer is essential to help students develop a moral code, and modernists argue that it is an intrusion on religious freedom and tolerance. The culture wars are intense because both groups wish for dominance in the political institution.

On the global scale, Lester Kurtz (2012) suggests that each of the world's major religions has something to offer to the effort to find a way for religious groups to peacefully coexist:

Hinduism: The idea that there are many paths to the same summit

Buddhism: The idea that the way to escape suffering is to treat all creatures with compassion

Judaism: The idea that we should be a light for others

Christianity: The ideas of loving one's enemies and bringing good news to the poor

Islam: The call for intensity of commitment

Given the clear evidence of the central importance of religion in the lives of billions of people in the world, social workers must become comfortable in assessing the role of religion and spirituality in the lives of their client systems at the individual, family, and community levels. We should not assume that all persons of a religious group hold the same beliefs regarding social issues. But we must be aware of religious beliefs—both our own and those of clients— when working with controversial social issues.

Trends in the Mass Media Institution

As she does her household chores, Leticia Renteria often watches television, but she has considered taking a break from TV. More often than not, she feels devalued, frightened, and dismayed by what she sees and hears about such political issues as the minimum wage and immigration policy. On the other hand, watching Telemundo (a U.S. network that broadcasts in Spanish with closed captions in both English and Spanish) helps her stay in touch with her Latino heritage and make connections between the English and Spanish languages.

The **mass media institution** is the primary institution for managing the flow of information, images, and ideas among all members of society. Mass media serves an entertainment role for society, but it also influences how we understand ourselves and the world. Mass media technology is the engine of globalization, giving people worldwide immediate access to other cultures and other markets. Rapid advances in electronic communication technology since the 1950s have resulted in widespread access to multiple forms of mass communication—"old media" such as newspapers, magazines, books, radio, television, and film and "new media" such as the Internet, digital television and radio, MP3 players, ever more elaborate multifunctional smartphones, and video games. Electronic media now allow two-way as well as one-way communication, and they can store and manipulate vast amounts of information. The mass media is thoroughly embedded in our daily lives and a larger focus of our leisure time than any other social institution (Devereux, 2013).

There are several important trends in the mass media landscape.

1. *Growth in media outlets and media products.* When the United States was founded, there was only one form of mass media: print. For much of the latter half of the 20th century, U.S. households had access to three television channels, but now there are hundreds of cable and satellite channels (Croteau, Hoynes, & Milan, 2012). New media products have been coming at a very fast clip, giving us new mobile devices (for example, smartphones, tablets, MP3 players, e-readers) and new Internet-based outlets (for example, Hulu, Netflix, iTunes, YouTube, Facebook, Twitter).

2. *More time and money spent on media products.* According to U.S. census data, U.S. households had an average of 8 radios and 2.8 television sets in 2010 (U.S. Census Bureau, 2010). In 2012, 81% of all U.S. households paid for some kind of cable, satellite, or telecom television (Farrell, 2013). In 2010, adults 18 and older spent an average of 4.4 hours a day viewing television (Croteau et al., 2012). However, from 2008 to 2012, about 3.7 million U.S. households, mostly composed of young adults, cut their cable, satellite, and other paid television subscriptions to use web-streaming sites or other over-the-air services. This does not mean less time spent on mass media, however. The typical Verizon customer has been reported to have seven Internet-connected devices in the household, and it is estimated that Americans

Photos 9.4a & 9.4b Mass media technology is the engine of globalization, and people around the world are saturated with images from multiple media forms. In Photo 9.4a, a man sits next to a billboard promoting Chinese wine in Chengdu. In Photo 9.4b, a woman logs in to her Facebook page.

© Liu Jin/AFP/Getty Images; © Karen Bleier/AFP/Getty Images

spend 1.7 hours per week watching video on smartphones and 8.2 hours watching on computers (Farrell, 2013). One study found that, by 2009, youth ages 8 to 18 averaged more than 7.5 hours a day engaged in entertainment media of some sort, including television, music, computers, and video games (Rideout, Foehr, & Roberts, 2010). The percentage of U.S. adults with home Internet access nearly doubled from 2000 to 2010, from 37% to 72% (Croteau et al., 2012). In 2013, 91% of U.S. adults were using cell phones (Rainie, 2013) and three quarters of the world's inhabitants had access to a mobile phone in 2012 (World Bank, 2012).

3. *Integration of media functions.* Increasingly, one media product is expected to provide several functions. Desktop and laptop computers can be used to word process, but they can also be used to surf the Internet; communicate by e-mail, instant message, social networking sites, or Skype; participate in chat rooms and blogs; shop; play music; stream audio and video presentations; or read online newspapers. Tablets and smartphones can perform most of these same functions, except word processing; in addition, they can take and transmit photographs and be used to make telephone calls or communicate by text message.

4. *Audiences as communicators and creators.* In the early days of the Internet, users formed an audience to read or watch content online. Certainly, we still use the Internet in this way, but now we can also have conversations and create content to share with others (Croteau et al., 2012; Hinton & Hjorth, 2013). Here are some examples: writing a review of a product on Amazon.com, updating our Facebook page or downloading material to share with our Friends, creating a video for YouTube, posting photos on Flickr, posting a blog entry, writing a tweet, or commenting on a news item.

5. *Globalization.* Media companies are increasingly targeting a global market to sell products. For example, Viacom International Media Networks reports that it includes many of the world's most popular multimedia brands seen globally in 700 million households in more than 160 countries and 37 languages. If you visit www.viacom.com/brands/pages/default.aspx, you can engage an interactive map that allows you to see the global span of each of its brands. You might be interested to note that Comedy Central and MTV have the largest global reach of the Viacom brands. Some critics suggest that the global reach of media companies based in North America and Europe, particularly in the United States, is a form of cultural imperialism through which U.S. cultural values are spread around the world (Croteau et al., 2012; Devereux, 2013).

6. *Concentration of ownership.* The mass media institution has been experiencing a merger mania. In 1983, the majority of all media products in the United States were controlled by 50 media companies. By 2004, although there were many new media products, five global conglomerates controlled the media business in the United States: Time Warner (U.S.), Disney (U.S.), News Corporation (Britain), Viacom (U.S.), and Bertelsmann (Germany) (Bagdikian, 2004). Since that time, these major conglomerates have continued to be involved in mergers, some successful and some not. Media companies were hit hard in the market crash in 2008 and have done some slimming down, and spin-offs of some parts of the conglomeration have become more common (*The Economist*, 2013).

In totalitarian societies, such as North Korea, the flow of information, images, and ideas is controlled by the government. In the United States, we have a long tradition of freedom of the press—a belief that the media must be free to serve as a public watchdog. Traditionally, the emphasis has been on the watchdog role in relation to the government and political institution—in other words, a press that is not controlled by the government. In the current era of media mergers and acquisitions, concerns have centered on media censorship by the economic institution. Critics suggest that powerful multinational media corporations censor the coverage of news to protect their economic or political interests. Organizations that analyze freedom of the press report that after 2 decades of improvement around the world, there was a decline in press freedom in recent years, and in 2013 only 14.5% of the world's citizens lived in countries with a free press (Freedom House, 2013). These organizations rated the United States as 32nd in freedom of the press in 2013, down from 21st in 2009. The highest marks went to the northern European countries (Freedom House, 2013; Reporters Without Borders, 2013).

In recent years, there is considerable concern about how the media abuses citizen privacy. There is concern about how social networking sites like Facebook violate users' privacy. There is concern about how commercial sites engage in information gathering, profiling, and data mining on "free" online platforms in order to market their products (Croteau et al., 2012). There is concern about how media companies hack phones to gather information for news stories. As this chapter is being written in late 2013, there is considerable concern in the United States about how the government uses a variety of technologies to mine data on its citizens.

It is estimated that there were about 2.4 billion Internet users around the world in June 2012, but there are great regional disparities in access to the Internet. The latest global analysis indicates that North America has the highest percentage of its population online (78.6%), compared with 67.6% in Oceania/Australia, 63.2% in Europe, 42.9% in Latin America/Caribbean, 40.2% in the Middle East, 27.5% in Asia, and 15.6% in Africa (Internet World Stats, 2012). By far, English and Chinese are the most used languages in Internet content, but Japanese and German speakers are much more likely than speakers of other languages to use the Internet. The greatest growth in Internet usage from 2000 to 2011 occurred among people who speak Arabic (2,501.2% increase), Russian (1,825.8%), and Chinese (1,478.7%) (Internet

World Stats, 2010). Going forward, the digital divide will play an important role in systems of inequality between and within countries and is an issue for social work advocacy.

Mass media critics suggest that control of the media by political and economic elites results in control of cultural meanings to benefit elites and silence dissident views.

Conflict perspective

The mass media in the United States has historically been controlled by White, middle- and upper-class men, who have presented their worldviews. Mass media owners are interested in attracting affluent consumers and choose content with this aim in mind (Croteau et al., 2012). Women, people of color, low-income people, sexual minorities, and people with disabilities are underrepresented in media presentations, and when they are represented, the images are often unflattering. There has been some improvement in this situation in the past 2 decades, but there is still a long way to go. Historically, nondominant groups have developed alternative media to compensate for their absence or poor treatment in the dominant media. That is still the case today and is becoming a much easier task with the new Internet-based media (Wilson, Gutiérrez, & Chao, 2013). Leticia Renteria is well aware of the negative images of immigrants that are often seen in the mass media in the United States. Social workers should be aware of how national and local media represent nondominant groups in their communities and collaborate with others to develop fairer representations.

Trends in the Family and Kinship Institution

You undoubtedly would agree that family and kinship relationships are a very important part of the unfolding story of Leticia Renteria and her family. Extended family members provided Leticia with a place to live and other types of support when she moved to the United States. Her cousins helped her return to the United States after she made a voluntary departure to avoid deportation. Her husband and children are the focus of her life. Family and kinship is the most basic social institution, and in simple societies it fulfills many of the functions assigned to other social institutions in complex societies. Although the functions of family and kinship have been the subject of some controversy in the contemporary era, most societies generally agree that the **family and kinship institution** is primarily responsible for the regulation of procreation, for the initial socialization of new members of society, and for the economic, emotional, and physical care of its members.

As the primary unit of every society, families are altered as the result of social change, and globalization is changing family life in some extraordinary ways around the world (Karraker, 2013). There are increasingly diverse ways of being a family around the globe, and there seems to be an exception for almost every family trend identified. However, we can identify three global trends in family life.

1. *Modified extended family form.* Historically, the extended family has been more important in Latin America, Asia, and Africa than in Europe and North America. Globalization appears to be leading to some convergence toward a *modified extended family*, a family system in which family members are highly involved with each other but maintain separate dwellings (Leeder, 2004). This is the current family form for Leticia Renteria's family, where family members maintain households across national lines, making them one of the growing numbers of *transnational families*. Within this general pattern, there are many variations. In wealthy advanced industrialized societies, governmental programs augment the care of dependent family members, but such programs are not typically available in nonindustrial or newly industrializing societies. Marriages continue to be arranged by elders in many parts of the world, particularly in African and Asian societies, but they are based on love matches in Western societies. *Monogamy*, or marriage to one person at a time, is the norm in Western societies, but *polygamy*, or marriage to multiple partners, is still followed in some parts of

the world. Increasingly, families are formed based on commitments that do not involve legal marriage (McGoldrick, Carter, & Garcia-Preto, 2011a; Walsh, 2012a).

2. *Mass migration.* Migration for a better life is not new; indeed, it is the history of the United States. From 1810 to 1921, 34 million people emigrated from Europe to the United States (McMichael, 2012). With economic globalization, many rural peasants in nonindustrialized and newly industrializing countries have been displaced by large agricultural corporations, many headquartered in the United States; some move to the cities in their own countries, and others immigrate to countries with greater economic opportunities. Many migrate because their labor became obsolete in a constantly reorganizing global market. Still others migrate to escape war or political persecution. By one account, 75% of refugees and displaced persons are women and children (McMichael, 2012). Often families are separated, with some members migrating and others staying behind, sometimes to migrate at a later stage. Migrants seek to earn money for families back home, and it is estimated that 100 million people globally depend on the remittances from family members who have migrated (McMichael, 2012). In affluent societies, such as the United States, some industries welcome the cheap labor of undocumented immigrants, and wealthy households welcome the access to cheap household servants. Yet an ongoing backlash and political fear campaigns have developed against immigrants from low-income nations. Anti-immigrant sentiment has been particularly strong in Europe in recent years (Nisbet, 2013).

3. *Feminization of wage labor.* In many parts of the world, women are increasingly involved in wage labor, in newly industrializing as well as highly industrialized societies (Karraker, 2013). For example, women make up 80% of the labor force in the export processing zones of Taiwan, the Philippines, Sri Lanka, Mexico, and Malaysia. In these export zones, women typically work longer hours at lower wages than men (McMichael,

2012). In the United States, families in which both parents work outside the home have become the norm, but from 2007 to 2011, during the recession, the percentage of married couples with two adult earners declined from 69% to 65%. This decline is explained by increased unemployment, which affected men as well as women (Payne & Gibbs, 2013). And yet there is a global gender wage gap. In the United States, the wage gap has been narrowing. In 2013, the median hourly earnings of women was 84% of the earnings of men, up from about 65% in 1980. Also in 2013, millennial women ages 25 to 34 earned 93% of what men of the same age earned. In interpreting these data, it is important to remember that millennial women were significantly more likely than their male same-age peers to have completed a bachelor's degree, 38% compared with 31%. The researchers noted that recent cohorts of women have fallen further behind their same-age male peers as they aged (Pew Research Social & Demographic Trends, 2013). Although the gender wage gap is somewhat lower in some European countries, it is much larger in many parts of the world (McMichael, 2012; Newman, 2012).

Three other trends are more characteristic of the United States and other late-industrial societies than of the preindustrial and newly industrializing societies but are occurring, nevertheless, in societies around the world (Adams & Trost, 2005).

1. *A rise in divorce rates.* An increase in divorce and separation is well documented in Argentina, China, Cuba, India, Iran, Kenya, and Kuwait (Adams & Trost, 2005). The divorce rate in the United States peaked in 1981 and has been declining gradually since then but still remains considerably higher than the 1960 rate. The United States has one of the highest divorce rates in the Global North countries (Ballantine & Roberts, 2014).

2. *Declining fertility.* Declining fertility has been documented in Argentina, India, Iran, Kenya, Kuwait, South Africa, and Turkey (Adams & Trost, 2005). The overall birthrate in the United States

declined to a record low in 2011, declining by 9% during the recession from 2007 to 2011. But hidden in this overall birthrate is a story about the changing pattern of maternal age at the time of childbirth. In 2011, the birthrate hit an all-time low among women in their teens and early 20s but rose to the highest rate in 4 decades among women in their early 40s (Pew Research Center, 2013).

3. *Increasing number of lone-parent families.* In 2012, 29.5% of all households with children in the United States were lone-parent family households. This is the highest rate among Global North countries. Northern European countries also have high rates of lone-parent households (for example, 25% in the United Kingdom and 21.7% in Denmark and Germany), but the southern European countries have low rates (for example, 5% in Spain and 7% in Italy) (Ritzer, 2013a). As noted earlier, lone-parent families are more likely to be poor than two-parent families.

Two other long-term trends in family relationships are likely to continue: greater valuing of autonomy and self-direction in children, as opposed to obedience and conformity, and equalization of power between men and women. These trends have been found to be almost universal, but they are more problematic in some societies than in others (Adams & Trost, 2005). Not all people agree that these trends are good, and some point to them as causes of the weakening of the family. Other people see these trends as providing possibilities for stabilizing the family in a time of great change in all major social institutions.

The average life expectancy is increasing in all of the advanced industrialized societies. In the United States, it increased from 68.2 years in 1950 to 79 years in 2011 (World Health Organization, 2013). This increase in longevity, added to the decrease in fertility, is changing the shape of families in the late-industrial societies. Families now have more generations but fewer people in each generation. The increase in longevity has also led to an increase in chronic disease and the need for families to provide personal care for members with disabilities.

Social service programs serving families, children, and older adults need to be responsive to these changing trends. The confluence of declining family size, increasing numbers of single parents, increasing numbers of women in the paid labor force, and an aging population calls for a reexamination, in particular, of our assumptions about family caregiving for dependent persons. Social workers should lead the way in discussions about social policies that can strengthen families and alleviate family stressors. We must pay particular attention to the needs of immigrant families like the family of Leticia Renteria. These issues receive greater attention in Chapter 10.

Critical Thinking Questions 9.4

What would life be like without the mass media? How would you find out about national and global events? Where would you get your ideas about social welfare, religion, and family? How would your daily life be different? What are some recent media images you have observed about the social welfare and family and kinship institutions? About immigration?

THEORIES OF SOCIAL INEQUALITY

Throughout this chapter, we have presented information on how social

Conflict perspective

inequality is created and maintained in eight interrelated major social institutions. **Social class** is the term generally used by sociologists to describe contemporary structures of inequality. Perhaps no question regarding the human condition has generated more intense and complex controversies and conflicts than the related issues of inequality and distributive justice. Unequal distribution of resources is probably as old as the human species and certainly has existed in all complex societies. Long before the discipline of sociology arose, thoughtful people constructed explanations and justifications for these inequalities (Lenski, 1966; Sernau, 2014). Although social class has been an important topic for sociology, by no means do sociologists agree about the role it plays in human behavior.

The contributing authors and I have presented inequality as a problem, but as you have probably noted, not everyone agrees with this view. Gerhard Lenski (1966) did a careful study of how societies over time have answered the question of whether inequality is a good or bad thing. He divided the way societies have responded to this question into a conservative thesis and a radical antithesis. In the **conservative thesis**, inequality is the natural, divine order, and no efforts should be made to alter it. In the **radical antithesis**, equality is the natural, divine order; inequality is based on abuse of privilege and should be minimized.

Classical Sociological Theories of Social Inequality

When social inequality is considered to be the natural order and divinely ordained, there is no need to search further for explanations of inequality. But as this traditional assumption gave way to a belief that human beings are born equal, persistent social inequalities required explanation and justification. Explanation of inequality and its relationship to human behavior became central to the emerging social and political sciences. Two classical theorists, Karl Marx (1818–1883) and Max Weber (1864–1920), have had lasting impact on the sociological analysis of social inequality.

Karl Marx was both a social theorist and a committed revolutionary. He was interested in explaining the social inequalities of industrial capitalism, but his interests went beyond explanation of inequality to promotion of a more just and equitable society. Marx (1887/1967) emphasized the economic determinants of social class relationships and proposed that class lines are drawn according to roles in the capitalist production system. Although he did not propose a strict, two-class system, he suggested a social class division based on a dichotomy of owners and controllers of production (bourgeoisie), on the one hand, and workers who must sell their labor to owners (proletariat), on the other. Marx saw the relationship between the classes to be based on exploitation and domination by the owners and controllers of production and on alienation among the workers. He saw social class as a central variable in human behavior and a central force in human history and believed that *class consciousness*—not only the awareness of one's social class but also hostility toward other classes—is what motivates people to transform society.

In contrast to Marx, who was a revolutionary, Weber argued for a value-free social science. Weber differed from Marx in other ways as well. Marx saw a class division based on production roles (owners of production and workers); Max Weber (1947) saw a class division based on "life chances" in the marketplace. *Life chances* reflect the distribution of power within a community, including economic power, social prestige, and legal power. Instead of Marx's dichotomous class system, Weber proposed that life chances fall on a continuum and that the great variability found along the continuum reflects the multiple sources of power. He suggested that social class is an important variable in human behavior but not, as Marx believed, the *primary* variable.

This difference in perspective on the causal importance of social class reflects the theorists' disagreement about the inevitability of class consciousness or class action. Marx saw class consciousness and communal action related to class as inevitable. Weber saw social class as a possible, but not inevitable, source of identity and communal action.

The Contemporary Debate

Attempts to determine the cause of persistent social inequalities have led to debate among sociologists who embrace functional theories and sociologists who embrace conflict theories. *Functional theories* of social stratification present structural inequality (social classes) as necessary for society. According to this view, unequal rewards for different types of work guarantee that the most talented persons will work hard and produce technological innovation to benefit the whole society. *Conflict theorists* (see Chapter 2 for more discussion of conflict theories), on the other hand, emphasize the role of power, domination, and coercion in the maintenance of inequality. According to this view, persons with superior wealth and income also hold superior social and political power and use that power to protect their privileged positions.

Sociological functionalism was dominant in U.S. sociology during the 1940s and 1950s, but it faded in importance after that. However, functionalism was the root for *modernization theory*, which attempted, in the 1960s, to explain on the global level why some countries are poor and others are rich (Rostow, 1990). These theorists suggested that poverty is caused by traditional attitudes and technology—by the failure to modernize. The conflict perspective counterargument to modernization theory was *dependency theory*, which argued that poor societies are created by worldwide industrial capitalism, which exploits natural resources and labor (Frank, 1967). These theorists emphasized the tremendous power of foreign multinational corporations to coerce national governments in poor nations. They called attention to colonial imperialism as the historical context of contemporary global inequalities (Sernau, 2014).

The recent debate has been between neoliberalism and the world systems perspective. *Neoliberalism* is based in classic economics and argues that free trade and free markets, with limited government interference, will result in a fair distribution of resources. As suggested earlier, this philosophy has been dominant across the world for the past few decades but is currently being challenged on several fronts. Economists at the World Bank and IMF have been strong voices in favor of neoliberalism, which informed the ideals of their structural adjustment program for dealing with the debts of impoverished nations. *Structural adjustment* called for poor countries to "clean house" by reducing government spending and bureaucracy and increasing exportation and entrepreneurship. To counter this view, the *world systems perspective*

suggests that inequality is created and maintained by economic globalization (Wallerstein, 1974, 1980, 1989). Under this perspective, the world is divided into three sectors: a *core sector* that dominates the capitalist world economy and exploits the world's resources, a *peripheral sector* that provides raw material to the core and is heavily exploited by it, and a *semiperipheral sector* that is somewhat independent but very vulnerable to the financial fluctuations of the core states. The core currently includes the United States, western Europe, and Japan; the periphery includes much of Africa, South Asia, and Latin America; and the semiperiphery includes such places as Spain, Portugal, Brazil, Mexico, Venezuela, and oil-producing countries in the Middle East (Leeder, 2004; McMichael, 2012). According to the world systems perspective, the hegemony of the core sector is reinforced by neocolonial practices of such transnational institutions as the World Bank, the IMF, and the WTO.

Structural Determinism Versus Human Agency

Will knowledge of my social class position help you to predict my attitudes and behaviors? That question has become a controversial one for contemporary social science. Social scientists who see human behavior as highly determined by one's position in the social class structure (*structural determinism*) are challenged by social scientists who emphasize the capacity of humans to create their own realities and who give central roles to human actors, not social structures (*human agency*).

Macro-oriented sociologists have taken Émile Durkheim's lead in arguing that human action is a by-product of social institutions external to human consciousness. Micro-oriented sociologists have taken Max Weber's lead in the counterargument that humans are proactive agents who construct meaning in interaction with others. In a position more consistent with the multidimensional framework of this book, Anthony Giddens (1979) has proposed *structuration theory*, a theory of the relationship between human agency and social structure. Giddens notes that social practices repeat themselves in patterned ways over time and in space, structured by the rules and resources embedded in social institutions. While acknowledging the constraints that rules and resources place on human action, he also notes that human agents have the ability to make a difference in the social world. Human actions produce social structure, and at all times human action is serving either to perpetuate or to transform social structure. You may recognize that this is very similar to the practice approach to culture presented in Chapter 8. Some critics have suggested that Giddens is too optimistic about how much agency humans have, but Giddens acknowledges that those with the most power have a disproportionate opportunity to reinforce institutional arrangements that perpetuate their positions of power.

Structuration theory is a good framework for social workers. It calls our attention to power arrangements that constrain the behaviors of some actors more than others in a way that perpetuates social injustice. But it also calls our attention to the possibilities for human action to transform social institutions. Mary Ellen Kondrat (1999) suggests that structuration theory poses two questions that, when raised, provide critical consciousness,

a necessary ingredient for progressive change agents. **Critical consciousness** can be defined as an ongoing process of reflection and knowledge seeking about mechanisms and outcomes of social, political, and economic oppression that requires taking personal and collective action toward fairness and social justice. The first question raised by Kondrat is, "How aware are we of the ways in which social institutions and social structure condition our behaviors?" The second question is, "How aware are we of the ways in which our day-to-day activities over time perpetuate or transform social structure?" Just as individual agency is essential for individual change, collective agency is essential for changing social institutions. That is the central point of the final chapter in this book, the chapter on social movements.

Critical Thinking Questions 9.5

Which social institutions have the greatest impact on your day-to-day life? What are some ways that your day-to-day activities perpetuate the existing social structure? What are some ways that your day-to-day activities have the potential to change social structure?

Implications for Social Work Practice

The trends in social institutions and social structure discussed in this chapter suggest several principles for social work practice. These practice principles have the greatest relevance for social work planning and administration, but some are relevant for direct social work practice as well.

- Develop adequate information retrieval skills to keep abreast of trends in the interrelated social institutions and the impact of these trends on human interdependence and dependence.
- Monitor the impact of public policies on poverty and inequality.
- Learn to use political processes to promote social services that contribute to the well-being of individuals and communities.
- Be particularly aware of the impact of trends in the economic institution on client resources and functioning.
- Collaborate with other social workers and human service providers to advocate for greater equality of opportunity in the educational institution.
- Work to ensure that the voices of poor and other oppressed people are included in ongoing public dialogue about health care reform.

- Consider the extent to which contemporary social welfare programs, especially those with which you are personally involved, are responsive to recent changes in the other major social institutions.
- Take the lead in public discourse about the fit between the current social welfare institution and trends in the other major social institutions.
- Be aware of the role religious organizations play in social service delivery and the role religion plays in the lives of clients.
- Collaborate with other social workers and human service providers to influence media coverage of vulnerable populations and patterns of social inequality.
- Review social service programs serving children, older adults, and other dependent persons to ensure they are responsive to changes in the family and kinship institution as well as the economic institution.

Key Terms

bifurcate
colonialism
conservative thesis
critical consciousness
economic institution
educational institution
family and kinship institution
Gini index

government and political
    institution
health care institution
mass media institution
neocolonialism
neoliberal philosophy
outsourcing
radical antithesis

religious institution
role
social class
social institution
social structure
social welfare institution
status
transnational corporation (TNC)

Active Learning

1. In the case study at the beginning of the chapter, Leticia Renteria is eager to legalize her immigrant status to ensure that she can stay in the United States rather than return to her native Mexico. One way to begin to understand her motivation to stay in the United States is to do a comparative analysis of social indicators in the two countries. To do this, you can make use of some of the many web resources that contain statistics on global well-being, including the following:

- *www.census.gov.* Official site of the U.S. Census Bureau. Under People, click on International Data Base (IDB). You can select specific countries and years and get key summary information about the social health of the countries.
- *www.unicef.org.* Official site of the United Nations Children's Fund. Click on Statistics and then on Country Statistics. You can select a specific country and access data on the status of children in that country.
- *www.undp.org.* Site of the United Nations Development Program. Click on Publications, and then click on the latest Human Development Report. You will get country-by-country information on the Human Development Index and the latest report on efforts to meet the millennium development goals.

Use these three resources, or other relevant resources, to prepare a statistical overview of the social health of the United States and Mexico. What are the areas of similarity? Main areas of difference? What indicators seem to be the most important in understanding Leticia Renteria's motivation to stay in the United States?

2. We have looked at the conservative thesis and the radical antithesis in an ongoing debate about the role of inequality in social life. Talk to at least five people about this issue, including at least one member of your family and at least one friend. Ask each person the following questions:

- Is inequality a good thing for a society? If not, why not? If so, in what way, and good for whom?
- If we accept inequality as inevitable, how much is necessary? Should society try to maximize or minimize the amount of inequality?
- On what criteria should we measure inequality?
- If we seek equality, is it equality of opportunity or of outcomes?

What kinds of positions did people take? How did they support their arguments? Did you find more support for the conservative thesis or the radical antithesis in the responses you heard?

Web Resources

**Center for Responsive Politics: www
.opensecrets.org**

Site maintained by the nonpartisan Center for Responsive Politics contains information on major organizational and individual contributors, the money collected and spent by major political candidates, and political news and issues.

**The Civil Rights Project: civilrightsproject
.ucla.edu**

Site presented by the Civil Rights Project, which was founded at Harvard University in 1996 and in 2007 moved to UCLA, presents data that track racial achievement gaps in the United States.

**Pew Research Internet Project: www
.pewinternet.org**

Site presented by the Pew Research Center's Internet Project presents reports on the impact of the Internet on families, communities, work and home, daily life, education, health care, and civic and political life.

**United Nations Children's Fund: www
.unicef.org**

Site contains cross-national information on the well-being of children.

U.S. Census Bureau: www.census.gov

Official site of the U.S. Census Bureau contains statistics on a wide variety of topics, including race and ethnicity, gender, education, birthrates, disabilities, and many other topics.

**World Health Organization (WHO): www
.who.int**

Site contains information on the health and the health care institutions of countries around the world.

Student Study Site

$SAGE edge™

Sharpen your skills with SAGE edge at **edge.sagepub.com/hutchisonpe5e**

SAGE edge for students provides a personalized approach to help you accomplish your coursework goals in an easy-to-use learning environment.

CHAPTER 10

Families

Elizabeth D. Hutchison

Chapter Outline

Key Ideas

As you read this chapter, take note of these central ideas:

1. How we define family shapes our view of family membership and our approach to working with different types of families.

2. From the earliest days of the United States as a nation, there has been a diversity of family structures and customs.

3. There is general agreement that the most pronounced change in family life in the United States in the past 50 years has been the change in gender roles.

4. A number of theoretical "lenses" for understanding families have been proposed, including the psychodynamic perspective, family systems perspective, family life cycle perspective, feminist perspective, family stress and coping perspective, and family resilience perspective.

5. Social workers encounter a diversity of family structures in their work with families, including nuclear families, extended families, cohabiting heterosexual couples, couples with no children, lone-parent families, stepfamilies, same-sex partner families, and military families.

6. In their work with families, social workers must be sensitive to their economic and cultural influences, as well as their experiences with immigration where relevant.

7. Contemporary families face many challenges, including family violence, divorce, and substance abuse, and often need assistance to cope with these issues.

CASE STUDY

The Sharpe Family's Postdeployment Adjustment

Bobby Sharpe's U.S. Army National Guard unit was deployed to Iraq in 2004 and to Afghanistan in 2010. Bobby suffered a relatively minor physical injury in Iraq and still has occasional nightmares about his tour in Afghanistan. He feels lucky, however, that he and his family have not suffered some of the traumatic postwar aftermath he has seen in the families of some members of his Guard unit.

Bobby Sharpe is a 40-year-old African American man who lives in a small southwestern town. He has been married to Vivian for 17 years, and they have a 16-year-old daughter, Marcie, and a 7-year-old son, Caleb, who has cerebral palsy. Back when Bobby finished high school, he served in the army for 4 years. He received some good training, enjoyed making friends with people from diverse backgrounds, and had two tours overseas but never served in a war zone. After 4 years, he was eager to return home to be near his close-knit family. Soon after returning home, he ran into Vivian, who had grown up in his neighborhood, and they were soon spending a lot of time together. A year later, they were married, and a year after that, Marcie was born.

Bobby wasn't sure what work he could do after he left the army, but a few months after he returned home, he got in touch with a high school friend who was working as a heating and air conditioning technician. After another technician was fired, Bobby got a job where his friend worked, and his friend helped him learn the technical aspects of the heating and air conditioning business. When Marcie was born, Vivian cared for her at home and also cared for her sister's small children while her sister, a single mother, worked. When Bobby's father had an automobile accident and had to miss work for 6 months, Bobby and Vivian provided some financial aid to Bobby's mother and younger siblings while his father was out of work. Finances were tight, and Bobby and Vivian were afraid they would not be able to keep up the mortgage on their house, which was a source of great pride to them. Bobby decided to join the army National Guard to bring in some extra money. He also looked forward to the type of camaraderie he had experienced in the army. He went to drills one weekend per month and took time off from work for a 2-week training each year. His unit was mobilized on two occasions to assist with floods in the state. The extra money helped to stabilize the family economics, and he enjoyed the friendships he developed, even though only one other person in his unit was from his small town. When Marcie entered public school, Vivian took a job in the cafeteria at her school, which allowed Bobby and Vivian to start a college fund for Marcie.

Bobby grew up in a close-knit family that included his mother and father and three younger sisters, as well as a maternal grandmother who lived with them. Several aunts, uncles, and cousins lived nearby. Both parents were hardworking people, and they created a happy home. Bobby's grandmother provided child care when the children were small and helped to keep the household running smoothly.

Vivian grew up a few blocks from Bobby. Her father died in Vietnam a few months before she was born, and her mother moved her two daughters back to the town where she had grown up. She struggled to raise her two daughters while working two jobs, with some help from her mother, who lived in town but also worked two jobs. Vivian was lucky that another neighborhood couple became her godparents and played an active role in her life. This couple was never able to have children of their own, and they were happy to include Vivian in their leisure activities. Vivian often turned to them for support and encouragement, and she continues to consider them family.

During Bobby's deployment to Iraq, Vivian and Marcie were able to get along fine, with the love and support of Bobby's family; Vivian's mother, sister, and godparents; and Bobby's boss. They missed Bobby and worried about him, but Marcie was very good about picking up more responsibilities to help Vivian with the chores usually performed by Bobby. When the furnace broke, Bobby's boss was generous about doing the repair. One of Bobby's sisters helped Vivian juggle taking Marcie to her afterschool activities and picking her up. Bobby was injured by shrapnel in his last week in Iraq and spent 2 weeks in the hospital in the nearest city when he returned home. The family and friend network took care of Marcie while Vivian juggled trips to the hospital with her work schedule.

But things were more complicated when Bobby was deployed to Afghanistan. Bobby's beloved grandmother had had a stroke 2 years before this deployment, and his mother and father were working opposite shifts at the

(Continued)

(Continued)

local nursing home so that someone was always home to care for her. Bobby's aunts, uncles, and cousins were taking turns providing a few hours of care so that his mom and dad could get a break and run errands. One of Bobby's sisters had stayed in the city after she completed college and had a busy life there. Another sister, a single mother of a 2-year-old daughter, was serving in the army in Iraq when Bobby left for Afghanistan. Her daughter was living with Bobby and Vivian while she was deployed. Bobby and Vivian's son Caleb is the joy of the family, but he requires extra care. While Bobby was deployed, Vivian's mother moved in with Vivian and cared for Caleb and the 2-year-old niece during the day while Vivian worked and then turned their care over to Vivian so that she could do a 6-hour shift caring for an older woman with dementia. To help stabilize the family finances, Vivian accepted the offer to take a supervisory position in the school department's lunch program. She was excited about the new responsibilities, but the demands of the new job were often too much during a time of great family upheaval. Vivian was especially concerned about monitoring Marcie's afterschool activities now that she was approaching adolescence, but her godparents were a great help with that, just as they had been for Vivian during her adolescent years. Vivian had heard that the National Guard had family support groups, but there was nothing in the small town where she lives. Vivian did reach out to the women's group at her church, who provided emotional support as well as occasional meals and transportation for Marcie. Marcie and Caleb missed their dad, and Marcie worried a lot about his safety, especially during the weeks when they did not know his whereabouts.

Bobby returned from Afghanistan with no physical injuries, but his best friend from the Guard lost a leg to a roadside bomb. When Bobby came home, Vivian, Marcie, and Caleb were thrilled and were eager to pick up life where they left off. Bobby wanted to spend a lot of time by himself, however, and Vivian realized that he was having trouble sleeping, sometimes had nightmares, and was easily startled by loud noises. She did some research on the Internet and decided that she needed to give Bobby time to readjust. She did her best to help Marcie and Caleb understand this also. She was pleased, but also worried, when Bobby began to go for long walks and to spend time with a new puppy. After 4 months, Bobby was able to talk about the guilt he felt about surviving when other Guard members had died. He gradually began to be more like his old self and was happy to get back to work. He still makes time to spend with his friend who lost a leg in Afghanistan. He and Vivian are preparing for, but dreading, the day when Marcie will leave for college.

FAMILY DEFINED _____

We know that families are one of the key institutions in almost every society, past and present. Perhaps no other relationships contribute as much to our identity and have such pervasive influence on all dimensions of our lives as our family relationships (Floyd & Morman, 2006). Families address personal needs, but they also contribute to the public welfare by caring for each other and developing responsible members of society (Newman, 2012).

Families in every culture address similar societal needs, but there are many variations in family structure, family customs, and power arrangements.

Around the globe, families are expected to provide economic security, emotional support, and a place in society for each family member; they also fulfill the critical social roles of bearing, providing for, and socializing children and youth. Families respond to these challenges in different ways, due in no small part to different cultures and different political and economic circumstances. Family situations and their access to resources differ as a function of their socioeconomic location. As suggested in Chapter 9, social, cultural, and economic globalization is changing families in the United States and around

> Social constructionist perspective

the world (Gardiner & Kosmitzki, 2011; Leeder, 2004).

So what is a family? We were all born into some sort of family and may have created a similar or different sort of family. Take a break from reading and think about who is family to you. Who is in your family, and what functions does your family perform for you? We hear a lot of talk about family and family values, but family means different things to different people. Even family scholars struggle to define how family is different from other social groups. White, Klein, and Martin (2015d) suggest that family differs from other social groups in degree only. They suggest that nonfamily groups such as friend networks and co-workers often have some of the same properties as families but usually to a lesser degree. Family research is hampered by the lack of consensus about how to define family (Baxter & Braithwaite, 2006). This lack of consensus was consistent in family science throughout the 20th century (Chibucos & Leite, 2005).

The family literature includes many different definitions of family, but the many definitions center on three ways to form a family: biologically, legally, or socially (Floyd & Morman, 2006; Lepoire, 2006). *Biologically*, family refers to people related by blood and genetically bound to each other, however distantly. Examples of biological family relationships include parents, children,

aunts, uncles, second cousins, grandparents, and great-grandparents. Families are created *legally* by marriage, adoption, or formalized fostering. There are many ways that families can be created *socially*, by social interaction, when there is no biological or legal relationship. Sometimes neighbors, godparents, or longtime friends are considered "family." These have been called "fictive kin," but I prefer to refer to them as chosen family. Vivian Sharpe clearly thinks of her godparents as family, and they have come to be family for Marcie as well. Family is increasingly being created by cohabiting romantic partners of either opposite sexes or the same sex. Family may also be created by informal fostering.

Definitions of family include different configurations of biological, legal, and social relationships. Exhibit 10.1 provides a selection of definitions developed by family scholars in the United States, as well as the definition used by the U.S. Census Bureau. It is very difficult to develop one definition that includes all forms of families, but family scholars have attempted to develop inclusive definitions. As you can see, the Census Bureau definition includes families formed biologically and legally but not those formed socially without legal sanction. Think about what types of family would not be considered family by this definition. In contrast to the Census Bureau, the definitions of family scholars Baxter and Braithwaite (2006); Galvin,

Exhibit 10.1 Selected Definitions of Family

Baxter & Braithwaite (2006)	A social group of two or more persons, characterized by ongoing interdependence with long-term commitments that stem from blood, law, or affection
Galvin, Bylund, & Brommel (2003)	Networks of people who share their lives over long periods of time bound by ties of marriage, blood, or commitment, legal or otherwise, who consider themselves as family and who share a significant history and anticipated future of functioning in a family relationship
Leeder (2004)	A group of people who have intimate social relationships and have a history together
Seccombe & Warner (2004)	A relationship by blood, marriage, or affection, in which members may cooperate economically, may care for any children, and may consider identity to be intimately connected to the larger group
U.S. Census Bureau (2013e)	A group of two or more people who reside together and who are related by birth, marriage, or adoption

Bylund, and Brommel (2003); and Seccombe and Warner (2004) include families formed socially along with families formed biologically and legally. Leeder (2004) goes even further with a purely social definition of family. Which of these definitions is the best fit for who you call family?

How do the definitions fit for Bobby and Vivian Sharpe's family? The Census Bureau definition would certainly include Bobby, Vivian, Marcie, and Caleb. It also could embrace Vivian's mother when she lived in the household during Bobby's deployment to Afghanistan. Did it still include Bobby while he was deployed and not living in the household? It is clear that he and other family members still thought of him as family. But what about Bobby's 2-year-old niece? Was she family in the time she spent in the household? Could Vivian sign permission forms if she needed medical care? Who do you think Bobby, Vivian, Marcie, and Caleb consider to be family? How would they define family?

For the purposes of our discussion, I will use the Baxter and Braithwaite (2006) definition of family: **Family** is "a social group of two or more persons, characterized by ongoing interdependence with long-term commitments that stem from blood, law, or affection" (p. 2). Increasingly, we exercise the freedom to use the word *family* to describe the social group with whom we have emotional closeness (a social definition). However, our freedom to define our own families is limited (Newman, 2012). We must interact with organizations that have their own definitions of family and sometimes have the power to impose those definitions on us. Local, state, and federal governments have definitions of family and also have the power to enforce those definitions when providing goods, services, and legal sanctions. Examples include legal standards about who can marry, who inherits from whom, who can benefit from filing joint tax returns, who receives survivor benefits, and who can make medical decisions for another person.

Conflict perspective

Restricted definitions of family have been used by local governments to discourage some groups of immigrant residents. For example, in December 2005, the city of Manassas, Virginia, amended the definition of family in the city code to include nuclear family only, essentially prohibiting extended families from living together. The stated purpose of the amendment was to combat overcrowding, but many critics saw it as a way to discourage Latino/Hispanic families from settling in the city. Under heavy criticism, the zoning amendment was suspended in 2006 (Equal Rights Center, 2007). In the United States and many other countries, the most contentious and public struggle over the tension between legal definitions and social definitions of family involve families formed by same-sex couples, a topic covered later in the chapter.

Many organizations in the private world also impose definitions of family. Health clubs define who can be included in a family membership, corporations decide which family members can receive health coverage, and hospitals decide who has visitation rights in intensive care units. As social workers, we should be most interested in whom a person considers to be family, because that is where social resources can be tapped, but we must also be alert to situations where legal definitions do not recognize a given form of family and how enforcement of those definitions impinges on the lives of particular individuals and families. This is an area that calls for social work activism.

In the United States, *monogamy*, or partnering with one spouse at a time, is the legal way to start a biological family. But anthropologists estimate that 75% of the world's societies prefer some type of *polygamy*, or having more than one spouse at a time (Newman, 2012). Polygamy can take the form of either polygyny (one man and multiple wives) or polyandry (one woman and multiple husbands). Polyandry is much less common than polygyny, however. Polygyny is found on every continent but is most common in Islamic countries, African countries, and parts of Asia (Gardiner & Kosmitzki, 2011). All societies allow monogamy, and, indeed, most people of the world cannot afford to support multiple spouses.

There are cultural variations in the process of mate selection. In most societies, mate selection is governed by both exogamy and endogamy rules. *Exogamy rules* require that mates must be chosen from *outside* the group. Most societies have either formal or informal rules prohibiting mating with specified family members, often referred to as the "incest taboo," but there are differences across cultures about which family members are prohibited. In the United States, 25 states prohibit marriage of first cousins, but 6 states allow it under some circumstances where the couple cannot reproduce, and North Carolina allows first-cousin marriage but prohibits double-cousin marriage (such as a sister and brother marrying cousins who are brother and sister; National Conference of State Legislatures, 2014a). There are also some informal exogamy taboos against mating with people within other groups, such as in the same university dorm (dormcest) and with people in the workplace (workcest) (Newman, 2012). *Endogamy rules*, on the other hand, require that mates should be selected from within the group on characteristics such as religion, race and ethnicity, and social class. Bobby and Vivian were honoring these rules when they chose each other, but endogamy rules are loosening in many places.

In the United States and other Western societies, mate selection is a culmination of romantic love, and it is often assumed that there is one true love in the world for each one of us. In many Eastern societies, marriages are arranged, and it is generally assumed that there are several possible mates with whom one can establish a successful long-term relationship. It is also assumed that parents will make wiser decisions than young people would make for themselves. In countries like Japan, however, love marriages are beginning to replace arranged marriages (Gardiner & Kosmitzki, 2011).

THE FAMILY IN HISTORICAL PERSPECTIVE

Social constructionist perspective; conflict perspective

I often hear people lament the demise of the family. Maybe you hear this as well. To understand whether there is reality in this lament, it is necessary to place the contemporary family in a historical context. This is a daunting task, however. For one thing, the family has never been a monolithic institution. The structure and functions of families always varied according to race, ethnicity, religion, sexual orientation, social class, and so on. Most of what has been written about the family historically was written from the perspective of dominant members of society. It is only since the 1960s, when the discipline of social history began to describe the lives of women and other marginalized groups, that we have a more complete understanding of the variety of ways families have adapted to the challenges they've faced in their lives. When people in the United States talk about the "golden age of the traditional family," they are typically talking about one particular group of families: White, middle-class, heterosexual, two parent families living in the 1950s. Social historians argue that the rosy picture usually painted about this group is really something that never existed. It is important to remember that a great diversity of family structures and functions has existed in the United States and around the world over time.

For another thing, in the United States, because we are a very young country, we tend to have a very short view of history. A longer-term tracing of the history of families worldwide would be the subject of multiple books. So, for

Exchange and choice perspective

the longer-term global view, I will simply note two important themes. First, it seems clear that families have adapted both their structures and their functions over time to cope with the changing nature of societies, as hunting and gathering societies gave way to horticultural societies, which gave way to agrarian societies, which gave way to industrial societies, and industrial societies are giving way to postindustrial societies focused on information, services, and technology. Second, a global understanding of the family in contemporary times must take account of the effects of colonialism. As the United States and European countries exploited local people in colonized countries, family life was directly impacted in both the colonizing and colonized countries. Most recently, families have been separated as some members relocate to find work, sometimes relocating from rural areas to cities within their own country and other times moving to wealthier countries where work is more plentiful. The case study in Chapter 13 provides an example of the impact of these relocations on both families and communities.

Any discussion of the history of the family in the United States should begin with the Native peoples who predated the White settlers from Europe. The Native peoples included more than 2,000 cultures and societies, each with its own set of family customs and lifestyles (Leeder, 2004). There were some similarities across these societies, however. As with other societies, social life was organized around the family. Affection was lavished on children, who were never spanked or beaten. Children were instructed and disciplined by numerous caregivers in the extended family. There was a clear gender division of labor, with women growing crops and caring for the home and property and men hunting, fishing, and waging war. In many Native societies, however, women were afforded a great deal of respect and power (Ho, Rasheed, & Rasheed, 2004).

The White settlers established small, privately owned agricultural enterprises, and families performed many of the functions that have since been turned over to other institutions such as hospitals, schools, and social welfare agencies. David Fischer's (1989) historical analysis found regional differences in the organization of family life among the White settlers. From 1629 to 1775, four major waves of English-speaking immigrants settled in what became the United States of America. Each wave of immigrants came from a different part of what is now the United Kingdom and brought their own family customs with them. Fischer argues that in spite of later waves of immigration and much interregional mobility, these regional differences in family customs have endured to some degree over time. See what you think.

1. *The Puritans.* The Puritans came from the east of England to Massachusetts from 1629 to 1640. They condemned the pursuit of wealth and avoided wealth inheritance by *partible inheritance*, meaning that property was divided among heirs rather than being passed on to one person. Marriage was highly valued, and family life was organized around a strong nuclear family, but the Puritans approved of divorce if the marriage covenant had been broken. They expected marriage to be based on true love. There was some gender inequality in family life, but women and men worked together, and husbands and wives were involved in mutual decision making. Women were protected from domestic violence by law, and there were high expectations for marital peace and harmony. Small children were seen as evil, and child rearing was based on "will breaking."

2. *The Virginia Cavaliers and indentured servants.* From 1642 to 1675, royalist elite and large numbers of indentured servants came from the south of England to Virginia. Their society was marked by a profoundly unequal distribution of wealth, and slavery was introduced to replace indentured servants who earned their freedom. Primogeniture inheritance, or inheritance of the full estate by the firstborn son, ensured the continued concentration of wealth. There was a lot of intermarrying among a small elite group, with cousin marriage allowed. Family life was organized around a strong sense of extended family, and they lived in neighborhoods based on kin. Much effort went into protecting family reputations. Marriage was highly valued but was expected to be based on social position rather than love. Divorce was not allowed, but there is evidence of much marital discord. Family life was male dominant, and rape was less severely punished than petty theft. Elite men expected servant women to yield to them sexually. Elite children were expected to exercise their will, but children of servants were expected to yield to hierarchy.

3. *The Quakers.* The Quakers came from Wales and the North Midland area of England to the Delaware Valley from 1675 to 1725. They embraced religious freedom, cultural pluralism, and nonviolence. Family life was child-centered

and nuclear. The Quakers had fewer children and more servants than the Puritans but more children and fewer servants than the Cavaliers. Family life was more egalitarian than for the Puritans or Cavaliers, and there were stiff penalties for sex crimes against women. Marriage was based on love, and cousin marriage was forbidden. Children were seen as harmless and innocent, and child rearing was based on the use of rewards.

4. *The Appalachians.* From 1718 to 1775, families left the borderlands between England and Scotland, where they had been the victims of one invasion after another, and settled in the Appalachian backcountry. On the whole, they were an impoverished group of farmers who hoped to improve their economic situation in the new land, but there was a highly unequal distribution of wealth among them. The small population of elite among them intermarried. The Appalachians had a strong sense of extended family and a weak sense of individual privacy. Marriage ties were weaker than blood ties, and families grew into clans. Marriage was full of both love and violence. Family life was male dominant, and women were expected to be hardworking, patient, and submissive. Male children were raised to be willful with a warrior's courage, and female children were raised to be industrious, obedient, patient, sacrificial, and devoted. Child rearing was permissive but punctuated by acts of anger and violence.

As you can see, from the earliest days of the United States as a nation, there were differences in family customs along several dimensions, including gender power arrangements, child-rearing practices, appropriate marriage partners, and nuclear versus extended family. Different attitudes about social inequality were also transmitted through the family. Subsequently, new waves of immigration increased the diversity of family customs.

During the industrial revolution, the economy of the United States and other newly industrializing nations shifted from the family-based economy of small, privately owned farms to a wage-based economic system of large-scale industrial manufacturing. The functions of the family changed to accommodate the changes in the economic system. In the upper and middle classes, men went out to work and women ran the household, but less advantaged women engaged in paid labor as well as family labor. By 1900, one fifth of U.S. women worked outside the home, and many children worked in mines, mills, and factories (Newman, 2012). The great majority of African American women engaged in paid labor, often serving as domestic servants in White households where they were forced to leave their own families and live in the employer's home. Women in other poor families took in piecework so they could earn a wage while also staying in the home. Poorer families also took in boarders to assist the family financially, something that also happened in the earlier agrarian period. Schools took over education, and family life began to be organized around segments of time: the workweek and weekends and summers off from school for children (Leeder, 2004). Rather than the center of work, the family home became a place to retreat from economic activities, and the primary role of the family was to provide emotional support to its members. A new ideal of marriage developed, based on sexual satisfaction, companionship, and emotional support. Family togetherness was never more emphasized than in the 1950s, a period of strong economic health in the United States.

Since the 1950s, personal fulfillment has become a major value in the United States and a number of other information/service/technology societies, but the great majority of people still view loving, committed relationships to be the most important source of happiness and well-being (Kamp Dush & Amato, 2005; Snyder & Lopez, 2007). Family members are often scattered across state and national lines, but the new technologies allow for continued connection. Recently, work and family time is once again comingled in many families, as the new technologies allow more work from home. Unfortunately, this often means that the workday is expanded.

As this discussion suggests, diversity of family structures is not new, but family forms have become increasingly varied in recent decades. Marriage and birthrates have declined, and more adults are living on their own. More children are born to unmarried parents. Divorce and remarriage are creating complex remarried families. Perhaps the biggest change in family structure in recent decades is the increase in dual-earner families, as women increased their involvement in paid labor (Walsh, 2012b).

There is general agreement that the most pronounced change in family life in the United States in the past 50 years is the change in gender roles. By 1960, one third of all workers were women (Gibbs, 2009), but employers typically paid women less than men performing the same job. In addition, as the cable TV series *Mad Men* illustrates, women were often treated in a demeaning manner at work. Females were about half as likely as males to go to college, and less than 10% of students playing high school sports were girls (Gibbs, 2009). When women needed surgery or other medical treatment, they often had to secure the signed consent of husbands or fathers. In many settings, they were not allowed to wear pants in public. (For a comprehensive review of the changes in gender roles in the United States since 1960, see Collins, 2009.) By 2011, women made up 47% of the labor force, and the unemployment rate was slightly higher for men (9.4%) than for women (8.5%). In that same year, 58.1% of women were in the labor force, including 70.9% of mothers with children younger than age 18. Unmarried mothers have higher rates of labor force participation than married mothers, 74.9% compared with 69.1%. Women working full time earned 82% of what men earned in 2011, up from 62% in 1979 (U.S. Bureau of Labor Statistics, 2013b). In Bobby's family, as in many African American families, women have always been in the paid labor force, often working more than one job. In fact, research indicates that gender roles in African American families have typically been applied flexibly to manage work and family demands.

There is evidence that attitudes about women in the labor force are changing. In 1977, 74% of men and 52% of women agreed with the statement that "men should earn the money and women should take care of the children and family"; in 2008, only 40% of men and 37% of women agreed with the statement (Galinsky, Aumann, & Bond, 2011, p. 9). The attitudes of men in dual-earner couples have changed the most. In 2010, 29% of wives in dual-earning couples earned more than their spouses, compared with 18% in 1987 (U.S. Bureau of Labor Statistics, 2013b). In the 2005–2006 academic year, women earned 58% of all bachelor's degrees and 60% of master's degrees (Galinsky et al., 2011). The rate of girls participating in high school sports is also approaching that of males. In addition, women have a larger presence in the public arena, serving in leadership positions in both the private and public sectors. However, women are still underrepresented on university faculties and in boardrooms and legislatures. They have also been charged higher insurance premiums than men, and this became a part of the debate about health care reform in 2009 (Gibbs, 2009). Although men are increasing their participation in child care and household labor, women still perform a larger share of this domestic work (Galinsky et al., 2011).

Unfortunately, business and government in the United States have been slow to respond to the changing needs of families who do not have a full-time mother at home. The Family and Medical Leave Act (FMLA) of 1993 requires employers with more than 50 employees to provide up to 12 weeks of *unpaid* sick leave per year for the birth or adoption of a child or to care for a sick child, parent, or spouse, excluding temporary and part-time workers. With the exemptions, about 40% of U.S. workers are not eligible for FMLA leave, but a good feature of the FMLA is that it covers both male and female workers (Ray, Gornick, & Schmitt, 2009). Compare this with the way that most other countries have responded to the increasing numbers of dual-earner families. One research project found that of 173 countries studied, 168 guarantee *paid* leave to women for childbirth and maternity, 98 countries guarantee at least 14 weeks of paid leave, and 66 guarantee paid paternity leave (Heymann, Earle, & Hayes, 2007). The combined leave employers must provide for both mothers and fathers in the five most generous countries ranges from 18 to 47 weeks. It is important to note, however, that the number of weeks of paid leave offered to fathers ranges from 2 to 7 in these same five countries (Ray et al., 2009).

Not all people in the United States agree that the changes in gender roles are a good trend. Certainly, around the world, there are many societies that have not embraced these changes, even though economic globalization has depended on the cheap labor of women in poor societies working long hours in low-wage jobs (McMichael, 2012).

Critical Thinking Questions 10.1

Where have you gotten your ideas about what it means to be family? Have those ideas changed over time? If so, what influenced those changes? What beliefs do you have about appropriate gender relationships, child-rearing practices, appropriate marriage partners, and nuclear versus extended family? How might those beliefs affect your ability to work with different types of families and families facing different types of challenges?

THEORETICAL PERSPECTIVES FOR UNDERSTANDING FAMILIES

With an understanding of societal trends affecting families as background, you can use a number of theoretical "lenses" to understand family functioning and avenues for positive change. This section introduces six of these theoretical perspectives: the psychodynamic perspective, family systems perspective, family life cycle perspective, feminist perspective, family stress and coping perspective, and family resilience perspective.

Psychodynamic Perspective and Families

> Psychodynamic perspective

Psychodynamic approaches to thinking about families are a mix of ideas from psychodynamic and social systems perspectives. Social workers who approach family situations from this perspective assume that current personal and interpersonal problems are the result of unresolved problems in the **family of origin**, the family into which we were born and/or in which we were raised (Nichols & Schwartz, 2006; Walsh, 2014). They suggest that these unresolved problems continue to be acted out in our current intimate relationships. Patterns of family relationships are passed on from generation to generation, and intergenerational relationship problems must be resolved to improve current problems.

Some social workers who employ the psychodynamic perspective draw heavily on Murray Bowen's (1978) concept of differentiation of self. Bowen suggested two aspects of **differentiation of self** in the family system (see McGoldrick, Carter, & Garcia-Preto, 2011b; Walsh, 2014):

1. *Differentiation between thinking and feeling.* Family members must learn to own and recognize their feelings. But they must also learn to think about and plan their lives rather than reacting emotionally at times that call for clear thinking. It is assumed that many family problems are based on family members' emotional reactivity to each other. This aspect of differentiation is very similar to Daniel Goleman's concept of emotional intelligence, which was discussed in Chapter 4.

2. *Differentiation between the self and other members of the family.* While recognizing their interdependence with other family members, individuals should follow their own beliefs rather than make decisions based on reactivity to the cues of others or the need to win approval. They should do this, however, without attacking others or defending themselves. A clear sense of self allows them to achieve some independence while staying connected to other family members. This aspect of differentiation is similar to Howard Gardner's concept of interpersonal intelligence, also discussed in Chapter 4.

Another key concept in the psychodynamic perspective on families is triangulation. **Triangulation** occurs when two family members (a family subsystem) inappropriately involve another family member to reduce the anxiety in the dyadic relationship. For example, if a couple is having marital problems, they may focus their energy on a child's school problems to relieve the tension in the marital relationship. The child's school problems then become the stabilizing factor in the marriage, and this problem will not improve until the parents look at their relationship problem (and the origins of it in their own families of origin). In recent years, proponents of this approach have noted that it is not always another family member that gets "triangulated in." It may be an addiction, an overinvolvement in work, or an extramarital affair—all used to ease tension in a dyadic relationship.

The psychodynamic perspective has been criticized for its Anglo American emphasis on individualism versus collectivism. To some, it pathologizes the value of connectedness that prevails in some cultures. There is some merit to this criticism if the theory is misused to interpret a strong sense of familial responsibility as seen in the Sharpe family, and many ethnic minority families, to be a sign of lack of differentiation. A strong separate self is not a value in many cultures. The psychodynamic perspective can alert us, however, to any problematic triangles that emerge when the parental subsystem is expanded in times of stress, such as when a parent in the military is deployed.

If you use a psychodynamic perspective for thinking about the Sharpe family, you might want to do a multigenerational **genogram**, or a visual representation of a family's composition and structure (see Exhibit 10.2), to get a picture

Exhibit 10.2   Sharpe Family Genogram

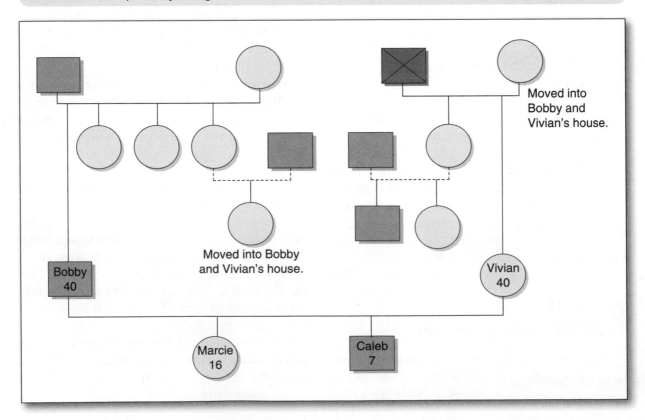

of the multigenerational family's patterns of relationships. (Females are indicated by circles, males by squares; lines indicate marriages and births.) The Sharpe genogram helps you to visualize the extended family relationships in Bobby Sharpe's family and Vivian's more limited extended family system in her family of origin. It may lead you to think about whether Bobby's deployments stirred unresolved grief about the loss of her father for Vivian and the loss of her husband for Vivian's mother.

Family Systems Perspective

A **family systems perspective** adds another lens—that of the family as a social system. As you might imagine, this approach requires a focus on relationships within the family rather than on individual family members. Persons are not thought of as individuals but as parts of overall patterns of roles and interactions (Galvin, Dickson, & Marrow, 2006). All parts of the family system are interconnected. Family members both affect and are affected by other family members; when change occurs for one, all are affected. Certainly, we can see that Bobby's and his sister's deployments and their grandmother's stroke affected the entire extended kinship system.

> Systems perspective

From the family systems perspective, families develop boundaries that delineate who is in the family at any given time. In the Sharpe family, the boundaries have shifted over time to cope with stressors of various kinds. Among members, families develop organizational structures and roles for accomplishing tasks, commonly shared beliefs and rules, and verbal and nonverbal communication patterns (White et al., 2015a). Like all systems, families have subsystems, such as a parental subsystem, sibling subsystem, or parent–child subsystem. When problems occur, the focus for change is the family system itself, with the assumption that changing the patterns of interaction between and among family members will address whatever problem first brought a family member to the attention of a social worker. Intervention may focus on helping to open communication across subsystems, helping the family explore the stated and unstated rules that govern interactions, or teaching members to communicate clearly with each other (Vetere, 2005; Walsh, 2014).

The **multilevel family practice model** (Vosler, 1996) widens the social worker's theoretical framework to include the larger systems in which the family system is embedded—including the neighborhood, local community, state, nation, and current global socioeconomic system. Thus, the multilevel model is broadly focused, acknowledging the economic, political, and cultural factors that affect resources available to the family and how family members view their current situation and future challenges. This model recognizes, as suggested in Chapter 9, that the family institution is interrelated with other social institutions—religious, political, economic, educational, social welfare, health care, and mass media. Among other things, this perspective would call our attention to how the Sharpe family is affected by terrorism and war, the global economic meltdown, and health and social welfare policies related to elder care and children with disabilities. They are also influenced by mass media coverage of race issues and the U.S. involvement in war.

A *family ecomap* can be used to assess the way the Sharpe family is connected to larger social systems. The **family ecomap** uses circles, lines, and arrows to show family relationships and the strength and directional flow of energy and resources to and from the family (Hartman & Laird, 1983; see also Vosler, 1996). Ecomaps help the social worker and the family to identify external sources of stress, conflict, and social support. Exhibit 10.3 is an example of an ecomap for the Sharpe family during Bobby's deployment to Afghanistan. It shows that Bobby and Vivian's nuclear family has both external stressors and external resources.

Family Life Cycle Perspective

The **family life cycle perspective** expands the concept of family system

> Developmental perspective

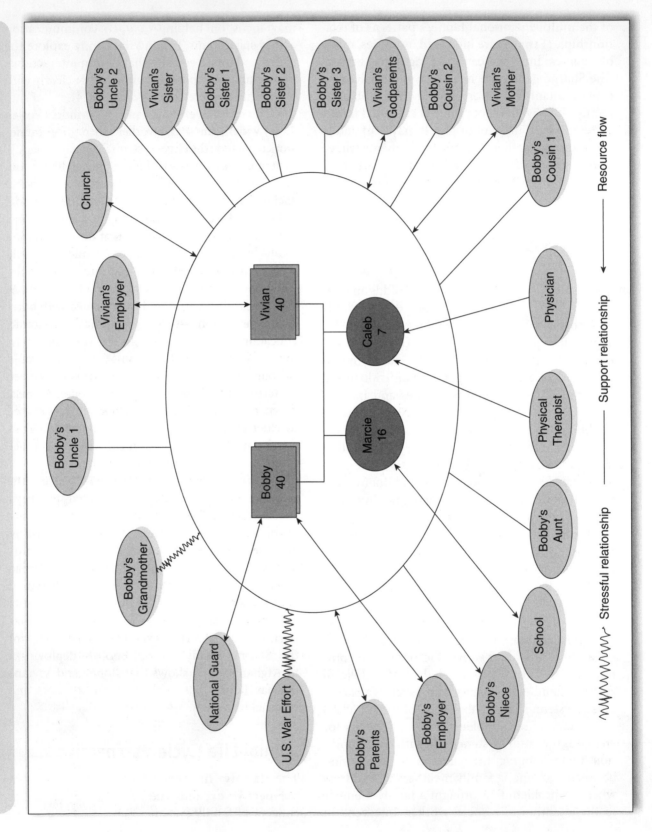

Exhibit 10.3 Sharpe Family Ecomap

Bobby's Uncle 2
Vivian's Sister
Bobby's Sister 1
Bobby's Sister 2
Bobby's Sister 3
Vivian's Godparents
Bobby's Cousin 2
Vivian's Mother

Church
Bobby's Cousin 1

Vivian's Employer
Physician

Vivian 40
Caleb 7

Bobby's Uncle 1
Physical Therapist

Marcie 16

Bobby 40
Bobby's Aunt

Bobby's Grandmother
School

National Guard
Bobby's Niece

U.S. War Effort
Bobby's Employer

Bobby's Parents

———— Resource flow

—→ Support relationship

∿∿∿∿∿∿ Stressful relationship

to look at families over time (McGoldrick et al., 2011a). Families are seen as multigenerational systems moving through time, composed of people who have a shared history and a shared future. Relationships in families go through transitions as they move along the life cycle; boundaries shift, rules change, and roles are constantly redefined. The family moving through time is influenced by cultural factors and by the historical era in which they live. The family life cycle perspective proposes that **transition points**, when the family faces a transition in family life stage or in family composition, are particularly stressful for families. Such transition points are especially stressful to those with a family or cultural history of trauma or disruption. McGoldrick et al. (2011a) recognize that contemporary families are undergoing changes and have many forms, but they delineate seven stages that many U.S. families seem to pass through: leaving home: emerging young adults, joining of families through marriage/union; families with young children; families with adolescents; launching children and moving on at midlife; families in late middle age; and families nearing the end of life. Each of these stages involves normative changes and challenging tasks, both for individual family members and for the family system as a whole. In this view, change is inevitable in families, and transitions offer opportunities for positive adaptation and growth. The identified life stages may not fit many of the families in today's society, however, including divorced and remarried families and families without children.

From the family cycle perspective, we can see that Bobby and Vivian's nuclear family was becoming a family with an adolescent and needed to open the family boundaries to allow for Marcie's growing relationships with peers during Bobby's deployment to Afghanistan. At the same time, they were a family with young children and needed to focus inward to ensure adequate care for two young children, including one with special care needs. This was happening as the family coped with the stressful transitions of Bobby's deployment and Vivian's new work responsibilities. The family life cycle perspective would alert us to the possibility that the family could struggle under the pressure of these stressful transitions.

Feminist Perspective and Families

Unlike the family systems perspective, the **feminist perspective on families** proposes that families should not be studied as whole systems, with the lens on the family level, because such attention results in failure to attend to patterns of dominance, subjugation, and oppression in families (Chibucos & Leite, 2005). As suggested in Chapter 2, the focus of the feminist perspective is on how patterns of dominance in major social institutions are tied to gender, with women devalued and oppressed. When applied to the family, the feminist perspective proposes that gender is the primary characteristic on which power is distributed and misused in the family (Allen, Lloyd, & Few, 2009). Although the Sharpe family, like many African American families, has relatively egalitarian approaches to enacting gender roles, they live in a world that gives men more power than women and are influenced by that bias. Men and women are both involved in nurturing care, but women are considered the primary caregivers. Bobby and Vivian have nieces and nephews whose fathers have taken no responsibility for their children, leaving the mothers to take full responsibility for their economic and emotional well-being.

The feminist perspective makes a distinction between sex and gender: Sex is biologically determined, but gender is socially constructed and learned from the culture. The feminist perspective questions how society came to assign male and female characteristics; seeks understanding of women's and children's perspectives on family life; analyzes how family practices create advantages for some family members and disadvantages for others; raises questions about caregiving responsibilities in families; and questions why the state should decide who should marry and receive a range of financial, legal, and medical rights (Wood, 2006). It argues that a diversity of family forms should be recognized and that the

Conflict perspective

strengths and weaknesses of each form should be thoughtfully considered. It calls attention to the family as a site of both love and trauma (Allen et al., 2009). Although gender is the starting point of the feminist perspective, most feminist theories focus on disadvantage based on other characteristics as well, including race, ethnicity, social class, sexuality, age, religion, nationality, and ability status (Lloyd, Few, & Allen, 2009).

The feminist perspective includes a variety of feminist theories—we should speak of *feminisms*, not feminism—such as liberal, radical, interpretive, critical, cultural, and postmodern feminism. These varieties of feminism may disagree on important issues. For example, liberal feminists support the inclusion of women in all military positions, because of their focus on equality of opportunity, while cultural feminists oppose women in the military because they see the valuing of life and nurturing, rather than destroying, as a central part of female culture (White et al., 2015e). Bobby Sharpe's sister does not consider herself a feminist, but she is among the many women taking advantage of career opportunities in the military.

The emerging **intersectionality feminist theory** is consistent with the multidimensional approach proposed in this book. Feminists of color introduced the concept of *intersectionality* to challenge the idea that gender is a monolithic category (Collins, 2000). They suggested that no single category is sufficient to understand social oppression, and categories such as gender, race, and class intersect to produce different experiences for women of various races and classes. Bobby Sharpe's sister could probably embrace this version of feminist theory, based on the observation that her e-mails from Iraq often included musings about what she was learning about how different her life experiences and life chances have been from other women in her unit, both White women and other African American women. She has also been shocked at the level of sexual harassment and sexual violence she has found in the military.

Intersectionality theory has also been used to look at other intersections in women's lives—for example, those related to sexuality, religion, disability, age, and nationality. From this perspective, a person may experience oppression based on gender or some other attribute but also experience privilege based on a different attribute. Some people may experience oppression related to several social categories. Intersectionality theory is being expanded to study transnational contexts, considering the consequences for women of colonialism and capitalism (Allen et al., 2009). Intersectionality theory would call attention to the ways that Bobby Sharpe and members of his family have experienced oppression related to race. But it would also suggest that Bobby has been able to build a middle-class life that has given him some class privilege compared with poor African American families. He also carries male privilege, heterosexual privilege, age privilege, and Christian privilege.

Family Stress and Coping Perspective

You read about theories of individual stress and coping in Chapter 5, and research in this area is incorporated into theorizing about stress and coping

> Systems perspective; psychodynamic perspective

at the family level. The primary interest of the family stress and coping perspective is the entire family unit (Price, Price, & McKenry, 2010). The theoretical foundation of this perspective is the **ABC-X model of family stress and coping**, based on Rueben Hill's (1949, 1958) classic research on war-induced separation and reunion. It theorizes that to understand whether an event (A) in the family system becomes a crisis (X), we also need to understand both the family's resources (B) and the family's definitions (C) of the event. The main idea is that the impact of stressors on the family (the X factor) is influenced by other factors, most notably the internal and external resources available and the meaning the family makes of the situation. With some updating, this theory continues to be the basis for examining family stress and coping (see Boss, 2006; Price et al., 2010).

Systems perspective

The ABC-X model describes a family transition process following a stressful event. A period of disequilibrium is followed by three possible outcomes: (1) *recovery* to the family's previous level of functioning; (2) *maladaptation*, or permanent deterioration in the family's functioning; or (3) *bonadaptation*, or improvement in the family's functioning over and above the previous level. Thus, under certain circumstances, a stressor event can actually be beneficial, if the family's coping process strengthens the family in the long term. They might, for instance, come together to deal with the stressors. Vivian and Marcie Sharpe often talk about how their relationship was strengthened by the way they pulled together during Bobby's deployments.

A more complex, *double* ABC X model incorporates the concept of **stress pileup** (McCubbin & Patterson, 1983). Over time, a series of crises may deplete the family's resources and expose the family to increasing risk of very negative outcomes (such as divorce, violence, or removal of children from the home). In this view, the balance of stressors and resources is an important consideration. Where there are significant numbers of stressors, positive outcomes depend on a significant level of resources being available to family members and the family as a whole. A **family timeline**, or chronology depicting key dates and events in the family's life (Satir, 1983; Vosler, 1996), can be particularly helpful in identifying times in the family's life when events have piled up. Family timelines can be used to identify the resources that have been tapped successfully in the past, as well as resource needs in the present. Exhibit 10.4 presents a family timeline for the Sharpe family. It suggests a pileup of stressors for the family in the period before, during, and after Bobby's deployment to Afghanistan; consequently, they needed a significant number of resources to allow for continued healthy individual and family functioning.

Two types of stressors are delineated in the ABC-X model (McCubbin & Figley, 1983). **Normative stressors** are the typical family life cycle transitions, such as the birth of a first child. **Nonnormative stressors** are potentially catastrophic events, such as natural disasters, medical trauma, drug abuse, unemployment, and family violence. These nonnormative events can quickly drain the family's resources and may leave family members feeling overwhelmed and exhausted. Lower-level but persistent stress—such as chronic illness or chronic poverty—can also create stress pileup, resulting in instability within the family system and a sense of being out of control on the part of family members.

Family Resilience Perspective

Humanistic perspective

The **family resilience perspective** extends the family stress and coping perspective by seeking to identify and strengthen processes that allow families to bear up under and rebound from distressing life experiences. From this perspective, distressed families are seen as challenged, not damaged, and they have the potential for repair and growth (Walsh, 2006). In her book *Strengthening Family Resilience*, Froma Walsh (2006) draws on existing research on risk and resilience to present a family resilience model for intervention and prevention, one that focuses on the family system as the target for intervention. She defines *resilience* as "the capacity to rebound from adversity strengthened and more resourceful" (p. 4). She describes this as "bouncing forward," rather than bouncing back. She assumes that all families face adversity, but resilient families "struggle well" and experience "both suffering and courage" (p. 6). She cautions social workers to avoid the tendency to pathologize the families they encounter in the midst of transitional distress, assessing families, instead, in the context of the situations they face and looking for family strengths.

Walsh (2006, 2012c) has taken the research on risk and resilience and organized the findings into a conceptual framework for targeting interventions to strengthen core processes of family resilience, whatever form the family takes. She organizes this framework into three dimensions: family belief systems, organizational patterns,

Exhibit 10.4   Sharpe Family Timeline

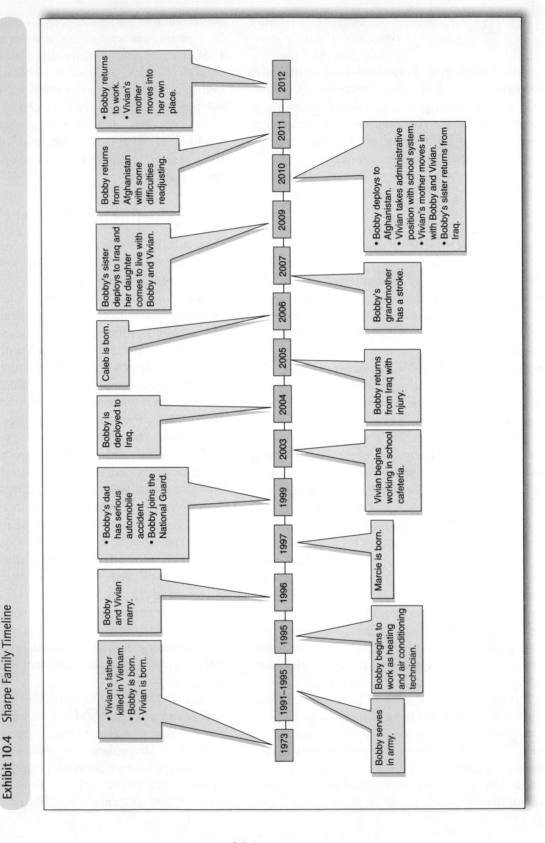

and communication processes. Each dimension is summarized here.

- *Family belief systems.* How families view problems and possibilities is crucial to how they cope with challenges. Resilient families make meaning of adversity by viewing it as a shared challenge. They find a way to hold on to a shared confidence that they can overcome the challenge. They act on this shared hope by taking initiative and persevering. They draw on a spiritual value system to see their situation as meaningful and to imagine future possibilities.

- *Organizational patterns.* Resilient families have organizational patterns that serve as shock absorbers. They maintain flexibility in family structure and are able to make changes in roles and rules to respond to the demands of the moment, but in the midst of change, they hold on to some rituals and routines to provide stability and continuity. Strong family leaders provide nurturance and protection to children and other vulnerable family members, but they also leave some room to negotiate rules and roles, based on the situation at hand, and exercise leadership with warmth. Resilient families provide mutual support and commitment while honoring individual differences. They are able to mobilize extended kin and community resources.

- *Communication processes.* Good communication is vital to family resilience. Resilient families send clear, consistent, and genuine messages. They share a wide range of feelings and show mutual empathy and tolerance for differences. They can use humor to lighten threatening situations. They also engage in collaborative problem solving, identifying problems and possible solutions, sharing decision making, and taking concrete steps.

Froma Walsh (2012b) cautions that

the concept of family resilience should not be misapplied to blame families that are unable to rise above harsh conditions, by simply labeling them as not resilient. Just as individuals need supportive relationships to thrive, families need supportive institutional polices, structures, and programs in workplace, health care, and other larger systems. (p. 412)

The Sharpe family has weathered a number of challenges along the way: health problems, war zone deployments for Bobby and his sister, the birth of a baby with special care needs, and intense elder care needs. According to Froma Walsh's model of family resilience, they are a resilient family. They view each adversity as a shared challenge for the extended kinship network, and they move forward with confidence that they can overcome each challenge. They take the initiative to devise plans for handling difficult situations, and they draw on a deeply held faith that makes meaning of their challenges. In terms of organizational patterns, they are flexible in the assignment of roles and resourceful in mobilizing extended care resources. They have made more use of family than community resources in the past, but Vivian was grateful for the support of their church during Bobby's deployment to Afghanistan. They communicate well, for the most part, often using humor to lighten stressful situations. Vivian, her sister, and her mother could benefit from more open communication about the struggles they had after Vivian's father was killed in Vietnam. They have never been able to talk about this, and it may well play a role in Vivian's sister's clinical depression and her mother's pervasive sadness.

Critical Thinking Questions 10.2

Which one of the preceding theoretical perspectives on families do you find most useful for thinking about the multigenerational Sharpe family? Which perspective do you think offers the least insight into this family? Which of the perspectives do you find most useful for thinking about your own family? The least useful? Explain your answers.

DIVERSITY IN FAMILY LIFE _____

One question that must be asked about each of the theoretical perspectives on families is how well it applies to different types of families. As suggested earlier, diversity has always existed in the structures and functions of families, but that diversity is clearly increasing, and the reality today is that a great deal of diversity exists among families, both in the United States and globally. There is diversity in family structures, as well as economic and cultural diversity.

Diversity in Family Structures

It is difficult, if not impossible, to catalog all of the types of family structures represented in the world's families. The following discussion is not meant to be exhaustive but rather to provide an overview of some relatively common structures that social workers might encounter.

Nuclear Families

There is a worldwide trend toward the nuclear family structure as societies become more industrialized and more people live in urban areas where smaller families are more practical (Ballantine & Roberts, 2014). The nuclear family is an adaptation to industrialization and urbanization. Some of the White settlers in the United States preferred the extended family structure, and others preferred the nuclear family, but the nuclear family has been the preferred family structure throughout most of U.S. history. Consequently, we would expect *nuclear family* to be easy to define. Actually, the family literature presents different definitions of this family structure. Some definitions specify that the nuclear family is composed of two parents and their biological or adopted offspring (LePoire, 2006). Others specify that a nuclear family is composed of at least one parent and one child (Leeder, 2004; Newman, 2012). This definition would include a broader brush of families, including lone-parent families and same-sex partners with children. But for the purpose of this discussion, we define the *nuclear family* as composed of two parents and their biological, adopted, or fostered offspring, because we think it is important to distinguish this idealized family structure from other family structures. Although, as mentioned, the nuclear family has been the

preferred model throughout U.S. history, it has always been an ideal that was difficult to accomplish (Hareven, 2000). Families in colonial days and later were often marked by unplanned pregnancies and untimely death. Early parental death led to remarriage and stepfamilies and to children being placed with extended family or in foster care or orphanages. Nonkin boarders were brought in to provide income and companionship.

In 2012, according to the U.S. Census Bureau (Vespa, Lewis, & Kreider, 2013), 20% of households in the United States were married couples with children, down from 40% in 1970. We don't know a lot about the functioning of nuclear families because they are not often studied, except to compare other types of families with them. For example, children in lone-parent families are often compared with children in two-parent families, with the finding that children benefit from the resources—material and social—that come with two parents (see Shore & Shore, 2009). Recent U.S. Census data indicate that adults in married-couple families are older, more likely to be college educated, more likely to own their own homes, and more likely to have higher incomes than lone-parent families (Vespa et al., 2013). Both government (through marriage initiative programs) and religious groups are actively involved in trying to promote more two-parent families. Some social scientists see risk in nuclear families as compared with extended families, suggesting that the family can easily become too isolated with too much pressure put on the spousal relationship to fill each other's needs (Walsh, 2012b).

The often idealized nuclear family has a father in the labor force and a stay-at-home mother. That type of nuclear family peaked in the 1950s but was already beginning to decline by 1960. In 2010, 54% of married couples with children younger than age 18 had two parents in the labor force, down from 66% in 2007 (U.S. Bureau of Labor Statistics, 2013b). From 2005 to 2011, a period that included a steep recession, the number of two-parent families with children younger than 18 who had at least one unemployed parent rose by 33% (Vespa et al., 2013). Having two parents in the labor force puts married couples at an economic advantage over

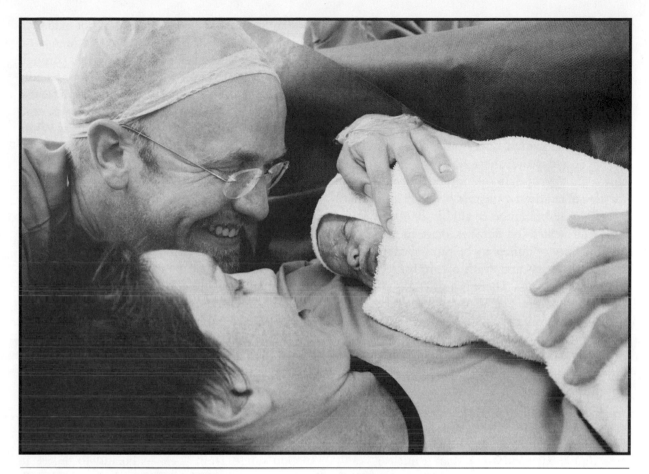

Photo 10.1   The birth of a first child is a major transition for a family system, calling for new roles and the management of new tasks.

© iStockphoto.com/Don Bayley

single parents but also raises concerns about who will provide child care and other domestic labor.

Nuclear families may include adopted and foster children (as may lone-parent families, same-sex partner families, and stepfamilies). The 2000 U.S. Census found that 2.5% of children younger than 18 were adopted, and 12.6% of those were foreign-born children (cited in Galvin, 2006). More recent data indicate that 25% of adopted children in the United States are international adoptions, 40% are transracial, and 37% are foster care adoptions (Statistic Brain, 2013). Adoptive families face the same challenges as other families, but they also face some additional ones. Every adopted child has two families, and disclosure about and navigation of this complexity must be addressed. The adoptive family must also develop a coherent story about how they came to be family and cope with issues of loss, grief, and attachment (Rampage et al., 2012).

Extended Families

An *extended family* is one in which the parent–child nuclear family lives along with other relatives, such as grandparents, adult siblings, aunts, uncles, or cousins. This is a common pattern in agricultural societies around the world. In the United States, this pattern exists in some rural families, as well as in some ethnic groups, particularly among Mexican Americans and some Asian American groups. This is financially practical, and it also allows family groups to practice their ethnic traditions (Ballantine & Roberts, 2014). However, there are some downsides to the extended family. Sometimes family members exploit the labor of other family members. In other cases, the emotional and economic obligations to the extended family may come at the expense of individual development (Leeder, 2004).

In recent years, there has been great debate about the appropriate role for extended family in the care of children orphaned by AIDS in southern Africa (see Mathambo & Gibbs, 2009). In societies where extended families share in the care of children, poor families are being challenged by the prolonged illness and death of family members at prime working age. There is a growing interest in the capacity of the extended family to care for the increasing number of children orphaned by AIDS. Some argue, however, that the extended family network is collapsing under the strain of the devastation caused by AIDS. Where resources are scarce, both support and misery are shared.

Some family scholars suggest it is more appropriate to speak of the contemporary family in the United States and other industrialized nations as a *modified extended family* than a nuclear family (Knodel, Kespichayawattana, Saengtienchai, & Wiwatwanich, 2010). Members of the extended family network may not reside together, but they are involved with each other in ongoing emotional and economic action. They stay connected. This is clearly the pattern in the Sharpe family. It is also the pattern in the current migrations across national lines. Family members are often separated across thousands of miles, but money is shared and the new technologies allow ongoing communication. Often immigrant groups travel together in kin networks and live very close to each other when not living together. The extended kin network is a source of support in times of crisis. For example, children may be transferred from one nuclear family to another within the extended kin network as need arises, as happened when Bobby and Vivian cared for their niece while her mother was deployed to a war zone. The extended kin system also influences values and behaviors. For instance, Vivian Sharpe has expectations that her extended kinship system will have a positive influence on Marcie's values and behaviors as she grows through adolescence. Extended family ties are usually stronger in Asian and Pacific Islander Americans, First Nations Peoples, African Americans, and Latino Americans than among middle-class White Americans (Ho et al., 2004).

Cohabiting Heterosexual Couples

Cohabiting is living together in a romantic relationship without marriage. This method of forming a romantic partnership has been on the increase in the United States and other Western societies since 1960. Cohabitation is now recognized as a family form by family scholars. Sociologists Patrick Heuveline and Jeffrey Timberlake (2004) examined data from almost 70,000 women from 17 nations to learn how nonmarital cohabitation in the United States compares with that in 16 other industrialized nations. They examined the percentage of women in each of the nations estimated to experience at least one cohabiting relationship before the age of 45 and found a very large cross-nation range, from 4.4% in Poland to 83.6% in France. Spain and Italy were at the low end, with less than 15% of women in each country reporting cohabitation. The United States fell in the middle of the range, with about 50% of women estimated to ever cohabit before age 45, and more recent data indicate that the United States continues to rank in the middle globally in terms of cohabitation (Social Trends Institute, 2012). Heuveline and Timberlake (2004) suggest that the cross-national differences in rates of cohabitation are influenced by a number of sociocultural factors, including religion, the economy, partnership laws and benefits, and availability of affordable housing. Besides differences in rates of cohabitation, they also found different types of cohabiting relationships occurring in different nations. For example, cohabitation can be a prelude to marriage or an alternative to marriage. Heuveline and Timberlake (2004) found that cohabiting relationships are less stable in the United States than in other countries.

Although the estimates vary, there is agreement that the rate of unmarried cohabiting partners in the United States has increased dramatically since the 1960s and that, currently, a majority of couples getting married are already living in a cohabiting relationship (Huang, Smock, Manning, & Bergstrom-Lynch, 2011). The increase in cohabitation is related to the increasing age at marriage. In the United States and other Western industrialized countries, cohabitation is most frequent among young adults ages 20 to 34 (OECD Family Database, 2013), but older adults are the fastest growing group of U.S. cohabitors as the baby boomers age (Vespa, 2012).

Qualitative research with a U.S. sample of cohabiting young adults identified three primary motives for cohabiting: wanting to spend more time together, wanting to share financial burdens, and wanting to test compatibility (Huang et al., 2011). There were gender differences in the perceived disadvantages of cohabitation. Women saw cohabitation as involving less commitment and less societal legitimacy than marriage, while men noted the loss of freedom involved in cohabitation. Both men and women reported that the benefits of cohabitation outweigh the disadvantages.

Another research team found that cohabitation is associated with greater economic well-being for adults with college degrees but not for adults without college degrees (Taylor et al., 2011). Adults without college degrees are more likely to cohabit than adults with college degrees, and college-educated cohabiters are more likely to marry within 3 years of moving in together than cohabiters without a college degree. Wealthier cohabiters are more likely than less wealthy cohabiters to report that cohabitation is a step toward marriage rather than a substitution for marriage.

As the age of marriage is pushed upward, researchers have begun to note the rise in *serial cohabitation*, defined as two or more cohabiting relationships over time, particularly among emerging adults (Cohen & Manning, 2010; Lichter, Turner, & Sassler, 2010). They have found that the majority of cohabiting unions dissolve, especially among economically disadvantaged cohabiting couples. Early sexual activity and teen childbearing are associated with serial cohabitation, and serial cohabiters are less likely than single-instance cohabiters to expect the cohabiting relationship to end in marriage. The researchers suggest that serial cohabitation is a new intensive form of dating among some emerging adults and an alternative to marriage among some older never-married women (Lichter et al., 2010). Another research team found that the unions of low-income mothers who were cohabiting at the time of giving birth were often dissolved; 46% dissolved within 3 years of giving birth and 64% dissolved within 5 years. Three quarters of these romantic relationships ended completely, but one quarter continued after cohabitation dissolution. Family stress and lack of human capital are associated with cohabitation dissolution, and mothers who have had more than one cohabitation partner are at special risk for cohabitation dissolution (Kamp Dush, 2011). Lichter and Qian (2008) speculate that serial cohabitation by women may "reflect demographic shortages of men who are good providers or companions (e.g., men with good jobs, who are faithful, or who are drug free)" (p. 874).

Couples With No Children

Over the past 3 decades, the United States and other wealthy nations have seen an increase in the proportion of married couples who are childless. Of note, relatively high rates of childlessness were experienced in these same societies from 1890 to 1920, followed by the lowest recorded prevalence of childlessness during the 1950s and early 1960s (Abma & Martinez, 2006; Kohli & Albertini, 2009). Thus, the current high rates of childlessness are a return to a trend started in the late 19th century. Couples may be temporarily or permanently childless. Permanently childless couples may be voluntarily or involuntarily childless. Although childlessness is a growing type of family structure, there is very little research on childless couples; the research that has been done focuses on childless women, with little or no attention to childless men (fertility of men is much harder to study) or to the childless couple system, except in cases of infertility. The research often does not distinguish between married and unmarried women.

The most comprehensive study of childless women in the United States to date was conducted by Joyce Abma and Gladys Martinez (2006) at the National Center for Health Statistics. Their study examined three types of childlessness: temporarily childless, voluntarily childless, and involuntarily childless. They studied both married and unmarried women and did not make distinctions between these two groups. They found that from 1976 to 2002, the percentage of women aged 35 to 39 who were childless increased from 11% to 20%, and the percentage of women aged 40 to 44 who were childless increased from 10% to 18%. The voluntarily childless was the largest group of childless women in 2002, making up 42% of all childless women; 30% were temporarily childless, and 28% were involuntarily childless. As might be expected, given declining fertility between the ages of 35 and 44, women who were temporarily childless were more likely to be in the younger cohort, ages 35 to 39, and women who were involuntarily childless were more likely to be in the older group, ages 40 to 44.

All three groups of childless women were found to have more egalitarian views on family relationships than the women who were parents. There were some differences in the profiles of these three groups of childless women, however. Consistent with earlier research, the voluntarily childless women, compared with parenting women and other childless women, were disproportionately White, tended to be employed full time, had the highest incomes, and were more likely to be nonreligious. However, from 1995 to 2002, the percentage of Black women among the voluntarily childless increased to where it was equivalent to their share of the total population of women ages 35 to 44. From 1976 to 2002, Hispanic women were consistently underrepresented among the voluntarily childless.

One finding from the Abma and Martinez (2006) study is that there was a slight downturn in the percentage of women who were voluntarily childless and a slight upturn in the percentage who were involuntarily childless from 1995 to 2002. They speculate that this change is probably related to the trend toward later marriage and childbearing, resulting in some couples discovering that they had fertility problems when they decided to become parents. Infertility can be caused by problems in the reproductive system of the man, the woman, or both. It is a global problem, but in countries with low resources it is most likely to be caused by sexually transmitted diseases, unsafe abortions, and home deliveries in unhygienic circumstances. Although there are many assistive technologies for dealing with fertility problems, these are inaccessible to most women in low-resource countries. In many countries of the world, childlessness is highly stigmatized, as well as an economic disadvantage where children are economic providers (Ombelet, 2014).

Research on the emotional impact of infertility indicates that it is a major source of stress. Infertility has been consistently associated with decreased scores in quality of life, affecting mental health, physical vitality, and social functioning (Drosdzol & Skrzypulec, 2008; El-Messidi, Al-Fozan, Lin Tan, Farag, & Tulandi, 2004; Lau et al., 2008). When couples experience similar levels of distress, they are more able to communicate about it and support each other (Peterson, Newton, & Rosen, 2003). However, it is not unusual for husbands and wives to have different reactions to infertility. The stressors related to infertility may go on over a long period of time. Treatments can be very costly and are often unsuccessful.

Although attitudes are changing, some social stigma is still attached to childlessness. Little is known about the lives of childless couples. In a recent attempt to understand the life trajectories of childless adults, an entire issue of the journal *Ageing & Society* was devoted to research on childless older adults. One researcher (Wenger, 2009) found that by the time they reached old age, childless people in rural Wales had made adaptations to their childless situation and developed closer relationships with kin and friends. This is the way Vivian Sharpe's godparents have adjusted to involuntary childlessness, and they draw great pleasure from being a part of the lively extended kin network in which Vivian and Bobby are embedded. On average, however, childless older adults in Wales entered residential care at younger ages than older adults who had children.

Lone-Parent Families

Lone-parent families are composed of one parent and at least one child residing in the same household. They are headed by either a divorced, a widowed, or an unmarried parent. Lone-parent families are on the increase in all wealthy industrialized nations but nowhere more than in the United States (U.S. Census Bureau, 2012). In 2012, nearly one third (32%) of children in the United States lived with only one parent, 27% with the mother only, and 5% with the father only (Vespa et al., 2013). This compares with less than 5% in Greece and Spain, 6% in Portugal, and 7% in Italy (U.S. Census Bureau, 2012). Around the world, lone mothers are the great majority of parents in lone-parent families. In the United States, 55% of non-Hispanic Black children, 31% of Hispanic children, 21% of non-Hispanic White children, and 13% of Asian American children live with one parent. The share of children living with one parent in the United States has tripled since 1970, when the rate was 11% (Shore & Shore, 2009). It is important to exercise caution with these statistics, however. Sometimes people who get counted as lone-parent families reside with other family members and/or may have the support of a romantic partner.

Single mothers around the world have some common challenges: They are playing the dual roles of mother and worker with no partner assistance, receive lower earnings than men, and receive irregular paternal support (Anderson, 2012). If they became lone parents after divorce, they and their children must cope with loss and grief, may have to relocate, and face on average a 37% decline in their standard of living (Stirling & Aldrich, 2008). Lone-parent families headed by mothers are especially vulnerable to economic insecurity and poverty. Cross-national differences in government policies result in different circumstances for single mothers and their children, however. Some countries provide universal child allowances, paid maternity leave, and free child care. Children of single mothers have higher rates of poverty than children from two-parent families around the world, but the poverty rates among children of single parents are much lower in countries that provide such supports.

In 2005, the poverty rate (based on 55% of median income) for single-mother families in the United States was 51%, compared with 8% in Denmark (Casey & Maldonado, 2012). This is a very large range and primarily reflects differences in child and family policies in the two countries. Three other countries had poverty rates of over 40% for single-mother families: Canada, Germany, and Ireland. At the other end of the continuum,

Photo 10.2 Family time: Mother spends quality time with her two daughters making breakfast.

© A. Inden/Corbis

three other countries had poverty rates of less than 15% for single-mother families: Norway, Finland, and Sweden.

In the United States, social policy has focused on two priorities to improve the living situation of children in lone-parent families, as well as to decrease public expenditures on these families: improved child support payment by the nonresidential parent and marriage of the lone parent. The first of these priorities is to step up the enforcement of child support payment by the nonresidential parent. Research indicates that if nonresidential parents pay the child support required, the economic situation of residential children does indeed improve, although not to the level they would experience if both parents resided together. However, for impoverished families, the payment of child support is not sufficient to bring them out of poverty (see Stirling & Aldrich, 2008).

The second policy direction proposed in the United States in recent years is to encourage marriage of the lone parent. Some policy analysts conclude that this would, indeed, improve the economic situation of children currently being raised in lone-parent families (see Rector, Johnson, & Fagan, 2008). Others conclude that while this might be a good solution for some lone-parent families, male unemployment and marginal employment present serious barriers to marriage for many low-income couples (Edin & Reed, 2005; Gibson-Davis, Edin, & McLanahan, 2005). These latter researchers have found that men and women in impoverished neighborhoods often value marriage highly but do not see themselves as economically stable enough to have a viable marriage. Impoverished lone mothers have reported that they do not have a pool of attractive marriage partners who are economically stable, not addicted to drugs and alcohol, not involved with the criminal justice system, and able to be loving and kind parents to their children (Edin, Kefalas, & Reed, 2004).

It is important to note that in wealthy nations, the number of lone-parent families is growing across all socioeconomic groups, and in the United States, many affluent and well-educated women and men are choosing to become lone parents because they want to be a parent but do not have a partner with whom to share parenting (Anderson, 2012). These lone parents have the resources to afford full-time child care, private schools, and other domestic assistance.

One more point is important. Much of the research on lone-parent families has taken a deficit approach in looking at family interaction and functioning. Other researchers have attempted to look at lone parents from a strengths perspective and document how they function to adapt to the challenges they face. One example of this is a qualitative research project that asked low-income African American mothers and members of their families (who were sometimes not biologically related to them) to identify components of effective and ineffective family functioning (McCreary & Dancy, 2004). They found that all but 1 of the 40 respondents reported that they see or talk daily with at least one family member other than their children, a coping strategy that increases the effectiveness of family functioning by preventing isolation.

Stepfamilies

Stepfamilies have always been a relatively common family form in the United States, but they have changed over time. In colonial days, stepfamilies were typically the result of one parent dying and the other parent remarrying. Today, most stepfamilies are formed after biological parents divorce or dissolve their relationship and go on to form new romantic partnerships. We don't have good current data on the number of stepfamilies in the United States, but it is estimated that 10% to 20% of children younger than age 18 reside in stepfamilies (National Healthy Marriage Resource Center, 2009). The U.S. Census Bureau defines stepfamilies as those with two adults and children, where one adult is not the biological parent (cited in Pasley & Lee, 2010). Stepfamilies can be of several types. The most common is the stepfather family in which the mother has children from a previous relationship in the household. Another type is the stepmother family in which the father has children from a previous relationship in the household. Some stepfamilies have children from both partners' prior relationships living in the household. Any of these family forms can become more complex when children are born to the new partnership. Stepfamilies are also formed by same-sex partners where one or both partners have children from prior relationships living in the household. Although not counted by the U.S. Census Bureau as living in stepfamilies, many children reside with a single mother and make visits to the biological father and his new wife.

Stepfamilies are complex family structures. They involve complicated networks of relationships that include biological parents; stepparents; perhaps siblings and stepsiblings; and multiple sets of grandparents, aunts, uncles, and cousins. Children in stepfamilies may move back and forth between two homes and maintain connections with the nonresident parent. There are a number of subsystems in the stepfamily, including the new couple, the parent–child, the stepparent–stepchild, the child–nonresidential parent, the biological parents, the parent–stepparent–nonresidential parent, and sometimes the sibling or stepsibling subsystem. The parent–child subsystem is a more long-standing form than the new couple subsystem.

The new stepfamily must negotiate rules, roles, rituals, and customs. Things as simple as foods served in the household, bedtimes, chores, and methods of discipline may become points of tension. This works best when the issues and expectations are made explicit. It is quite common for loyalty conflicts to arise involving several subsystems, with family members feeling torn and caught between people they love (Pasley & Lee, 2010). The biological parent often feels torn between loyalty to the child(ren) and love for the new spouse or partner. Children may aggravate this situation by testing the biological parent's loyalty to them. Children may feel a conflict between their loyalty to the nonresidential parent and the need to form a relationship with the stepparent. Children can easily get triangulated into conflict between the parent and stepparent, between the residential parent and the nonresidential parent, or between the stepparent and the nonresidential

parent. Events such as Parent Night at school can become a knotty situation.

The more children in the stepfamily situation, the more complicated the negotiations can become. First-marriage couples report that the biggest source of stress is finances, followed by child rearing. For stepfamilies, the biggest sources of stress are reversed, with child rearing coming first, followed by finances (Stanley, Markman, & Whitton, 2002). Stepparents are often treated as outsiders by children, and this is a difficult position from which to attempt to parent. Research indicates that stepfathers are less likely than stepmothers to try to engage in active parenting of stepchildren, no doubt because of expectations of gendered behavior; consequently, stepfathers tend to be perceived more positively than stepmothers (Pasley & Lee, 2010). Stepdaughters have been found to be more difficult to parent than stepsons (Hetherington & Kelly, 2002).

Same-Sex Partner Families

There is evidence that long-term relationships, even marriage, between same-sex partners were relatively common in premodern Europe (Boswell, 1994), but same-sex marriage is a new phenomenon in modern times (Chamie & Mirkin, 2011). In the 1990s, same-sex marriages were not legally recognized anywhere in the world. In 1989, Denmark was the first country to give legal rights to same-sex couples but did not allow them to marry. In 2001, the Netherlands became the first country to allow same-sex marriage, and by March 2014, 17 countries allowed same-sex marriage, up from 7 in December 2009 (Pew Research Religion & Public Life Project, 2014). A number of other countries have some sort of federal civil union laws that grant partner registration and some rights and benefits of marriage. In the United States, in March 2014, same-sex marriage was legal or soon would be in 17 states and the District of Columbia, up from 5 states plus the District of Columbia in May 2010. In 2013, the U.S Supreme Court struck down part of the Defense of Marriage Act, which was enacted in 1996, resulting in the requirement that the federal government recognize same-sex marriages from the states where they are legal (Pew Research Religion & Public Life Project, 2014). Three states provide the equivalent of spousal rights to same-sex couples, and one other state provides some spousal rights to same-sex couples. In addition, in March 2014, 29 states had constitutional amendments restricting marriage to one man and one woman, and 4 other states had state laws restricting marriage to one man and one woman (Human Rights Campaign, 2014). Given the current state of debate about same-sex marriage, it is quite likely there will be other actions by nations and states by the time you read this.

It is important to remember that the preponderance of research about same-sex partner families was done in a time when such partnerships were not legally recognized. Most of the early research was based on convenience samples of White, middle-class families in lesbian partnerships, but in the past 10-plus years, researchers have begun to investigate the diversity in same-sex couple families and to consider the gay male family (Biblarz & Savci, 2010).

Same-sex partnerships share many characteristics with heterosexual partnerships, but they also are unique: the partners are of the same gender, they must often navigate a social world that continues to stigmatize same-sex relationships, and in many places they lack legal recognition. Some researchers have found that same-sex partners report about the same frequency of arguments as heterosexual couples (Peplau & Fingerhut, 2007), but others have found that same-sex couples report less conflict than heterosexual couples, more relationship satisfaction, and better conflict resolution (Balsam, Beauchaine, Rothblum, & Solomon, 2008). There is evidence that both same-sex and heterosexual partners tend to disagree about similar topics, such as sex, money, and household tasks (Kurdek, 2006). Some studies find that members of same-sex partnerships are more likely than married heterosexual couples to separate when they are unhappy, but the one longitudinal study that has followed the first same-sex partners to take advantage of Vermont's civil union laws found that same-sex couples in civil unions are less likely to separate than same-sex couples not in legally recognized unions (Balsam et al., 2008). Same-sex partners have been found to engage in less traditional division of labor than heterosexual married couples, even though heterosexual couples have become more egalitarian over time. Both same-sex and heterosexual couples reported greater commitment to monogamy in 2000 than in 1975 (Gotta et al., 2011).

Many lesbians and gay men became parents in earlier heterosexual relationships, before coming out as gay or lesbian. Increasingly, lesbians and gay men are also becoming parents in the context of their same-sex partner relationships, with the assistance of reproductive technology or by adoption (Green, 2012). Recent research indicates that, in the United States, more than 111,000 same-sex couples are raising an estimated 170,000 biological, step-, or adopted children. Same-sex couples are four times as likely to adopt as heterosexual couples and six times as likely to raise foster children. Half of children younger than 18 living with same-sex couples are non-White, and indeed, same-sex couples of color are more likely than White same-sex couples to be raising children. The median household income of same-sex couples with children is lower than the median for heterosexual couples with children, probably because the preponderance of these couples are lesbian (Gates, 2013). Lesbian couples may choose artificial insemination, and gay male couples may choose to use a surrogate mother; each method results in the child sharing a bloodline with one partner but not the other. There is very little research on gay men who become fathers via surrogacy, but one study found that these fathers reported greater closeness with their families of origin after becoming fathers and also reported heightened self-esteem (Bergman, Rubio, Green, & Padrón, 2010). Other research has found that when lesbian couples use artificial insemination, the biological mother is likely to be the primary child care provider and to have a somewhat closer relationship with the child (Bos, van Balen, & van den Boom, 2007).

Considerable research attention has been given to the question of how children fare in families of same-sex partners. This research, most of it conducted with children of lesbian couples, consistently finds that children who grow up with same-sex parents do not differ in any important way from children raised in families of heterosexual couples. They have similar emotional and behavioral adjustment; no differences are found in self-esteem, depression, or behavioral problems (Biblarz & Savci, 2010). This is remarkable, given the stigma such families often have to face. Children of same-sex parents have also been found to be no more likely than children of heterosexual couples to identify as homosexual. The school setting may present challenges, however; the children may face harassment, and their parents may find that they are not accepted on parent committees (Goldberg, 2010).

Military Families

Military families may have any of the family structures already discussed. They are included in this discussion of diversity of family structures, however, because of some special challenges they face in times of deployment to war zones. In the United States, military members may serve in either the active-duty or reserve components of the military. Active-duty members serve in the U.S. Army, Navy, Marine Corps, or Air Force. Reservists serve either in the Army National Guard or Air National Guard. Compared with other recent conflicts, deployments to Afghanistan and Iraq were more frequent and lengthier, usually lasting 12 to 15 months.

Approximately one third of both active-duty and reservist members have children; children of reserve members are a little older, on average, than children of active-duty members. The circumstances of reservist families are different in some ways from those of active-duty families. Active-duty military families typically live on or near military installations where the active-duty member receives daily military training. Reservist families live and work in a civilian community and receive military training one weekend per month (Faber, Willerton, Clymer, MacDermid, & Weiss, 2008).

Research indicates that active-duty families usually cope well with temporary separations during peacetime (Flake, Davis, Johnson, & Middleton, 2009). Active-duty military spouses are accustomed to managing as single parents for periods of time and then readjusting to operating in their predeployment family structure again when the deployment ends. Reservists and their families, on the other hand, are accustomed to occasional brief deployments to respond to state, local, and even national emergencies. They are not as prepared to deploy quickly for long periods of time and must deal with the break in civilian employment, as well as prepare the family for the coming separation. Consequently, active-duty families and reservist families face both similar and different challenges.

Spouses of both active-duty soldiers and reservists have reported loneliness, loss of emotional support, role overload, and worry about the safety and well-being of the deployed spouse (Padden & Agazio, 2013). Parents who are spouses or partners of soldiers deployed to war zones report higher levels of stress than the national average for parents. Communication with the military member in the war zone is spotty at best, as the deployed soldier is in and out of the range of adequate communications systems (Wadsworth & Southwell, 2011). During his deployment to Iraq, Bobby Sharpe was able to have only infrequent contact with his family, but he was able to have fairly regular contact by e-mail and Skype much of the time he was in Afghanistan. Both the family members at home and the deployed family member may try to avoid alarming each other about what is happening in their worlds, and together they must gauge how involved the deployed family member can be in making decisions about what is happening at home. Bobby Sharpe did not know his furnace was broken until he returned home from his first deployment, because Vivian did not want to bother him with that kind of family problem. She also avoided telling him that she was overwhelmed with the demands of work and family while he was in Afghanistan.

As the end of the deployment draws near, family members report that they begin to worry about what to expect when the soldier returns, in terms of possible war wounds or personality or behavior changes (Faber et al., 2008). Marcie Sharpe had

Photo 10.3 This father and son share a moment of joy during a welcome home ceremony when the Arkansas National Guard's 39th Infantry Brigade Combat Team returns from deployment to Iraq.

© Staff Sgt. Chris A. Durney

heard scary stories of parents coming home with completely changed personalities. She worried a lot about this during Bobby's second deployment. Although it is often a joyous time, the military member's return home can be very stressful for families. Family members have to readjust to one another and realign family roles. Three out of four military families report that the first 3 months after coming home can be the most stressful period of the deployment process (Flake et al., 2009). Soldiers have to reacclimate to life away from the war zone and renegotiate roles, responsibilities, and boundaries with family members who had made adjustments in their absence (Faber et al., 2008). This readjustment is particularly difficult when there have been physical or mental injuries, such as

traumatic brain injury or post-traumatic stress disorder (Martin & Sherman, 2010). Families tend to stabilize over time, but many families have needed to prepare for another deployment that can come in as quickly as 1 year.

Children of both active-duty and reservist families involved in the Iraq and Afghanistan wars have been found to be at increased risk for a range of problems in psychosocial functioning. In the time just before a parent's deployment, children may become withdrawn or engage in regressive behavior. Early in the deployment, they may be overwhelmed, sad, and anxious and have more somatic (physical) symptoms, but these symptoms usually diminish once children adjust to the deployment. They are usually excited and relieved when the soldier parent comes home but may experience conflict about the readjustments being made at home (Flake et al., 2009). One study of children of deployed National Guard members found that they reported missing their deployed parent as the biggest difficulty of the deployment. Their biggest worry was that their deployed parent would be injured or killed. The biggest change in their lives involved increased responsibility at home, more chores, and more responsibility for younger siblings. They reported concern about trying to avoid upsetting the parent at home. The children also described some positive aspects of deployment. Some reported being proud of what their deployed parents were doing for the country, although this pride was tempered when they heard talk from television, classmates, and other sources suggesting that the war is bad. Some children also reported pride in themselves for their ability to be more responsible while the deployed parent was away (Houston et al., 2009).

There is one important difference in the experiences of active-duty and reservist families. A large portion of active-duty military families continues to live in or near military installations during the family member's deployment. This allows them to have ongoing support from other military families as well as from military programs. Reservist families, on the other hand, are scattered across all 50 states and the U.S. territories, many of them living in rural communities. This is especially the case for National Guard members because the National Guard has a strong tradition in rural communities, where it serves as a point of pride as well as a supplement to the low wages often found in these communities (Martin & Sherman, 2010). Sometimes a National Guard family will be the only one in their area experiencing deployment at a given time. This is problematic because of the lack of access to other families facing similar experiences. Children of deployed reservists have reported that a chance to talk to other children with a deployed parent would be a big help (Houston et al., 2009). Likewise, the returning reservist soldier may be isolated from other returning soldiers, as well as from some of the medical and psychiatric resources available in and near military installations.

Operation Iraqi Freedom ended in September 2010, and Operation Enduring Freedom (the War in Afghanistan) is winding down as this is written in March 2014. It is hard to say what the outcome of these wars is, but it is clear that the military families involved, both active-duty and reservist families, will continue to experience multiple challenges in the aftermath of the wars. According to a large-scale study sponsored by the RAND Corporation, many service members from the wars in Iraq and Afghanistan underwent prolonged periods of combat stress (Tanielian & Jaycox, 2008). In the aftermath of the trauma, many service members and veterans are experiencing horrific combat injuries; others are experiencing substance abuse, PTSD, relationship problems, and work problems (Wadsworth & Southwell, 2011). Social workers in all practice settings should be alert to possibilities for engaging these families in supportive services.

Critical Thinking Questions 10.3

Which, if any, of the family structures discussed did you grow up in? What do you see as the major strength of this type of family structure? The major challenge? Which, if any, of these family structures are you living in now? If this is different from the type of family structure you grew up in, what do you consider to be its major strength and major challenge?

Economic and Cultural Diversity

Family structure is influenced by economic and cultural patterns, as well as immigration status. As you read the following sections on economic diversity, cultural diversity, and immigrant families, think about how your family structure is affected by the family's position in the economic structure; cultural heritage; and experience with immigration, where relevant.

Economic Diversity

Economic inequality exists in all societies, historical and contemporary, but the number of social classes and the amount of inequality vary from society to society. As indicated in Chapter 9, the United States has less inequality than some nations of the world, but it has more inequality than any other advanced industrialized nation. And, unfortunately, since 1970, the gap between the richest and poorest U.S. citizens has been growing. During the worst recession in the United States since the Great Depression of the 1930s, which began in December 2008, the national unemployment rate climbed to 10%. A number of wealthy families lost millions, even billions, of dollars in fraud schemes and investments gone bad. Middle-class families were devastated by job cutbacks, home foreclosures, and high debt, with middle-class men older than age 55 being particularly hard hit by job cutbacks. The poorest of families barely survived, not able to meet basic needs for food and shelter. Large numbers of U.S. families reported feeling a sense of financial insecurity (Bartholomae & Fox, 2010).

The question to be addressed here is, what impact do economic resources have on family life? How do family economic circumstances affect parental relationships, parent–child relationships, and child development? A large volume of research has found that individual physical and mental health, marital relationships, parent–child relationships, and child outcomes decline as economic stress increases. Two theoretical models have been proposed to explain the connection between economic resources and individual and family functioning: the family economic stress model and the family investment model.

The family economic stress model is based on Glen Elder's (1974) research on the impact of the Great Depression on parents and children. This research found that severe economic hardship disrupted family functioning in ways that negatively affected marital quality, parenting quality, and child outcomes. Similar results have been found in more recent studies of Iowa farm families facing a severe downturn in the agricultural economy in the 1980s (Conger & Elder, 1994) and of economic pressure in African American families (Conger et al., 2002). In the **family economic stress model** based on this research, economic hardship leads to economic pressure, which leads to parent distress, which leads to disrupted family relationships, which leads to child and adolescent adjustment problems (see Exhibit 10.5; Conger & Conger, 2008).

There is a great deal of research to support the family economic stress model. Economic stress, such as unemployment, low income, and high debt, has been found to have negative effects on the physical and mental health of parents (Kahn & Pearlin, 2006; Mckee-Ryan, Song, Wanberg, & Kinicki, 2005). Research has also found that psychological distress about economic pressures takes its toll on marital quality (Gudmunson, Beutler, Israelsen, McCoy, & Hill, 2007). Couple disagreements and fighting increase with financial strain. Parental psychological distress and marital conflict have been found to affect parenting practices, leading to less parental warmth and more inconsistent, punitive, and controlling discipline (Mistry, Lowe, Renner, & Chien, 2008; Waanders, Mendez, & Downer, 2007).

Family economic hardship has also been found to be associated with a number of child outcomes. Children in families experiencing economic hardship tend to have higher levels of depression and anxiety (Gutman, McLoyd, & Tokoyawa, 2005). They also have been found to demonstrate more aggressive and antisocial behaviors (Solantaus, Leinonen, & Punamaki, 2004). Economic disadvantage is associated with lower self-esteem and self-efficacy in children (Shek, 2003) and poorer school performance (Gutman et al., 2005). Adolescents who report worrying about the family's finances also report more somatic complaints, such as stomachaches, headaches, and loss of appetite (Wadsworth & Santiago, 2008).

Whereas the family economic stress model focuses on the impact of low income and economic hardship on family life, the **family investment model** focuses on the other end of the economic continuum, on how economic advantage affects family life and child outcomes. This theoretical model proposes that families with greater economic

Exhibit 10.5 Family Economic Stress Model

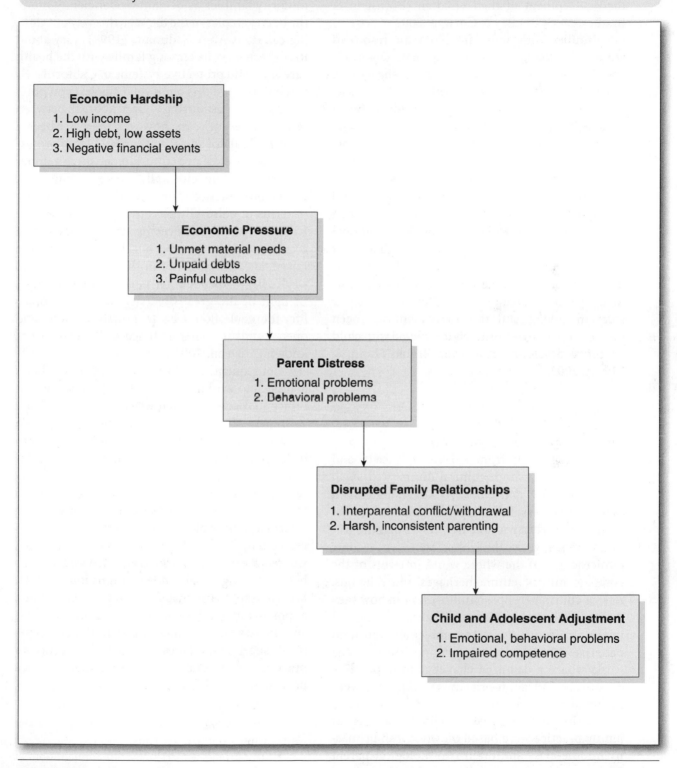

SOURCE: Conger & Conger, 2008, Figure 5.1, p. 67.

resources can afford to make large investments in the development of their children (Bornstein & Bradley, 2003; Bradley & Corwyn, 2002).

Families with abundant economic resources are able to make more learning materials available in the home; spend more time engaged in intellectually stimulating activities, such as visiting museums and traveling; secure education in enriched educational environments; secure outside assistance such as tutoring and specialized training; provide a higher standard of living in such areas as housing, clothing, nutrition, transportation, and medical care; and reside in a safe, clean, and roomy environment. They also are able to open doors to social networks that provide educational and career opportunities. This seems to go without saying, but there is empirical support for the proposal that family income affects the types of investments parents make in their children (Bradley & Corwyn, 2002), and this investment has been demonstrated to be positively associated with child cognitive development (Linver, Brooks-Gunn, & Kohen, 2002).

Cultural Diversity

The world over, we are living in a time when people are moving about from society to society and increasing the level of cultural diversity in small towns, suburbs, and cities. As suggested earlier, there has always been cultural diversity in the United States, but with the new waves of immigration in recent years, the United States has become a microcosm of the whole world in terms of the complex mix of ethnic heritages and religions. Across cultural groups, families differ in how they define family; in how they organize family life; and in their customs, traditions, and communication patterns (McGoldrick & Ashton, 2012). Social workers face a daunting challenge in responding sensitively and appropriately to each and every family they encounter.

In the past, many of the clinical models for family practice were based on work with primarily middle-class and often two-biological-parent European American families. Working from these models often led to thinking of racial and ethnic minority families as deviant or deficient. One of the best examples of the damage this way of thinking can do is Anne Fadiman's (1998) story about the experience of a Hmong family with the health care and child protective systems in California. (If you haven't read this book yet, I suggest you put it on your to-do list during your next break between terms.) In recent years, however, there has been a concerted call for social workers and other professionals to practice in a culturally sensitive manner that moves from culturally aware to culturally competent practice (Lum, 2011). I prefer to talk in terms of culturally sensitive practice, because I doubt that we can ever be truly competent in a culture other than the one in which we were raised, and certainly not in the multiple cultures we are likely to encounter in our work over time. In light of the great diversity in contemporary life, the goal should be to remain curious and open-minded, taking a stance of "informed not knowing" (Dean, 2001).

Consequently, I do not present a cookbook approach to working with cultural differences but rather a process by which we can develop cultural awareness about the family groups with which we work. The first step, as suggested earlier, is to develop an intense understanding of the limitations of our own cultural perspective and a healthy respect for the integrity of all cultures. Starting from this position, we can set out to become as well informed as possible about the cultural groups represented by the families we serve. One thing social workers are particularly good at, when we are at our best, is putting people and situations into context. We will want to use that strength to learn as much as possible about the context of the culturally variant families we encounter. Juliet Rothman (2008, p. 38) suggests the types of knowledge needed to practice in a culturally sensitive manner; they are presented in modified form here:

- The group's history prior to arriving in the United States, if relevant
- The group's experience with immigration, if relevant

Photo 10.4 It is important for social workers to understand ethnic differences in family beliefs, rules, communication patterns, and organizational norms.

© iStockphoto.com/Cliff Parnell

- The group's experience with settlement in the United States, if relevant
- The group's experience with oppression, discrimination, bias, and prejudice
- The group's relationship to the country of origin, if relevant
- The group's relationship to the country of residence
- The group's worldviews and beliefs about child rearing, family relationships, dating and marriage, employment, education, recreation, health and illness, aging, death and bereavement, and other life course issues
- Variations and differences within the group, particularly those related to social class
- Generational issues about acculturation within the group, if relevant

Some of this information may be more important for specific practice situations. There are a number of ways to learn this information: through Internet research, history books, biographies and autobiographies of group members, films and documentaries about the group, conversations with friends or colleagues who are members of the group, attendance at cultural festivals, and by asking your clients what you need to know to be helpful to them.

Even though we want to learn as much as we can about the cultural group, we must realize that there are many variations within all cultural groups. When I need to avoid stereotypical application of knowledge about a cultural group, it helps me to think about how many variations there are within my own cultural group and how well or poorly generalizations about my group apply to me. It is also helpful to hear different stories from members of the group, through books, videos, or personal conversations. It is particularly important to remember that there are social class differences among all cultural groups. You will want to consider whether the African American woman you are working with is middle class or working class and know something about her experiences with oppression. You will want to keep in mind that more than 500 distinct First Nations (or Native American) peoples exist within the United States, and they differ in language, religion, social structure, and many other aspects of culture (Weaver, 2011). You will want to know how a specific nation coped with attempts to eradicate their cultural practices. You will want to note whether the Latino immigrant family came from a rural or urban environment and what level of education they received in their home country; you will also want to note their country of origin and whether they are of documented or undocumented status. When working with an Asian or Pacific Island family, you will want to know not only the country of origin (out of 60 represented in the United States) but also the social class and education level of the family, religious beliefs, and when the family first immigrated to the United States. You will want to note how integrated the family from North Africa or the Middle East is into U.S. mainstream culture, as well as how traditional they are in religious and cultural beliefs. These are only a few examples of how you will need to individualize families while also putting them into cultural context.

Immigrant Families

The United States is built on successive waves of immigration and is currently the world's leader as a destination for immigrants. In 2011, approximately 40.4 million immigrants were living within the United States, making up 13% of the U.S. population (Pew Research Hispanic Trends Project, 2013). Immigrants are foreign-born people who plan to settle permanently in the United States. They may be economic migrants seeking better jobs and pay,

family migrants who come to join family members already here, or refugees involuntarily fleeing political violence or extreme environmental distress. Current immigrants to the United States are more diverse than earlier immigrants in terms of country of origin, language, religion, and socioeconomic status. The places from which immigrants come have changed over time, influenced by immigration policies. For example, 1965 amendments to the Immigration and Nationality Act of 1952 created a "family reunification" category and gave preference to immigrants who had family members already in the United States. The 1986 Refugee Assistance Extension Act made it easier for families facing political persecution and extreme environments in their home countries to enter the United States. The Immigration Act of 1990 shifted policy away from family reunification to individuals with specific education and credentials and to wealthy individuals who could invest in the U.S. economy (Bush, Bohon, & Kim, 2010).

Immigrants may be *first generation* (moved from another country to the United States), *second generation* (children of first-generation immigrants), or *third generation* (grandchildren of first-generation immigrants). In general, first-generation immigrants experience more loss and grief than second- and third-generation immigrants, but the reaction to immigration differs by the degree of choice about migration, accessibility to the country of origin, gender and age, stage of family life cycle, number of family members immigrating and left behind, community social supports, and experiences with discrimination in the country of origin and the country of adoption (Falicov, 2011). Many losses are involved with migration, including loss of the family members and friends left behind, loss of familiar language, and loss of customs and traditions. Involuntary immigrants often have been traumatized in their country of origin and have no option to visit home. Other immigrants are able to make frequent visits home and maintain transnational families who are in frequent contact. Families may migrate together or in sequential stages, whereby one or two family members immigrate first, followed by others at later times.

In cases of sequential migration, family roles and relationships must be reorganized over time.

The first immigrating family member must now perform some roles not carried out in the home country, whether those were domestic chores, paid labor, or managing finances. Likewise, the spouse left in the home country must now take on roles that had been filled by the immigrating family member. If the trailing spouse later immigrates, the spousal roles will have to be renegotiated, as happens when military families reunite. One difference in the reunifications of immigrant and military families is that sequential immigration may happen over a period of years and have unexpected delays, and the separations can be much longer than for military families. When children are left behind for a number of years, they may have trouble reattaching to the parents.

Immigrant families face a number of challenges. If they come from a non-English-speaking country, the language barrier will be a serious impediment to becoming comfortable in the new country. They will be unable to read street signs, job announcements and applications, food labels, and communications from the children's schools, unless they live where language translations are commonly used. Because children learn new languages more easily than adults, parent and child roles often are reversed as children become the language and cultural brokers. Children also learn the new cultural norms more quickly than parents, and this causes intergenerational tension about the appropriate level of acculturation, how much of the old to maintain and how much of the new to adopt. Parents may not understand the new culture's norms about child rearing and find themselves at odds with the school system and perhaps with the child protective system. Immigrant wives often come from cultures with traditional gender roles but need to engage in paid work in the United States to keep the family afloat. This often results in more independence and status for wives than they were accustomed to in their home countries and can cause marital conflict if men want to hold on to the traditional gender hierarchy. Research has found increased male-to-female violence in Asian families when wives earn as much or more than their husbands (Chung, Tucker, & Takeuchi, 2008). Many immigrant families come from collectivist cultures where harmony is valued over individual ambition and may feel a great deal of tension about how to respond to cultural pressures toward individualism. They may have had both the support and control of the extended family in the home country and find themselves struggling to maintain family stability with a much more limited support network.

CHALLENGES TO FAMILY LIFE

Contemporary families of all types face many stressful situations that challenge their ability to provide nurturance and the necessary resources for healthy development of family members. Every historical era and every culture presents its own set of challenges to families. In the following sections, we discuss three challenges to contemporary families: family violence, divorce, and substance abuse.

Family Violence

The family is the social group from whom we expect to receive our greatest love, support, nurturance, and acceptance. And yet family relationships are some of the most violent in many societies. It is estimated that wife beating occurs in about 85% of the world's societies, and husband beating occurs in about 27% (Newman, 2012). Children are even more vulnerable to violence within the family than adults. Children are abused by parents, but physical violence between siblings may be the most common form of family violence. Older adults are sometimes abused by their family caregivers, and teenage children sometimes abuse their parents, particularly their mothers (Gelles, 2010).

It is very difficult to produce accurate statistics about the amount of family violence in different categories because the family is the most intimate of social groupings; what happens in families is usually "behind closed doors," away from the watchful eyes of strangers, relatives, and neighbors. In addition, different definitions of violence are used by different researchers. The data presented here are the best available. According to the U.S. Department of Justice Statistics (Catalano, 2012), 775,650 women and 130,890 men in the United States were victims of intimate partner violence in 2009. This is a 64% decline since 1994. From 1994 to 2010, about 4 out of 5 victims of intimate partner violence were females. In 2012, an estimated 9.2 per 1,000 children were judged to be victims of child maltreatment by parents or other caregivers; of these situations where the type of maltreatment is known, 78% involved child neglect, 18.3% involved physical abuse, 9.3% involved sexual abuse, and 8.5% involved psychological maltreatment (U.S. Department of Health and Human Services, 2013b). National surveys find much higher numbers of child maltreatment than these official numbers (see Finkelhor, Ormrod, Turner, & Hamby, 2005). One research team found that 35% of 2,030 children in a national survey reported being physically assaulted by a sibling in the past year (Finkelhor et al., 2005). There are no official statistics on elder abuse, but one national incidence study found that 1 in 10 adults older than age 60 reported emotional, physical, or sexual mistreatment or neglect during the past year (Acierno et al., 2010). It is estimated that 750,000 to 1 million violent acts are committed against parents by their adolescent children each year (Gelles, 2010).

How is it that the social group assigned the societal task of providing love and nurturance becomes a setting for so much violence? Research indicates that family violence is multidetermined and identifies a number of associated factors. Stress, social isolation, economic distress, substance abuse, mental health problems, and intergenerational

Conflict perspective

modeling have all been found to increase the risk of family violence (Gelles, 2010; Newman, 2012). The United States is a relatively violent society, and violence is often seen as an appropriate way to resolve disputes (Hutchison, 2007). There are cultures of the world and subcultures in the United States that believe men have the right to beat women and parents have the right to beat children.

It can be argued that the very nature of family life makes it a breeding ground for conflict. Family members spend a great deal of time together and interact intimately in good times and bad. They tend to stir each other's most intense emotions, both positive and negative. If family members do not have good conflict resolution skills, they may not have a repertoire of behaviors other than violence to resolve conflicts.

Intervention in situations of family violence requires careful assessment, and even with the best assessment, it is difficult to predict future behavior. The decision that must be made is whether protective steps are necessary: Must children be removed? Are restraining orders necessary? Must the abused partner flee for safety? There are no ideal solutions. Removing children from abusive households may be necessary to protect them physically, but this solution carries its own risks. Children suffer emotional damage from the separation and loss and may blame themselves for the family disruption. They may be vulnerable to further abuse in the foster home if they have intense care needs. There are also risks to leaving children in homes where they have been abused, including the risk that the child will be killed. Unfortunately, the available resources are not often sufficient to meet a distressed family's needs. Clearly, no one solution fits every situation of child abuse.

The literature on domestic partner violence has proposed some useful typologies for thinking about intervention in such situations (Holtzworth-Munroe & Stuart, 1994; Johnson, 1995). Domestic partner violence can be one-way or mutual; mutual violence can be mutual fighting or involve self-defense or retaliation against a primary aggressor. It may be considered minor, involving shoving, pushing, grabbing, and slapping, or severe, involving choking, kicking, hitting with an object, beating up, or using a knife or gun. Mutual fighting tends to be less severe and more infrequent than other forms of intimate partner violence and does not usually escalate. It involves both partners who use physical means to resolve conflicts. On the other hand, one-sided use of severe forms of violence, sometimes called intimate terrorism, typically occurs more frequently and escalates over time. Many of the perpetrators of this type of violence are involved in other antisocial behaviors as well.

Just as with child abuse, different types of intervention are required for different types of domestic partner violence. Protective removal is imperative for intimate terrorism or any form of escalating violence. On the other hand, systemic couples work, in which couples are taught other methods of conflict resolution, may well be appropriate for couples who occasionally use mutual violence to resolve conflict. Support for this idea comes from a research project that looked at mutual and one-way spouse abuse in the army. The researchers found about even rates of these two types of intimate violence in 1998. After 4 years of prevention and education programs, mutual abuse had decreased by 58%, while one-way abuse had decreased by only 13% (McCarroll, Ursano, Fan, & Newby, 2004). This finding suggests that further attention to matching the intervention to the specific situation may be fruitful. The typologies discussed here do not cover every type of intimate partner violence situation, but they do make a good start at thinking about the multiple factors involved in family violence.

Divorce

Most people who get married do not anticipate that they will divorce, and yet divorce is very common. Almost all societies have mechanisms for dissolving marriages, whether it is divorce or civil or religious annulment. Worldwide, divorce rates tend to be higher in wealthier nations; for example, divorce rates are lower in the newly industrializing nations of Latin America and Asia than in the wealthy late-industrial nations of western Europe and North America (Newman, 2012). In the United States, however, the divorce rate is highest among low-income families.

There is much complexity in the analysis of divorce rates, but the divorce rate in the United States appears to have increased steadily from the mid-19th century through the 1970s, except for a sharp drop in the 1950s. It peaked in 1981 and has been dropping slightly since then but remains high compared with other wealthy industrialized countries (Greene, Anderson, Forgatch, Degarmo, & Hetherington, 2012). The lifetime probability of divorce in the United States still approaches 50% but appears to be lower for more recent marriages (Cherlin, 2010). Second and third marriages are more likely to end in divorce than first marriages. The average length of a marriage that ends in divorce is 8 years, and the average age of first divorce is 30 (Irvin, 2012). The likelihood of divorce is very small for couples that have been married for 35 or more years (divorcesource.com, n.d.).

It is thought that economic factors contribute to divorce. Wages have stagnated for non-Hispanic White men and have declined for African American men. Millions of lower-income wage earners are receiving poverty-level wages and are vulnerable to layoffs. Although women still earn less than men, they are becoming more economically independent, and about two thirds of divorces are initiated by women (Amato & Irving, 2006; Coleman, Ganong, & Warzinik, 2007). On the other hand, wives' earnings may reduce economic pressures and help to stabilize marriage (Fine, Ganong, & Demo, 2010).

There is a controversy in the empirical literature about the consequences of divorce for family members. Some researchers have found serious, long-term, postdivorce adjustment problems for both children and adults (Wallerstein & Blakeslee, 1990). Other researchers who use larger and more representative samples have found more modest and shorter-term effects for both adults and children (Barber & Demo, 2006; Braver, Shapiro, & Goodman, 2006).

Fine et al. (2010) suggest several reasons for the differences in findings. First, researchers tend to focus on one or two reactions to divorce and fail to measure other types of reactions. Second, few researchers have taken a longer-term longitudinal view of divorce adjustment, and consequently they are tapping reactions during the difficult acute adjustment phase. Third, researchers look for average reactions rather than for the variability of reactions to divorce. The feminist perspective, on the other hand, would emphasize that divorce is experienced and perceived differently by different family members and would be interested in these various perspectives. Fine et al. (2010) assert that the different conclusions about the effects of divorce on child and adult development may result partly from the fact that the effect sizes are often small and may vary with the nature and size of the sample, which would not happen if there was a stronger relationship between divorce and adjustment.

There is consistent evidence, however, that the economic well-being of women and children declines after divorce (Sayer, 2006). There are several reasons for this. Mothers devote more time to caring for children than fathers, and this restricts their time to devote to educational and occupational pursuits. Women do not earn as much as men. Moreover, many fathers do not comply fully with child support requirements (Pirog & Ziol-Guest, 2006), but even if they did, child support awards are typically too low to meet the costs of raising children (Stirling & Aldrich, 2008).

It seems clear that divorce is a crisis for most adults, lasting for approximately 2 years. Stress increases in the run-up to the divorce, during the divorce, and in the immediate aftermath. However, the stress level typically subsides within a year after divorce as families adjust relationships and routines (Demo & Fine, 2010). There is also evidence that African American women get more social support than White women following divorce (Orbuch & Brown, 2006).

After a careful review of the empirical evidence, Fine et al. (2010) agree with Emery (1999) on the following points about children's adjustment to divorce:

- Divorce is stressful for children.
- Divorce leads to adjustment and mental health problems for children.
- Most children are resilient and adjust well to divorce over time.
- Children whose parents divorce report pain, unhappy memories, and continued distress.
- Postdivorce family interaction has a great influence on adjustment to divorce.
- Children's adjustment is enhanced if they have a good relationship with at least one parent.

Substance Abuse

Substance abuse is often part of the fabric of family life and usually has an effect on the partner relationship and on child development. For the purposes of this discussion, substance abuse is defined as serious and persistent problems with alcohol and/or other substances and does not refer specifically to a clinical diagnosis. Substance abuse is often described as a family problem, not only because of its effect on the entire family system but also because of the growing evidence of a strong genetic component in the etiology of substance abuse (Bierut, 2011). The effect of substance abuse on the partner relationship and the impact of adolescent substance abuse on the family are discussed briefly here, followed by a larger discussion of the impact of parental substance abuse on children.

Kenneth Leonard and Rina Eiden (2007) reviewed the evidence about the impact of alcohol abuse on marital satisfaction and marital violence. They conclude that alcohol abuse has an adverse effect on marital satisfaction and stability, especially among couples where one partner is abusing alcohol and the other partner is not. They also conclude that there is evidence of a strong association between excessive alcohol consumption and intimate partner violence. Consistent with a family life cycle perspective, they found evidence that family transitions can affect patterns of alcohol use for both men and women, with excessive drinking declining in the transition to marriage and during pregnancy and increasing in the postnatal period. There is also strong evidence that excessive alcohol use increases after divorce but may decrease for women divorcing from spouses with alcohol problems.

Some evidence also exists that adolescent substance abuse problems change the nature of parent–child relationships, with parents changing their discipline methods in response to the substance abuse (Mezzich et al., 2007). There is also evidence that adolescent substance abuse increases parental stress and sometimes results in increased use of alcohol among parents (Leonard & Eiden, 2007). Parents may need family support and training in coping responses, as well as social policies that allow family leave from work when faced with an adolescent with substance abuse problems (Deater-Deckard, 2004).

By one estimate, one in four children in the United States is exposed to a family member's alcohol abuse, and one in six children live with parents who abuse illicit drugs (VanDeMark et al., 2005). Although research finds that parental substance abuse does not always lead to an unacceptable level of parenting (Coyle et al., 2009; Havnen, Breivik, Stormark, & Jakobsen, 2011; Street, Harrington, Chiang, Cairns, & Ellis, 2004), there is much empirical evidence that parental substance abuse often impairs parental functioning. Brynna Kroll (2004) reviewed the empirical literature on the experiences of children who grow up in families where adult use of alcohol and other substances is problematic. A number of negative effects on children were noted. In all the reviewed studies, secrecy and denial about the substance abuse were organizing features of family life, cutting the family off from extended family and community supports. Children often become afraid and mistrustful of outsiders who try to help, fearing being taken from their parent(s), among other fears.

Adult children of alcoholics report pervasive loss and grief, including loss of feeling loved, loss of a reliable parent, loss of a "normal" lifestyle, and loss of childhood itself. And while not all substance-abusing parents abuse their children, there is an increased risk of child maltreatment while using. Given that substance abuse is often characterized by cycles of relapse and recovery, parental substance abuse does not mean that everything falls apart, particularly during phases of abstinence or reduced use, but parental conflict and fighting do typically increase during periods of excessive substance use. Children's lives are often dominated by the needs, feelings, and behaviors of substance-abusing parents. The children sometimes become caregivers to their parents, putting them to bed when they are drunk or cleaning up after a parent who urinates on the floor. There is considerable evidence that substance-abusing parents engage in less monitoring of their children's behavior.

Research has also found parental substance abuse to be a risk factor for child behavior problems as well as depression and anxiety (Barnard & McKegaley, 2004). School performance often suffers in children of substance-abusing parents, as do peer relationships. Parental substance abuse during childhood is also associated with young-adult difficulties with romantic partnerships (Fischer, Lyness, & Engler, 2010).

Although parental substance abuse is a risk factor in child development, some substance-abusing parents are able to manage family life in a way that supports healthy child development. James Coyle and colleagues (2009) were interested in family functioning in families affected by parental alcohol abuse, particularly in the dimensions of family functioning that allowed these families to be resilient. Their statistical analysis identified families who were functioning at above-average, average, and below-average levels, according to standardized measures. Their research provides support for Froma Walsh's (2006) model of family resilience, in which aspects of belief systems, family organization, and communication processes allow families to be resilient in the face of adversity. They found that families who functioned well on one of these dimensions functioned well on all three. Levels of social functioning were not related to social class or parental education. They did find, however, that Black families with a substance-abusing parent were more likely to have above-average or average functioning than White and Native American families, even though the Black families were, overall, in the lower end of the range of economic resources and reported more stressful life events.

Other research that has looked at the strengths of substance-abusing parents has focused on those parents in treatment. This research finds that these parents are self-critical about their abilities to parent while abusing substances but also report making attempts to combine their substance abuse with efforts to ensure that the needs of their children were being met. The desire to look after their children properly or to get the children back from substitute care is a powerful motivator to stop using alcohol and/or other drugs (Fraser, McIntyre, & Manby, 2009; Tracy & Martin, 2007).

Some researchers report that substance-abusing mothers feel overwhelming guilt and shame about the impact their substance abuse has on their parenting (K. Cox, 2000). In a study of mothers in treatment, 68% of whom had "lost" children to substitute care, Tracy and Martin (2007) found that 90% of the mothers viewed their relationships with their children as close, and 84% reported that their children provide as much support for sobriety as the adults in their lives do. The emotional care provided by children of substance-abusing parents is often noted in the literature by such terms as "role reversal," "parental child," or "parentification," all of which suggest a negative impact on the child of providing such care. One research team (Godsall, Jurkovic, Emshoff, Anderson, & Stanwyck, 2004) examined the relationships between parental alcohol misuse and parentification and children's self-concept. They found that African American child participants scored higher on self-concept than European American children. They suggest that the concept of parentification, and similar concepts, may not be applicable to African American families and other collectivist-oriented families where close kinship networks are valued. They further suggest that considerable caregiving responsibilities in the context of close kinship ties may not have negative effects for children who are also receiving support and caring. Caregiving by children may be a part of a pattern of "filial responsibility" and not interpreted as unjust by the children.

In interpreting their finding that African American families with alcohol-abusing parents score better on family functioning than other such families, Coyle et al. (2009) note that Froma Walsh's (2006) model of family resilience indicates that flexibility in family structure in times of adversity serves as a shock absorber and fosters family resilience. Walsh (2006) also identifies family belief systems as sources for resilience, and Coyle et al. (2009) note that other researchers have found that cultural pride, kinship, spirituality, and high expectations for children are common in African American families. Coyle et al. (2009) suggest that struggling families may best be helped by identifying possible cultural beliefs, locating resources outside the nuclear family, becoming more flexible in family roles, and improving communication. You may recognize this as consistent with Walsh's model of family resilience that identifies belief systems, organizational patterns, and communication as the ingredients for family resilience.

Critical Thinking Questions 10.5

Three challenges to family life are discussed in the previous section: family violence, divorce, and substance abuse. If you were to be my coauthor on this chapter for the sixth edition of the book, what advice would you give me about the most important challenges facing families today? Are family violence, divorce, and substance abuse new or enduring challenges for families in the United States? Do these challenges appear to occur across cultural lines—across traditional, modern, and postmodern cultures (review Chapter 8 for descriptions of these three types of culture)?

Implications for Social Work Practice

This discussion of families and family life, in the context of larger social systems, suggests several practice principles:

- Assess families from a variety of theoretical perspectives. Given recent economic shifts, be particularly aware of the impact of changes in larger systems on families' resources and functioning.
- Recognize the diversity of family structures represented by the families with whom you work and be sensitive to the relative strengths and weaknesses of each of these family structures.
- Develop awareness of economic diversity among families and the different economic and other resources available to the families you serve.

- Develop awareness of cultural diversity among families and a commitment to culturally sensitive practice that involves ongoing learning both about and from families that are different from your own.
- Use appropriate family assessment tools, including the genogram, ecomap, and timeline, to help you develop a more comprehensive understanding of the families with which you work.
- Give families credit for struggling well in adverse circumstances.
- Understand policies and changes at the state and national levels and the ways they affect both your own work and the lives of all families—particularly lower-income, stressed families.
- Where appropriate, encourage family members to become involved in neighborhood, local, state, and national efforts for positive change.
- As appropriate, work toward your agency's becoming involved in policy and advocacy work on behalf of families, including development of needed programs and services.

Key Terms

ABC-X model of family stress and coping	family life cycle perspective	lone-parent families
cohabiting	family of origin	multilevel family practice model
differentiation of self	family resilience perspective	nonnormative stressors
family	family systems perspective	normative stressors
family ecomap	family timeline	stress pileup
family economic stress model	feminist perspective on families	transition points
family investment model	genogram	triangulation
	intersectionality feminist theory	

Active Learning

1. *Theory and your family.* We have used different theoretical lenses to look at the family of Bobby Sharpe. If you were a social worker working with a family similar to the Sharpes, you would want to be aware of how your own family experiences influence your practice with families. You can use theory to help you do that as well. To begin this process, reflect on the following questions related to your family of origin and your childhood:

- What value was placed on connectedness, and what value was placed on the differentiated self?
- What were the external boundaries—who was in and who was out of the family? What were the commonly shared beliefs? What roles did family members play? What were the patterns of communication?
- Were there any transition points that were particularly difficult for your family? What made those transitions difficult?
- How traditional were the gender roles in your family? How was power distributed?
- Can you recall any periods of stress pileup? If so, how did your family cope during those periods?
- How did your family use belief systems, organizational patterns, and communication to be resilient in the face of adversity?

After you have reflected on these questions, write a brief paper addressing the following points:

- Summarize your reflections on each question.
- How do you think your experiences in your family of origin might serve as a barrier or an aid in work with a family similar to the Sharpe family?

2. *Visualizing your family.* Sometimes we learn new things about families when we prepare visual representations of them. There are several tools available for doing this. You will use three of them here to visualize your own family.

- Referring to Exhibit 10.2, prepare a multigenerational genogram of your family, going back to your maternal and paternal grandparents.
- Referring to Exhibit 10.3, prepare a family ecomap of your current family situation.
- Referring to Exhibit 10.4, prepare a family timeline, beginning at the point of your birth or earlier if you think there were significant earlier events that need to be noted.

After you have prepared these materials, work in small groups in class to discuss how useful each tool was in helping you think about your family of origin. Were any new insights gained from using these visual tools? What is your overall reaction to using tools like these to understand your family?

Web Resources

Administration for Children & Families (ACF): www.acf.hhs.gov

Site of ACF, a government agency that is part of the U.S. Department of Health and Human Services, contains fact sheets about children and families and information about ACF programs such as child support enforcement, Head Start, and Temporary Assistance for Needy Families (TANF).

Council on Contemporary Families: www .contemporaryfamilies.org

Official site of the Council on Contemporary Families, a nonprofit organization that promotes an inclusive view of families, contains information and research on families, along with links to other Internet resources.

Families and Work Institute: www .familiesandwork.org

Site contains information on work–life research, community mobilization forums, information on the Fatherhood Project, and frequently asked questions.

Forum on Child and Family Statistics: www .childstats.gov

Official website of the Federal Interagency Forum on Child and Family Statistics offers easy access to federal and state statistics and reports on children and families, including international comparisons.

National Council on Family Relations (NCFR): www.ncfr.org

Site contains publications, news, and professional resources.

Student Study Site

⑤SAGE edge™

Sharpen your skills with SAGE edge at **edge.sagepub.com/hutchisonpe5e**

SAGE edge for students provides a personalized approach to help you accomplish your coursework goals in an easy-to-use learning environment.

CHAPTER 11

Small Groups

Elizabeth P. Cramer

Chapter Outline

- Small group work has become a common form of human service delivery. Why would work with small groups be an important form of social work practice in the current age of high mobility and concerns about cost containment?

- People find themselves a part of many different formal and informal small groups during their lifetimes. Why might it be helpful for a social worker to know about the groups to which a client belongs?

Key Ideas

As you read this chapter, take note of these central ideas:

1. Small groups are typically defined as two or more people who interact with each other because of shared interests, goals, experiences, and needs.

2. Types of social work groups include therapy, mutual aid, psychoeducational, self-help, and task groups. A group may be a combination of two or more types, and any of these types of groups can occur in either face-to-face or virtual formats.

3. Small groups in social work vary in how they develop, how long they last, and how they determine membership.

4. In determining group composition, small groups must resolve issues of heterogeneity versus homogeneity and related social justice issues.

5. To understand small group processes, social workers may draw on psychodynamic theory, symbolic interaction theory, status characteristics and expectation states theory, exchange theory, and self-categorization theory.

6. Both stage theories and process models have been used to understand how small groups develop.

7. Group dynamics are patterns of interaction, including factors such as leadership, roles, communication networks, and group cohesiveness.

8. Social workers often work in interdisciplinary teams with other professionals representing a variety of disciplines.

CASE STUDY

The Sexuality and Gender Group at a Women's Residential Substance Abuse Treatment Facility

The sexuality and gender group at the women's residential substance abuse treatment facility meets twice a month. This is a support group for lesbian, bisexual, and questioning women (those women who are unsure of their sexual orientation). Women who identify as transgender also attend the group. Women in the treatment facility are informed about the group by their counselors, and participation in the group is strictly voluntary. The facilitator is a licensed clinical social worker who is also a social work professor and a lesbian. The composition of the group can change each session because women are entering and exiting the facility regularly. Typically, 8 to 15 women attend the group. The duration of the treatment program is 90 days; however, some of the women choose to leave the program before treatment has been completed. Many of the women in the group are parents; some of them have brought their children into treatment with them because one of the treatment programs at this facility allows women and their children to come into residence. Most of the women in this group identify as African American or Hispanic and range in age from 19 to 50. The facilitator is Caucasian, Jewish, and in her early 40s. The following is an account of one of the group sessions. Pseudonyms for all the group members and facilitator are used in this case.

It's a hot day, and Deb is driving her non-air-conditioned car to the substance abuse treatment facility to facilitate the sexuality and gender group. She's been facilitating this group, which was the first of its kind at this facility, for about a year. It has been a good learning experience for her, and she has grown quite attached to the group. She particularly is impressed with the candidness of the group members and often refers to this population of women as superb "BS detectors," because they are not afraid to call each other out when denial or deceitfulness is surfacing. For a moment, Deb feels sorry for herself because she doesn't have air conditioning in her car and she lives in the South, but then she remembers that most of the women in group do not even own cars. That moment of self-pity quickly passes.

The group members are already in the lounge where group meets when Deb arrives. She smiles and acknowledges each of the group members through eye contact. She notices that out of the dozen women in the room, about eight of them were there for the last group session. Deb introduces herself and makes a point to say that she is a lesbian but not in recovery, although she has worked with many women who are in recovery. She mentions where she works and how long she has been facilitating this group. She then asks the women to introduce themselves using first names. In their introductions, some of the women mention why they have come to group or how long they've attended group. Two of the women share that they were curious about the group but don't identify as lesbian or bisexual; however, they have considered same-sex relationships and have had feelings of same-sex attraction. One of the group members notes that she has recently exited the prison system and had relationships with other women while she was incarcerated but never while "on the streets."

Deb describes the purpose of the group as a place for members to talk about sexual orientation, whether they are lesbian, bisexual, or questioning. Deb stresses that what is said in the room stays in the room and that members should refrain from sharing someone's story with others outside of the group. Confidentiality is especially important to emphasize in residential programs. Deb also mentions that the group is open and that members can freely discuss what they want to.

Deb usually has a loosely planned agenda for each group session but also waits to see what issues may get raised in the introductions and check-in at the beginning of the group. Today, she brought the documentary film *All God's Children* to show the group (Mosbacher, Reid, & Rhue, 1996). The film highlights the experiences of African American lesbians, gays, and bisexuals, particularly related to family, church, and community. It's a powerful film and reminds the group members that their sexual orientations are not experienced in a bubble; rather, the intersections of faith, neighborhood, geography, and other identities and characteristics influence how they experience their sexual orientations.

One part of the film seems to arouse much energy and discussion: whether a person is born gay or makes a decision or choice to be gay. Tamika, one of the younger women in group, strongly asserts that a person chooses

(Continued)

to be gay. She shuns the labels of "lesbian" and "bisexual"; instead, she prefers to allow herself to date or fall in love with whoever is attractive to her, whether that person is male, female, or transgendered. Monica, a woman in her early 50s, disagrees that sexual orientation is a choice. She shares a story of how she "knew" she was a lesbian when she was 12 and she fell head over heels for a girl in her neighborhood. She tried to suppress those feelings and pretended she was into boys all through middle school and the beginning of high school. By her junior year, she just couldn't pretend anymore. She secretly would date girls, but no one in her family or her church knew. To this day, many years later, she has never openly said to any of her family members that she is a lesbian. They all seem to know that she is, but it isn't discussed. She experienced a deep hurt at her church when her pastor delivered a sermon that Monica thought was very antigay. Her parents insisted that she attend church. She really didn't want to go to church after that sermon, but she also didn't want to tell her parents the reason why. That wasn't the first and last time that antigay remarks were made in her church. Gail, usually quiet in group, shares that her experience at church has been the opposite of Monica's. Her family attended a progressive church and persons of all sexual orientations were welcomed. She still hesitated to come out to her family members when she first began dating women but then eventually began to disclose to the family members to whom she felt closest. Their positive responses encouraged her to continue to disclose to other family members and close friends.

The discussion of the film moves the group into deeper core themes related to their sexual orientation and their addiction. As the facilitator, Deb looks for opportunities to work the parallel process in group—to note the similarities between the negative consequences of an addiction and the experience of being a sexual minority who is often discriminated against and ostracized. A few of these common issues include shame, fear, emotional dependence, and despair and loneliness. Shame is a particularly powerful emotion; the women in the group connect shame to experiences they've had as sexual minorities and the guilt and embarrassment about behaviors in which they've engaged while they were using drugs. Negative judgments from others about their sexual orientations and/or their addictions exacerbated the shame. One of the group members shares with the group about how she would get high in order to allow herself to be intimate with women. She thought it was the only way she could mask her fear and shame about her attraction to other women. Many of the group members struggle with feelings of internalized homophobia. In the group, Deb emphasizes how acceptance of oneself is important to group members' emotional health.

The group is coming to a close. Most of the women have spoken in group today. The film seemed to strike a chord with many of them. On the way back to her workplace, Deb thinks about all the group members and what they shared that day. She feels fortunate to be let in to the inner lives of the women during a time when they are working hard to heal.

SMALL GROUPS IN SOCIAL WORK

Much of human behavior takes place in small groups. The sexuality and gender group is a type of small group with special relevance to social work practice, but most people also become involved in other types of small groups: friendship groups, task groups at work, self-help groups, or sports teams, to name but a few. Donelson Forsyth (2011) reminds us that "people, no matter what they are doing—working, relaxing, studying, exercising, worshipping, or sleeping—are usually in a group rather than alone" (p. 19). We interact with others in many sizes of groups; the focus of this chapter is on small groups. We carry out our relationships with significant others in small groups, but it is important to remember that small groups also provide the structures on which communities, organizations, and the larger society are built.

In a mobile society, small groups serve a useful function. Exhibit 11.1 shows how group members may benefit from belonging to a small group. Small groups offer individuals an opportunity to meet others and work together to achieve mutual goals. They provide social support; they socialize us to the norms, values, behaviors, and skills for living in a given society; they provide a sense of belonging; they provide us with companionship and conversation; and they help us to connect to the wider world. Robert Putnam (2000) suggests that in our rapidly changing globalized society, small groups are an important source of *social capital*, or connections among individuals based on reciprocity and trustworthiness.

Small groups may be formally defined in a number of ways. A few scholarly definitions of small groups, along with examples from the sexuality and gender group, are displayed in Exhibit 11.2. Although these definitions differ, there is general agreement that small groups are more than a collection of individuals who may have similar traits or be in physical proximity. Persons who live on the same block may be in proximity but have little social interaction and not perceive themselves as a group. Thus, we may define a **small group** as "two or more people who interact with each other because of shared interests, goals, experiences and needs" (Ballantine & Roberts, 2014, p. 153).

A significant element of social work practice today is **group work**, which serves people's needs by bringing them together in small groups. Group work emerged in the United States in the late 1800s and early 1900s. Early group work took place within the settlement houses, YMCA/YWCA, Jewish community centers, and the Boy Scouts and Girl Scouts. These groups focused primarily on recreation, social integration, immigration issues, character building, and social reform. We are now seeing a resurgence in recreation and social skill–building groups, reminiscent of early group work (see Rosenwald et al., 2013). Social skills groups with elementary-age children (Lane et al., 2003); hoops groups (basketball) with adolescent males (Hansen, Larson, & Dworkin, 2003); and physical activity, reminiscence, and motivation groups for older adults (Hughes et al., 2005) are three examples.

By the 1930s and 1940s, formal organizations were promoting group work. In 1935, the Group Work Section of the National Conference on Social Work emerged, and in 1937, the American Association for the Study of Group Work formed. The American Association of Group Workers, which started in 1946, later merged with other organizations to become the National Association of Social Workers (NASW).

During World War II, group work became popular in hospitals and other clinical settings in the United States, resulting in some tension between group workers and caseworkers. Following the war, the philosophy of group work shifted from a strengths focus to a more problem-focused orientation. Nevertheless, group workers continued to attempt to influence the social work profession as a whole. During the 1960s and 1970s, social work education included courses on group work, and some students majored in group work. But then group work content declined as social work education shifted its focus to individuals and families. Ironically, at the same time, joining groups became more common in the United States. The 1980s and 1990s saw the rise of mutual aid groups (Gitterman & Shulman, 2005), today a popular type of social work group.

Exhibit 11.1   Benefits of Small Groups

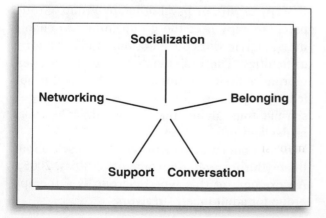

Exhibit 11.2 Definitions of Small Groups

Author(s)	Definition	Example
Newman (2012)	Set of people who interact more or less regularly and who are conscious of their identity as a unit	Members of the sexuality and gender group interact in this group twice a month and identify as a group of people with sexual orientations and/or gender identities that are different from the norm. They are able to use the group to become more accepting of their identities.
Ritzer (2013a)	A relatively small number of people who over time develop a patterned relationship based on interaction with one another	Members of the sexuality and gender group develop a culture within the group over time, which emphasizes open communication, confidentiality, and willingness to be truthful with each other.
Ballantine & Roberts (2014)	Two or more people who interact with each other because of shared interests, goals, experiences, and needs	The sexuality and gender group offers a space for the members to openly discuss what it is like to be a sexual minority and a recovering addict. Group members support each other in achieving recovery from their addiction and positive acceptance of their sexual orientation.

With today's concern about cost containment, groups are viewed as a financially prudent method of service delivery (Coyne, 2014). In addition, empirical studies have shown the effectiveness of groups in addressing a number of social, health, and emotional problems, such as mental illness and substance abuse (Drake, Mueser, Brunette, & McHugo, 2004; Lau, Chan, Li, & Au, 2010) and cancer (Spiegel & Classen, 2000). One researcher (Garrett, 2004) found that a small sample of school social workers make extensive use of group work methods. Group work content is coming back into the social work curriculum, and social work students are being exposed to group work through their field placements. Furthermore, graduating students have informed me that potential employers ask if they have had course content on group work.

A number of scholars have established classifications for groups encountered in social work (see, e.g., Kottler & Englar-Carlson, 2010; Toseland & Rivas, 2012; Zastrow, 2009). This chapter focuses on five: therapy groups, mutual aid groups, psychoeducational groups, self-help groups, and task groups. Exhibit 11.3 compares these five types of groups on several major features—purpose, leadership, size, duration—and gives examples of each. As you read about them, remember that groups may not fall exclusively into one category; rather, they may share elements of several group types. For example, a group for parents and friends of seriously mentally ill persons may include psychoeducational material about the nature of mental illness and its impact on family members, provide mutual aid to its members through discussion of taboo areas, and offer a therapeutic component in the examination of family patterns and dynamics. In recent years, all types of groups have been meeting in virtual format, and we take a look at this trend in this section.

Therapy Groups

One common type of group is known as the **therapy group**, or psychotherapy group. Group psychotherapy uses the group milieu to enable individuals to work out emotional and behavioral difficulties. The individuals in the group often reproduce their emotional and behavioral problems within the group setting, thus giving the leader and group members an opportunity to provide feedback about them (Burlingame, Kapetanovic, & Ross, 2005). An example of this type of group is a therapy group for adult incest survivors.

> Psychodynamic perspective

Exhibit 11.3 Types of Groups

Type of Group	Purpose	Leadership	Size	Duration	Examples
Therapy	Uses group modality to assist individuals to resolve emotional and behavioral problems	Typically led by a trained clinician or psychotherapist	Typically small, sometimes six or fewer members	Brief therapy groups usually meet for 6 weeks or less. Long-term psychotherapy groups can last years.	Groups for college students run by university counseling centers; groups for male adolescents who engage in sexual harm
Mutual aid	Uses mutual aid processes to create a helping environment within the group milieu	Typically led by a facilitator who may be a professional or layperson trained to lead the group. The leader may or may not have experienced the issue on which the group is focused.	These groups may be small (fewer than 5 persons) or large (12 or more), especially if run in a drop-in format.	Drop-in mutual aid groups may be ongoing for a number of years with members coming in and out of the group. Time-limited mutual aid groups typically run for 4 to 12 weeks.	Groups for cancer survivors; groups in schools for children whose parents are going through a divorce
Psychoeducational	Focuses on the provision of information about an experience or problem	Typically led by a trained professional	Limiting the group size is usually not as critical with these types of groups because of their purpose.	One-time meetings of psychoeducational groups may be offered on a regular schedule; they might be offered in a series of sessions (e.g., a 4-week educational series); or they might be offered on an as-needed basis.	Groups for couples preparing to adopt a child; groups to teach parents how to use adaptive equipment for children with disabilities
Self-help	Uses the commonality of the problem or issue to build social support among members	Typically led by a layperson who has experience with the problem (e.g., a person in recovery from alcohol and drug addiction)	Typically, since self-help groups operate on a drop-in basis, the group size is not limited.	Most often, self-help groups are run on a drop-in basis; however, some may be offered in a time-limited format.	Twelve-step groups (e.g., AA, ACOA, NA)
Task	Created to accomplish a specific task or to advocate around a particular social issue or problem	These groups may be led by professionals or nonprofessionals; leaders may be appointed or elected.	Often limited in size to successfully accomplish the task. When advocating for change, membership may be larger.	Meet until the task has been accomplished or the desired social change has been accomplished	A committee to examine low-income housing needs that is instructed to submit a report of their findings to the city council

387

Therapy groups typically have fewer members and meet for a longer duration than self-help, psychoeducational, or mutual aid groups. Such a group may have six or fewer members, may be led by a person who considers himself or herself to be a therapist, may meet weekly for a year or more, and may involve intrapsychic exploration of thoughts and emotions. Talk or verbal therapy groups are not the only type. Increasingly popular are art therapy groups, which have demonstrated the standard therapeutic factors of verbal therapy groups as well as some factors unique to art therapy (Wood, Molassiotis, & Payne, 2011). In addition, therapy groups do not necessarily meet for long periods. **Brief treatment models**, which usually last 6 weeks or less, are becoming more and more popular in a managed care environment.

Mutual Aid Groups

In **mutual aid groups**, members meet to help one another deal with common problems. The members of the group thus become as important to its success as the facilitator (Gitterman & Shulman, 2005; Lesser et al., 2004). In the sexuality and gender group, we witness many benefits of mutual aid groups:

- *Sharing data:* coming-out stories, events in the members' lives related to their sexual orientation and addiction

Photo 11.1   Therapy group—Members in therapy groups share experiences and obstacles they have encountered. Group therapy assists individuals in resolving emotional and behavioral problems.

© iStockphoto.com/JeanellNorvell

- *Engaging in a dialectical process of discovery:* theories about sexual orientation, insight into when one first felt one was not heterosexual
- *Discussing taboo subjects:* open discussion of intimacy, admitting shame or guilt about feelings or behaviors related to addiction and/or sexual orientation
- *Realizing that one is not alone (all in the same boat):* others who are not heterosexual and have had similar feelings regarding coming out and disclosure
- *Finding support:* a place to be oneself in a homophobic society
- *Making mutual demands:* challenges to internalized self-hatred, dishonesty about one's feelings and behaviors, and unhealthy coping mechanisms that lesbian and bisexual women may use as a way to live in two worlds
- *Problem solving:* disclosure decisions for individuals and the larger issue of self-disclosure of stigmatized identities (as a sexual minority and a recovering addict)
- *Rehearsing new behaviors:* role-playing of disclosure scenarios or confrontations with people who make antigay jokes
- *Finding strength in numbers:* reading literature and watching films that portray the lived experiences of "out" lesbian and bisexual women of various races, ethnicities, faiths, and abilities offers positive role modeling to group members

In general, mutual aid groups are led by someone, either a professional or a trained individual, who identifies with the population the group targets. For example, the facilitator of the sexuality and gender group self-identifies as a lesbian. In fact, some mutual aid groups form as an alternative to professionally led therapy groups. In this way, they may be similar in purpose to self-help groups. There is no requirement, however, that in order to be an effective leader, one must have "been there." The groups may be time-limited (for example, a 10-week group for siblings of children with disabilities) or ongoing (such as a weekly support group for incarcerated males).

Mutual aid groups also have the potential for activism. A group of people may meet initially to gain support and share concerns but may transform some of their healing energy into social change efforts. For instance, members of a mutual aid group for battered women may attend a Take Back the Night march (to protest violence against women) as a group and then courageously approach the microphone to speak about their own experiences of victimization and empowerment.

Psychoeducational Groups

Psychoeducational groups, in which social workers and other professionals share their knowledge and expertise to educate group members about a specific life problem or developmental issue, are

> Social behavioral perspective

becoming more common in the United States (Brown, 2005). The topics include problems such as substance abuse and divorce as well as more general interests, such as child development or the aging process. Those who participate are primarily looking for information rather than intervention for emotional and behavioral problems. Thus, the format of group meetings may be a lecture by the group leader or a guest speaker with minimal group discussion. The group could be a one-time workshop or it could last several sessions.

Although a psychoeducational group is not a therapy group, it can be therapeutic when members share feelings and concerns. An example is a one-time group meeting for family and friends of persons in a drug rehabilitation center. The stated purpose may be to provide education about the recovery process to family members and friends, but during the session, group members may share feelings about their loved one's addiction and how it has affected their lives.

Self-Help Groups

In general, **self-help groups** are not professionally led, although a professional may serve in the role of consultant. These groups are composed of people who voluntarily meet because of a common identity or life situation, thus offering members an opportunity to receive assistance from others who are also struggling with similar issues. An informal leader may emerge in a self-help group, or leadership may be rotated among the membership. Self-help groups are often used as a supplement to professional treatment. For example, someone who is receiving outpatient substance abuse treatment may be referred to Alcoholics Anonymous; someone in a family preservation program may be referred to Parents Anonymous. Self-help groups often have no limit on their life span and have rotating membership (people come and go from the group).

It appears that humans have developed and maintained self-help groups for ages (Teshome, Zenebe, Metaferia, & Biadgilign, 2012). Although there is no trustworthy estimate of the number of self-help groups in the United States and around the world, there is much evidence that both face-to-face and virtual self-help groups are numerous. Self-help groups have several benefits. People are able to offer help to others, as well as receive help, which produces psychological rewards (Zastrow, 2009). In addition, self-help groups can run with few resources. For example, a religious institution might donate space for meetings, and there generally are no costs for the group facilitators.

Photo 11.2 Mothers support group. Here, mothers join together to share stories, struggles, and insights about the adjustment of becoming a parent.

© Digital Vision/Thinkstock

Self-help groups offer their members some of the social functions mentioned in the beginning of this chapter—a chance to meet others and have meaningful interactions, a place to feel as though one belongs and to give support to others. In short, self-help groups offer a social support system. As discussed in Chapter 5, social support has been shown to help people prevent and overcome disease and to maintain good psychological health (Coker, Sanderson, Ellison, & Fadden, 2006). In addition, some believe that attending a self-help group is less stigmatizing than a "treatment" or "therapy" group, the latter being more often associated with those who are seriously ill or have major problems in living. Some people view self-help groups as a form of support by and for laypersons ("folks just like me"), and the idea of attending one can be much less intimidating than a therapy or mutual aid group. The absence of agency affiliation for many self-help groups is attractive to those who would rather think of themselves as getting support from people in similar situations than going to an agency for assistance. Yet others may find comfort in knowing that a particular self-help group has an affiliation with a national, state, or local organization (Wituk, Shepherd, Slavich, Warren, & Meissen, 2000). Self-help groups can demonstrate helping characteristics (e.g., universality, support, and communication of experiential knowledge) similar to those of mutual aid groups. In one study, however, self-help group members reported more satisfaction with the group and gave higher evaluations for most of the helping characteristics than mutual aid group members did (Schiff & Bargal, 2000).

Another benefit of self-help groups is their potential for activism. One study found that parents of children with cancer who were members of self-help groups were significantly more involved than other parents of such children in working to improve the medical system in which their children were involved (Chesney & Chesler, 1993). Another researcher (Tesoriero, 2006) found that women's self-help groups in India become active in community action projects and sometimes move their activism beyond the local community. A study of women's postpartum depression self-help groups (Taylor, 1999) found that these groups incorporate consciousness raising and advocacy with medical and mental health professionals and politicians to effect change in institutional responses to women experiencing postpartum depression.

Task Groups

Most of us have been involved in task groups, such as a committee at school or work or a task force in the community.

> Exchange and choice perspective

It appears that the use of task groups is increasing in the workplace (Kottler & Englar-Carlson, 2010). In social work practice, task groups are often short term and formed to accomplish specific goals and objectives. Task groups are used frequently by social workers involved in planning, administration, community organizing, and social action roles but are much less common in other social work roles. An example is a needs assessment committee formed at an agency to determine the problems and concerns of the population the agency serves. Although members of other types of groups may take on tasks (e.g., researching a subject and presenting it to the group), the **task group** is created with the express purpose of completing some specific task.

Task groups are often formally led by professionals appointed or elected to chair the group. Leaders may be chosen because of their position in the agency or their expertise in the area. Task groups formed in the community to advocate for change may be led by community members or co-led by professionals and community (lay) members.

In task groups as well as other kinds of groups, members fulfill what are commonly referred to as "task and maintenance" roles. The task specialist focuses on the goals set by the group and the tasks needed to accomplish them. These may include providing information to aid group discussion, giving directions for how to proceed with a task, or summarizing members' ideas. Maintenance roles refer to those that enhance the social and emotional bonding within the group. These include inquiring about how close members feel to each other, encouraging open and respectful discussion of conflicts, and inviting reluctant members to participate in group discussion (Coyne, 2014).

Critical Thinking Questions 11.1

In what types of small groups have you participated? What benefits have you derived from participating in small groups? What frustrations have you faced from participation in small groups?

Virtual Groups

Virtual groups are those where members do not meet face-to-face, meeting instead by telephone or through the Internet. Any of the discussed group types can and has used technology, either as the primary format for running the group or as a supplement to a group that meets face-to-face. Technological advances have made it possible to have telephone conversations among a number of people at very little cost. During the past 2 decades, some social workers and other helping professionals have been using the telephone to offer therapeutic and support groups (Toseland & Larkin, 2010; Toseland & Rivas, 2012). During this same time period, computer-mediated support groups have proliferated in the United States and around the world (Jones & Meier, 2011). We'll look first at telephone-mediated groups and then at computer-mediated groups.

Telephone-mediated groups have not been rigorously evaluated to date, but a number of good case studies have been reported. Toseland and Rivas (2012) reviewed 19 studies of telephone support groups. They found that these groups are most often used with persons with chronic and long-term illnesses or with caregivers of frail older adults. Their review found both advantages and disadvantages of telephone-mediated groups, but the findings were overwhelmingly positive for the types of groups noted earlier. Some researchers found that in some situations, telephone-mediated

groups are more cohesive than face-to-face groups. They found that in telephone groups members no longer focus on personal features such as skin color or other social status cues. Other advantages of telephone groups include convenience of meeting in one's own home, reduced time needed to participate because of no travel time, ability to reach people in rural areas and across greater distances, ability to reach people who are homebound or caring for someone who can't be left alone, and greater levels of self-disclosure. Disadvantages of telephone groups include difficulty for leaders to track individual participation and interpret subtle verbal cues; difficulty for group members to gauge each other's reactions because of the lack of visual cues; and distortions related to technological problems or background noise. Some researchers noted more hostility in telephone-mediated groups than in face-to-face groups, and others noted less hostility. Toseland and Larkin (2010) provide useful guidelines for developing and leading telephone groups. They suggest that social group workers use the same skills in telephone-mediated groups as with face-to-face groups but need to to be more active to ensure clear communication because of the lack of visual cues.

Computer technology offers several potential support group outlets, including e-mail-based groups, chat rooms, news groups, videoconferencing, and discussion forums. Computer-mediated support is particularly attractive to younger people for whom electronic communication is their primary means of communication. Computer-mediated groups may provide benefits to some of the same groups of people that benefit from telephone-mediated groups: people living in rural areas, people who are homebound, and caregivers who cannot leave their care recipients (Jones & Meier, 2011). As with telephone-mediated groups, some researchers have found that computer-mediated groups can speed up the process of group cohesiveness and heighten the sense of interdependence among members (Michinov, Michinov, & Toczek-Capell, 2004). Group identity and group cohesiveness do not appear to require member co-presence. On the other hand, miscommunication has been found to be more frequent in computer-mediated team meetings (Levi, 2014). Jones and Meier (2011) note that like face-to-face groups, computer-mediated groups must develop "coherent and compelling missions, recruit and retain members, establish and enforce group norms, and mange conflict" (p. 103).

Some people enjoy the anonymity of web-based groups. In some of these groups, the use of pseudonyms and withholding other identifying information is appealing for persons who desire support but don't want to feel too vulnerable. Social workers who refer clients to web-based groups may want to first discuss the potential negative consequences of using such groups. For example, because of the anonymity of the site, participants may engage in hostile or bullying behavior to an extent they would not do in person. A good group moderator will intervene in such behavior. Also, *cyberstalking* is another danger for those who desire to participate in web-based groups (Hitchcock, 2006).

It is a challenge for social workers to stay current with constant technological advances. Jones and Meier (2011) provide a case study of a computer-mediated support group that demonstrates the need to adapt to changing technology. They studied an online support group called Parents of Suicides (POS). The group started in 1998 as an e-mail-based mailing list of about 10 people. In the beginning, the group stayed small and developed quick bonding and a strong sense of identity. In the first year, however, the group grew substantially and lost some of its intimacy. In 2000, new technology allowed POS to add a web-based discussion forum to its e-mail-based list. A separate website was developed to create a memorial wall to honor members' deceased children. Along the way, an online newsletter was developed and then a chat room. As the group numbers grew into the hundreds, conflict and complaints grew. These new challenges were addressed through formalized rules and the formation of subgroups. This case study reminds us that many online support groups are quite large and are better characterized as e-communities than as e-groups. E-communities are discussed in Chapter 13.

In deciding whether to use virtual groups, social workers must also give thought to groups that do not have access to telephone and computer technology or who do not have the skills to use the technologies (Mann, Belchior, Tomita, & Kemp, 2005). The digital divide is shrinking but still exists. Students facilitating groups using social network sites need to be particularly careful of potential ethical issues, especially personal privacy, boundaries, safety, and client confidentiality (Barsky, 2013; Judd & Johnston, 2012). Students should act differently on their professional social network sites than their personal ones; on a professional social network site, students need to be especially aware of "the presentation of a professional self" (Judd & Johnston, 2012, p. 7). The picture you thought was hilarious of you during spring break in Cancun may not sit well with clients. Therefore, privacy settings on students' personal social network sites should be monitored in case clients happen upon their personal sites.

DIMENSIONS OF GROUP STRUCTURE

The sexuality and gender group serves a variety of functions. But that one group cannot provide for all of the group members' needs. Group members are also involved in friendship circles, 12-step groups, and educational classes. Each group plays a unique part in group members' lives. For example, friendship circles are important to maintaining recovery when those friends reinforce the attitudes and behaviors that support staying clean and sober. But all these groups are obviously structured quite differently. They can be categorized along three dimensions.

1. *How they develop.* The types of groups encountered in social work have typically been organized for a purpose. Such **formed groups** have a defined purpose and come about through the efforts of outsiders, such as an agency (Toseland & Rivas, 2012). Examples of formed groups include not only therapy groups, mutual aid groups, psychoeducational groups, self-help groups, and task

groups but also such groups as college classes, PTAs, and choirs. **Natural groups**, in contrast, "come together spontaneously on the basis of naturally occurring events, interpersonal attraction, or the mutually perceived needs of members" (Toseland & Rivas, 2012, p. 13). Families, peer groups, street gangs, and a group of patients who have befriended each other in a psychiatric hospital are examples of natural groups.

2. *How long they last.* A **time-limited group** is one with a set time for termination; an **ongoing group** has no defined end point. Both formed and natural groups may be time limited or ongoing, short or long term. A formed group, for example, may last for a 2-hour period (e.g., a focus group) or for months or years (e.g., the sexuality and gender group noted in the case example). A natural group may last a lifetime (a group of close friends from high school) or just through some event (tablemates at a workshop).

3. *How they determine membership.* Finally, both natural and formed groups may be open or closed or may fluctuate between open and closed. **Open groups** permit the addition of new members throughout the group's life. In **closed groups**, the minimum and maximum size of the group is determined in advance, before the group begins or as it is being formed, and others are prohibited from joining once that limit is reached. A group can start off open and then become closed. An example is a group of people who have been attending a drop-in support group for women in abusive relationships who decide after a few months that they would like to close the group to do some more intensive work in group sessions. Alternatively, a closed group may open up, as when the number of members has decreased considerably and new members are needed to keep the group going.

These three dimensions of group structure interact in complex ways. The sexuality and gender group is a formed group, yet it is open and ongoing. Attendance has ranged from 8 to 15 persons, and the group may continue indefinitely. An example of a closed natural group is an informal group of

middle school girls who call themselves the "lunch bunch." The five girls eat lunch together every day and have let it be known among their peers that no others are welcome. An example of a formed, time-limited, closed group is a 12-week group for men and women going through a divorce. Interested persons must register prior to the group's beginning, and once the first session begins, no new members are permitted.

An example of an ongoing, open, formed group is a bereavement group that meets every Tuesday evening at the local hospital and allows anyone who would like support to join the group on any Tuesday. Another example is a group that spontaneously meets at the basketball courts on Sunday afternoons to play ball. Whoever shows up can get into a game, with no predetermined limit to the number of people allowed to play.

GROUP COMPOSITION

Another important element of small groups is their composition—the types of people who are members. Natural groups often have implicit or explicit rules about who gets to belong and who doesn't. Take the previous example of the lunch bunch: The girls determined who would belong. Formed groups have rules of membership, too. A sorority or fraternity establishes a process to select who will belong. Sometimes social workers work with naturally occurring groups and do not make decisions about group composition. But for many groups facilitated by social workers, the social worker decides which members are included in the group. Space constraints and personnel issues may determine the size of the group, but the social worker must still make decisions about who gets to belong. One of the most important issues is how to manage diversity in the composition of the group.

Heterogeneity Versus Homogeneity

Diversity is becoming more common in the workplace, schools, and the community, and social work groups are increasingly heterogeneous. The degree of heterogeneity or homogeneity of groups may vary along several dimensions, such as age, race, sexual orientation, gender, level of education, skills, coping style, religion, socioeconomic status, disabilities, and problem areas or strengths. In natural groups, heterogeneity or homogeneity may be affected by such variables as the location (some geographic areas are highly homogeneous), preferences of group members (people tend to form natural groups with those with whom they feel some connection), and social norms and values (acceptance or condemnation of mixed groups).

Usually social work groups are homogeneous on one or a few of these dimensions and heterogeneous on the rest. For example, the sexuality and gender group is homogeneous regarding sexual orientation and substance abuse but quite heterogeneous on other dimensions, including race, age, socioeconomic status, disabilities, educational status, occupation, age at first awareness of sexual orientation, and amount of disclosure of sexual orientation to others.

Which is better for group work, heterogeneity or homogeneity? The best answer is "It depends." First, there is much agreement that homogeneity in the members' purposes for joining the group is essential. Beyond that, Magen and Mangiardi (2005) recommend two principles of composition that seem to have widespread acceptance. The first principle, which they attribute to Fritz Redel, is that "groups should be homogeneous in enough ways to insure their stability and heterogeneous in enough ways to insure their vitality" (Magen & Mangiardi, 2005, p. 355). The second principle, the Noah's ark principle, they attribute to Irvin Yalom. This principle recommends that group composition should not isolate any member on an important characteristic, such as age, race, or gender. Differences among people may be overridden by the overall purpose of the group, however. I am reminded of a friend who spoke to me of her experiences attending a support group for family members who had lost their loved ones. As the only African American group member, she said she felt like a "fly in a milk carton," but her fellow group members were the only people she knew who truly understood her grief.

Often heterogeneity/homogeneity is a matter of perception. For example,

Conflict perspective

in several studies of racially mixed groups, European American group members had a different perception from African American members regarding the racial balance of the group (Davis, 1984). If the group was in proportion to the population of African Americans in the geographic area, then the European American members perceived the group as balanced. If the group had equal numbers of White and Black members, the Black members viewed the group as balanced. The White members, however, perceived the group as imbalanced because the number of African Americans exceeded the psychological threshold of tolerance for European American members. In another study conducted by the same researcher and colleagues (Davis, Strube, & Cheng, 1995), the researchers tested perceptions of African American and White male participants in task groups with three racial mixtures: 25% African American, 50% African American, and 75% African American. They found that the harmony of the group atmosphere, the success of the group, and the perceived satisfaction with group decisions were all more favorable when either African Americans or Whites were in the majority and least favorable in groups in which neither African Americans nor Whites were in the majority (50% White, 50% African American). Most important, both the African American and White group members had similar reactions to the three racial configurations. In another study, Asian persons showed higher levels of participation and leadership skills in work groups that were racially balanced or all Asian compared with Asians in White-dominated groups (Li, Karakowsky, & Siegel, 1999).

Group workers must also give serious thought to whether to have gender homogeneity or gender heterogeneity in group membership. Clearly some group purposes call for gender homogeneity, but gender heterogeneity is often seen to be of value to maximize the range of ideas generated in a group. Research indicates that gender composition is an important variable in group interaction. Researchers have found that women speak more often and have greater influence in groups with gender homogeneity than in groups that include men (Karpowitz, Mendelberg, & Shaker, 2012). One research team found that women speak less than their equal share when they are in the minority in a group and at equal rates when they are in a large majority (Karpowitz et al., 2012). Women gained greater influence as their numbers grew. These researchers also found that when group decisions are made unanimously rather than by majority vote, women are not disadvantaged in either voice or authority when they are in the minority. Another research team (Toosi, Sommers, & Ambady, 2012) found that racial diversity in group composition changed the gender dynamics. In racially homogeneous groups, White women spoke less than White men and had less influence, but in racially diverse groups, White women spoke as much as men and had as much influence. These researchers emphasize that no social identity stands alone, and researchers and group workers must consider how identities interact with each other.

Contemporary research indicates that group composition may be more complex than once thought. But in the group work literature there is still strong support for Yalom's observation that for "long-term intensive interactional group therapy," heterogeneous groups appear to be better (Yalom, 1995, p. 255). Yalom is speaking here of homogeneity or heterogeneity of psychological problems. Homogeneous groups are generally not beneficial for long-term psychotherapeutic work that involves personality change, because they tend to remain at superficial levels and don't challenge individuals' behavioral patterns and dynamics as much as heterogeneous groups. Homogeneous groups, on the other hand, are often better for "support or symptomatic relief over a brief period" and "for individuals with monosymptomatic complaints or for the noncompliant patient" (Yalom, 1995, p. 255). Homogeneous groups tend to build commitment more quickly, offer more immediate support to members, and

> Psychodynamic perspective

have better attendance and less conflict. And given the research cited earlier, there are good reasons to consider composing groups segregated by race and ethnicity to allow for more intensive exploration of common problems.

An interesting research finding is that the heterogeneity/homogeneity issue takes on less importance the briefer and more structured the group. Compositional issues are more significant in groups that are less structured and that focus on group interaction (Yalom, 1995). In the sexuality and gender group, the homogeneity of sexual orientation and recovery from addiction provides the safety and support to explore the heterogeneous aspects of the group.

For task or work groups, heterogeneity has been shown to positively influence group productivity. Among the 42 student project groups examined in one study, racial/ethnic diversity was positively associated with group efficacy (Sargent & Sue-Chan, 2001). Another study of work groups assessed diversity by race, age, sex, and functional background in their contribution to quality of innovation (the usefulness of an idea or the impact it might have on a business) and quantity of innovation (the number of new ideas the group produces) (Cady & Valentine, 1999). These four dimensions of diversity had no significant impact on quality of innovation. There were significant differences in *quantity* of innovation, however. As gender diversity increased, the number of new ideas decreased, and conversely, when racial diversity increased, the number of new ideas increased. Another study found that increasing the dimensions of diversity in work group membership mitigates the negative effects of tensions between majority and minority group members based on a single trait such as gender or race (Valenti & Rockett, 2008).

Homogeneity/Heterogeneity in Group Composition: Social Justice Issues

As social group workers think about group composition, they do so in the contexts of an increasingly diverse society and a profession committed to the promotion of social justice. At the most basic level, that means social group workers will recognize the equal rights of all people in their communities to access social work groups. Promotion of social justice may, at times, mean the development of groups that are homogeneous on an important identity dimension, where people can speak about common experiences, receive social support, and develop solidarity. Such groups can lead to empowerment, and social group workers can support self-advocacy while also advocating for the group when appropriate.

At other times, promotion of social justice will mean being intentional about having a group that is heterogeneous on important social identity issues, while being homogeneous on group purpose. In developing such heterogeneous groups, the group worker should avoid having a token member of a marginalized community group (the Noah's Ark principle). When working with heterogeneous groups, the group worker must work to ensure that all members have a voice and are treated with dignity and respect, paying particular attention to power dynamics that members bring into the group from the world beyond the group. It is important for social workers to consider the potential for social work groups to create a safe place to discuss topics of diversity, oppression, and privilege that are avoided in most places of human interaction. For example, Richards-Schuster and Aldana (2013) describe one program that fosters youth dialogues on race and ethnicity. This type of program is a great opportunity for social workers to promote social justice.

Critical Thinking Questions 11.2

We live in an increasingly diverse world. What experiences have you had with small groups that were heterogeneous in race or ethnicity? What experiences have you had with small groups that were heterogeneous in gender? What did you see as the benefits of heterogeneity? What challenges were presented by heterogeneous membership?

BASIC GROUP PROCESSES

To be effective, group workers need tools for understanding the group processes in which they participate. Group processes are those unique interactions between group members that result from being in a group together. How people behave in groups is of interest to us because we spend much of our time in groups, and groups have a strong influence on our behaviors.

Theories of Group Processes

The fields of social psychology and sociology have been in the forefront of empirical research on group processes. Five of the major theories of group processes are discussed in this section: psychodynamic theory, symbolic interaction theory, status characteristics and expectation states theory, exchange theory, and self-categorization theory. Each one helps us understand, among other things, why and how certain members of a group develop and maintain more power than other members to influence the group's activities.

Psychodynamic Theory

You were introduced to the psychodynamic theoretical perspective in Chapter 2.

> Psychodynamic perspective

When applied to small groups, psychodynamic theory "focuses on the relationship between the emotional unconscious processes and the rational processes of interpersonal interaction" (McLeod & Kettner-Polley, 2005, p. 63). It is assumed that understanding the emotional processes in a group is essential for accomplishing the group's task. The psychodynamic theoretical perspective is especially important to therapy groups where understanding emotional processes is the central task of the group, but some group leaders argue that it is an important perspective for increasing the effectiveness of any type of group. Small groups can be challenging because they satisfy our need to belong, and yet they also arouse our fears about social acceptance and social competence (Geller, 2005).

McLeod and Kettner-Polley (2005) identify three broad assumptions of psychodynamic theory for understanding small groups:

1. Emotional, unconscious processes are always present in every group.

2. Emotional, unconscious processes affect the quality of interpersonal communication and task accomplishment.

3. Group effectiveness depends on bringing emotional, unconscious processes to group members' conscious awareness.

Group leaders in a psychodynamic therapy group would look for opportunities to assist group members to identify how their interactions within the group may mirror their patterns of interactions with others outside of the group; in other words, the group experience becomes a microcosm of members' lives outside the group. For example, a female group member who tends to defer to the opinions of male group members and who is afraid to confront them may be demonstrating a general theme in her life of being intimidated by males because of childhood experiences of severe physical abuse by her father.

Symbolic Interaction Theory

Social constructionist perspective

In Chapter 4, you read about symbolic interaction theory and how it is used to understand the self. This theory is also used to understand what happens in small groups. According to symbolic interaction theory, humans are symbol-using creatures. We make meaning of the world by interacting with others through symbols—words, gestures, and objects. Some small group theorists find it helpful to think about the small group as a place where symbols are created, exchanged, and interpreted and to think about individual and social change happening as meanings are made and changed through the use of symbols (Frey & Sunwolf, 2005). In fact, they think

that a "group" is itself a symbol used to describe a relationship people understand themselves to have with each other. Group members create a sense of being a "group" through their symbolic actions with each other, through their language and their behaviors over time. Groups may use such symbols as metaphors, stories, and rituals to communicate and build cohesion. In this way, they also build a culture with its own symbols and meanings. The symbols provide group identity and stimulate commitment to struggle with the tensions of group life.

The symbols used in a group, and the meaning made of those symbols, are influenced by the environments in which the group is embedded (Frey & Sunwolf, 2005). Group members are also members of other groups and bring symbolic meanings with them from these groups. This may lead to tension and conflict in the group as members struggle to develop shared meaning about who they are as a group, what their goals are, and how they will operate as a group.

An example of symbolic interaction within a group is a ritual developed by the chapter author and a co-facilitator for a support group for incarcerated battered women. At the beginning and end of each session, the group would light five candles and recite five affirmations related to the group's theme, loving and healing ourselves: "I am worthy of a good life," "I am worthy of positive friendship," "I am a loveable person," "I desire inner healing," and "I will recognize the good things about myself and others." The lighting of the candles symbolized bringing to awareness the inner strength and healing power of each woman in the group.

Status Characteristics and Expectation States Theory

Status characteristics and expectation states theory proposes that the influence and participation of

Exchange and choice perspective

group members during initial interactions are related to their status and to expectations others hold about their ability to help the group accomplish tasks (Fisek, Berger, & Moore, 2002; Oldmeadow, Platow, Foddy, & Anderson, 2003). **Status characteristics** are any characteristics evaluated in the broader society to be associated with competence; they may be either specific or diffuse. Let's look first at an example of a specific status characteristic. Joan and Bob are both members of a task force formed in a housing project community to increase healthy social interactions among the children and beautify the grounds. Joan, who is known to be artistic, makes a suggestion that the group involve children in painting murals on communal buildings and then hold a contest for the best mural. Bob, who is not known to be artistic, suggests that the group solicit volunteer contributions from local artists who would donate paintings and other artwork to display on the inside of buildings. It can be expected that group members will be more willing to go along with Joan's idea than with Bob's because of Joan's greater perceived expertise in artistic matters. Their **performance expectations**—predictions of how well an act will accomplish a group's task—are influenced by this specific status characteristic.

In the sexuality and gender group, Beverly carries some influence. She has attended group sessions for almost 3 months and is one of the core members who come to the group consistently. As an influential member, she is expected to articulate and enforce the group's rules and to assist new members in acclimating to the group. Group members expect Beverly to share her insights about the coming-out process and recovery from addiction, and they perceive her as a knowledgeable person, especially when discussing issues faced by African American lesbians.

Now let's look at an example of a diffuse status characteristic. In the sexuality and gender group,

Social constructionist perspective

Beverly is perceived as a knowledgeable person regarding coming out and the unique issues faced by African American lesbians. But in another setting, the color of Beverly's skin might negatively influence how she is perceived by other people.

Stereotypes about African Americans may cause other people to question Beverly's interests, skills, or values. Such stereotypes are the basis of *diffuse status characteristics* whereby the power and prestige of group members are correlated with their status in the external world, regardless of their specific characteristics relative to the task at hand.

For example, if people expect that someone using a wheelchair is incapable of playing basketball for a charity fund-raiser, then they will act as if a person using a wheelchair is unable to play basketball. They may disqualify that person from playing, thereby demoralizing the individual with the disability and preventing the person from contributing to the success of the fund-raiser.

Gender is an influential diffuse status characteristic in our society, perhaps because it can often be easily discerned. In mixed-gender groups, males have greater participation and influence than females, and males or females with traditionally masculine personality traits are likely to exhibit more dominant behavior (Karpowitz et al., 2012; Toosi et al., 2012). In same-sex groups, gender is not an initial status differential; instead, members develop expectations of each other based on other status characteristics, such as education, race, or experience. Regardless of gender, a person's perceived ability also affects performance expectations. For example, a female may be perceived as incapable of handling a complex mechanical problem in a work group, but she may be able to develop influence if she shows she can accomplish the task successfully (Schneider & Cook, 1995).

One assumption of status characteristics and expectation states theory is that people rely on their stereotypes in the absence of proof that those characteristics are irrelevant. In the psychological literature, this phenomenon is often referred to as "self-fulfilling stereotypes" (Snyder, 2014). In our example of assumptions people may make about persons using wheelchairs, the burden of proof would be on the persons using wheelchairs to demonstrate that they could indeed play basketball, thus establishing the inapplicability of others' assumptions about the disability.

Exchange Theory

Exchange and choice perspective

Sometimes in coming-out groups, those who have been out for the longest time have implicit power over those newly out, the baby dykes. A "let me show you the ropes and tell you what this is about" attitude can be used to gain power and influence over another person and to create dependency: "You need me to help you understand what you are getting yourself into." But social power can also be used in a positive way in a coming-out group, as when those who have been in the lesbian community for a long time offer support and information to others with the intention of providing mutual aid. To understand power as a social commodity, we can look to exchange theory (Lovaglia, Mannix, Samuelson, Sell, & Wilson, 2005), which assumes that human interactions can be understood in terms of rewards and costs.

According to exchange theory, social power is what determines who gets valued resources in groups and whether those resources are perceived as being distributed in a just manner. Conflicts within the group often revolve around power issues among members—those who want the power in the group, those who have power and don't want to give it up, and those who don't want others to have power over them.

Groups are particularly vulnerable to conflicts over power because social power arises within the context of the group itself rather than being an innate quality of an individual. Power not only determines the distribution of group resources but also influences people's expectations of others' abilities, even when the power results from structural conditions and not from innate personal ability (Lovaglia, 1995). Emotion also has an impact on perceived power and influence, regardless of status. If a person has negative emotions toward a high-status person, the power of the high-status person will lessen (Lovaglia, 1995).

Power differences among group members can create status differences but don't necessarily have to. Group members may rate more highly the abilities and influences of high-power members, which may in turn influence expectations for high-power members, but negative feelings toward high-power members may mitigate their influence.

The exercise of social power often brings with it a concern about justice, fairness, and equality. Most of us would agree that power should not be exercised to the special benefit or detriment of some group members. However, justice is a relative rather than absolute term. Any two persons may have quite different ideas about what constitutes justice. For some, justice would be an equal distribution of resources; for others, justice would be an equitable (but not necessarily equal) distribution.

How persons evaluate the equity of a situation depends on such factors as cultural values, self-interest, the situation, the relationships between those affected, and per-

Conflict perspective

sonal characteristics (Hegtvedt, 1994). People tend to operate more from self-interest in impersonal conditions than when they have personal bonds with others. The status of the person for whom justice claims are being considered also affects the definition of justice, the perception of injustice, and the resolution of injustices. In addition, what may be perceived as fair on an individual level may be perceived as unfair when viewed from a group perspective. For example, suppose a group member is in crisis and asks for extended time in the group. The other five group members agree to give the person an extra 10 minutes because of the crisis. This extension, however, requires each group member to give up 2 minutes of his or her floor time. Giving one individual an extra 10 minutes may not seem like much, but that one action has a cost for five other group members. And what if one group member decides that he or she has a pressing issue to discuss and does not want to give up the 2 minutes? How the group would resolve this dilemma relates to its spoken and unspoken guidelines for handling matters of justice within the group.

Self-Categorization Theory

Self-categorization theory builds on social identity theory, which, as discussed in Chapter 5, is a stage theory of socialization that articulates the process by which we come to identify with some social groups and develop a sense of difference from other social groups. **Self-categorization theory** expands social identity theory by suggesting that in this process, we come to divide the world into *in-groups* (those to which we belong) and *out-groups* (those to which we do not belong). We begin to stereotype the attributes of in-groups and out-groups by comparing them with each other, with bias toward in-groups. When we encounter new group situations, we are more likely to be influenced by in-group members than by out-group members. We give more credence to those similar to us than to those different from us, particularly when situations are conflicted or unclear. Doing so is consistent with our categorization schemes, but it also helps us maintain distinctive and positive social identities (Abrams, Hogg, Hinkle, & Otten, 2005; Hogg, 2005). So, in this approach, we are influenced in group situations by members of our in-groups, whether or not they hold high status in society.

An example of this is Katie, a member of the sexuality and gender group, who was raised in an evangelical Protestant church. Katie struggled with her sexuality and what she was taught in church about homosexuality. Katie received approval from her counselor to go into the community on a day pass so that she could accompany her sponsor to a Metropolitan Community Church service. She immediately "felt at home" there. She felt she had found a place where both her sexual orientation and faith could be affirmed—a place where she could belong.

Researchers have studied the impact of both status characteristics and self-categorization on social influence in group settings, recording who agrees with whom and who defers to whom. They have found that group members are influenced by both status characteristics and social identity. More specifically, they found that group members are more highly influenced by high-status members who also belong to the in-group than by either a low-status in-group member or a high-status out-group member (Kalkhoff & Barnum, 2000).

Critical Thinking Questions 11.3

The psychodynamic perspective on groups proposes that emotional processes in the small group affect the effectiveness of the group. Some proponents of this perspective argue that dealing with the emotional processes in the group is important in any type of group, not just therapy groups. What do you think about this argument? How important are emotional processes to mutual aid groups, psychoeducational groups, self-help groups, and task groups? Can you think of an example where unconscious emotional processes interfered with task accomplishment in a task group of which you were a member?

Group Development

To understand the unique nature of groups and why they are effective in helping people, we need to examine the ways groups develop. Two common ways of viewing group development are by the stages the group passes through and by the processes that facilitate the work of a group. This section provides a brief overview of stage theories and models and then discusses an example of the analysis of processes that facilitate the work of groups.

Stage Theories and Models

A variety of scholars have attempted to delineate the life cycle of small groups.

> Developmental perspective

Both progressive stage models and cyclical models have been proposed (Coyne, 2014). *Progressive stage models* propose stages that are sequential, with each stage building successively on accomplishments in prior stages. *Cyclical models* suggest that groups may move back and forth in group processes in a cyclical rather than linear manner (Donigian & Malnati, 2005). Most small group scholars recognize that groups do not always progress in a linear fashion but find progressive models to be helpful when thinking about group development. Researchers who focus on the stages of group development have reached no consensus as to how many stages there are, the order in which they appear, or the nature of those stages. Exhibit 11.4 displays five progressive models commonly cited in the group work literature. Note, however, that controlled experiments investigating group stages are rare. Most theories of group stages have been developed by observing patterns and changes in groups, usually after the group has disbanded. Because most of the stage theories have been based on studies of time-limited, closed groups, they may not be applicable to open-ended or ongoing groups.

Most progressive stage theorists agree, however, on some basic principles: Groups don't necessarily move through each stage in order, groups may revert to an earlier stage, stages are not distinct entities but may be a blend or combination, the group's development is influenced by the leader and the members, and groups do not need to reach the most advanced developmental stage in order to be effective (Coyne, 2014).

Exhibit 11.4 Stage Models of Group Development

Author(s)	Number of Stages	Stages
Garland, Jones, & Kolodny (1976)	Five	Preaffiliation Power and control Intimacy Differentiation Separation
Tuckman & Jensen (1977)	Five	Forming Storming Norming Performing Adjourning
Northen (1988)	Five	Planning and intake Orientation Exploring and testing Problem solving Termination
Brabender & Fallon (2009)	Five	Formation and engagement Conflict and rebellion Intimacy and unity Integration and work Termination
Kottler & Englar-Carlson (2010)	Four	Induction Experimental engagement Cohesive engagement Disengagement

Photo 11.3 Small group. This exercise class is an example of a small group that comes together to accomplish a goal: fitness.

© iStockphoto.com/Tomaz Levstek

Process Models

If stage theories are inadequate for explaining how groups develop, what are we to use instead? The chief alternative is process models, which identify what goes on in groups and how those processes affect group members and their interactions. The advantage of process analysis is that it focuses on the interactions among group members rather than creating norms for development.

A good example of a process model is that developed by Irving Yalom, one of the best-known group psychotherapists. Yalom (1995) describes 11 factors that shape the functioning of therapeutic groups. These factors are listed and defined in Exhibit 11.5.

Some of Yalom's therapeutic factors may operate to a degree in groups other than therapy groups. For example, universality and imparting of information are two of the mutual aid processes described earlier in this chapter. In addition, certain factors may be more significant at particular stages of group development than at others. One study of 12 time-limited outpatient psychotherapy groups found that the development of cohesion varied according to the stage (or phase) of psychotherapy (Budman, Soldz, Demby, Davis, & Merry, 1993). For example, in the earliest stage

> Psychodynamic perspective; social behavioral perspective; humanistic perspective

Exhibit 11.5   Therapeutic Factors Involved in Group Development

Therapeutic Factor	Definition
Instillation of hope	Confidence and optimism in the ability of the group and individual members to resolve issues and grow
Universality	Sense that others share similar problems and feelings and that one is not alone
Imparting of information	Leader's and group members' sharing of information and guidance around problems and concerns
Altruism	Benefits experienced when one realizes that one has helped another person
Corrective recapitulation of primary family group	(Re)experience of relationship patterns like those in one's family of origin while learning different approaches to relationships
Development of socializing techniques	Examination of patterns of interacting with others and acquisition of new social skills
Imitative behavior	Observation of how other group members handle their problems and feelings and recognition of how those methods apply to one's own situation
Interpersonal learning	Process of learning about oneself through interaction with others
Group cohesiveness	Sense of belonging that group members have and sense of acceptance and support they feel in the group
Catharsis	Sharing of deep and sometimes painful emotions with nonjudgmental acceptance from group members
Existential factors	Search for meaning and purpose in one's life

of the group, members sharing issues about their lives outside the group built cohesion; however, too much focus on the therapist during this stage tended to be countercohesive. In the sexuality and gender group, several therapeutic factors are evident at different times. When group members feel they can trust each other, catharsis and interpersonal learning are likely. When new members attend the group, they often desire to experience an instillation of hope, universality, imparting of information, and development of socializing techniques.

Group Dynamics

The overall development of the group is overlaid with patterns of interactions that can be characterized as **group dynamics**—such issues as how leaders are appointed or emerge, which roles members take in groups, how communication networks affect interactions in groups, and how groups develop cohesiveness.

Formal and Informal Leadership

Formal leaders are appointed or elected to lead the group by virtue of such characteristics as their position in the organization or community and their interest or expertise in relation to the group's focus. Informal leaders may emerge in groups where no formal leader exists or where formal leaders are established. In the latter case, a group member may feel more comfortable in a helper or leader role than as a client in the group, thereby mimicking the actions of the formal leader.

Both formal and informal group leaders have a binary focus: the individuals in the group and the group as a whole. **Task-oriented leaders** facilitate problem solving within the context of the group; **process-oriented leaders**, also known as social-emotional leaders, identify and manage group relationships (Myers & Anderson, 2008). Any given leader usually fluctuates from one role to the other, although people tend to be either more task oriented or more process oriented.

In natural groups, leaders may be formal or informal. A friendly softball game at the diamond on a Saturday morning may evolve into a complex hierarchy of leaders and followers as various activities are negotiated—who is on what team, who bats first, how long the game will last, who will decide batting order, and so on—and such process issues as team morale and cohesiveness are promoted.

Leaders of formed groups also take on various roles, depending on the purpose and structure of the group. A facilitator of a group for children with ADHD is a formal leader who may provide structured activities, support, and guidance for the children. Similarly, the leader of a one-time debriefing group may provide support and information to rescue workers after a fire. Informal leaders of formed groups might include a person who evolves into a leadership role in a work group assigned to some project.

Groups often have co-leaders, or one appointed leader and one or more group members who serve as self- or group-appointed co-leaders. At times, co-leaders may offer the group a nice balance of facilitation styles with one person having a more process-oriented style and the other person having a task orientation. Good communication and processing skills between co-leaders is essential to effective group leadership.

Gender, class, and race influence leadership (both who takes leadership and the perception of leaders by group members). Status differences based on gender influence the behaviors of both male and female group members, including their reactions to male and female group leaders (Karpowitz et al., 2012; Toosi et al., 2012). Both males and females tend to respect male leadership more quickly and easily. Males in a female-led group tend to challenge the leader(s)

Conflict perspective

and expect female leaders to be more nurturing than male leaders. Persons of color may distrust White leaders "from the system" (Davis, 1995, p. 49), because such leaders may be perceived as not being sensitive or responsive to minorities' needs. In addition, the significant difference in life experiences of persons of color and Whites may create a wide gap between White leaders and group members who are persons of color. White leaders of groups that include minorities may want to prepare themselves for three questions: "1. Are we people of goodwill? 2. Do we have sufficient mastery/skills to help them? 3. Do we understand their social realities?" (Davis, 1995, p. 53). White group leaders should also remember that their behavior should be purposeful, and they should demonstrate respect, examine their own attitudes and beliefs regarding clients who are different from them, use culturally appropriate techniques, know the resources that exist in the larger society that may be of help to their group members, make every effort to "get off to a good start," and expect success (Davis, 1995, p. 55). These same principles apply when middle-class group workers work with groups who are poor.

For at least 60 years, researchers have investigated the psychological traits of people who emerge as leaders in groups without a formal leader, and a number of traits have been identified. One research team (Ensari, Riggio, Christian, & Carslaw, 2011) reported on meta-analyses of the research on leadership emergence in leaderless groups. They found several traits associated with informal leadership in these groups: extraversion, intelligence, and social skills. They further found that men who appear authoritarian and self-confident are likely to emerge as leaders but that men are no more effective leaders than women. Using a large database of twins from Sweden, another research team (Chaturvedi, Zyphur, Arvey, Avolio, & Larsson, 2012) investigated the often-asked question, Are leaders born or made? They found that genetics explained approximately 40% of the variance in leadership emergence for both men and women. They also found that the contribution of genetics to leadership emergence in women varied across the female life course, being highest in the period of midcareer. This preliminary research suggests that, like other aspects of human behavior, informal leadership is related to both nature and nurture.

Formal and Informal Roles

In addition to formal and informal leadership roles within the group, group members fill a variety of other roles. Those roles serve a purpose for the group as a whole and simultaneously fulfill group members' personal needs (Myers & Anderson, 2008). Formal roles are assigned and may include leader, recorder, and adviser. Informal roles emerge through group interaction. They may be an outgrowth of a group member's self-concept, cultural background, or gender, but they are also based on expectations members have of each other. A group role can be defined as "a repeatable pattern of communicative behaviors that members come to expect from each other" (Myers & Anderson, 2008, p. 267). Roles can continue to evolve as the work of the group changes over time.

Roles of group members allow for division of labor but may have both positive and negative aspects. Group members may play useful task roles such as information seeker, information provider, summarizer, and technical adviser. They may also play important socioemotional roles such as encourager, process observer, gatekeeper who helps other members participate, and tension releaser. Sometimes these same roles can become dysfunctional for the group. The peacemaker, for example, may serve the function of reducing conflict and anxiety within the group—but perhaps at the cost of suppressing efforts to work through or resolve conflict within the group. The clown or jester reduces anxiety and stress in the group by joking but also enables the group to avoid a painful subject.

In the course of group interactions, members may develop roles that have been variously referred to as dysfunctional (Coyne, 2014), deviant (Myers & Anderson, 2008), and "problem

> Systems perspective

members" (Yalom, 1995). Such roles include the monopolizer, the silent member, the aggressor, the boring member, the help-rejecting complainer, the scapegoat, the avoider, the rescuer, and the recognition seeker. These problematic roles, like functional ones, are negotiated between the member and the group and may be attempts by both the member and the group to cope with underlying feelings about being in the group. Group leaders must help individual members and the group as a whole find more useful ways of interacting.

Roles are a social construction. They reflect group members' expectations and both produce and reproduce elements of the social structure. Roles are not necessarily fixed and rigid. Rather, they develop through give-and-take within the group (Myers & Anderson, 2008). Myers and Anderson (2008) suggest that members of healthy groups play a variety of roles and avoid role rigidity. Group leaders may need to assist members to broaden their role repertoire.

> Social constructionist perspective

Communication Networks

Groups function more effectively when members are able to communicate easily and with competence. Social workers who lead groups can set the tone for the group by being clear, direct, and compassionate in their own communication. The free flow of ideas among members enhances productivity, particularly in task groups.

Communication networks are the links among members—who talks to whom, how information is transmitted, and whether communication between members is direct or uses a go-between. *Sociograms* may be used to depict the physical arrangement of these communication channels. Typically, the formal leader occupies the central position in a communication network, like the hub at the center of spokes on a wheel (Toseland & Rivas, 2012). However, an informal leader may take the role of information giver and controller.

> Systems perspective

Group members' satisfaction with a group tends to be higher in group-centered "web" networks, where information passes freely among all group members, than in leader-centered "wheel" networks (Exhibit 11.6 diagrams these patterns). Leader-centered networks are the more efficient configuration for task groups addressing simple problems, however. Decentralized networks are more effective if the group is attempting to solve more complex problems (Levi, 2014). Group-centered communication patterns are associated with increased social interaction, group morale, goal commitment, and creativity (Toseland & Rivas, 2012).

Communication patterns may also be affected by whether the group meets face-to-face or uses telephone or computer technology. Enhancing the leaders' and members' auditory skills for group participation may be important for telephone groups because of the absence of visual cues and in-person interaction. An active leader role in telephone and computer groups may be necessary to confront monopolizers and encourage those who are silent (Toseland & Larkin, 2010).

Group Cohesiveness

Group cohesiveness is a dynamic process reflected in the tendency for the group to stick together and be unified in the pursuit of its objectives and the satisfaction of member emotional needs (May et al., 2008). Small group researchers examine two dimensions of group cohesiveness: *task cohesion* is the degree to which group members work toward a common goal, and *social cohesion* is the level of intimacy and positive regard among group members. Groups that are cohesive tend to have higher rates of attendance, participation, and mutual support. But cohesiveness does not mean the absence of conflict or dislike among group members. Even a cohesive group may sometimes experience bickering, frustration, or alienation. Cohesion is thought to be dynamic: It changes in extent and form throughout the life of a group. Thus, measuring the degree of group cohesiveness across contexts can be a challenge (Carron & Brawley, 2000). It is important for group leaders to try to prevent heterogeneous groups from splitting into coalitions that are not committed to the interest of the whole group (Jones, 2005).

The group leader can foster group cohesion by listening to members, validating their experiences, modeling genuine concern for each member, and recognizing members' supportive interactions and constructive participation (Toseland & Rivas, 2012). Some groups may develop rituals or habits to increase cohesiveness among members. For example, a gang member may receive a tattoo as an initiation rite, the group may name itself (the "lunch bunch"), a member who has been in the group for 6 months may receive a pin, or a group member may be expected to call another member when he or she is having difficulty.

Exhibit 11.6 Common Communication Patterns in Groups

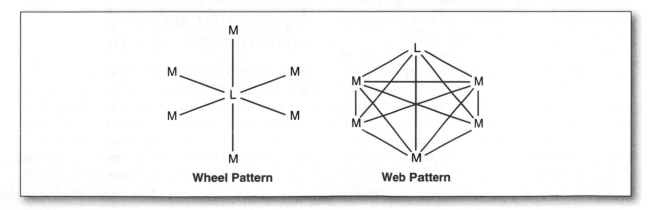

Wheel Pattern Web Pattern

The American Psychological Association systematically evaluated the factors involved in intervention effectiveness and found cohesion in group therapy to be demonstrably effective (Norcross & Wampold, 2011). Cohesive teams have also been found to be more effective than teams with low levels of cohesion (Kogler Hill, 2013). However, there can be negative effects of group cohesion if it leads to pathological conformity that sacrifices individuality, a phenomenon known as "group think" (Toseland & Rivas, 2012).

Critical Thinking Questions 11.4

Think about a small group in which you have participated that was particularly effective. What aspects of group dynamics do you think contributed to this effectiveness? Now, think of a small group in which you have participated that was particularly ineffective. What aspects of group dynamics do you think contributed to this ineffectiveness?

INTERDISCIPLINARY TEAMS AND LEADERSHIP

In recent years, many organizations, including those where social workers work, have implemented organizational team structures to respond to rapidly changing conditions (Levi, 2014). "A team is a specific type of group composed of members who are interdependent, who share common goals, and who must coordinate their activities to accomplish these goals" (Kogler Hill, 2013, p. 287). Because it is anticipated that work teams will continue to be a part of organizational structure for the near future, it is important for social workers to understand what makes a team successful. Many scholars argue that team leadership is the primary ingredient of team success, and social workers will need to be prepared to function as team leaders.

Interdisciplinary Teams and Social Work

Social workers may be involved, on a regular or occasional basis, in a special type of group known as an interdisciplinary team. **Interdisciplinary teams** are composed of a group of professionals representing a variety of disciplines, working in organized collaboration to solve a common set of problems (Oliver & Peck, 2006). They may include consumers or clients. Examples include Child Study and Early Intervention teams (Kropf & Malone, 2004), medical teams in hospital units (Kitchen & Brook, 2005), geriatric care teams (Cummings, 2008), end-of-life teams (Day, 2012), child abuse and neglect teams (Lalayants & Epstein, 2005), and coordinated community response (CCR) teams to address domestic violence and sexual assault (Mederos & Perilla, 2003). Interdisciplinary teams are not new, but federal policies and regulations are now requiring their use in a number of service sectors in the United States and other countries. Teams may be formed formally or informally and may have representatives from within or outside of an agency. It is important that social workers have a good understanding of other professions and the roles of other members of interdisciplinary teams. In addition, social workers must educate other team members about their own areas of expertise. Learning to work well with team members regardless of differing perspectives and job responsibilities enables social workers to better achieve their desired outcomes (Reese, 2011).

The Social Worker's Role on Interdisciplinary Teams

There is a very large social work literature, going back more than 2 decades, on social work participation in interdisciplinary teams. This literature is much too large to summarize here, and this discussion is limited to selected literature on interdisciplinary teams in hospice and child welfare settings. Two major themes in this literature are discussed:

How effective are interdisciplinary teams, and what are the special problems social workers face on interdisciplinary teams?

There are very few controlled studies of the effectiveness of interdisciplinary teams. In one survey of hospice interdisciplinary teams, Reese and Raymer (2004) found that a higher level of team functioning was correlated with fewer hospitalizations, lower home health costs, lower labor costs, and lower overall hospice costs. Lalayants and Epstein (2005) reviewed the research on child abuse and neglect teams. Although they found no rigorous controlled studies, they did find that referral sources, team members, and service recipients perceived a number of advantages of such teams: increased coordination and collaboration between agencies, increased information exchange, a broader range of viewpoints being heard, enhanced communication, and increased moral support and confidence.

The research on child abuse and neglect teams also reports a number of problems or challenges faced by these teams, including difficulty developing shared goals and objectives, conflicting theories and ideologies about child maltreatment, turf disputes, power struggles, agency territorialism, confusion about leadership roles, and more time-consuming decision making (Lalayants & Epstein, 2005). The research literature on social work participation in hospice teams has suggested that social workers are underused and underappreciated on these teams and that turf issues are a major barrier. Recent research suggests, however, that hospice directors have experienced a considerable increase in their understanding of and respect for the role of social workers on the hospice team over the past 25 years (Reese, 2011). Hospice social workers report that the most important factor in effective hospice teams is communication, both formal communication and informal "getting to know you" types of communication. Team-building exercises have been reported to improve communication and mutual appreciation (Oliver & Peck, 2006). Olshever (2011) proposes that hospice teams need to do a better job of integrating patients

and families into the team. She also suggests that social workers with knowledge and skills for working with small groups can be helpful in managing team dynamics.

Social Workers and Leadership

Social workers may at times be elected or appointed to lead interdisciplinary teams. While there are many definitions of **leadership**, the definition by Northouse (2013) is "a process whereby an individual influences a group of individuals to achieve a common goal" (p. 5). Northouse's definition acknowledges that leadership is a process rather than a particular trait of an individual, it involves inspiring others, and it takes place within the context of groups working toward goal achievement. Social workers can bring their unique social work values, ethics, and training in interpersonal communication to bear on their leadership styles. While relational skills can be useful in leading interdisciplinary teams, a task orientation can also be beneficial for enacting the work of the team. Social work leaders need to know how to manage conflict and power dynamics in the team, attend to individuals' needs and strengths, and establish group norms (Toseland & Rivas, 2012). In recent years, there has been a call for social workers to assume more leadership in interdisciplinary collaboration in several fields, including developmental disabilities (Kropf & Malone, 2004), legal services (Maidenberg & Golick, 2001), adolescent health services and other medical settings (Mizrahi & Abramson, 2000; NASW Virginia, 2003), and failing to thrive in infants and children (Marino, Weinman, & Soudelier, 2001).

There is some evidence that social workers in leadership positions on interdisciplinary teams would benefit from an understanding of corporate management functions, namely planning, organizing, coordinating, encouraging, monitoring, and evaluating (Veeder & Dalgin, 2004). In one study, the presence of five management outcome variables, including coordinating an interdisciplinary team, predicted successful cases (Veeder

& Dalgin, 2004). Social workers might also find it useful to use a self-analysis of leadership traits, such as the Leadership Trait Questionnaire, to measure their personal characteristics of leadership or to examine their leadership style using an instrument such as the Leadership Style Questionnaire to assess task and relationship factors (Northouse, 2013).

While social workers may find themselves naturally gravitating to certain leadership styles, one approach to leadership has been termed *situational.* Proponents of this approach note that "different situations demand different kinds of leadership. From this perspective, to be an effective leader requires that a person adapt his or her style to the demands of different situations" (Northouse, 2013, p. 99). Leaders using the situational approach would balance directive and supportive roles given the changing competence and commitment of members to carry out a task. There are times when the leader may need to assume a more directive style, whereas in other situations, the leader may find that a more supportive role would be appropriate. "Effective team leaders need a wide repertoire of communication skills to monitor and take appropriate action" (Kogler Hill, 2013, p. 290); they focus constantly on both task and socioemotional aspects of the group. There are many other theories of leadership with which social workers can familiarize themselves (see Northouse, 2013).

Research on team effectiveness suggests that effective teams have these traits:

- Clear, motivating goals
- Results-driven structure

- Competent team members
- Unified commitment
- Collaborative climate
- Standards of excellence
- External support and recognition
- Principled leadership (Kogler Hill, 2013)

Additionally, highly effective interdisciplinary teams demonstrate respect for the knowledge and contributions of members, positive regard for members' personal characteristics and their working styles, a high degree of trust of each other, and a communication style that promotes consensus decision making (Supiano & Berry, 2013).

It is important to note that many of the functions just noted need not be carried out exclusively by the formal leader. Teams may have a cadre of experienced and competent members who take on and share leadership activities. In other situations, teams have no designated formal leader, and the group works as a self-managed team. The important issue is that teams develop processes for monitoring progress toward goals and executing necessary actions (Kogler Hill, 2013).

Critical Thinking Questions 11.5

We have all had experience working in task groups of one type or another. We have also had an opportunity to observe different leadership styles and the impact leaders have on group effectiveness. From your experiences, how would you describe what makes someone a good leader? How would you describe what makes someone a bad leader?

Implications for Social Work Practice

The overview of formed and natural groups in this chapter suggests a number of principles for social work assessment, intervention, and evaluation:

- In the assessment process with individuals or families, identify any natural or formed groups to which the person or family belongs. Ecomaps or sociograms may be used to identify such groups.

- In the assessment process, determine whether the group modality or another intervention modality would be most appropriate for the client.
- In the assessment process with a potential group member, gather background information such as the motivation for joining the group, the expectations the person has of the leader and other group members, the strengths the person could offer the group, and previous experience with groups.
- Be aware of various groups in your community for referral and networking purposes.
- Develop and implement small groups when it is clear that a group would benefit the population you serve. Determine what type(s) of groups would be most appropriate for that population. Consider groups for prevention when appropriate.
- Collaborate with colleagues from other disciplines to co-facilitate groups in interdisciplinary settings.
- Seek to build alliances with natural and self-help groups that reinforce or supplement the services you are providing.
- In the groups you facilitate, understand the stated and unstated purposes and functions of the group and pay careful attention to issues of group structure, development, composition, and dynamics.
- Develop a plan for evaluating the effectiveness of a group prior to its formation, if possible. Use the information from ongoing evaluation to make needed changes in the group.
- Be aware of how managed care and technology affect the use of groups as a practice modality and carefully consider ethical implications.

Key Terms

brief treatment model
closed group
communication networks
formed group
group cohesiveness
group dynamics
group work
interdisciplinary team
leadership

mutual aid group
natural group
ongoing group
open group
performance expectations
process-oriented leader
psychoeducational group
self-categorization theory
self-help group

small group
status characteristics
status characteristics and
    expectation states theory
task group
task-oriented leader
therapy group
time-limited group

Active Learning

1. Compare and contrast the sexuality and gender group with a small group of which you are a member in terms of how it developed, its duration, how membership was determined, heterogeneity versus homogeneity, cohesiveness, and leadership.

2. In a small group formed by your instructor, attempt to solve this problem: Draw a square. Divide it into four identical squares. Remove the bottom left-hand square. Now divide the resulting shape into four identical shapes. Work on the problem for 15 minutes. Observe the overall process in the group, the diversity of membership in the group, and the roles of each member while engaged in problem solving. Write up your observations.

3. In personal reflection, think about your behavior and roles in important groups throughout your life, groups such as your family of origin, friendship groups, social groups, sports teams, work groups, therapy groups, and so on. What roles have you played in these different groups? Are there any patterns to the roles you have played across various types of groups? Do you notice any changes in your roles over time or in different types of groups? How do you understand both the patterns and the changes?

American Self-Help Group Clearinghouse, Self-Help Group Sourcebook: www.mentalhelp.net/selfhelp

Provides a guide to locate self-help and support groups in the United States and other countries.

Association for Specialists in Group Work (ASGW): www.asgw.org

Site maintained by a division of the American Counseling Association that promotes quality in group work training, practice, and research.

Google Groups: Groups.google.com

Site for creating or finding groups on the Internet, including support-related groups.

International Association for Group Psychotherapy and Group Processes: www.iagp.com

Site contains information about the association, contact information for the board, membership information, and an electronic forum.

International Association for Social Work with Groups (IASWG): http://iaswg.org

Formerly the Association for the Advancement of Social Work with Groups, this professional organization promotes group work practice, research, and education. Information about state chapters, conferences, and group work projects is available on the site as well as a resources page, which includes information on group-related journals, IASWG practice standards, sample group work course syllabi, and member publications.

ⓈSAGE edge™

Sharpen your skills with SAGE edge at **edge.sagepub.com/hutchisonpe5e**

SAGE edge for students provides a personalized approach to help you accomplish your coursework goals in an easy-to-use learning environment.

Formal Organizations

Elizabeth D. Hutchison

CASE STUDY

Changing Leadership at Beacon Center

Beacon Center (BC) has a short but proud history of providing innovative services to persons who are homeless in River Run, the midsize midwestern city where it is located. It was established in 1980, thanks to one woman, Martha Green, and her relentless pursuit of a vision.

While serving as executive director of the YWCA, Martha became increasingly concerned about the growing homeless population in River Run. During the late 1960s and 1970s, she had worked in several positions in

River Run's antipoverty agency, and she was well-known throughout the city for her uncompromising advocacy efforts for families living in poverty. Martha was also a skilled advocate and service planner, and she soon pulled together supporters for a new social service agency to address the special needs of homeless persons. A mix of private and public (both federal and local) funds were secured, and BC opened with Martha Green as director, working with the assistance of one staff social worker. The agency grew steadily, and within a decade it had a staff of 15, as well as several subcontracted programs.

Martha valued client input into program development and made sure that client voices were heard at all levels: at city council meetings, in community discussions of program needs, in BC discussions of program needs and issues, in staff interviews, and at board meetings. She remained uncompromising in advocacy efforts and often angered city officials because she was unyielding in her demands for fair treatment of homeless persons. She advocated for their right to receive resources and services from other social service organizations as well as for their right to congregate in public places.

By the same token, Martha and the staff consistently reminded clients of their obligations as citizens and, gently but firmly, held them to those obligations. Clients were sometimes angered by this call for responsible behavior, but they appreciated the tireless advocacy of Martha and the staff. They also appreciated that they were kept fully informed about political issues that concerned them, as well as about actions taken by BC in relation to these issues.

Martha also had a vision regarding staff relationships. She was committed to working collaboratively, to trusting frontline workers to make their own decisions, and to securing the participation of all staff on important policy decisions. This commitment was aided by the fact that Martha and her staff came from similar backgrounds and had deep family roots in River Run. Rules were kept to a minimum, and staff relationships were very personal. For example, a staff member needing to keep a medical appointment would make informal arrangements with another staff member to exchange an hour of service, with no need to "go through channels" or invoke formal sick leave. Martha believed in hiring the best-trained and most experienced staff for frontline positions and, over the years, hired and retained a highly skilled, committed core staff. She had high expectations of her staff, but she was also a nurturing administrator who was concerned about the personal well-being and professional development of each staff member. She established a climate of mutual respect where people could risk disagreeing.

Martha spent some time every week working in each program area to ensure that she understood the agency's programs as they were experienced by clients and frontline staff. She kept staff fully informed about economic and political pressures faced by BC and about her actions in regard to these issues. She regularly sought their input on these issues, and decisions were usually made by consensus. On occasion, however, around really sensitive issues—such as the choice between forgoing a salary increase and closing a program—she asked staff to vote by secret ballot to neutralize any potential power dynamics.

Martha had a vision, as well, about how a board of directors can facilitate a successful client-centered program. She saw the board as part of the BC system, just as staff and clients were part of the system. She worked hard to ensure that members chosen for the board shared the BC commitment to the rights of homeless persons, and she developed warm, personal relationships with them. She kept the board fully informed about issues facing BC and was successful in securing their support and active involvement in advocacy and resource development activities.

Over the years, BC became known as an innovative, client-centered service center, as well as a hardheaded advocacy organization. Staff and board members took pride in being part of what they considered to be a very special endeavor—one that outstripped other social service organizations in its expertise, commitment, and compassion.

(Continued)

(Continued)

Clients were not always satisfied with the services but generally acknowledged among themselves that they were lucky to have the dedication of BC.

Reactions from the community were more mixed, however. The respect offered up was, in many circles, a grudging one. Many city officials as well as staff of other social service organizations complained about the self-righteous attitudes and uncompromising posture of Martha and the staff at BC. These detractors acknowledged that the tactics of BC staff were successful in countering discrimination against homeless persons but suggested that BC succeeded at much cost of goodwill. Although Martha believed in keeping staff, clients, and board members informed about the economic and political pressures faced by BC, she saw it as her job to carry the major responsibility for responding to, and absorbing, those pressures, to protect staff energy for serving clients.

Martha retired almost 20 years ago and relocated with her husband to be closer to their children. An acting director was appointed at BC while a search for a permanent director was under way. The acting director had worked several years at BC and shared much of Martha's administrative and service philosophy. She was not as good, however, at juggling the multiple demands of the position. Staff and clients felt a loss of support, board members lost some of their enthusiasm and confidence, and antagonists in the community saw an opportunity to mute some of BC's advocacy efforts. Staff maintained a strong commitment to the rights of homeless persons, but they lost some of their optimism about making a difference.

After 8 months, Helen Blue, a former community college administrator, was hired as the new executive director. Like Martha Green, she was of European American heritage, but she had only lived in River Run for a few years. She was excited about this new professional challenge but had a vision for BC that was somewhat different from Martha's. She was concerned about the alienation that had resulted, in some circles, from BC's hard-hitting advocacy stance, and she favored a more conciliatory approach. For example, after meeting with city officials, she assigned staff social workers the task of convincing clients to stop congregating in the city park near BC and to stay out of the business district during business hours. After meeting with directors of other social service organizations, she directed staff to be less demanding in their advocacy for clients. Helen was also concerned about the lack of rules and the looseness of attention to chain of command, and she began to institute new rules and procedures. Staff meetings and open community meetings with clients became presentations by Helen. Staff were no longer allowed to attend board meetings and were not informed about what happened at them. Frontline staff often found their decisions overturned by Helen. When the first staff resignation came, Helen hired the replacement with no input from staff, clients, or board members.

Helen stayed a few years at BC and then decided to return to community college administration. Since she left, BC has had three executive directors, two that stayed for only a short time. The current CEO, Roderick Wallace, has been with BC for 12 years and has guided it through a major funding and program expansion. When he came to BC, the organization was floundering. He spent time with different groups of stakeholders—staff, board members, clients, community leaders, and representatives of other social service organizations—to learn their vision for the organization. He invited the staff to begin to attend board meetings again. Working collaboratively with other organizations, he brought in some new federal and local funds to expand health care coverage for homeless persons. His meetings with stakeholding groups identified two issues for BC: (1) the need for a more ethnically diverse staff and board (Roderick is African American) and (2) the need to improve information technology to support administrative functions and program accountability. Roderick has had some success in both areas, but the introduction of greater ethnic diversity of the staff has introduced new tensions that continue to bubble up from time to time.

In the recession of 2009, as funding streams became more restricted at a time of growing homelessness caused by home foreclosures and a weakened economy, Roderick encouraged the board to begin a strategic planning process to ensure financial stability and continued service quality, with some success on both fronts. In the past 2 years, BC has forged new partnerships in the community and expanded the comprehensiveness of its health care services. Roderick depends on a dedicated professional staff to ensure the quality of the programs. As the organization has grown, he has maintained much of the structure developed by Helen Blue, but he emphasizes to all stakeholders the importance of staying flexible in a highly volatile environment.

A DEFINITION OF FORMAL ORGANIZATIONS

You were probably born in a hospital. There is a good chance that you began to attend a house of worship at an early age. You may have been enrolled in a child care or education center by the age of 4. You have, by now, spent close to 2 decades in school. Along the way, you may have joined organizations such as Girl Scouts, Boy Scouts, YMCA, YWCA, or other athletic clubs. You may also have participated in programs offered by civic and social service organizations as a member, recipient of services, or volunteer. You probably manage your finances with the assistance of a bank or credit union, and you meet your basic survival needs as well as fulfill your consumer wants through a variety of business organizations. You depend on your telecommunications provider to stay connected to friends, family, school, work, news, consumer products, and much more. You may have been, or currently are, a member of a sorority or fraternity, and you may be a student member of the National Association of Social Workers (NASW). You probably have been a paid employee of at least one formal organization, and you most likely are enrolled, or soon will be, in a field practicum in a social service organization like Beacon Center. When you die, a news organization may announce your death, a public organization will issue a death certificate, and your loved ones will probably seek the service of several other organizations to plan your funeral.

For those of us who live in contemporary complex societies, formal organizations are pervasive in our lives, a most important but usually taken-for-granted part of life. But what, exactly, are they? A **formal organization** is a collectivity of people with a high degree of formal structure, working together to meet common goals. This definition, like most found in the organization literature, has three key components: a collectivity of people, a formal structure, and the common purpose of working together to meet common goals.

This definition leaves a lot of room for variation. Formal organizations differ in size, structure, culture, and goals. They also perform a variety of functions in contemporary society and influence human behavior in many ways. Keep in mind that formal organizations are intricately woven into the fabric of life in contemporary society, that formal organizations can be both functional and dysfunctional for society or for specific groups, and that some members of organizations benefit more than others from organizational goals and structure. They meet our needs, help us fulfill goals, and nurture our development. They also make stressful demands, thwart our goals, inhibit our holistic development, and constrain our behavior.

The purpose for introducing theory and research about formal organizations in this chapter is threefold: (1) to help you understand the pervasive and multifaceted influence of formal organizations on human behavior—yours as well as your clients', (2) to assist you in understanding the organizations in which social workers practice, and (3) to help you work for positive change in your professional organizations.

Photo 12.1   Formal organizations are defined as a collectivity of people with a high degree of formality, working together to meet common goals.

© Ned Frisk Photography/Brand X Pictures/Thinkstock

PERSPECTIVES ON FORMAL ORGANIZATIONS_____

Three decades ago, the ways of thinking about organizational life in the United States had grown so numerous, and so fragmented, one observer noted that the state of organization theory can be described as "more of a weed patch than a well-tended garden" (Pfeffer, 1982, p. 1). That is still an apt description of current theorizing about organizations (Walsh, Meyer, & Schoonhoven, 2006). Likewise, the research on organizations and the related prescriptions for organizational administration reflect great variety. Nevertheless, three generalizations can be made about the abundant multidisciplinary literature on formal organizations in the United States.

1. The preponderance of early theories of organizations assumed that a rational organization structure (bureaucracy) would ensure the effective and efficient accomplishment of organizational goals, which were assumed to be clear and specific. Contemporary theories challenge the rationality of formal organizations, but the image of the modern organization as a rational instrument (machine) of efficiency and predictability has had a lasting influence on theories of organizations (Godwyn & Gittell, 2012).

2. Early theories focused on what happens inside organizations and ignored all aspects of their external environments. In contrast, contemporary theories generally propose some sort of relationship

> Exchange and choice perspective

between organization and environment (Garrow & Hasenfeld, 2010). Attention to the effects of the physical environment, both external and internal, on organizational life has been lacking, suggesting a possible new direction for organizational theory and research.

Systems perspective

3. Most organizational theory has been biased toward the interests of owners and managers rather than those of workers (Morgan, 2006). In recent years, critical theorists have challenged this one-sided view of organizations and raised questions about domination and oppression in organizational life (Garrow & Hasenfeld, 2010; Morgan, 2006).

Conflict perspective

Before going further, it is important to recognize that national culture has a great influence on theories developed, and this is nowhere more true than in theorizing about formal organizations. Geert Hofstede (2010) argues that nationality has a large influence on organization theories, noting particularly that European organization theory shares some commonalities with that of the United States, but there are also some striking differences. Indeed, Hofstede suggests philosophical differences in the way scholars in different European countries theorize about organizations. In his analysis, Hofstede (2001) asserts that organization theory is always constructed according to a worldview about where organizations come from, the foundation on which they are built. This worldview, he argues, is tied up in culture and varies from nation to nation. Here is what he suggests as the worldview undergirding organization theory in selected countries:

- Britain: systems
- China: the family
- Eastern Europe: efficiency
- France: power
- Germany: order
- Japan: Japan
- Netherlands: consensus
- Nordic countries: equality
- United States: the market

Organization theorists have suggested the possibility of developing a more globally relevant theory of organizations (see Soulsby & Clark, 2007). They note that existing theories of organizations have been developed and studied in stable-market economic systems, usually in North America and Europe. They propose that study of the transformation of organizations in former socialist countries as they transitioned to market economies is a fruitful area for beginning to develop a more globally relevant theory (see Uhlenbruck, Meyer, & Hitt, 2003). However, at the moment, it appears that around the world, in Asia, Arab countries, eastern Europe, and Russia, business schools are using translations of North American books on organization theory (Czarniawska, 2007). It is possible that scholars in other countries will develop original theory as they try to adapt existing theory to fit their unique situations.

As noted earlier, Hofstede (2010) suggests that organization theory in the United States is strongly influenced by the high reverence for the market expressed in U.S. culture. You will probably note the market theme in some of the dominant organization theories in the United States. Often for social workers, particularly as we navigate human service organizations, this worldview is alienating and seems at odds with our ethic of care. Indeed, this is a major challenge to U.S. social workers, and perhaps increasingly to social workers in other countries in a globalized economy: how to provide caring services in organizations operating within a societal context that reveres the market.

Please keep the important role of culture in mind as you read the discussion of theoretical perspectives in this chapter, which focuses primarily on organization theory developed in the United States. There has been little cross-pollination of organization theory across national lines. Several people have attempted to organize the weed patch of U.S. organizational theory into a garden—to bring some order to the diversity of viewpoints without denying the complexity and multifaceted nature of contemporary formal organizations (e.g., Garrow & Hasenfeld, 2010; Greenwald, 2008; Morgan, 2006). Here we use a classification system that includes four perspectives: the rational perspective, systems perspective, interactionist/interpretive perspective, and critical perspective. None of these perspectives, taken individually, accounts for all functions of organizations, but taken together, they elaborate the multifaceted nature of organizations reflected in those functions. Each perspective encompasses both classical and contemporary theories, and each has relevance for social work practice. Although I have tried to organize the weed patch of organizational theories in this chapter, I warn you that even though I discuss only a small portion of existing theories, you most likely will feel overwhelmed by the number of theories discussed in this chapter. When you feel overwhelmed, I suggest you stop and ask, "Do I know any organizations that operate like this?"

As you read about these perspectives, you may want to keep in mind one author's suggestion (Walsh et al., 2006) that to be useful, contemporary research on organization theory needs to address three basic questions: (1) How can we understand current changing organizations (the theory question)? (2) How can we live *in* these organizations? (3) How can we more healthily live *with* these organizations? James Walsh and colleagues (2006) argue that existing theories of organizations fail to consider the powerful impact that contemporary organizations have on human "social and material lives and on our planet's ecosystem" (p. 661) and that new theorizing is needed that takes these issues into account (see Marti, Etzion, & Leca, 2008, for a similar argument). This argument is consistent with social work's interest in social justice, and in the following discussion, I have tried to incorporate contemporary theories that are beginning to address these issues. The rational perspective is presented first because of its dominance in the study of organizations (Godwyn & Gittell, 2012).

Critical Thinking Questions 12.1

Think of a formal organization of which you have been a part, for which you have positive feelings.

What words come to mind when you think of this organization? Now, think of a formal organization of which you have been a part, for which you have negative feelings. What words come to mind when you think of this organization?

Rational Perspective

When Helen Blue became the executive director at Beacon Center, she was concerned about the lack

Exchange and choice perspective

of administrative formality, the lack of rules, and the ambiguous chain of command, among other things. She also wanted greater authority over planning and decision making. These concerns reflect the **rational perspective on organizations**, which views the formal organization as a "goal-directed, purposefully designed machine" (Garrow & Hasenfeld, 2010, p. 34). It assumes organizations can be designed with structures and processes that maximize efficiency and effectiveness, concepts that are highly valued in this perspective. *Efficiency* means obtaining a high ratio of output to input, achieving the best outcome from the least investment of resources. *Effectiveness* means goal accomplishment. Exhibit 12.1 summarizes the central theories in this perspective.

The Ideal-Type Bureaucracy

In the modern era, formal organization is often equated with bureaucracy. Indeed, Max Weber (1947), the German sociologist who formulated a theory of bureaucracy at the beginning of the 20th century, saw bureaucracy and capitalism as inseparable. Although he had concerns about the negative impact of bureaucracies, Weber proposed a **bureaucracy** as the most efficient form of organization for goal accomplishment. The characteristics of Weber's ideal-type bureaucracy are presented in Exhibit 12.2.

Weber (1947) was enthusiastic about the advantages of the ideal-type bureaucracy over

Exhibit 12.1 The Rational Perspective on Formal Organizations

Major theme: The organization is a goal-directed, purposefully designed machine (closed system).	
Theory	**Central Idea**
The ideal-type bureaucracy (Weber, 1947)	Formal rationality—rules, regulations, and structures—is essential to goal accomplishment.
Scientific management (Taylor, 1911)	The most effective organizations maximize internal efficiency, the "one best way."
Human relations theory (Mayo, 1933)	Human relationships are central to organizational efficiency and effectiveness.
Management by objectives (Drucker, 1954)	Managers should focus on the desired outcome (objectives) and create an organizational design to achieve that outcome; strategic planning is key to organizational success.
Decision-making theory (March & Simon, 1958)	Organizational rationality has limits.

Exhibit 12.2 Weber's Ideal-Type Bureaucracy

Ideal-Type Bureaucracy

Clear hierarchy and chain of command

Clear division of labor based on specialized skills

Formal rules of operation

Formal and task-oriented communications

Merit-based recruitment and advancement

Keeping of files and records for administrative action

other ways of organizing for goal accomplishment, but he did not see bureaucracies as problem free. (Note: Weber did not use "ideal-type" to mean superior; instead he used it to mean an abstract model against which other organizations could be compared.) He was concerned about the dehumanizing potential of bureaucracies—their potential to become an **iron cage of rationality**, trapping people and denying many aspects of their humanity. Researchers have noted that excessive use of rules and procedures often limits the efficiency and effectiveness of bureaucratic organizations.

Despite the potential negative effects of bureaucracies, they continue to be the predominant form of organization in contemporary modern and postmodern societies, and the goal of maximization of efficiency is taken for granted. There is evidence, however, that some newer organizations are using less bureaucratic structures. This is true for human service organizations as well as organizations formed for other purposes (Hasenfeld, 2010a). Indeed, as Mary Katherine O'Connor and Ellen Netting (2009) suggest, most organizations that employ social workers have been influenced by the rational perspective but do not typically operate purely from this perspective. Moreover, as is the case with other types of organizations, their research has found that newer social service organizations are less likely than older ones to have traditional bureaucratic cultures. This means that a rational perspective will be less useful in understanding these newer organizations than it might be for understanding older social service organizations. How closely do the social work organizations you have worked in fit the ideal-type bureaucracy? How much emphasis is put on efficiency? Helen Blue and the executive directors who followed her wanted to move Beacon Center closer to the ideal-type bureaucracy than it was under Martha Green's leadership.

Martha Green, Helen Blue, and Roderick Wallace might all be interested in one researcher's findings that client satisfaction decreased as the level of bureaucracy increased in transitional housing programs for homeless families (Crook, 2001). In addition, conflict among residents increased as the level of organizational bureaucracy increased. The indirect impact of organizational bureaucracy on clients is called *trickle-down bureaucracy*. How about for you? Do you think of bureaucracy as a good or bad way to organize? There is no doubt that bureaucracy has gotten a bad name in many circles.

Scientific Management

Another early 20th-century approach to formal organizations has had lasting influence. Frederick W. Taylor's (1911) **scientific management**, sometimes referred to as Taylorism, was directed toward maximizing internal efficiency. The set of principles Taylor developed to guide the design of organizations was widely adopted by both industry and government, first in the United States and then worldwide. These principles are listed in Exhibit 12.3.

Exhibit 12.3 Taylor's Scientific Management

Scientific Management

Time and motion studies to find the "one best way" to perform each organizational task

Scientific selection and training of workers

Training focused on performing tasks in the standardized one best way

Close managerial monitoring of workers to ensure accurate implementation of task prescriptions and to provide appropriate rewards for compliance

Managerial authority over planning and decision making, with no challenge from workers

---

In his provocative book *The McDonaldization of Society*, George Ritzer (2013b) proposes that McDonald's Corporation is a prototype organization, whose organizational style is coming to dominate much of the world. This relatively new type of organization, which operates on the combined principles of bureaucratization and scientific management, has four key traits:

1. *Efficiency*, which is valued in a fast-paced society

2. *Calculability*, with an emphasis on quantity rather than quality of products and services

3. *Predictability*, with the assurance that a Big Mac will be the same in San Francisco as it is in Washington, DC, or Hong Kong

4. *Control*, with workers trained to do a limited number of things exactly as they are told to do them and with maximum use of nonhuman technology

Ritzer gives many examples of the proliferation of the McDonald's model, including shopping malls; packaged tours; managed medical care; the criminal justice system; weight loss organizations; the "junk-food journalism" of *USA Today*; the use of machine-graded, multiple-choice examinations; reliance on GPAs, PSATs, SATs, and GREs for evaluating educational potential; franchised hotels; planned communities; and franchised child care centers.

Principles of scientific management are frequently followed in social service organizations. For example, some organizations undertake task and workload analyses to improve effectiveness and efficiency, and managers develop procedures, regulations, and decision trees to be implemented by direct service workers. The recent emphasis on *best practices* and *evidence-based practice* is derivative of scientific management thinking, but these practices do not typically conceive of "one best way." Have you encountered any of these in your field setting? Although Helen Blue initiated more procedures and regulations and believed in managerial authority over planning and decision making, she did not share scientific management's enthusiasm for "one best way" of delivering services. The same can be said for Roderick Wallace.

Human Relations Theory

Human relations theory introduced a new twist on maximizing organizational efficiency and

Photo 12.2 Formal organizations have important influences on human behavior—think about the impact McDonald's has had on human eating behaviors and our concept of "fast" food.

© Richard T. Nowitz/Corbis

effectiveness. The theory grew out of a series of studies conducted by Elton Mayo (1933) and associates at the Hawthorne plant of the Western Electric Company in the 1920s and 1930s. Seeking to improve the rationality of the organization, the researchers were studying the effects of working conditions, such as intensity of lighting, on productivity. As expected, the researchers found that productivity increased as the lighting intensity increased. To their surprise, however, productivity continued to increase even when they began to dim the lights in an attempt to confirm their findings. The researchers concluded that technical rationality—the development of rational structures, procedures, and processes—is not sufficient to ensure maximum productivity. Social factors, they concluded, are as important as, if not more

important than, technical factors in accomplishing organizational goals. They based this conclusion, which became the central proposition of a new theory, on their observation that productivity appeared to be related to worker morale and sense of social responsibility to the work group.

This interpretation of the research findings has been criticized on the basis of the **Hawthorne effect**—the tendency of experimental participants to perform in particular ways simply because they know they are being studied. In other words, critics have suggested that the participants in the study may have become more productive simply because they knew their behavior was being studied.

Regardless of the validity of the initial findings, subsequent research led to the human relations theory of organizational management, which emphasized the heretofore unrecognized importance of human interaction in organizational efficiency and effectiveness. As the theory developed, it also proposed that democratic leadership is more effective than authoritarian management in securing worker cooperation.

The human relations approach has been a favorite theory in social service organizations because it calls attention to how staff attitudes about the work situation can influence how they relate to clients (see Garrow & Hasenfeld, 2010). The social workers at Beacon Center did indeed respond more cooperatively to Martha Green's democratic leadership than to Helen Blue's more authoritarian leadership. Furthermore, it appears that staff cohesion did "trickle down" to improve consumer satisfaction as well.

It is important to note, however, that human relations theory is still in the rational tradition.

Conflict perspective

Like scientific management, it focuses on maximizing efficiency and effectiveness, and it endorses the interests of owners and managers. Managers must become leaders capable of securing the cooperation of workers, but they are still in control of the organization. Although the consideration of human interaction opens the possibility of nonrational factors in organizational life, human relations theorists still assume that, with "leadership skills," human interactions can be as rationally managed as structures and procedures.

After losing ground during the 1950s, human relations theory was rein-

Humanistic perspective

vigorated in the 1960s by **organizational humanism** and a subfield called organizational development. These theories suggest that organizations can maximize efficiency and effectiveness while also promoting individual happiness and well-being. Douglas McGregor (1960), for example, a proponent of organizational humanism, identified two opposing sets of assumptions from which managers view workers (summarized in Exhibit 12.4). McGregor suggested that *Theory X* calls for directive management, but *Theory Y* calls for greater democratization of decision making in organizations. In your work experiences, have you encountered either of these theories about workers? If so, how did you react as a worker?

Management by Objectives (MBO)

In the 1950s, Peter Drucker (1954) suggested that organizational goals and objectives should be the primary concern of organizational managers. Managers should focus on the desired outcome (objectives) and create an organizational design to achieve that outcome. The planning process, known as *strategic planning*, is the key to organizational success. Both short-range and long-range planning are seen as important, although most organizations that follow the MBO approach have

Exhibit 12.4   Assumptions of Theory X and Theory Y

Assumptions of Theory X	Assumptions of Theory Y
Workers have an inherent dislike of work.	Workers see work as a natural activity.
Workers prefer to be told what to do.	Workers are self-directed when working on projects to which they are committed.
Workers respond to money as the primary motivator.	Workers seek responsibility when organizational goals are congruent with their needs. They have more creative contributions to make than organizations generally allow.

SOURCE: Based on McGregor, 1960.

not gone beyond short-range planning. You may recall that Roderick Wallace saw strategic planning as the way to manage the challenge of the economic recession.

Decision-Making Theory

In the 1950s, another group of organizational theorists in the rational tradition began to write about the limits to organizational rationality. Herbert Simon (1957) presented a **decision-making theory** of organizations, focusing on how decisions of individuals in organizations affect the organization as a whole.

James March and Simon (1958) argued that administrators cannot be perfectly rational in their decision making, because they face many constraints that limit their alternatives: incomplete information about alternatives for action, incomplete understanding of the consequences of those actions, and the incapacity to explore more than a limited number of alternatives at a time. March and Simon used the term **bounded rationality** to describe this limited rationality of organizational actors. They also suggested that bounded rationality leads administrators and other organizational actors to **satisfice** rather than maximize when making decisions—to seek satisfactory rather than perfect solutions and to discontinue the search for alternatives when a satisfactory solution is available. Cognitive psychologist Daniel Kahneman (2011) has presented research from several disciplines to support the argument that human rationality is much more limited than usually assumed.

Although the rational perspective on organizations has been dominant in the design of organizations, including social service organizations, and has had some positive impact on productivity, it has been criticized on a number of grounds. It fails to consider external pressures on organizational decision makers. As suggested by decision-making theory, it overstates the rational capacity of organizational actors. It fails to attend to the issue of power in organizational life. Garrow and Hasenfeld (2010) suggest that the rational perspective fails to take the moral basis of human service organizations into account.

Systems Perspective

Martha Green and Helen Blue had different styles of managing what happened

> Systems perspective

inside Beacon Center, but they also had different styles of managing external pressures and resources. Martha focused on giving homeless persons a voice in efforts to secure political and economic resources for Beacon Center; Helen focused on conciliation with community and political leaders. In her own way, however, each was attentive to Beacon Center's relationship with its environment, and Roderick Wallace has continued to pay attention to the multifaceted environment. He recognized the challenge that the recession presented to social service organizations, and he has been diligent in seeking community partners for expanding services for homeless persons in River Run. In this respect, they all have negated the rational perspective's view of the organization as a closed system that can be controlled by careful attention to internal structure and processes. During the 1950s and 1960s, the rationalist view of organizations was challenged by the systems perspective. All subsequent theorizing about organizations has been influenced by the systems perspective.

The **systems perspective on organizations** builds on the fundamental principle that the organization is in constant interaction with its multiple environments—social, political, economic, cultural, technological—and must be able to adapt to environmental change. Some systems theorists suggest mutual influence between organizations and their environments; other theorists see the influence as unidirectional, with organizational structure and processes being determined by the environment. A second important principle of the systems perspective is that organizations are composed of interrelated subsystems that must be integrated in order to achieve the organization's goals and meet environmental demands. Finally, in contrast to the rational approach, the systems perspective holds that there are many different ways, rather than one best way, to reach the same ends. The idea that a system can attain its goals in a variety of ways is known as *equifinality*.

Several systems theories of organizations have been developed over time, but we look at only two here: the political economy model and the learning organization theory. These two theories are summarized in Exhibit 12.5.

Political Economy Model

The **political economy model** focuses on the dependence of organizations on their environments for necessary resources and on the impact of organization–environment interactions on the internal structure and processes of the organization (Wamsley & Zald, 1973). More specifically, it focuses on two types of resources necessary to organizations: political resources (legitimacy and power) and economic resources. The greater the dependence of the organization on the environment for either of these types of resources, the greater the influence the environment will have on the organization. Likewise, the greater control one unit of the organization has over resources, the more power that unit has over the organizational processes. Researchers have recently applied the political economy model to study China's transition to a market economy and have found that political connections can substitute for market connections as organizations attempt to innovate and survive in the new economy (Nee & Opper, 2010; Zhou, 2013).

The political economy model is particularly potent for clarifying how social service organizations resolve such important issues as which clients to serve, which services to provide, how to organize service provision, and how to define staff and client roles (Garrow & Hasenfeld, 2010). Both Martha Green and Helen Blue were trying to read their political and economic environments as they made these kinds of decisions, but their different ways of thinking led them to attend to different aspects of the environment. Roderick Wallace appears to be taking a broad look at the agency's political and economic environments. The political economy model recognizes clients as resources and as potential players in the political arena. Social workers have an important role to play in facilitating their inclusion in the political process, a role that was part of Martha Green's vision for Beacon Center.

Learning Organization Theory

The **learning organization theory** was developed on the premise that rational planning is not sufficient for an organization to survive in a rapidly changing environment such as the one in which we live. Formal organizations must become complex systems capable of constant learning (Argyris, 1999; Argyris & Schön, 1978, 1996; Senge, 1990). The learning organization is one that can

- *Scan the environment, anticipate change, and detect "early warning" signs of trends and patterns. In a social work context, this facility means*

Exhibit 12.5   The Systems Perspective on Formal Organizations

Major theme: The organization is in constant interaction with multiple environments.	
Theory	**Central Idea**
Political economy model (Wamsley & Zald, 1973)	The organization depends on the environment for political and economic resources.
Learning organization theory (Argyris & Schön, 1978)	The organization must be able to learn and change in a rapidly changing environment.

understanding services from the points of view of clients as well as those of a variety of actors in the environment. It seems that Martha Green was more tuned in to the points of view of clients than Helen Blue was. On the other hand, Helen Blue seemed more sensitive to the points of view of some collaborating agencies. Roderick Wallace was attuned to the warning signs in the economic environment during the recession, but he also depends on the clinical staff at Beacon Center to stay attuned to the points of view of clients.

- *Question, challenge, and change customary ways of operating.* Certainly, Helen Blue, like many new administrators, was questioning and challenging Martha Green's customary ways of operating. The important issue, however, was whether she was developing ways of operating that allowed and encouraged ongoing questioning, challenging, and changing. Roderick Wallace was hopeful that the strategic planning process would lead to questioning customary ways of operating. Ongoing growth requires dialogue, expression of conflicting points of view, and some risk taking. Martha Green tried to develop a climate that allowed such dialogue, but the lack of staff diversity may have limited the nature of that dialogue.

- *Allow the appropriate strategic direction to emerge.* The learning organization needs vision, norms, values, and limits to guide organizational behavior (Morgan, 2006). But these should serve as guideposts, not straitjackets. Even these guideposts must be open for questioning. Ironically, both Martha Green's egalitarian vision and Helen Blue's vision of a more hierarchical organization had the potential to become straitjackets. Organizations need to be willing to look at both the benefits and the downside of their favored ways of operating—and to alter their strategic direction accordingly. Gareth Morgan (2006) emphasizes the importance of organizational limits, the "thou shalt nots" that guide organizational behavior. He suggests that Western organizations have put great emphasis on developing goals and objectives but have downplayed the limits needed to guide the actions taken to achieve those goals. There have

been many reports of corporate misbehavior in the beginning years of the 21st century, in both the private and public sectors, including social welfare organizations. Perhaps that is why we have been seeing an increasing call for "strong ethical leadership" in both sectors (Northouse, 2013). There is growing concern that organizations have established too few limits on behavior as they compete in a globalized and increasingly competitive and complex world.

- *Evolve designs that support continuous learning.* The challenge is to avoid anarchy on one hand and overcentralization on the other. The learning organization develops methods for shared decision making and avoids overdefining its members' actions. From this perspective, Beacon Center was more likely to be a learning organization under the leadership of Martha Green and Roderick Wallace than under the leadership of Helen Blue.

Theories in the systems perspective have advanced organizational understanding by calling attention to the influence of the external environment on organizations. They provide useful concepts for considering how organizations survive in turbulent environments, and, indeed, Uhlenbruck et al. (2003) suggest that learning organization theory is an appropriate theoretical approach for understanding how organizations in former socialist countries successfully adapted to the transition to market economies. But the systems perspective has little to say about the moral purposes of social service organizations or how organizations can be positive rather than negative forces in society. Recently, however, Stephen Gill (2010) has proposed learning organization theory as an appropriate model for nonprofit organizations. As we can see from the experience of Beacon Center, we live in a world that values the kind of order Helen Blue wants to bring to Beacon Center, and there can be much environmental resistance to the development of learning organizations. As Beacon Center continues to grow, Roderick Wallace is attempting to balance the need for order with the need to be open to new environmental conditions. If nothing else, the idea of the learning organization serves as a bridge between the systems perspective and the interactional/interpretive perspective.

> ### Critical Thinking Questions 12.2
>
> Think back to your earlier ideas about the characteristics of an organization for which you have positive feelings. Can you use specific theoretical concepts from the rational or systems perspective to talk about that organization? Now, think of your ideas about the characteristics of an organization for which you have negative feelings. Can you use specific theoretical concepts from the rational or systems perspective to describe that organization?

Interactional/Interpretive Perspective

Social constructionist perspective

As I have been suggesting, when Helen Blue became executive director at Beacon Center, she wanted to introduce more "rational order" and have fewer internal voices speaking about the kind of place the center should be. It might be said that she found Martha Green's vision for Beacon Center to be too interactional and interpretive. Theories of organizations within the **interactional/interpretive perspective on organizations** are quite diverse, but they all share two basic premises: (1) Organizations provide members with a sense of connection and meaning; and (2) organizations reflect the worldviews of the creators; they are social constructions of reality created by ongoing interactions and emerging relationships (Godwyn & Gittell, 2012).

Although the rational perspective on organizations has received the most attention in the organizational literature, the interactional/interpretive approach is actually older. In the early 1900s, Mary Parker Follett (1918) suggested that organizational reality is created by relationships; she did not focus on either workers or managers but on the relationships that connected them. Her philosophy took account of both mutual influence and egalitarianism.

The interactional/interpretive perspective rejects both the rational and the systems perspectives. Contrary to the rational perspective, the interactional/interpretive perspective focuses on processes rather than goals, emphasizes flexibility rather than control and reason, and is interested in a diversity of approaches rather than one right way. From this perspective, organizations are seen as increasingly fragmented into multiple realities, and they should be studied through multiple voices rather than through the unitary voice of the manager. Contrary to the systems perspective, the interactional/interpretive perspective emphasizes human agency in creating organizations and challenges the constraining influence of external forces.

Different interactional/interpretive theorists focus on different themes in relation to the basic premises just stated. The three separate approaches summarized in Exhibit 12.6 provide some sense of these differences.

Exhibit 12.6   The Interpretive Perspective on Formal Organizations

Major theme: The organization is a social construction of reality.	
Theory	**Central Idea**
Social action model (Silverman, 1971)	The organization is defined by individual actors.
Organizational culture model (Schein, 1992)	Organizations are cultures with shared experiences and shared meanings.
Managing diversity model (Cox, 1993)	Organizational systems and practices should maximize the potential advantages of diversity in organizational membership.

Social Action Model

One of the most influential contributions to the interactional/interpretive study of organizations is that of British sociologist David Silverman, presented in his 1971 book *The Theory of Organizations: A Sociological Framework*. Criticizing both rational and systems perspectives, Silverman proposed an approach that emphasizes the active role of individual organizational actors in creating the organization—an approach known as **Silverman's social action model**. He proposed a set of questions, presented in Exhibit 12.7, to ask when studying a specific organization.

In a more recent work, Silverman (1994) criticized the singular emphasis on organizational actors in his earlier model. He suggested that in reacting against deterministic theories of environmental constraints, he failed to acknowledge the influence of history and social structure. He further suggested that his portrayal of human behavior as free and undetermined failed to acknowledge the influence of cultural scripts and the tendency of humans to see their behavior as freer than it is. This self-critique is consistent with other criticisms of the limitations of the interactional/interpretive perspective, but Silverman's theory has had a large impact on European theorizing about organizations (Scott, 2014).

Exhibit 12.7 Silverman's Questions for Studying a Specific Organization (Social Action Model)

Who are the principal actors in the organization?

What goals are the actors trying to achieve?

How are the different actors involved in the organization?

What strategies do they use to achieve their goals?

What are the consequences of their actions for each other and for the development of interactional patterns in the organization?

SOURCE: Silverman, 1971.

Organizational Culture Model

In contrast to Silverman's de-emphasis on culture, Edgar Schein (1992) focuses on organizations as cultures whose members have shared experiences that produce shared meanings, or interpretations. Organizations, therefore, exist as much in the heads of their members as in policies, rules, and procedures. The **organizational culture model** views organizations as ongoing, interactive processes of reality construction, involving many organizational actors. Organizational culture is made up of language, slogans, symbols, rituals, stories, and ceremonies (Morgan, 2006) but also of mundane, routine, day-to-day activities. For example, under Martha Green's leadership, the slogan "client input" was an important feature of the Beacon Center culture, buttressed by the day-to-day practice of soliciting client opinions.

When we become new members of an organization, some aspects of its culture are immediately obvious. But other aspects are more difficult to decipher, causing us to feel uncomfortable and confused. For example, after one day in a field practicum agency, we may understand the cultural norms about casual versus professional dress and extended versus brief lunch hours, but it may take us several weeks to decipher whether we are in a cooperative or competitive culture. There may be a clear slogan about commitment to clients, but it may take some time to decipher how that commitment is implemented, or whether it is.

Organizational culture is always evolving, and it is not always unitary. In many organizations, competing beliefs and value systems produced subcultures. Given the evolution of organizational culture and rapid societal changes, it is not unusual to find a split between the old and new guard or to find cultural divisions based on organizational function. For example, fund-raisers in social service organizations may speak a different language from clinicians in the same agency. The result may be cultural fragmentation or cultural warfare.

According to the organizational culture approach, organizations choose their environments and interact with them based on their interpretive schemes. It could be said that when Martha Green was executive director, Beacon Center saw itself as more humane than, and therefore superior to, other organizations serving homeless persons. Founders, staff, and board members had certain definitions of other agencies and of their client group that they used to influence referring agencies, funding sources, and clientele. They clearly saw themselves as proactive, capable of influencing their environments. This interpretive scheme could serve as a motivating factor, but it could also create barriers to their effective work with clients or other organizations. Indeed, other agencies often felt a certain resentment toward the arrogance and self-righteousness of Beacon Center under Martha Green's leadership. Under Helen Blue, on the other hand, clients and staff resented not being included in decisions. Roderick Wallace sees his biggest challenges as managing issues related to staff diversity and keeping the organization open to continuous learning.

Criticisms of the organizational culture approach are twofold (Morgan, 2006). One criticism is leveled at theorists who write about managing organizational culture. These theorists are sometimes criticized for being biased in favor of management and potentially exploitative of employees. They are also criticized for overstating managers' potential to control culture, negating the role of multiple actors in the creation of shared meaning. The second criticism of the organizational culture approach is that it fails to take account of the fact that some members have more power than others to influence the construction of culture.

Managing Diversity Model

In the 1990s, organizational theorists developed an approach to organizational management called the **managing diversity model**. Given the trend toward greater diversity in the labor force, several social scientists (e.g., Cox, 1993, 2001; Kossek, Lobel, & Brown, 2006; Mor Barak, 2014; Mor Barak & Travis, 2010) have suggested that contemporary organizations cannot be successful unless they learn to manage diverse populations. Diversity is a permanent, not transitory, feature of contemporary life.

The purpose in managing diversity is to maximize the advantages of diversity while minimizing its disadvantages. Taylor Cox (1993), a leading proponent of the model, says, "I view the goal of managing diversity as maximizing the ability of all employees to contribute to organizational goals and to achieve their full potential unhindered by group identities such as gender, race, nationality, age, and departmental affiliation" (p. 11). He argues that this goal requires that a new organizational culture must be institutionalized, a culture that welcomes diversity (Cox, 2001).

Mor Barak and Travis (2010) analyzed a decade of research about the linkages between organizational diversity and organizational performance. This research can be divided into the study of individual outcomes, work group outcomes, and organizational outcomes. The results were mixed in terms of individual outcomes, with some researchers finding that job satisfaction improves when workers find a higher proportion of people similar to themselves in values and ethnicity and other researchers finding no such association. Likewise, mixed results were found in regard to diversity and work group outcomes. Some researchers found that the quality of ideas produced by work groups increased as racial and ethnic diversity increased, other researchers found that racially diverse groups had more emotional conflict than racially homogeneous work groups, and still other researchers found no relationship between extent of diversity of work group cohesion and performance. The results were also mixed regarding the relationship between diversity and organizational performance, but the majority of studies report positive relationships in both the corporate sector and the human service sector, meaning that organizational performance improves as diversity in the workforce increases. Roderick Wallace recognizes some of the tension related to ethnic diversity in the Beacon Center staff, but he has also seen new ideas and new understandings come out of the tension.

Management of diversity is still a young idea and a long distance from the one right way of the rational perspective, which has dominated modern thinking about organizations. Pioneering organizations in the United States have begun to develop specific tools to assist organizations to become more effective at managing diversity. They emphasize a vision that values the reflection of diversity in hiring and promotion policies, diversity training, language training, use of identity-based advisory groups, incorporating minority perspectives into organizational norms and culture, affirmative action programs, mentoring programs, and company-based social events (Cox, 2001). Mor Barak (2014) emphasizes the need to recognize different cultural expectations about interpersonal relationships in the workplace. Mor Barak and Travis (2010) note that social service organizations have historically served a diverse client population but have not historically hired a diverse workforce. Although the workforce in social service organizations has been gradually becoming more diverse, it lags behind the diversity of the clients served.

Critical Perspective

Although it may appear that Martha Green administered Beacon Center from an interactional/interpretative perspective,

Conflict perspective

it is probably more accurate to describe her worldview as a **critical perspective on organizations**. She tried to minimize the power differences in her organization, and when she asked her staff to vote on sensitive issues, she invoked the secret ballot to neutralize any possible power dynamics. Critical theorists share the interactional/interpretive perspective's bias about the role of human interaction and meaning making in human behavior, but critical theory undertakes, as its central concern, a critique of existing power arrangements and a vision for change suggested by this critique. More specifically, critical theories see organizations as instruments of exploitation and domination, where conflicting interests are decided in favor of the most powerful members. This focus distinguishes the critical perspective from the interactional/interpretive perspective, which generally ignores

or negates issues of power and the possibility that people in power positions can privilege their own versions of reality and marginalize other versions, thus controlling the organizational culture.

The critical perspective has roots in Robert Michels's work in the early 20th century. Michels (1911/1959) wrote about the "iron law of oligarchy" (rule by the few), arguing that as bureaucracies grow, they always end up under the control of a very narrow, elite group. The elite make decisions with an eye toward preserving their own power, and other voices are suppressed (Morgan, 2006). Gareth Morgan draws on the work of a diverse group of theorists and researchers to identify several ways in which organizations serve as "instruments of domination":

- Formal organizations create and continually reproduce patterns of social inequality through organizational hierarchies.
- Employees are exposed to work conditions that are hazardous to their health and welfare—such as working with toxic materials or dangerous equipment—and to work expectations that interfere with personal health maintenance and family life.
- Employees experience mental health problems caused by job insecurity in a downsizing and globalizing economy.

The critical perspective on organizations has been more popular in Europe than in the United States. Exhibit 12.8 summarizes two contemporary critical approaches to formal organizations discussed here: organizations as multiple oppressions and nonhierarchical organizations.

Organizations as Multiple Oppressions

Have you ever felt oppressed—voiceless, powerless, abused, manipulated, unappreciated—in any of the organizations of which you have been a member? Do you think that whole groups of people have felt oppressed in any of those organizations? In the contemporary era, the critical perspective has taken a more focused look at who is oppressed in organizations and the ways in which

Exhibit 12.8   The Critical Perspective on Formal Organizations

Major theme: Organizations are instruments of domination.	
Theory	**Central Idea**
Organizations as multiple oppressions (Hearn & Parkin, 1993)	Organizations exclude and discriminate against multiple groups.
Nonhierarchical organizations (Follett, 1924)	Organizations run by consensus, with few rules and with informality, are least likely to oppress employees.

they are oppressed. This approach was influenced by feminist critiques, during the 1970s and 1980s, of the failure of traditional organization theories to consider gender issues (Hearn & Parkin, 1993). Feminist critiques led to the recognition that other groups besides women had also been marginalized by formal organizations and by organization theory.

Jeff Hearn and Wendy Parkin (1993) recommend viewing **organizations as multiple oppressions**—social constructions that exclude and discriminate against some categories of people. According to these authors, oppression happens through a variety of processes, including "marginalization, domination and subordination, degradation, ignoring, harassment, invisibilizing, silencing, punishment, discipline and violence" (p. 153). These processes may also be directed at a variety of organizational actors, including "staff, members, employees, residents, patients and clients" (p. 153). Organizational domination can become compounded by multiple oppressions. Hearn and Parkin cite the example of a children's home where children were being sexually abused by male staff, and female staff were dissuaded, by intimidation, from reporting the situation. This idea that multiple oppressions are usually embedded in organizational life has also been addressed in a book by Sharon Kurtz (2002), who argues that addressing the situation of only one oppressed group will never get to the heart of the matrix of domination in organizations.

According to Hearn and Parkin (1993), frequently oppressed groups include women, younger and older people, persons with disabilities, those of lower economic class, persons of color, and sexual minorities. These groups may be excluded from organizations; admitted only in subordinate roles as clients, patients, or students; or admitted but discriminated against within the organization. If groups that are excluded or otherwise oppressed form their own organizations, dominant groups construct a hierarchy of organizations that maintains the oppression, as when a Black organization is viewed as inferior to similar White organizations.

Critical theory, with its focus on domination and oppression, reminds us that mainstream organizational theory is theory for the elite and not theory for the exploited. Therefore, our understanding of organizations is incomplete and biased. If you have felt somewhat alienated in reading about other theories in this chapter, you may be reacting to this bias. However, critical theory has been criticized for being ideological, giving priority to the voices of oppressed persons, just as Martha Green was criticized for giving too strong a voice to homeless persons. Critical theorists reply that their focus is no more ideological than is recognizing only the voices of the elite.

The critical perspective on organizations has special relevance to social workers. It helps us recognize the ways in which clients' struggles are related to oppressive structures and processes in the formal organizations with which they interact. It can help us to understand the ways in which social service organizations are gendered, with women constituting the majority of human service workers and men assuming key administrative roles. It also calls our attention to the power imbalance between clients and social workers and helps us think critically about how we use our power. We must be constantly vigilant about the multiple oppressions within the organizations where we work, as well as those with which we interact, as we try to promote social justice.

Nonhierarchical Organizations

Helen Blue preferred a more hierarchical organizational structure than the one developed at Beacon Center under Martha Green's leadership. A constant theme in critical theory is that hierarchical organizational structures lead to alienation and internal class conflict. Critical theorists directly challenge the rational perspective argument that hierarchy is needed to maximize efficiency; they point out that in fact hierarchy is often inefficient but is maintained because it works well to protect the positions of those in power. For example, the staff at Beacon Center wasted much time and energy trying to find ways to thwart Helen Blue's decisions. Design professionals argue that it is difficult to do creative work within a hierarchical organization (Johansson & Woodilla, 2008).

Humanistic perspective

The idea of the **nonhierarchical organization** is not new. Mary Parker Follett (1924) proposed that organizations, like other human collective efforts, should be based on nonhierarchical power, on energy that comes from the egalitarian interactions of people and ideas. Human relations theorists have recommended "participatory management," which involves lower-level employees in at least some decision making, for several decades. Historical evidence indicates that since the 1840s, experiments with nonhierarchical organizations have accompanied every wave of antimodernist social movements in the United States (Rothschild-Whitt & Whitt, 1986). There have also been unsuccessful experiments with power sharing in French organizations (Hofstede, 1996). Beginning in the 1970s, feminist critiques of organizational theory helped to stimulate renewed interest in nonhierarchical organizations (Kravetz, 2004). Nevertheless, such organizations constitute only a small portion of the population of formal organizations, and research on nonhierarchical organizations constitutes a very small part of the massive body of research on organizations (Garrow & Hasenfeld, 2010; Iannello, 1992).

Exhibit 12.9 lists the traits of a model of nonhierarchical organization that Kathleen Iannello (1992) calls the consensual model. Studies of nonhierarchical organizations summarize some of the special challenges, both internal and external, faced by consensual organizations (Ferree & Martin, 1995; Kravetz, 2004; Rothschild-Whitt & Whitt, 1986). Internal challenges include increased time needed for decision making, increased emotional intensity due to the more personal style of relationships, and difficulty incorporating diversity. External challenges are the constraints of social, economic, and political environments that value and reward hierarchy (Garrow & Hasenfeld, 2010).

On the basis of her study of two successful feminist organizations, Iannello (1992) proposed that the internal challenges of the nonhierarchical

Exhibit 12.9	Traits of a Consensual Model of Formal Organizations

Authority vested in the membership rather than in an elite at the top of a hierarchy

Decisions made only after issues have been widely discussed by the membership

Rules kept to a minimum

Personal, rather than formal, relationships among members

Leadership based on election, with rotation of leadership positions

No financial reward for leadership roles

No winners and losers in decision making—decisions made based on unchallenged "prevailing sentiment" (consensus)

SOURCE: Iannello, 1992.

organization could be addressed by what she calls a "modified consensual organization" model. Critical decisions continue to be made by the broad membership, but routine decisions are made by smaller groups; members are recognized by ability and expertise, not by rank and position; and there are clear goals, developed through a consensual process. Similarly, reporting on the life course of five feminist organizations initiated in the 1970s, Diane Kravetz (2004) found that these organizations developed "modified hierarchies" as they grew and faced new external challenges. They gradually delegated authority to individuals and committees but retained some elements of consensus decision making.

The two most prominent contemporary examples of organizations based on consensus are feminist organizations and Japanese firms. Both types of organizations typically feature a strong shared ideology and culture, which should lead to relatively easy consensus. However, the available evidence suggests that feminist organizations in which membership crosses either ideological or cultural lines have not been successful in operating by consensus (Barnoff & Moffatt, 2007). Under Martha Green's administration, most decisions at Beacon Center were made by consensus, but Martha was sometimes criticized for building a staff with little ideological or cultural diversity. Roderick Wallace has been very intentional about increasing staff diversity and encourages staff and client input, but Beacon Center cannot be considered a nonhierarchical organization under his leadership.

One trend to watch is toward worker-owned corporations, in both the United States and Europe. Sometimes these corporations are not truly democratic, with strong worker input into decisions, but evidence indicates they are moving toward greater democratization (Alperovitz, 2005). The fact that the number of worker-owned companies in the United States increased from 1,600 in 1975 to 11,000 in 2003 seems to be a sign that the idea of shared leadership is gaining in popularity (Alperovitz, 2005). In their recent book *The Citizen's Share*, Blasi, Freeman, and Kruse (2013) report on their 10-year study of profit-sharing and employee-owned businesses and argue that these arrangements offer a viable path for rebooting the U.S. economy and restoring the middle class.

Given the increasing diversity of the workforce in the United States, management of difference and conflict can be expected to become an increasing challenge in organizational life. This is as true for social work organizations as for others. The literature on consensual organizations has failed to address the difficult challenges of diverse ideological and cultural perspectives among organizational members—issues that are the focus of the managing diversity model. This is an area in which social work should take the lead.

In Canada, one notable exception has occurred. Feminist critiques of social service organizations have led to growing interest in *anti-oppressive* social work practice at both the direct practice and organizational practice levels. The anti-oppression model seeks to develop social service organizations free from all types of domination and privilege (Barnoff & Moffatt, 2007). This is not an easy task, and researchers have identified some barriers to these efforts. First, they have found that when groups of women encounter each other, they develop a *hierarchy of oppression*, in which women in different identity groups engage in ongoing competition about which group is most oppressed, with the different groups failing to look beyond their own experience to recognize the plight of other oppressed groups. Second, tension often develops between White women and women of color when White women try to control the agenda but lack awareness of how they are using White privilege to advance their own positions in the organization. Lisa Barnoff and Ken Moffatt (2007) conclude that anti-oppressive social work practice can be advanced only when privilege is a central concept in the discussion of oppression. Members of different identity groups need to recognize their own sources of privilege and give serious thought to how exercise of that privilege results in the subordination of others.

Critical Thinking Questions 12.3

Think back to your earlier ideas about the characteristics of an organization for which you have positive feelings. Can you use specific theoretical concepts from the interactional/interpretive or critical perspective to talk about that organization? Now, think of your ideas about the characteristics of an organization for which you have negative feelings. Can you use specific theoretical concepts from the interactional/interpretive and critical perspective to describe that organization?

BURNOUT: A NEGATIVE ORGANIZATIONAL OUTCOME

It was suggested at the beginning of this chapter that formal organizations meet our needs, assist us to fulfill goals, and nurture our development—but that they also make stressful demands, thwart our goals, inhibit our holistic development, and constrain our behavior. Robert T. Golembiewski (1994) used more colorful language to talk about the negative effects of organizations, suggesting that "organizational life bends people out of shape, and may even make them crazy" (p. 211).

In the past 4 decades, researchers have attempted to answer the question of whether organizational membership is hazardous to your health. The answer is that organizational membership is *often* hazardous to health, and burnout is the identified hazard. **Burnout** is a "prolonged response to chronic emotional and interpersonal stressors on the job, and is defined by the three dimensions of exhaustion, cynicism, and inefficacy" (Maslach, Schaufeli, & Leiter, 2001, p. 397). The study of burnout has appeal because it can give voice to individuals who are dominated or exploited in organizations, providing "organizational theory for the exploited," as recommended by Gareth Morgan (2006).

Burnout is most often studied using the Maslach Burnout Inventory (MBI) (Maslach & Jackson, 1981). The MBI, first developed for use with human service workers and later revised for use with teachers, analyzes three dimensions of burnout: (1) emotional exhaustion, or a feeling of being near the end of one's rope; (2) depersonalization, or a strong tendency to distance oneself from others, thinking of them as things or objects; and (3) reduced personal accomplishment, which refers to perceptions of doing well on a worthwhile project. In recent years, the MBI has been revised for use in occupations other than human services and education that are not as people oriented. The three dimensions of burnout have been conceptualized in the broader terms found in the previous definition of burnout: exhaustion, cynicism, and inefficacy (reduced personal accomplishment).

Burnout was introduced as a concept in North America but has now been found in research around the world. The concept was introduced by researchers in western Europe and Israel in the 1980s; in eastern Europe, Asia, the Middle East, Latin America, Australia, and New Zealand in the 1990s; and in Africa, China, and the Indian subcontinent in the 21st century (Schaufeli, Leiter, & Maslach, 2009). International research has noted high levels of burnout among public sector workers, social workers, teachers, workers in business organizations, and physicians and other health care providers (Kim, Ji, & Kao, 2011; Peterson et al., 2008; Tomic & Tomic, 2008; Yeh, Cheng, & Chen, 2009). The high level of hazard in so many settings suggests that social workers need to be attuned to symptoms of job-related burnout in their clients and in themselves.

Burnout has been found to be associated with absenteeism, turnover, lower productivity and effectiveness at work, decreased job satisfaction, reduced commitment to the job or organization, and deterioration in physical and mental health. Burnout can be contagious, causing interpersonal conflict and disrupting work. It is hazardous to both the individual and the organization. Sweden and the Netherlands have established medical diagnoses for burnout (Schaufeli et al., 2009).

After the first 25 years of research on the subject, researchers found six dimensions of work life to be associated with burnout (Maslach et al., 2001):

1. *Workload.* Work overload makes too many demands and exhausts people's capacity to recover. Workload has been found to be directly related to the exhaustion dimension of burnout. Cross-national comparisons have found that workers in North America have higher levels of burnout than workers in western Europe, particularly higher levels of exhaustion and cynicism (Maslach et al., 2001).

2. *Control.* People may have inadequate control over the resources needed to do their work, or they may be given responsibilities without the authority to do the work. These situations are associated with inefficacy (reduced personal accomplishment). The social workers at Beacon Center missed Martha Green's trust in them to make their own decisions, and they chafed at their diminishing control over their work and the direction of the organization after Helen Blue became the administrator. Roderick Wallace has attempted to return authority to line staff.

3. *Reward.* Organizations may fail to provide appropriate rewards for the work people do. There may be inadequate financial rewards, but social rewards, such as recognition and appreciation for contributions made, may also be missing. In addition, the work itself may not have intrinsic rewards because it does not feel important and useful. Lack of reward is associated with inefficacy.

4. *Community.* In some organizations, people do not have a sense of positive connections to others. People may work in isolation from others, their interactions may be impersonal, or there may be chronic and unresolved conflict with others on the job. Social support from supervisors has been found to be particularly important.

5. *Fairness.* There may be inequity of workload or pay, or work evaluations and promotions may be handled unfairly. Feelings of being treated unfairly are associated with exhaustion as well as with cynicism about the workplace.

6. *Values.* Sometimes people face situations where the job requires them to compromise their ethical standards. Or they may find a discrepancy between what the organization says it values and the day-to-day activities in the organization. Increasingly, human service organizations face a conflict between the competing values of high-quality service and cost containment. Little research has been done on the role of values in burnout. The original social workers at Beacon Center put high value on advocating for their homeless clients, and they were alienated by Helen Blue's request that they become more moderate in those efforts.

Research indicates that organizational factors play a bigger role in burnout than individual factors. And yet greater attention has been given to individual-oriented approaches to preventing burnout than to changing aspects of organizations. In the 21st century, researchers have focused on two major contributors to burnout: work demands and resources. Burnout is predicted when there is an imbalance in work demands with the resources for performing the work.

It has been suggested that social work is an occupation with above-average risk of burnout, but research has not supported this suggestion. One research team compared the burnout profiles for five occupational groups—teaching, social services, medicine, mental health, and law enforcement—in the United States and Holland (Schaufeli & Enzmann, 1998). They found that the comparisons differed by nation. In the United States, the levels of cynicism were higher for social service workers and mental health workers than for the other occupational groups, but they were about average in Holland. Other than that, the levels of burnout were about average for social service workers in both countries. In the United States, researchers have been particularly interested in burnout among child welfare workers, who are thought to be especially vulnerable to burnout. One researcher (Kim, 2011) found that public child welfare workers experience higher levels of burnout than child welfare workers in private settings but do not differ from other groups of social workers in the study. Another research team found that job stress and work–family conflict are associated with emotional exhaustion among public child welfare workers, and age of worker, work–family conflict, and organizational support are associated with depersonalization. Younger workers were more vulnerable to burnout than older workers, and burnout decreased as perceived organizational support increased (Lizano & Mor Barak, 2012). We know that our work as social workers has many satisfactions as well as many stressors, but further research is needed to discover which way the balance tilts and why.

Mary Guy and colleagues (Guy, Newman, Mastracci, & Maynard-Moody, 2010) have examined the relationship between emotional labor and burnout. They define **emotional labor** as "the engagement, suppression, or evocation of the worker's emotions necessary to get the job done" (p. 292). They argue that emotional labor is the key feature of the therapeutic relationship between social worker and client. Their research indicates that emotional labor can lead to burnout, but it can also lead to job satisfaction. When it leads to burnout, the worker feels emotional exhaustion, stress, cynicism, and lack of effectiveness. When emotional labor leads to job satisfaction, the worker feels energetic, involved, and a sense of accomplishment. Guy et al. (2010) found that social workers are more likely to experience burnout if they have to fake their emotional expressions in the course of their work and if they lack confidence in their ability to perform emotional work.

One small-scale research project attempted to discover the balance of job satisfaction and burnout among one sample of child welfare social workers. David Conrad and Yvonne Kellar-Guenther (2006) investigated burnout among child protection workers in Colorado. They sought to understand the relationship between *compassion fatigue* (reduced capacity for empathy caused by an overexposure to suffering), burnout (emotional exhaustion, depersonalization, and inefficacy), and *compassion satisfaction* (fulfillment from helping others and from positive collegial relationships). They found that about 50% of their sample suffered from compassion fatigue, only 7.7% suffered from burnout, and 75% had high levels of compassion satisfaction. Furthermore, they found that the respondents with

higher compassion satisfaction had lower levels of burnout and compassion fatigue than respondents with lower levels of compassion satisfaction. This is consistent with the findings of Guy et al. (2010) that emotional labor can lead to job satisfaction as well as burnout, and it may help to explain earlier findings that social workers are not much more prone to burnout than people in other occupations. These findings suggest that the concept of compassion satisfaction is worthy of further attention by social work researchers.

SOCIAL WORK AND FORMAL ORGANIZATIONS

You have probably learned already that social work is a diverse profession; we use diverse methods to address a diversity of social problems—and we work in diverse types of organizations. We work in hospitals, outpatient health and mental health clinics, in-home programs, nursing homes and other residential programs, crisis shelters, prisons and jails, government social service agencies, private family and children's agencies, schools, the workplace, community centers, social movement organizations, research centers, planning organizations, social entrepreneurial organizations, and private practice, among other places.

We can think about the differences among the organizations in which social workers are found in several ways. One is to divide them into host organizations, social work–oriented organizations, and human service organizations (Popple & Leighninger, 2011). In *host organizations*—such as schools, the workplace, correctional facilities, the military, and hospitals—social service is not the primary purpose of the organization. Social workers in these settings work with other disciplines to meet organizational goals, and they often serve as mediators between clients and the organization. In contrast, *social work–oriented organizations* have social service delivery as their purpose and are staffed primarily by social workers. Family and children's agencies and government social service programs are examples of social work–oriented organizations. Social workers also work in *human service organizations*, whose staff come from a variety of disciplines but work in a coordinated fashion to provide an array of services. Community health centers and drug treatment programs are examples of human service organizations.

Another way to think about formal organizations in which social workers work has traditionally been to divide them into public and private organizations. *Public social service organizations* are those funded and administered by local, state, or federal government; *private social service organizations* are privately funded and administered. This distinction made some sense in earlier eras, but it is not very useful in the contemporary era. Today, many public agencies contract programs out to private organizations, and many private organizations, like Beacon Center, receive public as well as private funding. The Social Security Act of 1935 ushered in an era of government dominance in both the funding and administering of social service programs, but for the past few decades, we have seen increasing **privatization** of social services, shifting the administration of programs back to private organizations (Karger & Stoesz, 2014). This trend is based on a belief that privatization will lead to more efficient and effective service delivery. It has been estimated that more than half of public social service dollars are contracted to private organizations (O'Connor & Netting, 2009).

Among private service organizations, the distinction between *nonprofit* and *for-profit* organizations is increasingly important but also increasingly blurred. Social workers have a long history with nonprofit organizations, also called *voluntary agencies* and *nongovernmental organizations* (NGOs), but their extensive involvement in for-profit organizations is more recent and has been increasing steadily since the 1970s. In the past 2 decades, corporations have played an increasing role in Medicaid, the State Children's Health Insurance Program, child welfare, and mental health (Karger & Stoesz, 2014). Large for-profit organizations have had the resources to move quickly into new markets and have become serious competitors

for nonprofit organizations in vying for government contracts. Some nonprofit organizations are responding by developing partnerships with for-profit organizations; others are changing to for-profit status. Indeed, many nonprofits use some profit-making programs, such as thrift stores, to shore up their income base. There is general agreement that for-profit organizations will continue to have a large presence in the social service landscape in the future. This is the case even though current research indicates that they have not met their promise to cut costs (Karger & Stoesz, 2014).

The entry of for-profit organizations into the social service arena poses questions raised by many observers: Will for-profit organizations, in search of profitable business opportunities, voluntarily serve the common good? Will they engage in advocacy and community-building activities that are the hallmark of the social work profession and the history of nonprofit organizations? Will they deny service as a cost-cutting measure, particularly service to clients with the most entrenched problems? Will they cut staff to increase profit? Historically, social service agencies funded advocacy and community-building activities out of surplus from other programs. Social workers will need to be vigilant to see that these important social work functions do not disappear. There is also some fear that very large for-profit organizations will have undue influence on social welfare policy in a way that protects their own interests (Karger & Stoesz, 2014).

Organizations in which social workers work have not been immune to the economic trends discussed in Chapter 9. Downsizing and the resulting "do more with less" climate have increased work-related stressors, and increasing economic inequality is producing stubborn social problems that must be addressed with shrinking resources. Social workers, like other workers, are increasingly involved in "contingent" labor situations—that is, in part-time, temporary, and contractual arrangements. There is increasing evidence that social service organizations are favoring clients who can pay, or who qualify for payment by a third party, and they are failing to serve people who are poor

Photo 12.3 The 100,000-square-foot Children and Family Services Center in Charlotte, North Carolina, is an innovative marriage of public and private sector organizations.

© AP Photo/Chuck Burton

or have the most challenging problems (Karger & Stoesz, 2014). Unfortunately, social welfare organizations, particularly in the nonprofit sector, have not been immune to the fraud and scandal that have embroiled many large corporations in the past decade. Given these challenges, a solid grounding in organizational theory can be an important tool in the social work survival kit.

Social service organizations, like other organizations, are trying to survive in turbulent, complex times. They must continuously adjust their services in response to changing societal trends, such as growing diversity in the population and lifestyles and growing inequality. In recent times, they have had to adapt to a political environment that shifted from thinking of social service organizations in

terms of social care to an emphasis on the market and personal responsibility (Hasenfeld, 2010a). It is unclear whether recent failures in the market will undermine popular reverence for the market model.

Two types of human service organizations are becoming more prominent in the social service landscape: hybrid organizations and social entrepreneurial organizations. **Hybrid organization** is the name given to organizations that combine political advocacy and service provision in their core identity (Minkoff, 2010). This type of social service organization has a history in organizations developed by women, Blacks, and other ethnic groups in the 1960s. These organizations make a strong commitment to service to typically underserved populations, but they also engage in advocacy work that is often focused on changing the perspectives of political figures and the general public on specific social problems. For example, homeless service organizations like Beacon Center have attempted to change public perception of homelessness, pushing for a framework that focuses on homelessness as the failure of housing policy rather than a consequence of personal failings. Advocacy work by nonprofit organizations has been steadily increasing in the past few decades (Meyer, 2010).

A **social entrepreneurial organization** is one formed by a social entrepreneur who recognizes a social problem and uses ideas from business entrepreneurs to organize, create, and manage a new venture to bring about social change related to that problem. The most famous social entrepreneurial organization is the Grameen Bank developed by Muhammad Yunus, a Bangladeshi economist who was the winner of the 2006 Nobel Peace Prize. The idea of using social entrepreneurship to solve social problems is spreading around the world (O'Connor & Netting, 2009).

Yeheskel Hasenfeld (2010b) has asked the question, "What is different about human service organizations?" In answering it, he identifies six attributes that set human service organizations apart from other organizations:

1. They engage in moral work, making judgments about what constitutes good behavior and a good society.

2. They get their legitimacy from the broader institutional society.

3. They must negotiate different interest groups that have different goals for the organization.

4. Client–staff relationships are the primary vehicle of service provision.

5. Emotional labor is their primary resource and must be harnessed through recruitment, training, and supervision.

6. They are gendered organizations where women are the majority of the frontline workers, matching the societal ideology that emotional work is women's work.

Technology and Social Service Organizations

The "information and communication revolution" has presented new challenges and opportunities to social service organizations. Information and communication technology (ICT) is an integral part of most social service organizations, but the literature on the topic is sparse. One researcher found that the costs of ICT are prohibitive for many small and economically poor social service organizations, while technically sophisticated organizations benefit from great access to government resources (Mano, 2009). Another researcher reviewed the applications of nonprofit organizations for technology innovation grants in the state of Georgia and found that social service organizations proposed a higher number of ICT innovations than other types of nonprofit organizations (Jaskyte, 2012). They were proposing to use innovations in ICT for both administrative and service activities. In the administrative area, they were proposing to upgrade their ability to use ICT for donor, member, client, and volunteer databases; internal communication and scheduling; online outcome databases; online donations; streamlining communication with community partners; and online surveys and assessments. In the service area, they were proposing to upgrade their ability to use ICT for online client education and to provide counseling and other services online. They expected ICT to help them increase the number of clients served, attract more donors and volunteers, and improve their communications with community partners.

There is a growing research literature on the use of Internet and wireless-supported mental health interventions, with most of the research addressing online counseling and psychotherapy, psychoeducational websites, and online support groups. The results of this research indicate positive outcomes of these technologically supported interventions but raise questions of confidentiality and access (Barak & Grohol, 2011). Here are two examples of recent innovations in the use of ICT to enhance service provision. Twenty veterans in outpatient treatment for alcohol abuse and dependence at a veterans hospital were given an iPod loaded with recovery-related audio podcasts. Most participants indicated that they used the device regularly, thought it was useful, and wished they had access to this type of support earlier (Shaw, Sivakumar, Balinas, Chipman, & Krahn, 2013). Another organization investigated the interest in an online coping skills training program for women living with a partner with a drinking problem and found that interest was high (Rychtarik, McGillicuddy, & Barrick, 2013). Both of these innovations were seen as an adjunct to ongoing face-to-face service provision.

Critical Thinking Questions 12.4

Were you surprised to read that some researchers have found that social workers are no more likely than workers in other fields to experience burnout? Explain your answer. What do you think of the concept of compassion satisfaction? How have you seen information and communication technologies used in human service organizations? What is one idea you have about a way for social workers to make good use of these technologies?

SOCIAL WORK LEADERSHIP IN FORMAL ORGANIZATIONS

With the pervasive influence of formal organizations in complex societies, attention has turned to a fascination with organization leadership. Books are being written, academic programs in leadership studies are being developed, and professional associations are developing "leadership initiatives." This intense focus on leadership seems to be driven by a frustration with the performance and impact of formal organizations as well as by a hope that we can engineer and manage them better—in such a way as to minimize their adverse effects and magnify their positive ones (Northouse, 2013). This concern applies to the formal organizations where social work is practiced, as well as to other formal organizations that affect our lives and those of our clients.

In Chapter 11, we presented Northouse's (2013) definition of leadership: a process whereby an individual influences a group of individuals to achieve a common goal. Northouse made a distinction between assigned leadership and emergent leadership. Assigned leaders occupy organizational positions that carry with them formal authority to influence others toward a common goal. They might be in a position called director, department head, administrator, supervisor, committee chair, or team leader. An emergent leader, on the other hand, is someone whose influence is recognized by others regardless of position; the emergent leader has personal authority rather than formal authority.

As social workers carry out their work in formal organizations, they may act sometimes as assigned leaders and sometimes as emergent leaders. I agree with O'Connor and Netting's (2009) premise that every social worker carries leadership responsibility in the organizations where he or she works; such responsibility goes with being a social worker. They define leadership as "an attitude about responsibilities in an organization based on professional skills and a set of values that compel an individual to act" (p. 29).

There are a number of theories of leadership (see, e.g., Northouse, 2013), and different perspectives on organizations call for different approaches to leadership. Certainly, you can imagine how the approach to thinking about leadership from a scientific management perspective is different from the approaches of an interactional/interpretive or critical perspective. In addition, it seems obvious that the nature of the organization itself will render some ways of leading more effective than others. Social work leaders pay attention to all of this. In spite of the complexity, some core leadership competencies can be identified. They include the following: problem-identification, problem-solving, and solution-generating skills; the ability to critically analyze our own beliefs and attitudes; the ability to critically analyze the beliefs and attitudes of others; the ability to forgo early judgments; the ability to conceptualize and articulate a vision and a plan; and good written, verbal, and nonverbal communication skills. In the contemporary, globalized, multicultural world, social work leaders must be able to live with change and flux, live with ambiguity, and recognize multiple perspectives on situations. We must know how to maneuver bureaucracies and complex systems, manage diversity, and recognize and struggle against the multiple oppressions we encounter in our own and other organizations. Every social worker is responsible to build this set of capabilities.

Globalization is leading to a need to develop and maintain effective organizations that cross national borders. Increasingly, social workers work in and provide leadership to transnational service and advocacy organizations (Cox & Pawar, 2013). Hofstede, Deusen, Mueller, and Charles (2002) suggest that transnational organizations are often unsuccessful because of cultural differences in attitudes about goals and appropriate traits of leaders. What is needed in such organizations are leaders who can become competent in cross-cultural awareness and communication. To that end, Robert House and colleagues (2004) have engaged in study of the attitudes about leadership in 62 societies. They have found that societies vary in their attitudes about leadership on a number of identified dimensions: uncertainty avoidance, power sharing, collective spirit and action, gender egalitarianism, assertiveness, future orientation, performance orientation, and humane orientation. For U.S. social workers working in transnational organizations, it is important to know that in this research the Anglo cluster of societies—which includes the United States, Australia, Ireland, the United Kingdom, White South Africa, and New Zealand—puts much more value on performance orientation and

much less value on collectivism than respondents in other societies.

CULTURALLY SENSITIVE CARE SYSTEMS

Issues of diversity, and managing diversity, are important for all formal organizations, but they take on special urgency in social service organizations. Social workers have a commitment to provide competent service to diverse populations. (We take a broad view of diversity, including, but not limited to, gender, race, ethnicity, social class, religion, disability, age, and sexual orientation.) In recent years, a growing body of literature has recommended ways of providing culturally competent practice (e.g., Lum, 2011). When I lived in Washington, DC, in an area where one public school might serve a student body representing well over 100 national heritages, I came to think in terms of providing *culturally sensitive practice*, rather than culturally competent practice. As Ruth G. Dean (2001) so aptly stated, to work effectively across cultural lines typically requires that we begin with a recognition that we are not competent in the culture of another, and from this position of "informed not knowing" (Laird, 1998), we establish a goal to understand.

Although there is much an individual social worker can do to provide more culturally sensitive practice, individual efforts will not go far unless the vision of cultural sensitivity is encoded into the fabric of social service organizations. Some effective guidelines for developing a culturally sensitive system of care can be gleaned from a number of sources. As you read these traits, keep in mind that some social service organizations serve a multicultural population, while others target a specific cultural group.

- The organization is located where it is accessible to the targeted population, and it is decorated in a manner appealing to the population. Particular attention is paid to the accessibility of the physical environment for people with a variety of disabilities.

- A name is chosen for the organization that is acceptable to the targeted population. For example, for some ethnic groups, "mental health services" carries a social stigma, and these words should be avoided when naming the organization. A name like Beacon Center carries no such stigma.

- The agency website is user-friendly for diverse populations.

- Diversity is reflected in the board of directors, administrators, and professional and non-professional staff, in accordance with the targeted population. The organization is engaged in an ongoing audit of the diversity represented at all levels, from clients to the board of directors.

- The organization conducts or supports ongoing training and communication about diversity issues and multicultural communication. A collection of resource materials on culturally diverse groups is available to staff.

- Ongoing efforts are made to create a climate where people can recover from multicultural miscommunications. This is especially important where there is a multicultural staff and multicultural client population.

- The ability to work cross-culturally is included in job descriptions and in the hiring process.

- Ongoing efforts are made to involve minority staff members in information networks and decision-making processes.

- Staff are actively engaged in learning about the community and its norms, values, and formal and informal resources, as well as the ways in which it is changing. They use what they learn in ongoing program planning. They pay particular attention to the cultural understanding of and preferences for caregiving and care receiving.

- Staff engage in active outreach, attending local functions, giving talks at community organizations, and so forth, particularly when the targeted population is not inclined to use formal social services. Outreach activities will help build credibility.

- The staff maintains working relationships with other organizations that serve the same population, such as ethnic agencies, agencies for sexual minority clients, or disability service centers.

Critical Thinking Questions 12.5

What does it mean to be a leader? What makes a "bad leader"? A "good leader"? How might ideas about good and bad leaders be influenced by culture? Why do you think there has been so much fascination with the issue of organizational leadership in recent years?

Implications for Social Work Practice

Several principles for social work action are recommended by this discussion of formal organizations:

- Be alert to the influence of formal organizations on the client's behavior. Be particularly alert to the ways in which the social service organization where you work, as well as other social service organizations to which you frequently refer clients, influences the client's behavior.
- Develop an understanding of the organizational goals of the social service organization where you work and how the tasks you perform are related to these goals.
- Develop an understanding of the shared meanings in the social service organization where you work and of the processes by which those meanings are developed and maintained.

- Develop an understanding of the forces of inertia and other constraints on rational decision making in the social service organization where you work.
- Develop an understanding of the social, political, economic, cultural, and technological environments of the social service organization where you work.
- Develop an understanding of the sources of legitimacy, power, and economic resources for the social service organization where you work and an understanding of how they influence internal decisions.
- Collaborate with colleagues at the social service organization where you work to understand and enhance the creative use of diversity.
- Collaborate with colleagues at the social service organization where you work to facilitate the inclusion of clients in the political process, internally as well as externally.
- Collaborate with colleagues at the social service organization where you work to develop an understanding of multiple oppressions within the organization.
- Be attuned to the symptoms of job-related burnout in yourself, your colleagues, and your clients.
- Collaborate with colleagues to create a culturally sensitive care system.

Key Terms

bounded rationality
bureaucracy
burnout
critical perspective on
    organizations
decision-making theory
emotional labor
formal organization
Hawthorne effect
human relations theory
hybrid organization

interactional/interpretive
    perspective on organizations
iron cage of rationality
learning organization theory
managing diversity model
nonhierarchical organization
organizational culture model
organizational humanism
organizations as multiple
    oppressions
political economy model

privatization
rational perspective on
    organizations
satisfice
scientific management
Silverman's social action model
social entrepreneurial organization
systems perspective on
    organizations

Active Learning

1. In the case study at the beginning of the chapter, you read about the transition in leadership at Beacon Center. You have also read about four theoretical perspectives on formal organizations. Imagine that you, and not Roderick Wallace, are the current CEO at Beacon Center. In small groups of four or five, talk about the following points: What vision would you have for Beacon Center? What would you want to keep the same as it had been, and what would you want to change? Use theory to back up your position.

2. Examine aspects of diversity in your workplace, your field practicum agency, or another organization you are familiar with. What can you observe or discover about diversity in the organization on the following variables: gender, age, social class, religion, ethnicity, race, and disability? Compare the diversity found among management to that among the line workers and clientele. Write a brief paper describing what you found and addressing the following points: How does diversity (or the lack of it) appear to affect organizational effectiveness? What changes would you suggest for the organization in terms of diversity? (Questions are based on Strom-Gottfried & Morrissey, 1999.)

Alliance for Nonprofit Management: www .allianceonline.org

Site contains resources, affinity groups, and webinars.

ARNOVA: www.arnova.org

Site presented by the Association for Research on Nonprofit Organizations and Voluntary Action contains a member directory, conference information, publications, and a job center.

Center on Nonprofits and Philanthropy: www .urban.org/center/cnp

Site maintained by the Center on Nonprofits and Philanthropy at the Urban Institute contains publications, a press room, events, and resources.

Student Study Site

⊛SAGE edge™

Sharpen your skills with SAGE edge at **edge.sagepub.com/hutchisonpe5e**

SAGE edge for students provides a personalized approach to help you accomplish your coursework goals in an easy-to-use learning environment.

CHAPTER 13

Communities

Elizabeth D. Hutchison and Soon Min Lee

Chapter Outline

CASE STUDY

Filipina Domestic Workers Creating Transnational Communities

Filipina domestic workers scattered around the globe read the multinational magazine *Tinig Filipino*, now on Facebook and Twitter, and many contribute articles describing the realities of their lives as overseas domestic workers. Sometimes their children back in the Philippines write articles about the pain of separation from their mothers or about the heroic sacrifices their mothers make to provide much-needed economic resources to their families back home. Filipino women (Filipinas) work as domestic workers in more than 130 countries, working in elder care, child care, and housecleaning. They are among the ranks of service workers of globalization.

Globalization has created both a pull and a push for Filipinas to become global domestic workers. It has created a heightened demand (pull) for low-wage service workers in major global cities of affluent nations to maintain the lifestyles of professional and managerial workers. It has also produced large geographical economic inequalities, and many poor countries, like the Philippines, are depending on the export of labor to help with debt repayment (push). More than 6 million Filipinos work overseas as contract workers, and the money and goods these workers send home to families, known as remittances, are an important source of revenue at home. In 2013, the Philippines ranked third among countries receiving the largest remittances from overseas workers, with remittances amounting to $26 billion (World Bank, 2013d). The large outflow of labor also helps to decrease very high unemployment and underemployment rates.

Since the early 1990s, women have made up over half of Filipino contract workers. Filipino men work as seamen, carpenters, masons, and mechanics, many in the Middle East. Two thirds of migrant Filipinas are domestic workers, and they work in cities around the world. Many of them have a college education, but they earn more as domestic workers in affluent nations than they would as professional workers in the Philippines. They migrate for economic gain but also, in many instances, to escape domestic violence or other domestic struggles. Most migrate alone. The Philippine government has applauded the legion of female migrant workers as "modern-day heroes." The remittances they send home allow families to buy houses, computers, and college educations for siblings, children, and other relatives.

The two most popular destinations for Filipina domestic workers are Rome and Los Angeles. The community life of the Filipina domestic workers in these two cities is alike in a number of ways; most important, both groups see themselves as simultaneously members of more than one community. They see themselves as part of a global community of Filipina domestic workers across geographic territories. They see themselves as part of their Philippine communities and only temporarily part of their receiving communities, referring to their sending communities as "home." While they are doing domestic work for class-privileged women in their receiving communities, they sometimes purchase the domestic services of even lower-paid women left behind in the Philippines to help care for their own families. They leave children, who are often very young, at home to be cared for by the extended family that benefits from the remittances they send. In 2008 they were keeping contact with their families in the Philippines by telephone, text messaging, e-mail, airmail letters and packages, and joint bank accounts. In both Rome and Los Angeles, they face anti-immigrant sentiment in their receiving communities, but the hostility is more severe in Rome.

There are great differences, however, in the local cultures of community life among Filipina domestic workers in Rome and Los Angeles. These differences seem to reflect the larger social and political contexts of the migration experience. Let's look first at the community of domestic workers in Rome. There, residence requirements restrict Filipina migrants to domestic work, and they live segregated lives in a society that is not welcoming. Consequently, they have built a community of much solidarity that congregates in multiple private and public gathering places. The domestic workers are residentially dispersed throughout the city, and gathering places are likewise geographically dispersed. Specific gathering places are associated with specific regions of the Philippines.

On their days off, the workers tend to congregate in private gathering places in church centers and apartments. Several churches, mostly Catholic, have opened day-off shelters or church centers where the workers can spend time watching television or listening to music, visiting, and purchasing Filipino food. These centers are often developed out of the joint efforts of local churches in the Philippines and in Rome. The Filipino Chaplaincy, a coalition of 28 Roman Catholic churches, is the strongest advocate for Filipino workers in Rome. It publishes a directory of religious, government, and civic organizations relevant to the Filipino workers. The Santa Prudenziana parish, besides offering regular spiritual activities, also provides a variety of social services, including job placement referrals, free medical care, legal assistance, and Italian language classes. The migrant workers can also participate in choirs, dance groups, and a theater group.

(Continued)

(Continued)

Apartments are another site of private gathering for the Filipinas in Rome. Domestic workers who can navigate the barriers to rent their own apartments sometimes rent out rooms or beds to other migrant workers. They also rent access to their apartments to live-in workers on their days off. Apartments are furnished with televisions and equipment for watching Filipino movies, and at night, renters congregate in the kitchen, eating and relaxing, playing card games and mahjong.

There are also particular train stations and bus stops that are known as public gathering places for Filipinos in Rome. However, the city authorities have discouraged congregating in such public places. After much harassment at one bus stop, the Filipino migrants moved to a spot under an overpass, near the Tiber River. They subsequently turned the spot into a shopping bazaar that includes food shops, restaurants, hair salons, and tailoring shops.

These gathering spots allow for network building, sharing information, and providing a variety of assistance to new migrants. The domestic workers often discuss their problems at work and share information about housing. There is an ethic of mutual assistance and solidarity, although occasionally, some migrants take advantage of others in activities such as money lending.

The community of Filipina domestic workers in Los Angeles is not nearly as cohesive as the one in Rome. In contrast to Rome, the Los Angeles Filipino population is class stratified. There has been a long stream of migration from the Philippines to the United States, going back a century, and many earlier streams involved professional workers, particularly in the medical professions. Although many of the Filipina domestic workers have connections to more economically privileged Filipinos in Los Angeles, often securing work through these connections, they perceive the class distinctions as impeding cohesion and do not feel supported by the middle-class Filipino community. This is so even though they often spend their days off with relatives or friends in middle-class homes, or even live alongside middle-class neighbors. The domestic workers perceive the Filipino enclaves as middle-class spaces.

A subcommunity of Filipina domestic workers does seem to form from time to time, however. Live-in workers often congregate in the parks and playgrounds of the wealthy communities where they work. The minority who work as day workers rather than live-in workers often meet on the buses traveling to and from work. Like their counterparts in Rome, they talk about work situations, but these gatherings are neither as large nor as regular as they are in Rome. The domestic workers also often participate in parties in the homes of middle-class Filipinos, but these associations do not seem to lead to the type of solidarity that occurs among the workers in Rome (Parreñas, 2001, 2008).

A DEFINITION OF COMMUNITY

Rhacel Salazar Parreñas (2001, 2008) first chronicled the lives of Filipina domestic workers from June 1995 to August 1996, a period before the wide use of the Internet and cell phones. By 2008, the workers were using these new technologies to keep connection with their multiple communities. We can imagine how even newer technologies, such as Facebook, YouTube, Twitter, and Instagram, are now supporting these connections. Although the circumstances of their lives are different in some important ways, the Filipinas in Rome and Los Angeles both appear to see themselves as members of multiple communities. But exactly what is community? This question has not been an easy one for social scientists. In fact, George Hillery's 1955 review of the sociological literature found 94 distinct definitions of *community*. Twenty years later, Seymour Sarason (1974) struggled to define the related concept of *sense of community* and concluded that even though sense of community is hard to define, "you know when you have it and when you don't" (p. 157).

How should we interpret the fuzziness of the concepts of community and sense of community? Some suggest that any concept with so many meanings is unscientific, and its potential utility is therefore highly suspect. On the other hand, Larry Lyon (1987) suggests that the multiplicity of definitions of community is evidence that the concept is meaningful to scholars with diverse interests and perspectives. More recently, Robert Chaskin (2013) noted that the concept of community is both ubiquitous and ambiguous. We would certainly agree with Lyon and Chaskin that a concept such as community should not be discarded simply because it has been hard to define. Over the past 3 decades, sociologists have in fact worked to develop greater agreement about the meaning of community, and community psychologists have been equally diligent about developing greater clarity for sense of community. Both lines of inquiry are relevant to social work.

Sociological attempts to reach agreement on the definition of community have centered on the report that approximately three fourths of the 94 definitions found in the sociological literature included the same three elements: geographic area, social interaction, and common ties (Hillery, 1955). The Filipina domestic workers' understanding of community seems very similar, but they would, most likely, suggest that community can be built across geographical distance. Historically, community did have a geographic meaning in sociology. More recently, however, two different sociological meanings of community have developed: community as a geographic or territorial concept and community as an interactional or relational concept. In this chapter, we discuss both meanings of community because both appear to have relevance for human behavior in the contemporary era. Recently, researchers are finding more similarities than differences in these two types of community (Obst & White, 2004; Obst, Zinkiewicz, & Smith, 2002a, 2002b). We use the following definition to cover both territorial and relational communities: **Community** is people bound either by geography or by webs of communication, sharing common ties, and interacting with one another.

Does it appear to you that the Filipina domestic workers in Rome have a sense of community with other domestic workers in the city? What about the Filipina domestic workers in Los Angeles? In 1974, Seymour Sarason proclaimed the enhancement of the "psychological sense of community" as the mission of community psychology. He saw the basic characteristics of **sense of community** as

> the perception of similarity with others, an acknowledged interdependence with others, a willingness to maintain this interdependence by giving to or doing for others what one expects from them, the feeling that one is part of a larger dependable and stable structure. (p. 157)

These characteristics of sense of community are very similar to the "common ties" element of the definition of community. The elements of community and sense of community are presented in Exhibit 13.1. We look more closely at the concept of sense of community in a later section.

Exhibit 13.1   Essential Elements of Community and Sense of Community

Community (from community sociology literature)

Linked by geography or webs of communication

Common ties

Interaction

Sense of Community (from community psychology literature)

Similarity with others

Interdependence

Mutual exchanges to fulfill needs

Sense of belonging

SOURCES: Based on Hillery, 1955; Sarason, 1974; Wellman, 1999.

TERRITORIAL COMMUNITY AND RELATIONAL COMMUNITY _____

Some would argue that community in the contemporary era is based on voluntary interaction (**relational community**), not on geography or territory (**territorial community**). For the Filipina domestic workers, community seems to be both relational and territorial. They are a part of a growing trend of transnational families who are also creating *transnational communities*. They maintain a sense of community connection to their sending communities in the Philippines as well as to other Filipina domestic workers in their territorial communities. In addition, they imagine themselves as part of a global community of Filipina domestic workers, especially when they read magazines such as *Tinig Filipino*. Their sense of belonging to this global community is based on common ties but does not include much interaction. They do, however, draw support from feeling a part of this community. What about for you? Are your strongest supports based on territorial or relational community?

In premodern times, human groups depended, by necessity, on the territorial community to meet their human needs. But each development in communication and transportation technology has loosened that dependency somewhat. Electronic communication now connects people over distant spaces, with a high degree of both immediacy and intimacy. The development of the World Wide Web in the early 1990s allowed rapid growth in the use of e-mail; beginning in the mid-1990s, hundreds of millions of people around the world began to use e-mail to communicate with other individuals and to develop e-mail discussion groups. Toward the end of 2004, Web 2.0 technologies, a second generation of the World Wide Web that allows people to collaborate and share information online, came to prominence. Web 2.0 includes blogs, wikis, podcasting, multimedia sharing sites, and social networking sites (SNSs). By 2008, a major research study of the use of digital technologies by adults in 17 industrialized nations found an average one third of leisure time spent using these technologies (Harrison & Thomas, 2009). The SNS Facebook reportedly has more than 1.3 billion users worldwide communicating in 70 different languages, with more than 600 million users accessing the site by mobile devices (Statistic Brain, 2014). Other SNSs have sprung up in specific countries—for example, Cyworld (Korea), Hyves (Holland), LunarStorm (Sweden), Mixi (Japan), Orkut (Brazil), QQ (China), and Skyrock (France), but some have closed down or become gaming sites only because of competition from Facebook. SNSs have been defined as web-based services that allow individuals to "construct a public or semi-public profile within a bounded system, articulate a list of other users with whom they share a connection, and view and traverse their list of connections and those made by others within the system" (Boyd & Ellison, 2008, p. 211). This definition is consistent with the aspects of the earlier definition of community: linked by webs of communication, common ties, and interaction. Recently, a boom in the growth of mobile social network applications, such as Foursquare, has been connecting virtual and territorial communities (Zhang, Wang, Vasilakos, & Ma, 2013).

Since the last edition of this book (2011), first author Lib Hutchison has continued to enjoy e-mail conversations with former students; former colleagues at three universities; contributing authors in three countries and eight states plus the District of Columbia; her editor in Los Angeles; former colleagues from a national committee spread across the United States and Canada; members of a local environmental justice task force; and numerous friends and relatives. She is struck by how much larger her e-mail network has grown since she worked on the first edition of this book in the late 1990s. Increasingly over the past few years, she has used text messaging as a way to keep connection with friends, relatives, and service providers, both near and far. She finds great pleasure in the videos of grandchildren sent to her by e-mail and text messaging. She has continued to enjoy keeping up on Facebook with a growing community of friends scattered around the world. She is recognizing that many members of her Facebook community now prefer Facebook communication to e-mail and also make regular use of text messaging and Twitter (sending "tweets"). You can follow Lib at @ehutch2014. Lib also makes use of Skype and Facetime to keep in touch with children and grandchildren as well as to coordinate some volunteer activities. No doubt, new technological innovations will continue to provide new ways of building community. Lib is also recognizing that members of her Facebook community are struggling with issues of privacy and have had to deal with unsettling situations in which their Facebook communications, especially those that were political, were responded to in different ways in different sectors of their Facebook communities.

The second author (Soon Min) also enjoys using SNSs. For example, she communicates daily with her sister in Australia through Band, Korean social networking services. She reconnected with her old friend in the United States via Kakao talk, another popular Korean mobile SNS. She was able to send a picture, stored in her smartphone, of her newborn baby to her old friend without accessing a computer. Also, she had a regular meeting with her Japanese friend via Google Chat, in order to discuss and collaborate on a research paper. SNSs have become an important part of Soon Min's life, so much so that it is hard to separate them from her life.

Due to privacy issues, Soon Min uses different SNSs depending on the purpose of the communication. For example, she uses Band for more private communications with her family, such as sharing her children's pictures, because people can be grouped in Band and the communication can stay within the arranged group. However, she uses Facebook or Kakao talk for more official communication with her colleagues or students, because people can find Soon Min with her e-mail address or phone number on Facebook or Kakao talk and her contact information can be easily accessed.

Despite people's concerns about privacy issues, SNSs emerge as a main communication medium. Soon Min's friend who has a school-age child uses a SNS to connect with other parents of her child's classmates. She participates in group chats among parents in Kakao talk. Once she is in the group chatting, she knows what is going on in school and what topics are discussed among parents. Although she is sometimes annoyed with the alarm sound of her smartphone that beeps whenever a new comment is posted in the group chat, she is glad she can be involved with mothers of her child's classmates. She thinks she might be isolated without the SNS because she is a working mother who does not have many opportunities to meet or communicate with other mothers in person. Another friend of Soon Min's, who does not use SNSs because of privacy issues, has seriously considered using SNSs after his colleagues arranged a hangout via SNS and he was not informed of it. He began to think that people using SNSs build another community among themselves. For Soon Min, SNSs help people to easily maintain their social relationships and enhance their relational community with those at a distance as well as in the same region.

For a number of years, researchers have been finding that local ties make up a decreasing portion of our social connections, interpreting that finding to mean that territorial community is no longer important in our lives (Hunter & Riger, 1986; Wellman, 1982; Wellman & Wortley, 1990). A more careful look at this research suggests, however, that even highly mobile people continue to have a lot of contacts in their territorial communities. One study in Toronto (Wellman, 1996) found that if we study *ties*, the number of people with whom we have connections, it is true that the majority are nonterritorial. However, when we study *contacts*, our actual interactions, two thirds are local, in the neighborhood or work setting. This may well be the case for the Filipina domestic workers who often complain about how isolating their domestic work is.

When technology opens the possibilities for relational communities, it does not spell the death of territorial community, but there have been conflicting findings about this. One research team found that Internet-wired suburbanites were more likely than their nonwired neighbors to engage in "active neighboring," actually using the Internet to support neighboring (Hampton &

Photos 13.1a and 13.1b Communities are linked together by geography and webs of communication, common ties, and interaction. Contrasted here are two types of neighborhoods, a suburban neighborhood in the United States and the village of Cantondougou on the Ivory Coast.

© iStockphoto.com/Tony Tremblay; © Kambou Sia/AFP/Getty Images

Wellman, 2003). A widely publicized 2006 study by McPherson et al. (2006) found the opposite. This study found that from 1985 to 2005, people in the United States became more socially isolated, the size of their discussion networks declined, and the diversity of their networks decreased. More specifically, the researchers found that people had fewer close ties in their neighborhoods and with voluntary associations (e.g., clubs, neighborhood associations). They suggested that use of the Internet and mobile phones pulls people away from neighborhood and other locally based social settings. Using the same database, with data collected 2 years later, DiPrete and colleagues (DiPrete, Gelman, McCormick, Teitler, & Zheng, 2011) found that people in the United States are not as isolated as suggested by the data used by McPherson, but their social networks are increasingly segregated along racial, social class, religious, and political lines.

To address the inconsistencies in prior research, the most comprehensive study of social isolation and new technology in the United States was reported by researchers with the Pew Internet & American Life Project (Hampton, Sessions, Her, & Rainie, 2009). These researchers undertook a study to compare the social networks of people who use particular technologies with those of demographically similar people who do not use these technologies. Here are their major findings about the trends in social networks since 1985. In interepreting these data, it is important to remember that the use of these technologies is changing rapidly and data are quickly outdated.

- There has been a small to modest drop in the number of people reporting that they have no one to talk to about important matters; 6% of adults report they have no one with whom they can discuss such matters.

- The average size of people's core discussion networks has declined, with a drop of about one confidant.
- The diversity of people's core discussion network has markedly declined.

However, the research also indicates that use of technology is not the driving force behind these changes. Here are their findings about the relationship between new technology and social networks:

- People who own a cell phone and use the Internet for sharing photos and messages have larger core discussion networks than those who do not use this technology.
- People who use these technologies have more nonkin in their networks than people who do not.
- People who use the Internet to share photos are more likely to have discussion partners that cross political lines.
- People who use Internet social networking sites have social networks that are about 20% more diverse.
- In-person contact remains the most frequent way to have contact in the geographical community.
- The mobile phone has replaced the landline as the most frequently used medium for communication.
- Text messaging tied with the landline as the third most popular way to communicate, but it is likely that this ranking no longer holds in 2014.
- Those who use SNSs are 25% less likely to use neighbors for companionship, but use of other technologies is associated with higher levels of neighborhood involvement.
- Internet users are less likely to depend on neighbors to provide concrete services.

Wendy Griswold (2013) proposes that people can have ties to both relational and territorial communities at the same time, and this does seem to be the case for the Filipina domestic workers in both Rome and Los Angeles. They maintain relationships with their sending communities while also building community in local gathering places in their receiving communities. Griswold recognizes the possibility that new technologies will simply allow us to develop and maintain a larger network of increasingly superficial relationships. But she also points out the possibility that the new capacity to be immediately and intimately connected across space could help us to develop more shared meanings and become more tolerant of our differences. Jeffrey Boase (2008) found that people who draw heavily on all types of available technology have larger and more diverse personal networks than people who make less use of available technology.

As social workers concerned about social justice, however, we must understand the multiple implications of inequality of access to new technologies. These technologies open opportunities for relational community and the multitude of resources provided by such communities. Skill in using new technologies is also increasingly rewarded in the labor market. Unless access to these technologies is equalized, however, territorial community will remain central to the lives of some groups—most notably, young children and their caregivers; older adults; poor families; and many persons with disabilities, who have their own special technological needs. On the other hand, new technologies may make it easier for some people with disabilities to gain access to relational community, even while inaccessible physical environments continue to block their access to territorial community. One of my former students who is African American has told me that she likes the Internet because it is color blind, and she can have encounters of various kinds without feeling that race gets in the way.

Although both territorial and relational communities are relevant to social work, social work's commitment to social justice has led to continued concern for territorial communities. That same commitment also requires social workers to work toward equalization of access to both territorial and relational community.

SOCIAL WORKERS AND COMMUNITIES: OUR HISTORY

From the earliest history of social work in the United States, social workers have been interested in the health of communities and in the influence of community on individual behavior (Brueggemann, 2013). Social work grew from two different approaches to social problems, one of which—the settlement house movement—was community focused. (The other was the social casework approach, which focused on individual and family adjustment.) Social workers in the settlement houses provided a wide range of services to help individual poor families cope with the challenges of poverty, including day nurseries, employment bureaus, a place to take a shower, English classes for immigrants, health clinics, pasteurized milk, information on workers' compensation, legal assistance, and emergency financial assistance. Their interests went beyond helping individual families, however; they were also interested in identifying and addressing community conditions that jeopardized the health and well-being of neighborhood families. They campaigned for social reforms such as tenement protection, improved sanitation, and labor reform. In addition, the settlement house social workers were interested in building a sense of mutual support in the poor neighborhoods where

they were located. They developed dance, drama, and arts classes; sports and hobby clubs; summer camps; cultural events; and libraries. During this same period, African American social work pioneers developed settlement houses and engaged in active community work to "improve the collective social functioning of their racially segregated communities" (Carlton-LaNey, 1999, p. 312).

Social work's interest in community has ebbed and flowed since then, with more interest shown in some periods than in others. Stanley Wenocur and Steven Soifer (1997) suggest three peak periods of intense social work interest in community in the United States: the Progressive Era at the turn of the 20th century, the Depression years of the 1930s, and the civil rights era of the 1960s. Contemporary critiques of social work suggest that the profession replaced its original focus on community with a preoccupation with personality problems of individuals (Reisch, Ife, & Weil, 2013; Thompson, 2002). The social work literature, however, reflects a recent expansion in community practice in the United States and around the world (Weil, Reisch, & Ohmer, 2013a). It is hard to say what mix of societal trends has produced this expanded interest in community practice, but some have credited the far-reaching impact of economic and cultural globalization, growing social inequality, massive movements of refugees, the devolution of policy decisions about social welfare programs to the state and local levels in the United States, and social work's renewed commitment to the goal of social justice (Brueggemann, 2013).

THEORETICAL APPROACHES TO COMMUNITY

Social workers traditionally have turned to *community sociology* for theory and research on community. During the 1950s and 1960s, however, community theory and research were scant—almost nonexistent—in the United States and Europe (Lyon, 1987; Puddifoot, 1995). Although this decline in academic interest in community sociology probably had multiple causes, sociologists suggest it was related in large part to the rising prominence of the concept of mass society (Lyon, 1987; Woolever, 1992). **Mass society** is standardized and homogenized—a society that has no ethnic, class, regional, or local variations in human behavior. Standardized public education, mass media, and residential mobility are cited as the primary mechanisms by which societies become standardized and homogenized. If we assume that mass society has no local or group-based variations in norms, values, and behavior, then community, which is local and group based, loses its relevance to the study of human behavior.

Just as the rising prominence of the concept of mass society contributed to the eclipse of community theory and research, recognition of the limits of mass society as a way of understanding human behavior contributed to the revitalization of community sociology. Beginning in the late 1960s, it became apparent that even though some standardization and homogenization had occurred, mass society had not eradicated ethnic, class, regional, and local variations in human behavior. In the 1980s, a more balanced view of community developed within sociology, a view that recognizes the contributions that both community and mass society make to human behavior (Cuba & Hummon, 1993; Flanagan, 1993; Keane, 1991; Lyon, 1987; Woolever, 1992). In this view, some standardization is present, but local variations still occur. Certainly, we note similarities in the experiences of the Rome and Los Angeles Filipinas, but there are also many differences.

More recently, scholars in a variety of disciplines have been interested in how globalization interacts with local cultural norms in the development, maintenance, and deterioration of community (Francescato & Tomai, 2001). They have been particularly interested in social inequalities and conflicts between communities of competing interests in a globalized, postmodern world. These scholars identify strong and hotly contested group-based variations in norms, values, and behavior.

At the same time the concept of community was regaining prominence in sociology, it also emerged as an important concept in psychology. In the midst of concern about the ineffectiveness of existing psychotherapeutic methods, the concept of community was discovered—or rediscovered—by the community mental health movement. The field of community psychology developed and became Division 27 of the American Psychological Association in the United States (Heller, 1989). During the 1980s, community psychology was also established as a division in some European countries, and in 1995, the European Network of Community Psychologists was formed (Francescato & Tomai, 2001). Like social workers, community psychologists have turned to the sociological literature for community theory, but they have also developed their own theory of psychological sense of community.

In a 1979 paper presented to the Community Section of the American Sociological Association, Roland Warren (1988) suggested that theorizing about community, like sociological theory in general, includes multiple perspectives. He recommended that multiple theoretical approaches be used to understand communities because each approach explains particular aspects of community. More than 3 decades later, it still seems wise for social workers to follow Warren's advice and use multiple theoretical approaches for understanding multidimensional community. That approach is, of course, consistent with the multidimensional approach of this book.

Five perspectives on community seem particularly relevant for social work: the contrasting types approach, spatial arrangements approach, social systems approach, social capital approach, and conflict approach. The second of these, the spatial arrangements approach, applies only to territorial communities, but the other four can be applied equally well to both relational and territorial communities. In combination, these five approaches to community should enable you to scan more widely for factors contributing to the problems of living among vulnerable populations, to recognize community resources, and to think more creatively about possible interventions. Using approaches that are not only varied but even discordant should assist you in thinking critically about human behavior and prepare you for the often ambiguous practice situations you will encounter.

Contrasting Types Approach

The Filipina domestic workers in Rome and Los Angeles are concerned about commitment, identification, and relationships within their communities. The Los Angeles Filipinas seem especially concerned about the nature of their relationship to the wider Filipino community in their area. This concern is at the heart of the oldest theory of community, Ferdinand Tonnies's (1887/1963) concepts of *gemeinschaft* and *gesellschaft* (translated from the German as *community* and *society*). Actually, Tonnies was trying to describe contrasting types of societies, rural preindustrial societies (gemeinschaft) versus urban industrial societies (gesellschaft), but his ideas continue to be used by community sociologists today to understand differences between communities, both spatial and relational (Ballantine & Roberts, 2014; Memmi, 2006; Ritzer, 2013a). In **gemeinschaft** communities, relationships are personal and traditional; in **gesellschaft** communities, relationships are impersonal and contractual. The defining characteristics of gemeinschaft and gesellschaft communities are listed in Exhibit 13.2.

Tonnies (1887/1963) saw gemeinschaft and gesellschaft as ideal types that will never exist in reality. However, they constitute a hypothetical dichotomy against which the real world can be compared. Although Tonnies's work is more than a century old, the gemeinschaft/gesellschaft dichotomy has proven to be a powerful analytical construct, and it continues to be used and validated in community research. It is also reflected in later typological theories. For example, Charles Cooley (1902) proposed that the social world can be defined in terms of *primary groups* (intimate, face-to-face groups to which we form attachments) and *secondary groups* (less intimate, more impersonal groups). Mark Granovetter (1973) made a distinction between strong ties and weak ties. *Strong ties* entail frequent contact between members, emotional intensity in interactions, and cohesion. *Weak ties* are impersonal and superficial, connecting acquaintances rather than friends. Some theorists have envisioned more of a continuum than a dichotomy, such as Robert Redfield's (1947) folk/urban continuum and Howard Becker's sacred/secular (1957) continuum.

Tonnies (1887/1963) shared the view of other early European sociologists, such as Max Weber and Émile Durkheim, that modernization was leading us away from gemeinschaft and toward gesellschaft. Capitalism, urbanization, and industrialization have all been proposed as causes of the movement toward gesellschaft. Many typology theorists lament the "loss of community" that occurs in the process. But some theorists suggest that electronic technology is moving us into a third type of community—sometimes referred to

Exhibit 13.2 Gemeinschaft and Gesellschaft Communities

Gemeinschaft	Gesellschaft
Strong identification with community	Little identification with community
Authority based on tradition	Authority based on laws and rationality
Relationships based on emotionalism	Relationships based on goal attainment and emotional neutrality
Others seen as whole persons	Others seen as role enactors

SOURCE: Based on Lyon, 1987.

as a *postgesellschaft*, or postmodern, community—characterized by diversity and unpredictability (Griswold, 2013; Lyon, 1987; Smith, 1996). This view has become more prominent with increasing globalization, and it is well illustrated by the Filipina domestic workers and their families back in the Philippines. Back home in their rural, newly industrializing sending communities, children, relatives, and friends talk about the loss of emotional intimacy in their relationships with the migrant workers. Although the Filipina domestic workers feel the pain of separation from family and friends back home, they talk about relationships based on goal attainment—meeting the goal of improving the financial situation of their families.

Howard Becker (1957) sees the evolution of community in a different light. He suggests that modern society does not always move toward the secular but instead moves back and forth a great deal on the sacred/secular continuum. To Becker, the sacred is best characterized by reluctance to change (traditional authority in Tonnies's gemeinschaft), and the secular is best characterized by readiness to change (emotional neutrality in Tonnies's gesellschaft).

Tonnies and other theorists who have studied communities as contrasting types have focused their attention on territorial communities. Indeed, empirical research supports the idea that territorial communities vary along the gemeinschaft/gesellschaft continuum (Cuba & Hummon, 1993; Hunter & Riger, 1986; Keane, 1991; Woolever, 1992). More recently, however, Barry Wellman (1999) and research associates have attempted to understand contrasting types of relational communities that are based on networks of interaction rather than territory. In his early work, Wellman (1979) identified three contrasting types of communities:

1. *Community lost.* Communities that have lost a sense of connectedness, social support, and traditional customs for behavior

2. *Community saved.* Communities that have retained a strong sense of connectedness, social support, and customs for behavior

3. *Community liberated.* Communities that are loosely knit, with unclear boundaries and a great deal of heterogeneity

Wellman (1999) suggests that as societies change, community is not necessarily lost but becomes transformed, and new forms of community develop. Daniel Memmi (2006) argues that online communities are just another form of community and another example of the long-term evolution of looser social relationships. There are differences of opinion about whether community is lost or merely transformed in the exportation of labor around the world. As you ponder this question, think about this personal story told by Rhacel Salazar Parreñas (2008) in her book *The Force of Domesticity*. While she was doing fieldwork about the families of Filipina migrant domestic workers in a city in the Philippines, she ended up spending a night in jail with her cousin, Mimi, in a remote small town. She was surprised that word of their incarceration reached relatives in the United States before anyone in her Filipino household or neighborhood knew anything about it.

Wellman and associates have continued to study the idea of contrasting types of relational communities for more than 20 years, seeking to understand multiple dimensions of communities. Their work (e.g., Wellman & Potter, 1999) suggests that it is more important to think in terms of *elements* of communities rather than *types* of communities. Using factor analytic statistical methods, they have identified four important elements of community—contact, range, intimacy, and immediate kinship/friendship—described in Exhibit 13.3. These elements are configured in different ways in different communities and in the same community at different times.

Social workers might benefit by recognizing both the gemeinschaft and gesellschaft qualities of the communities they serve as well as the histories of those communities. Approaches like Wellman and Potter's multiple elements of communities could be helpful in this regard.

Exhibit 13.3 Four Elements of Communities

Contact	Level of interaction; how accessible community members are for contact and how much contact they actually have
Range	Size and heterogeneity of community membership
Intimacy	Sense of relationships being special; desire for companionship among members; interest in being together in multiple social contexts over a long period of time; sense of mutuality in relationships, with needs known and supported
Immediate kinship/ friendship	Proportion of community membership composed of immediate kin (parents, adult children, siblings) versus friends

SOURCE: Based on Wellman & Potter, 1999.

Spatial Arrangements Approach

If we think about the Filipina community in Rome in terms of spatial arrangements, we note the dispersed gathering places where they congregate. We think about how their gathering places are segregated from the public space of the dominant society. We also think about the crowded apartments that sometimes hold as many as four residents in a small room. If we think about the Filipinas in Los Angeles, we think about domestic workers isolated in houses in wealthy neighborhoods and visiting middle-class Filipino neighborhoods where they feel like outsiders on their days off. We also think about their lack of transportation to get beyond their live-in and day-off neighborhoods.

Beginning with Robert Park's (1936) human ecology theory, a diverse group of sociological theorists have focused on community as spatial arrangements. Their interests have included city placement; population growth; land use patterns; the process of suburbanization; the development of "edge" cities (newly developed business districts of large scale located on the edge of major cities); and the relationships among central cities, suburbs, and edge cities. They are also interested in variations in human behavior related to the type of spatial community, such as rural area, small town, suburb, or central city, and more recently, in how human health and well-being are related to physical features of the community (Sternberg, 2009).

Symbolic interactionists have studied how symbolic images of communities—the way people think about their communities—are related to spatial arrangements (Wilson & Baldassare, 1996). A survey of a random sample of Denver employees found that a large majority thought of themselves as either a "city person" or a "suburbanite" (Feldman, 1990). Participants largely agreed about the spatial attributes that distinguish cities from suburbs. On the whole, both city people and suburbanites reported a preference for the type of spatial community in which they resided. Recently, however, there is evidence that, after 50 years of movement from U.S. cities to the suburbs, many suburbanites no longer want suburban life. Cities and high-density inner suburbs are now growing faster than the suburbs (Gallagher, 2013). Two of the reasons for this trend are a desire to spend less time in the car and a desire to live where human interactions are more convenient. The future of this suburban to urban migration is unclear. Stay tuned.

One research team set out to discover the meanings that residents of seven distressed neighborhoods in one midwestern city make of the physical aspects of their neighborhoods (Nowell, Berkowitz, Deacon, & Foster-Fishman, 2006). They used a *photovoice* methodology, putting cameras in the hands of participants and asking them to use the cameras to tell a story about their community.

> Social constructionist perspective

Photo 13.2 Teenagers can often be characterized as a community held together via social bonds; they share a common spirit, trust, art, and emotional connection. In this case, they also share a common territory.

© iStockphoto.com

They found that physical aspects of the neighborhood carry many meanings for the residents. Positive physical landmarks, such as parks and monuments, communicate a message of pride and identity, but physical conditions such as dilapidated houses, graffiti, and overflowing garbage convey negative meaning that invites frustration and shame. The researchers concluded that community physical conditions are important because they carry symbolic meanings for the residents. We are reminded that the Los Angeles Filipina domestic workers interpret the middle-class neighborhoods where they visit on their days off as "middle-class spaces."

The multidisciplinary theory on human behavior and the physical environment, discussed in Chapter 7, has also been extended to the study of community as spatial arrangements. Social scientists have focused on elements of environmental design that encourage social interaction as well as those that encourage a sense of control and the motivation to look out for the neighborhood. They have identified such elements as large spaces broken into smaller spaces, personalized spaces, and spaces for both privacy and congregation. One research team that studied the spatial arrangements in a suburban region found that people who had a sense of adequate privacy from neighbors' houses also reported a greater sense of community (Wilson & Baldassare, 1996). Another researcher found that opportunities to visit

Systems perspective

nearby shared space and having views of nature from home are correlated with increased neighborhood satisfaction (Kearney, 2006). Still another researcher found that neighborhood physical environments that provide opportunity for physical activity are particularly valued by children and recommends that social work assessment with children should include aspects of the child–neighborhood relationship (Nicotera, 2005). Recently, new urbanist designers have been interested in aspects of community design that encourage physical activity for people of all ages; they are thinking of the health benefits that physical activity provides (see discussion in Chapter 7).

Early settlement house social workers at Hull House in Chicago developed color-coded community maps for assessing the spatial arrangements of social and economic injustices in local neighborhoods (Schoech, 2013). Social work planners and administrators have recently returned to the idea of geographical mapping, making use of advancements in **geographic information system (GIS)** computer technology, which can map the spatial distribution of a variety of social data. In recent years, GIS has been used to map (1) the distribution of supermarkets in areas of high concentration of diet-related deaths (Giang, Karpyn, Laurison, Hillier, & Perry, 2008); (2) where foster care children are placed in relation to schools, community services, transportation, and other types of community resources (Potter, 2005); (3) the geographical distribution of rates of child physical abuse, neglect, and sexual abuse (Ernst, 2000); and (4) the clustering of outdoor advertisements for unhealthful products near child-serving institutions in low-income and minority communities (Hillier et al., 2009). GIS is also being used to map public health risk factors and to examine the match of physicians to community needs (see Cervigni, Suzuki, Ishii, & Hata, 2008); to study residents' views of neighborhood scale (Coulton, Jennings, & Chan, 2013); to target neighborhoods for community-building initiatives (Huber, Egeren, Pierce, & Foster-Fishman, 2009); and to study race disparities in the national distribution of hazardous waste treatment, storage, and disposal facilities (Mohai & Saha, 2007). Huber

et al. (2009) emphasize that community resources and community risk factors can be identified through the use of GIS.

GIS holds much promise for future social work planning, administration, and research. Amy Hillier (2007), a leading proponent of the use of GIS by social workers, emphasizes the important role GIS can play in identifying where social work clients live in relation to both resources and hazards. She also argues that GIS has the potential to empower community groups, particularly disenfranchised groups, but that it is rarely used this way by social workers. One challenge for social service organizations is the lack of staff training in the use of GIS software and hardware (Hillier & Culhane, 2013). If you have access to GIS technology, you might want to do some mapping of your territorial community: its ethnic makeup, socioeconomic class, crime rate, libraries, parks, hospitals, social services, and so on. If you do not have access to GIS, you can accomplish the same task with a good map blowup and multi-colored pushpins.

Thinking about territorial communities as spatial arrangements can

| Systems perspective |

help social workers decide which territorial communities to target, for which problems, and with which methods. An interdisciplinary literature has recently focused on the compounding and interrelated nature of problems in deteriorating, impoverished neighborhoods in central cities. Philanthropic funders have responded with comprehensive community initiatives (CCIs) to fund multifaceted community-building programs that address the economic and physical conditions, as well as social and cultural issues, of these impoverished communities (Huber et al., 2009; Nowell et al., 2006). Typical elements of CCIs are economic and commercial development, education, health care, employment, housing, leadership development, physical revitalization, neighborhood security, recreation, social services, and support networks. Although CCIs have been thought of as a development strategy for impoverished urban neighborhoods, Lori Messinger (2004) argues that the model is also relevant for work in rural communities. She suggests, however, that in rural communities, it is particularly important to pay attention to both current and historical points of tension and conflict. Another development is that many communities are using neighborhood youth for neighborhood cleanup and revitalization (Delgado & Staples, 2013).

Social Systems Approach

Systems perspective

A third way to think about communities is as social systems with cultures and patterns of interactions. We have looked at some of the ways the cultures and patterns of interactions of the Filipina community in Rome are similar to and different from those in Los Angeles. A closer look at these communities as social systems might help us understand both the differences and similarities. The social systems perspective focuses on social interaction rather than on the physical, spatial aspects of community. Social interaction in a community can be understood in two ways: as culture and as structure (Griswold, 2013). Exhibit 13.4 shows the differences between these two aspects of community.

Exhibit 13.4   Aspects of Community Culture and Community Structure

Community Culture

Use of language

Pattern of meanings

Typical practices

Common knowledge

Symbols that guide thinking, feelings, and behaviors

Community Structure

Network of relationships

Institutions

Economic factors

Political factors

SOURCE: Based on Griswold, 2013.

Social constructionist perspective

For thinking about community in terms of its culture, symbolic interaction theory is promising because of its emphasis on the development of meaning through interaction. *Ethnography* is also particularly useful for studying community culture. The goal of ethnographic research is to understand the underlying rules and patterns of everyday life, in a particular location or among a particular group, from the native point of view rather than the researcher's point of view. One example of this is work by Italian community psychologists Donata Francescato and Manuela Tomai (2001). Their method of building a profile of a territorial community of interest combines demographic data with ethnographic methods that include "environmental walks, drawings, movie scripts, narratives, and telling jokes" (p. 376). For the movie script, they ask different groups in the community to develop a plot for a movie script about the future they imagine for the neighborhood; sometimes these different groups perform parts of their "movies" for each other. Francescato and Tomai have used the movie script method to build understanding between Blacks, Afrikaners, and Asian Indians in a college town in South Africa; old farmers and young students in an Austrian town; and immigrants and locals in several neighborhoods in Italy.

Community can also be studied in terms of its structure. Roland Warren (1963, 1978, 1987) made significant contributions to the understanding of patterns of interactions in communities. Warren pointed out that members of communities have two distinctive types of interactions. The first are those that create **horizontal linkage**, or interactions with other members of the community. The second are interactions that create **vertical linkage**, or interaction with individuals and systems outside the community. Warren suggested that healthy communities must have both types of interactions. Communities with strong horizontal linkage provide a sense of identity for community members, but without good vertical linkage they cannot provide all the necessary resources for the well-being of community members. Communities with strong vertical linkage but weak horizontal linkage may leave community members searching and yearning for a sense of community.

More recently, a similar distinction has been made by scholars who write about community as social capital (to be discussed later; see Putnam, 2000). They differentiate between bonding social capital and bridging social capital. **Bonding social capital** is inward looking and tends to mobilize solidarity and in-group loyalty, and it leads to exclusive identities and homogeneous communities. It may also lead to strong out-group hostilities. This type of social capital is often found in minority ethnic enclaves that provide psychological, social, and economic support to members. **Bridging social capital** is outward looking and diverse, and it links community members to assets and information across community boundaries. Robert Putnam (2000) describes the difference between the two types of social capital this way: "Bonding social capital constitutes a kind of sociological superglue, whereas bridging social capital provides a sociological WD-40" (p. 23). One research team (Ellison, Steinfield, & Lampe, 2007) found that the SNS Facebook is particularly useful for bridging social capital but much less useful for bonding social capital. Tomai et al. (2010) found that both bridging and bonding social capital were increased for youth who joined an online community of high school students outside Rome; however, increased intensity of use was associated with increased bridging social capital but not with increased bonding social capital.

Researchers have found support for the advantages and disadvantages of horizontal and vertical linkage. But consider also the experiences of the Filipina domestic workers in Rome and Los Angeles. We see much evidence that the workers in Rome have built strong horizontal linkages, but their opportunities to build vertical linkages are hampered by anti-immigrant sentiment. Unfortunately, the Filipina domestic workers in Los Angeles seem to be limited in both horizontal and vertical linkages, although middle-class Filipinos appear to be a source of bridging social capital for them.

For almost 3 decades, network theorists and researchers have been using network analysis to study community structure (Borgatti & Halgin, 2011). They suggest that communities, like small groups and organizations, should be thought of as networks of social interaction (Wellman, 1999, 2005). They have tended to define community as **personal community**, which is composed of ties with friends, relatives, neighbors, workmates, and so on. Community is personal because the makeup of community membership varies from person to person. Another name for personal community is **network**, which has been defined as "a set of actors with a set of ties of a specified type" (Borgatti & Halgin, 2011, p. 1169). Network theorists suggest that new communication technologies, particularly the Internet, have played a large role in transforming community from *solidarity community*, which seeks the participation of all members in an integrated fashion, to what Barry Wellman has called community as **networked individualism**, where individuals operate in large, personalized, complex networks (Boase, Horrigan, Wellman, & Rainie, 2006). Some network theorists value this transformation (see, e.g., Boase et al., 2006). Others argue that communication technologies, and particularly the Internet, can and should be used to develop solidarity community, which is friendlier, richer, and more socially binding than networked individualism, which they argue is a North American idea (see, e.g., Day & Schuler, 2004). It seems that both sides are correct. Certainly, we know that the Internet has been used to develop support groups as one form of solidarity community. It is interesting to note that the Los Angeles Filipina domestic workers seem to be closer to a network individualism model, while the Rome Filipinas seem to have built solidarity community.

In the mid-1990s, when Parreñas (2001) first did her study of Filipina domestic workers, the Internet was a tool accessible only to the technically elite, but a decade later, it was a part of everyday life for a large majority of people. That represents an unusually rapid diffusion of innovation, which has been accompanied by debates about whether it is helping to build or destroy community. In 2004–2005, the PEW Internet & American Life Project undertook a research project to study this question (Boase et al., 2006). Using a random-digit sample of telephone numbers in the United States, the researchers studied two types of connection people have in their social networks: *core ties*, or our closest relationships, and *significant ties*, or relationships that are only somewhat closely connected. They found surprisingly large networks among the respondents, a median of 15 core ties and 16 significant ties. There was no difference in the number of core ties between Internet users and nonusers, but Internet users were found to have larger numbers of significant ties. Although the digital divide has been narrowing over time, it continues to raise important concerns about equal access to virtual communities.

Network analysis has been used to study social ties in both territorial and relational communities. In doing so, researchers have found that for many people, community is based more on relationships than territory. One research team (Lee & Campbell, 1999) did find, however, that barriers of segregation and discrimination make neighborhood relationships more important for Blacks than for Whites. They found that Blacks have more intimate and long-standing ties with neighbors than Whites do in similar neighborhoods, and they engage in more frequent contact with neighbors. Similarly, it would seem that the network of relationships built in Filipina gathering places in Rome is highly important to the Filipinas, who face much segregation and anti-immigrant discrimination.

Critical Thinking Questions 13.2

If we put a camera in your hands, what story would you tell about your territorial community? What images would you capture, and what meaning would you make of those images? Would you classify your territorial community as gemeinschaft or gesellschaft? What are the communities of which you are a part? Think of the community most meaningful to you and list five words that describe the culture of that community. How would you describe the horizontal and vertical linkages of that community?

Social Capital Approach

When the Filipinas in Rome talk about solidarity in their migrant community, they are talking about the quality of the connections community members make with each other and the commitment they feel to one another. They are thinking about community as a social bond that unifies people. Similarly, when the Filipinas in Los Angeles talk about the lack of camaraderie in the Los Angeles Filipino community, they are talking about a lack of a social bond in the community.

In the midst of globalization, it is not unusual to hear both the general public and social scientists lamenting the weakening of community bonds and talking longingly about searching for community, strengthening community, or building a sense of community. These concerns have been consistently voiced in public opinion polls for some time in the United States, and they were the subject of Robert Putnam's (2000) best-selling book *Bowling Alone: The Collapse and Revival of American Community*. To be sure, concerns about the waxing and waning of community are not new, but the nature of those concerns has shifted over time. In the past decade or so, community psychologists and community sociologists have turned to the concept of social capital to conceptualize this social bond aspect of community.

In simplest terms, *social capital* is community cohesion, which is thought to be based in dense social networks, high levels of civic engagement, a sense of solidarity and equality among members, and norms of reciprocity and trustworthiness (see Kay, 2006; Putnam, 1993). In *Bowling Alone*, Putnam (2000) argues that for the first two thirds of the 20th century, social capital was expanding in the United States, but that tide reversed in the final decades of the century. He calls for reconnection and revitalization of networks, civic engagement, solidarity and equality, and reciprocity and trustworthiness. Putnam (2000) presents much empirical evidence to build a powerful argument for the loss of community in the United States.

While respecting his empirical analysis, network researchers are critical of Putnam's conceptual analysis. They argue that community has been changing rather than declining and that, while people in the United States may not be participating in group-based community activities to the same extent as in the past, their networks remain large and strong (Boase et al., 2006). They see no inherent disadvantage to the more fragmented nature of contemporary social networks, while Putnam (2000) suggests that it takes dense integrated networks that exist over time to build cohesion and trust. The work of Robert Sampson and colleagues (see Sampson, 2003; Sampson, Morenoff, & Earls, 1999) seems to support and expand this concern of Putnam's. They have proposed a theory of **collective efficacy**, which is "the capacity of community residents to achieve social control over the environment and to engage in collective action for the common good" (Sampson, 2003, p. S56). Collective efficacy involves a working trust, a shared belief in the neighborhood's ability for action, and a shared willingness to intervene to gain social control. Research indicates that as collective efficacy in a neighborhood decreases, a host of individual and social ills increase (Odgers et al., 2009; Sampson, 2003). It is important to note, however, that Sampson and colleagues (1999) have found that the spatial dynamics and quality of the physical environment of the neighborhood have an impact on collective efficacy. The Filipinos in Rome showed a great deal of collective efficacy when they developed their shopping bazaar by the Tiber River after the city authorities challenged their right to congregate in public spaces.

This idea of a social bond among community members is what Seymour Sarason (1974) had in mind when he declared the enhancement of a *psychological sense of community* (PSOC) as the mission of community psychology. We looked earlier at Sarason's definition of sense of community (see Exhibit 13.1). Community psychologists David McMillan and David Chavis (McMillan, 1996; McMillan & Chavis, 1986) turned to the literature on group cohesiveness to understand how to enhance the social bonds of community. They presented a theory of PSOC that identified four essential elements.

1. *Membership* is a sense of belonging, of being part of a collective, something bigger than oneself. Reading *Tinig Filipino* provides the Filipina domestic workers with this sense of belonging to something bigger than themselves. Membership is based on boundaries, emotional safety, personal investment, and a common symbol system. Boundaries clarify who is in and who is out, and they protect against threat. Personal investment in a community is enhanced when we feel that we have worked for membership. Common symbols facilitate integration of the community, in part by intentionally creating social distance between members and nonmembers. However, communities built on exclusion, rather than inclusion, contribute to the fragmentation of social life.

2. *Influence* is bidirectional. On the one hand, members are more attracted to a community where they have some sense of control and influence. On the other hand, to be cohesive, a community has to be able to exert influence over members. In this way, behavioral conformity comes from the need to belong, and conformity promotes cohesiveness. The Filipinas in Rome have established a clear set of expectations that members engage in mutual assistance; this expectation promotes a sense of belonging, and conformity to it promotes cohesiveness.

> Exchange and choice perspective

3. *Integration and fulfillment of needs* refers to individual reinforcement or reward for membership. The community must be rewarding to its members, but McMillan and Chavis (1986) conclude that "a strong community is able to fit people together so that people meet others' needs while they meet their own" (p. 13). Both in Rome and in Los Angeles, the Filipina domestic workers share information about jobs and job-related problems. In Rome, solidarity compels the women to support each other's day-off business ventures, such as working as vendors. There is a mutual understanding that "I will buy your wares if you buy

> Social behavioral perspective

mine." However, on occasion, some workers take advantage of others and violate the norm of integration and mutual meeting of needs.

4. *Shared emotional connection* is based on a shared history and identification with the community. It is enhanced when members are provided with "positive ways to interact, important events to share and ways to resolve them positively, opportunities to honor members, opportunities to invest in the community, and opportunities to experience a spiritual bond among members" (McMillan & Chavis, 1986, p. 14). The Filipinas in Rome and Los Angeles have found positive ways to interact with each other, and they feel camaraderie in their shared migrant experience. When they read the stories in *Tinig Filipino*, they also feel a shared emotional connection to Filipina domestic workers around the world.

Humanistic perspective

On the basis of this definition of PSOC, McMillan and Chavis (1986) developed a 12-item Sense of Community Index (SCI) that has been used extensively for research. PSOC is one of the most widely studied concepts in community psychology (Townley, Kloos, Green, & Franco, 2011). Sense of community has been found to be related to positive health behaviors, positive mental health, and citizen participation. Recently, researchers have suggested some need to make minor revisions to the SCI (Obst & White, 2004). Some research teams caution that the SCI was developed and validated in Western societies and may not be a good fit for the meaning of community for non-Western people, particularly those from collectivist societies (Mak, Cheung, & Law, 2009; Xu, Perkins, & Chow, 2010). Measures of sense of community have been developed for specific cultural groups, including gay men (Proescholdbell, Roosa, & Nemeroff, 2006), Italians (Prezza & Costantini, 1998), and individuals with serious mental illness (Townley & Kloos, 2011).

Photos 13.3a and 13.3b Two contrasting communities: (*top*) a tribal community in Ethiopia and (*bottom*) a member of the Second Life (online) community.

© iStockphoto.com/David Kerkhoff; © Robin Utrecht/AFP/Getty Images

An Australian research team (Obst et al., 2002a, 2002b) has used McMillan and Chavis's theory of PSOC to compare PSOC in territorial and relational communities. More specifically, the researchers asked 359 science fiction aficionados attending a World Science Fiction Convention to complete questionnaires rating PSOC both for their fandom community and for their territorial community. Research participants reported significantly higher levels of PSOC in their fandom communities than in their territorial communities. They also found that although the ratings on all dimensions of McMillan and Chavis's four theorized dimensions of PSOC were higher in the fandom communities than in the geographical communities, the dimensions received essentially the same rank ordering in both communities. The researchers also suggest that a fifth dimension, *conscious identification* with the community, should be added to McMillan and Chavis's theory of PSOC. They found this cognitive identification to be an important component of PSOC. Other researchers have found that social bonding and intimacy take time to mature in computer-mediated communication (Harrison & Thomas, 2009).

In a theoretical turn particularly useful for considering the situations of the Filipina migrants in Rome and Los Angeles, some community psychologists have introduced the concept of **multiple psychological senses of community (MPSOC)**. They note that people live in multiple territorial and relational communities, such as neighborhood, city, workplace, university, religious group, sports league, SNS, and so on, and have multiple senses of community representing each of these communities (Brodsky, 2009). This conceptualization helps us to think about the different senses of community experienced by the Filipina migrant workers with their sending communities, their receiving communities, and their global communities. Beard and Sarmiento (2010) chronicle how immigrants from Oaxaca, Mexico, to Southern California establish hometown associations to maintain a positive sense of community in both their sending community and their receiving community. The associations in Southern California hold social and cultural events, such as fiestas and danzas, to fund-raise for community-planning projects back in their hometowns in Oaxaca.

In recent years, the social work literature has paid attention to the issue of community building. This literature often focuses broadly on community revitalization, in terms of the economic and physical, as well as the social relationship dimensions of communities. The literature on youth leadership development is particularly noteworthy for its attention to building a sense of community among youth in neighborhoods. Recent social work literature on community youth development has returned to its settlement house roots, recommending the use of arts, humanities, and sports to build a sense of community, as well as to empower youth and help them build skills (Delgado & Staples, 2013; Tilton, 2009).

Social capital theorists acknowledge that social capital can be used for antisocial as well as prosocial purposes. Think of the elements of social capital and sense of community and you will have to agree

| Conflict perspective |

that they apply equally well to the Ku Klux Klan (KKK) and a neighborhood committee formed to welcome the influx of new immigrants. The literature on networks often suggests that birds of a feather flock together. It is quite possible, as the KKK example demonstrates, that groups can be socially cohesive and yet quite exclusionary, distrustful, and hostile (even violently so) to outsiders. That has led Putnam (2000) and others (Townley et al., 2011) to accede the dark side of social capital. Townley et al. (2011) note that both sense of community and the positive value of diversity are core values in community psychology, and these two values can conflict in community life. Fisher and Karger (1997) have made a similar observation about social work. Putnam (2000) notes that in the same time period that social capital was declining in the United States, social tolerance was growing. On another dark note, Australian public health educator Fran Baum (1999) states a fear that has also been presented by European community psychologists (see Riera, 2005):

Social capital may come to be seen as a short-hand way of putting responsibility on communities that do not have the economic, educational or other resources to generate social capital. Networks, trust and cooperation are not substitutes for housing, jobs, incomes and education even though they might play a role in helping people gain access to them. (p. 176)

We would suggest that the dark side of social capital calls for a conflict approach to understanding community.

Conflict Approach

Conflict perspective
The Filipina domestic workers in Rome and Los Angeles have confronted anti-immigrant sentiment. They often feel exploited by their privileged employers. They feel shut out of all sectors of the labor market except for low-status domestic work. In Los Angeles, they have felt marginalized by and alienated from middle-class Filipinos. Back in the Philippines, many were abused or abandoned by their husbands. They blame the Philippine government for providing so little security to its residents, but they seldom blame the inequities of economic globalization for their limited options. Conflict theory's emphasis on dissension, power, and exploitation adds another dimension to our understanding of their story.

Writing about how European approaches to community psychology differ from U.S. community psychology, Francescato and Tomai (2001) suggest that European theorizing is much more in the conflict tradition than U.S. theorizing. They propose that, particularly in continental Europe (Germany, Italy, Spain, and Portugal), the work of community psychologists shows that they "do not believe in the myth of the self-made man" (p. 372) that undergirds much of the work in the United States. They further suggest that the longer historical view in Europe leads to more critical emphases in European theory on social and economic inequalities, the historical interpretations that have been presented by power elites to legitimize existing social hierarchies, and the historical collective struggles by which groups of people have become empowered. Indeed, they report that European textbooks on community psychology typically devote chapters to historical social struggles that have led to greater empowerment for specific groups. Francescato and Tomai (2001) argue that Putnam's findings of declining social capital in the United States can be explained by U.S. fascination with neoliberal economics and individual success, which has led to increasing inequality. They insist that social capital cannot exist at the community level without state policy that supports it. In their view, community practice should involve strategies that focus on unequal power distribution and stimulate community participants to challenge community narratives that legitimize the status quo.

Writing from the United Kingdom, Isabelle Fremeaux (2005) criticizes the social capital approach on several fronts. She argues that it typically romanticizes community and fails to recognize the internal coercion and divisions often at play in communities. Failure to recognize the power politics operating in communities does damage to the least powerful members. And, much like Francescato and Tomai, she criticizes Putnam and other social capital theorists for neglecting to analyze the impact of the macro political and economic contexts on local networks. The story of the Filipinas in Rome and Los Angeles is an excellent example of the influence of macro political and economic contexts on social networks among migrant domestic workers.

Other European social scientists argue that community is "as much about struggle as it is about unity" (Brent, 1997, p. 83). Community workers are often faced with heterogeneous settings with diverse opinions, attitudes, and emotional attachments (Dixon, Dogan, & Sanderson, 2005). Carles Riera (2005), community development specialist from Spain, argues that managing the conflicts in such diversity should be the focus of community theorists and practitioners. Riera notes that European society, like U.S. society, is becoming more and more multicultural, caused by migrations from non-European countries as well as by the loosening of the borders of the European Union. Migrating groups often have strong internal cohesion, but the receiving communities are often fragmented. The task for community workers is to work for both inclusion and equality of opportunities in a framework of coexistence.

Riera (2005) describes a model of practice developed in Barcelona, Spain, called the Intercultural Mediation Programme. The program is three-pronged: It strives (1) to facilitate the resolution of intercultural community conflicts that occur in public spaces, (2) to facilitate the resolution of intercultural conflict situations among neighbors living in the same buildings, and (3) to provide information and advice to service professionals struggling with intercultural conflicts. The program is carried out by community mediator teams who use both linguistic and sociocultural interpreters. Perhaps such mediation could have helped when the Filipinos in Rome were being harassed to stop congregating in public spaces, and it might also be helpful to bridge divisions in the Los Angeles Filipino community.

Conflict theory is not new to U.S. social workers and social scientists, but its popularity has waxed and waned over time. Like European theorists, Robert Fisher and Eric Shragge (2000) argue that the worldwide spread of neoliberal faith in the free market (see discussion in Chapter 9) has "dulled the political edge" of community social workers (p. 1). They argue for renewed commitment to a form of community social work willing to build opposition and use a range of confrontational tactics to challenge privilege and oppression. Given economic globalization, Fisher and Shragge (2000) recommend that effective community organizing in the current era will need to be tied to a global social movement (social movements are the topic of Chapter 14). To work effectively with community conflict, social workers must be able to analyze the structure of community power and influence (Martinez-Brawley, 2000). They must understand who controls which types of resources and how power brokers are related to one another. That means understanding the power held internally in the community as well as the power that resides external to the community. This type of analysis allows social workers to understand both the possibilities and limits of community empowerment. Emilia Martinez-Brawley (2000) suggests that social workers working in small communities should keep in mind that memories are usually long in such places, and conflictual relationships established on one issue may have an impact on future issues. Historical understanding is important.

Contemporary life also calls for the type of mediation programs recommended by Riera (2005). In many areas of life, from race relations to family relations, the mediator role is becoming more prominent for social workers. We will have to become more comfortable with conflict if we are to take leadership roles in healing these social fractures. In recent years, some rural communities have faced sudden influxes of refugees from a particular trouble spot in the world. Some of these communities have responded in exclusionary and punitive ways, while others have responded in inclusive and collaborative ways. It is more than likely that communities in the United States and other affluent countries will continue to face such influxes, and social workers should be able to assist communities in managing such change. One suggestion is that restorative justice programs similar to the ones used in criminal justice could be used to heal friction and conflict within neighborhoods (Verity & King, 2007). Restorative justice gatherings would allow storytelling and dialogue about social fractures and allow communities to move toward a more just future. This suggestion is consistent with Riera's Intercultural Mediation Programme.

> ### Critical Thinking Questions 13.3
>
> Think of two different communities of which you are a part. Is social cohesion or social conflict more prominent in each of them? Explain. How diverse is each of them? How well is diversity tolerated in each of them?

SOCIAL WORKERS AND COMMUNITIES: CONTEMPORARY ISSUES _____

As suggested in Chapter 9, modernization, capitalism, industrialization, urbanization, and globalization have great costs for society as well as benefits. The profession of social work was developed as one force to minimize the costs—a communal force to correct for extremes of individualism. In its efforts to promote the general social welfare, social work has always been involved with communities in some way. But, as suggested earlier, there is expanding interest in community among social workers around the world. The expanded interest in the United States has been nurtured by the Association for Community Organization & Social Administration (ACOSA), formed in 1987, and by the journal started by ACOSA, *Journal of Community Practice*. The 2005 publication of *The Handbook of Community Practice* (Weil, 2005) was a major advance in knowledge building for community social work practice, and the second edition (Weil, Reisch, & Ohmer, 2013b) continues to elevate the social work discussion about community practice.

The nature of social work's relationships with communities has changed over time, however, and there are long-standing disagreements about appropriate roles for social workers in communities. Depending on the preferred community model or perspective, social workers can play a number of different roles in the community, such as guide, facilitator, expert, therapist, organizer, administrator, activist, broker, or educator. Here, we summarize the issues involved in four of these points of disagreement.

Community as Context for Practice Versus Target of Practice

Social workers who view community as a context for practice focus on working with individuals and families, although they recognize the ways in which communities provide opportunities and barriers for client behaviors and agency responses. They are most likely to enact the therapist role but may also engage in individual or family education. In contrast, social workers who view community as a target of practice focus on enhancing the health of the community. They are most likely to enact the organizer, activist, broker, and educator roles.

There seems to be a growing consensus that social work needs to recognize community as both context and target of practice (Chaskin, 2013; Weil et al., 2013a). During the 1990s, there was a reemergence of the idea of comprehensive multifocused community interventions (Mulroy, Nelson, & Gour, 2005). More recent initiatives to revitalize impoverished neighborhoods have combined resource development and individual asset building with efforts to strengthen sense of community (Padilla & Sherraden, 2005). Community agencies are working to help individual families and at the same time to help in building strong and caring communities. For example, the Wellbriety Movement in Native American communities in the United States is focusing on recovery from alcohol and other addictions at both the individual and community level (Coyhis & Simonelli, 2005). They use the metaphor of a "healing forest" to suggest that youth can't get well in an unhealthy community. A similar continuum of practice has been developed for community building with and care of older adults (Mulroy et al., 2005).

Even with a combined, or comprehensive, community practice model, questions still arise about when to intervene with individuals and families and when to focus on larger collectivities and groups. Many projects focus almost exclusively on capacity building at the community level. For example, around the world, communities are engaging in community capacity-building projects as a strategy to prevent family violence in distressed neighborhoods (see Chan, Lam, & Cheng, 2009). They attempt to develop a sense of community, stimulate a sense of mutual responsibility, activate a process of communal problem solving, and improve access to resources. In a similar vein, the asset-building movement focuses on creating asset-rich communities for children and youth. These projects seek to engage adults in building supportive relationships with neighborhood children and youth, mobilize youth to become active participants in community life, and stimulate resource development and collaborative problem solving (see Green & Haines, 2012). On the other hand, the majority of social work interventions continue to occur at the individual and family level, with far too little attention to the context of individual and family lives.

In a much-cited work, Harry Specht and Mark Courtney (1994) called for putting the "social" back in social work with a "community-based system of social care" and elimination of the psychotherapeutic role. We would not recommend that the psychotherapeutic role be eliminated from social work's repertoire, but social workers may have come to rely too heavily on this role. They may be using it for problems for which it is neither efficient nor effective. An integrated community practice should avoid an overreliance on one-to-one and family sessions, opting, where appropriate, for collective and group formats. Two promising models for this are family group conferencing and peacemaking circles used in child protection and youth services (see Boyes-Watson, 2005; Connolly, 2006).

Agency Orientation Versus Social Action

Community social work practice has roots in a **social action model** of community organization, which was developed by leaders of the settlement house movement. This model of community practice is political, emphasizing social reform and challenge of structural inequalities. But by the 1930s, this social action model had been replaced by an **agency-based model**, which promoted social agencies and the services they provided (Fisher & Karger, 1997). This model of community practice is nonpolitical and puts little or no emphasis on social change. It is based on the assumption that the best way to strengthen communities is to provide social services. Proponents of the agency-based model of community organizing often focus on coordination of services across agencies (see Mizrahi, Rosenthal, & Ivery, 2013).

Saul Alinsky (1971), founder of one of the best-known community organizing training centers, was critical of the agency-based model of community social work. He did not think social justice was ensured by providing social services. A contemporary African social worker, Tlamelo Mmatli (2008), makes a similar argument. Mmatli argues that the main problems facing people in Africa are "unemployment, poverty, inequality, illiteracy, homelessness, child streetism, ill-health, HIV/AIDS, abuse of human right and civil liberties, civil conflicts and official corruption" (p. 297). He further argues that these problems require political advocacy, not social services.

This suggestion by Mmatli is consistent with the focus on *policy practice* as a social work intervention by some U.S. social workers over the past 3 decades (Jansson, Heidemann, McCroskey, & Fertig, 2013). Policy practice includes efforts to influence legislation, participation in political campaigns, efforts to change agency policies, or other activities related to policy reform. Policy practitioners work in many arenas around the world, including "national, state, and local legislatures; public agencies; public administrative or oversight agencies . . . ; nongovernmental agencies; think tanks"; and special boards or commissions (Jansson et al., 2013, p. 404). They must be able to analyze, develop, and use power; manage conflict; develop proposals; make effective presentations; work collaboratively with multidisciplinary task groups; and collect and analyze data.

We suggest that agency-based provision of social services, and interagency coordination of services, often do contribute to the well-being of communities. We need social workers who will advocate for the retention of threatened services as well as the development of new services, but we also need good program evaluation to guide those advocacy efforts. We also agree with DeFilippis, Fisher, and Shragge (2009) that although community-based nonprofit organizations are growing in number and influence, too many focus narrowly on service delivery and have lost sight of social and economic justice. DeFilippis et al. (2009) argue that it is possible to engage in both service provision and social action and provide examples of community organizations doing this. An integrated approach to community social work practice enhances community-based services, builds a sense of community, and advocates for social reform.

Critical Thinking Questions 13.4

When you decided to be a social worker, how did you think about the role of community in social work practice? Did you think of community as context of practice, target of practice, or neither? How do you think about the role of community in social work practice now? If this has changed over time, what led to that change? Which do you think is a better orientation for social work practice: an agency orientation or a social action orientation? Explain.

Conflict Model of Practice Versus Collaborative Model

Conflict perspective

Over the years, social work has taken different positions on the question of whether social workers should lean toward conflict or collaboration, ebbing and flowing in its "tradition of nagging the conscience of America" (Fisher & Karger, 1997, p. 188). In liberal times, social work has been more willing to embrace conflict approaches; in conservative times, more collaborative approaches have been preferred (Fisher, 2005). In the early 1900s, social work reformers used social surveys to expose exploitive industries and disseminated the results widely in newspapers and magazines (Fisher & Karger, 1997). In the current era of transnational corporations and high transnational mobility, these methods might be revisited by contemporary social workers. Today, however, as suggested, the trend is away from challenging the establishment and toward creating partnerships among community groups, government agencies, and corporations (DeFilippis et al., 2009; Fisher, 2005).

In his historical review of community practice, Robert Fisher (2005) argues that the global context of contemporary community practice is dominated by a conservative, corporate-oriented ethos. In this climate, the market dominates, issues are seen as private and not public, and people are becoming more isolated from each other. In such a climate, social action approaches both inside and outside social work have been viewed as inappropriate. Social workers depend on political and financial support from governmental and private philanthropies, which have, for the most part, a heavy investment in the status quo (Mmatli, 2008).

The contemporary tension between conflict and collaborative models of practice is exemplified by two articles that appeared in the *Journal of Community Practice* in 2000. Robert Fisher, a social work educator from the United States, and Eric Shragge, a social work educator from Canada, contrast social action and community building approaches to practice (Fisher & Shragge, 2000). *Social action* works for social change by organizing people to put pressure on governments or private organizations. It challenges social inequalities. **Community development** is based on an assumption of shared interests, rather than conflicting interests. It seeks to bring together diverse community interests for the betterment of the community as a whole, with attention to community building and an improved sense of community. Fisher and Shragge (2000) acknowledge that many community practitioners interweave social action and community development. They suggest, however, that the community development approach to community practice has become dominant. They lament this turn of events, arguing that we are in an era of growing inequality that requires more, not less, social action.

An article by Elizabeth Beck and Michael Eichler (2000) argues the other side of the coin. They propose consensus organizing, based in feminist theory, as a practice model for community building. *Consensus organizing* has four basic assumptions:

1. Power does not have to be redistributed; it can be grown.

2. Human behavior is motivated by mutual self-interest, not just individual self-interest.

3. People are basically good, and power holders will make decisions that improve community well-being when given the opportunity.

4. The wealthy and the poor, the powerful and the powerless can be knit together rather than become adversaries.

Like Fisher and Shragge (2000), Beck and Eichler (2000) suggest that both social action and community development are needed, but they argue for an emphasis on community work that strengthens relationships. They claim that social action calls for a redistribution of power, but consensus organizing does not assert that redistribution of power is necessary to end oppression. Indeed, Beck and Eichler (2000) argue that conflict tactics often don't reach the goal of redistribution of power anyway.

Contemporary social trends call for a contemporary style of community practice that draws on both conflict and collaborative models (Ohmer & Brooks, 2013). Community social workers need skills for exposing and challenging social injustice as well as for resolving conflict and building coalitions. The choice of tactics will depend on the specific circumstance. Michael Reisch (2013) astutely observes that in conservative times, social workers can use opportunities to work in collaborative, community-based projects to help create a radical vision of justice and fairness.

Some situations call for community social workers to elevate community conflict for the purpose of challenging exploitation and oppression. Throughout this book, we emphasize the need for social workers to take a critical perspective that recognizes power and oppression as important factors in the negotiation of social life. A critical perspective also calls for social workers to challenge existing patterns of domination and oppression. With the trend toward devolution of government responsibilities to the local level, the local territorial community becomes increasingly important to these efforts. Social work research can identify and expose local patterns of exploitation. Community social workers can use consciousness-raising tactics to help oppressed groups think critically about their situations. They can use a variety of advocacy skills to make appeals for the rights and needs of oppressed groups. Many contemporary social critics "see grassroots community organizations as potentially the most effective progressive balance to the elite domination" (Fisher & Karger, 1997, p. 130).

Other situations call for community social workers to resolve community conflicts. Robert Fisher and Howard Karger (1997) remind us that "public life is about difference, and about learning to create a society by interacting with others who have different opinions and experiences" (p. 26). This notion seems to be left out of most of the community psychology literature on PSOC (Townley et al., 2011). Social work's professional organizations have taken a position that values diversity. But they should go beyond that position and value the conflict that accompanies diversity. Communities often need help in negotiating their differences. Social workers can help to develop a civil discourse on controversial issues, a discourse that includes the voices of people previously marginalized and excluded. Community social workers can use a variety of conflict resolution skills to help different community groups understand and respect each other's experiences and to engage in respectful and effective problem-solving activities.

There is considerable agreement among social work scholars that social workers should focus on helping to develop broad issues that can unite diverse groups in social reform efforts; one example of such issues is financial security in a global economy. Recently, actions of the antiglobalization movement have suggested that a spark of resistance is alive for this issue. But these efforts are less likely to succeed if they do not build greater solidarity between poor and middle-class people, something very much lacking even among immigrant groups like the Filipinas in Los Angeles. Coalitions across cultural groups are also increasingly desirable. For example, domestic workers from different ethnic backgrounds might benefit from working collaboratively rather than competitively. The social work literature is beginning to grapple with the complexities of coalition building (see Mizrahi et al., 2013).

Expert Versus Partner in the Social Change Process

Exchange and choice perspective

The traditional **social planning model** of community social work is based on the premise that the complexities of modern social problems require expert planners schooled in a rational planning model (Sager & Weil, 2013). In this model, the community power structure is the author of social change efforts. This is often referred to as a top-down approach to social change.

Community-building models of community social work take a different view: Community practice should support and enhance the ability of community members to identify their own community's needs, assets, and solutions to problems. These approaches are commonly called participatory community planning. Social workers work in partnership with community members and groups and remain open to learning from the community (Gamble, 2013). This approach is often referred to as a bottom-up approach to social change.

Many local community development corporations (CDCs) are experimenting with ways of building partnerships with community members for community revitalization. When one community intervention team encountered difficulties in getting community residents to focus on possibilities rather than problems, they borrowed the miracle question from solution-focused therapy:

> Imagine you've gone to sleep and while you're sleeping, you have a dream. And in your dream, Westlane becomes exactly the way you'd like to see it. . . . Keeping your eyes closed: What do you see that lets you know the goal has been accomplished, that your dream

has become a reality. (Hollingsworth, Allen-Meares, Shanks, & Gant, 2009, p. 334)

Laura Ross and Mardia Coleman (2000) provide one model for community partnerships, a model they call urban community action planning (UCAP). They have adapted this approach from participatory rural appraisal (PRA), a grassroots approach used in rural areas of Africa, Latin America, and Asia. The PRA model is based on three assumptions:

1. *Local knowledge.* Community members have knowledge about local problems, but they need help to organize it.

2. *Local resources.* Community members have resources, but these resources need to be mobilized.

3. *Outside help.* Outside resources are available, but they need to be matched to community-identified priorities.

Efforts at community building often rely heavily on indigenous leaders, or leaders who are indigenous to the targeted community, to facilitate meaningful community participation. These efforts do not always run smoothly. Community practitioners have had little guidance on how to identify indigenous leaders and how to prepare them to lead. Recent literature has begun to address this important issue, noting both aids and barriers to effective indigenous leadership (Gray, Coates, & Yellow Bird, 2010).

A traditional social planning model is appropriate for problems requiring specialized technical knowledge. Community members are the experts, however, about community needs and assets. They also have the capacity to be active partners in identifying solutions to community problems. The Generations of Hope intergenerational communities project, which forms intentional communities where older adults serve as resources to foster and adoptive families, is an example of a community intervention that makes a distinction between tasks for which the professional is the expert and tasks for which community members are the experts

(Eheart, Hopping, Power, Mitchell, & Racine, 2009). For example, staff are seen as the experts about who should live in the community, how to secure and manage financial resources and relationships with the external environment, and providing counseling and therapeutic support. But members of the community are considered to be the experts on the needs of families, and older adults in the community are the primary resources for children and families.

Critical Thinking Questions 13.5

What intercultural conflicts have you seen in or around your local territorial community or in your online community? What social justice issues are involved in those conflicts? What approaches to community practice do you think could be useful in helping to manage these conflicts?

Implications for Social Work Practice

The preceding discussion of community has many implications for social work practice:

- Be informed about the communities you serve; learn about their readiness to change, their spatial arrangements (for territorial communities), their cultures, their patterns of internal and external relationships, their social capital, and their conflicts.
- Avoid overreliance on individual and family sessions; make use of small- and large-group formats where appropriate.
- When working with individuals and families, assess their opportunities to be supported by and to make contributions to the community and assess the limits imposed by their territorial and relational communities.
- Recognize the central role of territorial community in the lives of many young persons and their caregivers, older adults, and poor families.
- If you are a social work planner or administrator, become familiar with computer-based geographical information systems for mapping social data.
- Where appropriate, strengthen interaction within the community (horizontal linkages) to build a sense of community and maximize the use of internal resources. Strengthen intercommunity interactions (vertical linkages) to ensure there are adequate resources to meet the community's needs.
- Where appropriate, advocate for the retention of threatened social services, the coordination of existing services, and the development of new services.
- Where appropriate, collaborate with others to challenge exploitation and oppression in communities. Use consciousness-raising tactics to help oppressed groups understand their situations.
- Where appropriate, assist communities to negotiate differences and resolve conflicts.
- Where appropriate, assist in the development of coalitions to improve the resource base for community problem solving.
- Involve community members in identification of community strengths and community problems, in goal setting, and in intervention activities.
- When working with impoverished communities, work with other individuals and organizations, both inside and outside these communities, to develop comprehensive, multidimensional, integrated strategies.

Key Terms

agency-based model
bonding social capital

bridging social capital
collective efficacy

community
community development

gemeinschaft
geographic information system
   (GIS)
gesellschaft
horizontal linkage
mass society

multiple psychological senses of
   community (MPSOC)
network
networked individualism
personal community
relational community

sense of community
social action model
social planning model
territorial community
vertical linkage

Active Learning

1. You have read about two communities with geographical properties, one based in Rome and one based in Los Angeles. Now think about your own geographic community. Compare and contrast it with the communities of Filipina domestic workers in Rome and in Los Angeles according to the following characteristics:

   - Sense of community
   - Physical environment
   - Horizontal and vertical linkages

2. One research team has found that the majority of our ties to other people are nonterritorial, but two thirds of our actual interactions are local, in the neighborhood or work setting. To test this idea, for one day keep a record of all contacts you have with other people and the time spent in such contacts—face-to-face contacts as well as telephone and electronic contacts. What percentage of your contacts occurs in your neighborhood, at work, or at school?

3. Visit a neighborhood house or center, a YMCA or YWCA, or another community action organization in your town or city. Interview the director or another staff member about the mission of the organization, asking him or her to address the following questions:

   - Is the focus on working with individuals and families or on enhancing the health of the community?
   - Is the focus of the work political, emphasizing social reform and challenge of structural inequalities, or is it on providing and coordinating services?
   - Are the methods used confrontational ("challenging the establishment") or collaborative ("creating partnerships")?
   - How involved are community members in planning and carrying out the change activities of the organization?

Web Resources

The Annie E. Casey Foundation: www.aecf.org

Site maintained by the Annie E. Casey Foundation, a grant-making organization that works to build better futures for disadvantaged children and their families, contains a description of initiatives and projects and publications.

Association for Community Organization & Social Administration (ACOSA): www.acosa.org

Site includes recent publications, recent grants, regional news, and initiatives.

National Community Action Foundation (NCAF): www.ncaf.org

Site maintained by NCAF, an advocacy group for community action agencies, contains news, events, and current issues.

National People's Action (NPA): www.npa-us .org

Site maintained by NPA, an advocacy organization that helps neighborhood people take on corporate America and political institutions, contains news and information about campaigns.

Social Psychology Network: Community Psychology: www.socialpsychology.org

This online guide to community psychology maintained by Scott Plous at Wesleyan University contains links to sites covering a wide range of community psychology issues.

United Neighborhood Houses of New York: www.unhny.org

Site maintained by United Neighborhood Houses of New York, a federation of 38 settlement houses in New York City, includes information about the settlement house movement, current activities of settlement houses in the United States, and job vacancies.

Student Study Site

$SAGE edge™

Sharpen your skills with SAGE edge at **edge.sagepub.com/hutchisonpe5e**

SAGE edge for students provides a personalized approach to help you accomplish your coursework goals in an easy-to-use learning environment.

CHAPTER 14

Social Movements

Elizabeth D. Hutchison

Chapter Outline

Key Ideas

As you read this chapter, take note of these central ideas:

1. Social movements are formed when people feel that one or more social institutions are unjust and need to be changed.

2. The profession of social work has its origins in the confluence of two social movements: the charity organization society movement and the settlement house movement.

3. Three theoretical perspectives on social movements have emerged in the past 2 decades: the political opportunities perspective, the mobilizing structures perspective, and the cultural framing perspective. None of these perspectives taken individually is sufficient for understanding social movements, but taken together, they provide a multidimensional understanding. Dissatisfaction with these three perspectives is leading to emerging theories of social movements.

4. Social movements are neither completely successful nor completely unsuccessful.

5. Recently, there has been a rise in transnational social movement organizations (TSMOs).

6. Contemporary social work, like historical social work, must manage a tension between professional services and social reform.

CASE STUDY

Fighting for a Living Wage

Greg Halpern was in his senior year at Harvard University in 1998 when Aaron Bartley, his labor activist room-mate and childhood friend, "dragged" him to a meeting of the Harvard Living Wage Campaign (Terkel, 2003). Greg remembers that he was in the lunch line a few days later when a friend made a joke about how bad the food was. Greg laughed, and then he looked up and exchanged glances with one of the young women working behind the lunch counter. He saw her anger and hurt. He was deeply embarrassed and realized that most Harvard students had never been taught about the people who clean the bathrooms, serve the food, or clean the classrooms. Greg became active in the living wage campaign at Harvard, attending weekly rallies and sending letters to the university president, calling for the custodians, security guards, and food service workers at Harvard to be paid a living wage. In March 1999, the campaign presented the university president with the "Worst Employer in Boston" award while he was addressing a group of high school students. At graduation, some students chartered an airplane to pull a sign behind it that read, "Harvard needs a living wage" (Tanner, 2002).

That same spring, in his final year at Harvard, Greg Halpern did an independent study in which he interviewed and photographed university workers. He decided to blow the interviews up on 10-foot pages and stick them up in the public space provided for students, so that other students could know the stories of the low-wage workers. Greg had never been an activist, but he was dismayed at what he was hearing from workers, and he remained active in the Harvard Living Wage Campaign after he graduated. The campaign had been holding rallies at Harvard for 3 years, but nothing was happening. During the spring of 2001, 2 years after Greg graduated from Harvard, there was growing interest among the members of the Harvard Living Wage Campaign to engage in a sit-in. As they discussed this option, Greg remembered the custodian he had interviewed 2 years earlier. Bill Brook, who cleaned the room in which they were meeting, was 65 years old, worked two full-time jobs, and slept 4 hours per night (Terkel, 2003).

Greg became one of the leaders of the Harvard Living Wage Campaign sit-in strike that occupied Massachusetts Hall, the president's building, for 21 days, demanding that the university raise the wages for 1,400 employees who were making less than a living wage. Throughout the strike, the students, who had never participated in such an event before, kept in touch with the media by cell phones and e-mail (sent and received on their laptops).

There were 50 students inside Massachusetts Hall and a growing group of students on the outside. Three hundred professors or more took out a full-page ad in the *Boston Globe* in support of the students. The dining hall workers and food workers began to deliver pizzas to the students on the inside, and many workers took the risk to wear buttons on the job that said "We Support the Living Wage Campaign." Every local labor union in Cambridge, Massachusetts endorsed the students, and national labor leaders came to speak. The AFL-CIO union sent one of its top lawyers to negotiate with the university administration. Several high-profile religious leaders made appearances to support the students. On the 15th day of the sit-in, the Cambridge mayor and city council, along with other sympathizers, marched from City Hall to Harvard Yard in support of the students. During the second week of the sit-in, 30 to 40 Harvard Divinity School students held a vigil, chanting, "Where's your horror? Where's your rage? Div School wants a living wage." On the last night of the sit-in, there was a rally of about 3,000 people outside Massachusetts Hall (Tanner, 2002; Terkel, 2003).

In the end, the Harvard administration agreed to negotiate higher wages with the unions. Higher wages were paid, but the students were not fully satisfied with the results of their campaign. Two of the student activists later coproduced an advocacy film based on the sit-in, *Occupation: The Harvard University Living Wage Sit-in*, narrated by Ben Affleck (Raza & Velez, 2002). The sit-in at Harvard was neither the beginning nor the end of the gathering living wage movement in the United States. The sit-in built on the momentum that had started in Baltimore, Maryland, in 1994, and it fueled new actions on other university campuses. It was one piece of a story of a rapidly growing social movement.

In 1993, religious groups in Baltimore were seeing an increase in use of soup kitchens and food pantries by the working poor (Quigley, 2001; Tanner, 2002). They were angry that private companies involved in the city's urban renewal projects were paying low wages in order to bid low to win contracts with the city. They took their concerns to Baltimoreans United in Leadership Development (BUILD), a coalition of 50 Baltimore churches that had been advocating for services and subsidies for Baltimore's poor residents since the 1980s (Snarr, 2007). BUILD decided to join forces with the American Federation of State, County, and Municipal Employees (AFSCME)

(Continued)

and low-wage service workers to create a local campaign to develop a law that would require businesses that had contracts with the city to pay their workers a "living wage," a pay rate that would lift a family of four over the federal poverty level. At the time, the federal minimum wage was $4.25 an hour, a wage that could not lift a family out of poverty. The living wage law was enacted in July 1996, requiring city contractors with municipal contracts over $5,000 to pay a minimum wage of $6.16 an hour in 1996, with increments to reach $7.70 an hour in 1999. The law is estimated to have affected 1,500 to 2,000 workers (Quigley, 2001; Tanner, 2002).

The BUILD coalition had no intention of sparking a national social movement, but their success helped to trigger a nationwide alliance of religious and labor groups that has come to be known as the living wage movement. Local grassroots coalitions of activists have used a variety of tactics, including lobbying, postcard campaigns, rallies, door knocking, leafleting, workshops, and sit-ins to achieve their goals in more than 120 localities. The policy solutions have varied from locality to locality, with some bolder than others, but all have established a wage above the federal minimum wage for some group of workers. Some of the local living wage ordinances, like the one in Baltimore, cover only municipal workers. Others have been more expansive in their approach, like the ones in San Francisco and San Jose that cover all workers, public and private (Roosevelt, 2013). The living wage movement has also helped to enact legislation at the state rather than local level. As of February 2014, a total of 23 states plus the District of Columbia have enacted minimum wage laws that set the minimum wage higher than the federal requirement (National Conference of State Legislatures, 2014b).

Each local coalition is different. In Alexandria, Virginia, the living wage campaign started with the Tenants' and Workers' Support Committee, which had formed in 1986 to fight evictions of residents in low-rent housing. They were eventually joined by seven religious congregations and 17 unions. In Los Angeles, the living wage campaign was orchestrated by the Los Angeles Alliance for a New Economy (LAANE), which was created by a coalition of the Hotel Employees and Restaurant Employees Union, Hispanic neighborhood groups, a tenant group, Communities for a Better Environment, and religious organizations (Bernstein, 2002).These campaigns benefited from much assistance from the Living Wage Resource Center established by the Association of Community Organizations for Reform Now (ACORN). ACORN developed a 225-page guide to assist local activists in organizing a successful living wage campaign, written by labor economist David Reynolds. ACORN, an organization that once had neighborhood chapters in more than 90 cities, organized national training conferences and also regularly dispatched staff to consult with local coalitions.

The living wage movement has drawn on stories of the impact of living wage ordinances on the lives of low-wage workers to ignite public support for new campaigns. Here are some of the stories told:

- A retail worker at the Los Angeles airport was able to drop one of her part-time jobs to enroll in a class to build career skills.
- A parking lot attendant in Alexandria, Virginia, was able to quit one of his three jobs to spend more time with his family.
- A security guard in Tucson, Arizona, could finally take care of some small car repairs and start a savings account.

In 2006, a documentary called *Waging a Living* (Weisberg, 2006), which chronicles the daily struggles of four low-wage workers, premiered on public television and became available for sale and rental.

Along the way, the living wage movement has benefited from the support of a number of organizations. The Economic Policy Institute developed a guide to living wage initiatives and their economic impacts on its website. The National Low Income Housing Coalition compiled a report that calculated the amount of money a household needs to afford a rental unit in specific localities. The Brennan Center for Justice, located at the New York University School of Law, provided assistance to design and implement living wage campaigns, including economic impact analysis, legislative drafting, and legal analysis and defense. Responsible Wealth, a national network of businesspeople, investors, and affluent citizens, developed a living wage covenant for businesses interested in economic fairness. The Political Economy Research Institute (PERI), at the University of Massachusetts at Amherst, collected a number of research reports on the effects of living wage laws.

One of the more promising developments in the living wage social movement was the entry of university and high school students into the movement. The Living Wage Action Coalition (LWAC), made up of university students and recent graduates who had participated in living wage campaigns around the country, was created in the summer of 2005. LWAC toured around colleges and universities in the United States, running workshops about strategies for successful living wage campaigns for low-wage workers on campus (Living Wage Action Coalition, n.d.).

The living wage movement started in the United States, but by 2001, it had crossed national lines to London, England, where it has spread to hospitals, finance companies, universities, art galleries, and hotels (Living Wage Foundation, 2014). In October 2009, Asia Floor Wage, a loose coalition of labor and other groups, was formed to propose a floor wage for garment workers in Asia. Activists in 11 European countries participated in events to demand that retailers pay a living wage to all garment workers in their supply chains; the events included leafleting, public debates, visiting corporate headquarters, and hosting film screenings. These events were organized by a coalition of activists involved in a "clean clothes campaign" (fighting for the rights of workers in the global garment industry) (Clean Clothes Campaign, 2009). In 2013, a coalition of community activists, faith-based organizations, and unions concerned about the growing gap between the rich and the poor in New Zealand began a campaign called Living Wage Aotearoa New Zealand (2014).

Back in the United States, 2014 has been marked by an energetic debate about growing income inequality and the plight of low-wage workers. Fast-food workers around the country demanded wages of $15 an hour. One small town in Washington state voted to set the wage floor at $15 an hour, instead of the $9 state minimum wage. President Obama recommended that the federal minimum wage be raised from $7.25 to $10.10 (Kelly, 2014). Minimum wage laws apply to all employers whereas living wage laws have typically applied only to employers in government-subsidized jobs. In December 2013, Liz Halloran, reporter for National Public Radio, noted that in the midst of rising agitation for increasing the minimum wage, the living wage movement hadn't been getting much attention lately. Paul Sonn of the National Employment Law Project (NELP) responded that living wage and minimum wage are part of the same policy movement to promote wage fairness (Halloran, 2013).

A DEFINITION OF SOCIAL MOVEMENTS

What happens when a group of people, like the many people involved in living wage campaigns, think that certain arrangements are unjust and need to be changed? Sometimes they work together to try to bring about the desired changes—not just for themselves but for a large group of people. These joint efforts are **social movements**—ongoing, large-scale, collective efforts to bring about (or resist) social change.

We can think of social movements as either proactive or reactive (Ballantine & Roberts, 2014). **Proactive social movements** seek to reform existing social arrangements and try out new ways of living together. The living wage, Occupy Wall Street, and marriage equality movements are examples of proactive social movements. **Reactive social movements**, on the other hand, seek to

Photo 14.1 Social movements can be categorized as proactive (trying out new ways of living and cooperating) or reactive (defending traditional values). The U.S. civil rights movement was an example of a proactive social movement.

© Bettmann/CORBIS

defend traditional values and social arrangements. Christian and Islamic fundamentalist and property rights movements are examples of reactive social movements. Both types of social movements are common today in the United States and across the world.

Mario Diani (della Porta & Diani, 2006) identifies the following properties that distinguish social movements from other social collectivities. They

- Are involved in conflictual relations with clearly identified opponents.
- Are linked by dense informal networks.
- Share a distinct collective identity. (p. 20)

It is protest that distinguishes social movements from other types of social networks, but a single episode of protest is not a social movement unless it is connected to a longer-lasting network of public action (Tilly & Wood, 2013).

SOCIAL MOVEMENTS AND THE HISTORY OF SOCIAL WORK

Like many of the world's religions, some nation-states, labor unions, the YMCA/YWCA, and the Boy Scouts and Girl Scouts, the profession of social work is generally considered to have its origin in social movements. More specifically, the social work profession developed out of the confluence of two social movements: the charity organization society movement and the settlement house movement. You have probably studied these social movements in some of your other courses, so they are not discussed in great detail here. But as social workers, we should recognize how intertwined the history of social work is with social movements.

Both the charity organization society movement and the settlement house movement emerged out of concern during the late 1800s about the ill effects of industrialization, including urban overcrowding and economic instability among low-paid workers. Both social movements developed in England and spread to the United States. But from the beginning, their orientations were very different.

The **charity organization society (COS) movement** developed because private charity organizations became overtaxed by the needs of poor people. Middle- and upper-class individuals were fearful that a coalition of unemployed people and low-paid workers would revolt and threaten the stability of established political and economic institutions. Leaders of the COS movement saw poverty as based in individual pathology and immorality and set the goal of coordinating charity giving to ensure that no duplication occurred. Volunteer "friendly visitors" were assigned to poor families to help them correct character flaws and develop strong moral fiber. Leaders of the COS movement believed in private, rather than public, charity. The provision of efficient and effective service was the primary agenda of the COS.

The **settlement house movement** was stimulated by the same social circumstances but was based on very different values and goals. Whereas COS leaders focused on individual pathology, leaders of the settlement house movement focused on environmental hazards. They developed settlement houses in urban neighborhoods where "settlers" lived together as "good neighbors" to poor families and were actively involved in research, service, and reform. The settlers supported labor activities, lobbied for safe and sanitary housing, provided space for local political groups, offered day care, and provided a variety of cultural and educational programs. They published the results of their research widely and used it to push for governmental reform. **Social reform**—the creation of more just social institutions—was the primary agenda of the settlement house movement.

Over time, workers from the two social movements began to interact at annual meetings of the National Conference of Charities and Corrections, and social work as an occupation took shape. With efforts to professionalize the occupation of social work and, later, to win acceptance for the public social welfare institution, the social reform agenda of the settlement house movement lost ground. Direct service became the focus—specifically, individual and family casework in health and welfare agencies and social work with groups in the settlement houses and YMCAs/YWCAs. This transition away from reform toward a service model is not an uncommon trajectory of social movements. However, almost a century later, social work continues to experience a tension between service and social reform.

Although social work emerged from social movements, it is now a profession, not a social movement. Some social workers work for social movement organizations, however, and the social work profession struggles with its relationship to a variety of social movements. For example, Chapter 13 discussed the tensions in community social work around issues of social action. With the profession's emphasis on social justice, we should understand how social movements emerge and become successful. That is why this chapter on social movements is included in this book and why the professional literature is beginning to make use of social movement theory and to call for greater social work involvement with social movements (see, e.g., Dudziak & Profitt, 2012; Reisch, 2008; Thompson, 2002).

Critical Thinking Questions 14.1

Have you participated in any social movement activities? If so, what were your reasons? If not, what have been the reasons? Are there particular historical social movements that you think have had a good impact on U.S. or global societies? Are there particular historical social movements that you think have had a detrimental impact on U.S. or global societies? Are there recent social movements you would like to know more about? If so, how might you go about learning about them?

PERSPECTIVES ON SOCIAL MOVEMENTS

Conflict perspective

Early social science literature on social movements was based on a relatively unified perspective, commonly called **strain theory**. According to this theory, social movements develop in response to some form of strain in society, when people's efforts to cope with stress become collective efforts. Different versions of strain theory focus on different types of social strains, such as strain due to rapid social change, social inequality, social isolation and lack of community, or conflicts in cultural beliefs (Buechler, 2011). Discussion in earlier chapters has built a case that each of these types of strain exists in the United States today.

Recent social science theory and research have been critical of social strain theory, however. Critics argue that strain is always present to some degree in all societies, but social movements do not always appear in response, and their intensity does not vary systematically with the level of strain (della Porta & Diani, 2006; Tilly & Wood, 2013). These critics suggest that social strain is a necessary but not sufficient condition to predict the development of a social movement. Any social movement theory must start, they insist, with the condition of social strain, but other theories are needed to understand why a particular social movement

develops when it does, what form that movement takes, and how successful the movement is in accomplishing its goals. Without the sense of outrage felt by religious leaders in Baltimore in 1994, BUILD would not have joined forces with other groups, and without a sense of outrage in many localities, the living wage movement could not have capitalized on the Baltimore momentum. But the situation of low-wage workers had not changed suddenly, so why did the social reform movement develop when it did?

Instead of focusing on social strains, some social psychologists have

Psychodynamic perspective

looked for psychological factors or attitudes that might explain which individuals are likely to get involved in social movements. A variety of psychological characteristics have been investigated, including authoritarian personality, emotional conflicts with parents, alienation, aggression, and relative deprivation. Empirical investigations have found very little support for a relationship between such psychological characteristics and social movement participation, however. Indeed, research indicates that social movement activists tend to be people who are rich in relational resources and well-integrated into their communities. Research also indicates that a great many people who never join social movements have similar attitudes about movement goals to those of active movement participants (della Porta & Diani, 2006). Recently, however, some social movement scholars have suggested it is time to take another look at what motivates people to participate in social movement activities (Castells, 2012). We examine some of those ideas later, under the discussion of emerging perspectives.

Theory and research about social movements have flourished in the past 4-plus decades, and in 2012 Roberta Garner and Mayer Zald suggested that the study of social movements is "hotter" than ever. I would agree that it is hotter than at any period since I started work on the first edition of this book in the mid-1990s. Throughout the 1970s, social movement scholars in the United States and Europe worked independently of each

Photo 14.2 Social work experiences a tension between service (helping those in need) and reform (changing organizational structures and systems). Here, workers fight for a living wage.

© Reuters/Corbis

other and developed different theories and different research emphases. In the past 25 years, however, U.S. and European social movement scholars have worked together and engaged in comparative analysis of social movements across place and time (della Porta, Kriesi, & Rucht, 2009). Originally, these collaborative efforts focused only on social movements in the United States and western Europe. After the momentous political events in eastern Europe in the late 1980s, however, eastern European social movements received extensive and intensive investigation. More recently, the protest movements of the Arab Spring of 2011 have captured the attention of social movement scholars.

Three major perspectives on social movements have emerged out of this lively interest. I refer to

these as the political opportunities perspective, the mobilizing structures perspective, and the cultural framing perspective. There is growing agreement among social movement scholars that none of these perspectives taken alone provides adequate tools for understanding social movements (Buechler, 2011; Edwards, 2014). Each perspective adds important dimensions to our understanding, however, and taken together they provide a relatively comprehensive theory of social movements. Social movement scholars recommend research that synthesizes concepts across the three perspectives. The recent social movement literature offers one of the best examples of contemporary attempts to integrate and synthesize multiple theoretical perspectives to give a more complete picture of social phenomena.

Political Opportunities Perspective

Many advocates have been concerned about the deteriorating economic situation of low-wage workers in the United States for some time. After Republicans regained control of Congress in 1994, advocates saw little hope for major increases in the federal minimum wage. The federal minimum wage was increased slightly, from $4.25 an hour to $5.15 an hour in 1996, with a Democratic president and a Republican Congress. However, under the circumstances, advocates of a living wage decided it was more feasible to engage in campaigns at the local rather than federal level to ensure a living wage for all workers. A shift occurred at the federal level when the Democrats regained control of Congress in November 2006. After being stalled at $5.15 for 10 years, the minimum wage received a three-step increase from Congress in May 2007, and Republican president George W. Bush signed the new wage bill into law. The law called for an increase of the federal minimum wage to $5.85 in the summer of 2007, to $6.55 in the summer of 2008, and to $7.25 in the summer of 2009 (U.S. Department of Labor, 2014). In early 2014, Democratic president Barack Obama recommended an increase in the federal minimum wage to $10.10, but this proposal was given little chance in a highly polarized Congress. In the meantime, state and local governments continue to consider the issue of fair wages. These observations are in line with the **political opportunities (PO) perspective**, whose main ideas are summarized in Exhibit 14.1.

Conflict perspective

The PO perspective begins with the assumption that social institutions—particularly political and economic institutions—benefit the more powerful members of society, often called **elites**, and disadvantage many. The elites typically have routine access to institutionalized political channels, whereas disadvantaged groups are denied access. Power disparities make it very difficult for some groups

Exhibit 14.1 Key Ideas of the Political Opportunities Perspective

- Social movements emerge when political opportunities are open.
- Political systems differ from each other, and change over time, in their openness to social movements.
- A given political system is not equally open or closed to all challengers.
- Success of one social movement can open the political system to challenges from other social movements.
- A given political system's openness to social movements is influenced by international events.
- Opportunities for social movements open at times of instability in political alignments.
- Social movements often rely on elite allies.

to successfully challenge existing institutions, but the PO perspective suggests that institutions are not consistently invulnerable to challenge by groups with little power. Social movements can at times take advantage of institutional arrangements vulnerable to challenge. The BUILD coalition was convinced that it was morally unjust for workers to receive wages that kept them below the federal poverty line, but they astounded even themselves by setting in motion a process that would spark a national social movement. Theories of social movements often underestimate the ability of challengers to mount and sustain social movements (Morris, 2004).

The political system itself may influence whether a social movement will emerge at a given time, as well as the form the movement will take. Social movement scholars have identified several influential dimensions of political systems and analyzed the ways in which changes in one or more of these dimensions make the political system either receptive or vulnerable to challenges (della Porta & Diani, 2006; Tarrow, 2006). Here, we examine four of those dimensions: openness of the political system, stability of political alignments, availability of elite allies, and international relations.

Openness of the Political System

It might seem reasonable to think that activists will undertake collective action when political systems are open and avoid such action when political systems are closed. The relationship of system openness or closure to social movement activity is not that simple, however. They have instead a curvilinear relationship: Neither full access nor its total absence encourages the greatest degree of collective action. Some resistance stimulates movement solidarity, but too much resistance makes collective action too costly for social movement participants (Meyer, 2004). The nature of the political structure will also affect the types of social movement activities that emerge in a given society. Researchers have found that France, with its highly centralized government and hostility to professional social movement organizations, is more prone to strikes, demonstrations, and collective violence than other European countries that are more fragmented and democratic in their governmental structures (Koopmans, 2004).

More generally, but in a similar vein, democratic states facilitate social movements and authoritarian states repress them (Tilly & Wood, 2013). Indeed, social movements as a form of collective action arose with the development of the modern democratic state (Marks & McAdam, 2009). However, because democratic states invite participation, even criticism, many challenging issues that might spark social movements are "processed" out of existence through electoral processes. It is hard to mount a social movement if it seems that the political system is easily influenced without serious collective action. On the other hand, the repression found in authoritarian states may serve to radicalize social movement leaders, as was evident during the Arab Spring uprisings of 2011 (Castells, 2012). Furthermore, as was evident in eastern Europe in the late 1980s, authoritarian states are not always effective in repressing challenges. The political leadership's efforts to appease the population by offering small liberties had a snowball effect. Relaxation of social control in a previously repressive political system often has the unintended consequence of fueling the fire of long-held grievances.

Social movement researchers are interested in how police handle protest events. They have identified two contrasting styles of policing: the escalated-force model and the negotiated control model. The *escalated-force model* puts little value on the right to protest, has low tolerance for many forms of protest, favors little communication between the police and demonstrators, and makes use of coercive and even illegal methods to control protests. The *negotiated control model* honors the right to demonstrate peacefully, tolerates even disruptive forms of protest, puts high priority on communication between police and demonstrators, and avoids coercive control as much as possible. Social movement scholars suggest that in Western societies, including the United States, the escalated-force model lost favor and the negotiated control model became prominent after the intense protest wave of the 1960s (della Porta & Diani, 2006). They also argue, however, that preference for the negotiated control model has proven fragile in the face of the new challenge of transnational protest movements. In the United States, political activists have been spied on and disrupted in the name of the war on terror since September 11, 2001. In February 2003, in the weeks leading up to the beginning of the Iraq War, New York City authorities refused march permits to United for Peace and Justice, a coalition of more than 800 antiwar and social justice groups. Later that same year, the Philadelphia police commissioner classified the Free Trade Area of America (FTAA) as outsiders who were coming to terrorize the city; this was done to allow the city to receive $8.5 million in war-on-terror money (Bornstein, 2009).

A given political system is not equally open or closed to all challengers at a given time; some social movements are favored over others. Even in a democracy, universal franchise does not mean equal access to the political system; wealth buys access not easily available to poor people's movements (Bornstein, 2009). Indeed, the rapid success and growth of the living wage movement has been a surprise to many who support it ideologically, because it has been hard to sustain poor people's movements in the past.

The success of one social movement can open the political system to challenges by other social movements. For example, successful legislative action by the Black civil rights movement during the 1960s opened the way for other civil rights movements, particularly the women's movement, which benefited from Title VII of the Civil Rights Act of 1964, which included prohibiting employment discrimination on the basis of sex (McAdam, 1996a). But the successful movement may also open the way for opponent movements, called **countermovements**, as well as for allied movements. The women's movement has been countered by a variety of antifeminist movements, including the antiabortionist movement and a set of interrelated movements that focus on traditional gender roles for family life. Indeed, the living wage movement has engendered opposition coalitions that have launched intensive lobbying campaigns to convince state legislators in several states to bar cities from establishing their own minimum wages (Murray, 2001; Quigley, 2001).

Stability of Political Alignments

PO theorists agree that the routine transfer of political power from one group of incumbents to another, as when a different political party takes control of the U.S. presidency or Congress, opens opportunities for the development or reactivation of social movements (Tarrow, 2006). At such times, some social movements lose favor and others gain opportunity. In the United States, in both the 1930s and the 1960s, changes in political party strength appear to have been related to increased social movement activity among poor people. Some observers note that social movements on the Left mobilized during the Kennedy and Johnson administrations, and social movements on the Right mobilized during the Reagan and George H. W. Bush administrations and again when the Republicans took over Congress in 1994 (McAdam,

McCarthy, & Zald, 1996); social movements on the Right also appear to have gained momentum when George W. Bush became president in 2000. That did not mean, however, that local grassroots movements for a living wage could not be mounted. Edwin Amenta and colleagues (Amenta, Caren, & Stobaugh, 2012) take a slightly different view of the relationship between political regimes and social movement activity. They agree that political regimes on the Left spur the mobilization of Left-oriented social movements and political regimes on the Right spur the mobilization of Right-oriented social movements, but their research also indicates that Left regimes incite Right-oriented social movements and even more so, Right regimes incite Left-oriented social movements.

Disruption of political alliances occurs at times other than political elections, for both partisan and nonpartisan reasons, and such disruptions produce conflicts and divisions among elites. When elites are divided, social movements can sometimes encourage some factions to take a stand for disenfranchised groups and support the goals of the movement. The Harvard Living Wage Campaign garnered the support of the mayor and city council in Cambridge, Massachusetts. Disruptions in political alliances also occur when different branches of the government—such as the executive branch and the legislative branch—are at odds with each other. Such conflict was the case at the federal level in the early days of the living wage campaign but may have had little effect on the campaign because it was being fought at the local level. New coalitions may be formed, and the uncertainty that ensues may encourage groups to make new or renewed attempts to challenge institutional arrangements, hoping to find new elite allies. The new local coalitions formed during the living wage campaigns have often breathed new life into local progressive advocates (Murray, 2001).

The events in eastern Europe in the late 1980s and the Arab Spring of 2011 represent another type of political opportunity—one that has received little attention by social movement scholars—the opportunity that opens when a political regime loses legitimacy with those it governs. As reported in Chapter 9, many political analysts suggest that the current era is marked by a reduced capacity of nations to govern and increasing cynicism on the part of citizens about the ability of governments to govern. Some social movement scholars suggest that this sort of instability is contributing to the global spread of social movement activity (Castells, 2012).

Availability of Elite Allies

Participants in social movements often lack both power and resources for influencing the political process. But they may be assisted by influential allies who play a variety of supportive roles. These elite allies may provide financial support, or they may provide name and face recognition that attracts media attention to the goals and activities of the movement. Research indicates a strong correlation between the presence of elite allies and social movement success (della Porta & Diani, 2006). The Harvard students, who mostly came from elite families themselves, were able to attract a number of elite allies, including Congressman Edward M. Kennedy, former Labor secretary Robert Reich, chairman of the NAACP Julian Bond, high-profile religious leaders, and actors Ben Affleck and Matt Damon. Michael Moore and Cornel West showed up to address the assembly of Occupy Wall Street in 2011.

Social movement participants often have ambivalent relationships with their elite allies, however. On the one hand, powerful allies provide needed resources; on the other hand, they may limit or distort the goals of the movement (della Porta & Diani, 2006). The early relationship between participants in the disability movement and actor Christopher Reeve is a good example of the tension that can develop between movement participants and their elite allies. When Reeve was paralyzed following an equestrian accident in 1995, the media quickly assigned him the role of star speaker for the disability community. Many in the disability movement were offended. Reeve's personal agenda was to find a cure for spinal cord injuries, but the movement's emphasis was on personal assistance for people with disabilities—on living with disability, not curing it. People in the disability movement were concerned that the emphasis on a cure would undermine their efforts to win public acceptance of their disabilities and to make their environments more accessible.

International Relations

Since the 18th century, social movements have diffused rapidly across national boundaries, and the fate of national social movements has been influenced by international events. In the 19th century, the antislavery movement spread from England to France, the Netherlands, and the Americas (Tarrow, 2006). The mid-20th-century Black civil rights movement in the United States was influenced by international attention to the gap between our national image as champion of human rights and the racial discrimination that permeated our social institutions (McAdam, 1996a). The fight for the right of women to vote was first won in New Zealand in the 1880s; the United States followed almost 40 years later, in 1920. It took some time, but gradually the movement for women's suffrage spread around the world (Sernau, 2014).

The recent revolution in communication technology is quickening the diffusion of collective action, as evidenced by recent democracy and justice movements. Democracy movements surged across the Arab world in 2011 after the successful democracy movements in Tunisia and Egypt. In the midst of the deep financial crisis that began in late 2007, unemployment reached 22% in Spain by 2011. After ignoring the severity of the situation for some time, the Spanish government, under pressure from Germany and the International Monetary Fund, instituted austerity policies that resulted in deep cuts in health, education, and social services. In protest, activists put out the call to occupy Barcelona's Catalunya Square on May 16, 2011, an action so successful it was followed up on in 100 other Spanish cities as well as 800 cities around the world. The Occupy Wall Street action that began in the United States in September 2011 was modeled on this social movement (Castells, 2012).

Tarrow (2006) suggests that the international spread of social movements was aided by two growing trends. First, there was a growing attitude, after the end of the Cold War, that it is acceptable for nations to interfere with the affairs of other nations. Second, the end of classical colonialism—a policy by which one nation maintains control over a foreign nation and makes use of its resources—left a large number of weak states in its wake. With these two trends working together, opportunities were opened for minorities who were dispossessed in one nation to appeal for support from allies in another nation. It is also important to note that global social movements have been aided by human rights legislation from multistate governments such as the United Nations (Bornstein, 2009).

Critical Thinking Questions 14.2

Think of a social justice issue that you have some passion about. Are there any social movements currently working on this issue? If so, what are they? How open is the political system (in the United States or internationally) to social action about the issue? What types of elite allies might be helpful with opening political opportunities for the issue?

Mobilizing Structures Perspective

Exchange and choice perspective

Most analysts would agree that much of the success of the living wage movement can be attributed to strong existing networks of local progressive advocates. The movement also benefited from strong advocacy organizations like ACORN that developed and provided resources to grassroots organizers. These views are consistent with the **mobilizing structures (MS) perspective**, which starts from this basic premise: Given their disadvantaged position in the political system, social movement leaders must seek out and mobilize the

resources they need—people, money, information, ideas, and skills—in order to reduce the costs and increase the benefits of movement activities. In the MS perspective, social movements have no influence without effective organization of various kinds of **mobilizing structures**—existing informal networks and formal organizations through which people mobilize and engage in collective action. Mobilizing structures are the collective building blocks of social movements. The main ideas of the MS perspective are summarized in Exhibit 14.2.

Exhibit 14.2 Key Ideas of the Mobilizing Structures Perspective

- Social movements must be able to mobilize various kinds of formal and informal networks.
- Resource mobilization theory focuses on the coordination of movement activities through social movement organizations (SMOs).
- The network model focuses on mobilization of the movement through informal networks.
- Mobilizing structures have a strong influence on the life course of social movements.
- To survive, social movements must be able to attract new members and sustain the involvement of current members.

Informal and Formal Structures

MS scholars agree that social movements typically do not start from scratch but build on existing structures. They disagree, however, on the relative importance of informal versus formal structures. The MS perspective has two theoretical building blocks, one that emphasizes formal mobilizing structures and another that emphasizes informal mobilizing structures.

Resource mobilization theory focuses on the organization and coordination of movement activities through formal organizations called **social movement organizations (SMOs)** (Davis, McAdam, Scott, & Zald, 2005). Theorists in this tradition are particularly interested in **professional social movement organizations** staffed by leaders and activists who make a professional career out of reform causes (della Porta & Diani, 2006; Morris, 2004). The professional staff engages in fundraising and attempts to speak for the constituency represented by the movement. There are advantages to professional SMOs, because social movements are more likely to meet their goals when they have a well-structured organization to engage in continuous fund-raising and lobbying. There are also problems, however. Professional SMOs must respond to the wishes of the benefactors who may be comfortable with low-level claims only. Theda Skocpol (2003) argues that professionalization can lead to movement defeat by taming protest. This may explain why the Occupy Wall Street movement (also known as the Occupy movement) was vehemently opposed to a leadership role for SMOs in their movement (Castells, 2012). Della Porta and Diani (2006) remind us that although social movements need organizations, organizations are not social movements. They insist that one thing that distinguishes social movements is that they are linked by dense informal networks.

Global social movements are being supported by growing numbers of **transnational social movement organizations (TSMOs)**, or social movement organizations that operate in more than one nation-state. The number of TSMOs grew each decade of the 20th century, with particularly rapid growth in the last 3 decades of the century. There were 183 in 1973 and 1,011 in 2003 (Tilly & Wood, 2013). Some examples of TSMOs are Green Peace and Amnesty International.

In contrast to the resource mobilization theory, the **network model** focuses on everyday ties between people, in grassroots settings, as the basic structures for the communication and social solidarity necessary for mobilization (della Porta & Diani, 2006; Tindall, 2004). The focus is thus on naturally existing networks based in family, work, religious, educational, and neighborhood relationships or such networks as those that can be found at alternative cafes and bookshops and social and cultural centers. Naturally existing social networks facilitate recruitment to movement activities and support continued participation. These natural networks are hard to repress and control because,

in a democratic society, people have the right to congregate in their private homes and other informal settings.

Some social movement scholars argue that the shift in the organization of work to home-based work, smaller factories, and offshore industrial production is limiting the development of work-based networks of activism. On the other hand, the increased presence of women in higher education and places of employment is facilitating new ties between women. Not only do people get involved in social movements because of previous connections but they also make new connections through their movement activities, connections that may generate continued loyalty. Proponents of the network model emphasize that individual, not just organizational, participation is essential for social movements, and they argue that social movements have participants, not members, and must find ways to keep participants involved. Although the benefits of informal networks are often noted in the social movement literature, some researchers are beginning to explore cases where networks do not lead to participation (della Porta & Diani, 2006; Tindall, 2004).

Although resource mobilization theory and the network model disagree about the relative merits of formal and informal structures, they do agree that the costs of mobilizing social movements are minimized by drawing on preexisting structures and networks (Davis et al., 2005; Tindall, 2004). The living wage campaign in Baltimore got its start in an existing coalition of religious leaders, and the growing living wage movement was able to generate support from existing social movement organizations and university students. This is very common in the life of social movements. Black churches and Black colleges played an important role in the U.S. civil rights movement (Hutchison, 2012). The student movements of the 1960s benefited from friendship networks among activists of the civil rights movement (Oberschall, 1992). The global justice movement depends on a broad coalition of organizations with a strong background in activism, including trade unions and other worker organizations, ethnic organizations, farmers, religious organizations, consumer groups, environmental groups, women's groups, and youth groups (della Porta & Diani, 2006; Tarrow, 2006). Research indicates that the vast majority of active participants in the Occupy movement in the United States had participated in other social movements and been involved in activist networks on the Internet (Castells, 2012).

Several social movement scholars have noted the particularly "religious roots and character of many American movements" (McAdam et al., 1996, p. 18; Wood, 2002). They suggest that this link is not surprising, given the higher rates of church affiliation and attendance in the United States than in other comparable Western democracies.

Gemma Edwards (2014) argues that the mobilizing structures perspective has not paid enough attention to the relational nature of social movements. Social movement mobilization depends on participants developing a sense of collective identity, and the collective identity becomes the defining nature of the social movement.

Information and Communication Technology (ICT)

Social movement leaders have always made use of new communication technologies to mobilize, using the telephone, radio, television, and computer as they became available (see Exhibit 14.3 for an overview of new communication technologies since the invention of the modern social movement). However, as new communication technologies became available, they did not replace previously existing technologies but were, instead, used alongside them. In recent years, the Internet and wireless communication networks have been used extensively in the mobilization of social movements, and the dynamic force of their use is the primary reason the study of social movements is so hot now. Here are some fascinating examples of recent use of these technologies to mount social movements around the world.

In May 2007, activists in the southern China city of Xiamen were fighting the construction of a chemical plant in their city. They sent out text messages from their cell phones encouraging recipients to participate in a protest at a particular location on June 1 at 8 a.m. Discussion of the hazards of the chemical plant was taken up by bloggers. On June 1, tens of thousands of protesters marched against the project, uploading photographs, videos, and text messages to blogging sites as they marched. When one blogging site was blocked, another blogger would pick up the material and distribute it. In December 2007, the Chinese government announced that the plant would be moved to another city, Guangzhou. In March 2008, residents of Guangzhou and nearby towns engaged in 3 days of protest against the decision to move the plant to their city. In one nearby town, the protesters staged a sit-in to block traffic on a main road. The local government sent loudspeakers to the street to deny that the plant would be moved to Guangzhou. In 2011, thousands of people used text messaging to organize protests against a similar plant in another part of China, and that plant was closed by local authorities (Tilly & Wood, 2013).

On December 17, 2010, street vendor Mohamed Bouazizi set fire to himself in front of a government building in a small town in Tunisia to protest the constant confiscation of his fruit and vegetables by the local police after he refused to pay them a bribe. A few hours later, hundreds of youth, sharing similar experiences, led a protest in front of the same building. Mohamed's cousin, Ali, recorded the protest and distributed the video over the Internet. A few days later, spontaneous demonstrations were held around the country and continued in spite of brutal repression by the police. When the French government removed its support from the dictator Ben Ali, he and his family fled Tunisia. The protesters were not satisfied, however, and the demonstrations continued. The protesters posted videos (of the protests and police brutality), messages, and songs on Facebook, YouTube, and Twitter. They used the Twitter hashtag #sidibouzid to debate and communicate. Bloggers played an active role, and Al Jazeera television broadcast images that had been posted on YouTube. The mobilization was not all digital, however. The protesters also occupied the Place du Gouvernement, the site of most government offices, and covered the walls of the government square with

Exhibit 14.3 A Selected History of the Development of New Information and Communication Technologies

Year	Technology
1835	Invention of the electric telegraph
1876	Invention of the telephone
1895	Invention of the Marconi radio
1923	Introduction of the first working television system
1962	Launching of the first active communication satellite
1971	First e-mail sent
1973	Introduction of first handheld cell phone
1977	Introduction of microcomputers and the personal computer modem
Early 1990s	Introduction of 2G digital cellular networks, allowing text messaging and access to media content
Mid-1990s	Appearance of first search engines for WWW
1995	Public Internet established in United States
2001	Introduction of 3G cellular networks with faster connectivity
2002	Friendster social networking site (SNS) launched
2004	Facebook launched
2005	YouTube launched
2006	Twitter launched
2007	Tumblr launched
2009	Introduction of 4G cellular telephone networks

slogans. Hundreds of cars converged on the capital. The Tunisian protesters continued their actions throughout 2011 and were rewarded with open elections on October 23, 2011 (Castells, 2012; Tilly & Wood, 2013).

Inspired by the action in Tunisia, Asmaa Mafhouz, a business student in Cairo, Egypt, posted a video blog (vlog) on January 18, 2011, asking people to gather on Tahrir Square on January 25. Someone uploaded the vlog to YouTube, and it went viral. Tens of thousands of people converged on Tahrir Square on January 25, and more than 2 million people participated in demonstrations there over time. Demonstrators recorded the protests with their mobile phones and shared the videos on YouTube and Facebook, often with live streaming. They debated and communicated by Facebook, coordinated actions on Twitter, and made extensive use of blogs. Al Jazeera television played a major role in communicating the action to the Egyptian population. From the beginning of the protests, the Egyptian government took action to block social media websites. On January 27, it blocked text messaging and BlackBerry messaging. The protesters responded by using the old technologies of fax machines, ham radio, dial-up modems, and landlines. Hackers and techies around the world came to the aid of the protesters. Google and Twitter engineers designed a system that automatically converted a voice mail left on an answering machine into a tweet (Castells, 2012; Russell, 2011).

Moving to the United States in 2011, there was widespread outrage about a number of issues: the massive loss of homes and real estate value when the real estate market crashed, the near collapse of the financial system caused by speculation and greed, the use of taxpayer money to bail out the financial institutions, and the payment of huge bonuses to millionaires who had caused the economic collapse—all coming after a presidential campaign that had created great hope among a large portion of the electorate, particularly young adults. This outrage was occurring in the context of energized social movements in other parts of the world, particularly the Arab Spring. On July 13, 2011, Adbusters posted a call on its blog for people to converge on lower Manhattan on September 17 and set up tents, kitchens, and so forth and occupy Wall Street. About 1,000 people showed up, demonstrated against Wall Street, and occupied nearby Zuccotti Park. Videos of police repression were posted on YouTube, which mobilized more protesters to show up. With images and messages spreading across the Internet, occupations developed spontaneously in other cities, with approximately 600 Occupy demonstrations occurring around the country. The message of the movement was spread both internally and externally by Twitter, using the hashtag #occupywallstreet. Twitter networks were used to alert participants when police action was threatened, to distribute other types of information, and to post photos, videos, and comments. Tumblr was used to humanize the movement, by providing a platform for personal, anonymous storytelling. As new Occupy camps developed around the country, most camps created their own websites with sections such as contact, how to get involved, supplies requested, resources, calendar of events and announcements, and message boards. Most camps also had a Facebook group.

Communication scholars suggest that the Internet and wireless communication technologies are a rich resource for social movements because they can be used to bypass mainstream media, which often ignores or distorts movement activity. Manuel Castells (2012), professor of communication technology at the University of Southern California, suggests that these technologies are a source of "mass self-communication," because the users can control the message they send. His research indicates that YouTube is probably the most powerful mobilizing tool in the early stages of a movement because the visual images arouse strong emotions in the viewer.

The widespread use of the Internet and wireless communication technologies in social movement mobilization is raising new questions for social movement scholars. Are dense, face-to-face networks still necessary to mobilize social movements? How essential is shared direct experience and face-to-face interaction to keep activists involved? The research on this question is still in the early stages, but evidence suggests that the greatest power comes from connecting virtual relationships with occupation of a shared physical space (Bennett, 2004; Castells, 2012). In recent large-scale social movements, new technologies have been used to call people to gather in specific physical spaces and to occupy those spaces over time. Castells (2012) suggests that these recent movements are creating a new hybrid form of *space*, "a mixture of space of places, in a given territory, and space of flows, on the Internet. One could not function without the other" (pp. 168–169).

The Life Course of Social Movements

Social movements are by definition fluid. The MS perspective asserts that

> Developmental perspective

mobilizing structures have a strong influence on the life course of a social movement, making time an important dimension. Although most social movements fade relatively soon, some last for decades. Movements typically have brief periods of intense activity and long latent periods when not much is happening. One pattern for the movements that persist is as follows: At the outset, the movement is ill defined, and the various mobilizing structures are weakly organized (Kriesi, 1996; Marx & McAdam, 1994). Once the movement has been in existence for a while, it is likely to become larger, less spontaneous, and better organized. The mature social

Photos 14.3a, b, c Both virtual and face-to-face networks helped to mobilize the Arab Spring protest movements of 2011.

© R. Byhre/Demotix/Corbis; © DYLAN MARTINEZ/Reuters/Corbis;
© David Mbiyu/Demotix/Corbis

movement is typically led by the SMOs developed in the course of mobilization. The living wage movement seems to be in this position currently, with several organizations, including some transnational ones, playing a major role, but it was not always so.

Social movement scholars disagree about whether the increasing role of formal organizations as time passes is good or bad. Many suggest that movements cannot survive without becoming more organized and taking on many of the characteristics of the institutions they challenge (Tarrow, 2006). On the other hand, this tendency of social movements to become more organized and less spontaneous has often doomed them—particularly poor people's movements—to failure (Skocpol, 2003). Organizations that become more formal commonly abandon the oppositional tactics that brought early success and fail to seize the window of opportunity created by the unrest those tactics generated. But that is not always the case. Sometimes SMOs become more radical over time, and most current large-scale social movements are strengthened by the support of many types of organizations (della Porta & Diani, 2006). One of the most important problems facing social movement organizers is to create mobilizing structures that are sufficiently strong to stand up to opponents but also flexible enough to respond to changing circumstances (Tarrow, 2006). The living wage movement appears to have managed that tension in its first 2 decades, but it is still a work in progress.

Jo Freeman (1995) asserts that there is "no such thing as a permanent social movement" (p. 403). She suggests that every movement, at some point, changes into something else, often into many other things, through three basic processes:

1. *Institutionalization.* Some movements become part of existing institutions or develop durable SMOs with stable income, staff, and routine operations. The profession of social

work is an example of a social movement that became institutionalized.

2. *Encapsulation.* Some social movements, or at least some parts of them, lose their sense of mission and begin to direct their activities inward, to serve members, rather than outward, to promote or resist change. That has been the trajectory of some labor unions (Clemens, 1996). Social work's history also includes periods of encapsulation, when social workers became more concerned about "professional advancement and autonomy, status, and financial security" than about social justice and the public welfare (Reamer, 1992, p. 12). This appears to be the current state of the social work profession.

3. *Factionalization.* Still other movements fall apart, often disintegrating into contentious, competing factions. This was the trajectory of the U.S. student protest movements after the violence at the 1968 Democratic Party convention in Chicago (della Porta & Diani, 2006; Tarrow, 1994).

It is too early to tell what the long-term trajectory of the living wage movement will be. One possibility is that it will merge with other movements focused on economic justice.

Critical Thinking Questions 14.3

Think again of a social justice issue you have some passion about. What existing networks might be available to organize change efforts regarding the issue? How could you use—or how have you used—the Internet and wireless communication technologies to participate in action about the issue?

Cultural Framing Perspective

> Social constructionist perspective

The **cultural framing (CF) perspective** asserts that a social movement can succeed only when participants develop shared understandings and definitions of the situation. These shared meanings develop through a transactional process of consciousness raising, which social movement scholars call cultural framing. **Cultural framing** involves "conscious strategic efforts by groups of people to fashion shared understandings of the world and of themselves that legitimate and motivate collective action" (McAdam et al., 1996, p. 6). Exhibit 14.4 summarizes the central ideas of the CF perspective.

Exhibit 14.4 Key Ideas of the Cultural Framing Perspective

- Social movements must be able to develop shared understandings that legitimate and motivate collective action.
- Social movements actively participate in the naming of grievances and injustices.
- Social movement leaders must construct a perception that change is possible.
- Social movements must articulate goals.
- Social movements must identify and create tactical choices for accomplishing goals.
- Contests over cultural frames are common in social movements.
- Social movements must be able to create cultural frames to appeal to diverse audiences.

Social movement leaders and participants engage in a delicate balancing act as they construct cultural frames. To legitimate collective action, cultural frames must impel people to feel aggrieved or outraged about some situation they consider unjust. But to motivate people to engage in collective action, cultural frames must be optimistic about the possibilities for improving the situation. Consider the chant developed by the divinity students at Harvard: "Where's your horror? Where's your rage? Div School wants a living wage." The chant dramatized the severity of the situation and the fairness of their cause, but it also expressed hope for a solution. Simultaneously, social movements want to draw heavily on existing cultural symbols so that the movement frame will resonate with people's cultural understandings while they add new frames to the cultural stock, thus sponsoring new ways of thinking about social conditions. The challenge of this balancing act is "how to put forward a set of unsettling demands for unconventional people in ways that will not make enemies out of potential allies" (Tarrow, 1994, p. 10). The BUILD coalition was wise in choosing to call their cause a "living wage" rather than a "minimum wage." The notion that workers should draw a wage that allows them to "live" is morally persuasive, and even those who oppose the living wage movement have suggested that it is hard to take a public stance that you are opposed to such an idea (Malanga, 2003).

Cultural frames are "metaphors, symbols, and cognitive cues that cast issues in a particular light and suggest possible ways to respond to these issues" (Davis et al., 2005, pp. 48–49). Exhibit 14.5 presents some cultural frames provided by recent social movements around the world. You may not be familiar with many of these cultural frames, and I suggest you consult the Internet to learn more about those not familiar to you. How well do you think these cultural frames serve both to legitimate and to motivate collective action?

A complication in the process of constructing frames is that frames attractive to one audience are likely to be rejected by other audiences. Social movement groups "must master the art of simultaneously playing to a variety of publics, threatening opponents, and pressuring the state, all the while appearing nonthreatening and sympathetic to the media and other publics" (McAdam, 1996b, p. 344). Activists have desired media attention because that is the most effective way to reach wide audiences, but they also know they cannot control the way the movement will be framed by the mass media. That is why some social movement scholars see so much promise in the use of the Internet and wireless communication technology that allow participants to control their own messages. The mass media are attracted to dramatic, even violent, aspects of a movement, but these aspects are likely to be rejected by other audiences (Stein, 2009). They are often more interested in scandal than in providing substantive information

---

Exhibit 14.5 Cultural Frames Used in Recent Social Movements Around the World

Chains of Debt   Si Se Puede   *Revolution for Liberty and Dignity*

We Are All Khaled Said   The Revolution Will Continue

Real Democracy Now   *Indignados*

Marriage Equality   We are the 99%

We Are Not Merchandise in the Hands of Politicians and Bankers

They Do Not Represent Us   *Democracy Not Corporatocracy*

SORRY FOR THE INCONVENIENCE, WE ARE TRYING TO CHANGE THE WORLD

Nothing About us Without us

on movement issues (della Porta & Diani, 2006). ACORN, an SMO that was very helpful to the living wage campaign in the United States, became the subject of a highly publicized scandal in September 2009 regarding a few local staff caught in reportedly unethical behavior on hidden camera (Farrell, 2009). This scandal led to loss of federal funding and private donations, and by March 2010, ACORN announced that it was closing its offices after 40 years of successful advocacy efforts (Urbina, 2010). Indeed, it was their success in fighting for the rights of poor people that led to a backlash from conservative forces that wanted to destroy them. That is a possibility with which successful social movements must always contend. It is not clear how ACORN's demise has affected the living wage movement.

Movement activists are particularly concerned about the impact of the mass media on their **conscience constituency**—people attracted to the movement because it appears just and worthy, not because they will benefit personally. The students at Harvard gave serious thought to whether a sit-in demonstration would cause them to lose some support for their cause. They also were aware that they could face repercussions, such as being expelled from the university.

Social movement framing is never a matter of easy consensus building, and intense **framing contests** may arise among a variety of actors, particularly in the later stages. Representatives of the political system and participants in countermovements influence framing through their own actions and public statements, and internal conflicts may become more pronounced. Leaders and followers often have different frames for the movement (Marx & McAdam, 1994), and there are often splits between moderate and radical participants. It is not at all unusual for movements to put forth multiple frames, with different groups sponsoring different frames. For example, Bill Hughes (2009) suggests that disability activism in the United Kingdom is splitting into two branches, the disabled people's movement (DPM) and the "biological citizens." The DPM takes the position that disability is a social phenomenon created by discrimination and oppression and suggests that impairment is irrelevant to disability. The "biological citizens" organize politically around specific diagnostic labels and embrace medical and scientific knowledge associated with their "condition," with the goal of enhancing their ability to exercise citizenship. When a movement captures mass media attention, there is often an intense struggle over who speaks for the movement and which cultural frame is put forward.

Qualitative analysis of social movement framing has been a popular topic in the social movement literature in recent years. This literature indicates that cultural framing provides language, ideology, and symbols for understanding that a problem exists, recognizing windows of opportunity, establishing goals, and identifying pathways for action (Polletta, 2004).

Frames for Understanding That a Problem Exists

Social movements are actively involved in the "naming" of grievances and injustices. They do so in part by drawing on existing cultural symbols, but they also underscore, accentuate, and enlarge current understanding of the seriousness of a situation. In essence, they call attention to contradictions between cultural ideals and cultural realities. For example, the living wage movement calls attention to the discrepancy between working and receiving a wage that does not allow a person to rise out of poverty. Calling attention to this discrepancy is important in the United States, where the public tends to believe that people are poor because they don't work. The international antiglobalization movement has used "globalization" as a catchword to symbolize the misery and exploitation caused by the dominance of market forces in contemporary life. Many of the ill effects of global markets, such as growing inequality, were present before antiglobalization activists were able to turn "globalization" into a negative symbol that could mobilize people to action. When 50,000 demonstrators protested against the WTO meeting in Seattle on November 30, 1999, they used a number of slogans to frame globalization as a problem (della Porta & Diani, 2006, p. 163):

- The world is not for sale.
- No globalization without representation.
- We are citizens, not only consumers.
- WTO = Capitalism without conscience.

Some of these themes have been echoed in slogans of more recent social movements, as demonstrated in Exhibit 14.5.

In the United States, movement frames are often articulated in terms of rights—civil rights, disability rights, GLBT rights, animal rights, children's rights. In Europe, where there is less emphasis on individual liberty, rights frames are far less common in social movements (Hastings, 1998;

Tarrow, 1998). Recently, equality has been a powerful frame in the United States: "We are the 99%" and "Marriage Equality." The GLBT rights movement made the wise choice to use equality as the slogan as they pushed for same-sex marriage rights.

In the past 2 decades, fundamentalist religious movements have sprung up in many countries, including the United States. These movements have used morality frames, focusing on good and evil rather than justice versus injustice. Compared with Europe, the United States has historically produced a high number of such movements (Marx & McAdam, 1994). Prohibition, abolition, anticommunism, and antiabortionism have all had religious roots. A contemporary religious frame that crosses national boundaries as well as liberal and conservative ideologies is "reverence for life,"

Photo 14.4 The Occupy Wall Street movement uses the slogan "We are the 99%" to have an impact on the public discourse about democracy and economic justice.

© Jon Hicks/Corbis

expressed in such disparate movements as the environmental, health, antiabortion, animal rights, antiwar, and anti–capital punishment movements.

Frames for Recognizing a Window of Opportunity

The perception of opportunity to change a troublesome situation is also culturally framed, to some extent (Castells, 2014; della Porta & Diani, 2006). On occasion, it is easy to develop a shared frame that opportunity exists or does not exist, but most situations are more ambiguous. Social movement leaders must successfully construct a perception that change is possible, because an opportunity does not exist unless it is recognized. They typically attempt to overcome concerns about the dangers and futility of activism by focusing on the risks of inaction, communicating a sense of urgency, and emphasizing the openness of the moment. They are intent on keeping hope alive.

Calibrating this type of frame is a difficult task. On the one hand, overstating an opportunity can be hazardous. Without "fortifying myths," which allow participants to see defeats as mere setbacks, unrealistically high expectations can degenerate into pessimism about possibilities for change (Voss, 1996). On the other hand, "movement activists systematically overestimate the degree of political opportunity, and if they did not, they would not be doing their job wisely" (Gamson & Meyer, 1996, p. 285). Unrealistic perceptions about what is possible can actually make change *more* possible. The Harvard students were not happy with the size of the worker raise that came out of their sit-in, but their expectations led to bold action, which brought some improvements in the lives of workers and has been an inspiration for students at other universities around the country.

Frames for Establishing Goals

Once it has been established that both problem and opportunity exist, the question of social movement goals arises. Is change to be narrow or sweeping, reformist or revolutionary? Will the emphasis be on providing opportunities for individual self-expression or on changing the social order? At least three goals have been adopted by different segments of the antiglobalization movement: rejection, opt out, and reform. The rejectionists reject capitalism as an ethical economic form. The "opt out" segment of the movement focuses on experiments in local sustainable economic development, which they hope will allow them to avoid participation in the global economic system dominated by large, transnational companies. The reformists see economic globalization as a potentially good thing but favor measures to reduce the power of transnational businesses (della Porta & Diani, 2006). U.S. social movements have generally set goals that are more reformist than revolutionary (Marx & McAdam, 1994). PFLAG National, the nation's largest organization of parents, families and allies united with LGBTQ people, is a fairly typical example of a contemporary U.S. social movement organization that has struck a balance between goals of individual change and changes in the social order. Exhibit 14.6 demonstrates how PFLAG strikes this balance in its statement of goals.

Typically, goals are poorly articulated in the early stages of a movement but are clarified through ongoing negotiations about the desired changes. Manuals for social activism suggest that modest and winnable objectives in the early stages of a movement help to reinforce the possibility of change (Gamson & Meyer, 1996). Indeed, the early goals for the living wage movement were quite modest. The wage increase secured by BUILD only covered 1,500 to 2,000 workers. By 2001, it was estimated that the combined efforts of all local living wage campaigns had brought the number to only about 100,000 workers. Some progressives were critical of a movement that was yielding so little, but other analysts argued that it was the modest and winnable nature of the early campaigns that neutralized opposition and built a momentum of success (Murray, 2001). Certainly, it is true that the movement has become more ambitious in its goals over time, moving from improving the wages of a small number of municipal contract workers to large-scale, citywide ordinances, as

One. Build the capacity of our organization at every level so that we may have all the resources, in the form of information, people and funding, necessary to move forward in our work with the greatest possible effect.

Two. Create a world in which our young people may grow up and be educated with freedom from fear of violence, bullying and other forms of discrimination, regardless of their real or perceived gender identity or sexual orientation or that of their families.

Three. Make our vision and our message accessible to the broadest range of ethnic and cultural communities, ending the isolation of families with lesbian, gay, bisexual and transgender family members within those communities.

Four. Work toward full inclusion of lesbian, gay, bisexual and transgender persons within their chosen communities of faith.

Five. Create a society in which all LGBT persons may openly and safely pursue the career path of their choice, and may be valued and encouraged to grow to their full potential in the workplace.

Six. Create a society in which all lesbian, gay, bisexual and transgender persons may enjoy, in every aspect of their lives, full civil and legal equality and may participate fully in all the rights, privileges and obligations of full citizenship in this country.

SOURCE: PFLAG, 2014.

well as to statewide minimum wage laws. Likewise, the European activists' demands that all garment workers in retail supply chains be paid a living wage would have far-reaching results across national lines (Clean Clothes Campaign, 2009).

Social workers Ray MacNair, Leigh Fowler, and John Harris (2000) suggest that progressive, or proactive, social movements have a three-pronged goal: (1) They must confront oppression, (2) they must attend to the damaged identities of oppressed persons, and (3) they must "renovate" the cultural roles of both oppressor groups and oppressed groups. The living wage movement has paid a lot of attention to the first two of these goals. It has named the oppression, and it has actively engaged low-wage earners in the struggle. It is not clear how much work is being done on the third goal, but the European activists for the garment workers may well be thinking in those terms.

Three "identity movements"—the Black civil rights movement, the women's movement, and the lesbian-gay-bisexual-transgender movement—demonstrate the process of goal setting (MacNair et al., 2000). Each of these movements has a long history of emerging, waning, and reemerging in the United States, changing its framing of the movement's goals along the way. For these three

social movements, the framing of goals followed an evolutionary path through six frames:

1. *Assimilation.* Persuade the mainstream to recognize the capabilities of the oppressed group while also working to uplift the oppressed group.

2. *Normative antidiscrimination.* Place the onus for change completely on oppressor groups and oppressive institutions. Take a confrontational approach of legal challenges and political lobbying. Recognize the positive attributes of the oppressed group.

3. *Militant direct action.* Reject the legitimacy of normal decision-making processes and attempt to disrupt them. Develop a "culture of rebellion" to energize disruptive actions (MacNair et al., 2000, p. 75).

4. *Separatism.* Avoid oppression by avoiding oppressor groups.

5. *Introspective self-help.* Focus on building a healthy identity.

6. *Pluralistic integration.* Appreciate themselves and promote connections to other cultures.

Before we leave the discussion of goal framing, it is important to consider the position on goals taken by the Occupy movement. One demand was put forward in the beginning, a presidential commission to separate money from politics, but that did not become the unifying goal of the movement. Each Occupy camp site developed its own proposals, or no proposal at all (Tarrow, 2011). The movement has been criticized for having no clear goal or goals, but George Lakoff (2011) aptly described the Occupy movement as a moral movement whose aim was to have an impact on the public discourse about democracy and economic justice. It appears that the movement had some success in this regard, stimulating greater public dialogue about a number of issues related to democracy and justice, including the issue of fair wages. Public opinion polls taken in November 2011 indicate that almost 50% of the public agreed with the ideas at the heart of the movement (Castells, 2012).

Frames for Identifying Pathways for Action

Some of the most important framing efforts of a social movement involve tactical choices for accomplishing goals. Social movement scholars generally agree that each society has a repertoire of forms of collective action that are familiar to social movement participants as well as the elites they challenge (Tarrow, 2006). New forms are introduced from time to time, and they spread quickly if they are successful. In the United States, for example, marches on Washington have come to be standard fare in collective action, and activist groups exchange information on the logistics of organizing such a march on the nation's capital. On the other hand, the sit-down strike is no longer as common as it once was, but occupying a physical space over time has been a hallmark of recent social movements. Contemporary social movements draw power from the large selection of forms of collective action currently in the cultural stock, and many movements have wisely used multiple forms of action (della Porta & Diani, 2006; Tarrow, 2006). The living wage movement has made use of lobbying, postcard campaigns, door-knocking campaigns, leafleting, rallies, sit-ins, workshops, newspaper ads, and advocacy videos.

The repertoire of collective action is handed down, but there is some improvisation by individual movements. For example, public marches are a standard part of the repertoire, but there have been innovations to the march in recent years, such as closing rallies and the incorporation of theatrical forms. Participants in the global justice movement are using some long-standing action forms such as petitions, reports and press releases, sit-ins, marches, lobbying, blockades, and boycotts. They are also using recent action innovations as well as developing new action forms. Their repertoire includes concerts, vigils, theatrical masks, puppets, electronic advocacy, documentaries, and "buycotts" (active campaign to buy the products) of fair trade products. Computer technology has been used in two forms of disruptive action. *Net striking* is an action form in which a large number of people connect to the same website at a prearranged time. This jams the site and makes it impossible for other users to reach it. *Mailbombing* is an action form in which large numbers of e-mails are sent to a web address or a server until it overloads (della Porta & Diani, 2006).

Just as social movement goals fall on a continuum from reform to revolution, forms of collective action can be arranged along a continuum from conventional to violent, as shown in Exhibit 14.7. Nonviolent forms of collective action are the core of contemporary U.S. movements, and nonviolence as a way of life was a cornerstone of the camp sites of the Occupy movement. Nonviolent disruption of routine activities is today considered the most powerful form of activism in the United States and in other Western democracies with relatively stable governments (della Porta & Diani, 2006). The power of nonviolent disruption is that it creates uncertainty and some fear of violence yet provides authorities in democratic societies with no valid argument for repression. Violent collective action, on the other hand, destroys public support for the movement. Martin Luther King was ingenious in recognizing that the best path for the U.S. civil rights movement was "successfully courting violence while restraining violence in his followers" (McAdam, 1996b, p. 349). Consequently, it was the

Exhibit 14.7 Forms of Collective Action

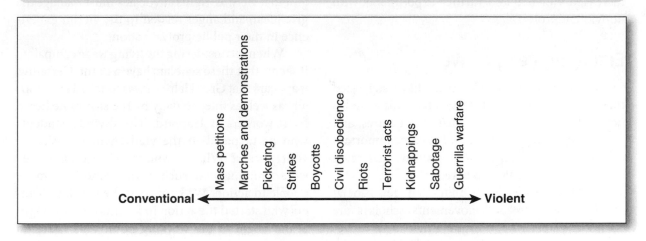

police who lost public favor for their brutality, not the demonstrators.

Some action forms, such as marches, petitions, and Net strikes, are used to demonstrate numerical strength. Other action forms, such as conferences, concerts, documentaries, and buycotts of fair products, are used to bear witness to the substantive issues. Still other action forms are designed to do damage to the parties reputed to be to blame for an unfair situation. Small-scale violence does this, as do boycotts. Not only do these latter action forms run the risk of escalating repression and alienating sympathizers, but boycotts also run the risk of harming workers (della Porta & Diani, 2006).

In an interesting development, a new organizing tactic has been used in peace and justice campaigns. The proponents of this tactic call it "creative play." They argue that "changing entrenched systems of oppression requires shifts in emotional as well as intellectual attitudes" (Shepard, 2005, p. 52). Furthermore, "culture-poems, songs, paintings, murals, chants, sermons, quilts, stories, rhythms, weavings, pots, and dances can make such emotional and visceral breakthroughs possible" (Si Kahn, 1995, cited in Shepard, 2005, p. 52). One global movement, Reclaim the Streets (RTS), used street parties as its organizing tool. During the 2004 presidential election, Billionaires for Bush used humor to lampoon the role of money in U.S.

politics. They appeared at both pro-Bush and anti-Bush rallies in tuxedos and top hats, and fake jewels and gowns, often carrying signs that read "Because Inequality Is Not Growing Fast Enough." Paul Bartlett, a member of the Billionaires group, suggests that "Performance with humor can disarm fear. When we laugh, we can listen, we can learn. . . . When people participate in a play, opportunities for new perspectives and transformation emerge" (cited in Shepard, 2005, p. 55).

Social movement scholars agree that for the past 200 years, social movement actions have become less violent (Tarrow, 2006). They also suggest, however, that beginning in the 1990s, violent social movements began to flourish again around the world. This trend was exemplified by White supremacist armed militias in the United States and militant Islamic fundamentalist movements in the Middle East, Central Asia, and Africa. Out of these two movements have come (respectively) the bombing of a state building in Oklahoma City and the somber events of September 11, 2001. It is unclear whether the increased violence of social movements will be a long-term trend and if so, whether existing theories of social movements will be relevant to the new forms of movement actions. The 2011 democracy movements in Tunisia and Egypt as well as the Occupy movement were nonviolent and experimented with new ways of peaceful protest. Perhaps the future will hold both increased violence and further experiments with nonviolent protest.

Emerging Perspectives

Some social movement scholars have suggested that the three dominant perspectives discussed—political opportunities, mobilizing structures, and cultural framing—fail to attend to some important dimensions of social movements. Two emerging perspectives are discussed here.

| Psychodynamic perspective |

First, a few social movements scholars are arguing that social movement researchers should take another look at the role of emotions in motivating people to participate in social movement activities. They contend that the social movement literature has fallen short by attending to rationality but not emotions of movement participants. Drawing on recent neuroscience research about the role of emotion in human behavior, Manuel Castells (2012) theorizes that the energy of a social movement "starts with the transformation of emotion into action" (p. 13). He suggests that anger is the triggering emotion in social activism, and extreme anger or outrage helps to override fear of the consequences of action. Enthusiasm and hope, which are generated in social interaction, also play an important role in overriding the fear of activism. Visual images are powerful stimulants of both anger and hope.

Deborah Gould (2004) applauds the rejection of earlier attempts to understand social movement actors in terms of psychopathologies but suggests that social movements are passionate political processes and emotions must be considered. She proposes that social movement researchers should study the role that emotions such as anger, indignation, hope, and pride play in motivating social movement involvement. She recounts her own qualitative research with lesbians and gays who participated in the AIDS activism group ACT UP, noting the important role that grief and anger about AIDS and the slow response to it played in moving participants to action. In another analysis,

Karen Stanbridge and J. Scott Kenney (2009) suggest that victims' rights advocates must manage the grief, fear, and anger related to the victim experience in their public protest action.

When reconsidering the living wage campaign, it seems that these scholars have a point. Certainly, it appears that Greg Halpern was touched emotionally as well as intellectually by the stories he heard from workers at Harvard. The divinity students who participated in the vigil chanted, "Where's your horror? Where's your rage?" Perhaps they were thinking that such strong emotions move people to action. We know that the religious leaders who started the action in Baltimore were angry at the plight of the working poor. This raises an important question for social movement leaders: Should they appeal to both emotional and intellectual understandings of injustice? If so, what are the best methods to do this?

Second, Richard Flacks (2004) suggests that the literature on resource mobilization has failed to consider the fundamental differences in the way different members participate in social movements. He asserts that there may be very different explanations for the participation of leaders, organizers, and mass participants. He thinks we should be more interested in why some people come to see societal change as a major priority in their lives while others don't and suggests that social movement scholars should study the biographies of activists to learn more about that. Studs Terkel was an activist, not a social movement scholar, but he was interested in exactly the same question that Flacks raises. For Terkel's (2003) book *Hope Dies Last*, he interviewed 55 activists about what motivated them to activism. As the title of the book indicates, he found hope to be a major motivator.

From another perspective, Robert Putnam (2000) notes that many people are participating at a very superficial level in contemporary social movements, responding to direct mail campaigns with a one-time contribution but making no greater commitment to the cause. Putnam argues that this type of involvement in social movements fails to build the social capital built in grassroots coalitions like those driving the living wage movement. There are, indeed, different ways to participate in social movements, and social movement leaders need to understand the different motivations involved.

Critical Thinking Questions 14.4

Think again of a social justice issue about which you have some passion. What are two or three cultural frames that would motivate people to engage in collective action on the issue? Review the cultural frames of recent social movements presented in Exhibit 14.5. Could any of those frames be extrapolated to motivate action on the issue about which you have some passion? How important do you think emotions are in motivating people to participate in social movement activity? Which, if any, of the cultural frames presented in Exhibit 14.5 arouse strong emotions in you? What types of emotions do they arouse?

SOCIAL MOVEMENT OUTCOMES

Because social movements are processes, not structures, they are not easy to research. The case study has been the predominant method used, with recent emphasis on comparative case studies. Unfortunately, one researcher may declare a particular movement a failure, while another researcher will see it as having succeeded. Often the impact of a movement cannot be determined until well past its heyday. Different analyses may be based, in part, on different guidelines for success, but the researchers may also be evaluating the movement from different time perspectives. This is a reminder, again, of the importance of the time dimension in changing person–environment configurations.

Like other human endeavors, social movements are neither completely successful nor completely unsuccessful. In general, however, the most successful social movements have outcomes far less radical than their proponents would like and far more radical than their opponents would like. Social movements rarely produce the major redistribution of power that activists desire and movement goals specify. The women's movement has not achieved its goal of equality and nondiscrimination for women. The conservative Christian movement has not reached its goal of restoring traditional family and gender roles. And yet social movements do have an effect on society. Thus, their success should perhaps be measured not by their survival but by the institutional changes they influence. For example, should any credit be given to the living wage movement for the 2007, 2008, and 2009 federal minimum wage increases in the United States? For minimum wage increases in a large number of states? These are hard questions to answer.

Sidney Tarrow (1998) suggests that the power of social movements is cumulative and can be appreciated only from a long-term historical perspective. Many of the gains of social movements get reversed, but "they often leave behind incremental expansions in participation, changes in popular culture, and residual movement networks" (p. 202). Castells (2012) suggests that the real legacy of a social movement is the cultural change it produces. Research on social movements documents a range of direct and indirect effects. Contemporary social movements have accomplished an impressive list of specific federal legislation, including the Civil Rights Act of 1964; Title IX, the federal law that prohibits gender-based discrimination in athletics and educational programs at institutions that receive federal funds; and the Americans with Disabilities Act of 1990. Considered by some scholars to be the most successful social movement in the United States since World War II, the Black civil rights movement has served as an organizing model, opened opportunities, and provided hope for other aggrieved groups. Because of social movements, the political system has become more open and responsive to previously ignored groups, and voicing grievances has become an expected part of life in a democratic country. New decision-making bodies, such as ad hoc committees and new governmental ministries, have been created in many nations (della Porta & Diani, 2006). Many SMOs have become a stable part of the social environment, and activist-oriented networks outlast the movements that spawned them. Research indicates that although individual activists are often temporarily disillusioned at the end of a social movement, in the long term, they are empowered and politicized by their participation (Tarrow, 1998).

Although the success of a given social movement depends on its unique configuration of political opportunities, mobilizing efforts, and cultural frames, social movement researchers have identified some factors that influence success or failure. Some of these factors are outside the control of the movement, but some of them can be successfully manipulated by movement leaders. The most obvious factor is the ability to attract a large number of participants. The most successful movements tap into existing networks and associations that have a shared culture, a strong sense of solidarity, and a common identity. These groups are the most likely to be willing to make sacrifices and remain committed over time and to have the shared symbols to frame the movement. Religious movements, for example, benefit from long-lasting and widely cherished religious symbols. Other forces, however, can serve as serious threats to the success of a social movement. Internal conflicts and factionalism weaken the chances for success, as does a strong opponent. Initial successes may stimulate strong countermovements, or a backlash may develop in reaction to the radical flank of a movement.

SOCIAL MOVEMENT TRENDS

Social movement scholars generally agree that social movements will continue to be a part of the social landscape in the foreseeable future (McMichael, 2012). In fact, some have predicted that we are entering an era of "movement societies," in which challenge and disruption of institutional arrangements will become a routine part of life (Tarrow, 2006). Della Porta and Diani (2006) predict that the antiglobalization movement will become a new political force in the world. They also see a trend toward the return of working-class movements and "mobilization by the dispossessed" (p. viii). They suggest that this may be happening because the size of social groups that lack full citizenship is growing around the world.

Tarrow (2006) suggests that the extraordinary international protests of the late 1990s and beginning years of the 21st century represent something new on the planet. Indeed, as suggested earlier, there has been a rapid expansion of TSMOs (McMichael, 2012). TSMOs have developed primarily in the areas of human rights, women's rights, environmental protection, antiglobalization, and peace (McMichael, 2012). One benefit of TSMOs is that they can include people who speak out about an issue in one country while people are silenced in other countries. TSMOs rarely use violent, or even seriously disruptive, methods. Many observers suggest that given the globalization of the economy, any successful labor challenge to growing inequality will have to be international in scope, and there is evidence that this is, indeed, happening. That is one aim of the antiglobalization movement, which is made up of a collection of labor activists as well as environmentalists and feminists (McMichael, 2012).

Another strong trend that began in the 1990s was a shift from single-issue organizing to multi-issue organizing by TSMOs (Tarrow, 2006). Traditionally, social movements and the SMOs that supported them focused tightly on a single issue, such as poverty or gender equality. The majority of TSMOs still focus on single issues, but the number of multi-issue TSMOs doubled in the 1990s, growing twice as fast as the overall TSMO population (Davis et al., 2005). Increasingly, for example, TSMOs are bridging labor issues with such other issues as the environment, gender equality, peace, and global justice (della Porta & Diani, 2006).

Finally, it seems likely that the trend of blending technology-based organizing with face-to-face interactions in occupied spaces will continue and perhaps escalate. As we have noted at other points in this book, technological inventions are coming at a fast clip, and it is impossible to foresee what new communication technologies will be used in future social movement mobilization. Given the time it takes to get a book like this into your hands, it is highly likely that you are aware of the use of new technologies not discussed in this chapter.

SOCIAL MOVEMENTS AND CONTEMPORARY SOCIAL WORK

Early in this chapter, I suggested that the professionalization of social work was accomplished by sacrificing the social reform fervor of its settlement house tradition. Some social movement scholars have found it difficult, if not impossible, to be both a profession and a reform movement (Freeman, 1995). Other social work scholars see a dual focus on professional service and social reform as achievable and even natural. The history of social work is one of tension between the goal of professional service and the goal of social reform. This tension has been quite obvious in recent years. On the one hand, social workers and their professional organizations have devoted a lot of resources to obtaining licensure for clinical social workers and to securing private and public reimbursement for clinical social work services. On the other hand, social work's leading professional organizations have in recent times revised documents, including the NASW Code of Ethics and CSWE's Curriculum Policy Statement, to add forceful language about the social justice goals of the profession.

Philip Popple (1992) suggests that each generation of social workers must struggle anew with the tension between a conservative mandate from society for efficient service that manages problems of dependency and a liberal or radical mandate from the profession to promote social justice. He also suggests that social workers experience this tension differently in different political eras. In conservative political times, there is great disparity between the societal mandate for social workers to act as social control agents and the profession's social reform tradition. In such times, the social reform goal is not prominent. In liberal political times, however, there is less tension between the two goals, and social work's social reform goal is more visible. Popple's analysis is consistent with a tenet of the PO perspective on social movements: Shifts in political alignments open or close opportunities for social movement activity. Even though the social work profession's emphasis on social reform at any given time is influenced by political opportunities, the valuing of social justice is a permanent feature of social work in the United States (Popple, 1992). Thus, all social workers should be familiar with developments in social movement theory and research.

Some social workers practice in **social movement service organizations (SMSOs)**, also known as *social movement agencies, alternative social agencies*, and *hybrid organizations*, which pursue social change while delivering services (Meyer, 2010). These organizations make a fundamental commitment both to social service provision and to advocacy efforts. They often attempt to provide revolutionary services oriented toward empowerment and cognitive liberation. Their advocacy efforts are often focused on reframing public understanding of social problems and their solutions. For example, SMSOs serving homeless persons have attempted to reframe homelessness as being a consequence of failed housing policies, rather than a consequence of individual failings. Likewise, rape crisis centers have focused on gaining public affirmation that rape is not the victim's fault (Hasenfeld, 2010b).

Megan Meyer (2010) identifies five characteristics of SMSOs:

1. They are driven by controversial values that they see as socially beneficial.

2. They closely integrate service provision and advocacy roles.

3. They develop a close sense of community among their clients.

4. They often mobilize their members to advocate for change.

5. They typically develop a hybrid structure that incorporates elements of both collective and bureaucratic forms of operation.

Some examples of SMSOs are feminist health and rape crisis centers, peace and conflict resolution organizations, and national women's and racial minority organizations. Unfortunately, there is very little research on SMSOs, and our knowledge of them and their impact is limited.

Critics of existing social movement theory have suggested that SMOs can be divided into a reform or moderate tradition and a radical tradition (Fitzgerald & Rodgers, 2000). Radical social movement organizations tend to be organized nonhierarchically and operate with little structure. Their goal is usually radical change in social institutions, rather than social reform. Exhibit 14.8 contrasts the characteristics of moderate and radical SMOs. As you can see, existing social movement theories are a better fit with moderate SMOs than with radical SMOs (Fitzgerald & Rodgers, 2000).

This model helps us understand the dimensions of contemporary SMOs but does not capture their changing trajectories over time. After studying six feminist SMOs, Cheryl Hyde (2000) suggested that many social movement agencies fall somewhere between the moderate and radical SMO. The six agencies she studied had begun as grassroots organizations with traits consistent with the description of radical SMOs. They changed in varying ways over the years, however, falling on a continuum from moderate to radical at the point she studied them.

We are living in a time of growing inequality, distrust of governments, hot spots of ethnic hatred, and activism based on social identity. It is easy to get overwhelmed and feel powerless about the situations we confront. Social movement theory is an important ingredient in our social work survival kit. It helps us see, as the title of Sidney Tarrow's (1998) book suggests, that there is "power in movement." It provides a conceptual base to reinvigorate our social reform mission. We may take inspiration from some contemporary examples of courage and conviction that led to social change:

- Rosa Parks, a tired seamstress on a public bus, helped launch the U.S. civil rights movement (Sernau, 2014).
- C. P. Ellis, a former Ku Klux Klan leader, started action that changed the racial climate of an entire community (Terkel, 1980).
- Craig Kielburger, a 12-year-old Canadian boy, began an international movement, Free

Exhibit 14.8 Characteristics of Moderate and Radical SMOs

	Moderate SMOs	Radical SMOs
Internal structure	Hierarchical leadership; formal bureaucratic organization; development of large membership base for resource generation	Nonhierarchical leadership; participatory democratic organization; egalitarian; "membership" based on involvement; indigenous leadership
Ideology	Reform agenda; emphasis on being a contender in the existing political system; national focus	Radical agenda; emphasis on structural change; flexible ideology; radical networks; global consciousness
Tactics	Nonviolent legal action	Nonviolent direct action; mass actions; innovative tactics
Communication	Mainstream media and communication channels	Either ignored or misrepresented by mainstream media; reliance on alternative forms of communication (music, street theater, pamphlets, newsletters, digital technology, cell phones, text messaging)
Assessment of success	Measured in terms of reform of existing political/economic system; longevity	Measured in terms of contribution to larger radical agenda; subject to intense opposition and government surveillance; may be purposefully short-lived

SOURCE: Based on Fitzgerald & Rodgers, 2000, Table 1.

the Children, to end child labor after reading a story about child workers in Pakistan (Sernau, 2014).

- In 1999, college students around the United States began a boycott of Reebok sports shoes, prompting improved conditions in that company's Indonesian factories (Ivins, 1999).
- After the three major Icelandic banks collapsed in 2008, the "kitchenware revolution" called for the government to resign and for new elections to be held. With pressure from the streets, the new government nationalized the three major banks, compensated consumers for the loss of their savings, and arrested leading figures in the banking sector (Castells, 2012).

These are just a few of the empowering stories we can recall in our most discouraged moments to give us hope.

Critical Thinking Questions 14.5

Do you see the goals of professional service and social reform as incompatible or as dual goals that can be fruitfully integrated? How prominent do you think the social reform goal is in the social work profession now? What factors do you think are influencing the current emphasis (or lack of emphasis) on social reform by the profession? How important are social movements in the search for social justice?

Implications for Social Work Practice

This discussion of social movements recommends several principles for social work activism:

- Become skillful in assessing political opportunities for social reform efforts.
- Become skillful in recognizing and mobilizing formal and informal networks for social reform activities.
- In conservative political eras, be vigilant about the temptation to encapsulate and lose sight of social work's social reform mission.
- Become skillful at attracting new recruits to social reform activities and sustaining the morale and commitment of current participants.
- Become skillful in managing internal movement conflicts and avoiding factionalism.
- Become skillful in developing cultural frames that legitimate and motivate collective action.
- Assist social workers in direct practice to assess the benefits and costs to clients of involvement in social movement activities.
- Assist social workers in the traditional social welfare institution to recognize the important role that reform social movements play in identifying new or previously unrecognized social injustices and social service needs.

Key Terms

charity organization society (COS) movement
conscience constituency
countermovement
cultural framing
cultural framing (CF) perspective elites
framing contests
mobilizing structures

mobilizing structures (MS) perspective
network model
political opportunities (PO) perspective
proactive social movement
professional social movement organizations
reactive social movement
resource mobilization theory

settlement house movement
social movement organizations (SMOs)
social movement service organizations (SMSOs)
social movements
social reform
strain theory
transnational social movement organizations (TSMOs)

1. You read about some of the early history of the living wage movement in the case study at the beginning of this chapter. This movement is 2 decades old. What, if anything, had you heard about this movement before reading the case study in the chapter? At this point, how do you evaluate its outcomes? How do you explain its successes? What challenges might lie ahead?

2. In this chapter, I suggested that successful social movements often open the way for countermovements. I also suggested that social movements may be either proactive or reactive. In considering these ideas, it is helpful to look at two social movements that hold competing views on issues related to women. Go to the websites of the National Organization for Women (NOW) at www.now.org and the National Right to Life Committee (NRLC) at www.nrlc.org. Study carefully the positions that each of these social movement organizations takes on the issue of abortion. What language and symbols does each organization use for framing the issue?

Web Resources

Amnesty International: www.amnesty.org

Site contains information about human rights by country, human rights by topic, human rights campaigns, and news.

Critical Social Work: www1.uwindsor.ca/criticalsocialwork

Site organized by the University of Windsor in Ontario, Canada, is an international, interdisciplinary e-journal whose goal is to promote dialogue about methods for achieving social justice.

Free the Children: www.freethechildren.com

Site maintained by the social movement organization developed by Craig Kielburger when he was 12 years old contains information about accomplishments, campaigns, planned activities and projects, conferences, and a speakers' bureau.

Greatergood.com: http://greatergood.com

Site maintained as part of a family of cause-related websites contains merchandise from more than 100 leading online merchants, with a portion of the purchase going to a charity of choice.

National Organizers Alliance (NOA): www.noacentral.org

Site maintained by NOA, a nonprofit organization with the mission to advance progressive organizing for social, economic, environmental, and racial justice, contains information about national gatherings, a job bank, a newsletter, a calendar of events, and links to other activist organizations.

New Organizing Institute (NOI): www.neworganizing.com

Site maintained by NOI, a grassroots program that trains young political organizers for progressive campaigns, contains information about training programs, internships, and jobs as well as a blog.

Student Study Site

$SAGE edge™

Sharpen your skills with SAGE edge at **edge.sagepub.com/hutchisonpe5e**

SAGE edge for students provides a personalized approach to help you accomplish your coursework goals in an easy-to-use learning environment.

REFERENCES

Abma, J., & Martinez, G. (2006). Childlessness among older women in the United States: Trends and profiles. *Journal of Marriage and Family, 68,* 1045–1056.

Abrams, D., Hogg, M., Hinkle, S., & Otten, S. (2005). The social identity perspective on small groups. In M. Poole & A. Hollingshead (Eds.), *Theories of small groups: Interdisciplinary perspectives* (pp. 99–137). Thousand Oaks, CA: Sage.

Abu-Lughod, L. (1999). The interpretation of culture(s) after television. In S. B. Ortner (Ed.), *The fate of culture: Geertz and beyond* (pp. 110–135). Berkeley: University of California Press.

Acierno, R., Hernandez, M., Amstadter, A., Resnick, H., Steve, K., Munoy, W., et al. (2010). Prevalence and correlates of emotional, physical, sexual, and financial abuse and potential neglect in the United States: The National Elder Mistreatment Study. *American Journal of Public Health, 100*(2), 292–297.

Acs, G., Braswell, K., Sorensen, E., & Turner, M. (2013). *The Moynihan Report revisited.* Urban Institute. Retrieved from www.urban.org/UploadedPDF/412839-The-Moynihan-Report-Revisted.pdf.

Adams, B., & Trost, J. (2005). *Handbook of world families.* Thousand Oaks, CA: Sage.

Adams, R., Boscarino, J., & Figley, C. (2006). Compassion fatigue and psychological distress among social workers: A validation study. *American Journal of Orthopsychiatry, 78*(1), 103–108.

Addams, J. (1910). *Twenty years at Hull House.* New York: MacMillan.

Adler, N., & Stewart, J. (2010a). Preface to the biology of disadvantage: Socioenomomic status and health. *Annals of the New York Academy of Sciences, 1186,* 1–4.

Adler, N., & Stewart, J. (2010b). Health disparities across the lifespan: Meaning, methods, and mechanisms. *Annals of the New York Academy of Sciences, 1186,* 5–23.

Aguilar, M. A. (2001). Catholicism. In M. Van Hook, B. Hugen, & M. Aguilar (Eds.), *Spirituality within religious traditions in social work practice* (pp. 120–145). Pacific Grove, CA: Brooks/Cole.

Ahmed-Mohamed, K. (2011). Social work practice and contextual systemic intervention: Improbability of communication between social work and sociology. *Journal of Social Work Practice, 25*(1), 5–15.

Ainsworth, M. S., Blehar, M. C., & Waters, E. (1978). *Patterns of attachment: A psychological study of the strange situation.* Oxford, UK: Erlbaum.

Albrecht, G. H. (2002). *Hitting home: Feminist ethics, women's work, and the betrayal of "family values."* London: Continuum.

Aldwin, C. M. (2007). *Stress, coping, and development: An integrative perspective* (2nd ed.). New York: Guilford Press.

Aldwin, C. M., & Yancura, L. A. (2004). Coping and health: A comparison of the stress and trauma literatures. In P. Schnurr & B. Green (Eds.), *Trauma and health: Physical health consequences of exposure to extreme stress* (pp. 99–125). Washington, DC: American Psychological Association.

Alinsky, S. (1971). *Rules for radicals.* New York: Vintage.

Allen, K., Lloyd, S., & Few, A. (2009). Reclaiming feminist theory, method, and praxis for family studies. In S. Lloyd, A. Few, & K. Allen (Eds.), *Handbook of feminist family studies* (pp. 3–17). Thousand Oaks, CA: Sage.

Almaas, A. H. (1995). *Luminous night's journey.* Berkeley, CA: Diamond Books.

Almaas, A. H. (1996). *The point of existence.* Berkeley, CA: Diamond Books.

Alperovitz, G. (2005). *America beyond capitalism: Reclaiming our wealth, our liberty, and our democracy.* Hoboken, NJ: Wiley.

Altman, I. (1975). *The environment and social behavior: Privacy, personal space, territory, and crowding.* Monterey, CA: Brooks/Cole.

Amaoka, T., Laga, H., Yoshi, M., & Nakajima, M. (2011). Personal space-based simulation of non-verbal communications. *Entertainment Computing, 2,* 245–261.

Amato, P., & Irving, S. (2006). Historical trends in divorce and dissolution in the United States. In M. Fine & J. Harvey (Eds.), *Handbook of divorce and relationship dissolution* (pp. 41–57). Mahwah, NJ: Erlbaum.

Amenta, E., Caren, N., & Stobaugh, J. (2012). Political reform and the historical trajectories of U.S. social movements in the twentieth century. *Social Forces, 90*(4), 1073–1100.

American Diabetes Association. (2013). *The cost of diabetes.* Retrieved from http://www.diabetes.org/advocate/resources/cost-of-diabetes.html.

American Heart Association. (2013a). *Heart disease and stroke statistics—2014 update: A report from the American Heart Association.* Retrieved from http://circ.ahajournals.org/content/early/2013/12/18/01.cir.0000441139.02012.80.citation.

American Heart Association. (2013b). *High blood pressure and African Americans.* Retrieved from http://www.heart.org/HEARTORG/Conditions/HighBloodPressure/UnderstandYourRiskforHighBloodPressure/High-Blood-Pressure-and-African-Americans_UCM_301832_Article.jsp.

American Heart Association. (2013c). *Statistical fact sheet 2013 update: High blood pressure.* Retrieved from https://www.heart.org/idc/groups/heart-public/@wcm/@sop/@smd/documents/downloadable/ucm_319587.pdf.

American Psychiatric Association. (2013). *Diagnostic and statistical manual of mental disorders* (5th ed.). Washington, DC: Author.

American Psychological Association. (2013). *Gun violence research: History of the federal funding freeze.* Retrieved from http://www.apa.org/science/about/psa/2013/02/gun-violence.aspx.

Amole, D. (2005). Coping strategies for living in student residential facilities in Nigeria. *Environment & Behavior, 37*(2), 201–219.

Anandarajah, G., & Hight, E. (2001). Spirituality and medical practice: Using the HOPE questions as a practical tool for spiritual assessment. *American Family Physician, 63*(1), 81–99.

Anderson, C. (2012). The diversity, strengths, and challenges of single-parent households. In F. Walsh (Ed.), *Normal family processes: Growing diversity and complexity* (4th ed., pp. 128–148). New York: Guildford.

Anderson, H. (2009). A spirituality for family living. In F. Walsh (Ed.), *Spiritual resources in family therapy* (2nd ed., pp. 194–211). New York: Guilford Press.

Anderson, K. F. (2013). Diagnosing discrimination: Stress from perceived racism and the mental and physical health effects. *Sociological Inquiry, 83*(1), 55–81.

Anderson, P. (2008). *The powerful bond between people and pets: Our boundless connections to companion animals.* Westport, CT: Praeger.

Anderson, R., & Carter, I. (1974). *Human behavior in the social environment: A social systems approach.* Chicago: Aldine.

Angell, G. B., Dennis, B. G., & Dumain, L. E. (1998). Spirituality, resilience, and narrative: Coping with parental death. *Families in Society, 79*(6), 615–630.

Angers, M. E. (2008). Psychoanalysis, politics, and "the repressed feminine": Toward a psychoanalytically informed sociology of knowledge. *Issues in Psychoanalytic Psychology, 30*(2), 137–155.

Aranda, M. P. (2008). Relationship between religious involvement and psychological well-being: A social justice perspective. *Health & Social Work, 33*(1), 9–21.

Argyris, C. (1999). *On organizational learning.* Cambridge, MA: Blackwell.

Argyris, C., & Schön, D. (1978). *Organizational learning: A theory of action perspective.* Reading, MA: Addison-Wesley.

Argyris, C., & Schön, D. (1996). *Organizational learning II: Theory, method, and practice.* Reading, MA: Addison-Wesley.

Asher, J., Michopoulos, V., Reding, K. M., Wilson, M. E., & Toufexis, D. (2013). Social stress and the polymorphic region of the serotonin reuptake transporter gene modify oestradiol-induced changes on central monoamine concentrations in female rhesus monkeys. *Journal of Neuroendocrinology, 25*(4), 321–328.

Ashford, J., LeCroy, C., & Lortie, K. (2010). *Human behavior in the social environment* (4th ed.). Belmont, CA: Cengage.

Ashkanani, H. R. (2009). The relationship between religiosity and subjective well-being: A case of Kuwaiti car accident victims. *Traumatology, 15*(1), 23–28.

Assagioli, R. (1965). *Psychosynthesis: A manual of principles and techniques.* New York: Viking.

Assagioli, R. (1973). *The act of will.* New York: Penguin.

Assagioli, R. (1989). Self-realization and psychological disturbances. In S. Grof & C. Grof (Eds.), *Spiritual emergency: When personal transformation becomes a crisis* (pp. 27–48). Los Angeles: Jeremy P. Tarcher.

Averill, J. R. (2012). The future of social constructionism: Introduction to a special section of *Emotion Review. Emotion Review, 4*(3), 215–220.

Bagdikian, B. (2004). *The new media monopoly* (5th ed.). Boston: Beacon Press.

Baker, E., Barton, P., Darling-Hammond, L., Haertel, E., Ladd, H., Linn, R., et al. (2010). *Problems with the use of student test scores to evaluate teachers.* Washington, DC: Economic Policy Institute.

Baker, M., Das, D., Venugopal, K., & Howden-Chapman, P. (2008). Tuberculosis associated with household crowding in a developed country. *Journal of Epidemiology and Community Health, 62*(8), 715–721.

Bal, S., Crombez, G., & Oost, P. V. (2003). The role of social support in well-being and coping with self-reported stressful events in adolescents. *Child Abuse & Neglect, 27*(12), 1377–1395.

Ballantine, J., & Roberts, K. (2014). *Our social world: Introduction to sociology* (4th ed.). Thousand Oaks, CA: Pine Forge.

Balsam, K., Beauchaine, T., Rothblum, E., & Solomon, S. (2008). Three-year follow-up of same-sex couples who had civil unions in Vermont, same-sex couples not in civil unions, and heterosexual married couples. *Developmental Psychology, 44*(1), 102–116.

Bandura, A. (1977a). Self-efficacy: Toward a unifying theory of behavioral change. *Psychological Review, 84*, 191–215.

Bandura, A. (1977b). *Social learning theory.* Englewood Cliffs, NJ: Prentice Hall.

Bandura, A. (1986). *Social foundations of thought and action: A social cognitive theory.* Englewood Cliffs, NJ: Prentice Hall.

Bandura, A. (2001). Social cognitive theory: An agentic perspective. *Annual Review of Psychology, 52*, 1–26.

Bandura, A. (2002). Social cognitive theory in cultural context. *Applied Psychology: An International Review, 51*(2), 269–290.

Banerjee, M. M., & Canda, E. R. (2009). Spirituality as a strength of African-American women affected by welfare reform. *Social Thought, 28*(3), 239–262.

Banerjee, M. M., & Canda, E. (2012). Comparing Rawlsian justice and the capabilities approach to justice from a spiritually sensitive social work perspective. *Journal of Religion & Spirituality in Social Work: Social Thought, 31*, 1–2, 9–31.

Banik, S., Gupta, A., Habib, M., & Mousumi, R. (2013). Determination of active personal space based on emotion when interacting with a service robot. *International Journal of Advanced Robotic Systems, 10*, 1–7.

Barak, A., & Grohol, J. (2011). Current and future trends in Internet-supported mental health interventions. *Journal of Technology in Human Services, 29*(3), 155–196.

Barber, B., & Demo, D. (2006). The kids are alright (at least, most of them): Links between divorce and dissolution and child well-being. In M. Fine & J. Harvey (Eds.), *Handbook of divorce and relationship dissolution* (pp. 289–311). Mahwah, NJ: Erlbaum.

Barker, R. G. (1968). *Ecological psychology: Concepts and methods for studying the environment of human behavior.* Palo Alto, CA: Stanford University Press.

Barnard, M., & McKeganey, N. (2004). The impact of parental drug use on children: What is the problem and what can be done to help? *Addiction, 99*, 552–559.

Barnekow, K., & Kraemer, G. (2005). The psychobiological theory of attachment: A viable frame of reference for early intervention providers. *Physical & Occupational Therapy in Pediatrics, 25*(1 & 2), 3–15.

Barnes, P. M., Bloom, B., & Nahin, R. (2008, December 10). Complementary and alternative medicine use among adults and children: United States, 2007. *National Health Statistics Report #12*, 1–23. Retrieved from www.ncbi.nlm.nih.gov/pubmed/19361005.

Barnoff, L., & Moffatt, K. (2007). Contradictory tensions in anti-oppression practice in feminist social services. *Affilia, 22*(1), 56–70.

Barret, R., & Barzan, R. (1996). Spiritual experiences of gay men and lesbians. *Counseling and Values, 41*, 4–15.

Barsky, A. (2013, March 18). Episode 115. Online social work with individuals, families, and groups: Ethical issues and responses.

inSocialWork Podcast Series. [Audio Podcast] Retrieved from http://www.socialwork.buffalo.edu/podcast/episode.asp?ep=115.

Bartholomae, S., & Fox, J. (2010). Economic stress and families. In S. Price, C. Price, & P. McKenry (Eds.), *Families & change: Coping with stressful events and transitions* (4th ed., pp. 185–209). Thousand Oaks, CA: Sage.

Bartholomew, R. E. (2000). *Exotic deviance: Medicalizing cultural idioms—From strangeness to illness.* Boulder: University Press of Colorado.

Barton, B. (2010). "Abomination"—Life as a Bible belt gay. *Journal of Homosexuality, 57,* 465–484.

Barton, J., & Pretty, J. (2010). What is the best dose of nature and green exercise for improving mental health? A multi-study analysis. *Environmental Science and Technology, 44,* 3947–3955.

Barton, P., & Coley, R. (2010). *The Black-White achievement gap: When progress stopped.* Princeton, NJ: Educational Testing Service.

Baskin, C. (2006). Aboriginal world views as challenges and possibilities in social work education. *Critical Social Work, 7*(2). Retrieved from www1.uwindsor.ca/criticalsocialwork/aboriginal-world-veiws-as-challenges-and-possibilities-in-social-work-education.

Baum, F. (1999). The role of social capital in health promotion. Australian perspectives. *Health Promotion Journal of Australia, 9*(3), 171–178

Baxter, L., & Braithwaite, D. (2006). Introduction: Metatheory and theory in family communication research. In D. Braithwaite & L. Baxter (Eds.), *Engaging theories in family communication: Multiple perspectives* (pp. 1–15). Thousand Oaks, CA: Sage.

BBC News. (2006, June 22). The popularity of "time" unveiled. Retrieved from news.bbc.co.uk/2/hi/5104778.stm.

Beard, V., & Sarmiento, C. (2010). Ties that bind: Transnational community-based planning in Southern California and Oaxaca. *International Development Planning Review, 32*(3–4), 207–224.

Beauchemin, K., & Hays, P. (1998). Dying in the dark: Sunshine, gender, and outcomes in myocardial infarction. *Journal of the Royal Society of Medicine, 91,* 352–354.

Beck, A. T. (1976). *Cognitive therapy and the emotional disorders.* New York: International Universities Press.

Beck, F., & Eichler, M. (2000). Consensus organizing: A practice model for community building. *Journal of Community Practice, 8*(1), 87–102.

Beck, J. S. (2005). *Cognitive therapy for challenging problems.* New York: Guilford Press.

Beck, U. (1992). *Risk society: Towards a new modernity.* Thousand Oaks, CA: Sage.

Becker, D. (2004). Post-traumatic stress disorder. In P. J. Caplan & L. Cosgrove (Eds.), *Bias in psychiatric diagnosis* (pp. 207–212). Lanham, MD: Jason Aronson.

Becker, D. (2005). *The myth of empowerment: Women and the therapeutic culture in America.* New York: New York University Press.

Becker, H. (1957). Current sacred–secular theory and its development. In H. Becker & A. Boskoff (Eds.), *Modern sociological theory in continuity and change* (pp. 137–185). New York: Dryden.

Beitel, M., Genova, M., Schuman-Olivier, Z., Arnold, R., Avants, S. K., & Margolin, A. (2007). Reflections by inner-city drug users on a Buddhist-based spirituality-focused therapy: A qualitative study. *American Journal of Orthopsychiatry, 77*(1), 1–9.

Belanger, K., Copeland, S., & Cheung, M. (2009). The role of faith in adoption: Achieving positive adoption outcomes for African American children. *Child Welfare, 87*(2), 99–123.

Belcher, J. R., Fandetti, D., & Cole, D. (2004). Is Christian religious conservatism compatible with the liberal social welfare state? *Social Work, 49*(2), 269–276.

Bell, K. (2012). Towards a post-conventional philosophical base for social work. *British Journal of Social Work, 42,* 408–423.

Bell, L. (2009). Mindful psychotherapy. *Journal of Spirituality in Mental Health, 11*(1–2), 126–144.

Bell-Toliver, L., & Wilkerson, P. (2011). The use of spirituality and kinship as contributors to successful therapy outcomes with African American families. *Journal of Religion & Spirituality in Social Work, 30*(1), 48–70.

Benavides, L. E. (2012). A phenomenological study of spirituality as a protective factor for adolescents exposed to domestic violence. *Journal of Social Service Research, 38*(2), 165–174.

Ben-David, V. (2011). Social constructions of reality and narratives of parental incapability in the process of adjudicating the adoption of minors in Israel. *Child and Family Social Work, 16,* 402–411.

Benedetti, F., Colombo, C., Barbini, B., Campori, E., & Smeraldi, E. (2001). Morning sunlight reduces length of hospitalization in bipolar depression. *Journal of Affective Disorders, 62*(3), 221–223.

Benedict, R. (1946). *The chrysanthemum and the sword.* Boston: Houghton Mifflin.

Benedict, R. (1989). *Patterns of culture.* Boston: Houghton Mifflin. (Original work published 1934)

Bennett, S., Sheridan, M. J., & Richardson, F. (2014). Caregiving as ministry: Perceptions of African Americans providing care for elders. *Families in Society: The Journal of Contemporary Social Services, 95*(1), 51–58.

Bennett, W. L. (2004). Communicating global activism: Strength and vulnerabilities of networked politics. In W. van de Donk, B. Loader, P. Nixon, & D. Rucht (Eds.), *Cyberprotest: New media, citizens and social movements* (pp. 109–126). London: Routledge.

Bentley, K. J., & Walsh, J. (2014). *The social worker & psychotropic medication: Toward effective collaboration with mental health clients, families, and providers* (4th ed.). Pacific Grove, CA: Brooks/Cole.

Berger, P. L. (1969). *The sacred canopy: Elements of a sociological theory of religion.* Garden City, NY: Doubleday.

Berger, P. L., & Luckmann, T. (1966). *The social construction of reality.* Garden City, NY: Doubleday.

Bergman, K., Rubio, R., Green, R., & Padrón, E. (2010). Gay men who become fathers via surrogacy: The transition to parenthood. *Journal of GLBT Family Studies, 6,* 111–141.

Berman, M., Kross, E., Krpan, K., Askren, M., Burson, A., Deldin, P., et al. (2012). Interacting with nature improves cognition and affect for individuals with depression. *Journal of Affective Disorder, 140,* 300–305.

Bernstein, J. (2002, May/June). Making a living: How the living wage movement has prevailed. *Shelterforce Online #123.* Retrieved from www.shelterforce.com/online/issues/123/makingaliving.html.

Berry, M. E. (2009). *The sacred universe: Earth, spirituality, and religion in the 21st century.* New York: Columbia University Press.

Bertalanffy, L. V. (1969). *General systems theory.* New York: George Braziller.

Berzoff, J. (2011). Why we need a biopsychosocial perspective with vulnerable, oppressed, and at-risk clients. *Smith College Studies in Social Work, 81,* 132–166.

Besthorn, F. H. (2001). Transpersonal psychology and deep ecology: Exploring linkages and applications for social work. In E. R. Canda & E. D. Smith (Eds.), *Transpersonal perspectives on spirituality in social work* (pp. 23–44). Binghamton, NY: Haworth Press.

Besthorn, F. H. (2012). Deep ecology's contributions to social work: A ten-year retrospective. *International Journal of Social Welfare, 21,* 248–259.

Besthorn, F. H. (2013). Radical equalitarian ecological justice: A social work call to action. In M. Gray, J. Coates, & T. Hetherington (Eds.), *Environmental Social Work* (pp. 31–45). New York: Routledge.

Biblarz, T., & Savci, E. (2010). Lesbian, gay, bisexual, and transgender families. *Journal of Marriage and Family, 72,* 480–497.

Bidart, C., & Lavenu, D. (2005). Evolutions of personal networks and life events. *Social Networks, 27*(4), 359–376.

Bierut, L. (2011). Genetic vulnerability and susceptibility to substance dependence. *Neuron, 69,* 618–627.

Bill and Melinda Gates Foundation. (2012). *Press room: Gates Foundation commits nearly $70 million to help fight neglected tropical diseases.* Retrieved from www.gatesfoundation.org/Media-Center/Press-Releases?2006–09/$70-Million-to-Help-Fight-Neglected-Tropical-Diseases.

Biorck, G. (1977). The essence of the clinician's art. *Acta Medica Scandinavica, 201*(3), 145–147.

Blacher, J., Begum, G., Marcoulides, G., & Baker, B. (2013). Longitudinal perspectives of child positive impact on families: Relationship to disability and culture. *American Journal on Intellectual and Developmental Disabilities, 118*(2), 141–155.

Blanchard, A. (2004). Virtual behavior settings: An application of behavior setting theories to virtual communities. *Journal of Computer-Mediated Communication, 9*(2). Retrieved from http://onlinelibrary.wiley.com/doi/10.1111/j.1083-6101.2004.tb00285.x/full.

Blasi, J., Freeman, R., & Kruse, D. (2013). *The citizen's share.* New Haven, CT: Yale University Press.

Blau, P. (1964). *Exchange and power in social life.* New York: Wiley.

Blumer, H. (1998). *Symbolic interactionism: Perspective and method.* Berkeley: University of California Press.

Boas, F. (1948). *Race, language and culture.* New York: Free Press. (Original work published 1940)

Boase, J. (2008). Personal networks and the personal communication system: Using multiple media to connect. *Information, Communication & Society, 11*(4), 490–508.

Boase, J., Horrigan, J., Wellman, B., & Rainie, L. (2006). *The strength of Internet ties: The Internet and email aid users in maintaining their social networks and provide pathways to help when people face big decisions.* Washington, DC: Pew Internet & American Life Project. Retrieved from www.pewinternet.org/files/old-media/Files/Reporrts/20067/PIP-Internet_ties.pdf.pdf.

Boddie, S. C., & Cnaan, R. A. (Eds.). (2006). *Faith-based social services: Measures, assessments, and effectiveness.* Binghamton, NY: Haworth Press.

Boddie, S. C., Hong, P. Y. P., Im, H., & Chung, S. (2011). Korean-American churches as partners in community development. *Social Work & Christianity, 38*(4), 395–416.

Bogovic, A., Mihanovic, M., Jokic-Begic, N., & Svagelj, A. (2013). Personal space of male war veterans with posttraumatic stress disorder. *Environment and Behavior.* Retrieved from eab.sagepub.com/content/early/2013/02/19/oo13916513477653.

Bohannan, P. (1995). *How culture works.* New York: Free Press.

Bonduriansky, R. (2012). Rethinking heredity, again. *Trends in Ecology & Evolution, 27*(6), 330–336.

Boonstra, H. (2010). Sex education: Another big step forward—and a step back. *The Guttmacher Policy Review, 13*(2), 27–28.

Booth, R., & O'Brien, P. J. (2008). An holistic approach for counsellors: Embracing multiple intelligences. *International Journal of Advising and Counselling, 30,* 79–92.

Borden, W. (2009). *Contemporary psychodynamic theory and practice.* Chicago: Lyceum.

Borgatti, S., & Halgin, D. (2011). On network theory. *Organization Science, 22*(5), 1168–1181.

Bornstein, A. (2009). N30 + 10: Global civil society, a decade after the Battle of Seattle. *Dialectical Anthropology, 33,* 97–108.

Bornstein, M., & Bradley, R. (Eds.). (2003). *Socioeconomic status, parenting, and child development.* Mahwah, NJ: Erlbaum.

Boroditsky, L., Fuhrman, O., & McCormick, K. (2011). Do English and Mandarin speakers think about time differently? *Cognition, 118,* 123–129.

Borysenko, J. (1996). *A woman's book of life: The biology, psychology, and spirituality of the life cycle.* New York: Riverhead Books.

Bos, H., van Balen, F., & van den Boom, D. (2007). Child adjustment and parenting in planned lesbian-parent families. *American Journal of Orthopsychiatry, 77,* 38–48.

Boss, P. (2006). *Loss, trauma, and resilience: Therapeutic work with ambiguous loss.* New York: Norton.

Boswell, J. (1994). *Same-sex unions in premodern Europe.* New York: Random House.

Bottoms, B. L., Nielsen, M., Murray, R., & Filipas, H. (2003). Religion-related child physical abuse: Characteristics and psychological outcomes. *Journal of Aggression, Maltreatment & Trauma, 8*(1/2), 87–114.

Bourdieu, P. (1977). *Outline of a theory of practice.* New York: Cambridge University Press.

Bowen, M. (1978). *Family therapy in clinical practice.* New York: Aronson.

Bowland, S., Biswas, B., Kyriakakis, S., & Edmond, T. (2011). Transcending the negative: Spiritual struggles and resilience in older female trauma survivors. *Journal of Religion, Spirituality & Aging, 23*(4), 318–337.

Bowler, D., Buyung-Ali, L., Knight, T., & Pullin, S. (2010). A systematic review of evidence for the added benefits of health and exposure to natural environments. *BMC Public Health, 10,* 456.

Boyd, D., & Ellison, N. (2008). Social network sites: Definition, history, and scholarship. *Journal of Computer-Mediated Communication, 13*(1), 210–230.

Boyes-Watson, C. (2005). Seeds of change: Using peacemaking circles to build a village for every child. *Child Welfare, 82*(2), 191–208.

Bozard, R. L., & Sanders, C. J. (2011). Helping Christian lesbian, gay, and bisexual clients recover religion as a source of strength: Developing a model for assessment and integration of religious identity in counseling. *Journal of LGBT Issues in Counseling, 5*(1), 47–74.

Brabender, V., & Fallon, A. (2009). *Group development in practice: Guidance for clinicians and researchers on stages and dynamics of change.* Washington, DC: American Psychological Association.

Bradley, R., & Corwyn, R. (2002). Socioeconomic status and child development. *Annual Review of Psychology, 53,* 371–399.

Bradshaw, Y., Healey, J., & Smith, R. (2001). *Sociology for a new century.* Thousand Oaks, CA: Pine Forge.

Brain Injury Association of America. (2013). *Brain injury facts.* Retrieved from http://www.biausa.org/glossary.htm.

Brandon, D. (1976). *Zen in the art of helping.* New York: Delta/ Seymour Lawrence.

Brantley, J., Doucette, D., & Lindell, A. (2008). Mindfulness, meditation, and health. In A. L. Strozier & J. E. Carpenter (Eds.), *Introduction to alternative and complementary therapies* (pp. 9–29). New York: Haworth Press.

Braude, A. (1997). Women's history is American religious history. In T. A. Tweed (Ed.), *Retelling U.S. religious history* (pp. 87–107). Berkeley: University of California Press.

Brautigam, D. (2009). *The dragon's gift: The real story of China in Africa.* Oxford: Oxford University Press.

Brave Heart, M. Y. H. (2001). Clinical interventions with American Indians. In R. Fong & S. Furuto (Eds.), *Cultural competent social work practice: Practice skills, interventions, and evaluation* (pp. 285–298). New York: Longman.

Braver, S., Shapiro, J., & Goodman, M. (2006). Consequences of divorce for parents. In M. Fine & J. Harvey (Eds.), *Handbook of divorce and relationship dissolution* (pp. 313–337). Mahwah, NJ: Erlbaum.

Brawley, E. (2006). *Design innovations for aging and Alzheimer's.* Hoboken, NJ: Wiley.

Brawley, E. (2009). Enriching lighting design. *NeuroRehabilitation, 25,* 189–199.

Breitman, B. E. (1995). Social and spiritual reconstruction of self within a feminist Jewish community. *Woman and Therapy: A Feminist Quarterly, 16*(2/3), 73–82.

Brent, J. (1997). Community without unity. In P. Hoggett (Ed.), *Contested communities: Experiences, struggles, policies* (pp. 68–83). Bristol, UK: Policy Press.

Brodsky, A. (2009). Multiple psychological sense of community in Afghan context: Exploring commitment and sacrifice in an underground resistance community. *American Journal of Community Psychology, 44,* 176–187.

Bronfenbrenner, U. (2005). *Making human beings human: Bioecological perspective on human development.* Thousand Oaks, CA: Sage.

Brown, D. R., Carney, J. S., Parrish, M. S., & Klem, J. L. (2013). Assessing spirituality: The relationship between spirituality and mental health. *Journal of Spirituality in Mental Health, 15*(2), 108–122.

Brown, G. (2009). NICU noise and the preterm infant. *Neonatal Network, 28*(3), 165–173.

Brown, G., Lawrence, T., & Robinson, S. (2005). Territoriality in organizations. *Academy of Management Review, 30*(3), 577–594.

Brown, K. A., Jemmott, F. F., Mitchell, H. J., & Walton, M. L. (1998). The Well: A neighborhood-based health promotion model for Black women. *Health and Social Work, 23*(2), 146–152.

Brown, L., Shepherd, M., Wituk, S., & Meissen, G. (2007). How settings change people: Applying behavior setting theory to consumer-run organizations. *Journal of Community Psychology, 35*(3), 399–416.

Brown, N. (2005). Psychoeducational groups. In S. Wheelan (Ed.), *The handbook of group research and practice* (pp. 511–529). Thousand Oaks, CA: Sage.

Brueggemann, W. (2013). History and context for community practice in North America. In M. Weil, M. Reisch, & M. Ohmer (Eds.), *The handbook of community practice* (2nd ed., pp. 27–46). Los Angeles: Sage.

Bryck, R. L., & Fisher, P. A. (2012). Training the brain: Practical applications of neural plasticity from the intersection of cognitive neuroscience, developmental psychology, and prevention science. *American Psychologist, 67*(2), 87–100.

Bucko, R. A., & Iron Cloud, S. (2008). Lakota health and healing. *Southern Medical Journal, 101*(6), 596–598.

Budman, S. H., Soldz, S., Demby, A., Davis, M., & Merry, J. (1993). What is cohesiveness? An empirical examination. *Small Group Research, 24,* 199–216.

Buechler, S. (2011). *Understanding social movements: Theories from the classical era to the present.* Boulder, CO: Paradigm.

Bullis, R. K. (1996). *Spirituality in social work practice.* Washington, DC: Taylor & Francis.

Bureau of Labor Statistics. (2013). *News release: Union members 2012.* Retrieved from www.bls.gov/new.release/pdf/union2.pdf.

Burke, M. T., Chauvin, J. C., & Miranti, J. G. (2005). *Religious and spiritual issues in counseling: Applications across diverse populations.* New York: Brunner/Routledge.

Burlingame, G., Kapetanovic, S., & Ross, S. (2005). Group psychotherapy. In S. Wheelan (Ed.), *The handbook of group research and practice* (pp. 387–406). Thousand Oaks, CA: Sage.

Burston, D., & Frie, R. (2006). *Psychotherapy as a human science.* Pittsburgh, PA: Duquesne University Press.

Burtless, G. (2012). *Life expectancy and rising income inequality: Why the connection matters for fixing entitlements.* Retrieved from http://www.brookings.edu/research/opinions/2012/10/23-inequality-life-expectancy-burtless.

Bush, K., Bohon, S., & Kim, H. (2010). Adaptation among immigrant families: Resources and barriers. In S. Price, C. Price, & P. McKenry (Eds.), *Families & change: Coping with stressful events and transitions* (4th ed., pp. 285–310). Thousand Oaks, CA: Sage.

Bussolari, C., & Goodell, J. (2009). Chaos theory as a model of life transitions counseling: Nonlinear dynamics and life's changes. *Journal of Counseling & Development, 87,* 98–107.

Buzzell, L., & Chalquist, C. (Eds.). (2009). *Ecotherapy: Healing with nature in mind.* San Francisco: Sierra Club Books.

Byoung-Suk, K., Ulrich, R., Walker, V., & Tassinary, L. (2008). Anger and stress: The role of landscape posters in an office setting. *Environment & Behavior, 40*(3), 355–381.

Cacioppo, J. T., Bernston, G. G., Sheridan, J. F., & McClintock, M. K. (2000). Multilevel integrative analysis of human behavior: Social neuroscience and the complementary nature of social and biological approaches. *Psychological Bulletin, 126*(6), 829–843.

Cady, S. H., & Valentine, J. (1999). Team innovation and perceptions of consideration: What difference does diversity make? *Small Group Research, 30*(5), 730–750.

Cairns, D. B. (2005). The journey to resiliency: An integrative framework for treatment for victims and survivors of family violence. *Social Work & Christianity, 32*(4), 305–320.

Cameron, J. (1992). *The artist's way: A spiritual path to higher creativity.* New York: Putnam.

Campbell, D. (1997). *The Mozart effect: Tapping the power of music to heal the body, strengthen the mind, and unlock the creative spirit.* New York: Harper Trade.

Canda, E. R. (1983). General implications of shamanism for clinical social work. *International Social Work, 26*(4), 14–22.

Canda, E. R. (1988). Conceptualizing spirituality for social work: Insights from diverse perspectives. *Social Thought, 14*(1), 30–46.

Canda, E. R. (1997). Spirituality. *Encyclopedia of social work: 1997 supplement* (19th ed.). Washington, DC: NASW Press.

Canda, E. R. (2001). Buddhism. In M. V. Hook, B. Hugen, & M. Aguilar (Eds.), *Spirituality within religious traditions in social work practice* (pp. 53–72). Pacific Grove, CA: Brooks/Cole.

Canda, E. R. (2005). The future of spirituality in social work: The farther reaches of human nature. *Advances in Social Work, 6*(1), 97–108.

Canda, E. R., & Furman, L. D. (1999). *Spiritual diversity in social work practice: The heart of helping.* New York: Free Press.

Canda, E. R., & Furman, L. D. (2010). *Spiritual diversity in social work practice: The heart of helping* (2nd ed.). New York: Oxford University Press.

Canda, E. R., Nakashima, M., & Furman, L. D. (2004). Ethical considerations about spirituality in social work: Insights from a national qualitative study. *Families in Society: The Journal of Contemporary Social Services, 85*(1), 27–35.

Canda, E. R., & Phaobtong, T. (1992). Buddhism as a support system for Southeast Asian refugees. *Social Work, 37,* 61–67.

Canda, E. R., Shin, S., & Canda, H. (1993). Traditional philosophies of human services in Korea and contemporary social work implications. *Social Development Issues, 15*(3), 84–104.

Canda, E. R., & Yellow Bird, M. J. (1996). Cross-tradition borrowing of spiritual practices in social work settings. *Society for Spirituality and Social Work Newsletter, 3*(1), 1–7.

Cannon, W. B. (1924). *Bodily changes in pain, hunger, fear, and rage.* New York: Appleton.

Cao, X., Mokhtarian, P., & Handy, S. (2009). Examining the impacts of residential self-selection on travel behavior: A focus on empirical findings. *Transport Reviews, 29*(3), 359–395.

Caplan, G. (1990). Loss, stress, and mental health. *Community Mental Health Journal, 26,* 27–48.

Caplan, G., & Caplan, R. B. (2000). The future of primary prevention. *Journal of Primary Prevention, 21*(2), 131–136.

Cappicci, A., Chadha, J., Bi Lin, M., & Snyder, F. (2012). Using critical race theory to analyze how Disney constructs diversity: A construction for Baccalaureate human behavior in the social environment curriculum. *Journal of Teaching in Social Work, 32*(1), 46–61.

Cardoso, C., Ellenbogen, M., Serravalle, L., & Linnen, A. M. (2013). Stress-induced negative mood moderates the relation between oxytocin administration and trust: Evidence for the tend-and-befriend response to stress? *Psychoneuroendocrinology, 38*(11), 2800–2804.

Carlton-LaNey, I. B. (1999). African American social work pioneers' response to need. *Social Work, 44*(4), 311–321.

Carlton-LaNey, I. B. (Ed.). (2001). *African American leadership: An empowerment tradition in social welfare history.* Washington, DC: NASW Press.

Carnes, R., & Craig, S. (1998). *Sacred circles: A guide to creating your own women's spirituality group.* San Francisco: HarperSanFrancisco.

Carnoy, M., & Rothstein, R. (2013). *What do international tests really show about U.S. student performance?* Washington, DC: Economic Policy Institute. Retrieved from www.epi.org/publications/us-student-performance-testing.

Carolan, M. T., Bagherinia, G., Juhari, R., Himelright, J., & Mouton-Sanders, M. (2000). Contemporary Muslim families: Research and practice. *Contemporary Family Therapy, 22*(1), 67–79.

Caron, S. L. (2011). *Sex around the world: Cross-cultural perspectives on human sexuality* (4th ed.). Upper Saddle River, NJ: Pearson/Prentice Hall.

Carroll, M. (1998). Social work's conceptualization of spirituality. *Social Thought, 18*(2), 1–14.

Carron, A. V., & Brawley, L. R. (2000). Cohesion: Conceptual and measurement issues. *Small Group Research, 31*(1), 89–106.

Carter, R. (2009). *The human brain book.* London: DK.

Casey, T., & Maldonado, L. (2012). *Worst off single-parent families in the United States: A cross-national comparison of single parenthood in the U.S. and sixteen other high-income countries.* Legal Momentum: The Women's Legal Defense and Education Fund. Retrieved from https://www.legalmomentum.org/sites/default/files/reports/worst-off-single-parent.pdf.

Castells, M. (2012). *Networks of outrage and hope.* Boston: Polity.

Castex, G. M. (1994). Providing services to Hispanic/Latino populations: Profiles in diversity. *Social Work, 39*(3), 288–296.

Catalano, S. (2012). *Intimate partner violence, 1993–2010.* U.S. Department of Justice. Retrieved from www.bjs.gov/content/pub/pdf/pv9310.pdf.

Cattich, J., & Knudson-Martin, C. (2009). Spirituality and relationship: A holistic analysis of how couples cope with diabetes. *Journal of Marital & Family Therapy, 35*(1), 111–124.

Center for Health Design. (2008). *A practitioner's guide to evidence-based design.* Concord, CA: Author.

Centers for Disease Control and Prevention. (2011). *Addressing the nation's leading killers: At a glance 2011.* Retrieved from http://www.cdc.gov/chronicdisease/resources/pubolications/AAG/dhdsp.htm.

Centers for Disease Control and Prevention. (2012a). *Sexual risk behavior: HIV, STD, & teen pregnancy prevention.* Retrieved from http://www.cdc.gov/HealthyYouth/sexualbehaviors.

Centers for Disease Control and Prevention. (2012b). *2011 YRBS results: Sexual behaviors that contribute to unintended pregnancy and sexually transmitted diseases, including HIV infection.* Retrieved from www.cdc.gov/healthyyouth/yrbs/slides/sexual_slides_yrbs.ppt.

Centers for Disease Control and Prevention. (2013a). *Injury prevention & control: Traumatic brain injury.* Retrieved from http://www.cdc.gov/traumaticbraininjury.

Centers for Disease Control and Prevention. (2013b). *Diagnoses of HIV infection in the United States and dependent areas, 2011. HIV Surveillance Report: Vol. 23.* Retrieved from http://www.cdc.gov/hiv/library/reports/surveillance/2011/surveillance_Report_vol_23.html.

Centers for Disease Control and Prevention. (2013c). *HIV in the United States: At a glance.* Retrieved from http://www.cdc.gov/hiv/statistics/basics/ataglance.html.

Centers for Disease Control and Prevention. (2013d). CDC health disparities and inequalities report—United States, 2013. *Morbidity and Mortality Weekly Report, 62*(Suppl. 3), 1–187.

Central Intelligence Agency. (2013a). *The world factbook: Country comparison: Distribution of income: Gini index.* Retrieved from https://www.cia.gov/library/publications/the-world-factbook/rankorder/2172rank.html.

Central Intelligence Agency. (2013b). *The world factbook: Country comparison: Life expectancy at birth*. Retrieved from https://www.cia.gov/library/publications/the-world-factbook/rankorder/2012rank.html.

Cervigni, F., Suzuki, Y., Ishii, T., & Hata, A. (2008). Spatial accessibility to pediatric services. *Journal of Community Health, 33,* 444–448.

Chamie, J., & Mirkin, B. (2011). Same-sex marriage: A new social phenomenon. *Population and Development Review, 37*(3), 529–551.

Chamiec-Chase, R. (2009). Developing a scale to measure social workers' integration of spirituality in the workplace. *Journal of Religion & Spirituality in Social Work, 28*(3), 284–305.

Chan, Y., Lam, G., & Cheng, H. (2009). Community capacity building as a strategy of family violence prevention in a problem-stricken community: A theoretical formulation. *Journal of Family Violence, 24,* 559–568.

Charmaraman, L., & Grossman, J. M. (2010). Importance of race and ethnicity: An exploration of Asian, Black, Latino and multiracial adolescent identity. *Cultural Diversity and Ethnic Minority Psychology, 16*(2), 144–152.

Charon, J. (1998). *Symbolic interactionism: An introduction, an interpretation, and integration* (6th ed.). Englewood Cliffs, NJ: Prentice Hall.

Chaskin, R. (2013). Theories of community. In M. Weil, M. Reisch, & M. Ohmer (Eds.), *The handbook of community practice* (2nd ed., pp. 105–121). Los Angeles: Sage.

Chaturvedi, S., Zyphur, M., Arvey, R., Avolio, B., & Larsson, G. (2012). The heritability of emergent leadership: Age and gender as moderating factors. *The Leadership Quarterly, 23,* 219–232.

Cheng, J., & Monroe, M. (2012). Connection to nature: Children's affective attitude toward nature. *Environment and Behavior, 44*(1), 31–49.

Cherlin, A. J. (2010). Demographic trends in the United States: A review of research in the 2000s. *Journal of Marriage and Family, 72,* 403–419.

Chesney, B. K., & Chesler, M. A. (1993). Activism through self-help group membership: Reported life changes of parents of children with cancer. *Small Group Research, 24,* 258–273.

Chibucos, T., & Leite, R. (2005). *Readings in family theory.* Thousand Oaks, CA: Sage.

Choi, G., & Tirrito, T. (1999). The Korean church as a social service provider for older adults. *Arete, 23*(2), 69–83.

Chong, J., Fortier, Y., & Morris, T. L. (2009). Cultural practices and spiritual development for women in a Native American alcohol and drug treatment program. *Journal of Ethnicity in Substance Abuse, 8*(3), 261–282.

Chung, D. K. (2001). Confucianism. In M. V. Hook, B. Hugen, & M. Aguilar (Eds.), *Spirituality within religious traditions in social work practice* (pp. 73–97). Pacific Grove, CA: Brooks/Cole.

Chung, G., Tucker, M., & Takeuchi, D. (2008). Wives' relative income production and household male dominance: Examining violence among Asian American enduring couples. *Family Relations, 57,* 227–238.

Chung, I. W. (2006). A cultural perspective on emotions and behavior: An empathic pathway to examine intergenerational conflicts in Chinese immigrant families. *Families in Society, 87*(3), 367–376.

Clammer, J. (2009). Sociology and beyond: Towards a deep sociology. *Asian Journal of Social Science, 37*(3), 332–346.

Clark, C. C. (2002). *Health promotion in communities: Holistic and wellness approaches.* New York: Springer.

Clark, J. L. (2007). Listening for meaning: A research-based model for attending to spirituality, culture and worldview in social work practice. *Critical Social Work, 7*(1). Retrieved from www.uwindsor.ca/criticalsocialwork/listening-for-meaning-a-research-based-model-for-attending-to-spirituality-culture-and-worldview-in-social-work-practice.

Clean Clothes Campaign. (2009, October 5). *Asia wage demand put to Euro retailers.* Retrieved from archives.cleanclothes.org/media-inquiries/press-releases/asia-wage-demand-put-to-euro-retailers.

Clemens, E. (1996). Organizational form as frame: Collective identity and political strategy in the American labor movement, 1880–1920. In D. McAdam, J. McCarthy, & M. Zald (Eds.), *Comparative perspectives on social movements* (pp. 205–226). New York: Cambridge University Press.

Cleveland Clinic. (2014). *Pulse and target heart rate.* Retrieved from http://my.clevelandclinic.org/heart/prevention/exercis/pulse-target-heart-rate.aspx.

Coates, J. (2003). *Ecology and social work: Toward a new paradigm.* Halifax, NS: Fernwood.

Coates, J. (2007). From ecology to spirituality and social justice. In J. Coates, J. R. Graham, B. Swartzentruber, & B. Ouelette (Eds.), *Spirituality and social work: Selected Canadian readings* (pp. 213–227). Toronto, Ont.: Canadian Scholars' Press.

Cockerham, W. (2012). Current direction in medical sociology. In G. Ritzer (Ed.), *The Blackwell encyclopedia of sociology* (pp. 385–401). Malden, MA: Blackwell.

Cohen, J., & Manning, W. (2010). The relationship context of premarital serial cohabitation. *Social Science Research, 39,* 766–776.

Cohen, S., Gottlieb, B. H., & Underwood, L. G. (2001). Social relationships and health: Challenges for measurement and intervention. *Advances in Mind–Body Medicine, 17*(2), 129–141.

Coholic, D. (2011). Exploring how young people living in foster care discuss spiritually sensitive themes in a holistic arts-based group program. *Journal of Religion & Spirituality in Social Work, 30*(3), 193–211.

Coker, A., Sanderson, M., Ellison, G., & Fadden, M. (2006). Stress, coping, social support, and prostate cancer risk among older African American and Caucasian men. *Ethnicity & Disease, 16*(4), 978–987.

Colby, I. C., Dulmus, C. N., & Sowers, K. M. (2012). *Social work and social policy: Advancing the principles of economic and social justice.* Somerset, NJ: Wiley.

Coleman, J. (1990). *Foundations of social theory.* Cambridge, MA: Belknap Press.

Coleman, M., Ganong, L., & Warzinik, K. (2007). *Family life in 20th-century America.* Westport, CT: Greenwood.

Coles, R. (1990). *The spiritual life of children.* Boston: Houghton Mifflin.

Collado, S., Staats, H., & Corraliza, J. (2013). Experiencing nature in children's summer camps: Affective, cognitive and behavioral consequences. *Journal of Environmental Psychology, 33,* 37–44.

Collins, G. (2009). *When everything changed: The amazing journey of American women from 1960 to the present.* New York: Little, Brown.

Collins, P. H. (2000). It's all in the family: Intersections of gender, race, and nation. In U. Narayan & S. Harding (Eds.), *Decentering the center: Philosophy for a multicultural, postcolonial, and feminist world* (pp. 156–176). Bloomington: Indiana University Press.

Collins, P. H. (2012). Looking back, moving ahead: Scholarship in service to social justice. *Gender & Society, 26*, 14–22.

Collins, R. (2004). *Interaction ritual chains*. Princeton, NJ: Princeton University Press.

Conger, R., & Conger, K. (2008). Understanding the processes through which economic hardship influences families and children. In D. R Crane & T. Heaton (Eds.), *Handbook of families & poverty* (pp. 64–81). Thousand Oaks, CA: Sage.

Conger, R., & Elder, G. (1994). *Linking economic hardship to marital quality and instability: Families in troubled times: Adapting to change in rural America*. New York: Aldine De Gruyter.

Conger, R., Wallace, L., Sun, Y., Simons, R., McLoyed, V., & Brody, G. (2002). Economic pressure in African American families: A replication and extension of the family stress model. *Developmental Psychology, 38*, 179–193.

Connolly, M. (2006). Fifteen years of Family Group Conferencing: Coordinators talk about their experiences in Aotearoa New Zealand. *British Journal of Social Work, 36*(4), 523–540.

Conrad, D., & Kellar-Guenther, Y. (2006). Compassion fatigue, burnout, and compassion satisfaction among Colorado child protection workers. *Child Abuse & Neglect, 30*, 1071–1080.

Conrad, P. (2007). *The medicalization of society: On the transformation of human conditions into treatable disorders*. Baltimore: Johns Hopkins University Press.

Cook, K. (Ed.). (1987). *Social exchange theory*. Newbury Park, CA: Sage.

Cook, K., Hardin, R., & Levin, M. (2005). *Cooperation without trust?* New York: Russell Sage Foundation.

Cooley, C. (1902). *Human nature and the social order*. New York: Scribner's.

Corbett, J. M. (1997). *Religion in America* (3rd ed.). Upper Saddle River, NJ: Prentice Hall.

Corcoran, J., & Walsh, J. (2010). *Clinical assessment and diagnosis in social work practice* (2nd ed.). New York: Oxford.

Coronado, V. G., McGuire, L. C., Sarmiento, K., Bell, J., Lionbarger, M. R., Jones, C. D., et al. (2012). Trends in traumatic brain injury in the U.S. and the public health response: 1995–2009. *Journal of Safety Research, 43*(4), 299–307.

Cortright, B. (1997). *Psychotherapy and spirit: Theory and practice in transpersonal psychotherapy*. Albany, NY: SUNY Press.

Coser, L. (1956). *The functions of conflict*. New York: Free Press.

Costa, M. (2012). Territorial behavior in public settings. *Environment and Behavior, 44*(5), 713–721.

Costas, O. E. (1991). Hispanic theology in North America. In L. M. Getz & R. O. Costa (Eds.), *Strategies for solidarity: Liberation theologies in tension* (pp. 63–74). Minneapolis, MN: Fortress Press.

Coulton, C., Jennings, M. Z., & Chan, T. (2013). How big is my neighborhood? Individual and contextual effects on perceptions of neighborhood scale. *American Journal of Community Psychology, 51*, 140–150.

Council for a Parliament of the World's Religions. (2013). *About us*. Retrieved from http://www.parliamentofreligions.org/index.cfm?n=1.

Council on Social Work Education. (2008). *Educational policy and accreditation standards*. Alexandria, VA: Author.

Cousins, L. (1994). *Community High: The complexity of race and class in a Black urban high school*. Unpublished doctoral dissertation, University of Michigan, Ann Arbor.

Cousins, L. (2008). Black students' identity and acting White and Black. In J. U. Ogbu (Ed.), *Minority status, oppositional culture and schooling* (pp. 167–189). New York: Routledge.

Cousins, L. (2013). Deservingness, children in poverty, and collective well being. *Children and Youth Services Review, 35*, 1252–1259.

Cousins, L., & Mabrey, T. (2007). Revisiting the regendering of social work practice with African American girls. In L. A. See (Ed.), *Human behavior in the social environment from an African American perspective* (2nd ed., pp. 235–252). New York: Haworth.

Cowley, A. S. (1993). Transpersonal social work: A theory for the 1990s. *Social Work, 38*, 527–534.

Cowley, A. S. (1996). Transpersonal social work. In F. J. Turner (Ed.), *Social work treatment: Interlocking theoretical approaches* (4th ed., pp. 663–698). New York: Free Press.

Cowley, A. S. (1999). Transpersonal theory and social work practice with couples and families. *Journal of Family Social Work, 3*(20), 5–21.

Cowley, A. S., & Derezotes, D. (1994). Transpersonal psychology and social work education. *Journal of Social Work Education, 30*, 32–39.

Cox, D., & Pawar, M. (2013). *International social work: Issues, strategies, and programs* (2nd ed.). Thousand Oaks, CA: Sage.

Cox, G. R. (2000). Children, spirituality, and loss. *Illness, Crisis & Loss, 8*(1), 60–70.

Cox, K. (2000). Parenting the second time around for parents in recovery: Parenting class using the twelve-step recovery model. *Sources, 10*, 11–14.

Cox, T., Jr. (1993). *Cultural diversity in organizations: Theory, research, and practice*. San Francisco: Berrett-Koehler.

Cox, T., Jr. (2001). *Creating a multicultural organization: A strategy for capturing the power of diversity*. San Francisco: Jossey-Bass.

Coyhis, D., & Simonelli, R. (2005). Rebuilding Native American communities. *Child Welfare, 84*(2), 323–336.

Coyle, J., Nochajski, T., Maguin, E., Safyer, A., DeWit, D., & Macdonald, S. (2009). An exploratory study of the nature of family resilience in families affected by parental alcohol abuse. *Journal of Family Issues, 30*(12), 1606–1623.

Coyne, R. (2014). *Group work leadership: An introduction for helpers*. Los Angeles: Sage.

Crabtree, S. A., Husain, F., & Spalek, B. (2008). *Islam and social work: Debating values, transforming practice*. Bristol, UK: Policy Press.

Cressey, T., & Lallemant, M. (2007). Pharmacogenetics of antiretroviral drugs for the treatment of HIV-infected patients: An update. *Infection, Genetics and Evolution, 7*(2), 333–342.

Crisp, B. (2010). *Spirituality and social work*. Burlington, VT: Ashgate.

Crocetti, E., Rubini, M., & Meeus, W. (2008). Capturing the dynamics of identity formation in various ethnic groups: Development and validation of a three-dimensional model. *Journal of Adolescence, 31*(2), 207–222.

Cronley, C. (2010). Unraveling the social construction of homelessness. *Journal of Human Behavior in the Social Environment, 20*(2), 319–333.

Crook, W. (2001). Trickle-down bureaucracy: Does the organization affect client responses to programs? *Administration in Social Work, 26*(1), 37–59.

Cross, W., Parham, T., & Black, E. (1991). The stages of Black identity development: Nigrescence models. In R. Jones (Ed.), *Black psychology* (3rd ed., pp. 319–338). Berkeley, CA: Cobb & Henry.

Croteau, D., Hoynes, W., & Milan, S. (2012). *Media/society* (4th ed.). Los Angeles: Sage.

Cuba, L., & Hummon, D. (1993). A place to call home: Identification with dwelling, community, and region. *Sociological Quarterly, 34*(1), 111–131.

Cummings, S. (2008). Treating older persons with severe mental illness in the community: Impact of an interdisciplinary geriatric mental health team. *Journal of Gerontological Social Work, 52*(1), 17–31.

Curra, J. (2011). *The relativity of deviance.* Thousand Oaks, CA: Pine Forge Press.

Czarniawska, B. (2007). Has organization theory a tomorrow? *Organization Studies, 28,* 27–29.

Datar, A., Liu, J., Linnemayr, S., & Stecher, C. (2013). The impact of natural disasters on child health and investments in rural India. *Social Science & Medicine, 76,* 83–91.

Davidson, R. J., & Begley, S. (2012). *The emotional life of your brain.* New York: Plume.

Davidson, R. J., Kabat-Zinn, J., Schumacher, J., Rosenkranz, M., Muller, D., Santorelli, S. F., et al. (2003). Alterations in brain and immune function produced by mindfulness meditation. *Psychosomatic Medicine, 65*(4), 564–570.

Davies, S. (2006). *Challenging gender norms: Five genders among the Bugis in Indonesia.* Belmont, CA: Wadsworth.

Davis, G., McAdam, D., Scott, W. R., & Zald, M. (2005). *Social movements and organization theory.* New York: Cambridge University Press.

Davis, L. E. (1984). Essential components of group work with Black Americans. *Social Work With Groups, 7*(3), 97–109.

Davis, L. E. (1995). The crisis of diversity. In M. D. Feit, J. H. Famey, J. S. Wodarski, & A. R. Mann (Eds.), *Capturing the power of diversity* (pp. 47–57). New York: Haworth.

Davis, L. E., Strube, M., & Cheng, L. (1995). Too many blacks, too many whites: Is there a racial balance? *Basic and Applied Social Psychology, 17*(1 & 2), 119–135.

Davis, M. (2000). *Magical urbanism: Latinos reinvent the U.S. city.* New York: Verso.

Davis, M. (2006). *Planet of slums.* London: Verso.

Day, M. (2012). Interdisciplinary hospice team processes and multidimensional pain: A qualitative study. *Journal of Social Work in End-of-Life & Palliative Care, 8*(1), 53–76.

Day, P., & Schuler, D. (2004). *Community practice in the network society: Local action/global interaction.* New York: Routledge.

De Fronzo, R. A., Ferrannini, E., Keen, H., & Zimmet, P. (Eds.). (2004). *International textbook of diabetes mellitus* (Wiley reference series in biostatistics) (Two volume set) (3rd ed.). Hoboken, NJ: Wiley.

Dean, R. G. (2001). The myth of cross-cultural competence. *Families in Society, 82*(6), 623–630.

Deater-Deckard, K. (2004). *Parenting stress.* New Haven, CT: Yale University Press.

DeFilippis, J., Fisher, R., & Shragge, E. (2009). What's left in the community? Oppositional politics in contemporary practice. *Community Development Journal, 44*(1), 38–52.

Delgado, M. (1988). Groups in Puerto Rican spiritism: Implications for clinicians. In C. Jacobs & D. D. Bowles (Eds.), *Ethnicity and race: Critical concepts in social work* (pp. 34–37). Silver Spring, MD: NASW Press.

Delgado, M., & Staples, L. (2013). Youth-led organizing, community engagement, and opportunity creation. In M. Weil, M. Reisch, & M. Ohmer (Eds.), *The handbook of community practice* (2nd ed., pp. 547–565). Los Angeles: Sage.

Dell'Amore, C. (2012, February 29). Women can make new eggs after all, stem-cell study hints finding may one day help delay menopause, improve fertility. *National Geographic News.* Retrieved from http://news.nationalgeographic.com/news/2012/02/120229-women-health-ovaries-eggs-reproduction-science.

della Porta, D., & Diani, M. (2006). *Social movements: An introduction* (2nd ed.). Malden, MA: Blackwell.

della Porta, D., Kriesi, H., & Rucht, D. (2009). *Social movements in a globalising world.* New York: Palgrave Macmillan.

Demo, D., & Fine, M. (2010). *Beyond the average divorce.* Thousand Oaks, CA: Sage.

DeNavas-Walt, C., Proctor, B., & Hill Lee, C. (2006). *Income, poverty, and health insurance coverage in the United States: 2005.* Washington, DC: U.S. Census Bureau.

DeNavas-Walt, C., Proctor, B., & Smith, J. (2013). *Income, poverty, and health insurance coverage in the United States: 2012.* Washington, DC: U.S. Census Bureau.

Denzin, N. K. (2001). *Interpretive interactionism.* Thousand Oaks, CA: Sage.

DePoy, E., & Gilson, S. F. (2004). *Rethinking disability: Principles for professional and social change.* Belmont, CA: Wadsworth.

DePoy, E., & Gilson, S. F. (2007). *The human experience: Description, explanation, and judgment.* New York: Rowman & Littlefield.

DePoy, E., & Gilson, S. F. (2011). *Studying disability: Multiple theories and responses.* Thousand Oaks, CA: Sage.

DePoy, E., & Gilson, S. F. (2012). *Human behavior theory and applications: A critical thinking approach.* Thousand Oakes, CA: Sage.

Derezotes, D. S. (2001). Transpersonal social work with couples: A compatibility-intimacy model. In E. R. Canda & E. D. Smith (Eds.), *Transpersonal perspectives on spirituality in social work* (pp. 163–174). Binghamton, NY: Haworth Press.

Derezotes, D. S. (2006). *Spiritually oriented social work practice.* Boston: Pearson Education.

Devereux, E. (2013). *Understanding the media* (3rd ed.). Thousand Oaks, CA: Sage.

Diamond, L. M., & Fagundes, C. P. (2010). Psychobiological research on attachment. *Journal of Social and Personal Relationships, 27*(2), 218–225.

DiPrete, T., Gelman, A., McCormick, T., Teitler, J., & Zheng, T. (2011). Segregation in social networks based on acquaintanceship and trust. *American Journal of Sociology, 116*(4), 1234–1283.

Disabled People's International. (2013). *About us.* Retrieved from http://dpi.org/AboutUs.

divorcesource.com. (n.d.). *U.S. divorce rates and statistics.* Retrieved from http://www.divorcesource.com/ds/main/u-s-divorce-rates-and-statiscs-1037.shtml.

Diwan, S., Jonnalagadda, S. S., & Balaswamy, S. (2004). Resources predicting positive and negative affect during the experience of stress: A study of older Asian Indian immigrants in the United States. *The Gerontologist, 44*(5), 605–614.

Dixon, J., Dogan, R., & Sanderson, A. (2005). Community and communitarianism: A philosophical investigation. *Community Development Journal, 40*(1), 4–16.

Dominelli, L. (2012). *Green social work: From environmental crises to environmental justice.* Cambridge, UK: Polity Press.

Donigian, J., & Malnati, R. (2005). *Systemic group therapy: A triadic model.* Belmont, CA: Wadsworth.

Donleavey, G. A. (2008). No man's land: Exploring the space between Gilligan and Kohlberg. *Journal of Business Ethics, 80,* 807–822.

Dosser, D. A., Smith, A. L., Markowski, E. W., & Cain, H. I. (2001). Including families' spiritual beliefs and their faith communities in systems of care. *Journal of Family Social Work, 5*(3), 63–78.

Drake, R. E., Mueser, K. T., Brunette, M. F., & McHugo, G. J. (2004). A review of treatments for people with severe mental illnesses and co-occurring substance use disorders. *Psychiatric Rehabilitation Journal, 27*(4), 360.

Drescher, K. D., Burgoyne, M., Casas, E., Lovato, L., Curran, E., Pivar, I., et al. (2009). Issues of grief, loss, honor, and remembrance: Spirituality and work with military personnel and their families. In S. M. Freeman, B. A. Moore, & A. Freeman (Eds.), *Living and surviving in harm's way: A psychological treatment handbook for pre- and post-deployment of military personnel* (pp. 437–466). New York: Routledge.

Drosdzol, A., & Skrzypulec, V. (2008). Quality of life and sexual function of Polish infertile couples. *European Journal of Contraceptive and Reproductive Health Care, 13,* 271–281.

Drucker, P. (1954). *The practice of management.* New York: Harper.

Duba, J. D., & Watts, R. E. (2009). Therapy with religious couples. *Journal of Clinical Psychology, 65*(2), 210–223.

Dudziak, S., & Profitt, N. (2012). Group work and social justice: Designing pedagogy for social change. *Social Work With Groups, 35,* 235–252.

Duran, E., & Duran, B. (1995). *Native American postcolonial psychology.* Albany: State University of New York Press.

Duvall-Early, K., & Benedict, J. (1992). The relationship between privacy and different components of job satisfaction. *Environment and Behavior, 24,* 670–679.

Dybicz, P. (2011). Anything goes? Science and social constructions in competing discourses. *Journal of Sociology & Social Welfare, 38*(3), 101–122.

Dylan, A., & Coates, J. (2012). The spirituality of justice: Bringing together the eco and the social. *Journal of Religion & Spirituality in Social Work, 31*(1–2), 128–149.

Eacott, M., & Easton, A. (2012). Remembering the past and thinking about the future: Is it really about time? *Learning and Motivation, 43,* 200–208.

Eagle, M., & Wolitzky, D. L. (2009). Adult psychotherapy from the perspectives of attachment theory and psychoanalysis. In J. H. Obegi & E. Berant (Eds.), *Attachment theory and research in clinical work with adults* (pp. 351–378). New York: Guilford Press.

Eberhard, J. (2008). *Brain landscape: The coexistence of neuroscience and architecture.* New York: Oxford University Press.

Eckerd, A., & Keeler, A. (2012). Going green together? Brownfield remediation and environmental justice. *Policy Science, 45,* 293–314.

The Economist. (2013, June 22). *Media conglomerates: Breaking up is not so very hard to do.* Retrieved from http://www.economist.com/new/busines/21579823-media-empires-are-becoming-more-focused-and-shareholders-it-breaking-up-not-so-very.

Edin, K., Kefalas, M., & Reed, J. (2004). A peek inside the black box: What marriage means for poor unmarried parents. *Journal of Marriage and the Family, 66,* 1007–1014.

Edin, K., & Reed, J. (2005). Why don't they just get married? Barriers to marriage among the disadvantaged. *The Future of Children, 15*(5), 117–137.

Edwards, G. (2014). *Social movements and protest.* New York: Cambridge University Press.

Eggerston, L. (2012). Hospital noise: Increasingly, it hinders communication and puts patients at risk. *Canadian Nurse, 108*(4), 28–31.

Eheart, B., Hopping, D., Power, M., Mitchell, E., & Racine, D. (2009). Generations of Hope Communities: An intergenerational neighborhood model of support and service. *Children and Youth Services Review, 31,* 47–52.

Elder, G. H., Jr. (1974). *Children of the Great Depression: Social change in life experience.* Chicago: University of Chicago Press.

Elder, G. H., Jr. (1998). The life course as developmental theory. *Child Development, 69*(1), 1–12.

Elder, G. H., Jr., & Giele, J. (Eds.). (2009). *The craft of life course research.* New York: Guilford Press.

Ellison, C. G., & Levin, J. S. (1998). The religion–health connection: Evidence, theory, and future directions. *Health, Education, and Behavior, 25*(6), 700–720.

Ellison, J. W., & Plaskow, J. (Eds.). (2007). *Heterosexism in contemporary world religion: Problem and prospect.* Cleveland, OH: Pilgrim Press.

Ellison, N., Steinfield, C., & Lampe, C. (2007). The benefits of Facebook "friends": Social capital and college students' use of online social network sites. *Journal of Computer-Mediated Communication, 12,* 1143–1168.

Ellsworth, P. C. (1991). Some implications of cognitive appraisal theories of emotion. In K. T. Strongman (Ed.), *International review of studies on emotion* (pp. 143–161). New York: Wiley.

El-Messidi, A., Al-Fozan, H., Lin Tan, S., Farag, R., & Tulandi, T. (2004). Effects of repeated treatment failure on the quality of life of couples with infertility. *Journal of Obstetrics and Gynaecology Canada, 26,* 333–336.

Emery, R. (1999). *Marriage, divorce, and children's adjustment* (2nd ed.). Thousand Oaks, CA: Sage.

Engel, R., & Schutt, R. (2013). *The practice of research in social work* (3rd ed.). Thousand Oaks, CA: Sage.

Engels, F. (1892). *The condition of the working class in England in 1844* (F. K. Wischnewtzky, Trans.). London: Sonnenschein.

Engels, F. (1970). *The origins of the family, private property and the state.* New York: International. (Original work published 1884)

Ensari, N., Riggio, R., Christian, J., & Carslaw, G. (2011). Who emerges as leader: Meta-analyses of individual differences as predictors of leadership emergence. *Personality and Individual Differences, 51,* 532–536.

Equal Rights Center. (2007). *Civil rights lawsuit filed against the city of Manassas, VA and its school system for discriminating against Hispanic residents.* Retrieved from http://www.equalrightscenter.org/site/DocServer/10.16.07_Civil_Rights_Lawsuit_Filed_Against_the City_of_pdf?docID=1124&AddInterest=1162.

Erera, P. (2002). *Family diversity: Continuity and change in the contemporary family.* Thousand Oaks, CA: Sage.

Erikson, E. (1963). *Childhood and society* (2nd ed.). New York: Norton.

Erikson, E. (1968). *Identity: Youth and crisis.* New York: Norton.

Ernst, J. (2000). Mapping child maltreatment: Looking at neighborhoods in a suburban county. *Child Welfare, 79,* 555–572.

Esbjörn-Hargens, S. (Ed.). (2010). *Integral theory in action: Applied, theoretical, and constructive perspectives on the AQAL model*. Albany, NY: SUNY Press.

European Commission: Employment, Social Affairs & Inclusion. (2013). *Social protection & social inclusion*. Retrieved from http://ec.europa.eu/social/main.jsp?catId=750.

Evans, C. J., Boustead, R. S., & Owens, C. (2008). Expressions of spirituality in parents with at-risk children. *Families in Society: The Journal of Contemporary Social Services, 89*(2), 245–252.

Evans, G., Lepore, S., & Allen, K. (2000). Cross-cultural differences in tolerance for crowding: Fact or fiction? *Journal of Personality and Social Psychology, 79*(2), 204–210.

Evans, G., & Saegert, S. (2000). Residential crowding in the context of inner city poverty. In S. Wapner, J. Demick, T. Yamamoto, & H. Minami (Eds.), *Theoretical perspectives in environment–behavior research: Underlying assumptions, research problems, and methodologies* (pp. 247–267). New York: Kluwer Academic.

Faber, A., Willerton, E., Clymer, S., MacDermid, S., & Weiss, H. (2008). Ambiguous absence, ambiguous presence: A qualitative study of military reserve families in wartime. *Journal of Family Psychology, 22*(2), 222–230.

Faculty of Public Health. (2010). *Great Outdoors! How our natural health service uses green space to improve well-being*. London: Faculty of Public Health. Retrieved from www.fph.org.uk/uploads/r_great_outdoors.pdf.

Fadiman, A. (1998). *The spirit catches you and you fall down: A Hmong child, her American doctors, and the collision of two cultures*. New York: Farrar, Straus and Giroux.

Fairbrother, M., & Martin, I. (2013). Does inequality erode social trust? Results from multilevel models of US states and counties. *Social Science Research, 42*, 347–360.

Falicov, C. (2011). Migration and the life cycle. In M. McGoldrick, B. Carter, & N. Garcia-Preto (Eds.), *The expanded family life cycle: Individual, family, and social perspectives* (4th ed., pp. 336–347). Boston: Allyn & Bacon.

Farmer, R. (2009). *Neuroscience and social work practice: The missing link*. Thousand Oaks, CA: Sage.

Farrell, M. (2009, September 19). ACORN scandal: How much federal funding does it get? *The Christian Science Monitor*. Retrieved from http://www.csmonitor.com/USA/2009/0919/p02s13-usgn.html.

Farrell, M. (2013, May 16). Many households cutting cable, but not their favorite TV shows. *BostonGlobe.com*. Retrieved from www.boston.globe.com/business/2013/05/15/rise-cord-cutter/CWuXxXnSdcsBUPQwZiz810/story/html.

Farrelly-Hansen, M. (2009). *Spirituality and art therapy: Living the connection*. London: Jessica Kingsley.

Faver, C. A., & Trachte, B. L. (2005). Religion and spirituality at the border: A survey of Mexican-American social work students. *Social Thought, 24*(4), 3–18.

Feldman, R. (1990). Settlement-identity: Psychological bonds with home places in a mobile society. *Environment and Behavior, 22*(2), 183–229.

Felsten, G. (2009). Where to take a study break on college campus: An attention restoration theory perspective. *Journal of Environmental Psychology, 29*, 160–176.

Ferguson, K. M., Wu, Q., Dryness, G., & Spruijt-Metz, D. (2007). Perceptions of faith and outcomes in faith-based programs for homeless youth: A grounded theory approach. *Journal of Social Service Research, 33*(4), 25–43.

Ferree, M. M., & Martin, P. Y. (1995). *Feminist organizations: Harvest of the new women's movement*. Philadelphia: Temple University Press.

Fine, M., Ganong, L., & Demo, D. (2010). Divorce: A risk and resilience perspective. In S. Price, C. Price, & P. McKenry (Eds.), *Families & change: Coping with stressful events and transitions* (4th ed., pp. 211–233). Thousand Oaks, CA: Sage.

Finger, W., & Arnold, E. M. (2002). Mind–body interventions: Applications for social work practice. *Social Work in Health Care, 35*(4), 57–78.

Finkelhor, D., Ormrod, R., Turner, H., & Hamby, S. (2005). The victimization of children and youth: A comprehensive national survey. *Child Maltreatment, 10*, 5–25.

Firestein, S. (2012). *Ignorance: How it drives science*. New York: Oxford University Press.

Fischer, D. (1989). *Albion's seed: Four British folkways in America*. New York: Oxford University Press.

Fischer, J., Lyness, K., & Engler, R. (2010). Families coping with alcohol and substance abuse. In S. Price, C. Price, & P. McKenry (Eds.), *Families & change: Coping with stressful events and transitions* (4th ed., pp. 141–162). Thousand Oaks, CA: Sage.

Fisek, M. H., Berger, J., & Moore, J. (2002). Evaluations, enactment, and expectations. *Social Psychology Quarterly, 65*(4), 329–345.

Fisher, R. (2005). History, context, and emerging issues for community practice. In M. Weil (Ed.), *The handbook of community practice* (pp. 34–58). Thousand Oaks, CA: Sage.

Fisher, R., & Karger, H. (1997). *Social work and community in a private world*. New York: Longman.

Fisher, R., & Shragge, E. (2000). Challenging community organizing: Facing the 21st century. *Journal of Community Practice, 8*(3), 1–19.

Fitzgerald, J. (1997). Reclaiming the whole: Self, spirit, and society. *Disability and Rehabilitation, 19*(10), 407–413.

Fitzgerald, K., & Rodgers, D. (2000). Radical social movement organizations: A theoretical model. *Sociological Quarterly, 41*(4), 573–592.

Flacks, R. (2004). Knowledge for what? Thoughts on the state of social movement studies. In J. Goodwin & J. Jasper (Eds.), *Rethinking social movements: Structure, meaning, and emotion* (pp. 135–153). Lanham, MD: Rowman & Littlefield.

Flake, E., Davis, B., Johnson, P., & Middleton, L. (2009). The psychosocial effects of deployment on military children. *Journal of Developmental & Behavioral Pediatrics, 30*(4), 271–278.

Flanagan, W. (1993). *Contemporary urban sociology*. New York: Cambridge University Press.

Flores-Gonzalez, N. (1999). Puerto Rican high achievers: An example of ethnic and academic identity compatibility. *Anthropology & Education Quarterly, 30*(3), 343–362.

Floyd, K., & Morman, M. (Eds.). (2006). *Widening the family circle: New research on family communication*. Thousand Oaks, CA: Sage.

Follett, M. P. (1918). *The new state: Group organization, the solution of popular government*. London: Longman, Green.

Follett, M. P. (1924). *Creative experience*. New York: Longman, Green.

Fordham, S. (1993). Those loud Black girls: (Black) women, silence, and gender "passing" in the academy. *Anthropology and Education Quarterly, 2*(1), 3–32.

Fordham, S. (1996). *Blacked out: Dilemmas of race, identity, and success at Capital High*. Chicago: University of Chicago Press.

Fordham, S., & Ogbu, J. (1986). Black students' school success: Coping with the "burden of 'acting white.'" *Urban Review, 18*(3), 176–206.

Forsyth, D. (2011). The nature and significance of groups: In R. Coyne (Ed.), *The Oxford handbook of group counseling* (pp. 19–35). New York: Oxford University Press.

Foucault, M. (1969). *The archaeology of knowledge and the discourse on language.* New York: Harper Colophon.

Fowler, J. F. (1981). *Stages of faith: The psychology of human development and the quest for meaning.* San Francisco: Harper.

Fowler, J. F. (1995). *Stages of faith: The psychology of human development and the quest for meaning.* New York: HarperCollins.

Fowler, J. F. (1996). *Faithful change: The personal and public challenges of postmodern life.* Nashville, TN: Abingdon Press.

Fox, M. (1994). *The reinvention of work: A new vision of livelihood for our time.* San Francisco: HarperSanFrancisco.

Frame, M. W. (2003). *Integrating religion and spirituality into counseling: A comprehensive approach.* Pacific Grove, CA: Brooks/Cole Thompson Learning.

Francescato, D., & Tomai, M. (2001). Community psychology: Should there be a European perspective? *Journal of Community & Applied Social Psychology, 11,* 371–380.

Francis, A. (2013). *Saving normal.* New York: HarperCollins.

Frank, A. (1967). *Capitalism and development in Latin America.* New York: Monthly Review Press.

Frankl, V. E. (1988). *The will to meaning: Foundations and applications of logotherapy.* New York: Meridian.

Franklin, R. M. (1994). The safest place on earth: The culture of Black congregations. In J. P. Wind & J. W. Lewis (Eds.), *American congregations* (Vol. 2, pp. 257–260). Chicago: University of Chicago Press.

Fraser, C., McIntyre, A., & Manby, M. (2009). Exploring the impact of parental drug/alcohol problems on children and parents in a Midlands county in 2005/06. *British Journal of Social Work, 39,* 846–866.

Freedberg, S. (2007). Re-examining empathy: A relational-feminist point of view. *Social Work, 52*(3), 251–259.

Freedom House. (2013). *Freedom of the press: 2013 freedom of the press data.* Retrieved from http://www.freedomhouse.org/report-types/freedom-press.

Freeman, D. R. (2006). Spirituality in violent and substance abusing African American men: An untapped resource in healing. *Social Thought, 25*(1), 3–22.

Freeman, E., & Couchonnal, G. (2006). Narrative and culturally based approaches in practice with families. *Families in Society: The Journal of Contemporary Social Services, 87*(2), 198–208.

Freeman, J. (1995). From seed to harvest: Transformations of feminist organizations and scholarship. In M. Ferree & P. Martin (Eds.), *Feminist organizations: Harvest of the new women's movement* (pp. 397–408). Philadelphia: Temple University Press.

Fremeaux, I. (2005). New labour's appropriation of the concept of community: A critique. *Community Development Journal, 40*(3), 265–274.

Freud, S. (1928). *The future of an illusion.* London: Hogarth Press and Institute of Psychoanalysis.

Freud, S. (1953). Three essays on the theory of sexuality. In J. Strachey (Ed. & Trans.), *The standard edition of the complete psychological works of Sigmund Freud* (Vol. 7, pp. 135–245). London: Hogarth Press. (Original work published 1905)

Freud, S. (1978). *The interpretation of dreams* (A. A. Brill, Trans.). New York: Modern Library. (Original work published 1899)

Frey, L., & Sunwolf. (2005). The symbolic-interpretive perspective of group life. In M. Poole & A. Hollingshead (Eds.), *Theories of small groups: Interdisciplinary perspectives* (pp. 185–239). Thousand Oaks, CA: Sage.

Fuchs, A. (2013). *Nonlinear dynamics in complex systems theory and applications for the life-, neuro- and natural sciences.* New York: Springer.

Fukuyama, M. A., & Sevig, T. D. (1999). *Integrating spirituality into multicultural counseling.* Thousand Oaks, CA: Sage.

Furman, L. E., & Chandy, J. M. (1994). Religion and spirituality: A long-neglected cultural component of rural social work practice. *Human Services in the Rural Environment, 17*(3/4), 21–26.

Gaard, G. (2011). Ecofeminism revisited: Rejecting essentialism and re-placing species in a material feminist environmentalism. *Feminist Formations, 23*(2), 26–53.

Galambos, C. (2001). Community healing rituals for survivors of rape. *Smith College Studies in Social Work, 71*(3), 441–457.

Gale, J. (2009). Meditation and relational connectedness: Practices for couples and families. In F. Walsh (Ed.), *Spiritual resources in family therapy* (2nd ed., pp. 247–266). New York: Guilford Press.

Galinsky, E., Aumann, K., & Bond, J. (2011). *Times are changing: Gender and generation at work and at home.* Washington, DC: Families and Work Institute. Retrieved from familiesandwork.org/downloads/TimesAreChanging.pdf.

Gallagher, L. (2013). *The end of the suburbs: Where the American dream is moving.* New York: Penguin.

Gallagher, M. (1996). *The abolition of marriage: How we destroy lasting love.* Washington, DC: Regnery.

Gallup. (2013). *Religion.* Retrieved from www.gallup.com/poll/1690/religion.aspx.

Gallup, G. H. (2002). *Americans feel need to believe.* Retrieved from http://www.gallup.com/poll/5617/americans-feel-need-believe.aspx.

Gallup, G. H., & Lindsay, D. M. (1999). *Surveying the religious landscape: Trends in U.S. beliefs.* Harrisburg, PA: Morehouse.

Galotti, K. M. (1989). Gender differences in self-reported moral reasoning: A review and new evidence. *Journal of Youth and Adolescence, 18,* 475–488.

Galvin, K. (2006). Joined by hearts and words: Adoptive family relationships. In K. Floyd & M. Morman (Eds.), *Widening the family circle: New research on family communication* (pp. 137–152). Thousand Oaks, CA: Sage.

Galvin, K., Bylund, C., & Brommel, B. (2003). *Family communication: Cohesion and change* (6th ed.). New York: Allyn & Bacon.

Galvin, K., Dickson, F., & Marrow, S. (2006). Systems theory: Patterns and wholes in family communication. In D. Braithwaite & L. Baxter (Eds.), *Engaging theories in family communication: Multiple perspectives* (pp. 309–324). Thousand Oaks, CA: Sage.

Gamble, D. (2013). Participatory methods in community practice. In M. Weil, M. Reisch, & M. Ohmer (Eds.), *The handbook of community practice* (2nd ed., pp. 327–343). Los Angeles: Sage.

Gamson, W., & Meyer, D. (1996). Framing political opportunity. In D. McAdam, J. McCarthy, & M. Zald (Eds.), *Comparative perspectives on social movements* (pp. 273–290). New York: Cambridge University Press.

Gannett, L. (2008). The Human Genome Project. *Stanford encyclopedia of philosophy.* Retrieved from http://plato.stanford.edu/entries/human-genome/#BriHisHumGenPro.

Garbarino, J., & Bedard, C. (1997). Spiritual challenges to children facing violent trauma. *Childhood: A Global Journal of Child Research, 3*(4), 467–478.

Garden, F., & Jalaludin, B. (2009). Impact of urban sprawl on overweight, obesity, and physical activity in Sydney, Australia. *Journal of Urban Health, 86*(1), 19–30.

Gardiner, H. W., & Kosmitzki, C. (2011). *Lives across cultures: Cross-cultural human development* (5th ed.). Boston: Pearson.

Gardner, H. (1999). *Intelligence reframed: Multiple intelligences for the 21st century.* New York: Basic Books.

Gardner, H. (2006). *Multiple intelligences: New horizons.* New York: Basic Books.

Garland, D. R., Myers D. M., & Wolfer, T. A. (2008). Social work with religious volunteers: Activating and sustaining community involvement. *Social Work, 53*(3), 255–265.

Garland, J., Jones, H., & Kolodny, R. (1976). A model for stages of development in social work groups. In S. Bernstein (Ed.), *Explorations in group work* (pp. 17–71). Boston: Milford.

Garner, R., & Zald, M. (2012). Now we are almost fifty! Reflections on a theory of the transformation of social movement organizations. *Social Forces, 91*(1), 3–11.

Garrett, K. (2004). Use of groups in school social work: Group work and group processes. *Social Work With Groups, 27*(2/3), 75–92.

Garrow, E., & Hasenfeld, Y. (2010). Theoretical approaches to human service organizations. In Y. Hasenfeld (Ed.), *Human services as complex organizations* (2nd ed., pp. 33–57). Thousand Oaks, CA: Sage.

Gates, G. (2013). *LGBT parenting in the United States.* The Williams Institute. Retrieved from williamsinstitute.law.ucla.edu/wp-content/uploads/LGBT-Parenting.pdf.

Geertz, C. (1973). *The interpretation of cultures.* New York: Basic Books.

Geertz, C. (1983). Common sense as a cultural system. In C. Geertz, *Local knowledge: Further essays in interpretive anthropology* (pp. 73–93). New York: Basic Books.

Geller, M. (2005). The psychoanalytic perspective. In S. Wheelan (Ed.), *The handbook of group research and practice* (pp. 87–105). Thousand Oaks, CA: Sage.

Gelles, R. (2010). Violence, abuse, and neglect in families and intimate relationships. In S. Price, C. Price, & P. McKenry (Eds.), *Families & change: Coping with stressful events and transitions* (4th ed., pp. 119–139). Thousand Oaks, CA: Sage.

George, L. (1993). Sociological perspectives on life transitions. *Annual Review of Sociology, 19*, 353–373.

Gerdes, K., & Segal, E. (2011). Importance of empathy for social work practice: Integrating new science. *Social Work, 56*(2), 141–148.

Gergen, K. (1985). The social constructionist movement in modern psychology. *American Psychologist, 40*, 266–275.

Germain, C. (1981). The physical environment and social work practice. In A. N. Maluccio (Ed.), *Promoting competence in clients* (pp. 103–124). New York: Free Press.

Germain, C., & Gitterman, A. (1996). *The life model of social work practice* (2nd ed.). New York: Columbia University Press.

Giang, T., Karpyn, A., Laurison, H., Hillier, A., & Perry, D. (2008). Pennsylvania's Fresh Food Financing Initiative. *Journal of Public Health Management and Practice, 14*, 272–279.

Gibbs, J. C., Basinger, K. S., Grime, R. L., & Snarey, J. R. (2007). Moral judgement development across cultures: Revisiting Kohlberg's universality claims. *Developmental Review, 27*, 443–500.

Gibbs, N. (2009, October 14). What women want now. *Time.* Retrieved from content.time.com/time/specials/packages/article/0,28804,1930277_1930145_1930309,00.html.

Gibson, M. (1988). *Accommodation without assimilation: Sikh immigrants in an American high school.* Ithaca, NY: Cornell University Press.

Gibson-Davis, C., Edin, K., & McLanahan, S. (2005). High hopes but even higher expectations: The retreat from marriage among low-income couples. *Journal of Marriage and Family, 65*(5), 1301–1312.

Giddens, A. (1979). *Central problems in social theory: Action, structure, and contradiction in social analysis.* Berkeley: University of California Press.

Giddens, A. (2000). *Runaway world: How globalization is reshaping our lives.* New York: Routledge.

Gifford, R. (2007). *Environmental psychology: Principles and practice* (4th ed.). Colville, WA: Optimal Books.

Gill, S. (2010). *Developing a learning culture in nonprofit organizations.* Thousand Oaks, CA: Sage.

Gilligan, C. (1982). *In a different voice.* Cambridge, MA: Harvard University Press.

Gilligan, C. (1988). Remapping the moral domain: New images of self in relationship. In C. Gilligan, J. V. Ward, & J. M. Taylor (Eds.), *Mapping the moral domain* (pp. 3–20). Cambridge, MA: Harvard University Press.

Gillis, J. (1996). *A world of their own making: Myth, ritual, and the quest for family values.* New York: Basic Books.

Gilson, S. F., & DePoy, E. (2000). Multiculturalism and disability: A critical perspective. *Disability & Society, 15*(2), 207–218.

Gilson, S. F., & DePoy, E. (2002). Theoretical approaches to disability content in social work education. *Journal of Social Work Education, 37*, 153–165.

Gitterman, A. (2009). The life model. In A. R. Roberts (Ed.), *Social workers' desk reference* (2nd ed., pp. 231–235).

Gitterman, A., & Germain, C. (2008). *The life model of social work practice: Advances in theory and practice* (3rd ed.). New York: Columbia University Press.

Gitterman, A., & Shulman, L. (Eds.). (2005). *Mutual aid groups, vulnerable and resilient populations and the life cycle* (3rd ed.). New York: Columbia University Press.

Gleason, P., Clark, M., Clark Tuttle, C., Dwoyer, E., & Silberberg, M. (2010). *The evaluation of charter school impacts.* Washington, DC: U.S. Department of Education. Retrieved from files.eric.ed.gov/fulltext/ED510573.pdf.

Gleick, J. (2008). *Chaos: Making a new science.* New York: Penguin.

Global Poverty Project. (2013). *1.4 billion reasons.* Retrieved from http://www.globalpovertyproject.com/pages/presentation.

Godsall, R., Jurkovic, G., Emshoff, J., Anderson, L., & Stanwyck, D. (2004). Why some kids do well in bad situations: Relation of parental alcohol misuse and parentification to children's self-concept. *Substance Use & Misuse, 39*(5), 789–809.

Godwyn, M., & Gittell, J. (2012). Introduction. In M. Godwyn & J. Gittell (Eds.), *Sociology of organizations: Structures and relationships* (pp. xi–xxiv). Thousand Oaks, CA: Sage.

Goffman, E. (1959). *Presentation of self in everyday life.* Garden City, NY: Archer.

Goggin, G. (Ed.). (2008). *Mobile phone cultures.* New York: Routledge.

Goldberg, A. (2010). Lesbian- and gay-parent families: Development and functioning. In S. Price, C. Price, & P. McKenry (Eds.),

Families & change: Coping with stressful events and transitions (pp. 263–284). Thousand Oaks, CA: Sage.

Goldman, J. (1996). *Healing sounds: The power of harmonics.* Rockport, MA: Element Books.

Goldstein, D. (1996). Ego psychology theory. In F. Turner (Ed.), *Social work treatment* (4th ed., pp. 191–217). New York: Free Press.

Goldstein, E. G. (1995). *Ego psychology and social work practice* (2nd ed.). New York: Free Press.

Goldstein, E. G. (2001). *Object relations theory and self psychology in social work practice.* New York: Free Press.

Goldstein, E. G. (2009). The relationship between social work and psychoanalysis: The future impact of social workers. *Clinical Social Work Journal, 37*(1), 7–13.

Goleman, D. (2005). *Emotional intelligence* (10th anniv. ed.). New York: Bantam.

Golembiewski, R. T. (1994). Is organizational membership bad for your health? Phases of burnout as covariants of mental and physical well-being. In A. Farazmand (Ed.), *Modern organizations: Administrative theory in contemporary society* (pp. 211–227). Westport, CT: Praeger.

Golsworthy, R., & Coyle, A. (1999). Spiritual beliefs and the search for meaning among older adults following partner loss. *Mortality, 4*(1), 21–40.

Goodenough, W. (1996). Culture. In D. Levison & M. Ember (Eds.), *Encyclopedia of cultural anthropology* (Vol. 1, pp. 291–298). New York: Holt.

Gordon, J. R., Pruchno, R. A., Wilson-Genderson, M., Murphy, W. M., & Rose, M. (2010). Balancing caregiving and work: Role conflict and role strain dynamics. *Journal of Family Issues, 33*(5), 662–689.

Gordon, M. (1964). *Assimilation in American life: The role of race, religion, and national origins.* New York: Oxford University Press.

Gordon, W., Zafonte, R., Cicerone, K., Cantor, J., Brown, M., Lombard, L., et al. (2006). Traumatic brain injury rehabilitation: State of the science. *American Journal of Physical Medicine & Rehabilitation, 85*(4), 343–382.

Gotham, K. (2013). Contrasts of carnival: Mardi Gras between the modern and the postmodern. In P. Kivisto (Ed.), *Illuminating social life: Classical and contemporary theory revisited* (6th ed., pp. 319–344). Los Angeles: Sage.

Gotta, G., Green, R., Rothblum, E., Solomon, S., Balsam, K., & Schwartz, P. (2011). Heterosexual, lesbian, and gay male relationships: A comparison of couples in 1975 and 2000. *Family Process, 50*(3), 353–376.

Gould, D. (2004). Passionate political processes: Bring emotions back into the study of social movements. In J. Goodwin & J. Jasper (Eds.), *Rethinking social movements: Structure, meaning, and emotion* (pp. 155–175). Lanham, MD: Rowman & Littlefield.

Granovetter, M. (1973). The strength of weak ties. *American Journal of Sociology, 78,* 1360–1380.

Gray, A. J. (2010). Whatever happened to the soul? Some theological implications of neuroscience. *Mental Health, Religion, and Culture, 13*(6), 637–648.

Gray, M., Coates, B., & Yellow Bird, M. (Eds.). (2010). *Indigenous social work around the world: Towards culturally relevant education and practice.* Surrey, UK: Ashgate.

Gray, M., Coates, J., & Hetherington, T. (2013). *Environmental social work.* New York: Routledge.

Greeff, A. P., & Fillis, A. J. (2009). Resiliency in poor single-parent families. *Families in Society: The Journal of Contemporary Social Services, 90*(3), 279–285.

Green, D., & McDermott, F. (2010). Social work from inside and between complex systems: Perspective on person-in-environment for today's social work. *British Journal of Social Work, 40,* 2414–2430.

Green, G., & Haines, A. (2012). *Asset building & community development* (3rd ed.). Los Angeles: Sage.

Green, R. (2012). Gay and lesbian family life: Risk, resilience, and rising expectations. In F. Walsh (Ed.), *Normal family processes: Growing diversity and complexity* (4th ed., pp. 172–193). New York: Guildford.

Greenberg, L. S. (2011). *Emotion-focused therapy.* Washington, DC: American Psychological Association.

Greene, G., & Lee, M. Y. (2011). *Solution-oriented social work practice: An integrative approach to working with client strengths.* New York: Oxford University Press.

Greene, M. L., Way, N., & Pahl, K. (2006). Trajectories of perceived adult and peer discrimination among Black, Latino, and Asian American adolescents: Patterns and psychological constructs. *Developmental Psychology, 42*(2), 218–238.

Greene, R. R., & Cohen, H. L. (2005). Social work with older adults and their families: Changing practice paradigms. *Families in Society, 86*(3), 367–373.

Greene, S., Anderson, E., Forgatch, M., Degarmo, D., & Hetherington, E. M. (2012). Risk and resilience after divorce. In F. Walsh (Ed.), *Normal family processes: Growing diversity and complexity* (4th ed., pp. 102–127). New York: Guildford.

Greenwald, H. (2008). *Organizations: Management without control.* Thousand Oaks, CA: Sage.

Griffin, B., Eibner, C., Bird, C., Jewell, A., Margolis, K., & Shih, R. (2013). The relationship between urban sprawl and coronary heart disease in women. *Health & Place, 20,* 51–61.

Griswold, W. (2013). *Cultures and societies in a changing world* (4th ed.). Thousand Oaks, CA: Sage.

Grof, S. (2003). Physical manifestations of emotional disorders: Observations from the study of non-ordinary states of consciousness. In K. Taylor (Ed.), *Exploring holotropic breathwork: Selected articles from a decade of The Inner Door.* Santa Cruz, CA: Hanford Mead.

Grof, S., & Bennett, H. Z. (1992). *The holotropic mind: The three levels of human consciousness and how they shape our lives.* New York: HarperCollins.

Grossman, P., Niemann, I., Schmidt, S., & Walach, H. (2004). Mindfulness-based stress reduction and health benefits: A meta-analysis. *Journal of Psychosomatic Research, 57*(1), 35–43.

Gudmunson, C., Beutler, I., Israelsen, C., McCoy, J., & Hill, E. (2007). Linking financial strain to marital instability: Examining the roles of emotional distress and marital interaction. *Journal of Family and Economic Issues, 28*(3), 357–376.

Gutierrez, L. (1990). Working with women of color: An empowerment perspective. *Social Work, 35*(2), 149–153.

Gutierrez, L. (1994). Beyond coping: An empowerment perspective on stressful life events. *Journal of Sociology and Social Welfare, 21*(3), 201–219.

Gutman, L., McLoyd, V., & Tokoyawa, T. (2005). Financial strain, neighborhood stress, parenting behaviors, and adolescent adjustment in urban African American families. *Journal of Research on Adolescence, 15*(4), 425–449.

Guttmacher Institute. (2012). *In brief: Facts on American teens' sources of information about sex.* Retrieved from http://www.guttmacher.org/pubs/FB-Teen-Sex-Ed.pdf.

Guttmacher Institute. (2013). *Facts on American teens' sexual and reproductive health.* Retrieved from http://www.guttmacher.org/pubs/FB-ATSRH.pdf.

Guy, M., Newman, M., Mastracci, S., & Maynard-Moody, S. (2010). Emotional labor in the human service organization. In Y. Hasenfeld (Ed.), *Human services as complex organizations* (2nd ed., pp. 291–309). Thousand Oaks, CA: Sage.

Haan, N. (1991). Moral development and action from a social constructivist perspective. In W. Kurtines & J. Gewirtz (Eds.), *Handbook of moral behavior and development: Theory* (Vol. 1, pp. 251–273). Hillsdale, NJ: Erlbaum.

Habermas, J. (1984). *The theory of communicative action: Vol. 1. Reason and the rationalization of society.* Boston: Beacon Press.

Habermas, J. (1987). *The theory of communicative action: Vol. 2. Lifeworld and system: A critique of functionalist reason* (T. McCarthy, Trans.). Boston: Beacon Press. (Original work published 1981)

Haddad, Y. Y. (1997). Make room for the Muslims? In W. H. Conser Jr. & S. B. Twiss (Eds.), *Religious diversity and American religious history: Studies in traditions and cultures* (pp. 218–261). Athens: University of Georgia Press.

Haig-Brown, C. (1988). *Resistance and renewal: Surviving the Indian residential school.* Vancouver, BC, Canada: Tillacum Library.

Hall, E. (1966). *The hidden dimension.* New York: Doubleday.

Halloran, L. (2013, December 24). "Living wage" effort eclipsed by minimum-pay battles. *NPR.* Retrieved from http://www.npr.org/2013/12/24/256879640/living-wage-effort-eclipsed-by-minimum-pay-battles.

Hames, A. M., & Godwin, M. C. (2008). The "out of control" balloon: Using spirituality as a coping resource. In C. F. Sori & L. L. Hecker (Eds.), *The therapist's notebook: More homework, handouts, and activities for use in psychotherapy* (pp. 171–176). New York: Routledge/Taylor & Francis.

Hampton, K., Sessions, L., Her, E. J., & Rainie, L. (2009, November 4). *Social isolation and new technology.* Washington, DC: Pew Internet & American Life Project. Retrieved from http://www.pewinternet.org/2009/11/04/social-isolation-and-new-technology.

Hampton, K., & Wellman, B. (2003). Neighboring in Netville: How the Internet supports community and social capital in a wired suburb. *City & Community, 2*(4), 277–311.

Handel, G., Cahill, S. E., & Elkin, F. (2007). *Children and society: The sociology of children and childhood socialization.* Los Angeles: Roxbury.

Hansen, D., Larson, R., & Dworkin, J. (2003). What adolescents learn in organized youth activities: A survey of self-reported developmental experiences. *Journal of Research on Adolescence, 13*(1), 25–55.

Hansen, J. E., & Lambert, S. M. (2011). Grief and loss of religion: The experiences of four rural lesbians. *Journal of Lesbian Studies, 15,* 187–196.

Hardie, E. A. (2005). Stress-coping congruence: A tripartite conceptual framework for exploring the health consequences of effective and ineffective coping. *Journal of Applied Psychology: Social Section, 1*(2), 26–33.

Hareven, T. K. (2000). *Families, history, and social change: Life-course and cross-cultural perspectives.* Boulder, CO: Westview Press.

Harrison, R., & Thomas, M. (2009). Identity in online communities: Social networking sites and language learning. *International Journal of Emerging Technologies & Society, 7*(2), 109–124.

Hart, J. (1970). The development of client-centered therapy. In J. T. Hart & T. M. Tomlinson (Eds.), *New directions in client-centered therapy* (pp. 3–22). Boston: Houghton Mifflin.

Hartman, A., & Laird, J. (1983). *Family-centered social work practice.* New York: Free Press.

Harvard Pluralism Project. (2005). *Native American religious and cultural freedom: An introductory essay.* Retrieved from pluralism.org/reports/view/176.

Hasenfeld, Y. (2010a). Introduction. In Y. Hasenfeld (Ed.), *Human services as complex organizations* (2nd ed., pp. 1–5). Thousand Oaks, CA: Sage.

Hasenfeld, Y. (2010b). The attributes of human service organizations. In Y. Hasenfeld (Ed.), *Human services as complex organizations* (2nd ed., pp. 9–32). Thousand Oaks, CA: Sage.

Hastings, M. (1998). Theoretical perspectives on social movements. *New Zealand Sociology, 13*(2), 208–238.

Hauser, M., Cushman, F., Young, L., Mikhail, J., & Jin, R. K. (2007). A dissociation between moral judgments and justifications. *Mind & Language, 22*(1), 1–21.

Havnen, K., Breivik, K., Stormark, K., & Jakobsen, R. (2011). Why do children placed out-of-home because of parental substance abuse have less mental health problems than children placed for other reasons? *Children and Youth Services Review, 33,* 2010–2017.

Hay, D., & Nye, R. (2006). *The spirit of the child* (Rev. ed.). London: Jessica Kingsley.

Hay, D., Nye, R., & Murphy, R. (1996). Thinking about childhood spirituality: Review of research and current directions. In L. J. Francis, W. K. Kay, & W. S. Campbell (Eds.), *Research in religious education* (pp. 47–71). Macon, GA: Smyth & Helwys.

Hayward, R., Miller, S., & Shaw, T. (2013). Social work education on the environment in contemporary curricula in the USA. In M. Gray, J. Coates, & T. Hetherington (Eds.), *Environmental social work* (pp. 246–259). New York: Routledge.

Healey, J. (2012). *Race, ethnicity, gender, and class: The sociology of group conflict and change* (6th ed.). Los Angeles: Sage.

Hearn, J., & Parkin, W. (1993). Organizations, multiple oppressions and postmodernism. In J. Hassard & M. Parker (Eds.), *Postmodernism and organizations* (pp. 148–162). Newbury Park, CA: Sage.

Hedberg, P., Brulin, C., & Alex, L. (2009). Experiences of purpose in life when becoming and being a very old woman. *Journal of Women & Aging, 21*(2), 125–137.

Hederman, R., & Rector, R. (1999). *Income inequality: How census data misrepresent income distribution.* Retrieved from http://www.heritage.org/research/reports/1999/09/income-inequality.

Hegtvedt, K. A. (1994). Justice. In M. Foshci & E. J. Lawler (Eds.), *Group processes: Sociological analyses* (pp. 177–204). Chicago: Nelson-Hall.

Heller, K. (1989). The return to community. *American Journal of Community Psychology, 17*(1), 1–14.

Henderson, L. (2000). The knowledge and use of alternative therapeutic techniques by social work practitioners: A descriptive study. *Social Work in Health Care, 30*(3), 55–71.

Henrich, J., Heine, S., & Norenzayan, A. (2010). The weirdest people in the world? *Behavioral and Brain Sciences, 33*(2–3), 61–83.

Hepworth, D., Rooney, R., Rooney, G. D., & Strom-Gottfried, K. (2013). *Direct social work practice: Theory and skills* (9th ed.). Independence, KY: Cengage Learning.

Herman, D. (Ed.). (2003). *Narrative theory and the cognitive sciences*. Chicago: Center for the Study of Language and Information.

Hetherington, E., & Kelly, J. (2002). *For better or worse*. New York: Norton.

Hetherington, T., & Boddy, J. (2013). Ecosocial work with marginalized populations: Time for action on climate change. In M. Gray, J. Coates, & T. Hetherington (Eds.), *Environmental social work* (pp. 46–61). New York: Routledge.

Heuveline, P., & Timberlake, J. (2004). The role of cohabitation in family formation: The United States in comparative perspective. *Journal of Marriage and Family, 66*, 1214–1230.

Heymann, J., Earle, A., & Hayes, J. (2007). *The work, family, and equity index. How does the United States measure up?* Boston: Project on Global Working Families, Harvard School of Public Health. Retrieved from www.mcgill.co/files/ihsp/WFEI2007.pdf.

Hickson, J., & Phelps, A. (1998). Women's spirituality: A proposed practice model. In D. S. Becvar (Ed.), *The family, spirituality, and social work* (pp. 43–57). Binghamton, NY: Haworth Press.

Hill, A. J., & Donaldson, L. P. (2012). We shall overcome: Promoting an agenda for integrating spirituality and community practice. *Journal of Religion & Spirituality in Social Work: Social Thought, 31*(1–2), 67–84.

Hill, R. (1949). *Families under stress*. Westport, CT: Greenwood.

Hill, R. (1958). Generic features of families under stress. *Social Casework, 49*, 139–150.

Hillery, G. (1955). Definitions of community: Areas of agreement. *Rural Sociology, 20*, 111–123.

Hillier, A. (2007). Why social work needs mapping. *Journal of Social Work Education, 43*(2), 205–221.

Hillier, A., Cole, B., Smith, T., Williams, J., Grier, S., Yancey, A., et al. (2009). Clustering of unhealthy advertisements around child-serving institutions: A three-city study. *Health and Place, 15*, 935–945.

Hillier, A., & Culhane, D. (2013). GIS applications and administrative data to support community change. In M. Weil, M. Reisch, & M. Ohmer (Eds.), *The handbook of community practice* (2nd ed., pp. 827–844). Los Angeles: Sage.

Hing, B. (2004). *Defining America through immigration policy*. Philadelphia: Temple University Press.

Hinton, S., & Hjorth, L. (2013). *Understanding social media*. Los Angeles: Sage.

Hitchcock, J. (2006). *Net crimes and misdemeanors: Outmaneuvering web spammers, stalkers, and con artists*. Medford, NJ: Cyber-Age Books.

Ho, M., Rasheed, J., & Rasheed, M. (2004). *Family therapy with ethnic minorities* (2nd ed.). Thousand Oaks, CA: Sage.

Hobfoll, S. E. (1996). Social support: Will you be there when I need you? In N. Vanzetti & S. Duck (Eds.), *A lifetime of relationships* (pp. 46–74). Belmont, CA: Thomson Brooks/Cole.

Hobsbawm, E. (1983). Introduction: Inventing tradition. In E. Hobsbawm & T. Ranger (Eds.), *The invention of tradition* (pp. 1–14). New York: Cambridge University Press.

Hodge, D. R. (2002). Does social work oppress evangelical Christians? A new class analysis of society and social work. *Social Work, 47*, 401–414.

Hodge, D. R. (2004). Working with Hindu clients in a spiritually sensitive manner. *Social Work, 49*(1), 27–38.

Hodge, D. R. (2005a). Social work and the House of Islam: Orienting practitioners to the beliefs and values of Muslims in the United States. *Social Work, 50*(2), 162–173.

Hodge, D. R. (2005b). Developing a spiritual assessment toolbox: A discussion of the strengths and limitation of five different assessment methods. *Health & Social Work, 30*(4), 314–323.

Hodge, D. R., Cardenas, P., & Montoya, H. (2001). Substance use: Spirituality and religious participation as protective factors among rural youths. *Social Work Research, 25*(3), 153–161.

Hofstede, G. (1996). An American in Paris: The influence of nationality on organization theories. *Organization Studies, 17*(13), 525–537.

Hofstede, G. (2001). *Culture's consequences: Comparing values, behaviors, institutions and organizations across nations* (2nd ed.). Thousand Oaks, CA: Sage.

Hofstede, G. (2010). *Cultures and organizations: Software of the mind* (3rd ed.). Boston: McGraw-Hill.

Hofstede, G., Deusen, C., Mueller, C., & Charles, T. (2002). What goals do business leaders pursue? A study in fifteen countries. *Journal of International Business Studies, 33*(4), 785–803.

Hogg, M. (2005). The social identity perspective. In S. Wheelan (Ed.), *The handbook of group research and practice* (pp. 133–157). Thousand Oaks, CA: Sage.

Holder, D. W., Durant, R. H., Harris, T. L., Daniel, J., Obeidallah, D., & Goodman, E. (2000). The association between adolescent spirituality and voluntary sexual activity. *Journal of Adolescent Health, 26*(4), 295–302.

Hollinghurst, S., Kessler, D., Peters, T., & Gunnell, D. (2005). Opportunity cost of antidepressant prescribing in England: Analysis of routine data. *British Medical Journal, 330*(7948), 999–1000.

Hollingsworth, L., Allen-Meares, P., Shanks, T., & Gant, L. (2009). Using the miracle question in community engagement and planning. *Families in Society, 90*(3), 332–335.

Holm, J., & Bowker, J. (Eds.). (1994). *Women in religion*. New York: Pinter.

Holtzworth-Munroe, A., & Stuart, G. (1994). Typologies of male batterers: Three subtypes and the differences among them. *Psychological Bulletin, 116*(3), 476–497.

Homans, G. (1958). Social behavior as exchange. *American Journal of Sociology, 63*, 597–606.

Hornsey, M. J. (2008). Social identity theory and self-categorization theory: A historical review. *Social and Personality Psychology Compass, 2*(1), 204–222.

House, R., Hanges, P., Javidan, M., Dorfman, P., Gupta, V., et al. (Eds.). (2004). *Culture, leadership, and organizations: The GLOBE study of 62 societies*. Thousand Oaks, CA: Sage.

Houston, J. B., Pfefferbaum, B., Sherman, M., Meison, A., Jeon-Slaughter, H., Brand, M., et al. (2009). Children of deployed National Guard troops: Perceptions of parental deployment to Operation Iraqi Freedom. *Psychiatric Annals, 39*(8), 805–811.

Hsu, S. H., Grow, J., Marlatt, A., Galanter, M., & Kaskutas, L. A. (Eds.). (2008). *Research on Alcoholics Anonymous and spirituality in addiction recovery*. New York: Springer Science.

Huang, P., Smock, P., Manning, W., & Bergstrom-Lynch, C. (2011). He says, she says: Gender and cohabitation. *Journal of Family Issues, 32*(7), 876–905.

Huber, M. S., Egeren, L., Pierce, S., & Foster-Fishman, P. (2009). GIS applications for community-based research and action:

Mapping change in a community-building initiative. *Journal of Prevention & Intervention in the Community, 27*, 5–20.

Hugen, B., & Venema, R. (2009). The difference of faith: The influence of faith in human service programs. *Journal of Religion & Spirituality in Social Work: Social Thought, 28*(4), 405–429.

Hughes, B. (2009). Disability activisms: Social model stalwarts and biological citizens. *Disability & Society, 24*(6), 677–688.

Hughes, S., Williams, B., Molina, L., Bayles, C., Bryant, L., Harris, J., et al. (2005). Characteristics of physical activity programs for older adults: Results of a multisite survey. *Gerontologist, 45*(5), 667–675.

Human Rights Campaign. (2014). *Equality from state to state 2013*. Retrieved from www.hrc.org/resources/entry/equality-from-state-to-state.

Hunler, O. S., & Gencoz, T. (2005). The effect of religiousness on marital satisfaction: Testing the mediator role of marital problem solving between religiousness and marital satisfaction relationship. *Contemporary Family Therapy, 27*(1), 123–136.

Hunter, A., & Riger, S. (1986). The meaning of community in community mental health. *Journal of Community Psychology, 14*, 55–71.

Hunter, J. D. (1994). *Before the shooting begins: Searching for democracy in America's culture wars*. New York: Free Press.

Hurdle, D. E. (2002). Hawaiian traditional healing: Culturally based interventions for social work practice. *Social Work, 47*(2), 183–192.

Hurst, J. (2007). Disability and spirituality in social work practice. *Journal of Social Work in Disability & Rehabilitation, 6*(1/2), 179–194.

Husain, S. A. (2012). Trauma, resiliency and recovery in children: Lessons from the field. *Psychiatria Danubina, 24*(Suppl. 3), 277–284.

Hutchison, E. (1987). Use of authority in direct social work practice with mandated clients. *Social Service Review, 61*(4), 581–598.

Hutchison, E. (2007). Community violence. In E. Hutchison, H. Matto, M. Harrigan, L. Charlesworth, & P. Viggiani (Eds.), *Challenges of living: A multidimensional model for social workers* (pp. 71–104). Thousand Oaks, CA: Sage.

Hutchison, E. (2012). Spirituality, religion, and progressive social movements: Resources and motivation for social change. *Journal of Religion & Spirituality in Social Work: Social Thought, 31*, 105–127.

Hutchison, E. (2014). Adult criminal justice system. In H. Matto, J. Strolin-Goltzman, & M. Ballan (Eds.), *Neuro-science for social work* (pp. 355–378). New York: Springer.

Hutchison, E., & Charlesworth, L. (2000). Securing the welfare of children: Policies past, present, and future. *Families in Society, 81*(6), 576–586.

Hutchison, E., Charlesworth, L., Matto, H., Harrigan, M., & Viggiani, P. (2007). Elements of knowing and doing in social work. In E. Hutchison, H. Matto, M. Harrigan, L. Charlesworth, & P. Viggiani (Eds.), *Challenges of living: A multidimensional working model for social workers* (pp. 13–33). Thousand Oaks, CA: Sage.

Huynh-Nhu, L., Ceballo, R., Chao, R., Hill, N., Murry, V., & Pinder-hughes, E. E. (2008). Excavating culture: Disentangling ethnic differences from contextual influences in parenting. *Applied Developmental Science, 12*(4), 163–175.

Hyde, C. (2000). The hybrid nonprofit: An examination of feminist social movement organizations. *Journal of Community Practice, 8*(4), 45–67.

Iannello, K. (1992). *Decisions without hierarchy: Feminist interventions in organization theory and practice*. New York: Routledge.

Imre, R. (1984). The nature of knowledge in social work. *Social Work, 29*, 41–45.

Ingstad, B., & Whyte, S. (Eds.). (1995). *Disability and culture*. Berkeley: University of California Press.

Institute for Innovation in Social Policy. (2013). *The index of social health*. Retrieved from http://iisp.vassar.edu/ish.html.

Interfaith Observer. (2012). *2014 Parliament of the World's Religions in Brussels cancelled*. Retrieved from http://theinterfaithobserver.org/journal-articles/2012/12/15/2014-parliament-of-the-worlds-religions-in-brusselss-cancelled.html.

International Institute for Democracy and Electoral Assistance. (2011). *Voter turnout*. Retrieved from www.idea.int/vt/countryview.cfm?id.

Internet World Stats. (2010). *Internet world users by languages*. Retrieved from http://www.internetworldstats.com/stats7.htm.

Internet World Stats. (2012). *Internet usage statistics: The internet big picture*. Retrieved from http://www.internetworldstats.com/stats.htm.

Irvin, M. (2012). *Shocking divorce statistics*. Retrieved from http://www.mckinleyirvin.com/blog/divorce/32-shocking-divorce-statistics.

Ivins, M. (1999, October 21). Way to go, college students! *Creators Syndicate, Inc*. Retrieved from http://www.creators.com/opinion/molly-ivins-october-21-1999-10-21.html.

Jackson, M. A. (2002). Christian womanist spirituality: Implications for social work practice. *Social Thought, 21*(1), 63–76.

James, R., & Gilliland, B. (2013). *Crisis intervention strategies* (7th ed.). Belmont, CA: Brooks/Cole.

James, W. (1890). *Principles of psychology*. New York: Holt.

Jandt, F. (2010). *An introduction to intercultural communication: Identities in a global community* (6th ed.). Thousand Oaks, CA: Sage.

Jansson, B., Heidemann, G., McCroskey, J., & Fertig, R. (2013). Eight models of policy practice: Local, state, national, and international arenas. In M. Weil, M. Reisch, & M. Ohmer (Eds.), *The handbook of community practice* (2nd ed., pp. 403–420). Los Angeles: Sage.

Jaskyte, K. (2012). Exploring potential for technology innovation in nonprofit organizations. *Journal of Technology in Human Services, 30*, 118–127.

Jeffers, E. (2013). Banking deregulation and the financial crisis in the US and France. *Comparative Economic Studies, 55*, 479–500.

Jenkins, R. (Ed.). (1998). *Questions of competence: Culture, classification and intellectual disability*. New York: Cambridge University Press.

Jenkins, W. (2008). *Ecologies of grace: Environmental ethics and Christian theology*. Oxford, UK: Oxford University Press.

Jenson, J., & Fraser, M. (2011). *Social policy for children and families: A risk and resilience perspective* (2nd ed.). Thousand Oaks, CA: Sage.

Johansson, U., & Woodilla, J. (2008). Designers dancing within hierarchies: The importance of non-hierarchical power for design integration and implementation. *The Design Journal, 11*(2), 95–118.

Johnson, G. R., Jang, S. J., Larsen, D. B., & De Li, S. (2001). Does adolescent religious commitment matter? A re-examination of the effects of religiosity on delinquency. *Journal on Research in Crime and Delinquency, 38*(1), 22–43.

Johnson, H. C. (2004). *Psyche and synapse expanding worlds: The role of neurobiology in emotions, behavior, thinking, and addiction for non-scientists* (2nd ed.). Greenfield, MA: Deerfield Valley.

Johnson, M. (Ed.). (1992). *People with disabilities explain it all for you*. Louisville, KY: Advocado Press.

Johnson, M. (1995). Patriarchal terrorism and common couple violence: Two forms of violence against women. *Journal of Marriage and the Family, 57*(2), 283–294.

Johnson, S. K. (1997). Does spirituality have a place in rural social work? *Social Work and Christianity, 24*(1), 58–66.

Johnstone, B., Yoon, D. P., Rupright, J., & Reid-Arndt, S. (2009). Relationships among spiritual beliefs, religious practices, congregational support and health for individuals with traumatic brain injury. *Brain Injury, 23*(5), 411–419.

Joint United Nations Programme on HIV/AIDS. (2013). *Global report: UNAIDS report on the global AIDS epidemic—2013*. Geneva, Switzerland: UNAIDS.

Jones, A., & Meier, A. (2011). Growing www.parentsofsuicide: A case study of an online support community. *Social Work With Groups, 34*, 101–120.

Jones, T. (2005). Mediating intragroup and intergroup conflict. In S. Wheelan (Ed.), *The handbook of group research and practice* (pp. 463–483). Thousand Oaks, CA: Sage.

Jorgensen, G. (2006). Kohlberg and Gilligan: Duet or duel? *Journal of Moral Education, 35*(2), 179–196.

Joseph, M. V. (1988). Religion and social work practice. *Social Casework, 69*, 443–452.

Joye, Y. (2007). Architectural lessons from environmental psychology: The case of biophilic architecture. *Review of General Psychology, 11*(4), 305–328.

Judd, R. G., & Johnston, L. B. (2012). Ethical consequences of using social network sites for students in professional social work programs. *Journal of Social Work Values & Ethics, 9*(1), 5–12.

Jung, C. (1933). *Modern man in search of a soul*. New York: Harcourt, Brace & World.

Jung, C. (1969). *The archetypes and the collective unconscious* (R. F. C. Hull, Trans.). Princeton, NJ: Princeton University Press. (Original work published 1959)

Kagan, J. (2007). *What is emotion? History, measures, and meanings*. New Haven, CT: Yale University Press.

Kahn, J., & Pearlin, L. (2006). Financial strain over the life course and health among older adults. *Journal of Health & Social Behavior, 47*(1), 17–31.

Kahneman, D. (2011). *Thinking fast and slow*. New York: Farrar, Straus and Giroux.

Kahneman, D., & Tversky, A. (1982). The psychology of preferences. *Scientific American, 246*, 160–173.

Kahneman, D., & Tversky, A. (1984). Choices, values, and frames. *American Psychologist, 39*, 341–350.

Kaitz, M., Bar-Haim, Y., Lehrer, M., & Grossman, E. (2004). Adult attachment style and interpersonal distance. *Attachment & Human Development, 6*(3), 285–304.

Kalkhoff, W., & Barnum, C. (2000). The effects of status-organizing and social identity processes on patterns of social influence. *Social Psychology Quarterly, 63*, 95–115.

Kamp Dush, C. (2011). Relationship-specific investments, family chaos, and cohabitation dissolution following a nonmarital birth. *Family Relations, 60*, 586–601.

Kamp Dush, C., & Amato, P. (2005). Consequences of relationship status and quality for subjective well-being. *Journal of Social and Personal Relationship, 22*(5), 607–627.

Kapit, W., Macey, R. I., & Meisami, E. (2000). *The physiology coloring book* (2nd ed.). Cambridge, MA: HarperCollins.

Kaplan, S., & Berman, M. (2010). Directed attention as a common resource for executive functioning and self-regulation. *Perspectives on Psychological Science, 6*(1), 43.

Karenga, M. (1995). Making the past meaningful: Kwanzaa and the concept of Sankofa. *Reflections: Narratives of Professional Helping, 1*(4), 36–46.

Karger, H., & Stoesz, D. (2014). *American social welfare policy: A pluralist approach* (7th ed.). Boston: Pearson.

Karls, J. M., & O'Keefe, M. (2008). *Person-in-environment system manual* (2nd ed.). Washington, DC: NASW Press.

Karlsson, M., Nilsson, T., Lyttkens, C., & Leeson, G. (2010). Income inequality and health: Importance of a cross-country perspective. *Social Science & Medicine, 70*, 875–885.

Karmanov, D., & Hamel, R. (2008). Assessing the restorative potential of contemporary urban environment(s): Beyond the nature versus urban dichotomy. *Landscape and Urban Planning, 86*, 115–125.

Karpowitz, C., Mendelberg, T., & Shaker, L. (2012). Gender inequality in deliberative participation. *American Political Science Review, 106*(3), 533–547.

Karraker, M. (2013). *Global families* (2nd ed.). Los Angeles: Sage.

Kasee, C. R. (1995). Identity, recovery, and religious imperialism: Native American women and the new age. *Women and Therapy: A Feminist Quarterly, 16*(2/3), 83–93.

Kay, A. (2006). Social capital, the social economy and community development. *Community Development Journal, 41*(2), 160–173.

Kaya, N., & Burgess, B. (2007). Territoriality: Seat preferences in different types of classroom arrangements. *Environment & Behavior, 39*(6), 859–876.

Kaya, N., & Weber, M. (2003). Territorial behavior in residence halls: A cross-cultural study. *Environment and Behavior, 35*(3), 400–414.

Keane, C. (1991). Socioenvironmental determinants of community formation. *Environment and Behavior, 23*(1), 27–46.

Kearney, A. (2006). Residential development patterns and neighborhood satisfaction: Impacts of density and nearby nature. *Environment and Behavior, 38*(1), 112–139.

Keefe, T. (1996). Meditation and social work treatment. In F. J. Turner (Ed.), *Social work treatment: Interlocking theoretical approaches* (4th ed., pp. 434–460). New York: Free Press.

Kelly, G. (2014, February 22). SeaTac: The small US town that sparked a new movement against low wages. *The Observer*. Retrieved from http://www.theguardian.com/world/2014/feb/22/setac-minimum-wage-increase-washington.

Kempes, M. M., Gulickx, M. M. C., van Daalen, H. J. C., Louwerse, A. L., & Sterck, E. H. M. (2008). Social competence is reduced in socially deprived rhesus monkeys. *Journal of Comparative Psychology, 122*(1), 62–67.

Kent, S. (1991). Partitioning space: Cross-cultural factors influencing domestic spatial segmentation. *Environment and Behavior, 23*, 438–473.

Keutzer, C. (1982). Physics and consciousness. *Journal of Humanistic Psychology, 22*, 74–90.

Kidd, S. M. (1996). *The dance of the dissident daughter: A woman's journey from Christian tradition to the sacred feminine*. New York: HarperCollins.

Kihlström, A. (2012). Luhmann's system theory in social work: Criticism and reflections. *Journal of Social Work, 12*(3), 287–299.

Kim, H. (2011). Job conditions, unmet expectations, and burnout in public child welfare workers: How different from other social workers? *Children and Youth Services Review, 33*, 358–367.

Kim, H., Ji, J., & Kao, D. (2011). Burnout and physical health among social workers: A three-year longitudinal study. *Social Work, 56*(3), 258–268.

Kinkade, K. (1973). *A Walden Two experiment: The first five years of Twin Oaks Community.* New York: Morrow.

Kissman, K., & Maurer, L. (2002). East meets West: Therapeutic aspects of spirituality in health, mental health and addiction recovery. *International Social Work, 45*(1), 35–43.

Kitchen, A., & Brook, J. (2005). Social work at the heart of the medical team. *Social Work in Health Care, 40*(4), 1–18.

Kivel, P. (1991). Men, spirituality, and violence. *Creation Spirituality, 7*(4), 12–14, 50.

Kjellgren, A., & Buhrkall, H. (2010). A comparison of the restorative effect of a natural environment with that of a simulated natural environment. *Journal of Environmental Psychology, 30,* 464–472.

Knodel, J., Kespichayawattana, J., Saengtienchai, C., & Wiwatwanich, S. (2010). How left behind are rural parents of migrant children? Evidence from Thailand. *Ageing and Society, 30*(5), 811–841.

Koenig, H. G. (1999). *The healing power of faith: Science explores medicine's last great frontier.* New York: Simon & Schuster.

Koenig, H. G. (2001). Religion and mental health II: Religion, mental health, and related behaviors. *International Journal of Psychiatry in Medicine, 31*(10), 97–109.

Koenig, H. G. (2005). *Faith and mental health: Religious sources for healing.* Philadelphia: Templeton Foundation Press.

Koenig, H. G., King, D. E., & Carson, V. B. (2012). *Handbook of religion and health* (2nd ed.). New York: Oxford University Press.

Koenig, H. G., Larson, D. B., & Larson, S. S. (2001). Religion and coping with serious medical illness. *Annals of Pharmacotherapy, 35*(3), 352–359.

Kogler Hill, S. (2013). Team leadership. In P. Northouse, *Leadership: Theory and practice* (6th ed., pp. 287–318). Los Angeles: Sage.

Kohlberg, L. (1969). *Stages in the development of moral thought and action.* New York: Holt, Rinehart and Winston.

Kohli, M., & Albertini, M. (2009). Childlessness and intergenerational transfers: What is at stake? *Ageing & Society, 29,* 1171–1183.

Kondrat, M. E. (1999). Who is the "self" in self-aware: Professional self-awareness from a critical theory perspective. *Social Service Review, 73*(4), 451–477.

Kondrat, M. E. (2008). Person-in-environment. In T. Mizrahi & L. Davis (Eds.), *Encyclopedia of social work* (20th ed., Vol. 3, pp. 349–354). New York: NASW Press/Oxford Press.

Koopmans, R. (2004). Political. Opportunity. Structure: Some splitting to balance the lumping. In J. Goodwin & J. Jasper (Eds.), *Rethinking social movements: Structure, meaning, and emotion* (pp. 61–73). Lanham, MD: Rowman & Littlefield.

Korosi, A., & Baram, T. Z. (2010). Plasticity of the stress response early in life: Mechanisms and significance. *Developmental Psychobiology, 52*(7), 661–670.

Kosmin, B., & Keysar, A. (2009). *American Religious Identification Survey (ARIS 2008).* Retrieved from http://commons.trincoll.edu/aris/2011/08/ARIS_Report_2008.pdf.

Koss, M., & Figueredo, A. (2004). Change in cognitive mediators of rape's impact on psychosocial health across 2 years of recovery. *Journal of Counseling and Clinical Psychology, 72*(6), 1063–1072.

Kossek, E., Lobel, S., & Brown, J. (2006). Human resource strategies to manage workforce diversity: Examining "the business case." In A. Konrad & J. Pringle (Eds.), *Handbook of workplace diversity* (Vol. 1, pp. 53–74). Thousand Oaks, CA: Sage.

Kottak, C. P. (1994). *Anthropology: The exploration of human diversity.* New York: McGraw-Hill.

Kottak, C. P. (1996). *Mirror for humanity: A concise introduction to cultural anthropology.* New York: McGraw-Hill.

Kottak, C. P. (2008). *Anthropology: The exploration of human diversity* (12th ed.). Boston: McGraw-Hill.

Kottak, C. P., & Kozaitis, K. (2008). *On being different: Diversity and multiculturalism in the North American mainstream.* Boston: McGraw-Hill.

Kottler, J., & Englar-Carlson, M. (2010). *Learning group leadership: An experiential approach.* Thousand Oaks, CA: Sage.

Kravetz, D. (2004). *Tales from the trenches: Politics and practice in feminist service organizations.* Lanham, MD: University Press of America.

Kriesi, H. (1996). The organizational structure of new social movements in a political context. In D. McAdam, J. McCarthy, & M. Zald (Eds.), *Comparative perspectives on social movements* (pp. 152–184). New York: Cambridge University Press.

Krill, D. F. (1996). Existential social work. In F. J. Turner (Ed.), *Social work treatment* (4th ed., pp. 250–281). New York: Free Press.

Kroeber, A., & Kluckhohn, C. (1963). *Culture: A critical review of concepts and definitions.* New York: Vintage.

Kroeber, A., & Kluckhohn, C. (1978). *Culture: A critical review of concepts and definitions.* Cambridge, MA: Peabody Museum. (Original work published 1952)

Kroll, B. (2004). Living with an elephant: Growing up with parental substance misuse. *Child and Family Social Work, 9,* 129–140.

Kropf, N., & Malone, D. M. (2004). Interdisciplinary practice in developmental disabilities. *Journal of Social Work in Disability & Rehabilitation, 3*(1), 21–36.

Kunkel, A., Hummert, M. L., & Dennis, M. R. (2006). Social learning theory: Modeling and communication in the family context. In D. Braithwaite & L. A. Baxter (Eds.), *Engaging theories in family communication: Multiple perspectives* (pp. 250–275). Thousand Oaks, CA: Sage.

Kupritz, V. (2003). Accommodating privacy to facilitate new ways of working. *Journal of Architectural and Planning Research, 20*(2), 122–135.

Kurdek, L. (2006). Differences between partners from heterosexual, gay, and lesbian cohabiting couples. *Journal of Marriage and Family, 68,* 509–528.

Kurlanski, S., & Ibay, A. (2012). Seasonal affective disorder. *American Family Physician, 86*(1), 1037–1041.

Kurtz, L. (2012). *Gods in the global village: The world's religions in sociological perspective* (3rd ed.). Los Angeles: Sage.

Kurtz, S. (2002). *Workplace justice: Organizing multi-identity movements.* Minneapolis: University of Minnesota Press.

Kurzweil, R. (2012). *How to create a mind: The secret of human thought revealed.* New York: Viking.

Kvarfordt, C. L. (2010). Spiritual abuse and neglect of youth: Reconceptualizing what is known through an investigation of practitioners' experiences. *Journal of Religion & Spirituality in Social Work: Social Thought, 29*(2), 143–164.

Kvarfordt, C. L., & Sheridan, M. J. (2007). The role of religion and spirituality in working with children and adolescents: Results of a national survey. *Social Thought, 26*(3), 1–23.

Kythreotis, A. (2012). Progress in global climate change politics? Reasserting national state territoriality in a post-political world. *Progress in Human Geography, 36*(4), 457–474.

LaDue, R. A. (1994). Coyote returns: Twenty sweats does not an Indian expert make. *Women & Therapy, 15*(1), 93–111.

Laird, J. (1998). Theorizing culture: Narrative ideas and practice principles. In M. McGoldrick (Ed.), *Revisioning family therapy* (pp. 20–36). New York: Guilford.

Lajoie, D. H., & Shapiro, S. I. (1992). Definitions of transpersonal psychology: The first twenty-three years. *Journal of Transpersonal Psychology, 4,* 79–98.

Lakey, B., & Orehek, E. (2011). Relational regulation theory: A new approach to explain the link between perceived social support and mental health. *Psychological Review, 118*(3), 482–495.

Lakoff, G. (2004). *Don't think of an elephant! Know your values and frame the debate: The essential guide for progressives.* White River Junction, VT: Chelsea Green.

Lakoff, G. (2006). *Whose freedom? The battle over America's most important ideas.* New York: Farrar, Straus and Giroux.

Lakoff, G. (2011). How Occupy Wall Street's moral vision can beat the disastrous conservative world view. *AlterNet.* Retrieved from www.alternet.org/story/152800/lakoff%3A_how_occupy_wall_street's_moral_vision_can_beat_the_disastrous_conservative_worldview.

Lalayants, M., & Epstein, I. (2005). Evaluating multidisciplinary child abuse and neglect teams: A research agenda. *Child Welfare, 84*(4), 433–458.

Lally, J. R. (2011). The link between consistent caring interactions with babies, early brain development, and school readiness. In E. Zigler, W. S. Gilliam, & W. S. Barnett (Eds.), *The pre-K debates: Current controversis and issues* (pp. 159–162). Baltimore: Paul H. Brooks.

Lane, C. (2007). *Shyness: How normal behavior became a sickness.* New Haven, CT: Yale University Press.

Lane, K. L., Wehby, J., Menzies, H. M., Doukas, G. L., Munton, S. M., & Gregg, R. M. (2003). Social skills instruction for students at risk for antisocial behavior. The effects of small-group instruction. *Behavioral Disorders, 28*(3), 229–248.

Lantz, J., & Walsh, J. (2007). *Short-term existential intervention in clinical practice.* Chicago: Lyceum.

Lau, J. T., Wang, Q., Cheng, Y., Kim, J., Yang, X., & Tsui, H. (2008). Infertility-related perceptions and responses and their associations with quality of life among rural Chinese infertile couples. *Journal of Sexual and Marital Therapy, 34,* 248–267.

Lau, J. Y. F., Eley, T. C., & Stevenson, J. (2006). Examining the state-trait anxiety relationship: A behavioural genetic approach. *Journal of Abnormal Child Psychology, 34*(1), 19–27.

Lau, W., Chan, C., Li, J., & Au, T. (2010). Effectiveness of group cognitive-behavioral treatment for childhood anxiety in community clinics. *Behavior Research and Therapy, 28,* 1067–1077.

Lawrence, C., & Andrews, K. (2004). The influence of perceived prison crowding on male inmates' perception of aggressive events. *Aggressive Behavior, 30*(4), 273–283.

Lazarus, R. S. (1999). *Stress and emotion: A new synthesis.* New York: Springer.

Lazarus, R. S. (2001). Relational meaning and discrete emotions. In K. R. Scherer, A. Schorr, & T. Johnstone (Eds.), *Appraisal processes in emotion: Theory, methods, research* (pp. 37–67). New York: Oxford University Press.

Lazarus, R. S. (2007). Stress and emotion: A new synthesis. In A. Monat, R. S. Lazarus, & G. Reevy (Eds.), *The Praeger handbook on stress and coping* (Vol. 1, pp. 33–51). Westport, CT: Praeger/Greenwood.

Le Brocque, R. M., Hendrikz, J., & Kenardy, J. A. (2010). The course of posttraumatic stress in children: Examination of recovery trajectories following traumatic injury. *Journal of Pediatric Psychology, 35*(6), 637–645.

Lee, B., & Campbell, K. (1999). Neighbor networks of Black and White Americans. In B. Wellman (Ed.), *Networks in the global village* (pp. 119–146). Boulder, CO: Westview Press.

Lee, J. (2001). *The empowerment approach to social work practice: Building the beloved community.* New York: Columbia University Press.

Lee, K. H. (2011). The role of spiritual experience, forgiveness, and religious support on the general well-being of older adults. *Journal of Religion, Spirituality & Aging, 23*(3), 206–223.

Lee, M. (2008). A small act of creativity: Fostering creativity in clinical social work practice. *Families in Society, 89*(1), 19–31.

Lee, M. Y., Ng, S., Leung, P. P. Y., & Chan, C. L. W. (2009). *Integrative body–mind–spirit social work: An empirically based approach to assessment and treatment.* New York: Oxford University Press.

Lee, Y. (2010). Office layout affecting privacy, interaction, and acoustic quality in LEED-certified buildings. *Building and Environment, 45,* 1594–1600.

Leeder, E. (2004). *The family in global perspective: A gendered journey.* Thousand Oaks, CA: Sage.

Leiby, J. (1985). Moral foundations of social welfare and social work: A historical view. *Social Work, 30,* 323–330.

Lengermann, P., & Niebrugge-Brantley, G. (2007). Contemporary feminist theories. In G. Ritzer (Ed.), *Contemporary sociological theory and its classical roots* (2nd ed., pp. 185–214). Boston: McGraw-Hill.

Lenski, G. (1966). *Power and privilege.* New York: McGraw-Hill.

Leonard, K., & Eiden, R. (2007). Marital and family processes in the context of alcohol use and alcohol disorders. *Annual Review of Clinical Psychology, 3,* 285–310.

LePoire, B. (2006). *Family communication: Nurturing and control in a changing world.* Thousand Oaks, CA: Sage.

Lesser, J., O'Neill, M., Burke, K., Scanlon, P., Hollis, K., & Miller, R. (2004). Women supporting women: A mutual aid group fosters new connections among women in midlife. *Social Work With Groups, 27*(1), 75–88.

Leung, P. P. Y., & Chan, C. L. W. (2010). Utilizing Eastern spirituality in clinical practice: A qualitative study of Chinese women with breast cancer. *Smith College Studies in Social Work, 80*(2–3), 159–183.

Leung, P. P. Y., Chan, C. L. W., Ng, S. M., & Lee, M. Y. (2009). Towards body-mind-spirit integration: East meets West in clinical social work practice. *Clinical Social Work Journal, 37*(4), 303–311.

Levi, D. (2014). *Group dynamics for teams* (4th ed.). Los Angeles: Sage.

Levine, S. (1999). Children's cognition as the foundation of spirituality. *International Journal of Children's Spirituality, 4*(2), 121–140.

Levinson, D. (1996). *The seasons of a woman's life.* New York: Knopf.

Lewandowski, C. A., & Canda, E. R. (1995). A typological model for the assessment of religious groups. *Social Thought, 18*(1), 17–38.

Lewicka, M. (2011). Place attachment: How far have we come in the last 40 years? *Journal of Environmental Psychology, 31*, 207–230.

Li, J., Karakowsky, L., & Siegel, J. (1999). The effects of proportional representation on intragroup behavior in mixed-race decision-making groups. *Small Group Research, 30*(3), 259–279.

Lichter, D., & Qian, Z. (2008). Serial cohabitation and the marital life course. *Journal of Marriage and Family, 70*, 861–878.

Lichter, D., Turner, R., & Sassler, S. (2010). National estimates of the rise of serial cohabitation. *Social Science Research, 39*, 754–765.

Lieberman, M. (2013). *Social: Why our brains are wired to connect.* New York: Crown.

Lightfoot, C., Lalonde, C., & Chandler, M. (Eds.). (2004). *Changing conceptions of psychological life.* Mahwah, NJ: Erlbaum.

Limb, G. E., & Hodge, D. R. (2008). Developing spiritual competency with Native Americans: Promoting wellness through balance and harmony. *Families in Society: The Journal of Contemporary Social Services, 89*(4), 615–622.

Lindsey, E. W., Kurtz, P. D., Jarvis, S., Williams, N. R., & Nackerud, L. (2000). How runaway and homeless youth navigate troubled waters: Personal strengths and resources. *Clinical and Adolescent Social Work Journal, 17*(2), 115–140.

Linver, M., Brooks-Gunn, J., & Kohen, D. (2002). Family processes as pathways from income to young children's development. *Developmental Psychology, 38*, 719–734.

Lippa, R. A. (2005). *Gender, nature, and nurture* (2nd ed.). Mahwah, NJ: Erlbaum.

Living Wage Action Coalition. (n.d.). *Student worker solidarity resource center.* Retrieved from http://www.livingwageaction.org.

Living Wage Aotearoa New Zealand. (2014). *About.* Retrieved from http://www.livingwagenx.org.nz/about.php.

Living Wage Foundation. (2014). *History.* Retrieved from http://www.livingwage.org.uk/history.

Lizano, E., & Mor Barak, M. (2012). Workplace demands and resources as antecedents of job burnout among public child welfare workers: A longitudinal study. *Children and Youth Services Review, 34*, 1769–1776.

Lloyd, S., Few, A., & Allen, K. (2009). Preface. In S. Lloyd, A. Few, & K. Allen (Eds.), *Handbook of feminist family studies.* Thousand Oaks, CA: Sage.

Logan, G. (2000). Information-processing theories. In A. E. Kazdi (Ed.), *Encyclopedia of psychology* (Vol. 4, pp. 294–297). Washington, DC: American Psychological Association.

Logan, S. L. (1997). Meditation as a tool that links the personal and the professional. *Reflections: Narratives of Professional Helping, 3*(1), 38–44.

Logan, S. L. (Ed.). (2001). *The Black family: Strengths, self-help, and positive change* (2nd ed.). Boulder, CO: Westview Press.

Loomis, E. (2013). The global water crisis: Privatization and neocolonialism in film. *Radical History Review, 116*, 189–195.

Lopez, R., & Hynes, P. (2006). Obesity, physical activity, and the urban environment: Public health research needs. *Environmental Health: A Global Access Science Source, 5*(1), 25. Retrieved from health-equity.pitt.edu/3813.

Lovaglia, M. J. (1995). Power and status: Exchange, attribution, and expectation states. *Small Group Research, 26*, 400–426.

Lovaglia, M., Mannix, E., Samuelson, C., Sell, J., & Wilson, R. (2005). Conflict, power, and status in groups. In M. Poole & A. Hollingshead (Eds.), *Theories of small groups: Interdisciplinary perspectives* (pp. 63–97). Thousand Oaks, CA: Sage.

Low, S., & Altman, I. (1992). Place attachment: A conceptual inquiry. In I. Altman & S. Low (Eds.), *Place attachment* (pp. 1–12). New York: Plenum.

Lowenberg, F. M. (1988). *Religion and social work practice in contemporary American society.* New York: Columbia University Press.

Lownsdale, S. (1997). Faith development across the lifespan: Fowler's integrative work. *Journal of Psychology and Theology, 25*, 49–63.

Lowry, B., Cao, J., & Everard, A. (2011). Privacy concerns versus desire for interpersonal awareness in driving the use of self-disclosure technologies: The case of instant messaging in two cultures. *Journal of Management Information Systems, 27*(4), 163–200.

Lubin, H., & Johnson, D. R. (1998). Healing ceremonies. *Family Networker, 22*(5), 38–39, 64–67.

Luhmann, N. (2011). *Introduction to systems theory.* New York: Polity Press.

Lum, D. (2011). *Culturally competent practice: A framework for understanding diverse groups and justice issues* (4th ed.). Belmont, CA: Thomson.

Lutz, A., Dunne, J. D., & Davidson, R. J. (2007). Meditation and the neuroscience of consciousness. In P. Zelazo, M. Moscovitch, & E. Thompson (Eds.), *The Cambridge handbook of consciousness* (pp. 499–552). Cambridge, UK: Cambridge University Press

Lyon, L. (1987). *The community in urban society.* Philadelphia: Temple University Press.

Lyotard, J. (1984). *The postmodern condition.* Minneapolis: University of Minnesota Press.

MacArthur Network on Mind–Body Interactions. (2001). *Vital connections: Science of mind–body interactions: A report on the interdisciplinary conference held at NIH, March 26–28, 2001.* Chicago: Author.

Mackay, G., & Neill, J. (2010). The effect of "green exercise" on state anxiety and the roles of exercise duration, intensity, and greenness: A quasi-experimental study. *Psychology of Sport and Exercise, 22*, 238–245.

MacKinlay, E. (Ed.). (2006). *Aging, spirituality and palliative care.* Binghamton, NY: Haworth Press.

MacNair, R., Fowler, L., & Harris, J. (2000). The diversity functions of organizations that confront oppression: The evolution of three social movements. *Journal of Community Practice, 7*(2), 71–88.

Mader, S., & Windelspecht, M. (2012). *Human biology* (12th ed.). New York: McGraw-Hill.

Madigan, S., Moran, G., & Pederson, D. R. (2006). Unresolved states of mind, disorganized attachment relationships, and disrupted interactions of adolescent mothers and their infants. *Developmental Psychology, 42*(2), 293–304.

Magai, C. (2001). Emotions over the life span. In J. E. Birren & K. W. Schale (Eds.), *Handbook of the psychology of aging* (5th ed., pp. 399–426). San Diego, CA: Academic Press.

Magen, R., & Mangiardi, E. (2005). Groups and individual change. In S. Wheelan (Ed.), *The handbook of group research and practice* (pp. 351–361). Thousand Oaks, CA: Sage.

Maggiolo, F., & Leone, S. (2010). Is HAART modifying the HIV epidemic? *The Lancet, 376*(9740), 14–20.

Maidenberg, M. P., & Golick, T. (2001). Developing or enhancing interdisciplinary programs: A model for teaching collaboration. *Professional Development: The International Journal of Continuing Social Work, 4*(2), 15–24.

Mak, W., Cheung, R., & Law, L. (2009). Sense of community in Hong Kong: Relations with community-level characteristics and residents' well-being. *American Journal of Community Psychology, 44,* 80–92.

Malanga, S. (2003, Winter). How the "living wage" sneaks socialism into cities. *City Journal.* Retrieved from http://www.city-journal .org/html/13_1_how_the_living_wage.html.

Maller, C., Townsend, M., Pryor, A., Brown, P., & St. Leger, L. (2005). Healthy nature healthy people: "Contact with nature" as an upstream health promotion intervention for populations. *Health Promotion International, 21*(1), 45–54.

Malti, T., Gasser, L., & Buchmann, M. (2009). Aggressive and prosocial children's emotion attributions and moral reasoning. *Aggressive Behavior, 35*(1), 90–102.

Mann, C. (2011). *1493: Discovering the new world Columbus created.* New York: Knopf.

Mann, S. (2011). Pioneers of U.S. ecofeminism and environmental justice. *Feminist Formations, 23*(2), 1–25.

Mann, W. C., Belchior, P., Tomita, M. R., & Kemp, B. J. (2005). Computer use by middle-aged and older adults with disabilities. *Technology and Disability, 17*(1), 1–9.

Manning, L. K. (2010). An exploration of paganism: Aging women embracing the divine feminine. *Journal of Religion, Spirituality & Aging, 22*(3), 196–210.

Manning, M., Cornelius, L., & Okundaye, J. (2004). Empowering African Americans through social work practice: Integrating an Afrocentric perspective, ego psychology, and spirituality. *Families in Society: The Journal of Contemporary Social Services, 85*(2), 229–235.

Mano, R. (2009). Information technology, adaptation and innovation in nonprofit human service organizations. *Journal of Technology in Human Services, 27,* 227–234.

Mapp, S. (2008). *Human rights and social justice in a global perspective: An introduction to international social work.* New York: Oxford University Press.

March, J., & Simon, H. (1958). *Organizations.* New York: Wiley.

Mardy, D. (n.d.). *Masters of chiasmus: Winston Churchill.* Retrieved from http://www.drmardy.com/chiasmus/masters/churchill1 .shtml.

Marecek, J., Kimmel, E. B., Crawford, M., & Hare-Mustin, R. T. (2003). Psychology of women and gender. In D. K. Freedheim (Ed.), *Handbook of psychology: History of psychology* (Vol. 1, pp. 249–268). Hoboken, NJ: Wiley.

Marino, R., Weinman, M. L., & Soudelier, K. (2001). Social work intervention and failure to thrive in infants and children. *Health and Social Work, 26*(2), 90–97.

Markovitzky, G., & Mosek, A. (2005). The role of symbolic resources in coping with immigration. *Journal of Ethnic & Cultural Diversity in Social Work, 14*(1/2), 145–158.

Marks, G., & McAdam, D. (2009). On the relationship of political opportunities to the form of collective action: The case of the European Union. In D. della Porta, H. Kriesi, & D. Rucht (Eds.), *Social movements in a globalising world* (pp. 97–111). New York: Palgrave Macmillan.

Markus, H., & Kitayama, S. (2003). Models of agency: Sociocultural diversity in the construction of action. In G. Berman & J. Berman (Eds.), *Cross-cultural differences in perspectives on the self* (pp. 2–57). Lincoln: University of Nebraska Press.

Markus, H., & Kitayama, S. (2009). Culture and the self: Implications for cognition, emotion, and motivation. In P. Smith & D. Best

(Eds.), *Cross-cultural psychology* (Vol. 1, pp. 265–320). Thousand Oaks, CA: Sage.

Marsh, V. R. (2005). Story sharing, voice fatigue, and moving forward after divorce: When women resist being defined by their tragedies. *Reflections: Narratives of Professional Helping, 11*(1), 86–91.

Marti, I., Etzion, D., & Leca, B. (2008). Theoretical approaches for studying corporations, democracy, and the public good. *Journal of Management Inquiry, 17,* 148–151.

Martin, E. P., & Martin, J. M. (2002). *Spirituality and the Black helping tradition in social work.* Washington, DC: NASW Press.

Martin, J. G. (1993). Why women need a feminist spirituality. *Women's Studies Quarterly, 1,* 106–120.

Martin, J. J. (2013). Benefits and barriers to physical activity for individuals with disabilities: A social-relational model of disability perspective. *Disability and Rehabilitation: An International, Multidisciplinary Journal, 35*(24), 2030–2037.

Martin, J., & Sherman, M. (2010). The impact of military duty and military life on individuals and families. In S. Price, C. Price, & P. McKenry (Eds.), *Families & change: Coping with stressful events and transitions* (4th ed., pp. 381–397). Thousand Oaks, CA: Sage.

Martinez-Brawley, E. (2000). *Close to home: Human services and the small community.* Washington, DC: NASW Press.

Martz, E. (2004). Do reactions of adaptation to disability influence the fluctuation of future time orientation among individuals with spinal cord injuries? *Rehabilitation Counseling Bulletin, 47*(2), 86–95.

Marx, G., & McAdam, D. (1994). *Collective behavior and social movements: Process and structure.* Englewood Cliffs, NJ: Prentice Hall.

Marx, J. (2012). *American social policy in the 60's and 70's: The Social Welfare History Project.* Retrieved from http://www .socialwelfarehistory.com/eras/american-social-policy-in-the-60s-andthe70s.

Marx, K. (1967). *Capital: A critique of political economy* (S. Moore & E. Aveling, Trans; Vol. 1). New York: International. (Original work published 1887)

Maslach, C., & Jackson, S. (1981). *Maslach Burnout Inventory: Research edition.* Palo Alto, CA: Consulting Psychologists Press.

Maslach, C., Schaufeli, W., & Leiter, M. (2001). Job burnout. *Annual Review of Psychology, 52,* 397–422.

Maslow, A. (1954). *Motivation and personality.* New York: Harper.

Maslow, A. (1962). *Toward a psychology of being.* New York: Van Nostrand.

Maslow, A. (1971). *Farther reaches of human nature.* New York: Viking.

Mason, M., Skolnick, A., & Sugarman, S. (Eds.). (2003). *All our families: New policies for a new century: A report of the Berkeley family forum.* New York: Oxford University Press.

Mathambo, V., & Gibbs, A. (2009). Extended family childcare arrangements in a context of AIDS: Collapse or adaptation? *AIDS Care, 21,* 22–27.

Matheson, L. (1996). Valuing spirituality among Native American populations. *Counseling and Values, 41,* 51–58.

Matthews, D. A., McCullough, M. E., Larson, D. B., Koenig, H. G., Swyers, J. P., & Milano, M. G. (1998). Religious commitment and health status: A review of the research and implications for family medicine. *Archives of Family Medicine, 7*(2), 118–124.

Matto, H., Berry-Edwards, J., Hutchison, E. D., Bryant, S. A., & Waldbillig, A. (2006). An exploratory study on multiple intelligences and social work education. *Journal of Social Work Education, 42*(2), 405–416.

Maxwell, L. (2003). Home and school density effects on elementary school children: The role of spatial density. *Environment and Behavior, 35*(4), 566–578.

May, A., Duivenvoorden, H., Korstjens, I., van Weert, E., Hoekstra-Weebers, J., van den Borne, B., et al. (2008). The effects of group cohesion on rehabilitation outcome in cancer survivors. *Psycho-Oncology, 17,* 917–925.

Maynard, M., & Taylor, C. (1996). A comparative analysis of Japanese and U.S. attitudes toward direct marketing. *Journal of Direct Marketing, 10*(1), 34–44.

Mayo, E. (1933). *The human problems of an industrial civilization.* New York: Macmillan.

Mayo Foundation for Medical Education and Research. (2012). *Multiple sclerosis: Symptoms.* Retrieved from http://www .mayoclinic.com/health/multiple-sclerosis/DS00188/ DSECTION=symptoms.

Mayo, K. R. (2009). *Creativity, spirituality, and mental health: Exploring connections.* Surrey, UK: Ashgate.

McAdam, D. (1996a). Conceptual origins, current problems, future directions. In D. McAdam, J. McCarthy, & M. Zald (Eds.), *Comparative perspectives on social movements* (pp. 23–40). New York: Cambridge University Press.

McAdam, D. (1996b). The framing function of movement tactics: Strategic dramaturgy in the American civil rights movement. In D. McAdam, J. McCarthy, & M. Zald (Eds.), *Comparative perspectives on social movements* (pp. 338–355). New York: Cambridge University Press.

McAdam, D., McCarthy, J., & Zald, M. (1996). Introduction: Opportunities, mobilizing structures, and framing processes: Toward a synthetic, comparative perspective on social movements. In D. McAdam, J. McCarthy, & M. Zald (Eds.), *Comparative perspectives on social movements* (pp. 1–20). New York: Cambridge University Press.

McAvoy, M. (1999). *The profession of ignorance: With constant reference to Socrates.* Lanham, NY: University Press of America.

McBee, L., Westreich, L., & Likourezos, A. (2004). A psychoeducational relaxation group for pain and stress management in the nursing home. *Journal of Social Work in Long-Term Care, 3*(1), 15–28.

McCarroll, J., Ursano, R., Fan, Z., & Newby, J. (2004). Patterns of mutual and nonmutual spouse abuse in the U.S. Army (1998–2002). *Violence and Victims, 19*(4), 453–468.

McCreary, L., & Dancy, B. (2004). Dimensions of family functioning: Perspectives on low-income African American single-parent families. *Journal of Marriage and Family, 66,* 690–701.

McCubbin, H. I., & Figley, C. R. (1983). *Stress and the family: Vol. 1. Coping with normative transitions.* New York: Brunner/Mazel.

McCubbin, H. I., & Patterson, J. M. (1983). The family stress process: The double ABCX model of adjustment and adaptation. In H. I. McCubbin, M. B. Sussman, & J. M. Patterson (Eds.), *Social stress and the family: Advances and developments in family stress theory and research* (pp. 7–37). New York: Haworth.

McDermott, M. L. (1997). Voting cues in low-information elections: Candidate gender as a social information variable in contemporary United States elections. *American Journal of Political Science, 41*(1), 270–283.

McGoldrick, M., & Ashton, D. (2012). Culture: A challenge to concepts of normality. In F. Walsh (Ed.), *Normal family processes: Growing diversity and complexity* (4th ed., pp. 249–272). New York: Guilford.

McGoldrick, M., Carter, B., & Garcia-Preto, N. (2011a). *The expanded family life cycle: Individual, family, and social perspectives* (4th ed.). Boston: Allyn & Bacon.

McGoldrick, M., Carter, B., & Garcia-Preto, N. (2011b). Self in context: Human development and the individual life cycle in systemic perspective. In M. McGoldrick, B. Carter, & N. Garcia-Preto (Eds.), *The expanded family life cycle: Individual, family, and social perspectives* (4th ed., pp. 20–41). Boston: Allyn & Bacon.

McGregor, D. (1960). *The human side of enterprise.* New York: McGraw-Hill.

McHale, S., Updegraff, K., Ji-Yeon, K., & Cansler, E. (2009). Cultural orientations, daily activities, and adjustment in Mexican American youth. *Journal of Youth and Adolescence, 38*(5), 627–641.

McIntosh, D., Poulin, M., Silver, R., & Holman, E. A. (2011). The distinct roles of spirituality and religiosity in physical and mental health after collective trauma: A national longitudinal study of responses to the 9/11 attacks. *Journal of Behavioral Medicine, 34,* 497–507.

McIntosh, P. (2007). White privilege: Unpacking the invisible knapsack. In P. Rothenberg (Ed.), *Race, class, and gender in the United States* (6th ed., pp. 163–168). New York: Worth.

McKee-Ryan, F., Song, Z., Wanberg, C., & Kinicki, A. (2005). Psychological and physical well-being during unemployment: A meta-analytic study. *Journal of Applied Psychology, 90*(1), 53–76.

McKnight, P., Snyder, C., & Lopez, S. (2007). Western perspectives on positive psychology. In C. Snyder & S. Lopez (Eds.), *Positive psychology: The scientific and practical explorations of human strengths* (pp. 23–35). Thousand Oaks, CA: Sage.

McLeod, P., & Kettner-Polley, R. (2005). Psychodynamic perspectives on small groups. In M. Poole & A. Hollingshead (Eds.), *Theories of small groups: Interdisciplinary perspectives* (pp. 63–97). Thousand Oaks, CA: Sage.

McMichael, P. (2012). *Development and social change: A global perspective* (5th ed.). Los Angeles: Sage.

McMillan, D. (1996). Sense of community. *Journal of Community Psychology, 24,* 315–325.

McMillan, D., & Chavis, D. (1986). Sense of community: A definition and theory. *Journal of Community Psychology, 14,* 6–23.

McPherson, M., Smith-Lovin, L., & Brashears, M. (2006). Social isolation in America: Changes in core discussion networks over two decades. *American Sociological Review, 71*(3), 353–375.

Mead, G. H. (1934). *Mind, self, and society.* Chicago: University of Chicago Press.

Mead, G. H. (1959). *The philosophy of the present.* LaSalle, IL: Open Court.

Mederos, R., & Perilla, J. (2003). *Community connections: Men, gender, and violence.* Retrieved from http://www.melissainstitute .org/documents/eighth/men_gender_violence.pdf.

Meisenhelder, J. B., & Marcum, J. P. (2009). Terrorism, post-traumatic stress, coping strategies, and spiritual outcomes. *Journal of Religion and Health, 48*(1), 46–57.

Melchert, T. (2013). Beyond theoretical orientations: The emergence of a unified scientific framework in professional psychology. *Professional Psychology: Research and Practice, 44*(1), 11–19.

Melton, J. G. (1993). *Encyclopedia of American religion.* Detroit, MI: Gale Research.

Memmi, D. (2006). The nature of virtual communities. *AI & Society: Journal of Knowledge, Culture and Communication, 20,* 288–300.

Menezes, P., Scazufca, M., Rodrigues, L., & Mann, A. (2000). Household crowding and compliance with outpatient treatment in patients with non-affective functional psychoses. *Social Psychiatry and Psychiatric Epidemiology, 35*(3), 116–120.

Messinger, L. (2004). Comprehensive community initiatives: A rural perspective. *Social Work, 49*(4), 529–624.

Meyer, C. (1993). *Assessment in social work practice.* New York: Columbia University Press.

Meyer, D. (2004). Tending the vineyard: Cultivating political process research. In J. Goodwin & J. Jasper (Eds.), *Rethinking social movements: Structure, meaning, and emotion* (pp. 47–59). Lanham, MD: Rowman & Littlefield.

Meyer, M. (2010). Social movement service organizations: The challenges and consequences of combining service provision and political advocacy. In Y. Hasenfeld (Ed.), *Human services as complex organizations* (2nd ed., pp. 533–550). Thousand Oaks, CA: Sage.

Mezzich, A., Tarter, R., Kirisci, L., Feske, U., Day, B., & Gao, Z. (2007). Reciprocal influence of parent discipline and child's behavior on risk for substance disorder: A nine-year prospective study. *American Journal of Drug and Alcohol Abuse, 33*(6), 851–867.

Michels, R. (1959). *Political parties: A sociological study of the oligarchical tendencies of modern democracy* (Eden & Cedar Paul, Trans.). New York: Dover. (Original work published 1911)

Michinov, N., Michinov, E., & Toczek-Capell, M. (2004). Social identity, group processes and performance in synchronous computer-mediated communication. *Group Dynamics: Theory, Research, and Practice, 8*(11), 27–39.

Middleton, K., & Craig, C. D. (2012). A systematic literature review of PTSD among female veterans from 1990 to 2010. *Social Work in Mental Health, 10*(3), 233–252.

Migration Policy Centre. European University Institute. (2013). *Syrian refugees: A snapshot of the crisis in the Middle East and Europe.* Retrieved from syrianrefugees.eu.

Migration Policy Institute. (2013). *Immigration data hub: Migration facts, stats, and maps.* Retrieved from http://www.migrationinformation.org/datahub.

Mijares, S. G., & Khalsa, G. S. (2005). *The psychospiritual clinician's handbook: Alternative methods for understanding and treating mental disorders.* New York: Haworth Reference Press.

Mikulas, W. L. (2002). *The integrative helper: Convergence of Eastern and Western traditions.* Pacific Grove, CA: Brooks/Cole Thomson Learning.

Miles, M. (1995). Disability in an Eastern religious context: Historical perspectives. *Disability and Society, 10,* 49–69.

Miller, L., Davies, M., & Greenwald, S. (2000). Religiosity and substance use and abuse among adolescents in the National Comorbidity Survey. *Journal of the American Academy of Child and Adolescent Psychiatry, 19*(9), 1190–1197.

Miller, S. D., Duncan, B. L., & Hubble, M. A. (2005). Outcome-informed clinical work. In J. C. Norcross & M. R. Goldfried (Eds.), *Handbook of psychotherapy integration* (2nd ed., pp. 84–102). New York: Oxford University Press.

Miller, W. D., Pollack, C. E., & Williams, D. R. (2011). Healthy homes and communities. *American Journal of Preventive Medicine, 40,* S48–S57.

Minkoff, D. (2010). The emergence of hybrid organizational forms: Combining identity-based provision and political action. In Y. Hasenfeld (Ed.), *Human services as complex organizations* (2nd ed., pp. 117–138). Thousand Oaks, CA: Sage.

Miringoff, M. L., & Opdycke, S. (2008). *America's social health: Putting social issues back on the public agenda.* Armonk, NY: M. E. Sharpe.

Mishel, L. (2013). *The CEO-to-worker compensation ratio in 2012 of 273 was far above that of the late 1990s and 13 times the ratio of 20.1 in 1965.* Economic Policy Institute. Retrieved from www.epi.org/publications/the-ceo-to-worker-compensation-ratio-in-2012-of-2731.

Mistry, R., Lowe, D., Renner, A., & Chien, N. (2008). Expanding the family economic stress model: Insights from a mixed-methods approach. *Journal of Marriage and Family, 70*(1), 196–209.

Mizrahi, T., & Abramson, J. S. (2000). Collaboration between social workers and physicians: Perspectives on a shared case. *Social Work in Health Care, 31*(3), 1–24.

Mizrahi, T., Rosenthal, B., & Ivery, J. (2013). Coalitions, collaborations, and partnerships: Interorganizational approaches to social change. In M. Weil, M. Reisch, & M. Ohmer (Eds.), *The handbook of community practice* (2nd ed., pp. 383–402). Los Angeles: Sage.

Mmatli, T. (2008). Political activism as a social work strategy in Africa. *International Social Work, 51*(3), 297–310.

Mohai, P., & Saha, R. (2007). Racial inequality in the distribution of hazardous waste: A national-level reassessment. *Social Problems, 54*(3), 343–370.

Mohamed, N., & Ahmad, I. (2012). Information privacy concerns, antecedents and privacy measure use in social networking sites: Evidence from Malaysia. *Computers in Human Behavior, 28,* 2366–2375.

Mor Barak, M. (2014). *Managing diversity: Toward a globally inclusive workplace* (3rd ed.). Thousand Oaks, CA: Sage.

Mor Barak, M., & Travis, D. (2010). Diversity and organizational performance. In Y. Hasenfeld (Ed.), *Human services as complex organizations* (2nd ed., pp. 341–378). Thousand Oaks, CA: Sage.

Moren-Cross, J. L., & Lin, N. (2006). Social networks and health. In R. H. Binstock & L. K. George (Eds.), *Handbook of aging and the social sciences* (6th ed., pp. 111–126). Amsterdam: Elsevier.

Morgan, G. (2006). *Images of organizations* (Updated ed.). Thousand Oaks, CA: Sage.

Morgan, J. P. (2002). Dying and grieving are journeys of the spirit. In R. B. Gilbert (Ed.), *Health care and spirituality: Listening, assessing, caring* (pp. 53–64). Amityville, NY: Baywood.

Morgan, P. (2010). Towards a developmental theory of place attachment. *Journal of Environmental Psychology, 30,* 11–22.

Morreale, D. (Ed.). (1998). *The complete guide to Buddhist America.* Boston: Shambhala.

Morris, A. (2004). Reflections on social movement theory: Criticisms and proposals. In J. Goodwin & J. Jasper (Eds.), *Rethinking social movements* (pp. 233–246). Lanham, MD: Rowman & Littlefield.

Morris, P. M. (2002). The capabilities perspective: A framework for social justice. *Families in Society, 83*(4), 365–373.

Mosbacher, D., Reid, F., & Rhue, S. (1996). *All god's children.* [Videorecording]. Available from Woman Vision, http://www.womanvision.org.

Mueller, P. C., Plevak, D. J., & Rummans, T. A. (2001). Religious involvement, spirituality, and medicine: Implications for clinical practice. *Mayo Clinical Proceedings, 76*(12), 1225–1235.

Mukhopadhyay, C. C., Henze, R., & Moses, Y. T. (2007). *How real is race: A sourcebook on race, culture and biology.* Lanham, MD: Rowman & Littlefield Education.

Mulligan, K., & Scherer, K. R. (2012). Toward a working definition of emotion. *Emotion Review, 4*(4), 345–357.

Mullings, L. (2005). Interrogating racism: Toward an antiracist anthropology. *Annual Review of Anthropology, 34,* 667–693.

Mulroy, E., Nelson, K., & Gour, D. (2005). Community building and family-centered service collaboratives. In M. Weil (Ed.), *The handbook of community practice* (pp. 460–474). Thousand Oaks, CA: Sage.

Murphy, M. J. (2004). *Cognitive and constructivist psychotherapies: Theory, research, and practice.* New York: Springer.

Murray, B. (2001). Living wage comes of age: An increasingly sophisticated movement has put opponents on the defense. *The Nation, 273*(4), 24.

Myers, B. K. (1997). *Young children and spirituality.* New York: Routledge.

Myers, S., & Anderson, C. (2008). *The fundamentals of small group communication.* Thousand Oaks, CA: Sage.

Nagai, C. (2007). Culturally based spiritual phenomena: Eastern and Western theories and practices. *Psychoanalytic Social Work, 14*(1), 1–22.

Naidoo, R., & Adamowicz, W. (2006). Modeling opportunity costs of conservation in transitional landscapes. *Conservation Biology, 20*(2), 490–500.

NASW Virginia. (2003, February). The social worker as part of an interdisciplinary team. *NASW Virginia Chapter News, 3*(1), 8.

Natale, S. M., & Neher, J. C. (1997). Inspiriting the workplace: Developing a values-based management system. In D. P. Bloch & L. J. Richmond (Eds.), *Connections between spirit and work in career development: New approaches and practical perspectives* (pp. 237–255). Palo Alto, CA: Davies-Black.

Nathanson, I. G. (1995). Divorce and women's spirituality. *Journal of Divorce and Remarriage, 22,* 179–188.

National Alliance to End Homelessness. (2013a). *Frequently asked questions.* Washington, DC: Author. Retrieved from http://www.endhomelessness.org/pages/faqs.

National Alliance to End Homelessness. (2013b). *Snapshot of homelessness.* Washington, DC: Author. Retrieved from http://www.endhomelessness.org/pages/snapshot_of_homelessness.

National Alliance to End Homelessness. (2013c). *Cost of homelessness.* Washington, DC: Author. Retrieved from http://www.endhomelessness.org/pages/cost_of_homelessness.

National Association of Social Workers. (2001). *NASW cautious about Bush's faith-based initiative.* Retrieved from http://www.socialworkers.org/pressroom/2001/021401.asp.

National Association of Social Workers. (2006). *Tell the president and Congress to oppose government-funded religious discrimination!* Retrieved from http://www.socialworkers.org/advocacy/alerts-012606.asp.

National Association of Social Workers. (2008). *Code of ethics* (Rev.). Washington, DC: Author.

National Center for Complementary and Alternative Medicine. (n.d.). *Complementary, alternative, or integrative health: What's in a name?* Retrieved from http://nccam.nih.gov/health/whatiscam.

National Center for Education Statistics. (2013). *Program for International Student Assessment (PISA): Selected findings from PISA 2012.* Retrieved from http://nces.ed/gov/surveys/pisa2012.

National Conference of State Legislatures. (2014a). *State laws regarding marriages between first cousins.* Retrieved from http://www.ncsl.org/research/human-services/state-laws-regarding-marriages-between-first-cousi.aspx.

National Conference of State Legislatures. (2014b). *State minimum wages.* Retrieved from http://www.ncsl.org/research/labor-and-employment/state-minimum-wage-chart.aspx.

National Healthy Marriage Resource Center. (2009). *Stepfamilies in the United States: A fact sheet.* Retrieved from www.healthymarriageinfo.org/resources-detail/index.aspx?id=3002.

National Human Genome Research Institute. (2013). *All about the Human Genome Project (HGP).* Retrieved from http://www.Genome.gov/10001772.

National Institute of Diabetes & Digestive & Kidney Diseases. (2011). *National Diabetes Information Clearinghouse: Fast facts on diabetes.* Retrieved from diabetes.niddk.nih.gov/dm/pubs/statistics/#fast.

National Institute of Neurological Disorders and Stroke. (2013). *Multiple sclerosis: Hope through research.* Retrieved from http://www.ninds.nih.gov/disorders/multiple_sclerosis/detail_multiple_sclerosis.htm#240043215.

National Institutes of Health. (2010). *Fact sheet: Human Genome Project.* Retrieved from http://report.nih.gov/nihfactsheets/Pdfs/HumanGenomeProject%28NHGRI%29.pdf.

National Multiple Sclerosis Society. (n.d.). *Epidemiology of MS.* Retrieved from http://www.nationalmssociety.org/about-multiple-sclerosis/what-we-know-about-ms/who-gets-ms/epidemiology-of-ms/index.aspx.

National Network of Libraries of Medicine. (2013). *Health literacy.* Retrieved from http://nnlm.gov/outreach/consumer/hlthlit.html.

National Religious Partnership for the Environment. (2014). *About.* Retrieved from http://www.nrpe.org/about.html.

Navarro, V., Muntaner, C., Borrell, C., Benach, J., Quiroga, A., Rodriguez-Manz, M., et al. (2006). Politics and health outcomes. *Lancet, 368*(9540), 1033–1037.

Neal, J. (2000). Work as service to the divine: Giving our gifts selflessly and with joy. *American Behavioral Scientist, 43*(8), 1316–1333.

Nechamkin, Y., Salganik, I., Moadai, I., & Ponizovsky, A. (2003). Interpersonal distance in schizophrenic patients: Relationship to negative syndrome. *International Journal of Social Psychiatry, 49,* 116–174.

Nee, V., & Opper, S. (2010). Political capital in a market economy. *Social Forces, 88*(5), 2105–2132.

Neff, K. D., & Helwig, C. C (2002). A constructionist approach to understanding the development of reasoning about rights and authority in cultural contexts. *Cognitive Development, 17,* 1429–1450.

Negy, C., Shreve, T. L., Jensen, B. J., & Uddin, N. (2003). Ethnic identity, self-esteem, and ethnocentrism: A study of social identity versus multicultural theory of development. *Cultural Diversity and Ethnic Minority Psychology, 9*(4), 333–344.

Nelson-Becker, H. B. (2006). Voices of resilience: Older adults in hospice care. *Journal of Social Work in End-of-Life & Palliative Care, 2*(3), 87–106.

Nesdale, D. (2004). Social identity processes and children's ethnic prejudice. In M. Bennett & M. Sani (Eds.), *The development of the social self* (pp. 219–245). New York: Psychology Press.

Netting, F. E., O'Connor, M. K., & Singletary, J. (2007). Finding homes for their dreams: Strategies founders and program initiators use to position and sustain faith-based programs. *Families in Society: The Journal of Contemporary Social Services, 88*(1), 19–29.

Neufeld, P., & Knipemann, K. (2001). Gateway to wellness: An occupational therapy collaboration with the National Multiple Sclerosis Society. *Occupational Therapy in Health Care, 12*(3/4), 67–84.

Newman, D. (2012). *Sociology: Exploring the architecture of everyday life* (9th ed.). Los Angeles: Sage.

Newport, F. (2011). *More than 9 in 10 Americans continue to believe in God.* Retrieved from http://www.gallup.com/poll/147887/Americans-Continue-Believe-God.aspx.

Newport, F. (2013). *In U.S., four in 10 report attending church in last week.* Retrieved from http://www.gallup.com/poll/166613/four-report-attending-church-last-week.aspx.

Nichols, M., & Schwartz, R. (2006). *Family therapy: Concepts and methods* (7th ed.). Boston: Allyn & Bacon.

Nicotera, N. (2005). The child's view of neighborhood: Assessing a neglected element in direct social work practice. *Journal of Human Behavior in the Social Environment, 11*(3/4), 105–133.

Niemann, S. (2005). Persons with disabilities. In M. T. Burke, J. C. Chauvin, & J. G. Miranti (Eds.), *Religious and spiritual issues in counseling: Applications across diverse populations* (pp. 105–133). New York: Brunner-Routledge.

Nisbet, R. (2013, October 14). The rise of Europe's anti-immigration parties. *Sky News.* Retrieved from http://news.sky.com/story/1153190/the-rise-of-europes-anti-immigration-parties.

Nobles, W. W. (1980). African philosophy: Foundations for Black psychology. In R. L. Jones (Ed.), *Black psychology* (2nd ed., pp. 23–36). New York: Harper & Row.

Noddings, N. (2002). *Starting at home: Caring and social policy.* Berkeley: University of California Press.

Noddings, N. (2005). *Educating citizens for global awareness.* New York: Teacher's College Press.

Norcross, J. C., & Wampold, B. E. (2011). Evidence-based therapy relationships: Research conclusions and clinical practices. *Psychotherapy, 48*(1), 98–102.

Northen, H. (1988). *Social work with groups* (3rd ed.). New York: Columbia University Press.

Northouse, P. (2013). *Leadership: Theory and practice* (6th ed.). Los Angeles: Sage.

Norton, C. (2009). Ecopsychology and social work: Creating an interdisciplinary framework for redefining person-in-environment. *Ecopsychology, 1*(3), 138–145.

Novak, G., Fan, T., O'Dowd, B. F., & George, S. R. (2013). Striatal development involves a switch in gene expression networks, followed by a myelination event: Implications for neuropsychiatric disease. *Synapse, 67*(4), 179–188.

Novelli, D., Drury, J., & Reicher, S. (2010). Come together: Two studies concerning the impact of group relations on "personal space." *British Journal of Social Psychology, 49,* 223–236.

Nowell, B., Berkowitz, S., Deacon, Z., & Foster-Fishman, P. (2006). Revealing the cues within community places: Stories of identity, history, and possibility. *American Journal of Community Psychology, 37*(1/2), 29–46.

Nussbaum, M. (2001). *Women and human development: The capabilities approach.* New York: Cambridge University Press.

Nussbaum, M. (2011). *Creating capabilities: The human development approach.* Cambridge, MA: The Belknap Press of the Harvard University Press.

Oberschall, A. (1992). *Social movements: Ideologies, interests, and identities.* New Brunswick, NJ: Transaction.

O'Brien, P. (1992). Social work and spirituality: Clarifying the concept for practice. *Spirituality and Social Work Journal, 3*(1), 2–5.

O'Brien, P. (2001). Claiming our soul: An empowerment group for African-American women in prison. *Journal of Progressive Human Services, 12*(1), 35–51.

Obst, P., & Tham, N. (2009). Helping the soul: The relationship between connectivity and well-being within a church community. *Journal of Community Psychology, 37*(3), 342–361.

Obst, P., & White, K. (2004). Revisiting the Sense of Community Index: A confirmatory factor analysis. *Journal of Community Psychology, 32*(6), 691–705.

Obst, P., Zinkiewicz, L., & Smith, S. (2002a). Sense of community in science fiction fandom: Part 1. Understanding sense of community in an international community of interest. *Journal of Community Psychology, 30*(1), 87–103.

Obst, P., Zinkiewicz, L., & Smith, S. (2002b). Sense of community in science fiction fandom: Part 2. Comparing neighborhood and interest group sense of community. *Journal of Community Psychology, 30*(1), 105–117.

Ochshorn, J., & Cole, E. (Eds.). (1995). *Women's spirituality, women's lives.* Binghamton, NY: Haworth Press.

O'Connor, M., & Netting, E. (2009). *Organization practice: A guide to understanding human service organizations* (2nd ed.). Hoboken, NJ: Wiley.

Odgers, C., Moffitt, T., Tach, L., Sampson, R., Taylor, A., Matthews, C., et al. (2009). The protective effects of neighborhood collective efficacy on British children growing up in deprivation: A developmental analysis. *Developmental Psychology, 45*(4), 942–957.

OECD Family Database. (2013). *Cohabitation rate and prevalence of other forms of partnership.* Retrieved from www.oecd.org/els/soc/SF3_3_Cohabitation_rate_and_prevalence_other_forms_of_partnerships_Jan2013.pdf.

Office of Faith-Based and Neighborhood Partnerships. (2009). *Preserving our constitutional commitments and values.* Retrieved from http://www.whitehouse.gov/administration/eop/ofbnp/values.

Ogbu, J. (2003). *Black American students in an affluent suburb: A study of academic disengagement.* Mahwah, NJ: Erlbaum.

Ohmer, M., & Brooks, F. (2013). The practice of community organizing: Comparing and contrasting conflict and consensus approaches. In M. Weil, M. Reisch, & M. Ohmer (Eds.), *The handbook of community practice* (2nd ed., pp. 233–248). Los Angeles: Sage.

Oldmeadow, J., Platow, M., Foddy, M., & Anderson, D. (2003). Self-categorization, status, and social influence. *Social Psychology Quarterly, 66*(2), 138–152.

Oliver, D., & Peck, M. (2006). Inside the interdisciplinary team: Experiences of hospice social workers. *Journal of Social Work in End-of-Life & Palliative Care, 2*(3), 7–21.

Olshever, A. (2011). Integration of groupwork theory and hospice interdisciplinary team practice: A review of the literature. *Groupwork, 21*(3), 22–61.

Ombelet, W. (2014). Is global access to infertility care realistic? The Walking Egg Project. *Reproductive BioMedicine Online, 28,* 267–272.

Orbuch, T., & Brown, E. (2006). Divorce in the context of being African American. In M. Fine & J. Harvey (Eds.), *Handbook of divorce and relationship dissolution* (pp. 481–498). Mahwah, NJ: Erlbaum.

O'Reilly, B. (2007). *Culture warrior.* New York: Broadway Books.

Organisation for Economic Co-operation and Development. (2011). Growing income inequality in OECD countries: What drives it and how can policy tackle it? Retrieved from http://www.oecd.org/els/47723414.pdf.

Organisation for Economic Co-operation and Development. (2012). *Key characteristics of parental leave systems.* Retrieved from www.oecd.org/social/soc/PF2.1_Parental_leave_systems%20-20%update%20%2018_July_2012.pdf.

Organisation for Economic Co-operation and Development. (2013a). *Education at a glance 2013: OECD indicators.* OECD Publishing. Retrieved from http://dx.doi.org/10.17871/eag-2013-en.

Organisation for Economic Co-operation and Development. (2013b). *OECD: StatExtracts: Trade union density.* Retrieved from stats.oecd.org/index.aspx?Queryld=20167.

Organisation for Economic Co-operation and Development. (2013c). *Health at a glance 2012: OECD indicators.* OECD Publishing. Retrieved from http://dx.doi.org/a0.1787/health_glance-2013-en.

Organisation for Economic Co-operation and Development. (2013d). *Dataset: Social expenditure—Aggregated data.* Retrieved from stats.oecd.org/Index.aspx?datasetcode=SOCX_AGG.

Ortner, S. B. (1984). Theory in anthropology since the sixties. *Comparative Studies in History and Society, 26*(1), 126–166.

Ortner, S. B. (1989). *High religion: A cultural and political history of Sherpa Buddhism.* Princeton, NJ: Princeton University Press.

Ortner, S. B. (1996). *Making gender: The politics and erotics of culture.* Boston: Beacon Press.

Ortner, S. B. (Ed.). (1999). *The fate of culture: Geertz and beyond.* Berkeley: University of California Press.

Ortner, S. B. (2006). *Anthropology and social theory: Culture, power, and the acting subject.* Durham, NC: Duke University Press.

Ozdemir, A. (2008). Shopping malls: Measuring interpersonal distance under changing conditions and cultures. *Field Methods, 20*(3), 226–248.

Ozorak, E. W. (1996). The power, but not the glory: How women empower themselves through religion. *Journal for the Scientific Study of Religion, 35*(1), 17–29.

Padden, D., & Agazio, J. (2013). Caring for military families across the deployment cycle. *Journal of Emergency Nursing, 39*(6), 562–569.

Padilla, Y., & Sherraden, M. (2005). Communities and social policy issues: Persistent poverty, economic inclusion, and asset building. In M. Weil (Ed.), *The handbook of community practice* (pp. 103–116). Thousand Oaks, CA: Sage.

Pals, D. L. (1996). *Seven theories of religion.* New York: Oxford University Press.

Panksepp, J. (2008). The affective brain and core consciousness: How does neural activity generate emotional feelings? In M. Lewis, J. M. Havilland-Jones, & L. F. Barrett (Eds.), *Handbook of emotions* (3rd ed., pp. 47–67). New York: Guilford Press.

Papell, D., & Prodan, R. (2011). *The statistical behavior of GDP after financial crises and severe recessions.* Paper prepared for the Federal Reserve Bank of Boston conference Long-Term Effects of the Great Recession, October 18–19, 2011. Retrieved from www.bostonfed.org/economics/conf/LTE2011/papers/Papell_Prodan.pdf.

Paradies, Y. (2006). A systematic review of empirical research on self-reported racism and health. *International Journal of Epidemiology, 35*(4), 888–901.

Parappully, J., Rosenbaum, R., van den Daele, L., & Nzewi, E. (2002). Thriving after trauma: The experience of parents of murdered children. *Journal of Humanistic Psychology, 42*(1), 33–70.

Pargament, K. I. (1997). *The psychology of religious coping: Theory, research, practice.* New York: Guilford Press.

Pargament, K. I. (2007). *Spiritually integrated psychotherapy: Understanding and addressing the sacred.* New York: Guilford Press.

Pargament, K. I. (2008). The sacred character of community life. *American Journal of Community Psychology, 41*(1–2), 22–34.

Pargament, K. I., Koenig, H. G., & Perez, L. M. (2000). The many methods of religious coping: Development and initial validation of the RCOPE. *Journal of Clinical Psychology, 56*, 519–543.

Parham, P. (2009). *The immune system* (3rd ed.). New York: Garland Science, Taylor & Francis.

Paris, P. J. (1995). *The spirituality of African peoples: The search for a common moral discourse.* Minneapolis, MN: Fortress Press.

Parish, S. L., Magana, S., & Cassiman, S. A. (2008). It's just that much harder: Multi-layered hardship experiences of low-income mothers with disabilities. *AFFILIA: Journal of Women and Social Work, 23*(1), 51–65.

Park, R. (1936). Human ecology. *American Journal of Sociology, 17*, 1–15.

Parkinson, B., Fischer, A. H., & Manstead, A. S. R. (2005). *Emotion in social relations: Cultural, group, and interpersonal processes.* New York: Psychology Press.

Parreñas, R. (2001). *Servants of globalization: Women, migration, and domestic work.* Palo Alto, CA: Stanford University Press.

Parreñas, R. (2008). *The force of domesticity: Filipina migrants and globalization.* New York: New York University Press.

Parrillo, V. (2009). *Diversity in America* (3rd ed.). Thousand Oaks, CA: Pine Forge.

Pasley, K., & Lee, M. (2010). Stress and coping within the context of stepfamily life. In S. Price, C. Price, & P. McKenry (Eds.), *Families & change: Coping with stressful events and transitions* (4th ed., pp. 235–261). Thousand Oaks, CA: Sage.

Paulino, A. (1995). Spiritism, santeria, brujeria, and voodooism: A comparative view of indigenous healing systems. *Journal of Teaching in Social Work, 12*(1/2), 105–124.

Paulino, A. (1998). Dominican immigrant elders: Social service needs, utilization patterns, and challenges. *Journal of Gerontological Social Work, 30*(1/2), 61–74.

Payne, K., & Gibbs, L. (2013). *Economic well-being and the great recession: Dual earner married couples in the U.S., 2006 and 2011.* (FP-13-05). National Center for Family & Marriage Research. Retrieved from http://ncfmr.gbsu.edu/pdf/family_profiles/file126564.pdf.

Payne, R. (2000). *Relaxation techniques: A practical handbook for the health care professional* (2nd ed.). Edinburgh, NY: Churchill Livingstone.

Pearson, J. (1996). *Discovering the self through drama and movement: The Sesame Approach.* London: Jessica Kingsley.

Pedrotti, J., Snyder, C., & Lopez, S. (2007). Eastern perspectives on positive psychology. In C. Snyder & S. Lopez (Eds.), *Positive psychology: The scientific and practice explorations of human strengths* (pp. 37–50). Thousand Oaks, CA: Sage.

Peplau, L., & Fingerhut, A. (2007). The close relationships of lesbians and gay men. *Annual Review of Psychology, 58*, 373–408.

Perkins, T. (2012). Women's pathways into activism: Rethinking the women's environmental justice narrative in California's San Joaquin Valley. *Organization & Environment, 25*(1), 76–94.

Perlman, F., & Brandell, J. (2011). Psychoanalytic theory. In J. Brandell (Ed.), *Theory & practice in clinical social work* (2nd ed., pp. 41–80). Thousand Oaks, CA: Sage.

Perry, A. V., & Rolland, J. S. (2009). The therapeutic benefits of a justice-seeking spirituality: Empowerment, healing, and hope. In F. Walsh (Ed.), *Spiritual resources in family therapy* (2nd ed., pp. 379–396). New York: Guilford Press.

Perry, B. G. F. (1998). The relationship between faith and well-being. *Journal of Religion and Health, 37*(2), 125–136.

Peteet, J., Lu, F., & Narrow, W. (2011). *Religious and spiritual issues in psychiatric diagnosis: A research agenda for DSM-V.* Washington, DC: American Psychiatric Publishing.

Peterson, B., Newton, C., & Rosen, K. (2003). Examining congruence between partners' perceived infertility-related stress and its relationship to marital adjustment and depression in infertile couples. *Family Process, 42,* 59–70.

Peterson, U., Demerouti, E., Bergstrom, G., Samuelsson, M., Asberg, M., & Nygren, A. (2008). Burnout and physical and mental health among Swedish healthcare workers. *Journal of Advanced Nursing, 62,* 84–95.

Pew Forum on Religion & Public Life. (2008). *U.S. religious landscape survey: Religious affiliation—diverse and dynamic.* Washington, DC: Author.

Pew Forum on Religion & Public Life. (n.d.). *Religion and public life.* Retrieved from http://www.pewtrusts.org/our_work_category.aspx?id=318.

Pew Research Center. (2009). *Views of religious similarities and differences: Muslims widely seen as facing discrimination.* Retrieved from http://www.pewforum.org/files/2009/09/survey0909.pdf.

Pew Research Center. (2013). *Birth rates hit record low for those under 25, still on the rise for those 40+.* Retrieved from http://www.pewreserach.org/fact-tank/2013/07/03/birth-rates-hit-record-low-for-those-under-25-still-on-the-rise-for-those-40.

Pew Research Center's Religion & Public Life Project. (2010). *World religion makeup.* Retrieved from http://www.globalreligiousfutures.org/explorer#/?subtopic=15&chartType=pie&year=2010&data_type=percentage&religious_affiliation=all&destination=to&countries=Worldwide.

Pew Research Center's Religion & Public Life Project. (2012). *"Nones" on the rise.* Retrieved from http://www.pewforum.org/2012/10/09/nones-on-the-rise.

Pew Research Center's Religion & Public Life Project. (2014, February 5). *Gay marriage around the world.* Retrieved from http://www.pewforum.org/2013/12/19/gay-marriage-around-the-world-2013.

Pew Research Hispanic Center. (2013). *Statistical portrait of the foreign-born population in the United States, 2011.* Retrieved from http://www.pewhispanic.org/files/2013/02/statistical-portrait-of-the-foreign-born-population-in-the-United-States-2011_Final.pdf.

Pew Research Hispanic Trends Project. (2013). *A nation of immigrants: A portrait of the 40 million, including 11 million unauthorized.* Retrieved from http://www.pewhispanic.org/2013/01/29/a-nation-of-immigrants.

Pew Research Social & Demographic Trends. (2013). *On pay gap, millennial women near parity—for now.* Retrieved from http://www.pewsocialtrends.org/2013/12/11on-pay-millennial-women-near-parity-for-now.

Pew-Templeton Global Religious Futures Project. (2014). Retrieved from http://www.globalreligiousfutures.org/explorer#/?subtopic=15&chartType=pie&year=2010&data_type=percentage&religious_affiliation=all&destination=to&countries=Worldwide.

Pfeffer, J. (1982). *Organizations and organization theory.* Boston: Pitman.

PFLAG. (2014). *About PFLAG.* Retrieved from http://community.pflag.org/page.aspx?pid=237.

Pharr, S. (1988). *Homophobia: A weapon of sexism.* Inverness, CA: Chardon Press.

Pickering, J., Kintrea, K., & Bannister, J. (2012). Invisible walls and visible youth: Territoriality among young people in British cities. *Urban Studies, 49*(5), 945–960.

Pinker, S. (2011). *The better angels of our nature: Why violence has declined.* New York: Viking.

Pirog, M., & Ziol-Guest, M. (2006). Child support enforcement: Programs and policies, impacts and questions. *Journal of Policy Analysis and Management, 25,* 943–990.

Plasse, B. R. (2001). A stress reduction and self-care group for homeless and addicted women: Meditation, relaxation and cognitive methods. *Social Work With Groups, 24*(3/4), 117–133.

Plutchik, R. (2005). The nature of emotions. In P. W. Sherman & J. Alcock (Eds.), *Exploring animal behavior: Readings from American Scientist* (4th ed., pp. 85–91). Sunderland, MA: Sinauer Associates.

Pokorná, J., Machala, L., Rezáčová, P., & Konvalinka, J. (2009). Current and novel inhibitors of HIV protease. *Viruses, 1*(3), 1209–1239.

Polletta, F. (2004). Culture is not just in your head. In J. Goodwin & J. Jasper (Eds.), *Rethinking social movements* (pp. 97–110). Lanham, MD: Rowman & Littlefield.

Pons, F., Laroche, M., & Mourali, M. (2006). Consumer reactions to crowded retail settings: Cross-cultural differences between North America and Middle East. *Psychology & Marketing, 23*(7), 555–572.

Popenoe, D. (1996). *Life without father: Compelling new evidence that fatherhood and marriage are indispensable for the good of children and society.* New York: Martin Kessler Books.

Popple, P. (1992). Social work: Social function and moral purpose. In P. Reid & P. Popple (Eds.), *The moral purposes of social work: The character and intentions of a profession* (pp. 141–154). Chicago: Nelson-Hall.

Popple, P., & Leighninger, L. (2011). *Social work, social welfare, and American society* (8th ed.). Boston: Pearson.

Postman, N. (1993). *Technopoly: The surrender of culture to technology.* New York: Vintage Books.

Potter, T. (2005, Fall). Bringing foster care management into the 21st century with GIS. *ArcNews Online.* Retrieved from http://www.esri.com/news/arcnews/fall05articles/bringing-foster.html.

Praglin, L. (2004). Spirituality, religion, and social work: An effort towards interdisciplinary conversation. *Social Thought, 23,* 67–84.

Prezza, M., & Costantini, S. (1998). Sense of community and life satisfaction: Investigation in three different territorial contexts. *Journal of Community and Applied Social Psychology, 8*(3), 181–194.

Price, S., Price, C., & McKenry, P. (2010). *Families & change: Coping with stressful events and transitions* (4th ed.). Thousand Oaks, CA: Sage.

Prichard, D. (2004). Critical incident stress and secondary trauma: An analysis of group process. *Groupwork, 14*(3), 44–62.

Procidano, M. E., & Smith, W. W. (1997). Assessing perceived social support: The importance of context. In G. R. Pierce, B. Lakey, & B. R. Sarason (Eds.), *Sourcebook of social support and personality* (pp. 93–106). New York: Plenum Press.

Proescholdbell, R., Roosa, M., & Nemeroff, C. (2006). Component measures of psychological sense of community among gay men. *Journal of Community Psychology, 34*(1), 9–24.

Puchalski, C., & Romer, A. L. (2000). Taking a spiritual history allows clinicians to understand patients more fully. *Journal of Palliative Medicine, 3*(1), 129–137.

Puddifoot, J. (1995). Dimensions of community identity. *Journal of Community & Applied Social Psychology, 5,* 357–370.

Putnam, R. (1993). *Making democracy work.* Princeton, NJ: Princeton University Press.

Putnam, R. (2000). *Bowling alone: The collapse and revival of American community.* New York: Simon & Schuster.

Quigley, B. (2001). The living wage movement. *Blueprint for Social Justice, 54*(9), 1–7.

Raanaas, R., Evensen, K., Rich, D., Sjostrom, G., & Patil, G. (2011). Benefits of indoor plants on attention capacity in an office setting. *Journal of Environmental Psychology, 31,* 99–105.

Raines, J. (1997). Co-constructing the spiritual tree. *Society for Social Work and Social Work Newsletter, 4*(1), 3, 8.

Rainie, L. (2013, June 6). *Cell phone ownership hits 91% of adults.* Retrieved from http://www.pewresearch.org/fact-tank/2013/06/06/cell-phone-onwership-hits-91-of-adults.

Ramirez, R. (1985). Hispanic spirituality. *Social Thought, 11*(3), 6–13.

Rampage, C., Eovaldi, M., Ma, C., Foy, C., Samuels, G., & Bloom, L. (2012). Adoptive families. In F. Walsh (Ed.), *Normal family processes: Growing diversity and complexity* (4th ed., pp. 222–246). New York: Guilford.

Rapoport, J., Jacobs, P., & Jonsson, E. (2009). *Cost containment and efficiency in national health systems.* Hoboken, NJ: Wiley-Blackwell.

Ravitch, D. (2010). *The death and life of the great American school system: How testing and choice are undermining education* (Revised and expanded). New York: Basic Books.

Ravitch, D. (2013). *Reign of error: The hoax of the privatization movement and the danger to America's public schools.* New York: Knopf.

Rawls, J. (1971). *A theory of justice.* Cambridge, MA: Harvard University Press.

Rawls, J. (2001). *Justice as fairness: A restatement.* Cambridge, MA: The Belknap Press of Harvard University.

Ray, O. (2004). How the mind hurts and heals the body. *American Psychologist, 59*(1), 29–40.

Ray, R., Gornick, J., & Schmitt, J. (2009). *Parental leave policies in 21 countries: Assessing generosity and gender equality.* Washington, DC: Center for Economic and Policy Research. Retrieved from www.lisdatacenter.org/wp-content/uplaids/parent-leave-report1.pdf.

Raza, M., & Velez, P. (Directors). (2002). *Occupation: The Harvard University living wage sit-in* [Motion picture]. Waterville, ME: EnMasse Films.

Reamer, F. (1992). Social work and the public good: Calling or career? In P. Reid & P. Popple (Eds.), *The moral purposes of social work: The character and intentions of a profession* (pp. 11–33). Chicago: Nelson-Hall.

Reardon, S. (2011). The widening academic achievement gap between the rich and the poor: New evidence and possible explanations. In G. Duncan & R. Murname (Eds.), *Whither opportunity? Rising inequality, schools, and children's life chances* (pp. 91–116). New York: Russell Sage Foundation.

Rector, R., Johnson, K., & Fagan, P. (2008). Increasing marriage would dramatically reduce child poverty. In D. R. Crane & T. Heaton (Eds.), *Handbook of families & poverty* (pp. 457–470). Thousand Oaks, CA: Sage.

Redfield, R. (1947). The folk society. *American Journal of Sociology, 52,* 293–308.

Redman, D. (2008). Stressful life experiences and the roles of spirituality among people with a history of substance abuse and incarceration. *Social Thought, 27*(1–2), 47–67.

Reese, D. J. (2011). Interdisciplinary perceptions of the social work role in hospice: Building upon the class Kulys and Davis study. *Journal of Social Work in End-of-Life & Palliative Care, 7*(4), 383–406.

Reese, D. J., & Kaplan, M. S. (2000). Spirituality, social support, and worry about health: Relationships in a sample of HIV+ women. *Social Thought, 19*(4), 37–52.

Reese, D. J., & Raymer, M. (2004). Relationships between social work services and hospice outcomes: Results of the National Hospice Social Work Survey. *Social Work, 49*(3), 415–422.

Reeves, T. C. (1998). *The empty church: Does organized religion matter anymore?* New York: Simon & Schuster.

Regoeczi, W. (2008). Crowding in context: An examination of the differential responses of men and women to high-density living environments. *Journal of Health and Social Behavior, 49*(3), 254–268.

Reichert, E. (2006). *Understanding human rights: An exercise book.* Thousand Oaks, CA: Sage.

Reilly, P. (1995). The religious wounding of women. *Creation Spirituality, 11*(1), 41–45.

Reinhardt, U., Hussey, P., & Anderson, G. (2002). Cross-national comparisons of health systems using OECD data, 1999. *Health Affairs, 21*(3), 169–181.

Reinhardt, U., Hussey, P., & Anderson, G. (2004). U.S. health care spending in an international context. *Health Affairs, 23*(3), 10–25.

Reisch, M. (2008). Social movements. In T. Mizrahi & L. Davis (Eds.), *Encyclopedia of social work* (20th ed., Vol. 4, pp. 52–56). New York: NASW Press and Oxford University Press.

Reisch, M. (2013). Radical community organizing. In M. Weil, M. Reisch, & M. Ohmer (Eds.), *The handbook of community practice* (2nd ed., pp. 361–381). Los Angeles: Sage.

Reisch, M., Ife, J., & Weil, M. (2013). Social justice, human rights, values, and community practice. In M. Weil, M. Reisch, & M. Ohmer (Eds.), *The handbook of community practice* (2nd ed., pp. 73–103). Los Angeles: Sage.

Reisch, M., & Jani, J. (2012). The new politics of social work practice: Understanding the context to promote change. *British Journal of Social Work, 42,* 1132–1150.

Reporters Without Borders. (2013). *Press Freedom Index 2013.* Retrieved from http://en.rsf.org/press-freedom-index-2013.1054.html.

Ressler, L. E., & Hodge, D. R. (2003). Silenced voices: Social work and the oppression of conservative narratives. *Social Thought, 22,* 125–142.

Reuther, R. (1983). *Sexism and God-talk: Toward a feminist theology.* Boston: Beacon Press.

Richards-Schuster, K., & Aldana, A. (2013). Learning to speak out about racism: Youth's insights on participation in an Intergroup Dialogues Program. *Social Work With Groups, 36*(4), 332–348.

Richman, J. M., Rosenfeld, L. B., & Hardy, C. J. (1993). The social support survey: A validation study of a clinical measure of the social support process. *Research on Social Work Practice, 3,* 288–311.

Richmond, M. (1917). *Social diagnosis.* New York: Russell Sage Foundation.

Rideout, V., Foehr, U., & Roberts, D. (2010). *Generation M2: Media in the lives of 8- to 18-year-olds.* Menlo Park, CA: Henry J. Kaiser Family Foundation.

Riera, C. (2005). Social policy and community development in multicultural contexts. *Community Development Journal, 40*(4), 433–438.

Ripley, A. (2013). *The smartest kids in the world: And how they got that way.* New York: Simon & Schuster.

Ritzer, G. (2013a). *Introduction to sociology.* Thousand Oaks, CA: Sage.

Ritzer, G. (2013b). *The McDonaldization of society* (20th anniv. ed.). Los Angeles: Sage.

Robbins, S., Chatterjee, P., & Canda, E. (2012). *Contemporary human behavior theory: A critical perspective for social work* (3rd ed.). Boston: Allyn & Bacon.

Roberson, W. W. (2004). *Life and livelihood: A handbook for spirituality at work.* Harrison, PA: Morehouse.

Roberts, K., & Yamane, D. (2012). *Religion in sociological perspective* (5th ed.). Los Angeles: Sage.

Robertson, R. (1992). *Globalization.* London: Sage.

Robinson, T. L. (2000). Making the hurt go away: Psychological and spiritual healing for African American women survivors of childhood incest. *Journal of Multicultural Counseling and Development, 28*(3), 160–176.

Robinson, T. R. (2010). *Genetics for dummies* (Kindle Locations 2036–2039). Hoboken, NJ: Wiley. Kindle Edition.

Roehlkepartain, E. C., King, P. E., Wagener, L., & Benson, P. L. (2006). *Spiritual development in childhood and adolescence.* Thousand Oaks, CA: Sage.

Rogers, C. R. (1951). *Client-centered therapy.* Boston: Houghton Mifflin.

Rogers, C. R. (1986). Carl Rogers on the development of the person-centered approach. *Person-Centered Reviews, 1*(3), 257–259.

Rogers, R. K. (2009). Community collaboration: Practices of effective collaboration as reported by three urban faith-based social service programs. *Social Work & Christianity, 36*(3), 326–345.

Rogers-Sirin, L., & Gupta, T. (2012). Cultural identity and mental health: Different trajectories among Asian and Latino youth. *Journal of Counseling Psychology, 59*(4), 555–566.

Rollero, C., & Piccoli, N. (2010). Place attachment, identification and environment perception: An empirical study. *Journal of Environmental Psychology, 30,* 198–205.

Ronen, T., & Freeman, A. (Eds.). (2007). *Cognitive behavior therapy in clinical social work practice.* New York: Springer.

Roof, W. C. (1993). *A generation of seekers: The spiritual journeys of the baby boom generation.* San Francisco: HarperCollins.

Roof, W. C. (1999). *Spiritual marketplace: Baby boomers and the remaking of American religion.* Princeton, NJ: Princeton University Press.

Roosevelt, M. (2013, January 1). "Living-wage" movement growing in region. *Orange County Register.* Retrieved from http://www.ocregister.com/articles/wage-523783-living-long.htm.

Rosaldo, R. (1993). *Culture and truth: The remaking of social analysis.* Boston: Beacon Press.

Rose, S. (1992). *Case management and social work practice.* White Plains, NY: Longman.

Rose, S. (1994). Defining empowerment: A value-based approach. In S. P. Robbins (Ed.), *Melding the personal and the political: Advocacy and empowerment in clinical and community practice. Proceedings of the Eighth Annual Social Work Futures Conference, May 13–14, 1993* (pp. 17–24). Houston, TX: University of Houston Graduate School of Social Work.

Rosenwald, M., Smith, M., Bagnoli, M., Ricceli, D., Ryan, S., Salcedo, L., et al. (2013). Relighting the campfire: Rediscovering activity-based group work. *Social Work With Groups, 36*(4), 321–331.

Rosenzweig, S. M., Breedlove, N. V., & Watson, M. R. (2010). *Biological psychology: An introduction to behavioral, cognitive, and clinical neuroscience* (6th ed.). Sunderland, MA: Sinauer Associates.

Ross, L., & Coleman, M. (2000). Urban community action planning inspires teenagers to transform their community and their identity. *Journal of Community Practice, 7*(2), 29–45.

Rostow, W. (1990). *The stages of economic growth: A non-communist manifesto.* Cambridge, UK: Cambridge University Press.

Rothenberg, P. (2006). Preface. In P. Rothenberg (Ed.), *Beyond borders: Thinking critically about global issues* (pp. xv–xvii). New York: W. H. Freeman.

Rothenberg, P. (2010). *Race, class, and gender in the United States* (8th ed.). New York: Worth.

Rothman, J. (2008). *Cultural competence in process and practice: Building bridges.* Boston: Pearson.

Rothschild-Whitt, J., & Whitt, J. (1986). *The cooperative workplace.* Cambridge, UK: Cambridge University Press.

Rothstein, R. (2011). *Fact-challenged policy.* Economic Policy Institute. Retrieved from www.epi.org/publication/fact-challenged-policy.

Roulstone, A. (2004). Employment barriers and inclusive futures? In *Disabling barriers—enabling environments* (2nd ed., pp. 195–200). Thousand Oaks, CA: Sage.

Rudacille, D. (2005). *The riddle of gender: Science, activism, and transgender rights.* New York: Pantheon.

Russel, R. (1998). Spirituality and religion in graduate social work education. *Social Thought, 18*(2), 15–29.

Russell, A. (2011). Extra-national information flows, social media, and the 2011 Egyptian uprising. *International Journal of Communication, 5,* 1375–1405.

Rychtarik, R., McGillicuddy, N., & Barrick, C. (2013). Reaching women under stress from a partner's drinking problem: Assessing interest in online help. *Journal of Technology in Human Services, 31*(3), 185–196.

Saez, E. (2012). *Striking it richer: The evolution of top incomes in the United States (Updated with 2009 and 2010 estimates).* Retrieved from elsa.berkeley.edu/~saez/saez-UStopincomes-2010.pdf.

Sager, J., & Weil, M. (2013). Larger-scale social planning. In M. Weil, M. Reisch, & M. Ohmer (Eds.), *The handbook of community practice* (2nd ed., pp. 299–325). Los Angeles: Sage.

Sahgal, N., & Smith, G. (2009). *A religious portrait of African-Americans.* Pew Research Center's Forum on Religion & Public Life. Retrieved from http://www.pewforum.org/A-Religious-Portrait-of-African-Americans.aspx.

Sahlins, M. (1981). *Historical metaphors and mythical realities: Structure in the early history of the Sandwich Islands kingdom.* Ann Arbor: University of Michigan Press.

Saleebey, D. (2012). *The strengths perspective in social work practice* (6th ed.). Upper Saddle River, NJ: Pearson.

Sampson, R. (2003). The neighborhood context of well-being. *Perspectives in Biology and Medicine, 46*(3), S53–S65.

Sampson, R., Morenoff, J., & Earls, F. (1999). Beyond social capital: Spatial dynamics of collective efficacy for children. *Science, 277,* 918–924.

Sarafino, E. P., & Smith, T. W. (2010). *Health psychology: Biopsychosocial interactions* (7th ed.). New York: John Wiley & Sons.

Sarason, S. (1974). *The psychological sense of community: Prospects for a community psychology.* San Francisco: Jossey-Bass.

Sargent, L. D., & Sue-Chan, C. (2001). Does diversity affect group efficacy? The intervening role of cohesion and task independence. *Small Group Research, 32*(4), 426–450.

Satir, V. (1983). *Conjoint family therapy* (3rd ed.). Palo Alto, CA: Science and Behavior Books.

Sayer, L. (2006). Economic aspects of divorce and relationship dissolution. In M. Fine & J. Harvey (Eds.), *Handbook of divorce and relationship dissolution* (pp. 385–406). Mahwah, NJ: Erlbaum.

Scales, T. L., Wolfer, T. A., Sherwood, D. A., Garland, D. R., Hugen, B., & Pittman, S. W. (2002). *Spirituality and religion in social work practice. Decision cases with teaching notes.* Alexandria, VA: Council on Social Work Education.

Scannell, L., & Gifford, R. (2010a). Defining place attachment: A tripartite organizing framework. *Journal of Environmental Psychology, 30,* 1–10.

Scannell, L., & Gifford, R. (2010b). The relations between natural and civic place attachment and pro-environmental behavior. *Journal of Environmental Psychology, 30,* 289–297.

Scannell, L., & Gifford, R. (2013). Personality relevant climate change: The role of place attachment and local versus global message framing in engagement. *Environment and Behavior, 45*(1), 60–85.

Schackman, B. R., Gebo, K. A., Walensky, R. P., Losina, E. L., Muccio, T., Sax, P. E., et al. (2006). The lifetime cost of current human immunodeficiency virus care in the United States. *Medical Care, 44*(11), 990–997.

Schacter, S., & Singer, J. E. (1962). Cognitive, social, and physiological determinants of emotional states. *Psychological Review, 69,* 379–399.

Schamess, G., & Shilkret, R. (2011). Ego psychology. In J. Berzoff, L. M. Flanagan, & P. Hertz (Eds.), *Inside out and outside in: Psychodynamic clinical theory and psychopathology in contemporary multicultural contexts* (3d ed., pp. 62–96). Lanham, MD: Rowman & Littlefield.

Schaufeli, W., & Enzmann, D. (1998). *The burnout companion to study and practice: A critical analysis.* London: Taylor & Francis.

Schaufeli, W., Leiter, M., & Maslach, C. (2009). Burnout: 35 years of research and practice. *Career Development International, 14*(3), 204–220.

Schein, E. (1992). *Organizational culture and leadership* (2nd ed.). San Francisco: Jossey-Bass.

Schiff, M., & Bargal, O. (2000). Helping characteristics of self-help and support groups: Their contribution to participants' subjective well-being. *Small Group Research, 31*(3), 275–304.

Schiller, J., Lucas, J., & Peregoy, J. (2012). Summary health statistics for U.S. adults: National Health Interview Survey, 2011. *Vital and Health Statistics, 10*(256). Hyattsville, MD: U.S. Department of Health and Human Services: Centers for Disease Control and Prevention.

Schneider, J., & Cook, K. (1995). Status inconsistency and gender: Combining revisited. *Small Group Research, 26,* 372–399.

Schoech, D. (2013). Community practice in the digital age. In M. Weil, M. Reisch, & M. Ohmer (Eds.), *The handbook of community practice* (2nd ed., pp. 809–826). Los Angeles: Sage.

Scholz, R. W., Blumer, Y. B., & Brand, F. S. (2012). Risk, vulnerability, robustness, and resilience from a decision-theoretic perspective. *Journal of Risk Research, 15*(3), 313–330.

Schore, A. N. (2002). Dysregulation of the right brain: A fundamental mechanism of traumatic attachment and the psychopathogenesis of post-traumatic stress disorder. *Australian and New Zealand Journal of Psychiatry, 36,* 9–30.

Schuster, M. A., Stein, B. P., Jaycox, L. H., Collins, R. L., Marshall, G. N., Zhou, A. J., et al. (2001). A national survey of stress reactions after the September 11, 2001, terrorist attacks. *New England Journal of Medicine, 345*(20), 1507–1512.

Schutz, A. (1967). *The phenomenology of the social world* (G. Walsh & F. Lehnert, Trans.). Evanston, IL: Northwestern University Press. (Original work published 1932)

Schwalbe, M. (2006). Afterword: The costs of American privilege. In P. Rothenberg (Ed.), *Beyond borders: Thinking critically about global issues* (pp. 603–605). New York: Worth.

Schweinhart, L., Barnett, S., & Belfield, C. (2005). *Lifetime effects: The High/Scope Perry Preschool Study through age 40.* Ypsilanti, MI: High/Scope Press.

Scott, A. H., Butin, D. N., Tewfik, D., Burkhardt, A., Mandel, D., & Nelson, L. (2001). Occupational therapy as a means to wellness with the elderly. *Physical and Occupational Therapy in Geriatrics, 18*(4), 3–22.

Scott, M. (2005). A powerful theory and a paradox: Ecological psychologists after Barker. *Environment and Behavior, 37*(3), 295–329.

Scott, W. R. (2014). *Institutions and organizations: Ideas, interests, and identities* (4th ed.). Los Angeles: Sage.

Seabrook, J., & Avison, W. (2012). Socioeconomic status and cumulate disadvantage processes across the life course: Implications for health outcomes. *Canadian Review of Sociology, 49*(1), 50–68.

Seccombe, K., & Warner, R. (2004). *Marriages and families: Relationships in social context.* New York: Thomson Learning.

Segerstrom, S. S., & Miller, G. E. (2004). Psychological stress and the human immune system: A meta-analytic study of 30 years of inquiry. *Psychological Bulletin, 130*(4), 601–630.

Seidman, E. (2012). An emerging action science of social settings. *American Journal of Community Psychology, 50,* 1–16.

Seligman, M. (1998). *Learned optimism: How to change your mind and your life* (2nd ed.). New York: Pocket Books.

Seligman, M. (2002). *Authentic happiness: Using the new positive psychology to realize your potential for lasting fulfillment.* New York: Free Press.

Seliske, L., Pickett, W., & Janssen, I. (2012). Urban sprawl and its relationship with active transportation, physical activity and obesity in Canadian youth. *Health Reports, 23*(2), 1–9.

Selye, H. (1991). History and present status of the stress concept. In A. Monat & R. S. Lazarus (Eds.), *Stress and coping: An anthology* (3rd ed., pp. 21–35). New York: Columbia University Press.

Sen, A. (1992). *Inequality reexamined.* Cambridge, MA: Harvard University Press.

Sen, A. (1999). *Development as freedom.* New York: Anchor Books.

Sen, A. (2009). *The idea of justice.* Cambridge, MA: The Belknap Press of Harvard University.

Senge, P. (1990). *The fifth discipline.* New York: Doubleday.

Sernau, S. (2014). *Social inequality in a global age* (4th ed.). Los Angeles: Sage.

Severson, K. (2011, July 5). Systematic cheating is found in Atlanta's school system. *New York Times.* Retrieved from www.nytimes.com/2011/07/06/education/06atlanta.html.

Shaw, B., Sivakumar, G., Balinas, T., Chipman, R., & Krahn, D. (2013). Testing the feasibility of mobile audio-based recovery material as an adjunct to intensive outpatients treatment for veterans with substance abuse disorders. *Journal of Technology in Human Services, 31*(4), 321–336.

Shek, D. (2003). Economic stress, psychological well-being and problem behavior in Chinese adolescents with economic disadvantage. *Journal of Youth and Adolescence, 32*(4), 259–266.

Shepard, B. (2005). Play, creativity, and the new community organizing. *Journal of Progressive Human Services, 16*(2), 47–69.

Shepard, B. (2013). Community gardens, community organizing, and environmental activism. In M. Gray, J. Coates, & T. Hetherington (Eds.), *Environmental social work* (pp. 121–134). New York: Routledge.

Sheridan, M. J. (1995). Honoring angels in my path: Spiritually sensitive group work with persons who are incarcerated. *Reflections: Narratives of Professional Helping, 1*(4), 5–16.

Sheridan, M. J. (2002). Spiritual and religious issues in practice. In A. R. Roberts & G. J. Greene (Eds.), *Social workers' desk reference* (pp. 567–571). New York: Oxford University Press.

Sheridan, M. J. (2004). Predictors of use of spiritually-derived interventions in social work practice: A survey of practitioners. *Journal of Spirituality and Religion in Social Work: Social Thought, 23*(4), 5–25.

Sheridan, M. J. (2009). Ethical issues in the use of spiritually-based interventions in social work practice: What are we doing and why? *Social Thought, 28*(1/2), 99–126.

Sheridan, M. J. (2013). Elders caring for elders: The role of religious involvement and spiritual rewards on caregiver stress, resources, and health. *Journal of Religion & Spirituality in Social Work: Social Thought, 32,* 397–421.

Sheridan, M. J. (Ed.). (2014). *Connecting spirituality and social justice: Conceptualizations and applications for macro social work practice.* London, UK: Routledge.

Sheridan, M. J., & Amato-von Hemert, K. (1999). The role of religion and spirituality in social work education and practice: A survey of student views and experiences. *Journal of Social Work Education, 35*(1), 125–141.

Sheridan, M. J., & Bullis, R. K. (1991). Practitioners' views on religion and spirituality: A qualitative study. *Spirituality and Social Work Journal, 2*(2), 2–10.

Sheridan, M. J., Bullis, R. K., Adcock, C. R., Berlin, S. D., & Miller, P. C. (1992). Practitioners' personal and professional attitudes and behaviors toward religion and spirituality: Issues for social work education and practice. *Journal of Social Work Education, 28*(2), 190–203.

Sheridan, M. J., Wilmer, C., & Atcheson, L. (1994). Inclusion of content on religion and spirituality in the social work curriculum: A study of faculty views. *Journal of Social Work Education, 30,* 363–376.

Sherry, A., Adelman, A., Whilde, M. R., & Quick, D. (2010). Competing selves: Negotiating the intersection of spiritual and sexual identities. *Professional Psychology: Research and Practice, 41*(2), 112–119.

Shore, R., & Shore, B. (2009). *Increasing the percentage of children living in two-parent families.* Baltimore: The Annie E. Casey Foundation. Retrieved from http://www.aecf.org/~/media/Pubs/Initiatives/KIDS%20COUNT/K/KIDSCOUNTIndicatorBriefIncreasingthePercentag/Two%20Parent%20Families.pdf.

Shorey, H. S., & Snyder, C. R. (2006). The role of adult attachment styles in psychopathology and psychotherapy outcomes. *Review of General Psychology, 10*(1), 1–20.

Shu, L., & Li, Y. (2007). How far is enough? A measure of information privacy in terms of interpersonal distance. *Environment & Behavior, 39*(3), 317–331.

Shweder, R. (1995). Anthropology's Romantic rebellion against the Enlightenment, or there's more to thinking than reason and evidence. In R. Shweder & R. LeVine (Eds.), *Culture theory: Essays on mind, self, and emotion* (pp. 27–66). New York: Cambridge University Press. (Original work published 1984)

Sideridis, G. D. (2006). Coping is not an "either" "or": The interaction of coping strategies in regulating affect, arousal and performance. *Stress and Health: Journal of the International Society for the Investigation of Stress, 22*(5), 315–327.

Silverman, D. (1971). *The theory of organizations: A sociological framework.* New York: Basic Books.

Silverman, D. (1994). On throwing away ladders: Re-writing the theory of organizations. In J. Hassard & M. Parker (Eds.), *Towards a new theory of organizations* (pp. 1–23). New York: Routledge.

Simaika, J., & Samways, M. (2010). Biophilia as a universal ethic for conserving biodiversity. *Conservation Biology, 24*(3), 903–906.

Simon, H. (1957). *Administrative behavior* (2nd ed.). New York: Macmillan.

Sinetar, M. (2011). *Do what you love, the money will follow: Discovering your right livelihood.* New York: Random House.

Singh, G., & Hiatt, R. (2006). Trends and disparities in socioeconomic and behavioural characteristics, life expectancy, and cause-specific mortality of native-born and foreign-born populations in the United States, 1979–2003. *International Journal of Epidemiology, 35*(4), 903–919.

Singh, R. (2001). Hinduism. In M. V. Hook, B. Hugen, & M. Aguilar (Eds.), *Spirituality within religious traditions in social work practice* (pp. 34–52). Pacific Grove, CA: Brooks/Cole.

Sinha, S., & Mukherjee, N. (1996). The effect of perceived cooperation on personal space requirements. *Journal of Social Psychology, 136,* 655–657.

Sinha, S., & Nayyar, P. (2000). Crowding effects of density and personal space requirements among older people: The impact of self-control and social support. *Journal of Social Psychology, 140*(6), 721–726.

Siporin, M. (1986). Contribution of religious values to social work and the law. *Social Thought, 12*(4), 35–50.

Siragusa, N. (2001). *The language of gender.* Retrieved from www.hawaii.edu/hivandaids/The%20Language%20of%20Gender.pdf.

Skinner, B. F. (1948). *Walden Two.* New York: Macmillan.

Skocpol, T. (2003). *Diminished democracy: From membership to management in American civil life.* New York: Cambridge University Press.

Skocpol, T., & Williamson, V. (2012). *The Tea Party and the remaking of Republican conservatism.* New York: Oxford University Press.

Skolnick, A. (1997, May/June). Family values: The sequel. *American Prospect, 32,* 86–94.

Skye, W. (2002). E.L.D.E.R.S. gathering for Native American youth: Continuing Native American traditions and curbing substance abuse in Native American youth. *Journal of Sociology and Social Welfare, 24*(1), 117–135.

Slater, S., Ewing, R., Powell, L., Chaloupka, F., Johnston, L., & O'Malley, P. (2010). The association between community physical activity settings and youth physical activity, obesity, and body mass index. *Journal of Adolescent Health, 47*(5), 496–503.

Slee, N. M. (1996). Further on from Fowler: Post-Fowler faith development research. In L. J. Francis, W. K. Kay, & W. S. Campbell (Eds.), *Research in religious education* (pp. 73–96). Leominster, UK: Gracewing.

Smith, C., & Denton, M. L. (2005). *Soul searching: The religious and spiritual lives of American teenagers.* New York: Oxford University Press.

Smith, C. O., Smith, E. P., Levine, D. W., Dumas, J., & Prinz, R. J. (2009). A developmental perspective of the relationship of racial-ethnic identity to self-construct, achievement, and behavior in African American children. *Cultural Diversity and Ethnic Minority Psychology, 15*(2), 145–157.

Smith, E. D. (1995). Addressing the psychospiritual distress of death as reality: A transpersonal approach. *Social Work, 40,* 402–413.

Smith, G. (1996). Ties, nets and an elastic bund: Community in the postmodern city. *Community Development Journal, 31*(3), 250–259.

Smith, N. R. (2006). *Workplace spirituality: A complete guide for business leaders.* Lynn, MA: Axial Age.

Smith, R., Fortin, A., Dwamena, F., & Frankel, R. (2013). An evidence-based patient-centered method makes the biopsychosocial model scientific. *Patient Education and Counseling, 91,* 265–270.

Snarr, C. M. (2007). "Oh Mary, don't you weep": Progressive religion in the living wage movement. *Political Theology, 8*(3), 269–279.

Snipp, C. M. (1998). The first Americans: American Indians. In M. L. Andersen & P. H. Collins (Eds.), *Race, class, and gender: An anthology* (pp. 357–364). Belmont, CA: Wadsworth.

Snyder, C., & Lopez, S. (2007). *Positive psychology: The scientific and practical explorations of human strengths.* Thousand Oaks, CA: Sage.

Snyder, M. (2014). Self-fulfilling stereotypes. In P. S. Rothenberg (Ed.), *Race, class, and gender in the United States* (9th ed.). New York: Worth.

Snyder, S., & Mitchell, D. (2001). Re-engaging the body: Disability studies and the resistance to embodiment. *Public Culture, 13*(3), 367–389.

Social Trends Institute. (2012). *What do marriage & fertility have to do with the economy?* Retrieved from http://sustaindemographicdividend.org/wp-content-uploads/2012/07/SDD-2011-Final.pdf.

Society for Neuroscience. (2012). *Brain facts: A primer on the brain and nervous system.* Washington, DC: Author. Retrieved from www.sfn.org.

Solantaus, T., Leinonen, J., & Punamaki, R. (2004). Children's mental health in times of economic recession: Replication and extension of the family economic stress model in Finland. *Developmental Psychology, 40*(3), 412–429.

Sollod, R., Wilson, J., & Monte, C. (2009). *Beneath the mask: An introduction to theories of personality* (8th ed.). Hoboken, NJ: Wiley.

Solomon, B. (1976). *Black empowerment: Social work in oppressed communities.* New York: Columbia University Press.

Solomon, B. (1987). Empowerment: Social work in oppressed communities. *Journal of Social Work Practice, 2*(4), 79–91.

Sommer, R. (1969). *Personal space: The behavioral basis of design.* Englewood Cliffs, NJ: Prentice Hall.

Sommer, R. (2002). Personal space in a digital age. In R. Bechtel & A. Churchman (Eds.), *Handbook of environmental psychology* (pp. 647–660). New York: Wiley.

Sompayrac, L. M. (2012). *How the immune system works.* Hoboken, NJ: Wiley & Sons.

Soulsby, A., & Clark, E. (2007). Organization theory and the post-socialist transformation: Contributions to organizational knowledge. *Human Relations, 60*(10), 1419–1442.

Specht, H., & Courtney, M. E. (1994). *Unfaithful angels: How social work has abandoned its mission.* New York: Free Press.

Speybroeck, N., Konings, P., Lynch, J., Harper, S., Berkvens, D., Lorant, V., et al. (2010). Decomposing socioeconomic health inequalities. *International Journal of Public Health, 55*(4), 347–351.

Spiegel, D., & Classen, C. (2000). *Group therapy for cancer patients: A research-based handbook of psychosocial care.* New York: Basic Books.

Stanbridge, K., & Kenney, J. S. (2009). Emotions and the campaign for victims' rights in Canada. *Canadian Journal of Criminology & Criminal Justice, 51*(4), 473–509.

Stanley, S., Markman, H., & Whitton, S. (2002). Communication, conflict, and commitment: Insights on the foundations for relationship success from a national survey. *Family Process, 41,* 659–675.

Starhawk. (1979). *The spiral dance: A rebirth of the ancient religion of the great Goddess.* San Francisco: Harper & Row.

Statistic Brain. (2013). *Adoption statistics.* Retrieved from http://www.statisticbrain.com/adoption-statistics.

Statistic Brain. (2014). *Facebook statistics.* Retrieved from http://www.statisticbrain.com/facebook-statistics.

Stein, L. (2009). Social movement web use in theory and practice: A content analysis of US movement websites. *New Media & Society, 11*(5), 749–771.

Sternberg, E. (2009). *Healing spaces: The science of place and well-being.* Cambridge, MA: Belknap Press.

Stevens, R., & Brown, B. (2011). Walkable new urban LEED-Neighborhood-Development (LEED-ND) community design and children's physical activity: Selection, environmental, or catalyst effects? *International Journal of Behavioral Nutrition and Physical Activity, 8*(1), 139–148.

Stewart, C., Koeske, G., & Pringle, J. L. (2007). Religiosity as a predictor of successful post-treatment abstinence for African-American clients. *Journal of Social Work Practice in the Addictions, 7*(4), 75–92.

Stewart, J. (2001). Radical constructivism in biology and cognitive science. *Foundations of Science, 6*(1–3), 99–124.

Stiglitz, J. (2012). *The price of inequality: How today's divided society endangers our future.* New York: W. W. Norton.

Stirling, K., & Aldrich, T. (2008). Child support: Who bears the burden? *Family Relations, 57,* 376–389.

Stocking, G. W., Jr. (1968). *Race, culture, and evolution: Essays on the history of anthropology.* New York: Free Press.

Stokols, D., & Montero, M. (2002). Toward an environmental psychology of the Internet. In R. Bechtel & A. Churchman (Eds.), *Handbook of environmental psychology* (pp. 661–675). New York: Wiley.

Stone, D. (2012). *Policy paradox: The art of political decision making* (3rd ed.). New York: Norton.

Street, K., Harrington, J., Chiang, W., Cairns, P., & Ellis, M. (2004). How great is the risk of abuse in infants born to drug-using mothers? *Child Care, Health and Development, 30*(4), 325–330.

Streib, H. (2005). Faith development research revisited: Accounting for diversity in structure, content, and narrativity of faith. *International Journal for the Psychology of Religion, 15,* 99–121.

Streifel, C., & Servaty-Seib, H. L. (2009). Recovering from alcohol and other drug dependency: Loss and spirituality in a 12-step context. *Alcoholism Treatment Quarterly, 27*(2), 184–198.

Strier, R. (2013). Responding to the global economic crisis: Inclusive social work practice. *Social Work, 58*(4), 344–353.

Strom-Gottfried, K., & Morrissey, M. (1999). The organizational diversity audit. In K. Strom-Gottfried (Ed.), *Social work practice: Cases, activities, and exercises* (pp. 168–172). Thousand Oaks, CA: Pine Forge.

Stuart, R. (1989). Social learning theory: A vanishing or expanding presence? *Psychology: A Journal of Human Behavior, 26,* 35–50.

Stuening, K. (2002). *New family values: Liberty, equality, diversity.* Lanham, MD: Rowman & Littlefield.

Super, J. T., & Jacobson, L. (2011). Religious abuse: Implications for counseling lesbian, gay, bisexual, and transgender individuals. *Journal of LGBT Issues in Counseling, 5,* 180–196.

Supiano, K. P., & Berry, P. H. (2013). Developing interdisciplinary skills and professional confidence in palliative care social work students. *Journal of Social Work Education, 49,* 387–396.

Sutphin, S. (2010). Social exchange theory and the division of household labor in same-sex couples. *Marriage & Family Review, 46*(3), 191–206.

Swatos, W. H. (2005). Globalization theory and religious fundamentalism. In P. Kivisto (Ed.), *Illuminating social life: Classical and contemporary theory revisited* (3rd ed., pp. 319–339). Thousand Oaks, CA: Pine Forge.

Świątczak, B. (2012). Immune system, immune self: Introduction. *Avant: Journal of Philosophical-Interdisciplinary Vanguard, 3*(1), 12–18.

Swidler, A. (1986). Culture in action: Symbols and strategies. *American Sociological Review, 51,* 273–286.

Swift, D. C. (1998). *Religion and the American experience.* Armonk, NY: M. E. Sharpe.

Swinton, J. (2012). From inclusion to belonging: A practical theology of community, disability, and humanness. *Journal of Religion, Disability & Health, 16*(2), 172–190.

Tan, P. P. (2006). Spirituality and religious beliefs among South-East Asians. *Reflections: Narratives of Professional Helping, 12*(3), 44–47.

Tangenberg, K. M. (2008). Saddleback Church and the P.E.A.C.E. plan: Implications for social work. *Social Work & Christianity, 35*(4), 391–412.

Tangenberg, K. M., & Kemp, S. (2002). Embodied practice: Claiming the body's experience, agency, and knowledge for social work. *Social Work, 47*(1), 9–18.

Tanielian, T., & Jaycox, L. (Eds.). (2008). *Invisible wounds of war: Psychological and cognitive injuries, their consequences, and services to assist recovery.* Santa Monica, CA: RAND Corporation.

Tanner, J. (2002). Do laws requiring higher wages cause unemployment? *CQ Researcher, 12*(33), 769–786.

Tarrow, S. (1994). *Power in movement: Social movements, collective action, and politics.* New York: Cambridge University Press.

Tarrow, S. (1998). *Power in movement: Social movements and contentious politics* (2nd ed.). New York: Cambridge University Press.

Tarrow, S. (2006). *The new transnational activism.* New York: Cambridge University Press.

Tarrow, S. (2011). Why Occupy Wall Street is not the Tea Party of the Left. *Foreign Affairs, Snapshot.* Retrieved from http://www.foreignaffairs.com/articles/136401/sidney-tarrow/why-occupy-wall-street-is-not-the-tea-party-of-the-left.

Tausch, C., Marks, L. D., Brown, J. S., Cherry, K. E., Frias, T., McWilliams, Z., et al. (2011). Religion and coping with trauma: Qualitative examples from Hurricanes Katrina and Rita. *Journal of Religion, Spirituality & Aging, 23*(3), 236–253.

Taylor, A., & Kuo, F. (2009). Children with attention deficits concentrate better after walk in the park. *Journal of Epidemiology and Community, 56,* 913–918.

Taylor, F. W. (1911). *Principles of scientific management.* New York: Harper & Row.

Taylor, P., & Cohn, D. (2012). A milestone en route to a majority minority nation. Pew Research Center. Retrieved from http://www.pewsocialtrends.org/2012/11/07/a-mileston-en-route-to-a-majority-minority-nation.

Taylor, P., Fry, R., Cohn, D., Wang, W., Velasco, G., & Docterman, D. (2011). *Living together: The economics of cohabitation.* Pew Social & Demographic Trends. Retrieved from www.pewsocialtrends.org/files/2-11/06/pew-social-trends-cohabitation-06-2011.pdf.

Taylor, R. B. (1988). *Human territorial functioning: An empirical, evolutionary perspective on individual and small group territorial cognitions, behaviors, and consequences.* Cambridge, UK: Cambridge University Press.

Taylor, R. J., Chatters, L. M., & Levin, J. (2004). *Religion in the lives of African-Americans: Social, psychological, and health perspectives.* Thousand Oaks, CA: Sage.

Taylor, S. E., & Stanton, A. L. (2007). Coping resources, coping processes, and mental health. *Annual Review of Clinical Psychology, 3,* 377–401.

Taylor, V. (1999). Gender and social movements: Gender processes in women's self-help movements. *Gender & Society, 13*(1), 8–33.

Tebbe, E., & Moradi, B. (2012). Anti-transgender prejudice: A structural equation model of associated constructs. *Journal of Counseling Psychology, 59*(2), 251–261.

Teeple, G. (2000). *Globalization and the decline of social reform: Into the twenty-first century.* Aurora, Ont., Canada: Garamond Press.

Terkel, S. (1980). C. P. Ellis. In *American dreams: Lost and found* (pp. 200–211). New York: New Press.

Terkel, S. (2003). *Hope dies last: Keeping the faith in difficult times.* New York: The New Press.

Teshome, E., Zenebe, M., Metaferia, H., & Biadgilign, S. (2012). The role of self-help voluntary associations for women empowerment and social capital: The experience of women's *Iddirs* (burial societies) in Ethiopia. *Journal of Community Health, 37,* 706–714.

Tesoriero, F. (2006). Strengthening communities through women's self-help groups in South India. *Community Development Journal, 41*(3), 321–333.

Thomas, E., Wingert, P., Conant, E., & Register, S. (2010, March 5). Why we can't get rid of bad teachers. *Newsweek, 155*(11), 24–27.

Thomas, M. L. (2009). Faith collaboration: A qualitative analysis of faith-based social service programs in organizational relationships. *Administration in Social Work, 33*(1), 40–60.

Thomas, W. I., & Thomas, D. S. (1928). *The child in America: Behavior problems and programs.* New York: Knopf.

Thompson, N. (2002). Social movements, social justice and social work. *British Journal of Social Work, 32*, 711–722.

Thompson Coon, J., Boddy, K., Stein, K., Whear, R., Barton, J., & Depledge, M. (2011). Does participating in physical activity in outdoor natural environments have a greater effect on physical and mental wellbeing than physical activity indoors? A systematic review. *Environmental Science & Technology, 45*, 1761–1772.

Thomson, R. G. (Ed.). (1996). *Freakery: Cultural spectacles of the extraordinary body.* New York: New York University Press.

Thyer, B. A. (2005). The misfortunes of behavioral social work: Misprized, misread, and misconstrued. In S. A. Kirk (Ed.), *Mental disorders in the social environment: Critical perspectives* (pp. 330–343). New York: Columbia University Press.

Tilly, C., & Wood, L. (2013). *Social movements 1768–2012.* Boulder, CO: Paradigm.

Tilton, J. (2009). Youth uprising: Gritty youth leadership development and communal transformation. In L. Nybell, J. Shook, & J. Finn (Eds.), *Childhood, youth, & social work in transformation: Implications for policy & practice* (pp. 385–400). New York: Columbia University Press.

Timberlake, E. M., & Cook, K. O. (1984). Social work and the Vietnamese refugee. *Social Work, 29*(2), 108–114.

Tindall, D. (2004). Social movement participation over time: An ego-network approach to micro-mobilization. *Sociological Focus, 37*, 163–184.

Titone, A. M. (1991). Spirituality and psychotherapy in social work practice. *Spirituality and Social Work Communicator, 2*(1), 7–9.

Tomai, M., Veronica, R., Mebane, M., D'Acunti, A., Benedetti, M., & Francescato, D. (2010). Virtual communities in schools as tools to promote social capital with high school students. *Computers & Education, 54*, 265–274.

Tomic, W., & Tomic, E. (2008). Existential fulfillment and burnout among principals and teachers. *Journal of Beliefs & Values: Studies in Religion & Education, 29*(1), 11–27.

Tonnies, F. (1963). *Community and society* (C. P. Loomis, Ed.). New York: Harper & Row. (Original work published 1887)

Toosi, N., Sommers, S., & Ambady, N. (2012). Getting a word in group-wise: Effects of racial diversity on gender dynamics. *Journal of Experimental Social Psychology, 48*, 1150–1155.

Torrez, E. (1984). *The folk-healer: The Mexican-American tradition of curanderismo.* Kingsville, TX: Nieves Press.

Toseland, R. W., & Larkin, H. (2010). Developing and leading telephone groups. *Social Work With Groups, 34*(1), 21–34.

Toseland, R. W., & Rivas, R. F. (2012). *An introduction to group work practice* (7th ed.). Boston: Allyn & Bacon.

Townley, G., Kloos, B., Green, E., & Franco, M. (2011). Reconcilable differences? Human diversity, cultural relativity, and sense of community. *American Journal of Community Psychology, 47*, 69–85.

Townley, G., & Kloos, B. (2011). Examining the psychological sense of community for individuals with serious mental illness residing in supported housing environments. *Community Mental Health Journal, 47*, 436–446.

Tracy, E., & Martin, T. (2007). Children's roles in the social networks of women in substance abuse treatment. *Journal of Substance Abuse Treatment, 32*, 81–88.

Tripses, J., & Scroggs, L. (2009). Spirituality and respect: Study of a model school–church–community collaboration. *School Community Journal, 19*(1), 77–97.

Troiden, R. (1989). The formation of homosexual identities. *Journal of Homosexuality, 17*, 43–73.

Tucker, M. (2011). *Standing on the shoulders of giants: An American agenda for education reform.* Washington, DC: National Center on Education and the Economy.

Tuckman, B., & Jensen, M. (1977). Stages of small group development revisited. *Group and Organizational Studies, 2*, 419–427.

Turkle, S. (2011). *Alone together: Why we expect more from technology and less from each other.* New York: Basic Books.

Turner, R. P., Lukoff, D., Barnhouse, R. T., & Lu, F. G. (1995). Religious or spiritual problem: A culturally sensitive diagnostic category in the DSM-IV. *Journal of Nervous and Mental Disease, 183*, 435–444.

Tweed, T. T. (1997). Asian religions in the United States. In W. H. Conser Jr. & S. B. Twiss (Eds.), *Religious diversity and American religious history: Studies in traditions and cultures* (pp. 189–217). Athens: University of Georgia Press.

Uchino, B. N. (2009). Understanding the links between social support and physical health: A life-span perspective with emphasis on the separability of perceived and received support. *Perspectives on Psychological Science, 4*(3), 236–255.

Uchino, B. N., Holt-Lunstad, J., Smith, T. W., & Bloor, L. (2004). Heterogeneity in social networks: A comparison of different models linking relationships to psychological outcomes. *Journal of Social & Clinical Psychology, 23*(2), 123–139.

Uhlenbruck, K., Meyer, K., & Hitt, M. (2003). Organizational transformation in transition economies: Resource based and organizational learning perspectives. *Journal of Management Studies, 40*, 257–282.

Ulrich, R. (1984). View through a window may influence recovery from surgery. *Science, 224*, 420–421.

Ulrich, R. (2006). Evidence-based health-care architecture. *Lancet, 368*, 538–539.

Ulrich, R., Simons, R., Losito, B., Fiorito, E., Miles, M., & Zelson, M. (1991). Stress recovery during exposure to natural and urban environments. *Journal of Environmental Psychology, 11*, 201–230.

Ulrich, R., & Zimring, C. (2005). *The role of the physical environment in the hospital of the 21st century: A once-in-a-lifetime opportunity.* Retrieved from http://www.healthdesign.org/chd/research/role-physical-environment-hospital-21st-century.

UNAIDS. (2013). *Global report on the global AIDS epidemic 2013.* Retrieved from www.unaids.org/en/media/unaids/contentassets/documents/epidemiology/2013/UNAIDS_Global_Report_2013_en_pdf.

UNESCO. (2012). *EFA global monitoring report 2012: Youth and skills: Putting education to work.* Paris: Author.

UNICEF. (2012). *Measuring child poverty.* Florence, Italy: UNICEF Innocenti Research Center. Retrieved from www.unicef-irc.org/publications/pdf/rc10_eng.pdf.

UNICEF. (2013a). *End child trafficking.* Retrieved from http://www.unicefusa.org/work/protection/child-trafficking/?gclid=CK2yt_-CorsQlafgodqlARw.

UNICEF. (2013b). *MDG related facts and figures.* Retrieved from http://www.unicef.org/media/media_45485.html.

United Nations. (1948). *The universal declaration of human rights*. Retrieved from www.un.org/en/documents/udhr.

United Nations Development Programme. (2013). *Human development report 2013*. New York: Author.

United Nations Enable. (2013). *Convention on the Rights of Persons with Disabilities*. Retrieved from http://www.un.org/disabilities/default.asp?id=150.

United States v. Windsor. No. 12-307. June 26, 2013.

Urbina, I. (2010, March 23). Acorn to shut all offices by April 1. *New York Times*, p. A17.

U.S. Bureau of Labor Statistics. (2013a). *Persons with a disability: Labor force characteristics summary*. Retrieved from http://www.bls/gov/news.release/disabl.nr0.htm.

U.S. Bureau of Labor Statistics. (2013b). *Women in the labor force: A databook*. Retrieved from www.bls.gov/cps/wlf-databook-2012.pdf.

U.S. Census Bureau. (2010). *Statistical abstract of the United States*. Washington, DC: Government Printing Office.

U.S. Census Bureau. (2012). *Statistical abstract of the United States, 2012*. Retrieved from https:www.census.gov/compendia/stattab/2012edition.html.

U.S. Census Bureau. (2013a). *Asians fastest-growing race or ethnic group in 2012*. Retrieved from www.census.gov/newsroom/releases/archieves/population/cb13-112.html.

U.S. Census Bureau. (2013b). *American Community Survey*. Retrieved from http://www.census.gov.

U.S. Census Bureau. (2013c). *America's foreign born in the last 50 years*. Retrieved from http://www.census.gov/how/infographics/foreign_born.html.

U.S. Census Bureau. (2013d). *American Community Survey Reports: The foreign-born population in the United States: 2010*. Washington, DC: Government Printing Office.

U.S. Census Bureau. (2013e). *Current population survey (CPS)—Definitions*. Retrieved from www.census.gov/cps/about/cpsdef.html.

U.S. Commission on Human Rights. (1998). Indian tribes: A continuing quest for survival. In P. S. Rothenberg (Ed.), *Race, class and gender in the United States: An integrated study* (4th ed., pp. 378–382). New York: St. Martin's Press.

U.S. Department of Health and Human Services. (2013a). *Key features of the Affordable Care Act by year*. Retrieved from http://www.hhs.gov/healthcare/facts/timeline/timeline-text.html.

U.S. Department of Health and Human Services. (2013b). *Child maltreatment 2012*. Washington, DC: Government Printing Office. Retrieved from www.acf.hhs.gov/sites/default/files/cb/cm2012.pdf.

U.S. Department of Housing and Urban Development. (2011, December 5). Homeless Emergency Assistance and Rapid Transition to Housing Program; Defining "homeless." *Federal Register: The Daily Journal of the United States Government*, p. 75994. FR DOC # 2011-30942.

U.S. Department of Labor. (2014). *Federal minimum wage*. Retrieved from http://www.dol.gov/elaws/esa/flsa/minwage.htm.

Vaillant, G. (2002). *Aging well*. Boston: Little, Brown.

Valenti, M., & Rockett, T. (2008). The effects of demographic differences on forming intragroup relationships. *Small Group Research, 39*(2), 179–202.

VanDeMark, N., Russelol, L., O'Keefe, M., Finkelstein, N., Noether, C., & Gambell, J. (2005). Children of mothers with histories of substance abuse, mental illness, and trauma. *Journal of Community Psychology, 33*, 445–459.

Van de Werfhorst, H., & Salverda, W. (2012). Consequences of economic inequality: Introduction to a special issue. *Research in Social Stratification and Mobility, 30*, 377–387.

Van Hook, M., Hugen, B., & Aguilar, M. (Eds.). (2001). *Spirituality within religious traditions in social work practice*. Pacific Grove, CA: Brooks/Cole.

Veeder, N. W., & Dalgin, R. E. (2004). Social work as management: A retrospective study of 245 hospital care management practice outcomes. *Journal of Social Service Research, 31*(1), 33–58.

Verity, F., & King, S. (2007). Responding to intercommunal conflict—What can restorative justice offer? *Community Development Journal, 43*(4), 470–482.

Vespa, J. (2012). Union formation in later life: Economic determinants of cohabitation and remarriage among older adults. *Demography, 49*, 1103–1125.

Vespa, J., Lewis, J., & Kreider, R. (2013). *America's families and living arrangements: 2012*. U.S. Census Bureau. Retrieved from https://www.census.gov/prod/2013pubs/p20-570.pdf.

Vetere, A. (2005). Structural family therapy. In T. Chibucos & R. Leite (Eds.), *Readings in family theory* (pp. 293–302). Thousand Oaks, CA: Sage.

Vickrey, B. G., Strickland, T. L., Fitten, L. J., Admas, G. R., Ortiz, F., & Hays, R. D. (2007). Ethnic variations in dementia caregiving experiences: Insights from focus groups. *Journal of Human Behavior in the Social Environment, 15*(2/3), 233–249.

Vlahov, D., Galea, S., & Freudenberg, N. (2005). The urban health "advantage." *Journal of Urban Health, 82*(1), 1–4.

Vohra-Gupta, S., Russell, A., & Lo, E. (2007). Meditation: The adoption of Eastern thought to Western social practices. *Social Thought, 26*(2), 49–61.

Voronin, Y., & Phogat, S. (2010). HIV/AIDS: Vaccines and alternate strategies for treatment and prevention. *Annals of the New York Academy of Sciences, 1205*(Suppl. 1), E1–E9.

Vosler, N. R. (1996). *New approaches to family practice: Confronting economic stress*. Thousand Oaks, CA: Sage.

Voss, K. (1996). The collapse of a social movement: The interplay of mobilizing structures, framing, and political opportunities in the Knights of Labor. In D. McAdam, J. McCarthy, & M. Zald (Eds.), *Comparative perspectives on social movements* (pp. 227–258). New York: Cambridge University Press.

Voss, R. W., Douville, V., Little Soldier, A., & Twiss, G. (1999). Tribal and shamanic-based social work practice: A Lakota perspective. *Social Work, 44*(3), 228–241.

Vranic, A. (2003). Personal space in physically abused children. *Environment and Behavior, 35*(4), 550–565.

Vryan, K. D., Adler, P. A., & Adler, P. (2003). Identity. In L. T. Reynolds & N. J. Herman-Kinney (Eds.), *Handbook of symbolic interactionism* (pp. 367–390). Walnut Creek, CA: AltaMira Press.

Waanders, C., Mendez, J., & Downer, J. (2007). Parent characteristics, economic stress and neighborhood context as predictors of parent involvement in preschool children's education. *Journal of School Psychology, 45*(6), 619–636.

Wadsworth, M., & Santiago, C. (2008). Risk and resiliency processes in ethnically diverse families in poverty. *Journal of Family Psychology, 22*(3), 399–410.

Wadsworth, S., & Southwell, K. (2011). Military families: Extreme work and extreme "work-family." *The Annals of the American Academy of Political and Social Science, 638*, 163–183.

Wagner, R. (1981). *The invention of culture*. Chicago: University of Chicago Press.

Walch, J., Day, R., & Kang, J. (2005). The effect of sunlight on post-operative analgesic medication use: A prospective study of patients undergoing spinal surgery. *Psychosomatic Medicine, 67*, 156–163.

Walker, D. F., Reid, H. W., O'Neill, T., & Brown, L. (2009). Changes in personal religion/spirituality during and after childhood abuse: A review and synthesis. *Psychological Trauma: Theory, Research, Practice, and Policy, 1*(2), 130–145.

Wallerstein, I. (1974). *The modern world system: Capitalist agriculture and the origins of the European world economy in the 16th century*. New York: Academic Press.

Wallerstein, I. (1979). *The capitalist world economy*. London: Cambridge University Press.

Wallerstein, I. (1980). *The modern world-system: Mercantilism and the consolidation of the European world economy, 1600–1750*. New York: Academic Press.

Wallerstein, I. (1989). *The modern world-system: The second great expansion of the capitalist world-economy, 1730–1840's*. San Diego, CA: Academic Press.

Wallerstein, I. (2004). *World systems analysis: An introduction*. Durham, NC: Duke University Press.

Wallerstein, J., & Blakeslee, S. (1990). *Second chances*. New York: Ticknor & Fields.

Walsh, F. (2006). *Strengthening family resilience* (2nd ed.). New York: Guilford Press.

Walsh, F. (2009a). Integrating spirituality in family therapy: Wellsprings for health, healing, and resilience. In F. Walsh (Ed.), *Spiritual resources in family therapy* (2nd ed., pp. 31–61). New York: Guilford Press.

Walsh, F. (2009b). Spiritual resources in family adaptation to death and loss. In F. Walsh (Ed.), *Spiritual resources in family therapy* (2nd ed., pp. 81–102). New York: Guilford Press.

Walsh, F. (2012a). *Normal family processes* (4th ed.). New York: Guilford.

Walsh, F. (2012b). The new normal: Diversity and complexity in 21st-century families. In F. Walsh (Ed.), *Normal family processes: Growing diversity and complexity* (4th ed., pp. 3–27). New York: Guilford.

Walsh, F. (2012c). Family resilience: Strengths forged through adversity. In F. Walsh (Ed.), *Normal family processes: Growing diversity and complexity* (4th ed., pp. 399–427). New York: Guilford Press.

Walsh, J. (2000). *Clinical case management with persons having mental illness: A relationship-based perspective*. Pacific Gove, CA: Brooks/Cole.

Walsh, J. (2014). *Theories for direct social work practice* (3rd ed.). Belmont, CA: Wadsworth.

Walsh, J., Meyer, A., & Schoonhoven, C. (2006). A future for organization theory: Living in and living with changing organizations. *Organization Science, 17*(5), 657–671.

Wamsley, G., & Zald, M. (1973). *The political economy of public organizations*. Lexington, MA: Heath.

Wanyeki, I., Olson, S., Brassard, P., Menzies, D., Ross, N., Behr, M., et al. (2006). Dwellings, crowding, and tuberculosis in Montreal. *Social Science & Medicine, 63*(2), 501–511.

Warner, S. R. (1993). Work in progress: Toward a new paradigm for the sociological study of religion in the United States. *American Journal of Sociology, 98*, 1044–1093.

Warren, R. (1963). *The community in America*. Chicago: Rand McNally.

Warren, R. (1978). *The community in America* (2nd ed.). Chicago: Rand McNally.

Warren, R. (1987). *The community in America* (3rd ed.). Chicago: Rand McNally.

Warren, R. (1988). Observations on the state of community theory. In R. Warren & L. Lyon (Eds.), *New perspectives on the American community* (5th ed., pp. 84–86). Chicago: Dorsey.

Warwick, L. L. (1995). Feminist Wicca: Paths to empowerment. *Women and Therapy: A Feminist Quarterly, 16*(2/3), 121–133.

Waterhouse, L. (2010). Multiple intelligences, the Mozart effect, and emotional intelligence: A critical review. *Educational Psychologist, 41*(4), 207–225.

Watters, E. (2010). *Crazy like us: The globalization of the American psyche*. New York: Free Press.

Watts, J. (2013, August 16). Ecuador approves Yasuni national park oil drilling in Amazon rainforest. Retrieved from http://www.theguardian.com/world/2013/aug/16/ecuador-approves-yasuni-amazon-oil-drilling.

Weaver, H. (2011). Cultural competence with First Nations peoples. In D. Lum (Ed.), *Culturally competent practice: A framework for understanding diverse groups and justice issues* (4th ed., pp. 223–247). Belmont, CA: Thomson.

Weber, M. (1947). *The theory of economic and social organization*. New York: Free Press.

Weber, M. (1958). *The Protestant ethic and the spirit of capitalism* (T. Parsons, Trans.). New York: Scribner's. (Original work published 1904–1905)

Weil, M. (Ed.). (2005). *The handbook of community practice*. Thousand Oaks, CA: Sage.

Weil, M., Reisch, M., & Ohmer, M. (2013a). Introduction: Contexts and challenges for 21st century communities. In M. Weil, M. Reisch, & M. Ohmer (Eds.), *The handbook of community practice* (2nd ed., pp. 3–25). Los Angeles: Sage.

Weil, M., Reisch, M., & Ohmer, M. (Eds.) (2013b). *The handbook of community practice* (2nd ed.). Los Angeles: Sage.

Weisberg, R. (Producer/Director). (2006). *Waging a living* [Motion picture]. New York: Public Policy Productions.

Weitz, R. (2013). *The sociology of health, illness, and health care: A critical approach* (6th ed.). Boston: Wadsworth.

Wellman, B. (1979). The community question. *American Journal of Sociology, 84*, 1201–1231.

Wellman, B. (1982). Studying personal communities. In P. Marsden & N. Lin (Eds.), *Social structure and network analysis* (pp. 61–80). Beverly Hills, CA: Sage.

Wellman, B. (1996). Are personal communities local? A Dumptarian reconsideration. *Social Networks, 18*, 347–354.

Wellman, B. (1999). The network community: An introduction. In B. Wellman (Ed.), *Networks in the global village* (pp. 1–47). Boulder, CO: Westview Press.

Wellman, B. (2005). Community: From neighborhood to network. *Communications of the ACM, 48*(10), 53–55.

Wellman, B., & Potter, S. (1999). The elements of personal communities. In B. Wellman (Ed.), *Networks in the global village* (pp. 49–81). Boulder, CO: Westview Press.

Wellman, B., & Wortley, S. (1990). Different strokes from different folks: Community ties and social support. *American Journal of Sociology, 96*, 558–588.

Welwood, J. (2000). *Toward a psychology of awakening: Buddhism, psychotherapy, and the path of personal and spiritual transformation.* Boston: Shambhala.

Wenger, G. C. (2009). Childlessness at the end of life: Evidence from rural Wales. *Ageing and Society, 29*(8), 1243–1259.

Wenocur, S., & Soifer, S. (1997). Prospects for community organization. In M. Reisch & E. Gambrill (Eds.), *Social work in the 21st century* (pp. 198–209). Thousand Oaks, CA: Pine Forge.

Werbart, A., Levin, L., Andersson, H., & Sandell, R. (2013). Everyday evidence: Outcomes of psychotherapies in Swedish public health services. *Psychotherapy, 50*(1), 119–130.

Wethington, E., Moen, P., Glasgow, N., & Pillemer, K. (2000). Multiple roles, social integration, and health. In K. Pillemer, P. Moen, & N. Glasgow (Eds.), *Social integration in the second half of life* (pp. 48–71). Baltimore: Johns Hopkins University Press.

Wheeler, H. (Ed.). (1973). *Beyond the punitive society.* San Francisco: Freeman.

White, J., Klein, D., & Martin, T. (2015a). The systems framework. In *Family theories* (4th ed., pp. 141–174). Thousand Oaks, CA: Sage.

White, J., Klein, D., & Martin, T. (2015b). The conflict framework. In *Family theories* (4th ed., pp. 175–206). Thousand Oaks, CA: Sage.

White, J., Klein, D., & Martin, T. (2015c). The rational choice and social exchange framework. In *Family theories* (4th ed., pp. 39–69). Thousand Oaks, CA: Sage.

White, J., Klein, D., & Martin, T. (2015d). *Family theories: An introduction* (4th ed.). Thousand Oaks, CA: Sage.

White, J., Klein, D., & Martin, T. (2015e). The feminist framework. In *Family theories* (4th ed., pp. 207–238). Thousand Oaks, CA: Sage.

White, M., Pahl, S., Ashbullby, K., Herbert, S., & Depledge, M. (2013). Feelings of restoration from recent nature visits. *Journal of Environmental Psychology, 25,* 40–51.

Whitehead, B. (1997). *The divorce culture.* New York: Knopf.

Wicker, A. (2012). Perspectives on behavior settings: With illustrations from Allison's ethnography of a Japanese Hostess Club. *Environment and Behavior, 44*(4), 474–492.

Wilber, K. (1977). *Spectrum of consciousness.* Adyar, India: Quest Books.

Wilber, K. (1995). *Sex, ecology, spirituality: The spirit of evolution.* Boston: Shambhala.

Wilber, K. (1996). *A brief history of everything.* Boston: Shambhala.

Wilber, K. (1997a). *The eye of spirit: An integral vision for a world gone slightly mad.* Boston: Shambhala.

Wilber, K. (1997b). An integral theory of consciousness. *Journal of Consciousness Studies, 4*(1), 71–93.

Wilber, K. (2000a). *Integral psychology: Consciousness, spirit, psychology, therapy.* Boston: Shambhala.

Wilber, K. (2000b). *Sex, ecology, spirituality: The spirit of evolution* (2nd ed.). Boston: Shambhala.

Wilber, K. (2001). *A theory of everything: An integral vision for business, politics, science, and spirituality.* Boston: Shambhala.

Wilber, K. (2006). *Integral spirituality.* Boston: Integral Books.

Williams, C. (2006). The epistemology of cultural competence. *Families in Society: The Journal of Contemporary Social Services, 87*(2), 209–220.

Williams, D., Mohammed, S., Leavell, J., & Collins, C. (2010). Race, economic status, and health: Complexities, ongoing challenges, and research opportunities. *Annals of New York Academy of Sciences, 1186,* 69–101.

Williams, M., Teasdale, J. D., Segal, Z., & Kabat-Zinn, J. (2007). *The mindful way through depression: Freeing yourself from unhappiness.* New York: Guilford Press.

Williams, R. (1977). *Marxism and literature.* Oxford, UK: Oxford University Press.

Williams, R. (1983). *Key words: A vocabulary of culture and society* (Rev. ed.). New York: Oxford University Press.

Williamson, J. S., & Wyandt, C. M. (2001). New perspectives on alternative medicines. *Drug Topics, 145*(1), 57–66.

Wills, T. A., Yaeger, A. M., & Sandy, J. M. (2003). Buffering effect of religiosity for adolescent substance abuse. *Psychology of Addictive Behaviors, 17*(1), 24–31.

Wilson, C., Gutiérrez, F., & Chao, L. (2013). *Racism, sexism, and the media: Multicultural issues into the new communications age* (4th ed.). Los Angeles: Sage.

Wilson, E. (2007). Biophilia and the conservation ethic. In D. Penn & I. Mysterud (Eds.), *Evolutionary perspectives on environmental problems* (pp. 249–257). New Brunswick, NJ: Transaction.

Wilson, G., & Baldassare, M. (1996). Overall "sense of community" in a suburban region: The effects of localism, privacy, and urbanization. *Environment and Behavior, 28*(1), 27–43.

Winant, H. (2004). *The new politics of race: Globalism, difference, justice.* Minneapolis: University of Minnesota Press.

Winnicott, D. W. (1975). *Collected papers: From paediatrics to psychoanalysis.* New York: Basic Books.

Winston, C. A. (2006). African American grandmothers parenting AIDS orphans: Grieving and coping. *Qualitative Social Work, 5*(1), 33–43.

Wisniewski, C. (2008). Applying complementary and alternative medicine practices in a social work context: A focus on mindfulness meditation. *Praxis, 8,* 13–22.

Wittine, B. (1987, September/October). Beyond ego. *Yoga Journal,* 51–57.

Wituk, S., Shepherd, M. D., Slavich, S., Warren, M. L., & Meissen, G. (2000). A topography of self-help groups: An empirical analysis. *Social Work, 45*(2), 157–165.

Wolsko, C., & Hoyt, K. (2012). Employing the restorative capacity of nature: Pathways to practicing ecotherapy among mental health professionals. *Ecopsychology, 4*(1), 10–24.

Wood, J. (2006). Critical feminist theories: A provocative perspective on families. In D. Braithwaite & L. Baxter (Eds.), *Engaging theories in family communication: Multiple perspectives* (pp. 197–212). Thousand Oaks, CA: Sage.

Wood, M., Molassiotis, A., & Payne, S. (2011). What research evidence is there for the use of art therapy in the management of symptoms in adults with cancer? A systematic review. *Psycho-Oncology, 20,* 135–145.

Wood, R. (2002). *Faith in action: Religion, race, and democratic organizing in America.* Chicago: University of Chicago Press.

Woolever, C. (1992). A contextual approach to neighbourhood attachment. *Urban Studies, 29*(1), 99–116.

World Bank. (2012, July 17). *Press release. Mobile phone access reaches three quarters of planet's population.* Retrieved from http://www.worldbank.org/en/news/press-release/2012/07/17/mobile-phone-access-reaches-three-quarters-planets-population.

World Bank. (2013a). *GDP per capita.* Retrieved from http://data.worldbank.org/indcator/NY.GDO.PCAP.CD.

World Bank. (2013b). *Mortality rate, under 5 (per 1,000 live births).* Retrieved from http://data.worldbank.org/indicator/SH.DYN.MORT.

World Bank. (2013c). *World Bank launches initiative on migration, releases new projections on remittance flows.* Retrieved from http://www.worldbank.org/en/news/press-release/2013/04/19/world-bank-launches-initiative-on-migration-releases-new-projections-on-remittance-flows.

World Bank. (2013d). *Developing countries to receive over $410 billion in remittances in 2013, says World Bank.* Retrieved from http://www.worldbank.org/en/news/press-release/2013/10/02/developing-cvountries-remittances-2013-world-bank.

World Health Organization. (2012a). *Human trafficking.* Retrieved from www.who.int/iris/bitstream/10665/77394/1/WHO_RHR_12.42_eng.pdf.

World Health Organization. (2012b). *Why are some tropical diseases called "neglected"?* Retrieved from http://www.who.int/features/qa/53/en.

World Health Organization. (2013). *World health statistics 2013.* Geneva: Author.

Wright, V. H. (2005). *The soul tells a story: Engaging spirituality with creativity in the writing life.* Downers Grove, IL: InterVarsity Press.

Wronka, J. (2008). *Human rights and social justice: Social action and service for the helping and health professions.* Thousand Oaks, CA. 3age.

Wuthnow, R. (2001). *Creative spirituality: The way of the artist.* Berkeley: University of California Press.

Wuthnow, R. (2003). Studying religion, making it sociological. In M. Dillon (Ed.), *Handbook of the sociology of religion* (pp. 17–30). Cambridge, UK: Cambridge University Press.

Xu, Q., Perkins, D., & Chow, J. (2010). Sense of community, neighboring, and social capital as predictors of local political participation in China. *American Journal of Community Psychology, 45,* 259–271.

Yalom, I. D. (1995). *The theory and practice of group psychotherapy* (4th ed.). New York: Basic Books.

Yanagisako, S. J. (2002). *Producing culture and capital: Family firms in Italy.* Princeton, NJ: Princeton University Press.

Yarhouse, M. A., & Carr, T. L. (2012). MTF transgender Christians' experiences: A qualitative study. *Journal of LGBT Issues in Counseling, 6,* 18–33.

Yeh, W. Y., Cheng, Y., & Chen, C. J. (2009). Social patterns of pay systems and their associations with psychosocial job characteristics and burnout among paid employees in Taiwan. *Social Science & Medicine, 68,* 1407–1415.

Yellow Bird, M. J. (1995). Spirituality in First Nations story telling: A Sahnish-Hidatsa approach to narrative. *Reflections: Narratives of Professional Helping, 1*(4), 65–72.

Yeung, D., Fung, H., & Kam, C. (2012). Age difference in problem solving strategies: The mediating role of future time perspective. *Personality and Individual Differences, 53,* 38–43.

Yost, C. (2012, May 23). 3 reasons why card-carrying capitalists should support paid family leave. *Forbes.* Retrieved from http://www.forbes.com/sites/work-in-progress/2012/05/23/3-reasons-why-card-carrying-capitalists-should-support-paid-family-leave.

Zastrow, C. H. (2009). *Social work with groups: A comprehensive workbook* (7th ed.). Belmont, CA: Brooks/Cole.

Zeisel, J. (2006). *Inquiry by design: Environment/behavior/neuroscience in architecture, interiors, landscape, and planning* (Rev. ed.). New York: Norton.

Zeisel, J. (2009). *I'm still here: A breakthrough approach to understanding someone living with Alzheimer's.* New York: Penguin Group.

Zhang, B., Wang, T., Vasilakos, A., & Ma, J. (2013). Mobile social networking: Reconnect virtual community with physical space. *Telecommunication Systems, 54,* 91–110.

Zhou, W. (2013). Political connections and entrepreneurial investment: Evidence from China's transition economy. *Journal of Business Venturing, 28,* 299–315.

Zimbardo, P. (2007). *The Lucifer effect.* New York: Random House.

Zimbardo, P., & Boyd, J. (2008). *The time paradox.* New York: Free Press.

Zinnbauer, B., Pargament, K., Cole, B., Rye, M., Butter, E., & Belavich, T. (1997). Religion and spirituality: Unfuzzying the fuzzy. *Journal for the Scientific Study of Religion, 36,* 549–564.

Zunkel, G. (2002). Relational coping processes: Couples' response to a diagnosis of early stage breast cancer. *Journal of Psychosocial Oncology, 20*(4), 39–55.

Zyskinsa, J., & Heszen, I. (2009). Resources, coping with stress, positive emotions, and health. Introduction. *Polish Psychological Bulletin, 40*(1), 1–5.

GLOSSARY

ABC-X model of family stress and coping A way of viewing families that focuses on stressor events and crises, family resources, family definitions and beliefs, and outcomes of stress pileup.

Accommodation (cognitive) The process of altering a schema when a new situation cannot be incorporated within an existing schema.

Accommodation (cultural) Process of partial or selective cultural change in which members of nondominant groups follow the norms, rules, and standards of the dominant culture only in specific circumstances and contexts.

Acculturation A process of changing one's culture by incorporating elements of another culture; a mutual sharing of culture.

Acquired immunodeficiency syndrome (AIDS) Disease caused by human immunodeficiency virus (HIV); involves breakdown of the immune system.

Adaptation A change in functioning or coping style that results in a better adjustment of a person to his or her environment.

Affect The physiological manifestation of a feeling.

Agency The capacity to intentionally make things happen.

Agency-based model A model of community social work practice that focuses on promoting social agencies and the services they provide.

Antibodies Protein molecules that attach to the surface of specific antigens in an effort to destroy them.

Antigens Foreign substances such as bacteria, fungi, protozoa, and viruses that cause the immune system to react.

Assimilation (cognitive) In cognitive theory, the incorporation of new experiences into an existing schema.

Assimilation (cultural) The process of change whereby individuals of one society or ethnic group are culturally incorporated or absorbed into another by adopting the patterns and norms of the host culture.

Assistive technology Technology developed and used to assist individuals with disabilities to perform functions that might otherwise be difficult or impossible.

Assumption Something taken to be true without testing or proof.

Atria The two upper, thin-walled chambers of the heart.

Attribution theory A theory of emotional behavior asserting that the experience of emotion is based on conscious evaluations people make about their physiological sensations in particular social settings.

Autoimmune disease Disease that occurs when the immune system wrongly attacks systems it should be protecting.

Axon A conduction fiber that conducts impulses away from the body of a nerve cell.

Behavior settings Settings where particular kinds of activities are performed. For example, a school classroom is a behavior setting where learning/teaching activities are performed.

Behavior settings theories Theories proposing that consistent, uniform patterns of behavior occur in particular places, or behavior settings.

Bicultural socialization Process whereby members of nonmajority groups master both the dominant culture and their own culture.

Bifurcate Divide into two branches, as in labor force bifurcation into a core of stable, well-paid labor and a periphery of casual, low-wage labor.

Biological determinism Defining and differentiating social behavior on the basis of biological and genetic endowment.

Biophilia A genetically based need of humans to affiliate with nature.

Biopsychosocial approach An approach that considers human behavior to be the result of interactions of integrated biological, psychological, and social systems.

Blood pressure Measure of the pressure of the blood against the wall of a blood vessel.

Bonding social capital Community relationships that are inward looking and tend to mobilize solidarity and in-group loyalty; they lead to exclusive identities and homogeneous communities.

Boundary An imaginary line of demarcation that defines which human and nonhuman elements are included in a given system and which elements are outside the system.

Bounded rationality The limited rationality of organization decision makers in decision-making theory of formal organizations.

Brain injury (BI) Damage to the brain arising from head trauma (falls, automobile accidents), infections (encephalitis), insufficient oxygen (stroke), or poisoning.

Bridging social capital Community relationships that are outward looking and diverse and that link community members to assets and information across community boundaries.

Brief treatment model A type of practice modality characterized by a brief time period for intervention (usually 6 weeks or less) and practice techniques that are solution focused.

Built environment The portion of the physical environment attributable solely to human effort.

Bureaucracy A form of organization, considered by Max Weber to be the most efficient form for goal accomplishment, based on formal rationality.

Burnout A process in which a previously committed worker disengages from his or her work in response to stress and strain experienced in the job.

Cardiovascular system Biological system made up of the heart and the blood circulatory system.

Chaos theory A theory that emphasizes systems processes that produce change, even sudden, rapid change.

Charity organization society (COS) movement A social movement, brought to the United States from England in the late 1800s, that emphasized the delivery of services through private charity organizations.

Classical conditioning theory A theory in the social behavioral perspective that sees behavior as the result of the association of a conditioned stimulus with an unconditioned stimulus.

Closed group A natural or formed group that is open to certain persons and closed to others based on such characteristics as age, gender, geographic location, or type of problem/issue; a natural or formed group that opens its membership for a certain time period and then closes the group when the ideal number of members has been reached or the time period has elapsed.

Cognition Conscious thinking processes; mental activities of which the individual is fully aware. These processes include taking in information from the environment, synthesizing that information, and formulating plans of action based on that synthesis.

Cognitive mediation The influence of thinking between the occurrence of a stimulus and one's response to the stimulus.

Cognitive operations Use of abstract thoughts and ideas that are not tied to sensory and motor information.

Cognitive social learning theory A theory in the social behavioral perspective that sees behavior as learned by imitation and through cognitive processes.

Cohabiting When a couple lives together in a romantic relationship without marriage.

Collective efficacy The ability of community residents to engage in collective action to gain control of the neighborhood.

Colonialism The practice of dominant and powerful nations going beyond their boundaries; using military force to occupy and claim less dominant and powerful nations; imposing their culture, laws, and language on the occupied nation through the use of settlers.

Common sense Shared ways of perceiving reality and shared conclusions drawn from lived experience; an organized body of culture-bound beliefs that members of a community or society believe to be second nature, plain, obvious, and self-evident.

Communication networks The organization and pattern of communication among group members.

Community People bound either by geography or by webs of communication, sharing common ties and interacting with one another.

Community development A collaborative model of community social work that seeks to bring together diverse interests for the betterment of the community as a whole, with attention to community building and improved sense of community.

Concept A word or phrase that serves as an abstract description, or mental image, of some phenomenon.

Conflict perspective An approach to human behavior that draws attention to conflict, dominance, and oppression in social life.

Conscience constituency People attracted to a social movement because it appears just and worthy, not because they will benefit personally.

Conservative thesis A philosophy that inequality is the natural, divine order and no efforts should be made to alter it.

Control theories Theories that focus on the issue of how much control we have over our physical environment and the attempts we make to gain control.

Conventional morality In Kohlberg's theory of moral development, a stage in which moral decisions are based on adherence to social rules.

Coping A person's efforts to master the demands of stress, including the thoughts, feelings, and actions that constitute those efforts.

Countermovement A social movement that arises to oppose a successful social movement.

Crisis A major upset in psychological equilibrium as a result of some hazardous event, experienced as a threat or loss, with which the person cannot cope.

Critical consciousness The ongoing process of reflection and knowledge seeking about mechanisms and outcomes of social, political, and economic oppression; requires taking personal and collective action toward fairness and social justice.

Critical perspective on organizations A perspective that sees formal organizations as instruments of domination.

Critical race theory A theory proposed by legal scholars who wanted to draw attention to racial oppression in law and society, calling attention to microaggressions, brief, everyday exchanges that send denigrating messages and insults to people of color or members of any other minority identity group.

Critical theorists Theorists who argue that as capitalism underwent change, people were more likely to be controlled by culture and their consumer role than by their work position.

Critical thinking Engaging in a thoughtful and reflective judgment about alternative views and contradictory information; involves thinking about your own thinking and the influences on that thinking, as well as a willingness to change your mind.

Crowding Unpleasant experience of feeling spatially cramped.

Cultural conflict Conflict over the meaning of cultural symbols.

Cultural framing A conscious effort by a group of people to develop shared understandings of the world and themselves.

Cultural framing (CF) perspective An approach to social movements asserting that they can be successful only when participants develop shared understandings and definitions of some situation that impels participants to feel aggrieved or outraged, motivating them to action

Cultural hegemony The all-encompassing dominance of particular structures in society. Not limited to political control but includes a way of seeing the world that includes cultural and political dominance.

Cultural innovation A process of adapting, modifying, and changing culture through interaction over time.

Cultural relativism The position that behavior in a particular culture should not be judged by the standards of another culture.

Culture Shared cognitive and emotional frames and lenses that serve as the bases for an evolving map for living. It is constructed from the entire spectrum of human actions and the material circumstances of people in societies as they attempt to create order, meaning, and value.

Culture of poverty A term coined by Oscar Lewis to describe the unique culture and ways of those who are impoverished; it has been used over time to look at impoverished people as having cultural deficits.

Customs Beliefs, values, and behaviors, such as marriage practices, child-rearing practices, dietary preferences, and attire, that are handed down through generations and become a part of a people's traditions.

Daily hassles Common occurrences that are taxing; used to measure stress.

Decision-making theory A theory that sees organizational decision makers as constrained and limited in their capacity for rational decision making.

Deductive reasoning A method of reasoning that lays out general, abstract propositions used to generate specific hypotheses to test in unique situations.

Deep ecology A theory and a social movement that emphasizes the total interconnectedness of all elements of the natural and physical world and the inseparability of human well-being and the well-being of planet Earth; it argues for the intrinsic value of all life forms.

Defense mechanisms Unconscious, automatic responses that enable a person to minimize perceived threats or keep them out of awareness entirely.

Defensible space Newman's theory that certain physical design features can reduce crime and fear of crime in neighborhoods by enhancing residents' motivation to defend their territory.

Density Ratio of persons per unit area of a space.

Determinism A belief that persons are passive products of their circumstances, external forces, or internal urges.

Developmental perspective An approach that focuses on how human behavior changes and stays the same across stages of the life cycle.

Diabetes mellitus A disease of the endocrine system resulting from insulin deficiency or resistance to insulin's effects.

Differential emotions theory A theory asserting that emotions originate in our neurophysiology and that our personalities are organized around affective biases.

Differentiation of self In family systems theory, the process of learning to differentiate between thoughts and feeling and to follow one's own beliefs rather than making decisions based on reactivity to the cues of others or the need to win approval.

Dimension A feature that can be focused on separately but that cannot be understood without considering its embeddedness with other features.

Diversity Patterns of group differences.

Ecocentric Perspective that the ecosphere and everything on earth has its own intrinsic worth and should be valued and cared for, including Earth (Gaia) itself; recognition that humans are only one part of the interconnected web of life.

Ecocritical theories Theories that call attention to the ways human behavior degrades and destroys the natural world, the unequal burden of environmental degradation on different groups, and ethical obligations humans have to nonhuman elements of the natural environment.

Ecofeminism A feminist approach to environmental ethics; sees the oppression of women and the domination of nature as interconnected.

Economic institution The social institution with primary responsibility for regulating the production, distribution, and consumption of goods and services.

Ecotherapy Exposure to nature and the outdoors as a component of psychotherapy.

Educational institution The social institution responsible for passing along formal knowledge from one generation to the next.

Efficacy expectation In cognitive social learning theory, the expectation that one can personally accomplish a goal.

Ego A mental structure of personality responsible for negotiating between internal needs of the individual and the outside world.

Ego psychology A theory of human behavior and clinical practice that views activities of the ego as the primary determinants of behavior.

Elites The most powerful members of a society.

Emotion A feeling state characterized by one's appraisal of a stimulus, changes in bodily sensations, and expressive gestures.

Emotional intelligence A person's ability to process information about emotions accurately and effectively and consequently to regulate emotions in an optimal manner.

Emotional labor A form of emotion regulation wherein workers are expected to engage, suppress, or evoke emotions as part of their job.

Emotion-focused coping Coping efforts in which a person attempts to change either the way a stressful situation is attended to (by vigilance or avoidance) or the meaning of what is happening. Most effective when situations are not readily controllable by action.

Empirical research A careful, purposeful, and systematic observation of events with the intent to note and record them in terms of their attributes, to look for patterns in those events, and to make one's methods and observations public.

Empowerment theories Theories that focus on processes by which individuals and collectivities can recognize patterns of inequality and injustice and take action to increase their own power.

Endocrine system A body system involved in growth, metabolism, development, learning, and memory. Made up of glands that secrete hormones into the blood system.

Ethnic identity Feelings, beliefs, and behaviors associated with membership in an ethnic group that are based on common relations such as kinship, language, religion, geographic location, and historical experience.

Ethnocentrism Considering one's own culture as superior and judging culturally different practices (beliefs, values, behavior) by the standards and norms of one's own culture.

Ethos The moral and aesthetic tone, character, and quality of a people's life; their underlying feelings toward themselves and the world.

Evidence-based design Architectural design that reflects findings on physiological and health-outcome measures on the health benefits of specific design features.

Exchange and choice perspective A category of behavioral science theory that shares the common focus on the processes whereby individual and collective actors seek and exchange resources and the choices made in pursuit of those resources.

Faith As defined in Fowler's theory of faith development, a generic feature of the human search for meaning that provides a centering orientation from which to live one's life. May or may not be based in religious expression.

Faith stages Distinct levels of faith development, each with particular characteristics, emerging strengths, and potential dangers. Fowler identifies seven faith stages in his theory of faith development.

Family A social group of two or more persons, characterized by ongoing interdependence with long-term commitments that stem from blood, law, or affection.

Family and kinship institution The social institution primarily responsible for the regulation of procreation, for the initial socialization of new members of society, and for the economic, emotional, and physical care of its members.

Family ecomap Visual representation of how a family is connected to other individuals and social systems; uses circles, lines, and arrows to show family relationships and the strength and directional flow of energy and resources to and from the family.

Family economic stress model A model of family stress suggesting that economic hardship leads to economic pressure, which leads to parent distress, which leads to disrupted family relationships, which leads to child and adolescent adjustment problems.

Family investment model Theoretical model proposing that families with greater economic resources can afford to make large investments in the development of their children.

Family life cycle perspective An approach that looks at how families change over time and proposes normative changes and tasks at different stages.

Family of origin The family into which we were born and in which we were raised, when the two are the same.

Family resilience perspective An approach to family that seeks to identify and strengthen family processes that allow families to bear up under and rebound from distressing life experiences.

Family systems perspective A way of understanding families that focuses on the family as a social system, with patterns of interaction and relationships, and on changes in these patterns over time.

Family timeline A visual representation of important dates and events in a family's life over time.

Feedback control mechanism The mechanism by which the body controls the secretion of hormones and therefore their actions on target tissues.

Feedback mechanism A process by which information about past behaviors in a system are fed back into the system in a circular manner.

Feminist perspective on families A perspective proposing that families should not be studied as whole systems, with the lens on the family level, but rather as patterns of dominance, subjugation, and oppression, particularly as those patterns are tied to gender.

Feminist theories Theories that focus on male domination of the major social institutions and present a vision of a just world based on gender equity.

First force therapies Therapies based on dynamic theories of human behavior, with the prime concern being solving instinctual conflicts by developing insights.

Formal organization A collectivity of people, with a high degree of formality of structure, working together to meet a goal or goals.

Formed group A group formed for a specific purpose, such as a group for substance abusers, a therapy group for women with eating disorders, or a self-help group for gamblers.

Four quadrants From Wilber's integral theory, the four most important dimensions of existence; the upper-left quadrant represents the interior of individuals, or the subjective aspects of consciousness or awareness; the upper-right quadrant represents the exterior of individuals, including the objective biological and behavioral aspects; the lower-left quadrant represents the interior of collectives, or the values, meanings, worldviews, and ethics shared by groups of individuals; the lower-right quadrant represents the exterior, material dimensions of collectives, including social systems and the environment.

Fourth force therapies Therapies that specifically target the spiritual dimension, focusing on helping the person let go of ego attachments and transcend the self through various spiritually based practices.

Framing contests Competition among factions of a social movement to control the definition of the problem, goals, and strategies for the movement.

Fulcrum In Wilber's full-spectrum model of consciousness, a specific turning point in development, where the person must go through a three-step process of fusion/differentiation/integration in order to move from one level of consciousness to another.

Gemeinschaft A community in which relationships are personal and traditional.

General adaptation syndrome The physical process of coping with a stressor through the stages of alarm (awareness of the threat), resistance (efforts to restore homeostasis), and exhaustion (the termination of coping efforts because of the body's inability to sustain the state of disequilibrium).

Genogram A visual representation of the multigenerational family system, using squares, circles, and relationship lines.

Geographic information system (GIS) Computer-based system for mapping the spatial distribution of a variety of social data.

Gesellschaft A community in which relationships are impersonal and contractual.

Gini index An index that measures the extent to which the distribution of income within a country deviates from a perfectly equal distribution; scores range from 0 (perfect equality) to 100 (perfect inequality).

Globalization The process by which the world's people are becoming more interconnected economically, politically, environmentally, and culturally.

Government and political institution The social institution responsible for how decisions are made and enforced for the society as a whole.

Group cohesiveness A tendency for a group to stick together and be unified in the pursuit of its objectives and the satisfaction of members' emotional needs.

Group dynamics The patterns of interaction that emerge in groups, including group leadership, roles, and communication networks.

Group work A recognized social work method that involves teaching and practicing social work with groups.

Hawthorne effect Tendency of participants in an experimental study to perform in particular ways simply because they know they are being studied.

Health care institution The social institution with primary responsibility for promoting the general health of a society.

Heterogeneity Individual-level variations; differences among individuals.

Hierarchy of needs Abraham Maslow's humanistic theory suggesting that higher needs cannot emerge until lower needs have been satisfied; the hierarchy runs from physiological needs at the bottom, to safety needs, belongingness and love needs, and esteem needs, with self-actualization needs at the top.

High blood pressure (hypertension) Blood pressure greater than 140/90; the leading cause of strokes and a major risk factor for heart attacks and kidney failure.

Homeostasis Equilibrium; a positive, steady state of biological, psychological, or social functioning.

Horizontal linkage Interaction within a community.

Human immunodeficiency virus (HIV) The virus that causes acquired immunodeficiency syndrome (AIDS).

Humanistic perspective An approach that sees human behavior as based on freedom of action of the individual and focuses on the human search for meaning.

Human relations theory A theory that focuses on the role of human relationships in organizational efficiency and effectiveness.

Hybrid organization An organization that combines political advocacy and service provision in its core identity.

Hypotheses Tentative statements to be explored and tested.

Ideology (cultural) The dominant ideas within a culture about the way things are and should work, derived from a group's social, economic, and political interests.

Ideology (personal) A particular body of ideas or outlook; a person's specific worldview.

Immune system Organs and cells that interact and work together to defend the body against disease.

Information processing theory A sensory theory of cognition that sees information as flowing from the external world through the senses to the nervous system, where it is coded.

Interactional/interpretive perspective on organizations A perspective that sees formal organizations as social constructions of reality, providing members with a sense of connection and reflecting the worldviews of the creators.

Interdisciplinary team A special type of task group composed of professionals representing a variety of disciplines; it may also include consumers or clients.

Interpretist perspective Ways of understanding human behavior that share the assumption that reality is based on people's definition of it.

Intersectionality feminist theory A feminist theory suggesting that no single category is sufficient to understand social oppression and that categories such as gender, race, and class intersect to produce different exprinces for women of various races and classes.

Intersectionality theory A pluralist theory of social conflict that recognizes numerous vectors of oppression and privilege, including but not limited to gender, class, race, global location, sexual orientation, and age; recognizes that individuals often hold cross-cutting and overlapping memberships in different status groups.

Iron cage of rationality Max Weber's term for the dehumanizing potential of bureaucracies.

Leadership A process of influencing a group to achieve a common goal.

Learned helplessness In cognitive social learning theory, a situation in which a person's prior experience with environmental forces has led to low self-efficacy and efficacy expectation.

Learning organization theory A theory of formal organizations developed on the premise that rational planning is not sufficient for an organization to survive in a rapidly changing environment such as the one in which we live, and that formal organizations must become complex systems capable of constant learning.

Levels of consciousness From Wilber's integral theory, overall stages of awareness and being; moving from the prepersonal to the personal and transpersonal phases, each with multiple levels of development.

Linear time Time based on past, present, and future.

Lines of consciousness From Wilber's integral theory, the approximately two dozen relatively independent developmental lines or streams that can evolve at different rates, with different dynamics, and on different time schedules; examples include cognitive, moral, interpersonal, self-identity, and socioemotional capacity.

Lone-parent families Families composed of one parent and at least one child residing in the same household, headed by either a divorced or unmarried parent.

Lymphocytes White blood cells.

Managing diversity model An approach to formal organizations that focuses on the need to maximize the potential advantages, and minimize the potential disadvantages, of diversity in organizational membership.

Mass media institution In a democratic society, the social institution responsible for managing the flow of information, images, and ideas.

Mass society A society that is standardized and homogenized, with no ethnic, class, regional, or local variations in human behavior.

Mobilizing structures Existing informal networks and formal organizations that serve as the collective building blocks for social movements.

Mobilizing structures (MS) perspective An approach to social movements that suggests that they develop out of existing networks and formal organizations.

Mood A feeling disposition that, in contrast to an emotion, is more chronic, less intense, and less tied to a specific situation.

Multidetermined behavior A view that human behavior is developed as a result of many causes.

Multidimensional Having several identifiable dimensions.

Multilevel family practice model A way of viewing a family that focuses on stress from and resources provided (or not provided) by patterns and institutions within larger social systems, including the neighborhood, local community, state, nation, and global socioeconomic system.

Multiple intelligences The eight distinct biopsychosocial potentials, as identified by Howard Gardner, with which people process information that can be activated in cultural settings to solve problems or create products of value in the culture.

Multiple psychological senses of community (MPSOC) The idea that individuals participate in multiple communities and consequently have multiple senses of community.

Musculoskeletal system Muscles that are attached to bone and cross a joint. Their contraction and relaxation are the basis for voluntary movements.

Mutual aid group A formed group of persons who use the support, encouragement, and feedback from other persons in the group to work on certain problems they have in common.

Narrative theory A theory proposing that all of us are engaged in an ongoing process of constructing a life story.

Natural environment That part of the environment made up of all living and nonliving things naturally occurring.

Natural group A group that occurs naturally, without external initiative, such as a group of peers or co-workers.

Neocolonialism The practice of dominant and powerful nations going beyond their boundaries, using international financial institutions such as the World Bank and the International Monetary Fund to exert influence over impoverished nations and to impose their culture, laws, and language on the occupied nations through the use of financial incentives (loans) and disincentives.

Neoliberal philosophy A philosophy that governments should keep their hands off the economic institution.

Nervous system The biological system responsible for processing and integrating incoming sensory information; it influences and directs reactions to that information.

Network A set of relationships and ties among a set of actors.

Network model A social movement theory in the mobilizing structures perspective that focuses on the role of grassroots settings in the development and maintenance of social movements.

Networked individualism A way of thinking about community in which individuals operate in large, personalized, complex networks.

Neural plasticity The capacity of the nervous system to be modified by experience.

Neuron Nerve cell that is the basic working unit of the nervous system. Composed of a cell body, dendrites (receptive extensions), and an axon.

Neurotransmitters Messenger molecules that transfer chemical and electrical messages from one neuron to another.

Nonhierarchical organization An organization run by consensus, with few rules, characterized by informality.

Nonnormative stressors Unexpected stressful events that can quickly drain a family's resources.

Nonspecific immunity Immunity that includes physical barriers to infection, inflammation, and phagocytosis. Does not include antibodies or cell-mediated immunity.

Norm Culturally defined standard or rule of conduct.

Normative stressors The stressors families face as a result of typical family life cycle transitions.

Objective reality The belief that phenomena exist and have influence, whether or not we are aware of them.

Ongoing group A natural or formed group that is set up without a particular time limit and that meets until the group is disbanded.

Open group A natural or formed group that includes any person who would like to become a member; a natural or formed group that accepts persons who meet the group's criteria after the group has begun and throughout its existence.

Operant conditioning theory A theory in the social behavioral perspective that sees behavior as the result of reinforcement.

Organizational culture model An approach to formal organizations that sees them as cultures with shared experiences and shared meanings.

Organizational humanism An approach to formal organizations that assumes organizations can maximize efficiency and effectiveness while also promoting individual happiness and well-being.

Organizations as multiple oppressions A theory of organizations that views them as social constructions that exclude and discriminate against some categories of people.

Othering Labeling people who fall outside of one's own group as abnormal, inferior, or marginal.

Outsourcing In the economic institution, the relocation of goods and services production from one place to another as a strategy for cost reduction.

Performance expectations The expectations group members have of other group members in terms of how they will act or behave in the group or how well they will perform a task.

Personal community Networks of social interaction composed of friends, relatives, neighbors, workmates, and so on.

Personal network Those from the social network who provide a person with his or her most essential support resources.

Personal space The physical distance we choose to maintain in interpersonal relationships.

Person-in-environment (PIE) classification system A classification system developed for the purpose of social work assessment. Assessment is based on four factors: social functioning problems, environmental problems, mental health problems, and physical health problems.

Phenomenal self An individual's subjectively felt and interpreted experience of "who I am."

Place attachment A process in which individuals and groups form bonds with places.

Place identity A process in which the meaning of a place merges with one's self-identity.

Political economy model A model of formal organizations that focuses on the organization's dependence on its environments for political and economic resources and, more specifically, on the influence of political and economic factors on the internal workings of the organization.

Political opportunities (PO) perspective An approach to social movements that suggests they develop when windows of political opportunity are open.

Positive psychology An approach to psychology that focuses on people's strengths and virtues and promotes optimal functioning of individuals and communities.

Positivist perspective The perspective on which modern science is based. Assumes objective reality: that findings of one study should be applicable to other groups, that complex phenomena can be studied by reducing them to some component part, and that scientific methods are value-free.

Postconventional morality In Kohlberg's theory of moral development, a stage in which moral decisions are based on moral principles that transcend those of one's own society.

Postmodernism A term used to describe contemporary culture as a postindustrial culture in which people are connected across time and place through global electronic communications; emphasis is on the existence of different worldviews and concepts of reality.

Postpositivism A philosophical position that recognizes the complexity of reality and the limitations of human observers; proposes that scientists can never develop more than a partial understanding of human behavior.

Post-traumatic stress disorder (PTSD) A set of symptoms experienced by some trauma survivors that includes reliving the traumatic event, avoidance of stimuli related to the event, and hyperarousal.

Practice orientation A way of thinking about culture that recognizes the relationships and mutual influences among structures of society and culture, the impact of history, and the nature and impact of human action.

Preconscious Mental activity that is outside of awareness but can be brought into awareness with prompting.

Preconventional morality In Kohlberg's theory of moral development, a stage in which moral decisions are made on the basis of avoiding punishment and receiving rewards.

Primary emotions Emotions that developed as specific reactions and signals with survival value for the human species. They serve to mobilize an individual, focus attention, and signal one's state of mind to others; examples include anger, fear, sadness, joy, and anticipation.

Primary territory A territory that evokes feelings of ownership, that we control on a relatively permanent basis, and that is vital to our daily lives.

Privacy Selective control of access to the self or to one's group.

Privatization Shifting the administration of programs from government to nongovernment organizations.

Privilege Unearned advantage enjoyed by members of some social categories.

Proactive social movement A social movement with the goal of changing traditional social arrangements.

Problem-focused coping Coping efforts in which the person attempts to change a stress situation by acting on the environment. Most effective when situations are controllable by action.

Process-oriented leader A leader who identifies and manages group relationships.

Professional social movement organizations Organizations staffed by leaders and activists who make a career out of reform causes.

Programs In behavior settings theories, the consistent, prescribed patterns of behavior developed and maintained in particular behavior settings.

Proposition An assertion about a concept or about the relationship between concepts.

Psychoanalytic theory A theory of human behavior and clinical intervention that assumes the primacy of internal drives and unconscious mental activity in determining human behavior.

Psychodynamic perspective An approach that focuses on how internal processes motivate human behavior.

Psychoeducational group A formed group focused on providing information and support concerning a particular problem area or issue; such groups usually meet over a short period of time.

Psychology The study of the mind and mental processes.

Public territory A territory open to anyone, to which we generally make no attempt to control access.

Qualitative methods of research Research methods that use flexible methods of data collection, seek holistic understanding, present findings in words rather than numbers, and attempt to account for the influence of the research setting and process on the findings.

Quantitative methods of research Research methods, based on the tenets of modern science, that use quantifiable measures of concepts, standardize the collection of data, attend only to preselected variables, and use statistical methods to look for patterns and associations.

Race A system of social identity based on biological markers such as skin color that influences economic, social, and political relations.

Racism Discriminatory thoughts, beliefs, and actions based on the assignment of an individual or group to a racial classification.

Radical antithesis Philosophy that equality is the natural, divine order and that inequality is based on abuse of privilege and should be minimized.

Rational perspective on organizations A perspective that sees formal organizations as goal-directed, purposefully designed machines that maximize efficiency and effectiveness.

Reactive social movement A social movement with the goal of defending traditional values and social arrangements.

Reciprocity A norm that receiving resources in social exchange requires giving resources of relatively equal value, proposed by social exchange theory.

Relational community A community based on voluntary association rather than geography.

Relational coping Coping that takes into account actions that maximize the survival of others as well as oneself.

Relational theory A theory proposing that the basic human tendency is relationships with others and that our personalities are formed through ongoing interactions with others.

Religion A systematic set of beliefs, practices, and traditions experienced within a particular social institution over time.

Religious institution The social institution with primary responsibility for answering questions about the meaning and purpose of life.

Resource mobilization theory A social movement theory in the mobilizing structures perspective that focuses on the role of formal organizations in the development and maintenance of social movements.

Role A set of usual behaviors of persons occupying a particular social status or position.

Role strain Problems experienced in the performance of specific roles. Used by sociologists to measure stress.

Satisfice In organizational theory, to seek satisfactory rather than perfect solutions and to discontinue the search for alternative solutions when a satisfactory solution is available.

Schema (plural *schemata*) An internalized representation of the world, including systematic patterns of thought, action, and problem solving.

Science A set of logical, systematic, documented methods for answering questions about the world.

Scientific management A set of principles developed by Frederick Taylor to maximize the internal efficiency of formal organizations; it is focused on finding the "one best way" to perform every organizational task.

Second force therapies Therapies based on behavioral theories; they focus on learned habits and seek to remove symptoms through various processes of direct learning.

Secondary emotions Emotions that are socially acquired. They evolved as humans developed more sophisticated means of learning, controlling, and managing emotions to promote flexible cohesion in social groups. Examples include envy, jealousy, anxiety, guilt, shame, relief, hope, depression, pride, love, gratitude, and compassion.

Secondary territory A territory less important to us than primary territories, control of which does not seem essential.

Self An essence of who we are that is more or less enduring.

Self-categorization theory A theory of small groups proposing that in the process of social identity development, we come to divide the world into in-groups (those to which we belong) and out-groups (those to which we do not belong) and to be biased toward in-groups.

Self-efficacy A sense of personal competence.

Self-help group A formed group, which may or may not be professionally led, composed of persons who share a common life situation.

Self-system In Wilber's full-spectrum model of consciousness, the active self or person who moves through the stages of consciousness and mediates between the basic and transitional structures of development.

Sense of community A feeling of belonging and mutual commitment.

Settlement house movement A social movement, brought to the United States from England in the late 1800s, that turned attention to the environmental hazards of industrialization and focused on research, service, and social reform.

Silverman's social action model A model of formal organizations that focuses on the active role of individual actors in creating the organization.

Small group Two or more people who interact with each other because of shared interests, goals, experiences, or needs.

Social action model (community organization) A model of community social work practice that emphasizes social reform and the challenge of structural inequalities.

Social behavioral perspective An approach that sees human behavior as learned when individuals interact with their environments.

Social capital Connections among individuals that provide potential sources of a number of types of resources.

Social class A particular position in a societal structure of inequality.

Social constructionist perspective An approach that focuses on how people learn, through their interactions with each other, to classify the world and their place in it.

Social entrepreneurial organization An organization formed by a social entrepreneur who recognizes a social problem and uses ideas from business entrepreneurs to organize, create, and manage a new venture to bring about social change related to that problem.

Social exchange theory A theory in the exchange and choice perspective that sees human behavior as based on the desire to maximize benefits and minimize costs in social interactions.

Social identity theory A stage theory of socialization that articulates the process by which we come to identify with some social groups and develop a sense of difference from other social groups.

Social institutions Patterned ways of organizing social relations in a particular sector of social life.

Social movement organizations (SMOs) Formal organizations through which social movement activities are coordinated.

Social movement service organizations (SMSOs) A type of social agency that has the explicit goal of social change and accomplishes this goal through the delivery of services.

Social movements Large-scale collective actions to make change, or resist change, in specific social institutions.

Social network The people with whom a person routinely interacts; the patterns of interaction that result from exchanging resources with others.

Social network theory A developing theory in the exchange and choice perspective that focuses on the pattern of ties that link persons and collectivities.

Social planning model A model of community social work based on the premise that the complexities of modern social problems require expert planners schooled in a rational planning model; also referred to as a top-down approach.

Social reform Efforts to create more just social institutions.

Social structure A set of interrelated social institutions developed by humans to support and constrain human interaction for the purpose of the survival and well-being of the collectivity.

Social support The interpersonal interactions and relationships that provide people with assistance or feelings of attachment to others they perceive as caring.

Social welfare institution The social institution in modern industrial societies that is concerned with allocating goods, services, and opportunities to enhance social functioning of individuals and contribute to the social health of the society.

Socioeconomic status (SES) Social, economic, and political relations developed around education, economic, and occupational status; social class.

Sociofugal spaces Physical designs that discourage social interaction.

Sociopetal spaces Physical designs that encourage social interaction.

Specific immunity Immunity that involves cells (lymphocytes) that not only respond to an infection but also develop a memory of that infection and allow the body to defend against it rapidly during subsequent exposure.

Spiritual bypassing Use of spiritual beliefs or practices to avoid dealing in any significant depth with unresolved issues and related emotional and behavioral problems; includes attempts to prematurely transcend the ego.

Spirituality A search for purpose, meaning, and connection among oneself, other people, the universe, and the ultimate reality, which can be experienced within either a religious or nonreligious framework.

Staffing In behavior settings theories, the participants in a particular behavior setting.

State A personality characteristic that changes over time, depending on the social or stress context.

States of consciousness From Wilber's integral theory, an understanding of experience that includes both ordinary (waking, sleeping, and dreaming) and nonordinary experiences (peak experiences, religious experiences, altered states, and meditative or contemplative states).

Status A specific social position.

Status characteristics In status characteristics and expectation states theory, any characteristics evaluated in the broader society to be associated with competence.

Status characteristics and expectation states theory A theory of basic group process assuming that the influence and participation of group members during initial interactions are related to their status and to expectations others hold about their ability to help the group accomplish tasks.

Stimulation theories Theories that focus on the physical environment as a source of sensory information necessary for human well-being.

Strain theory An approach to social movements that sees them as developing in response to some form of societal strain.

Stress Any biological, psychological, or social event in which environmental demands or internal demands, or both, tax or exceed the adaptive resources of the individual.

Stress pileup When a series of crises over time depletes a family's resources and exposes the family to increasing risk of very negative outcomes.

Subjective reality The belief that reality is created by personal perception and does not exist outside that perception; the same as the interpretist perspective.

Symbol Something verbal (language, words) or nonverbal (such as a flag) that comes to stand for something else; a way of expressing meaning.

Symbolic interactionism A theory stressing that we develop a sense of meaning in the world through interaction with our physical and social environments and interpretation of symbols.

Synapse In the nervous system, the gap between an axon and a dendrite; the site at which chemical and electrical communication occurs.

Systems perspective An approach that sees human behavior as the outcome of reciprocal interactions of persons operating within linked social systems.

Systems perspective on organizations A perspective that focuses on formal organizations in constant interaction with multiple environments.

Task group A group formed for the purpose of accomplishing a specific goal or objective.

Task-oriented leader A leader who facilitates problem solving within the context of the group.

Technology The tools, machines, instruments, and devices developed and used by humans to enhance their lives.

Territorial community A community based on geography.

Territoriality A pattern of behavior of a group or individual that involves marking or personalizing a territory to signify ownership and engaging in behaviors to protect it from invasion.

Testes Male gonads, primarily responsible for producing sperm (mature germ cells that fertilize the female egg) and secreting male hormones called androgens.

Theory An interrelated set of concepts and propositions, organized into a deductive system, that explains relationships among aspects of our world.

Therapy group A formed group that uses an intensive group format to promote growth in its members and to assist its members in resolving emotional and behavioral problems.

Third force therapies Therapies rooted in experiential/humanistic/existential theories that focus on helping a person deal with existential despair and that seek the actualization of the person's potential through techniques grounded in immediate experiencing.

Time-limited group A natural or formed group whose members or leader establish a certain length of time that they will meet as a group.

Time orientation The extent to which individuals and collectivities are invested in three temporal zones: past, present, and future.

Tradition A process of handing down from one generation to another particular cultural beliefs and practices. In particular, a process of ratifying particular beliefs and practices by connecting them to selected social, economic, and political practices.

Trait A stable personality characteristic.

Transition points Time when families face a transition in family life stage or in family composition.

Transnational corporation (TNC) A very large company that carries on production and distribution activities in many nations.

Transnational social movement organizations (TSMOs) Social movement organizations that operate in more than one nation-state.

Transpersonal approach An approach to human behavior that includes levels of consciousness or spiritual development that move beyond rational-individuated-personal personhood to a sense of self that transcends the mind/body ego—a self-identity also referred to as transegoic.

Traumatic stress Stress associated with events that involve actual or threatened severe injury or death of oneself or significant others.

Triangulation A process that occurs when two family members (a family subsystem) inappropriately involve another family member to reduce the anxiety in the dyadic relationship.

Ultimate environment Conceptualizations of the highest level of reality, understood differently by persons at various levels of spiritual development or consciousness.

Unconscious Mental activities of which one is not aware but that influence behavior.

Uterus Also called the womb; serves as the pear-shaped home for the fetus for the 9 months from implantation to birth.

Ventricles The two lower, thick-walled chambers of the heart.

Vertical linkage Interaction with systems external to the community.

Voluntarism The belief that persons are free and active agents in the creation of their behaviors.

Worldcentric Identification beyond the "me" (egocentric), or the "us" (ethnocentric), to identification and concern for "all of us" (worldcentric), or the entire global human family; a moral stance characteristic of higher levels of spiritual development.

Worldview A cognitive picture of the way things—nature, self, society—actually are.

INDEX

ABC-X model of family stress, 352–353
ABI (acquired brain injury), 88
Abma, Joyce, 360
Abnormal coping, 169–174
Accessible environments, 227–228, 252–254, 254 (exhibit)
Accommodation, cognitive, 119
Accommodation, cultural, 280
Acculturation, 280, 283
    See also Ethnic identity
Acetylcholine (ACh), 90
ACh (acetylcholine), 90
ACORN organization, 482, 492, 500
Acquired brain injury (ABI), 88
Active personal space (APS), 233
Activism, 389, 391
    See also Social movements
ADA (Americans with Disabilities Act), 252–254
Addams, Jane, 18, 228, 237, 265
ADD (attention deficit disorder), 239
Adler, Nancy, 111
Adoptive families, 357
Affect, 118
    See also Emotion
Affluence and families, 368–370
African Americans
    case studies, 181, 258–260
    community, 465
    culture of, 265, 266, 270, 273, 275, 281, 282, 284–285, 287
    education, 313
    empowerment of, 59
    ethnic identity, 154–155, 156
    families, 362, 378
    mortality rates, 316
    physical environment, 235, 251
    poverty rates, 300
    slavery, 263, 344, 345
    small group compositions, 395
    spirituality, 206–207
    substance abuse, 378
Age
    chronological, 16–17
    disabilities and, 253–254
    personal space and, 231
    spirituality and, 212
Agency-based model of community organization, 472–473

Agoraphobia, 137
AIDS. See HIV/AIDS
Ainsworth, M. S., 149
Aldana, A., 397
Alienation, 46
Alinsky, Saul, 472
All God's Children (film), 383–384
Almaas, A. H., 203–204
Alone Together (Turkle), 245
Altman, Irwin, 230, 233
Altruistic behavior, 50
Amenta, Edwin, 490
American privilege, 19–20
Americans with Disabilities Act (ADA), 252–254
Amino acids, 91
Amygdala, 130, 151–152
Anderson, C., 406
Anderson, Ralph, 13
Anorexia nervosa, 137
ANS (autonomic nervous system), 88, 99, 128
Antibodies, 96
Antigens, 95
Anti-oppressive model of social work, 434
Anxiety disorders, 65
Anxious-ambivalent attachment style, 149
Appalachians, 345
APS (active personal space), 233
Arab Spring protest movements, 46, 487, 489–490, 497 (photo)
Archetypes, 191
ART (attention restoration theory), 238
Arteries, 99
Asian Americans, 153, 154–155, 207–208, 235
Assagioli, Robert, 191
Assimilation, cognitive, 119
Assimilation, cultural, 280
Assistive technology, 103–104, 246, 246 (exhibit)
Assumptions (defined), 27
Attachment styles and personal space, 231
Attachment theory, 57, 149–150
Attention deficit disorder (ADD), 239
Attention restoration theory (ART), 238
Attribution theory of cognition, 133
Authoritarian systems, 301
Autoimmune diseases, 95

Case knowledge, 23–24
Case studies
    biological person, 80–84
    community, 448–450
    culture, 258–260
    family, 338–340
    formal organizations, 414–417
    physical environment, 226–228
    psychological person, 116–118
    psychosocial person, 146–147
    small groups, 382–384
    social movements, 480–483
    social structure and social institutions, 292–294
    spiritual person, 178–183
    theoretical perspectives, 36–38
Castells, Manuel, 496, 506, 507
Catholic faith case study, 180
Causal level of consciousness, 200
CBT (cognitive-behavioral therapy), 66, 127
Cell phones and culture, 275–276
Censorship, 328
Centers for Disease Control and Prevention, 87, 94–95, 104
Central nervous system (CNS), 88, 91, 102
Cerebellum, 89
Cerebral cortex, 88, 89, 89 (exhibit)
CF (cultural framing) perspective of social movements, 498–507, 498 (exhibit), 499 (exhibit)
Challenges as stressful, 155
The Changing Life Course (Hutchison), 17
Chaos theory, 41, 42, 43
Charity organization society (COS) movement, 485
Chaskin, Robert, 451
Chavis, D., 466
Child Guidance Clinic, 71
Childhood
    morality, 299
    mortality, 315–316
    personality development, 57, 58
    physical environment, 235, 250–251
    poverty, 300, 323
    spiritual capacities, 202
    See also Families
Childlessness, 359–361
Child welfare workers and burnout, 436–437
Chinese activists, 494
Chosen family, 341
Christian faith case study, 178–179
Chromosomes, 106
Chronological age, 16–17
The Citizen's Share (Blasi, Freeman and Kruse), 434
Civic place attachment, 250–251
Clammer, John, 42
Clark, J. L., 203
Classical conditioning theory, 64–65

Clock time cultures, 15–16
Closed groups, 394
Closed systems, 40
Clusters of social support, 166
CNS (central nervous system), 88, 91, 102
Code of Ethics, 20, 25, 25 (exhibit), 211, 271–272, 509
Cognition
    attribution theory, 133
    cognitive theory, 119–120, 119 (exhibit), 126
    definitions, 118–119
    emotional "disorders," 136–137
    emotions influencing, 129
    information processing theory, 120
    moral reasoning theories, 123–125, 124 (exhibit)
    multiple intelligences theory, 121–123, 122 (exhibit)
    social learning theory, 65–66, 120–121
    social work practice and theories, 125–127
Cognitive-behavioral therapy (CBT), 66, 127
Cognitive mediation, 120–121
Cognitive structure, self as, 139
Cognitive theory, 119–120, 119 (exhibit), 126
Cohabitation, 358–359
Coherence and conceptual clarity of theories
    conflict perspective, 46–47
    developmental perspective, 62
    exchange and choice perspective, 51
    humanistic perspective, 70
    psychodynamic perspective, 57–58
    social behavioral perspective, 66
    social constructionist, 54
    systems perspective, 42–43
Cohesiveness of small groups, 407–408
Coleman, J., 49
Coleman, Mardia, 475
Coles, Robert, 24
Coley, Richard, 313
Collaborative versus conflict model of community, 473–475
Collective action repertoire, 504–506, 505 (exhibit)
Collective agency, 66
Collective behavior, 7
Collective efficacy, 466
Collective spirituality, 215–217
Collectivism versus individualism, 348
Collins, Randall, 50, 51
Colonialism, 301, 307, 343–344, 492
Common Core standards, 313–314
Common sense, 277
Communication, 139, 231, 355, 406–407, 407 (exhibit)
Communities
    case study, 448–450
    conflict perspective, 468, 469–470, 473
    contemporary issues, 471–476
    context versus target of practice, 471–472
    country comparisons, 449–450

Walsh, Joseph, 55
Warner, R., 341 (exhibit)
Warren, Roland, 457, 463–464
Watson, John B., 65
Watson (computer), 244
Weber, Max, 44, 45, 333, 420–422, 421 (exhibit), 458
Web resources
  biological person, 114
  communities, 477–478
  culture, 290
  families, 380
  formal organizations, 445
  general sites, 34
  psychological person, 143
  psychosocial person, 176
  search engines, 33
  small groups, 412
  social movements, 512
  social structure/institutions, 336
  spirituality and religion, 221
  theoretical perspectives, 75–76
WEIRD (Western, educated, industrialized, and democratic) societies, 31
Wellbriety Movement, 471
Wellman, Barry, 459, 464
Wells-Barnett, Ida B., 265
Welwood, John, 201
Wenocur, Stanley, 456
Western, educated, industrialized, and democratic (WEIRD) societies, 31
White, J., 341

White Americans
  culture, 282
  ethnic identity, 154–155
  impact of child with disabilities, 264
  mortality rates, 316
  physical environment, 235, 251
  poverty rates, 300
  small group compositions, 395
White blood cells, 95–96
Wicker, Allan, 235–236
Wilber's integral theory of consciousness, 192, 197–204, 197 (exhibit)
Williams, D. R., 87
Williams, Raymond, 263
Worker/client relationship, 149
Work overload, 436
Workplace arrangements, 231
World Bank, 303–304, 307, 309
Worldcentric way of being, 196
World Trade Organization (WTO), 303–304
Worldview and culture, 270
WTO (World Trade Organization), 303–304

Yalom, Irvin, 395, 396, 403

Zald, Mayer, 486–487
Zambardo, Philip, 15–16
Zimbardo Time Perspective Inventory (ZTPI), 16
Zimring, Craig, 248
ZTPI (Zimbardo Time Perspective Inventory), 16

ABOUT THE AUTHOR

Elizabeth D. Hutchison, MSW, PhD, received her MSW from the George Warren Brown School of Social Work at Washington University in St. Louis and her PhD from the University at Albany, State University of New York. She was on the faculty in the Social Work Department at Elms College from 1980 to 1987 and served as chair of the department from 1982 to 1987. She was on the faculty in the School of Social Work at Virginia Commonwealth University from 1987 to 2009, where she taught courses in human behavior and the social environment, social work and social justice, and child and family policy; she also served as field practicum liaison. She has been a social worker in health, mental health, aging, and child and family welfare settings. She is committed to providing social workers with comprehensive, current, and useful frameworks for thinking about human behavior. Her other research interests focus on child and family welfare. She lives in Rancho Mirage, California, where she is active in environmental justice issues facing farm workers in East Coachella Valley.

ABOUT THE CONTRIBUTORS

Megan Beaman is a community-based civil rights attorney representing primarily low-income and immigrant clients and communities around Southern California, particularly in the Coachella Valley, and also leading and participating in community advocacy toward policy and systems change outside of the traditional legal context. Ms. Beaman is a longtime advocate for the rights of workers, immigrants, women, and low-income communities—and the combination of any or all of those groups. Her career and passion are rooted in her own rural, working-class upbringing, as well as the experiences she has shared with diverse communities and leaders around the country, all united in their commitments to justice and better lives.

Leanne Wood Charlesworth, LMSW, PhD, is associate professor in the Department of Social Work at Nazareth College of Rochester. She has practiced within child welfare systems, and her areas of service and research interest include poverty and child and family well-being. She has taught human behavior and research at the undergraduate and graduate levels.

Linwood Cousins, MSW, MA, PhD, is professor in the School of Social Work at Western Michigan University. He is a social worker and an anthropologist who has practiced in child welfare and family and community services. His research, teaching, and practice interests include the sociocultural manifestations of race, ethnicity, and social class as well as other aspects of human diversity in the community life and schooling of African Americans and other ethnic and economic minorities.

Elizabeth P. Cramer, MSW, PhD, LCSW, ACSW, is professor in the School of Social Work at Virginia Commonwealth University. Her primary scholarship and service areas are domestic violence, lesbian and gay male issues, and group work. She is editor of the book *Addressing Homophobia and Heterosexism on College Campuses* (2002). She teaches in the areas of foundation practice, social justice, oppressed groups, and lesbian and bisexual women.

Cory Cummings, LCSW, is a doctoral student in the School of Social Work at Virginia Commonwealth University. He has worked in community mental health, providing individual and group interventions, case management, and administrative services for a number of years. His research interests include health disparities, health equity, and community-engaged interventions for people affected by serious and persistent mental health problems. Cory has adjunct teaching experience with social work methods and has participated in the design, development, and delivery of numerous in-service clinical trainings.

Stephen French Gilson, MSW, PhD, is professor and coordinator of interdisciplinary disability studies at the Center for Community Inclusion and Disability Studies; professor at the School of Social Work at the University of Maine; and senior research fellow at Ono Academic College Research Institute for Health and Medical Professions, Kiryat Ono, Israel. After he completed his undergraduate degree in art, he shifted his career to social justice, pursuing a masters in social work. Realizing that knowledge of human biology and physiology was foundational to his work, he completed a PhD in medical sciences. Synthesizing the diversity and richness of this scholarly background, Dr. Gilson engages in research in disability theory, disability as diversity, design and access, social justice, health and disability policy, and the atypical body. He serves on the board of directors of the Disability Rights Center of Maine and is chair of the Disability Section of the American Public Health Association. He teaches courses in disability as diversity, policy, and human behavior from a legitimacy perspective. Along with his wife, Liz DePoy, Stephen is the owner of an adapted rescue farm in Maine. Living his passion of full access, the barn and farm area have been adapted not only to better assure human access and animal caretaking but also to respond to the needs of the disabled and medically involved animals that live on the farm. Two other major influences on Dr. Gilson's writing, research, and work include his passion for and involvement in adaptive alpine skiing and dressage.

Beverly B. Koerin, MSW, PhD, is associate professor emerita in the School of Social Work at Virginia Commonwealth University (VCU). She practiced in public social services at the local and state levels. At VCU she taught policy, macro practice, and diversity courses and served as BSW program director, MSW program director, and associate dean. For more than 10 years, she has been involved in research and service related to family caregiving. For many years she cofacilitated a caregiver support group for the Richmond Alzheimer's Association. She currently volunteers with Jewish Family Services in aging-related programs and serves on the Advisory Council of the Richmond, Virginia, Retired Senior Volunteer Program (RSVP).

Soon Min Lee, MSW, LSW, PhD, is assistant professor in the School of Social Work at Sejong Cyber University, Seoul, Korea. Her major areas of interest include adjustment to college among students with visual impairments, e-learning for blind students, social work supervision, and ethics of social workers.

Michael J. Sheridan, MSW, PhD, is an associate professor at the National Catholic School of Social Service (NCSSS) of The Catholic University of America. Her practice experience includes work in mental health, health, corrections, and youth and family services. Her major areas of interest are spirituality and social work and issues related to diversity, oppression, and social and economic justice. She teaches courses on diversity and social justice, spirituality and social work, transpersonal theory, human behavior, international social development, research methods and statistics, and conflict resolution and peacebuilding at the MSW and doctoral levels. She is also the director of NCSSS's Center for Spirituality and Social Work.

Joseph Walsh, MSW, PhD, LCSW, is professor in the School of Social Work at Virginia Commonwealth University. He was educated at Ohio State University and has worked for 35 years in community mental health settings. His major areas of interest are clinical social work, serious mental illness, and psychopharmacology. He teaches courses in social work practice, human behavior and the social environment, and research while maintaining a small clinical practice.

⊛SAGE researchmethods

The essential online tool for researchers from the world's leading methods publisher

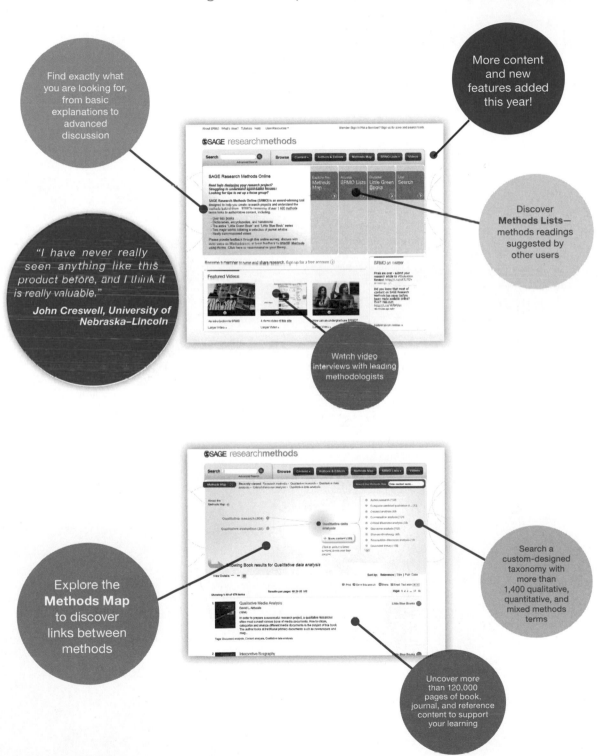

Find exactly what you are looking for, from basic explanations to advanced discussion

More content and new features added this year!

"*I have never really seen anything like this product before, and I think it is really valuable.*"

John Creswell, University of Nebraska–Lincoln

Discover **Methods Lists**—methods readings suggested by other users

Watch video interviews with leading methodologists

Explore the **Methods Map** to discover links between methods

Search a custom-designed taxonomy with more than 1,400 qualitative, quantitative, and mixed methods terms

Uncover more than 120,000 pages of book, journal, and reference content to support your learning

Find out more at
www.sageresearchmethods.com